LIVES
OF THE
LORD CHANCELLORS OF ENGLAND.

LIVES

OF

THE LORD CHANCELLORS

AND

KEEPERS OF THE GREAT SEAL

OF

ENGLAND

FROM THE EARLIEST TIMES TILL THE REIGN OF QUEEN VICTORIA

BY

LORD CAMPBELL.

SEVENTH EDITION.

ILLUSTRATED.

VOL. X.

WILDSIDE PRESS

CONTENTS

OF

THE TENTH VOLUME.

CHAP.	PAGE
CCXIV.—Lord Lyndhurst's Early Life, ...	1
CCXV.—At the Bar till he was appointed Solicitor-General, .	11
CCXVI.—Solicitor-General.—Attorney-General.—Master of the Rolls, ...	24
CCXVII.—Lord Chancellor under Canning, Lord Goderick, and the Duke of Wellington, ...	47
CCXVIII.—Lord Chief Baron, ...	64
CCXIX.—Lord Chancellor during the 100 days, and ex-Chancellor during the Administration of Lord Melbourne, ...	90
CCXX.—Lord Chancellor under Sir Robert Peel, . . .	126
CCXXI.—Out of Office, ...	155
CCXXII.—The Russian War, ...	180
CCXXIII.—Lord Brougham's Early Life, ...	202
CCXXIV.—Life of Lord Brougham from his removal to England to the death of George III., ...	236
CCXXV.—Attorney-General to Queen Caroline, ...	275
CCXXVI.—From the Death of Queen Caroline till he became Lord Chancellor	313
CCXXVII.—Lord Chancellor, ...	35
CCXXVIII.—"The One Hundred Days" till the Final Resignation of Lord Melbourne, ...	443

CHAP.	PAGE
CCXXIX.—From the Resignation of Lord Melbourne till the Resignation of Sir Robert Peel,	49
CCXXX.—From the Beginning of the Session of 1847, till the Overthrow of the Derbyites,	523
CCXXXI.—Conclusion,	551

LIVES

OF THE

LORD CHANCELLORS OF ENGLAND.

CHAPTER CCXIV.

LORD LYNDHURST'S EARLY LIFE.

MANY of my contemporaries have sunk into the tomb, but Lord Lyndhurst, considerably my senior, survives, in the full enjoyment of his intellectual powers.[1] He is a noble subject for biography, from his brilliant talents—from the striking vicissitudes of his career—from the antagonistic qualities which he displayed—and from the quick alternation of warm praise and severe censure which must, in fairness, be pronounced upon his actions. Having known him familiarly above half a century, both in public and in private life, I ought to be able to do him justice; and notwithstanding a hankering kindness for him with all his faults, I think I can command sufficient impartiality to save me in this Memoir from confounding the distinctions of right and wrong. All rivalry between us has long ceased, and I am sure I can never be induced to disparage or to blame him from resentment or envy.

Half in jest, half in earnest, he has prayed that in writing his Life I would be merciful to him; and I have promised that if he would supply me with materials I would do my best for him as far as my conscience would allow. He has replied, "Materials you shall have *none* from me; I have already burned every letter and paper which could be useful to my biographer, therefore he is at liberty to follow his own inclination."[2]

[1] This Memoir was begun March, 1853.—Ed.
[2] Lord Lyndhurst has since asked me, "How are you getting on with my

When I have proceeded a little way, Law Reports, Parliamentary Debates, and my own testimony, will furnish me with abundant materials for my narrative. But, in starting, I have only uncertain rumors as to the origin of Lord Lyndhurst and his infancy. I thought that Debrett's, Lodge's, or Burke's 'Peerage,' would at least have given me a pedigree, which I might have adopted; but instead of telling us how the first Copley, under the name of *De Couplé*, came in with the conqueror, and tracing the Chancellor up to him, they do not even mention the Chancellor's father, for they all begin with his own birth on the 21st of May, 1772, as if he had then sprung from the earth, without even telling us what region of the world witnessed this wonderful vegetation. The account of himself which he sent to these genealogists seems to disclose a weakness,—that he was very unreasonably ashamed of his family. Although not descended from De Veres, Bohuns, or Bigods, he might have been proud to be the son of an eminent artist, whose pencil had worthily commemorated some of the most striking events in English history: Charles I. ordering the arrest of the five Members in the House of Commons; the seige of Gibraltar; the Victory of Wolfe, and the Death of Chatham. Lord Lyndhurst, when in the zenith of his power, was much hurt by a speech delivered at a public dinner by the Honorable James Stuart Wortley, now Recorder of London, himself of royal descent. In demonstrating the superior good qualities of the Tories over the rival party, he dwelt particularly on the alleged aristocratic exclusiveness of the Whigs, by which, when they were in power, Burke and Sheridan had been banished from the Cabinet; "whereas," said he, "we glory in having as our leader, in the one House, the son of a cotton-spinner; and in the other, the son of a painter." Offense might have been justly taken at the expression by which the art of the Chancellor's father was thus referred to,—intimating, to a person before unacquainted with the truth, that the Chancellor's sire was an *operative*, or, at any rate, not better than a sign-painter.

Life?" and has offered to correct the proof sheets, adding, "I can surely judge better than any one of the accuracy of your statements." This reminds me of a married lady, against whom a scandalous story had got abroad, and who said to a friend of mine, "You have my authority positively to contradict it; and surely I ought to know whether it be true or false."

I have not been able to trace this line of the Copleys
farther back than the Chancellor's grandfather, who, being
an Englishman by birth, married in Ireland Mary Singleton, and went with her to Boston, in America. Here was
born John Singleton Copley, the Chancellor's father.
Ireland has been claimed as the birthplace of the distinguished artist; but there seems to be no doubt that,
before he saw the light, his parents had emigrated to the
new world. In the year 1782, when he had acquired great
reputation by his pencil in London, he was thus addressed
by an American patriot at Boston:—"I trust, amidst this
blaze of prosperity, that you don't forget your dear native
country, and the cause it is engaged in, which I know lay
once near your heart, and I trust does so still." So, when
he sent copies of the print of his painting of "The Death
of Chatham" to WASHINGTON and ADAMS, the one
replied, "This work, highly valuable in itself, is rendered
more estimable in my eye when I remember that America
gave birth to the celebrated artist who produced it;" and
the other, "I shall preserve my copy, both as a token of
your friendship and as an indubitable proof of American
genius."[1] There can not be conceived a more unpromis-
ing soil for the cultivation of the fine arts than the retreat
of the "Pilgrim Fathers," whose descendants had made
little progress in wealth, and still fostered a puritanical
distaste for all that was elegant or imaginative. Yet
almost at the same hour America produced, amid her
deserts and her trading villages, two eminent painters,
WEST and COPLEY, who, unknown to each other, were
schooling themselves in the rudiments of art, attempting
portraits of their friends one day, and historical compositions the next; studying nature from the "naked Apollos
of the wilderness," as some one called the Indian chiefs,
and making experiments on all manner of colors, primi-
tive and compound; in short, groping through inspiration
the right way to eminence and fame. West's progress was
more rapid, and from the patronage of George III. he
gained the higher position; but Copley was more favored
by the public, and his productions are in much greater
estimation than those of his countryman, once much
prized for their skillful drawing and academical correctness. While Copley continued at Boston, he not only

[1] Cunningham's "Lives of British Painters," vol. v., p. 174.

was considered a prodigy,—making an income of £300 a year by drawing portraits at fourteen guineas apiece,—but he sent over paintings for the Exhibition of the Royal Academy in Somerset House. Some of these attracted considerable notice, and he was strongly advised to push his fortune on this side the Atlantic. To one of these counsellors he answered: "I would gladly exchange my situation for the serene climate of Italy, or even that of England; but what would be the advantage of seeking improvement at such an outlay of time and money? I am now in as good business as the poverty of this place will admit. I make as much as if I were a Raphael or a Coreggio; and three hundred guineas a year, my present income, is equal to nine hundred a year in London. With regard to reputation, you are sensible that fame can not be durable where pictures are confined to sitting-rooms, and regarded only for the resemblance they bear to their originals. Were I sure of doing as well in Europe as here, I would not hesitate a moment in my choice; but I might, in the experiment, waste a thousand pounds and two years of my time, and have to return baffled to America. My ambition whispers me to run this risk, and I think the time draws nigh that must determine my future fortune." According to the precept of Sir Joshua Reynolds to artists, he had continued a bachelor till the meridian of life; but about the year 1770 he entered the married state, uniting himself to a young lady said to be of high respectability and of great intellectual accomplishments. I have not been able to discover her maiden name, or the exact time of their union. But it rests on the most undoubted authority that, on the 21st day of May, 1772, they were made happy by the birth of their first-born son, named JOHN SINGLETON, after his father, and destined to be four times Lord High Chancellor of Great Britain.

Before entering upon the career of the son, the reader may wish to be informed of the subsequent adventures of the sire. In the beginning of the year 1774 he set sail from Boston for England, dreading that, if he deferred the voyage longer, it might be effectually prevented by hostilities between the mother-country and her colonies. But he by no means then resolved on seeking a new domicile, for he left his mother, his wife, and his child with all his unsold pictures and his household gods, behind him;

in the hope that, having had a glimpse of Europe, in all probability he should rejoin them, and find all disputes amicably adjusted. A final separation between the two countries was then as little thought of as that the earth should be severed from the solar system. After a short stay in London, where he said, "he met with few *friends* and many *advisers*," he impatiently set off for Rome, the object of his aspiring wishes since he first drew a likeness on the wall with a piece of chalk. There is no account of the impression made upon him by the wonders of the Vatican, but in May, 1775, we find him thus writing to an acquaintance in London:—

"Having seen the Roman school and the wonderful efforts of genius exhibited by Grecian artists, I now wish to see the Venetian and Flemish schools. There is a kind of luxury in seeing as well as there is in eating and drinking; the more we indulge the less are we to be restrained, and indulgence in art I think innocent and laudable. Art is in its utmost perfection here; the Apollo, the Laocoon, &c., leave nothing for the human mind to wish for. More can not be effected by the genius of man than what is happily combined in those miracles of the chisel."

This artistic tour gave a new impulse to Copley's genius, and strengthened his confidence in his own powers. On his return to London, in the end of the year 1775, he resolved boldly to establish himself as an artist in this great metropolis, trusting to portrait-painting as his steady means of subsistence, but not despairing of being able to enhance his fame by original compositions commemorating interesting events in English history. These, he wisely thought, offered him a fairer hope than "Holy Families," "Last Suppers," or "Crucifixions," to which his countryman West was devoting himself. Accordingly he set up his easel 25, George Street, Hanover Square, the very house which his son, when Lord High Chancellor, inhabited, and still—an octogenarian Ex-Chancellor—inhabits.

His success fully justified his anticipations, and his "Death of Chatham," though liable to severe criticism in some of its details, being received with unbounded applause, placed him in the first rank of his profession. He was elected a Royal Academian, and lived much respected by his brother artists and by the public. Once, and once only, he figured as a party in a court of justice. A rich citizen of Bristol came to Copley, and had himself, his wife, and seven children, all included in a family piece. "It wants but one thing," said the head of the family, "and that is the portrait of my first wife, for this one is my second." "But," said the artist, "she is dead, you know, Sir: what can I do? She is only to be admitted as an angel." "Oh no, not at all," answered the other; "she must come in as a woman; no angels for me." The portrait of the first wife was added; but, while the picture remained in the studio, the citizen returned with a stranger lady on his arm. "I must have another cast of your hand, Mr. Copley," said he; "an accident befell my second wife; this lady is my third, and she is come to have her likeness included in the family group." The painter complied, and the husband looked with a glance of satisfaction on his three spouses. Not so the living lady. On this occasion she remained silent, but afterwards she called by herself and remonstrated. "Never was such a thing heard of: it was unchristian that a man should have three wives at once; her character would be gone if she submitted to it; out her predecessors must go." And she solemnly declared that she had her husband's full authority for the alteration. The artist yielded, and immediately sent the picture home, that he might have no more trouble with it. But the enraged trigamist, without sending it back, refused to pay for it, and, being sued, set up as a defense that it was not according to order. The Judge before whom the action was tried left it to the Jury, "whether they did not believe that, under the circumstances, the third wife had the authority of the defendant for directing the ejection of the first and second wife;" and the plaintiff recovered a verdict for the full amount of his demand.

Sir Thomas Lawrence arose, to supersede for a time all rivals in portrait-painting, although his reputation has since sadly declined: but Copley, by successive historical pieces, continued to maintain a high position as an artist till his death, in the year 1815.

At this period his son, the subject of the present memoir, was in the meridian of life, and, notwithstanding extraordinary talents and acquirements, had gained little public distinction. His mother lived to see him in the robes of Lord Chancellor, but his father could hardly have hoped that he would ever reach so high as the dignity of a puisne judge.

We must now trace his career, and analyze the "mixture of good and evil arts" by which he reached the lofty eminence he still commands.

When Copley, the father, sailed from America, as I have related, his wife and son were left behind him, and I have not been able to ascertain the exact time when they followed him to England. Some have said that the youth continued to reside at Boston, after the treaty of peace recognizing the independence of America, so long as indelibly to fix upon himself the stamp of American citizenship. When Lord Chancellor Lyndhurst indiscreetly denounced the Irish as "*aliens* in blood, language, and religion," Daniel O'Connell retorted that the Chancellor himself was an alien, and liable to be reclaimed as a refugee Yankee. But there is clearly no foundation for this surmise; his father must be considered domiciled in England when the treaty of independence was concluded; the Chancellor himself was certainly transferred to this country while *in statu pupillari;* and he never again set foot on American soil except as a tourist.[1]

In the year 1786, young Copley appears to have been at school at Clapham, in the county of Surrey, and precociously both a lover and a poet. The author of " Literary Lawyers," after noticing Sir William Jones, and a few others, from the short list of those who have been celebrated both in Westminster Hall and Paternoster Row, thus proceeds:—

"Lord Lyndhurst, too, has wooed the Muse. While he was at a school kept by a Mr. Franks, a circumstance occurred which will serve to show how early the ardent temperament and ready talent, which have distinguished his public career, developed itself in this remarkable man. At Clapham there was a young ladies' school, which was attended by the same dancing-master as that employed at Mr. Franks'; and, previous to his annual ball, the two

---

[1] I have heard him express himself in terms of affection for his native land, and speak proudly of distinguished Americans as his countrymen. In early life, when there seemed so little prospect of his burning ambition ever being gratified, he must have regretted that he had lost the chance of becoming President of the United States.

schools used frequently to meet together for the purpose of practicing. At one of these agreeable *reunions* young Copley, then not more than fourteen years of age, was smitten with the charms of a beautiful girl; and at their next meeting slipped into her hand a letter containing a locket with his hair, and a copy of verses of which the following is a transcript. They were entitled:—

' *Verses addressed by J. Copley to the most amiable* ——.

' Thy fatal shafts unerring move,
I bow before thine altar, love;
I feel thy soft, resistless flame
Glide swift through all my vital frame;
For while I gaze my bosom glows,
My blood in tides impetuous flows;
Hope, fear, and joy alternate roll,
And floods of transport whelm my soul.
My faltering tongue attempts in vain
In soothing murmurs to complain;
My tongue some secret magic ties,
My murmurs sink in broken sighs;
Condemned to nurse eternal care,
And ever drop the silent tear,—
Unheard I mourn, unheard I sigh,
Unfriended live, unpitied die.

' I beg you will do me the honor to accept of the trifle which accompanies it, and you will oblige
    ' Your affectionate admirer,
            ' J. S. COPLEY, JUN.
' P. S.—Pray excuse the writing.'

"It is only necessary to add that the lady to whom these verses were addressed still survives, and retains in her possession both the letter and its contents."

The lines, closely imitated from a well-known translation of Horace, I suspect to have been copied for the occasion from a scrap-book; for the professed lover has never since been known to versify.

From Clapham he was removed to a school at Chiswick. Here he was taught first by the Rev. Mr. Crawford, afterwards by the Rev. Dr. Horne, father of the present Sir William Horne, once my colleague as law officer of the Crown, now a Master in Chancery. I have not been able to obtain any authentic account of young Copley's proficiency or demeanor at this school; but at this time he must have laid the foundation of his classical knowledge, which is reckoned very considerable.

He next entered on a field in which he acquitted himself most creditably. The following is a copy of the entry of his admission at Trinity College, Cambridge:—

"1790, July 8.—Admissus est Pensionarius Johannes Singleton Copley, filius Johannis Singleton Copley de Boston in America, a schola apud Chiswick in Middlesexia sub præsidio Doctoris Horne. Annos nat. 18."

From his wonderful quickness of comprehension and strength of memory he was able to make a given portion of time devoted to study more available than any man in the University, and he would occasionally affect to be an idler and a man of pleasure; but his solid acquirements must have been the result of steady application.

When he was to take his Bachelor's degree, in a good year, he came out second wrangler, and he proved his proficiency not only in mathematics, but in classics and general learning, by obtaining a Trinity fellowship the first time he sat for this highly creditable honor.[1]

The tremendous struggle produced by the French Revolution between the defenders of old institutions, however defective, and those who contended that all existing governments ought to be overturned, was now at its height; and young Copley's mind being from infancy imbued with republican principles, he took what in American phrase he called the "go-a-head side" so warmly and openly, as to run some risk of serious animadversion. He gradually became more cautious, but, till many years afterwards when he was tempted to join the Tory ranks by an offer of a seat in parliament and the near prospect of the office of Chief Justice of Chester, he thought a democratic revolution would be salutary, and he is said to have contemplated without dismay, the possible establishment of an Anglican Republic.

The law was the profession by which on this, as on the other side of the Atlantic, such ambitious dreams were to be realized. He had no appetite for the necessary drudgery, but to gain an object which he had at heart he could for a season submit to intense application. For his means of subsistence he depended chiefly upon his fellowship; his father, having lived rather ex-

[1] 1795. October, 2: Joannes Singleton Copley, juratus et admissus in socium minorem.
1797, July 5: Joannes Singleton Copley, juratus et admissus in socium majorem.
He took his degree of M.A. 1797, and was created LL.D. in 1835.

pensively, had accumulated little for him. But the aspiring youth hoped that before the time when, by the rules of the College, he must take orders or forfeit his fellowship, he should have made sufficient progress at the bar to enable him to dispense with all adventitious aid.

On the 19th day of May, 1794, he was admitted a member of the Honorable Society of Lincoln's Inn by the name and designation of "John Singleton Copley of Trinity College, Cambridge, Gentleman, eldest son of John Singleton Copley of George Street, Hanover Square, in the county of Middlesex, Esq." His residence, however, was in the Temple, which is chiefly haunted by the students of the Common Law, the branch of the profession to which he was destined. As soon as he had finally left Cambridge he took chambers in Crown Office Row.

He soon after became a pupil of Mr. Tidd, the famous Special Pleader, and having diligently worked in his chambers till he was well conversant with everything, from the Declaration of the Surrebutter, he commenced Special Pleader under the bar on his own account.

Now was the time when I made his acquaintance. He still kept up a friendly intercourse with Tidd, and attended a debating club which was held at his chambers in King's Bench Walk. When I entered here as a pupil, and was admitted a member of this club, I had the honor of being presented to Mr. Copley, to whom I looked up with the most profound reverence and admiration. He was a capital speaker, but rather too animated for dry juridicial discussion. I remember once he was so loud and long upon a question arising out of the law of libel that the porters and laundresses gathered round the window, in great numbers, listening to his animated periods. At last a cry of fire being raised from the crowd, the Temple fire-engine was actually brought out, and had the effect of putting an end to the flaming oration by raising a general laugh at the expense of the incendiary. He was very kind to me, and although of much older standing and much courted from his university reputation, he would ask me to call upon him. In those days I never met him in private society, but I did meet him not unfrequently at public dinners of a political complexion. In after life he asserted that he had never been a Whig—

which I can testify to be true. He was a Whig *and something more*, or in one word a *Jacobin*. He would refuse to be present at a dinner given on the return of Mr. Fox for Westminster, but he delighted to dine with the "Corresponding Society," or to celebrate the anniversary of the acquittal of Hardy and Horne Tooke.

As a Special Pleader under the bar, his eloquence being of no service, and a constant attendance at chambers being expected, which was very distasteful to him, he had not the success which he expected; and he determined on being called to the bar. But before commencing his forensic career he embarked for America, having a strong desire to revisit his native country, and to renew an intimacy with some relations whom he had left there. With a view to this ramble he had solicited and obtained at Cambridge the appointment of Traveling Bachelor, and in compliance with the statutes he remitted to the Vice-Chancellor an ample account of Transatlantic cities and manners. This I have in vain attempted to see, and I am afraid it is lost forever.[1] His narrative must be exceedingly interesting if it detailed his personal adventures; for he paid a visit of some days to the illustrious Washington, and he traveled some weeks in company with Louis Philippe—afterwards King of the French—then a refugee in the United States.

CHAPTER CCXV.

AT THE BAR TILL HE WAS APPOINTED SOLICITOR-GENERAL.

AS soon as possible after his return from America, Copley was called to the bar by the Benchers of Lincoln's Inn, and he became a candidate for business in the Court of King's Bench and on the Midland Circuit. His professional progress was extremely slow. It used to be said that there were four, and only four, ways in which a young man could get on at the bar: 1.

[1] On my application to his College and to the University authorities, search was made for these letters, but I was informed that they could nowhere be found.

By *huggery.* 2. By writing a law book. 3. By quarter sessions. 4. By a miracle.

The first was successfully practiced by that great nisi prius leader, Tom Tewkesbury, the hero of " The Pleaders' Guide," who not only gave dinners at his chambers to the attorneys, but suppers to their clerks:—

> " Nor did I not their clerks invite
> To taste said venison hashed at night :
> For well I knew that hopeful fry
> My rising merit would descry."

But Copley, although by no means scrupulous about principle, was above any sort of meanness, and always comported himself as a gentleman. Although he behaved to attorneys and their clerks with courtesy, and would talk very freely with them, as with all the rest of mankind, he never would flatter them, or court them, or make interest with them to obtain business. 2. Park's book on the " Law of Insurance," and Abbott's on the " Law of Shipping," had recently acquired for their respective authors the reputation of deep mercantile lawyers, and filled their bags with briefs at Guildhall. But Copley had always a great contempt for authorship, and would rather starve than disgrace himself by it. 3. He took to Quarter Sessions very cordially, and had success in poor-law cases, as well as in defending prisoners charged with petty larcenies, but this did not extend his fame beyond the limits of a single county, and even here, when the assizes came round, he found himself postponed to juniors who had won reputation as successful special pleaders in London. 4. The *miracle* consists in the conjunction of an opportunity to make a great speech in some very popular cause, with full ability to improve the advantage. Such an opportunity, at last (as we shall see), did arrive to Copley, and his fortune was made, although with the utter sacrifice of his character for political consistency.

Meanwhile, finding that, after having been nine years at the bar, his progress was very slow in a stuff gown, and that he was not likely soon to gain such a position as entitled him to ask to be made a King's Counsel, he resolved to take the dignity of Sergeant-at-Law, supposed to be open *suo periculo* to any barrister of fair reputation and seven years' standing. Accordingly he was *coifed*, and gave gold rings, choosing for his motto "Studiis vigilare severis," which some supposed was meant as an intimation that he had sown his wild oats, and that he was now to become a plodder.

He remained, however, for a considerable time unchanged, particularly in his devoted attachment to republican doctrines. Strange to say, his hero was Napoleon the Great, who had established pure despotism in France, and wished to extinguish liberty in every other country. But Copley still worshiped him, and when he was denominated by Mr. Pitt "the child and the champion of Jacobinism," and fostered some vague idea that when once all the existing governments of Europe had been overturned, free institutions might follow. He loudly deplored the disasters of the Russian campaign in 1812, and felt deep sympathy with the fallen conqueror, whose dominions had afterwards shrunk within the narrow limits of the Isle of Elba. What, then, must have been his raptures when he heard that Napoleon had escaped, had landed at Cannes, and was marching triumphantly to Paris! It is said that Copley, hearing the news while walking in the street, enthusiastically tossed his hat in the air, and exclaimed, "*Europe is free!*" Nevertheless I doubt not that he rejoiced sincerely in the battle of Waterloo, for he has always been solicitous for the interests and the glory of his country.

At this period of his life he mixed little in general society. The Tory leaders he utterly eschewed. He did make acquaintance with some eminent Whigs, but thought poorly of them, as their notions of reform were so limited. Although he would not mix with the Radicals of the day, who were men of low education and vulgar manners, he thought they might be made useful, and by rumor, he was so far known to them that they looked forward to his patronage should they be prosecuted by the Crown for sedition or treason.

At last arrived the crisis of Copley's fate, when a new and brilliant career was opened to him, which he entered upon, throwing aside the "Burden of his Principles" as joyfully as Christian, in the "Pilgrim's Progress," got rid of the "Burden of his Sins."

The general pacification of 1815 was by no means immediately followed by the prosperity anticipated from it.

The exhaustion of capital during the war was severely felt; the derangement in the monetary system, occasioned by the Act of 1797 for sanctioning an inconvertible paper circulation, operated most mischievously both upon commerce and agriculture; and, the artificial stimulus of exorbitantly high prices being suddenly withdrawn, a general paralysis of industry was the consequence. Bad legislation and an unwise severity in the executive government aggravated these evils. With a view to keep up rents, the importation of foreign corn was prohibited, and the system of Protection, now happily exploded, was rigorously acted upon.

The laboring classes were thus thrown out of employment, and general discontent prevailed among them. Instead of remedying the evil by allowing a free interchange of commodities with foreign countries, penal laws were passed forbidding public meetings and seeking to fetter the liberty of the Press.

This was the time for demagogues to flourish. Instead of seeking a constitutional remedy in Parliament, or trying to enlighten the public mind, they strove to gain eminence and influence by exaggeration, misrepresentation, and the application of physical force. One of these " Patriots" was a certain Dr. Watson, a physician without patients, who collected large assemblages of people in the Spa Fields, near London, and by speeches and placards was the cause of a dangerous riot. He was apprehended, and brought to trial for high treason, the charge mainly relied upon being, that he had "levied war against the King."

The prosecution was ill-advised, as the proper course clearly would have been to have indicted him for a misdemeanor, in which case he must inevitably have been convicted, and severely punished by fine and long imprisonment. But Lord Liverpool and his colleagues thought it would strengthen the government if they could make this out to be a case of high treason, and so exhibit a spectacle of hanging and beheading. The utmost importance was attached to the result of the prosecution, and the ministers confessed that they could hardly expect to survive a defeat.

The leading counsel for the Crown were the Attorney-General, Sir Samuel Shepherd, a very sound lawyer, who, had it not been for the infirmity of deafness, would have filled the highest judicial stations, and the Solicitor-General, Sir Robert Gifford, who, on account of his supposed extraordinary merit, had been lately appointed to that office, while wearing a stuff gown behind the bar.

Their opponents were curiously selected and matched The leader was Sir Charles Wetherell, a high-minded but furious ultra-Tory, then breathing vengeance against the government, because he had been disappointed in obtaining the post of Solicitor-General, to which, from his standing, his talents, and his services, he had a strong claim. The other was Mr. Sergeant Copley, generally understood to entertain pretty much the opinions professed by the prisoner, though with prudence sufficient not to act upon them till there should be a fair prospect of their success.

The trial was at the bar of the Court of King's Bench at Westminster, before Lord Ellenborough and his colleagues, and began on the 9th of June, 1817. Among the distinguished men who sat on the Bench as auditors was Lord Castlereagh, then leader of the House of Commons and the most efficient member of Lord Liverpool's Cabinet.

A clear case of aggravated riot was made out, and, if a spy was to be believed, there had been an organized plot to take the Tower and to bring about a revolution. But this spy, upon his own showing, was a man of infamous character, and he was contradicted by credible witnesses on the most material parts of his testimony. Sir Charles Wetherell asked the jury—

"Will you suffer the purity of British jurisprudence to depend upon the credit of that indescribable villain? Will you add to the blood-money he has already earned? Will you encourage the trade and merchandise of a man who lives on blood? Will you—the guardians and protectors of British law—will you suffer death to be dealt out by him as he pleases? Will you suffer a human victim to be sacrificed on the testimony of that indescribable villain? But if *you* suffer it, I must add, will the British public suffer it? Will the people permit it? Will they tolerate or endure it?"

The learned counsel had been too abrupt in his declamation, and had not carried along with him the sympathies of the jury, who seemed rather disposed to return an unpropitious answer to these interrogatories.

Sergeant Copley, who followed, was much more calm, persuasive, and successful. I heard his speech with great delight, and I consider it one of the ablest and most effective ever delivered in a court of justice. Yet, on re-perusing it, I found much difficulty in selecting any passage which would convey to the reader an idea of its merit. The whole is a close chain of reasoning on the evidence as applicable to the charge. Thus quietly does he begin:—

"I have been called upon to assist as counsel in a cause which in the circumstances with which it is attended, and in the consequences to which it may lead, is one of the most important that has ever occurred in the history of the jurisprudence of this country; a cause of infinite importance to the prisoner at the bar, whose life and character—everything that can be valuable to him as a man and as a member of the community—are at issue and depend upon your verdict."

After taking a softened view of the tumultuous proceedings which the prisoner had instigated and sanctioned, he conceded that they might amount to a riot:—

"But," said he, "let me again remind you that although there might have been a riot and a dangerous riot, it does not follow that war has been levied against the King in his realm. In order to constitute a treasonable riot there must have been a deliberate purpose and design to overturn the Government. Under Lord George Gordon there were forty or fifty thousand men marching in columns with colors flying and military music up to the doors of the House of Commons, and afterwards maintaining their possession of the capital for a fortnight. Lord George Gordon was indeed tried for treason, but he was acquitted because, however improper or mischievous his conduct, the jury were of opinion (and it was put fairly to them by Lord Mansfield) that he had in view no treasonable object."

When Sergeant Copley observed that, by his skillful treatment of a part of the case most relied upon by the Crown, he had made a deep impression on the jury, he added, with an air of seeming humility and sincerity,—

"I wish I could state it with half the strength with which I feel it. But the prisoner in selecting me as one of his counsel on this occasion gives the strongest evidence of the conviction he feels of the goodness of his cause. He must have known that I possessed no powers of eloquence, and little of the skill of an advocate. He must have known that I could only proceed in a straightforward course, pursuing the subject in a plain way, and holding up the facts truly to the jury, leaving them to draw their own conclusion in favor of his innocence."

Having gone over all the topics which the defense presented, seemingly without any plan, but according to the most consummate rules of art, he conformed to the Rubric, which in the " Service for High Treason " requires a final prayer that the jury may be directed by Heaven to a right verdict ; but he made it short and pithy :—

" Let me then conclude by fervently praying that Providence which enlightens the minds of men and pours the spirit of truth and justice into their hearts, will dispense that light and spirit to you in the discharge of the great duty which is cast upon you. From the attention you have paid to the evidence I can only anticipate a favorable result, and although you can not approve of all the prisoner has said or done, you will without hesitation acquit him of this weighty and unfounded charge."

The Solicitor-General made a clever reply, and Lord Ellenborough summed up strongly for a conviction; but the jury, after a short deliberation, found a verdict of *Not Guilty*.

Lord Castlereagh, who had remained in court in a state of great anxiety till the conclusion of the trial, declared to the witty Jekyll, whom he met accidentally the following day, that " if Sergeant Copley had been for the Crown, the prosecution would have succeeded ; " and expressed a wish that he might never be against the Crown again. The answer was : " Bait your rat-trap with Cheshire cheese, and he will soon be caught." The objection to the joke is that it was rather obvious ; for the office of Chief Justice of Chester had been so often successfully used to induce adventuring lawyers to leave their party, that a man of much inferior powers might have given the same recipe for catching Copley.

Lord Castlereagh, who was a matter-of-fact man, took the advice in good earnest ; and, having consulted Lord Liverpool, the Premier, obtained his sanction for opening a negotiation to secure Copley to the Government. Lord

Eldon, the Chancellor, was not consulted on the subject; and it is a curious circumstance that, notwithstanding his great power in making and unmaking ministries, he never interfered in the appointment of the law officers of the Crown.[1]

A communication was immediately made to Copley, through the medium of an eminent solicitor with whom he was intimate. In the overture, nothing was said about Chester or any other appointment; but a seat in the House of Commons, for a Government borough, was proposed, without any express condition or promise as to services or reward; nevertheless, with the clear reciprocal understanding that the *convertite* was thenceforth to be a thick and thin supporter of the Government, and that everything in the law, which the Government had to bestow, should be within his reach.

This was a terrible temptation into which he was led. The chance of a Jacobinical revolution had passed away, and there did not seem a possibility of the Whigs coming into office during the life of the Regent, who heartily hated them, having basely betrayed them. The Sergeant was ambitious, and he was conscious of possessing great powers if he should have an opportunity of displaying them in Parliament. But, *per contra*, this would be considered a very flagrant case of *ratting*, because his opinions on the Liberal side were known to be extreme, although he had never formally attached himself to any party, whereas the existing Government was conducted on very arbitrary principles, so that the defense of its measures must require a considerable sacrifice of conscience.

In the seventeenth year of the reign of Queen Victoria, when party distinctions are almost obliterated, it is difficult to understand the state of feeling in the end of the reign of George III., when conflicting political creeds were nearly as well defined as religious, and the transit of a man of any eminence from the opposition to the government side caused as great a sensation as the perversion of a popular Protestant divine to the Church of Rome. Copley

---

[1] When Copley afterwards was actually sworn in Solicitor-General, Lord Eldon declared that he had never before spoken to him or seen him.

According to another statement circulated in Westminster Hall, Lord Castlereagh is supposed to have said spontaneously at the conclusion of Copley's speech, "I can discover in him something of the *rat*, and I will set my trap for him, baited with Cheshire cheese."

must have been well aware of the odium, of the animadversions, of the sarcasms, of the railleries, which awaited him. Another Regulus, he braved them all,—with this difference, that he had to consider not what *duty*, but what *interest* demanded.

Out of decency, he asked a little time to deliberate. Although very free spoken upon almost all subjects, this is a passage of his life which he always shuns, and it would be vain to conjecture whether he had any and what internal struggles before he yielded.

When the negotiation had been completed, he had a formal interview with Lord Liverpool, the Prime Minister, and without a shilling being put into his hand, or anything being said about his *kit*, he was enlisted and attested a soldier in the Tory army.

Soon after, the "London Gazette," announced that "John Singleton Copley, Esq., sergeant-at-law, was returned to serve in Parliament for Yarmouth, in the Isle of Wight." This was a borough then under the influence of the Treasury, and afterwards disfranchised by the Reform Act. Not having been before in Parliament, he escaped the disgrace of walking across the floor of the House, and fronting his former associates. For some time he prudently avoided any display to attract notice, and he made no "maiden speech." He first broke silence in the House by a few observations in support of the practice, now abandoned and universally condemned, of giving rewards to witnesses upon the conviction of offenders:—"He entered his protest against the broad assertion hazarded by an honorable member that the system of granting rewards had been productive of great confusion throughout the country. He himself," he said, "had been engaged for fourteen years on the Midland Circuit, and had never known a single instance to justify such a statement."[1]

However, he soon showed that he was resolved to consider only how he could best please his employers. A Bill was pending to continue the Alien Act, whereby the Government was authorized, at their free will and without assigning any cause, to send out of the country all who were not natural born subjects, however long or however peaceably they might have resided under the allegiance

[1] 38 Hansard, 510.

of the English crown. The measure was strongly opposed by Sir Samuel Romilly and Sir James Mackintosh as arbitrary, unconstitutional, and in time of peace wholly unnecessary. However, Ministers having staked their existence on carrying it, thus was it defended by him who had hitherto been the professed admirer and eulogist of the French Revolution :—

"Let the House examine for a moment what sort of persons they were about to admit, if they rejected the Bill. They were about to harbor in this country a set of persons from the continent, who were educated in and who had supported all the horrors of the French Revolution :—persons who were likely to extend in this country that inflamed and turbulent spirit by which they themselves were actuated—persons who did not possess either morality or principle, and who could not be expected to respect those qualities in this country."

There seems to have been a tempest of ironical cheers from the opposition benches, prompted by some knowledge of the antecedents of the orator. This was a very critical moment for him—but his audacity triumphed.

"I have expressed," said he, in a calm and lowered voice, "and I will repeat the opinions which I have deliberately formed, and which I conscientiously entertain on this question. I am aware that these opinions are distasteful to some honorable Members on the other side of the House, who perhaps think that our institutions might be improved by a little Jacobinical admixture. [Loud cheers and counter-cheers.] I repeat that I express myself as I feel, and I shall never be disturbed by any clamor raised on the other side of the House meant to question my sincerity; for there is not any one who truly knows me but is aware that the observations I have made are the result of my conviction as to the line of conduct which ought to be pursued on this occasion. If no Alien Bill existed there might and probably would be an influx of persons whose principles and views are alarming to all who love the regulated freedom which we enjoy. I know that the great mass of the English population are well affected to the laws of England ; but all in the House must be aware—and if not, the eyes and ears of Members are shut—that there still exist in England disaffected persons ready to disturb its quiet,—persons who, forming a junction with disaffected foreigners, may be stimulated and encouraged to acts of disturbance and outrage. I am not so hazardous a politician as to throw an additional quantity of combustible matter into the country in order to see how much we can bear without exploding. I do not wish to make the experiment as to the quantity of fresh poison which may be inhaled without destroying the constitution. In 1793 similar arguments to those of the honorable gentlemen opposite had been used, but Parliament by disregarding them saved us from those horrors which a reckless clamor for liberty had conjured up in another country."[1]

The implied promise for such services was duly performed, and Best, afterwards created Lord Wynford, who had previously been rewarded for deserting his party by the Chief Justiceship of Chester, having resigned that office on being raised to the bench in Westminster Hall, it was conferred on the new renegade, who had already had a slight foretaste of ministerial favor in being created a King's sergeant.

"The statesman we abhor, but praise the judge."

Immediately proceeding on the circuit, he displayed those extraordinary powers and qualities which might have made him the very greatest magistrate who has presided in an English court of Justice during the present century. But, admired and praised by all who saw and heard him clothed in scarlet and ermine, Copley cared for none of these things, and he was impatient to finish his business in Denbighshire, Flintshire, and Cheshire, that he might get back to St. Stephen's to prosecute his ambitious schemes, for which the times seemed so propitious. His name is now to be found in the list of the ministerial majority in every division, and he could be relied upon in every emergency of debate, doubtless saying to himself, "the sailor who looks for high salvage and prize money must be ready to go out in all weathers."

As a matter of course, upon the first vacancy he was made Solicitor-General to the King, and he regularly became a member of Lord Liverpool's government. He talked rather licentiously of his chief and of his colleagues, but he very steadily co-operated with them in all

[1] 38 Hansard, 820.

their measures, good or bad. From the beginning Lord Eldon had an instinctive dislike to him, and seems to have had a presentiment that the man had at last appeared who was to turn him out of office. The worthy old-fashioned Peer, who had been a sincere and bigoted Tory all his life, could not look with benignity on one who, he was credibly informed, had danced round the Tree of Liberty to the tune of *Ca ira*, and he declared that he had no faith in political conversions. Copley always behaved to him respectfully, but showed no earnestness to cultivate him, knowing that he did not hold of the Chancellor, and that the Chancellor's long tenure of office must of necessity ere long come to a conclusion.

Mr. Solicitor's great mortification was to find himself serving under Gifford, the Attorney-General, his junior in standing and greatly his inferior in acquirements and oratory. He now transferred himself from the Court of Common Pleas, where he had practiced since he became a sergeant, to the Court of King's Bench, where there is more profitable business. But, although he had precedence here, Gifford having stationed himself in the Court of Chancery as a school for the woolsack, he had not the first practice. This was retained by Scarlett, who (take him for all and all) was the most formidable champion for his opponent I have ever known at the English bar, and who was at this time irresistible from the entire ascendancy he had acquired over Lord Chief Justice Tenterden, the presiding Judge.

Mr. Solicitor's position, however, now appeared very prosperous. His spirited and noble bearing had secured him a favorable hearing in the House of Commons, and his very agreeable manners had made him popular with all branches of the profession of the law. Nor did he seem to suffer from any unpleasant consciousness of having acted questionably, or from any suspicion that he might be ill thought of by others. His gait was always erect, his eye sparkling, and his smile proclaiming his readiness for a jest.

How different his fate from that of poor Charles Warren, who had only been "a Whig *and nothing more.*" After being for years petted by the Whigs, their destined Attorney-General, and possessed of such celebrity as a

"diner out" that he would not accept an invitation till he had a list of the company he was to meet,—in an evil hour he too afterwards *ratted*, being made Chief Justice of Chester; but he could not stand the reproachful looks and ironical cheers of his former friends in the House of Commons, and he soon died of a broken heart—
"Ille crucem pretium sceleris tulit, hic diadema."

I am now to present Sir John Copley in a new light—as a man of fashion. Hitherto his converse with the gay world had been very limited; he had seldom been in higher society than at a Judge's dinner in Bedford-square; he himself generally dined at a coffee-house, and when the labors of the day were over he solaced himself in the company of his friends in Crown Office Row. But he now fell in love with a beautiful young widow, whose husband, Lieut.-Colonel Thomas, had been killed in the battle of Waterloo. She was the niece of Sir Samuel Shepherd, the late Attorney-General, at whose house he first met her. She received his attentions favorably, and they were married on the 13th of March, 1819.

Forthwith he set up a brilliant establishment in his father's old house, George-street, Hanover-square, which he greatly enlarged and beautified. Lady Copley was exceedingly handsome, with extraordinary enterprise and cleverness. She took the citadel of Fashion by storm, and her concerts and balls, attended by all the most distinguished persons who could gain the honor of being presented to her, reflected back new credit and influence on her enraptured husband. There were afterwards jealousies and bickerings between them, which caused much talk and amusement; but they continued together on decent terms till her death at Paris in 1834—an event which he sincerely lamented. He was sitting as Chief Baron in the Court of Exchequer when he received the fatal news. He swallowed a large quantity of laudanum and set off to see her remains. But his strength of mind soon again fitted him for the duties and pleasures of life.

CHAPTER CCXVI.

SOLICITOR-GENERAL.—ATTORNEY-GENERAL.—MASTER OF THE ROLLS.

SIR JOHN COPLEY continued Solicitor-General five years, doing his official duty in Court very ably and unexceptionably, but supporting all the measures of Government in Parliament with an ostentatious contempt of public opinion. He was quite satisfied with the consolation that the Goverment was strong, and that while it lasted his promotion was secure.

During this long period the only great State prosecution was that which arose out of the Cato-street Conspiracy, which looked like a travesty of "Venice Preserved," but was a real and very detestable plot, to begin with the murder of all the fifteen members of the Cabinet when assembled at a Cabinet dinner. Thistlewood, a half-pay officer, who induced a number of mechanics and clowns to join with him in his scheme of *liberation*, was first brought to trial, and a clear case was made out against him. Mr. Solicitor-General replied, and satisfied himself with calmly and clearly recapitulating the evidence, and showing that it substantiated the charge of high treason. In some of the other cases he opened the prosecution to the jury in the same tone as if he had been conducting an action for "goods sold and delivered," to which no defense could be set up. Convictions were obtained without difficulty, and five of the prisoners actually suffered death according to the sentence pronounced upon them.

This is the last instance of capital punishment being actually inflicted for the crime of high treason in these realms. Frost and his associates were convicted of high treason at Monmouth when I was Attorney-General, they having engaged in a very formidable armed insurrection and taken the town of Newport by storm. I succeeded, against the opinion of several members of the Cabinet, in having their sentence commuted to transportation for life, because a question had been raised upon which the Judges were nearly equally divided, as to the regularity of the procedure preparatory to their trial. Again, Smith

O'Brien was convicted of high treason in Ireland when I was a member of the Cabinet, guiding the deliberations of the Government in such matters. He was clearly guilty in point of law and fact, too; but his rebellion was so ludicrously absurd that I thought it would take away all dignity and solemnity from the punishment of death if it should be inflicted upon him, and my advice was followed in offering him a pardon on condition of transportation. So foolish was he, that he denied the power of the Crown to commute the sentence without his consent; and he insisted on being immediately liberated,—or hanged, beheaded, and quartered. I was actually obliged to bring in and push a Bill through Parliament (against which he petitioned) to sanction the conditional pardon; and under this he is still an exile in the southern hemisphere.[1] But, upon a satisfactory conviction in a real and serious case of high treason, I am clearly of opinion that capital punishment is proper. The temptation to ambitious and unprincipled men to engage in revolutionary plans which may at once give them power and fame is not adequately met by the mere dread of lengthened imprisonment in case of failure, and one of the conditions on which resistance may be justifiable is that it is successful.

I must now submit to the painful task of exhibiting Mr. Solicitor Copley as a politician. Antigallican Toryism —generated by the French Revolution—although near its end, was still in morbid vigor, and exhibited most alarming and revolting symptoms. The old genuine Tories I very much respect. They carried to excess their desire of defending what they considered the just privileges of the Church and prerogative of the Crown, but they were by no means hostile to an improvement in our institutions. They stood up for triennial Parliaments, and from the Treaty of Utrecht to that concluded by Mr. Pitt with France, in 1787, they always supported the cause of " free trade " against the Protectionist Whigs.

The terror of innovation inspired by the French Revolution entirely changed the nature of the Tories, and made them passionately cherish every abuse. Lord Eldon, the Chancellor, was the venerable impersonation of this perverted Toryism; and he still held uncontrolled sway.

[1] August, 1858. He has since received a free pardon, and been permitted to return to Ireland, where on account of his folly, he is harmless.

The consequence was, a violent conflict between public opinion and the authority of the Government. Discontent sometimes broke out in licentious publications from the press, and sometimes in tumultuary assemblages of the people. These were met, not by concession and reform, but by a furious extension of the criminal law and by military execution. Now came the "Manchester Massacre," or the "Battle of Peterloo,"[1] when a meeting which was certainly unlawful was as certainly dispersed by unlawful means and with unnecessary cruelty. However, all the excesses of magistrates and soldiers were defended and eulogized by the Secretary of State, and Parliament was suddenly summoned to pass new laws in restraint of public liberty. In the debate on the Address to the Prince Regent Mr. Solicitor took a prominent part, boldly justifying all that had been done at Manchester by the civil and military authorities, and asking whether it could be supposed that his learned friend the Attorney-General and himself had advised his Majesty's ministers to resort to martial violence against the people? Mr. Scarlett calmly answered, that "from all he had known of his honorable and learned friend he believed him incapable of such conduct, *unless, indeed, his opinions had lately undergone a very material change.*"[2]

The famous SIX ACTS were passed. Fortunately, they have all long ago either expired or been repealed. While they were upon the Statute-Book the Constitution was suspended, oral discussion was interfered with not only at county meetings but in debating clubs and philosophical societies, and no man could venture to write upon political or theological subjects except at the peril of being transported beyond the seas as a felon.

These Acts were carried through the House of Commons by Copley. Gifford was still Attorney-General, but had not nerve for heading the encounter, he, too, having in his youth professed liberal principles, although with much more moderation than his colleague. On the second reading of "The Seditious Meetings Prevention Bill," they resorted to the expedient of Mr. Solicitor apologizing for his coming forward as leader to explain and support it in a very elaborate speech, by pretending that the task unexpectedly de-

[1] So called from the place near Manchester where the meeting was held.
[2] 41 Hansard, 173.

volved upon him from the sudden indisposition of his honorable and learned colleague, which he had only heard of since he came into the House. On this occasion, Mr. Solicitor resorted to that which had become his favorite theme—the horrors of the French Revolution :—

"It had been said by some honorable gentlemen that the disease was merely local. Good God! was it possible that those by whom such an assertion was made had entirely forgotten what had already occurred in the world? Was all the experience derived from the course and progress of the French Revolution to be lost to the world? Who did not know that at the commencement of that revolution a large part of France was not alienated from the existing Government? Who did not know that it was only in the great manufacturing and populous districts in France that disaffection originally manifested itself, and that to the inertness of the friends of monarchy in the other parts of that kingdom the deplorable consequences that followed were attributable?"

Having observed that the anti-revolutionary measures proposed by the Government could only be judged of properly when viewed as a whole, he went over all the SIX *seriatim*, lauding them as mild when compared with the evils which they were to remedy. Thus he concluded :—

"The gentlemen on the other side were always advising the Ministry to try the effects of conciliation. There was every disposition on the part of Ministers to conciliate the honest, the well-disposed, and the loyal; there was no disposition to exercise coercion on them. But how were Ministers to conciliate these reformers who were drawing the sword against Constitutional authority? It would be weakness to attempt it. They were not men to be conciliated. To offer conciliation would be to succumb—would be to give a triumph to the disaffected, and an encourgement to them to rally round the banners of sedition."[1]

In a subsequent debate on what was called " The Blasphemous Libel Bill," the Marquis of Tavistock alluded to the manner in which the Solicitor-General in his *former*, perhaps he might call them his *less prudent days*, had indulged in expressing his feelings:—

[1] 41 Hansard, 607.

Mr. Solicitor-General.—" I would ask the noble Lord on what grounds he brings charges against me for my former conduct? Why am I taunted with inconsistency? I never, before my entrance into this House, belonged to any political society, or was in any way connected with politics; and even if I had intended to connect myself with any party, I confess that during my short parliamentary experience I have seen nothing in the *views* of the gentlemen opposite to induce me to join them." [1]

This harangue was delivered from the Treasury Bench, and was received with derision by the Whig leaders to whom it was addressed. At the conclusion Mackintosh whispered to Lord John Russell, who sat next to him, " The last sentence, with the change of one word for a synonyme, would have been perfectly true. But, instead of quarreling with our *views*, he should have said that he did not like our *prospects*." [2]

Although what Copley said of his not being actually an admitted member of any political party before he entered Parliament was true to the letter, he was aware that all who heard him knew he was gainsaying all the opinions and sentiments which he had before entertained and expressed; and that he would have supported with equal zeal measures, if possible, more obnoxious at the will of the Minister. He was accordingly compared to the mercenary soldier, ready to obey every command of his superior officer, and exclaiming :—

" Pectore si fratris gladium juguloque parentis
   Condere me jubeas . . .
     . . . invita peragam tamen omnia dextra."

The Bills were all carried by large majorities, and for a time we could not be said to live in a free country. But an explosion was at hand, which, when it burst forth, caused the Six Acts to be forgotten.

On the 30th of January, 1820, died George III., in the sixtieth year of his reign. As he had long been civilly dead,—although his effigy was still placed upon the coin, and the government was administered in his name,—this event would have caused little sensation, and would hardly have produced any change in the aspect of public affairs, had it not been that, while the power of the Regent

---
[1] 41 Hansard, 1438.
[2] Lord John Russell's preface to vol. vi. of his " Life of Moore."

(become George IV.) remained as it was, Caroline of Brunswick was now Queen of England, and, unless some proceedings were instituted against her, entitled to all the rights and privileges of that exalted station.

Her husband, who would sooner have renounced his throne than shared it with her, had been collecting evidence to prove her guilty of conjugal infidelity, and now intimated that this would immediately be brought forward against her, unless she would consent to live abroad, as a private individual, upon a liberal allowance to be settled upon her. Having rejected this offer with contempt, she entered London amidst the plaudits of the populace, and his Majesty declared war against her by laying a green bag, containing the crimnatory evidence, on the table of both Houses of Parliament.

In the scandalous and ill-judged proceedings which followed, Copley was not at all to blame. He was not consulted on the expediency of bringing the Queen to an open trial; he never spoke upon the subject in the House of Commons, and when the Divorce Bill was introduced into the House of Lords, he strictly confined himself to his professional duty as an advocate, in trying to prove the allegation of adultery which the preamble of the Bill contained. The Queen's Attorney and Solicitor-General having obtained leave from the House of Commons to appear at the bar of the House of Lords as advocates against the Bill, similar leave was given to the King's Attorney and Solicitor-General to support it.

In the forensic contest which ensued, Copley appeared to great advantage compared with Gifford, his colleague, who, though naturally acute and shrewd, now lamentably exposed his defective education, and proved that his sudden and unexpected rise was a mere frolic of fortune.[1]

Copley chiefly distinguished himself in the reply. This, upon the whole, greatly delighted the King, although his Majesty was somewhat offended by the banter and *persiflage* in which the counsel occasionally indulged to a degree hardly suitable to the solemnity of the occasion and the dignity of the royal personages on whose conduct

---

[1] I regret to be obliged to speak thus slightingly of a very amiable man. To him no blame was to be imputed in any part of his career. He received his various promotions without solicitation or intrigue, and although they were *jobs*, they were the jobs of others, to whom his elevation was convenient.

he commented. His chief resource was to excite the jaded attention, and to chase the growing ennui of his hearers, by humorous quotations and striking analogies. In pressing the topic of the rapid promotion of Bergami, by the Queen, from being a common courier, wearing livery, to a high office in her household, he asked:—

"Is it possible that we can shut our eyes to the inference which must of necessity be drawn? What are the services thus rewarded? One of the best dramatic authors, in speaking upon subjects of this kind, has given us this solution; for your Lordships will find that it is put into the mouth of a Roman Empress in a situation, and under circumstances, which I will not describe:—

> ' Thread-bare chastity
> Was poor in the advancement of her creatures;
> Wantonness—magnificent.' "

In commenting upon the fact that, in traveling, Bergami's room in the hotels they visited was always next hers, and on the explanation of her counsel, that it was for her protection, and to guard against surprise, Copley thus raised a rather indecorous laugh:—

"Oh! all this was intended to guard against surprise against some danger with which she was threatened. Are we to be led away by the confident assertions of counsel? I look around to see whether I can possibly discover to what my learned friend refers, or from what source he takes the idea of a 'surprise.' I have not been able to discover it, except in a grave author with whose writings I know him to be very conversant. In Foote's 'Trip to Calais,' I see something like a hint for this. *Miniken*, the chambermaid, and *O'Donovan*, the Irish chairman, are discussing the extraordinary friendship of Sir Henry Hornby for their mistress, and the *protection*, he afforded her, which had caused much scandal, but which thus he explains away:—

"'My Lord was obliged to go about his affairs into the North for a moment, and left his disconsolate lady behind him in London.'

"*Miniken*.—'Poor gentlewoman!'

"*O'Donovan*.—'Upon which his friend Sir Henry used to go and stay there all day, to amuse and divert her!'

"*Miniken*.—'How good-natured that was in Sir Henry!'

O'Donovan.—'Nay; he carried his friendship much

farther than that; for my Lady, as there were many highwaymen and footpads about, was afraid that some of them should break into the house in the night, and so desired Sir Henry Hornby to be there every night.'

"*Miniken.*—'Good soul! and I suppose he consented.' "

The Solicitor-General's speech, which lasted two days, was thus concluded:—

"In retiring from your Lordships' bar we should be guilty of the greatest ingratitude if we did not make to your Lordships our acknowledgments for the kindness which we have experienced at your Lordships' hands. Never came a cause into a Court of Justice in which there was so much anxiety with respect to every step in its progress, and with respect to its final result. Every passion has been successfully appealed to in the conduct of the defense by my learned friends on the other side. They have well and faithfully discharged their duty to their illustrious client. We make no complaint of their conduct. We rejoice to see such talents exercised in the defense of a Queen of England. My Lords, my learned friends have endeavored to awaken successively all the sympathies and all the passions of your nature. They have even appealed to the basest of all passions—the passion of fear. In his high and august assembly, the *élite*, if I may so express myself, of a nation renowned for its firmness and intrepidity, my learned friends have appealed to the passion of fear. You are told by one of my learned friends that if you pass this Bill into a law, you will commit an act of suicide. Another of my learned friends tells you that 'you are to pass the Bill at your peril!' These words hung upon the lips of my learned friend for a time sufficiently long to be understood; and they were afterwards affectedly withdrawn. I know, my Lords, that you will not dare to do anything that is unjust. At the same time I know that what justice requires you will do, without regard to any personal consideration that may affect yourselves. But, my Lords, it is not in this place alone that these arts have been resorted to. The same course has been pursued out of doors; the same threats have been held out, and every attempt has been made to overawe and intimidate the decision of your Lordships. Even the name of her Majesty herself has been profaned for this purpose. In her name, but undoubtedly without her sanction, attacks of the most direct nature have been made against all that is sacred and venerable in this empire—against the constitution—against the sovereign —against the hierarchy—against all orders of the State. My Lords, this could not proceed from her Majesty. Her name must have been made use of by persons aiming, under the sanction and shield of that name, at some dark and pernicious designs. Believing otherwise, my Lords, we must imagine that her Majesty was aiming at the overthrow of the government of the country, to be replaced by revolutionary anarchy —

> —— dum Capitolio
> Regina dementes ruinas,
> Funus et imperio parabat

might in that case become a new era with our posterity. My Lords, if, having considered the whole case, you should have the strongest conviction on your minds that the Queen is guilty of the charges which are imputed to her in this Bill, but you should think that in strictness there is not legal proof on which you can judicially act, I admit that you must adopt the language suggested by my learned friend Mr. Denman, and say, 'GO AND SIN NO MORE.' But, my Lords, if, bending your minds earnestly to the contemplation of the evidence, and drawing from it as Judges, as men of understanding and men of honor, its just and legitimate conclusion, the case is made out so strongly, so fully, and in a manner so satisfactory as to leave no reasonable doubt upon your Lordships' minds, then, my Lords, knowing what I do of the tribunal I am now addressing, I am sure you will pronounce your decision on this momentous question with that firmness which is consonant with your exalted station."[1]

I need not mention that, although the second reading of the bill was carried by a small majority, it was afterwards withdrawn by the ministers, to the great disgust of the Sovereign, who had ever after a grudge against them, and a liking for Copley, in return for his vigorous support of it.[2]

---

[1] Hansard, N. S., vol. iii. See "Lives of Chancellors," vol. vii. chap. 204.
[2] On the reassembling of Parliament in January, 1821, Copley further showed his zeal on the King's side, by a speech against the motion to censure the omission of the Queen's name from the Liturgy, saying, "His impression was, that no person could agree with the present motion without being alike an enemy to the monarch and the monarchy." A motion was made to take

No change took place in the law offices under the Government for the three following years. During this period Copley spoke in the House of Commons not unfrequently, but it was only officially, as was expected of an Attorney or Solicitor-General in the old *régime*, in defending all arbitrary acts of the executive Government, and opposing all attempts to improve our laws. He was particularly zealous in denouncing Sir James Mackintosh's Bill for taking away capital punishment from the offense of forgery; and in an elaborate speech he tried to prove that such a measure would be fatal to paper credit, and to the commerce of the country.[1] Than such an exhibition nothing can more strikingly illustrate the odiousness of the system of government which happily was then drawing to a close, for Copley himself was enlightened and humane, and when he was at liberty to act according to his own feelings, without offending his superiors or endangering his own advancement, he was disposed to take the liberal side on every question, and to assist in mitigating the barbarous severity of our penal code.

At last, on Gifford succeeding Sir Vicary Gibbs as Chief Justice of the Common Pleas, Copley became Attorney-General. Since the time of Thurlow and Wedderburn no Attorney-General has been in the House of Commons so prominent a member of the Government. Yet, after a diligent search in Hansard, I can find no speech of his at this period of his career which would now be found interesting.

The topic which then agitated the public, and on which the people, and the Parliament, and the Cabinet were nearly equally divided, was "Catholic Emancipation." This topic Copley as yet had cautiously avoided, uncertain which side was likely to prevail. There were very contradictory rumors respecting the private inclinations of George IV. The Duke of York, heir presumptive to the crown, had publicly made a vow that he never would consent to the measure—but his life was considered very precarious, and there was little chance of his surviving the reigning sovereign. Lord Liverpool, the Prime Minister, although he had steadily opposed further

---

down these words; but they were explained away so as, without spoiling their pith, to get rid of the charge of being disorderly.—*Hansard*, vol. iv. 199.

[1] Hansard, N. S., v. 895.

concession to the Catholics, had done so with much moderation, and he had allowed their admission to Parliament to be an "open question." Lords Eldon and Peel were staunch anti-Catholics; but the former was declining fast in political influence, and the latter had given alarming signs of a tendency to liberalism. On the other hand, Canning, leader of the House of Commons since the death of Lord Castlereagh, with a rising reputation, was a zealous and sincere emancipator. If Copley had acted according to his own secret wishes, he would have both voted and spoken for the bill to allow Roman Catholics to sit in Parliament, as well as for the more limited measure to allow Roman Catholic Peers to sit in the House of Lords. However, he considered the more prudent course to give an anti-Catholic vote, without committing himself by a speech,—taking care in private conversation to intimate that he had no decided opinions upon the subject, and that a change of circumstances might justify a change of policy.

He still resisted all reforms of the law proposed by opposition members. Thus the bill for allowing counsel to address the jury in cases of felony he denounced as unnecessary and dangerous. "At present," he said, "the Judge is of counsel for the accused in trials for felony. But if the counsel for the defense were to make a speech full of inflammation and exaggeration, which must inevitably happen, then it would be replied upon by the Judge in his charge, and he would thus become of counsel against the prisoner."[1] So he urged very forcibly all the fallacious arguments which in a subsequent stage of his career, when law reform had become popular, he as forcibly refuted, calling forth the remark that he had made the best speech against, and the best speech for the Bill.

During all the time that he was Attorney-General, he never filed a single information ex-officio for a libel. With Lord Castlereagh died the system of trying to govern by terror. Some of the Six Acts expired without any attempt to continue them, and the others became a dead letter. This change is to be ascribed mainly to the more enlightened views of Canning, who was now rapidly gaining the ascendant, being warmly supported by Huskisson, who had been introduced into the Cabinet to the

[1] Hansard, N. S., xi. 207; xv. 596.

great disgust of Lord Eldon, while Peel, the Home Secretary, was beginning himself to set up for a law reformer, and on all subjects except Catholic emancipation was alarming the *optimists*, who thought that our institutions at the close of the reign of George III. had reached a state of absolute perfection. If Copley had been directed to file as many criminal informations as Sir Vicary Gibbs, who placed widows and old maids on the floor of the Court of King's Bench to receive sentence for political libels published in newspapers which they had never read, because they received annuities secured on the profits of the newspapers aforesaid, I fear me he would have obeyed, and would have produced very plausible reasons to justify what he did ; but I believe that he had sincere pleasure in following the mild course towards the press which distinguished his Attorney-Generalship, being swayed both by his natural good-humor and by a reasonable conviction that, unless " libels " contain some direct insult to religion, or some direct incitement to violate the law, the state prosecutor had better leave them to be answered and refuted by the press, or quietly drop into neglect.

Chancery reform (as afterwards in 1852) was now the great subject of agitation. Lord Eldon, in his own court and in the judicial department of the House of Lords, had allowed arrears to accumulate which could not be cleared off in the lifetime of the litigants; and to expose this abuse the opposition were frequently moving for returns and for committees of inquiry. The staff of Judges to dispose of equity business was certainly insufficient, and much of the delay so grievously complained of arose from the absurd system, now happily exploded, of the Judge before whom a cause was heard referring it to another Judge, called a " Master in Chancery," with perpetual appeals and fresh references between them. Lord Eldon, however, was personally answerable for unnecessary and culpable " cunctation," as he called it, in protracting the arguments of counsel and in deferring judgment from day to day, from term to term, and from year to year, after the arguments had closed and he had irrevocably decided in his own mind what the judgment should be. His colleagues in the Cabinet were fully aware of his infirmity, and would have been well pleased to be rid of him. But they knew that he had great authority with the King, and that the "Church-and-King" party looked up to him as their head; so that any affront to him might be fatal to the existing administration. Copley had a nice game to play. The administration was to be upheld, for he would have been overwhelmed in in its ruins;· but Lord Eldon, as far as was consistent with that object, was to be *villipended*, so that at the first convenient opportunity he might be got rid of, and a fit successor might take his place. Lord Eldon, knowing that in spite of long cunctation, "that fell Sergeant Death" would, ere long, be "strict in his arrest," destined as his successor his humble favorite Gifford, and looked suspiciously on Copley, who not only had been a Jacobin, but had acquired a high position in the House of Commons as an anti-Jacobin, and was now ready, as pro-Catholic or anti-Catholic, to avail himself of the first favorable opportunity of clutching the Great Seal.

In private Mr. Attorney talked with the most undisguised and unmitigated scorn of the Lord Chancellor. In the House of Commons he applied to the "venerable Judge" all the epithets which courtesy required; but he only came forward in his defense when forced so to do by official etiquette, and then he lavished upon him praise strongly seasoned with sarcasm.

To stave off the repeated motions for Chancery reform, a commission had been appointed, which after sitting two years, had made a report recommending certain improvements in the procedure of the Court of Chancery. Copley's last performance in the House of Commons as Attorney-General was to introduce a Bill founded on this report. After a very luminous exposition of the flagrancy of the existing system—irresistibly suggesting the question, *Why had it been allowed to exist so long?*—he said, " He would not venture to expatiate upon the merits of the present Chancellor, a theme above his power; he would content himself with reminding the House of the panegyric lately pronounced on the noble and learned Lord by a learned member, who had eloquently dwelt upon the artlessness and simplicity of his mind and of his manners, his singular disinterestedness, and his readiness to sacrifice his love of retirement to the discharge of his official duties." [1] The Bill, having been read a first time,

[1] Hansard, N. S., vol. xv. p. 1228.

was allowed to languish till Lord Eldon had resigned the Great Seal to Lord Lyndhurst.

But we have still some notice to take of our hero before he reached this elevation. While Attorney General he continued the second in practice in Westminster Hall, though still at a long distance from Scarlett, who, by his own merits and the partiality of Lord Tenterden, was decidedly the first. At this time no state trial nor *cause célèbre* of any sort arose, and I have in vain looked for any further producible specimen of Copley's forensic eloquence. He was wonderfully clear and forcible; but he could not make the tender chords of the heart vibrate, having nothing in unison with them in his own bosom. He was more solicitous about the effect he might produce while speaking than about the ultimate result of the trial. Therefore he was unscrupulous in his statement of facts when opening his case to the jury, more particularly when he knew that he was to leave the court at the conclusion of his address, on the plea of attending to public business elsewhere. I was often his junior, and on one of these occasions, when he was stating a triumphant defense, which we had no evidence to prove, I several times plucked him by the gown and tried to check him. Having told the jury that they were bound to find a verdict in his favor, he was leaving the court; but I said, "No! Mr. Attorney, you must stay and examine the witnesses; I can not afford to bear the discredit of losing the verdict from my seeming incompetence: if you go, I go." He then dexterously offered a reference—to which the other side, taken in by his bold opening, very readily assented.[1]

Strange to say, although he had an eye to the woolsack, he would not be tempted by any fee to go into the Court of Chancery as counsel, nor would he take a brief in Scotch appeals in the House of Lords. For gaining the

---

[1] It was related that Clarke, the leader of the Midland Circuit (under whom Copley was reared), having in the middle of his opening speech observed a negotiation going on for the settlement of the cause, stated confidently an important fact which he had imagined at the moment. When all was over, his attorney afterwards said to him privately, "Sir, don't you think we have got very good terms? but you rather went beyond my instructions." "You fool," cried he, "how do you suppose you could have got such terms if I had stuck to your instructions?" But in the case in the text, Copley had entertained no ulterior view beyond making a dashing speech, and leaving poor Campbell to lose the verdict.

object of his ambition he trusted entirely to politics, and, if asked how he expected to be able to dispose of "demurrers for want of equity," and "exceptions to the Master's Report," and how he should know whether to affirm or reverse interlocutors of the Court of Session he would gayly exclaim, "*Alors comme alors.*"

About this time he was so much petted by the high Tories that he had some vague notion of cutting the profession of the law altogether and accepting a political office, in the hope that he might succeed Lord Liverpool; and, with the addition of fixed principles, he certainly would have been far better qualified than Perceval, who, to the satisfaction of his party, had become Prime Minister from being Attorney-General. Copley had a much better stock of general information and superior oratorical powers, with fascinating manners, which made him a general favorite. He now more than ever affected the man of fashion, and when he took a trip to Paris was flattered with any raillery which supposed that he indulged in all the gayeties of that dissipated capital. By driving himself about the streets of London in a smart cabriolet, with a "tiger" behind, he greatly shocked Lord Eldon, who exclaimed, " What would my worthy old master, George III., have thought of me, had he heard of his Attorney-General comporting himself like a prodigal young heir dissipating a great fortune?" I know not whether Copley had any view to the Foreign Office, for I never heard him say so; but he particularly cultivated the *corps diplomatique*, who were constantly to be seen at his table and at Lady Copley's receptions. She now weeded her visiting-book almost entirely of lawyers, and their wives and daughters; but he, by his *bonhomie*, or rather his *abandon*, contrived to keep up his popularity with all ranks. A proof of this was, that, becoming a candidate to represent the University of Cambridge in Parliament, he was warmly supported by lawyers—Tory, Whig, and Radical—and he was triumphantly returned. Luckily, he had not to make a speech, nor to publish addresses to the constituents; so that even when he took his seat as the representative of a body strongly opposed to Catholic emancipation, he was at liberty to espouse either side, without the open scandal of inconsistency.

But events were thickening which determined him to

declare himself a strong anti-Catholic. Lord Gifford, who had conformed himself in all things to Lord Eldon's views, had been the destined anti-Catholic Chancellor. But in the beginning of September, 1826, this worthy person, whose rise had been so extraordinary, suddenly died, making a vacancy in the office of Master of the Rolls, and in the reversion of anti-Catholic Lord Chancellor. Lord Eldon wished much that Sir Charles Wetherell, then Solicitor-General, whose notions about Church and State exactly agreed with his own, should succeed him. Of Copley, the bigoted ultra-Tory had an utter horror; for in dreams he had seen this rival snatching the Great Seal from his hand, and heard him delivering a harangue in favor of the Roman Catholics.

Lord Liverpool, full well knowing the Chancellor's sentiments on this subject, thus cautiously addressed him:—

"You will, of course, have heard the melancholy and unexpected death of Lord Gifford. He is a very great loss, at this time, both public and private. I promise you that I will speak to no one on the subject till I have seen you. Having, however, received an account, yesterday, of Lord Gifford's extreme danger, it was impossible I should not turn in my mind, during the night, what was to arise, if we were so unfortunate as to lose him. I confess to you, the present inclination of my mind is that the Attorney-General should be *made* to accept the Mastership of the Rolls. He has no competitor at the bar, at least on our side, nor any one on the Bench who can compete with him for the highest honors of the profession. Indeed, I know not what else can be done which would not increase all prospective difficulties to an immense degree.

"Do not return any answer to this letter; but turn it well over in your mind, and let us talk of it when we meet to-morrow."

Lord Eldon, in great consternation, wrote a "most private and confidential" letter to Sir Robert Peel, in which, after mentioning Lord Gifford's death, and observing that "the prejudice created against him in the public mind was generated by the industry of some who envied his rapid professional advancement, more than by any other assignable cause," he thus proceeds:—

"Of course the Minister is now looking for a successor

—he naturally looks to Copley. I doubt extremely whether he will accept the office of Master of the Rolls, even with the prospect of possessing the Great Seal. His professional emoluments must be very great—the object for him naturally to look to is the King's Bench, and report as to the health of the Chief Justice does not represent the prospect of obtaining that object as at a distance. I have stated to Lord Liverpool—who has conducted himself to me, as to this, very respectfully—my apprehensions that he will decline the Rolls. He ought not, perhaps—yet a man of his eminence in that part of the profession in which he has been engaged may probably feel unwilling to go into a Court of Equity as a Judge, never having been in one as a counsel, and especially in that Equity Court in which much business is rather business of form than requiring the exercise of a powerful intellect. He has always refused briefs in Scotch causes, which looks as if his views were directed to the King's Bench, and not to the office of Chancellor, who must hear so many Scotch causes."

The object of this letter was to persuade Sir Robert Peel that Copley was not fit for the office of Master of the Rolls, or of Chancellor, and to induce him to interfere to bring about another arrangement; but the attempt wholly failed, and in a subsequent letter to his confidant, Lord Eldon says:

"With respect to Copley he accepted the office, and, it appeared to me, without any doubt about accepting it. Indeed, though I doubted whether he would accept, as he never had been in a Court of Equity at all, and never would take a brief in a Scotch cause, yet, considering that the Chancellorship and the Chief Justiceship of the King's Bench may be soon open,—and on the other hand, the change of Administration may not be a thing so impossible in the meantime as to make the acceptance a foolish thing of an office and income worth £8,000 a-year for life, which may be accepted without prejudice to his moving to either of the above offices, if they happen to be vacant in due time,—I think he has acted very prudently, especially taking into the account that he goes to school in the lower form (the Rolls) to qualify him to remove into the higher, if he takes the Chancellorship."

In truth, Copley never did hesitate one moment in accepting the offer, although clogged with the condition that he must not for the present ask a peerage. Lord Eldon had pointed out the impossibility of his sitting, as Gifford had done, and presiding as Deputy Speaker in the decision of appeals. This point was conceded by Lord Liverpool to Lord Eldon, who undertook to get through the appeals with the assistance of Alexander, C.B., and Vice-Chancellor Leach. They were both well acquainted with Scotch law, and he suggested that, though commoners, they might be appointed to act as Deputy Speakers, and in fact give judgment in the name of the House, although they could not give any reason for the decision.[1] Copley felt that for him to have attempted to speak *ex cathedrâ* on the Scotch tenure "*a me vel de me*" would only have exposed him to ridicule, whereby his power of supplanting Lord Eldon might be materially impaired; whereas, by remaining in the House of Commons as Master of the Rolls, he would acquire new weight there, and might be ready at any favorable moment to give the *coup de grace* to the condemned Chancellor.

On the first day of Michaelmas Term, 1826, he appeared at the Chancellor's levée in a gold-embroidered gown as Master of the Rolls. He looked a little abashed, for hitherto this office had generally been declined by aspiring Attorney-Generals as being considered rather a comfortable shelf for second-rate men; but he soon recovered his air of self-satisfaction and hilarity, conscious to himself that he was playing a deep and a sure game.

Of his judicial performances as Master of the Rolls hardly a vestige remains. They ought to be found in "Russell's Chancery Reports," but there, although his name is mentioned, no decision of his of the slightest importance is recorded. The gossip of the profession during the short period when he continued Master of the Rolls, was that "he sat as seldom as possible, and rose as early as possible, and did as little as possible." Yet he showed his tact and cleverness by avoiding all scrapes

---

[1] This attempt led to very anomalous and inconvenient consequences, and will never be repeated. Leach, as he could not make a speech in the House, used to get the counsel and solicitors into a committee-room, and there state to them his reasons for the judgment of the House. He might just as well have assembled a mob around him in Palace Yard and parodied the giving of a judgment or any other proceeding of the House of Lords.

into which he might have fallen, and by keeping the bar and the solicitors in good humor.

His whole energies were now absorbed in political intigue. The death of the Duke of York in January, 1827, after having vowed eternal hostility (whether as subject or sovereign) to Catholic emancipation, caused some doubts and misgivings to his Honor, the Master of the Rolls, who was further told that the life of George IV. had become very precarious, and that the Duke of Clarence, now heir presumptive, had come round to the side of the Roman Catholics. But a crisis unexpectedly arose to confirm the anti-Catholic propensities which his Honor had confidentially disclosed during his canvass for the University, and induced him publicly and solemnly to proclaim himself a determined and unchangeable anti-Catholic. In February, 1827, Lord Liverpool, the Prime Minister, was suddenly struck down by apoplexy, and although he continued to breathe for some months, it was known that his public career was at an end. A terrible collision immediately took place between pro-Catholics and anti-Catholics. The King laid down as the basis of the new government that there should be a majority of anti-Catholics in the Cabinet, and *that he should have an anti-Catholic keeper of his conscience*, but that emancipation should still be "an open question." This was acquiesced in by all parties, and it was absolutely settled that, whoever the Prime Minister might be, there was, at all events, to be an anti-Catholic Lord Chancellor. Copley said to himself and his intimates, "I am the man." The rivals for the premiership were Peel and Canning. The former, indeed, said he was willing to continue to serve as Home Secretary under some anti-Catholic peer if any one of sufficient reputation to succeed Lord Liverpool could be discovered—which he knew to be impossible. Canning openly and resolutely claimed the premiership, but Peel vowed that under a pro-Catholic premier he would not serve. Lady Conyngham, who now ruled the King, favored Canning, and a detachment of Whigs, on account of Canning's liberal principles, were ready to coalesce with him.

Although the struggle was going on many weeks, the business in parliament proceeded without any public notice being taken of Lord Liverpool's illness. Copley again brought in the Bill for reforming the Court of Chancery, in which no progress had been made during the last session, and he now took a bolder tone in pointing out existing abuses and in creating amazement that so consummate a Judge as Lord Eldon should so long have tolerated them,—insinuating the inference that they could only be remedied under other auspices.

But his Honor's great object was to show himself to the King and to the country, although no longer disinclined to reform our civil institutions, and so far in harmony with Canning and his Whig recruits, yet—in religion—a stern, uncompromising, and inflexible ultra-Protestant. A very favorable opportunity for this was afforded by Plunket's motion, on the 6th of March, for removing the disabilities of his Majesty's Roman Catholic subjects. Copley having taken immense pains to prepare himself, and resolutely determined to despise any sneers that might be excited by his sudden conversion from Jacobinism to bigotry, spoke at great length on the second night of the debate, immediately following Lord Eliot (afterwards the Earl of St. Germans and Lord-Lieutenant of Ireland), who had frankly declared that, although he had hitherto voted against the Catholics, he had from recent events come to the conclusion that their emancipation could no longer be withheld.

Master of the Rolls.—" I give the noble Lord who has just sat down the fullest credit for the manliness of conduct which he has displayed on this occasion. The manner in which the avowal has been made is as creditable to the noble Lord as the avowal itself. For myself, as the representative of a numerous and highly distinguished body of constitutents who have considered maturely and thought deeply, even intensely, in this crisis of our religion—I trust that I may be permitted to state to the House their opinions, in which I fully concur.[1] We are indeed standing in a great crisis. The eyes of the country are fixed upon the present deliberations. The great mass of the Protestant population of the empire are looking with deep anxiety to the result of

---

[1] This was very skillful and artistic,—to divert, if possible, the attention of the House from himself to his constituents, although he was obliged to say, *sotto voce*, that he concurred in their opinions.

these deliberations. The great mass of the Catholic population of Ireland are looking with still more intense feeling of anxiety to the result of these deliberations. Whatever the result may be—if it be arrived at by means of calm consideration and candid debate—by means of fair statement and cool examination—it will be entitled to the acquiescence of the country."

But he speedily alters this placid tone, and exclaims,—

"The Protestants of England are put upon their defense. We are the parties accused. We are charged with intolerance, with religious bigotry, with oppression. Who are our accusers? The professors of the Roman Catholic Religion. They do show that severe laws were made against them, but they altogether pass over the acts by which those laws were rendered necessary. Without wishing to excite any bad or angry feelings I must ask the House to consider the circumstances under which these laws were enacted. Was it upon mere speculation—upon conjectural fears—upon remote apprehensions of danger—that the Acts of Elizabeth were passed for keeping in subjection the Roman Catholics? The men by whom they were proposed and enacted had been observers of the short but eventful reign of Mary. Some of them had been sufferers from the religious violence of those times. All of them had been witnesses of the persecutions in the Netherlands and of the treacherous massacres in France. The Roman Catholics of that period were endeavoring day by day to undermine and overturn the constitution of this country, and, in concert with the most tyrannical and bigoted government that ever existed (I mean Spain), to introduce into England a thraldom which our ancestors successfully resisted, and to which I trust we, their descendants, will never submit."

He proceeded at great length to recapitulate the misdeeds of the Roman Catholics down to the Irish massacre of 1641, and asked if it was not natural to guard against the repetition of such outrages. He then came to the attempt to re-introduce Popery in the reign of James II., and justified the penal code of William III. Catholics having already full liberty of worship, he said the only question was "whether they should be admitted to the exercise of political power?" By-and-by he attempted to show the danger of the Inquisition being introduced among us.

"In 1798 the Inquisition was abolished in Spain, in consequence of the French Revolution; but now that cursed, that hated engine of misery and torture, that instrument of cruelty and revenge, was again established in all its original rigor and deformity in Spain and in Italy. I do not mean to say that the Inquisition will be established in Ireland: no; but nevertheless the Catholic religion is still unchanged, and the same power to effect mischief is still in existence. You are assembled by the King's writ commanding you to consider matters relating to the interests of the State and of the Protestant Church; and thus assembled, you are called upon to admit as members of a Protestant legislature, deliberating upon matters connected with the safety of the Church of England, a body of Roman Catholics hostile to that Church, and hostile to it from their principles as Roman Catholics. I regret to say there are in this House some lukewarm and indifferent to the interests of the established Church, and there are some in this House who are actuated by feelings of enmity towards the Church—although their number be small compared to those who cordially love and support it. But small as the number of enemies may be, is it prudent to add to their number? All who love the Church of England, therefore, are bound to reject this motion. Instead of tranquillizing, the measure, if carried, would convulse Ireland. The Catholics would triumph in their victory, and the Protestants would repine in the consciousness that they were subdued. A momentary calm would be followed by a frightful explosion, and by permanent anarchy. The Roman Catholic religion is a religion of encroachment, and there are circumstances connected with its existence in Ireland which increase the disposition to encroach. Then claim would be made after claim till Catholic ascendancy is completely established."

He concluded this speech, of which I have only given a few extracts and an imperfect outline, by boldly claiming credit for *sincerity!*

"It is not improbable," said he, "that I may be followed by my right honorable friend the Attorney-General for Ireland [Plunket]. There is not any man who pos-

sesses greater powers, or who can use them more forcibly
for the advantage of the cause which he espouses. I
admire the earnestness with which he has entered into
this question; but while I pay this deserved tribute to
his talent and his zeal, I trust that he will give me equal
credit for the *sincerity* with which I entertain the opinions
I have expressed." [1]

He sat down amidst some cheers and a great deal of
tittering.

In truth, if he had any opinions on the subject, they
were known to be on the other side of the question, and
he had now spoken literally, as at *Nisi Prius*, from a brief;
for all the historical facts and arguments which he had
used were to be found nearly in the same order in a very
able pamphlet recently published by Dr. Philpotts, then
Prebendary of Durham, now Bishop of Exeter. Before
Copley concluded, the plagiarism was detected by several
members, and a stanza from a well-known song was whispered through the House :—

> " Dear Tom, this brown jug which now foams with mild ale,
> Out of which I now drink to sweet Nan of the Vale,
> Was once Toby Philpotts'."

Before long, Copley spoke his own real sentiments in
supporting the Duke of Wellington's Bill for Catholic
emancipation. There is no denying that, on the present
occasion, he acted with a view to the Great Seal as his
immediate reward. And he succeeded. George IV.
set him down as a thorough anti-Catholic, and was quite
willing to surrender to him the keeping of his conscience.
Canning was a good deal shocked by some of the topics
which Copley had resorted to, but comforted himself with
the reflection that, when in a situation to carry emancipation, a rotatory Chancellor would be no obstacle in his
way.

The negotiations were still long protracted, but no reputable anti-Catholic peer being found for premier, the
King, on the 10th of April, commissioned Canning to form
a new administration. Lord Eldon, thinking that Can-

---

[1] 16 Hansard, N. S., 92. I still remained on very familiar terms with him,
and meeting him next evening, freely expressed to him my astonishment at
his speech. His only answer was, "You will see that I am quite right."
From this time our personal intercourse almost entirely ceased, till I myself
became a member of the House of Peers, when we talked together as freely
and recklessly as ever.

ning, the new minister, could not stand, tendered his resignation. This was immediately accepted, and Copley, without any affectation or coyness, frankly and joyfully agreed to be his successor. The Great Seal, however, remained some time in Lord Eldon's custody, that he might give judgment in various cases which had been argued before him.

Meanwhile, Copley was raised to the peerage by the title of Baron Lyndhurst of Lyndhurst, in the county of Southampton. Everyone, foe or friend, had a fling at him; but, on account of his brilliant talents and his delightful manners, the appointment was by no means unpopular.

CHAPTER CCXVII.

LORD CHANCELLOR UNDER CANNING, LORD GODERICH, AND THE DUKE OF WELLINGTON.

NEVER was there a greater contrast than between the *ousted* and *incoming* Chancellor, both in their intellectual faculties and in their acquirements; above all, with respect to what is called *humbug;*—for the one, thinking that mankind was governed by it, was always making professions of honesty and became his own dupe; while the other, being of opinion that by despising all pretenses to political principles he should best make his way in the world, affected to be worse than he really was, and excited doubts as to his faults by exaggerating them. Both these extraordinary men were too good-natured to foster actual hatred of each other, but that they formed a very low estimate of each other's moral qualities they took no pains to conceal. Yet the forms of courtesy were duly preserved between them. When Lord Eldon had delivered his judgments, he wrote a very respectful letter to Lord Lyndhurst, congratulating him on his elevation, and inquiring when it would be convenient that the transfer of the Great Seal should take place. The following was the becoming answer:—

"George Street, April 26th.

"My dear Lord,

"I thank your Lordship for your kind congratulations.

With respect to the change of the custody of the Seal, nothing more has been stated to me than a wish that it should take place before the meeting of the House of Lords.[1] I beg your Lordship will, in every particular, consult your own convenience, to which it will be my greatest pleasure to conform. If your Lordship will permit me, I will wait upon you after I have made the necessary inquiries, and inform your Lordship of the result.

"Believe me, my dear Lord (with the deepest sense of your uniform kindness to me), to remain, with unfeigned respect,   Your Lordship's faithful servant,

"LYNDHURST."

The transfer actually did take place at St. James's, on the 30th of April, 1827. Lord Eldon, having delivered it into the King's hands, withdrew—his Majesty expressing deep grief at the loss of such a dear councillor; and, Lord Lyndhurst being called in, received it from the King, with the title of Lord Chancellor, his Majesty expressing his high satisfaction at being able to place it in the hands of one in whom he placed entire confidence.[2]

The 2nd of May was the first day of Easter Term, and the day to which the House of Lords had been adjourned. At twelve o'clock the new Chancellor held a levée at his house in George Street, and went from thence to Westminster Hall, attended by a crowd of nobles, privy councillors, judges, and king's counsel, after the ancient form, except that it was a carriage procession instead of a *cavalcade*. In the Court of Chancery he took the oaths, the new Master of the Rolls holding the book. The oath being recorded, he boldly called over the bar. From his ignorance of the practice, motions might have been made which would have greatly perplexed him; but, according to the etiquette mentioned by Roger North, in his account of the inauguration of Lord Shaftesbury, in the reign of

---

[1] The House of Lords had been adjourned from the 12th April to the 2nd May.

[2] The ceremony is thus described in the "London Gazette:"—

"At the Court at St. James's, the 30th day of April, 1827.

"PRESENT, THE KING'S MOST EXCELLENT MAJESTY IN COUNCIL.

"HIS MAJESTY IN COUNCIL was this day pleased to deliver the Great Seal to the Right Honorable John Singleton Lord Lyndhurst, whereupon the oath of Lord High Chancellor of Great Britain was, by His Majesty's command, administered to his Lordship, and his Lordship took his place at the Board accordingly."

Charles II., nothing was stirred which could alarm a novice in the marble chair; and he rose, whispering with a triumphant smile: "You see how well I get on—Bah! there is nothing in it."

In another performance, which he had to go through immediately after, he was perfect. This was taking his place on the woolsack and being seated as a peer. Upon such occasions he was seen to great advantage; and although he would laugh at them when they were over, he played his part with seriousness and dignity.[1]

Henceforth he was a most distinguished member of this branch of the legislature, and he swayed its deliberations for good and for evil in very critical times. At first he affected to be shy, and he was very reserved. Only twice during the subsistence of Mr. Canning's government does he appear to have addressed their Lordships. The first was in support of a very anomalous measure, to which he was obliged to resort from his ignorance of Scottish jurisprudence. He was himself wholly unqualified to decide appeals from the Court of Session, and the House (at present so rich in law lords, having no fewer than four ex-Chancellors, besides the actual Lord Chancellor and the Chief Justice of the Queen's Bench[2]) could then furnish no law lord who could be asked to do this duty for him, as Lord Eldon could not, with dignity, have acted as the deputy of his successor. The expedient was, to have Alexander,

---

[1] *Extract from the Journals of the House of Lords, 2nd May, 1827:*—

"His Royal Highness the Duke of Clarence acquainted the House that his Majesty had been pleased to create the Right Honorable Sir John Singleton Copley, Knt., Lord Chancellor of that part of the United Kingdom of Great Britain and Ireland called Great Britain, a peer of these realms.

"Whereupon his Lordship, taking in his hand the purse with the Great Seal, retired to the lower end of the House, and, having there put on his robes, was introduced between the Lord Howard de Walden and the Lord King (also in their robes), the Gentleman Usher of the Black Rod, Garter King of Arms and Earl Marshal, and the Deputy Lord Great Chamberlain preceding. His Lordship laid down the patent upon the Chair of State, kneeling, and from thence took and delivered it to the clerk, who read the same at the table, which bears date the 25th day of April, in the eighth year of his present Majesty; whereby is granted to his Lordship and the heirs male of his body the style and title of Baron Lyndhurst, of Lyndhurst, in the County of Southampton. (Writ of Summons read.)

"Then his Lordship, at the table, took the oaths, and made and subscribed the declaration, and also made and subscribed the oath of abjuration pursuant to the statutes; and was afterwards placed on the lower end of the Barons' bench, and from thence went to the upper end of the Earls' bench, and sat there as Lord Chancellor, and then returned to the woolsack."

[2] A. D. 1853.

the Chief Baron, and Leach, the Master of the Rolls, to sit for him by turns, three days in the week; and a commission, authorizing them respectively to act as Speaker, in the absence of the Lord Chancellor, was granted. This practice being objected to by several peers as irregular, and unconstitutional, Lord Chancellor Lyndhurst delivered his maiden speech in defense of it. After showing the immense number of Scotch appeals pending, he said—"he could not devote his own time to them without injury to the suitors in the Court of Chancery. It was indispensably necessary that the Chancellor should sit two days a week in the House of Lords, to hear English and Irish appeals. This arrangement would give him four days for the Court of Chancery—which, he trusted, would be sufficient to keep down the business of that court. If their Lordships would grant him the indulgence which he asked, he pledged himself, before the next session, to perfect a plan with reference to his court which should secure the performance of its duties regularly, faithfully, and efficiently."[1]

This pledge smoothed over the difficulty; but it never was redeemed.[2]

On the other occasion of his speaking while Chancellor under Canning, he showed the liberal tendency which always guided him when he was not biassed by some interested or party motive. A bill was pending, which I had afterwards the satisfaction of carrying through Parliament, for allowing the marriages of Protestant Dissenters, who had conscientious objections to parts of the marriage service in the English liturgy, to be celebrated in their own places of religious worship and before their own pastors. This bill was of course opposed by Lord Eldon; and he denounced certain Bishops who approved of it as little better than infidels. But the new Lord Chancellor supported it very powerfully, showing that, till the Council of Trent, no religious ceremony nor intervention of a priest was necessary to constitute a valid marriage in any part of Europe; that to prohibit the King's subjects from contracting this relation without violating their conscience, was an infringement of their civil and religious rights, and

---

[1] 17 Hansard, N. S., 574.
[2] In his last Chancellorship I myself sat for him two days a week; but this was less objectionable, as I was a member of the House.

that all the State could justly enjoin respecting the ceremony of marriage, was that it be simple, certain, and capable of easy proof. He forcibly dwelt upon the impolicy of making the Establishment odious to a large class of the community, and concluded by observing that the measure would be a relief almost as much to the Church as to the Dissenters.[1] He consented, however, that the bill should stand over till another session.

It was thought cowardly in the Chancellor not to defend more strenuously his chief against the combined efforts of the Duke of Wellington and Lord Grey. The latter, notwithstanding his generally patriotic career, was on this occasion particularly vulnerable; for, although Canning was decidedly liberal both in his foreign and domestic policy, and was supported by Brougham and many Liberals, he was bitterly attacked by the avowed leader of the Whigs, apparently from the dread of being deserted by all the rest of the party. But the Chancellor quickly perceived that, with any exertion he could make to save it, the present Government could not last long, and he did not like to incur the enmity of those who would probably have to construct a new cabinet.

Even if Canning had lived, the combination against him would probably have been too strong to be resisted. Upon his lamented death it was seen that either the Duke of Wellington or Lord Grey must soon be Prime Minister.

Lyndhurst openly laughed at the scheme of setting up Lord Goderich as the nominal head of a government. Concurring in the freak of gazetting him as First Lord of the Treasury, yet, in prospect of the inevitable change at hand, the long-headed Chancellor labored to ingratiate himself with the King and those about the Court who were likely to have influence in the formation of the new arrangements.

How he was conducting himself in the meantime as a Judge in the Court of Chancery I must reserve for a future opportunity, when I shall deliberately discuss his judicial character. For the present it is enough to say that he showed capacity for becoming one of the greatest magistrates who ever filled the marble chair, but, alas! at the same time, utter indifference about his future judicial

[1] 17 Hansard, N. S. 1418.

fame,—doing as little business as he could without raising a loud clamor against him, shirking difficult questions which came before him in his original jurisdiction, and *affirming* in almost every appeal—satisfied with himself if he could steer clear of serious blunders, and escape from public animadversion.

Some of the duties of Chancellor he performed with vigor and *éclat*. Soon after he received the Great Seal he brought out a numerous batch of King's counsel, including all those whom Lord Eldon had long so improperly kept back; and, further, he gave dinners in the most splendid style, hightening the effect of the artistic performances of his French cook and Italian confectioner by his own wit and convivial powers. It was rumored that his band of attendants at table was sometimes swelled by sheriff's officers put into livery, there being frequent executions in his house; but I believe that for these stories, so generally circulated, there was no sufficient foundation. Notwithstanding all his gains as Attorney and Solicitor-General, he certainly was poor; for his private practice had not been very profitable, and he spent money as fast as he earned it. But I have heard him declare that he never had incurred debts which he had not the means of satisfying.

Lord Goderich (or "poor Goody," as the Chancellor called him) ere long lost his head altogether. His wisest act was the announcement of his own incapacity. Parliament was summoned for the middle of January; and he sat down to compose the King's speech, without being able to make any progress in it. No wonder, for he could not determine in his own mind with respect to any measure to be recommended, or any opinion to be expressed on any public question, domestic or foreign, which then engaged the public attention. He was particularly puzzled about the character to be given to the battle of Navarino, which his illustrious successor thought fit to call an "untoward event." But when he had got over several of these difficulties he was driven to commit suicide by a paltry difference between two of his subordinates, which upon an appeal to him, he was unable to adjust.

Late at night, on the 6th of January, he came to Lord Lyndhurst in a state of great agitation, and for some minutes walked about the room wringing his hands, without uttering any articulate sound. At last he exclaimed, " I deem it due to you to let the Lord Chancellor know that I have made up my mind to resign immediately." An explanation taking place, it turned out that, in reality, no new disaster had happened. The Chancellor tried to reassure him, and to advise him to meet Parliament, saying, that "after all, the session might pass off smoothly, and, at any rate, it would be more dignified to fall by an adverse vote than to tumble down with a confession of incapacity." He attempted no answer, but mopped the perspiration from his brows with his handkerchief, as he was used to do in debate when his ideas became very confused. He now merely said that his resolution was irrevocable, and that what he feared was to break the matter to the King, who must be much perplexed by being called upon to change his cabinet a few days before the meeting of Parliament. " As far as that goes," said the Chancellor, "instead of your writing a letter to his Majesty (about which there might be some awkwardness), if you do not like to face him in a private audience, I don't mind accompanying you to Windsor." This offer was joyfully accepted, and by a dexterous stroke of policy the Chancellor became master of the position which gave him the power of forming the new administration.

Next day they proceeded to Windsor together. The King had been prepared for their visit by reason of a secret communication to his private secretary, who was a fast friend of the Chancellor, and his Majesty received them very graciously and accepted the resignation. "But," said he, rather addressing himself to the Chancellor, "I ought to ask your advice about the person I ought to send for to consult about the formation of a new administration." "Sir," said the Chancellor, " I venture to mention the name which must have already presented itself to the mind of your Majesty, the Duke of Wellington." *King.*—" Let him come to me as soon as possible." Lord Lyndhurst, in relating the particulars of this conference, avers that his Majesty added, " But, remember, whoever is to be Minister, you, my lord, must remain my Chancellor." One would have thought it more probable that this appointment should have been suggested by the Duke of Wellington, when commissioned to submit to his Majesty the list of a new administration. Nevertheless it is certain that Lord Lyndhurst's retention of the Great Seal was absolutely determined upon very early in the negotiation for the new ministry, although this was carefully concealed for a fortnight from Lord Eldon, who, during the whole of that time, was impatiently expecting a summons to resume his former office. When he read in the newspapers the list of the new ministry, with "*Lord Lyndhurst*, CHANCELLOR," at the head of it, he was furious. He wrote to his daughter,—"A lady, probably, has had something to do with it;" but he added, "My opinions may have had something to do with it." In truth, the Duke of Wellington, entertaining a great respect for Lord Eldon, and as yet, knowing little of Lord Lyndhurst which he much liked, was shrewd enough to perceive (although he had then formed no distinct plan of concessions either to Dissenters or to Roman Catholics) that a Cabinet could stand no longer with a sturdy and conscientious member in it, who thought that all the antiquated principles of the ultra-Toryism generated by the French Revolution must be religiously adhered to. Lyndhurst had at times made speeches in a spirit quite as intolerant, but he was known to be more *open to conviction*. Peel, who was to be the leader of the House of Commons, dreaded still more than the Duke of Wellington the incumbrance of Lord Eldon, of whose blind resistance to all change he had complained under Lord Liverpool. Still, Peel had more scruples than the Duke of Wellington in agreeing to Lord Lyndhurst being Chancellor, for he had enjoyed better opportunities of marking his career, and he reposed no confidence in his sincerity. It is a curious fact, that, although Lyndhurst and Peel sat together in the Cabinet so long, and, after the formation of the Duke of Wellington's Government, never had an open difference, even down to the repeal of the corn laws;—they always entertained a considerable personal dislike of each other, which they took very little pains to conceal.

The Chancellor now filled a larger space in the public eye than at any former time. He was reputed to have had the principal hand in forming the new Government, and he had high credit for his address in contriving to hold the Great Seal under three premiers in one year. It was supposed that he might be a little embarrassed by the new view to be taken of Turkish politics, and of the battle of Navarino, which had been hailed as a glorious victory; but when the 29th of January came, he, as one of the Lords Commissioners who addressed the two Houses of Parliament in his Majesty's name, read the ollowing passage without any faltering in his voice or blush upon his cheek:—

"Notwithstanding the valor displayed by the combined fleet, His majesty deeply laments that this conflict should have occurred with the naval force of an ancient ally; but he still entertains a confident hope that this *untoward event* will not be followed by further hostilities."

The great measure of this Session was Lord John Russell's Bill for repealing the Corporation and Test Acts, to which Sir Robert Peel had assented on behalf of the Government in the House of Commons. When it came up to the Lords it was strongly opposed by Lord Eldon; but as his arguments were chiefly drawn from Lord Lyndhurst's famous anti-Catholic speech in the House of Commons, when he was Master of the Rolls, and did not now make much impression, the refutation of that speech by Lord Lyndhurst was reserved for another opportunity.

In the committee on the bill, a discussion arose upon the *declaration* substituted for the sacramental test,—a declaration which, I think, ought to have been omitted altogether; for it has been of no service whatever to the Church,—being superfluous if meant to be confined to obedience to existing law, and clearly not binding if meant to extend to future legislation. Lord Eldon having proposed an amendment of the declaration which would have confined the benefit of the bill to Protestants, the Chancellor accused him of "exercising his talents, his zeal, and his influence mischievously in thus trying to defeat the bill."

Lord Eldon.—"Strange that such a charge should be brought against me, and from such a quarter! I have served my country to the best of my abilities, and if I am now engaged in anything calculated to be *mischievous*, I pray God that I may be forgiven. I cast back the imputation which has been sought to be thrown upon my conduct by the noble and learned Lord on the woolsack, with all the scorn of a man who feels himself injured."

Before long, the Marquis of Lansdowne brought forward "Catholic emancipation," in the shape of a resolution that "it is expedient to consider the laws affecting our Roman Catholic fellow-subjects, with a view to such a conciliatory adjustment as might be conducive to the peace and strength of the United Kingdom." This policy was as yet disagreeable to the Government, and was therefore opposed by the Chancellor, who strenuously contended that our constitution was made essentially Protestant at the Revolution of 1688; and he justified all the laws then passed for that purpose. Having thus established his premises, he then asked: " What change had taken place in the position or condition of Ireland which required that the conduct of this country should be altered towards the Catholics of Ireland? It was too true there were persons in Ireland exercising a sway and authority which was altogether unknown to the constitution. They demanded, for the Catholics of Ireland, admission to seats in this Protestant House; they demanded admission to offices of State, thereby rendering this House no longer a Protestant House of Peers, and the Government no longer a Protestant Government. Exercising the best judgment he could, he did not think that the concessions now demanded would have the effect of tranquillizing Ireland. For the last seven years the priesthood had increased its authority there to a degree unprecedented, and this would only be increased and rendered more dangerous by the concessions which were meditated. As long as this religion continued to be the religion of Ireland, no such concessions could succeed in composing that agitated country." [1]

The motion was negatived by a majority of forty-four, and the subject was not again debated during that session.

But, before Parliament met again, the Government (including Lord Lyndhurst) had resolved that, although the Roman Catholic religion continued the religion of Ireland, the fatal concessions should be granted. I do not think that the Chancellor was at all consulted before the measure of Catholic emancipation was finally determined upon by the Duke of Wellington and Sir Robert Peel; but when it was mentioned to him he very readily

[1] 19 Hansard, N. S., 1246.

acquiesced in it. Not only was he influenced by the consideration that if he did not acquiesce he must resign the Great Seal, but I make no doubt that he inwardly approved of the new policy of the Government. It was, to be sure, a sudden change for him, and he was more obnoxious to the charge of interested conversion than his anti-Catholic colleagues; for they had always, from early youth till now, been of the same opinion, and it was admitted that hitherto they had entertained that opinion with sincerity, while his apparent bigotry had been recently assumed. Whatever his motives or his reasoning with himself might be, he at once became a zealous *emancipationist*—nor did he recoil from or much dread the invectives, the taunts, and the sarcasms to which he knew he must be exposed—prepared to turn them off with a laugh, and boldly to retaliate on all who should assail him.

In the royal speech, at the opening of the memorable Session of 1829, he, on behalf of his Majesty, after complaining of the Catholic Association, and asking for powers to put it down, thus proceeded in a firm tone and with a steady aspect: " His Majesty recommends that, when this essential object shall have been accomplished, you should take into your deliberate consideration the whole condition of Ireland, and that you should review the laws which impose civil disabilities on his Majesty's Roman Catholic subjects."

While the Catholic Relief Bill was making progress in the House of Commons, there were, from the commencement of the Session, nightly skirmishes in the House of Lords on the presentation of petitions for and against the measure. The Chancellor sometimes mixed in these, and received painful scratches. Lord Eldon, presenting an anti-Catholic petition from the Company of Tailors at Glasgow, the Chancellor, still sitting on the woolsack, said in a stage whisper, loud enough to be heard in the galleries:—" What! do *tailors* trouble themselves with such *measures?*"

Lord Eldon.—" My noble and learned friend might have been aware that *tailors* can not like *turncoats*." [A loud laugh.]

On a subsequent day, the Chancellor charged Lord Eldon with *insidiously* insinuating, when presenting petitions against the Roman Catholics, that they were not loyal subjects, and that they were unwilling to swear that they would support the Protestant succession to the Crown.

Lord Eldon.—" My Lords, I am not in the habit of *insinuating*—what I think, I avow. And, my Lords, I am an *open*, not an *insidious* enemy, when I feel it my duty to oppose any measure or any man. My character, known to my country for more than fifty years, is, I feel, more than sufficient to repel so unfounded a charge. It is equally unnecessary that I should criticise the career of my accuser." [1]

The grand struggle was in the debate upon the second reading of the bill. Lord Eldon's friends wished to give him the advantage of following his rival, whom they at last forced up by personal appeals to him. No man in a deliberative assembly was ever placed in a more trying position, for he really rose to answer Dr. Philpott's pamphlet against the measure—on which pamphlet he himself had spoken very recently in the other House of Parliament. He acquitted himself very dexterously by abstaining from any professions of sincerity, by quietly trying to show that he had been a very consistant politician, by assuming a tone of ribaldry, and by bringing a charge of inconsistency against Lord Eldon, who often proclaimed himself, and was generally considered by others, if one of the most bigoted, at all events the most consistent of all living politicians.

"If," said the Chancellor, "after the gracious recommendation from the Throne at the commencement of the Session—if, after this Bill has passed through the other House of Parliament, with a majority so commanding, expressing, in a manner so marked and decided, the opinion of the representative body of the nation; if, after this, owing to any circumstance, the Bill do not pass and become part of the law of the land, it is impossible that the firmest mind or the stoutest heart can contemplate the consequences without something approaching to dismay. The noble and learned lord at the table—I call him *the noble and learned lord*, because he has declared that he will not allow me to call him *my noble and learned friend*—directed me on a former night to vindicate my consistency. My lords, I readily accept the challenge."

[1] 20 Hansard, N. S., 1827.

He then stoutly asserted that he had never attacked the principle of Catholic emancipation, and that he had always declared that it was a question of expediency—the Catholics having an equal right with Protestants to the enjoyment of all civil rights, if such equality would not endanger the constitution. Feeling that this was a ticklish topic, and observing some sceptical smiles and shrugs, notwithstanding the extreme gravity and decorum ever preserved among their lordships, he rapidly passed on to a supposed charge against him, which he feigned for the purpose of answering it—of having violated the oath he had taken truly to counsel the King.

Said he: "I have deeply considered the obligation this oath has imposed upon me, and, after much deliberation, the result has been that I came to a firm conclusion in my own mind that if the stability of the empire were to me, as it ought to be, an object of deep and intense interest, Ireland must be tranquillized, and that it was impossible for me not to give the counsel which I have given to my Sovereign. Have I, then, violated the oath I took? Yet the most bitter opprobrium has been cast upon me. I have been assailed by revilings in the most unmeasured and in the coarsest terms, because I wish to put an end to the grievous discontents which have so long prevailed in Ireland. Since I recently became a responsible adviser of the Crown, I have possessed the means of arriving at information which I did not before possess, and which has enabled me to discharge my duty as a faithful counsellor. But the noble and learned lord at the table, had been twenty-five years the responsible adviser of the Crown, with the same means of information—during all that time he saw the distracted state of Ireland and he applied no remedy to the evil. He did not suggest any considerate line of policy which was suitable to the manifold disorders of that afflicted country; and now he assails that which is brought forward by his successors. He was contented to sit in a divided cabinet that could not fairly consider the Catholic question, and whose resolve, as a body, was to grant no further concession to the Catholics. This, I think, was acting contrary to the peace of the country, and contrary to the principles of the constitution. I allow that, before the noble and learned lord was a member of the Cabinet, he supported measures fo:

the relief of the Catholics of Ireland, which might have given a much greater alarm to Protestantism than the Bill now proposed; for this Bill only completes, with a small addition, the system then begun.

"While he was Attorney-General in 1791 and 1792, all disabilities, with a trifling exception, were suddenly removed from Roman Catholics; they were allowed to become magistrates; the army and navy, and all professions, were thrown open to them; and the elective franchise was conferred upon them. The noble and learned lord was a member of the Cabinet when a measure, on which he had turned out the Whigs in 1806, quietly passed, for allowing the highest military commissions to be held by Roman Catholic officers. The noble lord should not be envious of seeing fully accomplished the work which he so auspiciously had begun and carried forward.

"The noble and learned lord's fears are vain; for Catholics sat in both Houses long after the Reformation, without any danger to the reformed faith. This is proved by a speech of Colonel Birch, who in the course of his argument in the House of Commons, in the reign of Charles II., said, ' *Will you at one step turn out of both Houses of Parliament so many members?*' evidently alluding to the Roman Catholics. I state this as one of the many facts that never were disputed, to show that the Roman Catholics sat in Parliament under our Protestant Government."

Lord Eldon.—" Did the noble and learned lord know that last year?"

Chancellor.—" I confess that I did not; but, my lords, I have since been prosecuting my studies; I have advanced in knowledge; and, in my humble opinion, even the noble and learned lord might improve himself in the same way."

This sally set the House in a roar; and being understood as a good-humored abandonment of character, procured a favorable hearing for the Chancellor during the rest of his speech. This speech for the Catholics was as able as that which he had delivered against them, although he was said to be " pitching it too strong," when he urged that emancipation would bring about a conversion of the Catholics to the reformed faith, which he so dearly loved. He thus concluded:—

"I care not for the personal obloquy which may be cast upon me for advocating this measure; I have discharged

my duty fearlessly and conscientiously, and to the best of
my ability, and my most anxious desire, as it would be
my greatest consolation, is to be associated with your lordships in carrying this Bill into a law, and thereby to secure
upon a permanent basis the happiness and tranquillity of
the United Kingdom."

Lord Eldon.—" I ceased to call the noble and learned
Lord on the woolsack *my noble and learned friend*, because
he accused me of ' *disingenuous insinuations*,'—language
which I felt to be extremely disrespectful. But if the noble lord can reconcile himself in the House of Commons
with himself as a member of your Lordships' House, I am
ready to be reconciled to him, and to forget all that has
passed. I feel, in making these remarks, that there is a
sort of indecorum in such a dispute between a Chancellor
and an ex-Chancellor; but I cannot refrain from expressing my astonishment that the noble and learned lord
should attempt to show that he himself had been *consistent*, by preferring a charge of *inconsistency* against me. I
have read the speech of the noble and learned lord delivered a few months ago in the House of Commons, and
from that speech I have drawn all the arguments I have
used in this House against the repeal of the Corporation
and Test Acts, and against what is called the 'Catholic
Relief Bill.' Since that speech of the honorable and
learned lord, there has been no change in the circumstances
of the country, although there is a great change in the circumstances of the noble and learned lord. His sudden
conversion may be sincere and disinterested, but surely he
is not the man to taunt me with inconsistency. Laying
my account with obloquy while I was in office, I hoped
to have escaped it when I retired into private life, but I
regret to find that it is still thought a pleasant thing in
Parliament to have a slash at the ex-Chancellor." [1]

The bill was passed by a large majority, and we all
laughed very much at the ex-Chancellor's fears and proph-
ecies. I by no means regret what was then done; and with
a perfect foreknowledge of all that has since happened, I
would still have taken the same course; but I am sorry to
say that we have not derived from the measure all the
benefits which reasonable men expected from it, and some
color has been given to the objections of its opponents.

[1] 21 Hansard, N. S., 190.

Many Roman Catholics in Ireland, not contented with equality, have aimed at ascendency, and have shown that with power they would be intolerant, denying to others the religious liberty which they had so loudly claimed for themselves. But we can now resist Roman Catholic aggression more effectually than if we had continued liable to the reproach of tyranny and oppression.

Lord Lyndhurst at last carried through his bill for improving the procedure of the Court of Chancery, and the session closed. Goverment had seemed very strong in both houses, but Lord Lyndhurst declared that he had great apprehensions for the future. The party of the Tories, to which he had attached himself, was rent assunder; a large section of them were eager for revenge upon the authors of the Emancipation Bill at any price, and the cry resounded *Nusquam tuta fides*. Still the Whigs were in sad disrepute, and George IV, who had been for many years their leader,and under whom they had expected to enjoy uninterrupted sway, closed his career as Regent and as King, without once having admitted them to office.

A session of Parliament had been begun on the 4th of February, 1830, but nothing of much interest occurred in it, for his Majesty was understood to be laboring under a mortal malady, and parties were preparing their measures and mustering their forces with a view to a new reign. The current now running powerfully towards law reform, the Chancellor proposed several schemes for mitigating the severty of the criminal code, and for improving the procedure of the courts of equity and common law; but the only bill of any importance which passed was that which he introduced to authorize the use of a stamp instead of the King's sign manual for the purpose of testifying the King's assent to acts of state. The Chancellor took the opportunity to lament very tenderly the necessity for such a departure from constitutional form on account of his Maesty's extreme bodily weakness; and he was no doubt very sincere on this occasion, for he had been a marked favorite at Court ever since his famous speech against Queen Caroline, and the inclinations of the heir to the throne were now supposed to be rather in favor of the party in opposition.

Prudent management might have saved the existing Government. The ultra Tories were exceedingly hostile to it; but many of the Whigs were disposed to support it, and, with a few concessions to public opinion, it might have permanently stood. William IV. was contented with the Duke of Wellington and Peel, and neither expressed nor felt any desire for a change.

It has ever been a wonder to me that Lyndhurst, who well knew the state of the popular mind, and who himself inwardly approved of liberal measures, should not have striven to induce the Duke of Wellington to accept the aid of that party who had enabled him to carry Catholic emancipation. The Duke thought that any further concession would be mischievous; and his ill-judged policy now was, by assuming a high-Tory tone, to win back those who had been alienated from him by his removal of the disabilities of the Dissenters and the Roman Catholics. In this policy the Lord Chancellor implicitly acquiesced. He abstained from making any public declarations by which he might afterwards be hampered; but in private he admitted the extreme difficulty which any Government must encounter in now trying to resuscitate the doctrines of *political optimism*.

Although upon a dissolution of Parliament the elections ran considerably in favor of the Whigs, still the Iron Duke's resolution was maintained to set them at defiance.

One symptom of a liberal tendency was at this time openly exhibited by Lyndhurst. He always declared the doctrine, and acted upon it, that the holder of the Great Seal has the exclusive right of appointing the puisne judges, and ought *proprio marte* to take the pleasure of the Sovereign upon their appointment, without any communication with the Prime Minister or any other of his colleagues. Two years before, although a notorious Whig, I had been placed at the head of the Real Property Commission. This was Peel's doing; but now Lyndhurst, in a very handsome manner, addressed to me a laudatory epistle, offering to make me a puisne judge of the Court of King's Bench. I had recently been returned to the House of Commons for the borough of Stafford, and from my position at the bar, I was not prepared to be so shelved. But I was nevertheless obliged to him, and I accompanied my refusal of the offer with very warm thanks for his kindness.

The public remained in suspense as to the policy of the government till the delivery of the King's speech on the opening of the session, and the inference drawn from this was fatally confirmed by the Duke of Wellington's memorable declaration that the existing state of parliamentary representation did not require and did not admit of any improvement. The ultra-Tories were in no degree appeased, and they loudly vociferated that they would sooner see in office men who had always consistently supported Whiggism than men who had treacherously paltered with their vows to defend Church and King. The Duke of Wellington's government was therefore doomed to destruction, and it ingloriously fell by a division on a trifling motion in the House of Commons for a committee to inquire into the expenditure of the civil list.

CHAPTER CCXVIII.

LORD CHIEF BARON.

LYNDHURST, who had already been Chancellor under three successive premiers holding very opposite opinions, was not without hopes that he might have continued to hold his office under a fourth, and he would have been very ready to coalesce with the new Whig Government, pleading as his excuse that it was to comprise his old chief Lord Goderich, now Earl of Ripon, the Duke of Richmond, who had been a conspicuous Tory, and the once Tory Lord Palmerston, with other associates of Canning. Strange to say, Lord Grey was by no means disinclined to this arrangement. He expressed high respect for the talents of the Duke of Wellington's Chancellor—particularly as displayed in his exposition of the Regency Bill, which was still pending in the House, and which "it was desirable he should carry through." This bill Lord Lyndhurst had introduced in the House of Lords the very same night in which the disastrous division had taken place in the House of Commons on the Civil List. The object of it was to make the Duchess of Kent Regent in case William IV. should die before the Princess Victoria, then heir presumptive to the crown, and only twelve years old, should have completed her eighteenth year.

In laying it on the table the Chancellor certainly did take a most masterly view of the constitutional law upon the subject,—illustrated by very interesting allusions to what had been done in this and other countries on similar occasions. He likewise alluded, with much delicacy, to the contingency of the Queen being *enceinte* at the death of the King, and giving birth to a child after the Princess Victoria should be placed upon the throne. However, there was little difference of opinion as to the fitness of the measure; and it might easily have been carried through its subsequent stages, even if it had been opposed by its versatile author. Lord Grey's real motive, I believe, was, that he might avoid handing over the Great Seal to Brougham, of whose temerity and insubordination he had a most distressing anticipation. Some alleged that, not insensible in old age to the influence of female charms, the venerable Whig Earl had been captivated by the beauty and lively manners of Lady Lyndhurst, and that her bright eyes were new arguments shot against the transfer of the Great Seal. However this may be, it is certain that he offered Brougham the office of Attorney-General, meaning to soften the proposal with an enumeration of some of the illustrious men who had held the office, and a representation of the importance to the new Government that the newly elected member for the county of York should remain in the House of Commons. But Brougham burst away from Lord Grey with indignation; and this being the very day fixed, by a notice which he had given in the House of Commons before the Duke of Wellington's resignation, for his motion on parliamentary reform, he hurried down to St. Stephen's with the determination of immediately bringing it on. As such a step would have destroyed the new Government while yet in embryo, he was earnestly entreated to desist from his purpose; and he yielded, but making use of language which clearly indicated that he would only consent to become a supporter of Lord Grey's administration on his own terms:—

"I beg it to be understood that what I do, I do in deference to the wishes of the House. And further, *as no change that can take place in the administration can by any possibility affect me*, I beg to be understood that, in putting off the motion, I will put it off until the 25th of this month, *and no longer.* I will then, and at no more distant period, bring forward the question of parliamentary reform, *whatever may be the condition of circumstances, and whosoever may be his Majesty's Ministers.*"[1]

I know not if Lord Grey exclaimed, as I once heard him do upon a similar "flare up" of the same person, "The fat is all in the fire;" but he instantly renounced all notion of Lyndhurst being his Chancellor, and before "the 25th of the month," when the question of Parliamentary Reform was without fail to have been brought forward in the House of Commons by the honorable member for the county of York, "*whosoever might be his Majesty's Ministers,*" the Right Honorable Henry Lord Brougham and Vaux took his seat on the woolsack in the House of Lords.

Still, the object of attaching the Tory ex-Chancellor to the Whig Government was by no means abandoned. He was asked by the new Premier to continue to take charge of the Regency Bill, with many compliments to his eloquence and ability, which were very complacently received. A scheme was soon after devised and carried out, which it was thought would take off all danger of Lyndhurst's active opposition, if he should not be quite contented with his new position. Alexander, the Chief Baron of the Exchequer, was asked to resign. He was willing to do so on condition of having a peerage, to which he had no just pretension. This would have caused some scandal; and a hint was thrown out to Alexander, by a friend of the new Government, that some notice was threatened in the House of Commons of his unfitness to continue on the bench by reason of his age and infirmities. Alexander thereupon agreed to resign unconditionally; and his office was offered to Lyndhurst. Hitherto there never had been an instance of a Lord Chancellor or Lord Keeper, after resigning the Great Seal, becoming a common law Judge; but there was no objection to it in point of law, nor would the supposed breach of etiquette be blamed by any one whose opinion was worth regarding. Lyndhurst had sufficient confidence in his own powers to support his dignity; and the offer of a place

---
[1] Hansard, i. 562. Henceforth the 3rd series of Hansard is to be understood as quoted.

for life, with a salary of 7,000*l.* a year, was very tempting to him, for although he could contrive to prevent executions being put into his house, he was exceedingly poor, and the retired allowance for a Chancellor was then only 4,000*l.* a year,—an income quite inadequate to support Lady Lyndhurst's fashionable establishment. Accordingly, on the first day of Hilary Term, 1831, the ex-Chancellor took his seat on the Bench as Chief Baron of the Court of Exchequer. I ought to state that, accepting this office, he gave no pledge whatever to support Lord Grey's government. No doubt great disappointment was felt when he suddenly became the leader of the Opposition in the House of Lords; but in all the bitter struggles that followed, and amidst the many provocations he gave by the violent and unfair means he resorted to for the purpose of defeating the measures of the Whigs, I never heard, either in public or private, any taunt thrown out against him on the supposition that the course he took was contrary to good faith.

He continued to preside in the Court of Exchequer four years, again showing that, if he had liked, he might have earned the very highest reputation for judicial excellence. I did not regularly practice before him but I often went into his court, particularly in revenue causes, after I became a law officer of the Crown, and as often I admired his wonderful quickness of apprehension, his forcible and logical reasoning, his skillful commixture of sound law and common sense, and his clear, convincing, and dignified judgments. He was a great favorite with the bar on account of his general courtesy, although he has told me that he acted upon the principle that "it is the duty of a Judge to make it disagreeable to counsel to talk nonsense." He regularly went circuits, saying that "he thought it pleasanter to try larcenies and highway robberies than to listen to seven Chancery lawyers on the same side upon exceptions to the Master's report." He declared that he was even pleased with what Judges generally find intolerable—the duty of receiving the country gentlemen at dinner, when the labors of the day are supposed to be over; but he averred that he not only could make *himself* entertaining to *them*, but that he could make *them* entertaining to *himself* in return.

Still he would not heartily give his mind to his judicial

business. His opinion was, and is, of small weight in Westminster Hall; and I do not recollect any case being decided on any judgment or dictum of his. It was only while he was in court that he cared for or thought of the causes he had to dispose of. The rest of his time he spent in attending the debates of the House of Lords, or in forming cabals with his political partisans, or at the festal board. He had for a puisne Bayley, who, having been a Judge of the King's Bench, had come into the Exchequer, from being tired of Lord Tenterden. On this learned and laborious coadjutor Lyndhurst relied entirely. The pure law so supplied he knew how to extract from the quartz in which it was mixed up, and to exhibit as if he himself had dug it up resplendent from the mine, or had long held it in his private purse.

I never suspected him of partiality, except on the trial of a cause of *Dicas* v. *Lord Brougham*. This was an unfounded action for false imprisonment, brought by a blackguard attorney against Lord Chancellor Brougham, at a time when there was a great enmity (followed by a strict friendship) between the noble defendant and the judge. I must say I thought the latter on this occasion showed a strong inclination to push his rival into a scrape; but, if this inclination actually existed, it might have proceeded from a love of *fun* rather than from rancor or *malice*. I myself was sued by the same attorney, in the Court of Exchequer, for defamation in my speech against him as counsel for the defendant in this very cause, and I must confess I was rather uneasy at the thought of my trial coming on before the Lord Chief Baron, as I dreaded lest, to have a laugh against me, he might leave this question to the jury in such a way as to induce them to find a verdict against me. Luckily my antagonist had not the courage to proceed to trial, and at last I had "judgment against him as in case of a nonsuit."

In the time of Lord Chief Baron Lyndhurst the Exchequer was a court of equity as well as a court of law; but the equity business was disposed of by a single judge, and, caring little about it, the Chief Baron generally handed it over to Mr. Baron Alderson. One equity case, however, he was required to hear on account of its magnitude (*Small* v. *Attwood*), and it turned out *heavier*

(in legal phrase) than any case ever tried in England; for
the hearing, from first to last, occupied a greater number
of hours than the trial of Mr. Hastings. It arose out of
a contract for the sale of iron-mines in the county of
Stafford; and the question was, whether the contract was
not vitiated by certain alleged fradulent representations
of the vendor. The leading counsel had a brief, endorsed
with a fee of 5,000 guineas; many days were occupied in
reading the depositions, and weeks in the comments upon
them. The Chief Baron paid unwearied attention to the
evidence and the arguments, and at last delivered (by all
accounts) the most wonderful judgment ever heard in
Westminster Hall. It was entirely oral, and, without
even referring to any notes, he employed a long day in
stating complicated facts, in entering into complex calculations, and in correcting the misrepresentations of the
counsel on both sides. Never once did he falter or hesitate, and never once was he mistaken in a name, a figure,
or a date. Nevertheless, it was finally held that he had
come to a wrong conclusion on the merits. The decree
being that the contract was void, an appeal was brought
in the House of Lords, the hearing of which lasted nearly
a whole session. Time for consideration was taken till
the following session; and then Lord Cottenham, Chancellor, and Lord Brougham, ex-Chancellor, declared their
opinion to be that the decree must be reversed. Lord
Lyndhurst adhered to his original opinion, and defended
it in a speech which again astounded all who heard it, by
the unexampled power of memory and lucidness of arrangement by which it was distinguished. But this final
judgment was not pronounced till many years after the
era to which I had brought my narrative,—viz. the commencement of Lord Grey's administration, and to this I
must now revert.

It would appear that from the moment Lyndhurst was
appointed Chief Baron he had resolved to go into opposition, and I must confess that I think the Whigs were very
silly in expecting his support. The Great Seal being in
the grasp of one of them, who it was supposed must hold
it as long as they were in power, no further promotion was
open to the supposed new ally, except to the office of
Chief Justice of the King's Bench. For this he would
have been admirably well suited, and its increased salary

would have pleased him; but he shrunk from the heavy and responsible duties belonging to it, which he could not cast upon another, and which would have interfered, not only with his social enjoyment, but with his political intrigues. There was a strong probability of the Duke of Wellington and Sir Robert Peel being soon restored to office, for Lord Grey and his colleagues, at starting, by no means enjoyed public confidence, and they had committed some financial blunders which made it be supposed that their reign would be very short. Nor could it be said that honor forbade Lyndhurst to follow the course which interest pointed out to him, for, in accepting a purely judicial office, he could not be considered as changing his politics, so as to entitle his former associates to renounce him as a renegade, or his new patrons to claim him as a convert. He was very moderate and reserved, however, till the Reform Bill was brought forward. Then he led, and thenceforth he long continued to lead, the most violent and factious opposition I have ever known or read of in our party annals.

During the first half of the session he confined himself in the House of Lords to commenting upon certain bills proposed by the Lord Chancellor for reforming the Court of Chancery, and for establishing new local courts and a new Court of Bankruptcy—doing the best he could to disparage all these measures, but in a tone of great moderation and courtesy. Meanwhile, he was privately taken into council by the opponents of the Reform Bill, from its introduction into the House of Commons; and they were chiefly guided by his advice till he committed a gross blunder, by which the bill was passed in the most obnoxious form given to it by its authors; whereas, by more skillful management, it might have been materially altered according to the wishes of its enemies.

General Gascoigne's resolution against reducing the number of English representatives, of which Lyndhurst approved, was a very deterous move, but was turned to the decided advantage of the Reformers by an immediate dissolution of Parliament.

This *coup* was wholly unexpected by Lord Lyndhurst, and he left the bench of the Court of Exchequer in seeming consternation on hearing that, without any previous notice, the King was on his way to announce it from the throne.

He hurried to the House of Lords, which he found in a state of confusion unexampled since the dispersion of the Long Parliament by Oliver Cromwell. According to Hansard, four lords having simultaneously risen *to order*, " Lord Lyndhurst also rose, but the noise in the House was so great that it was almost impossible to hear what the noble lord said. He was understood to object to the conduct of the Duke of Richmond, one of the four who had been speaking to order at the same time, saying 'there was nothing in their lordships' proceedings so disorderly as the interference of the noble Duke.' The Duke of Richmond moved that the standing order should be read against the use of offensive language by noble lords in that House. The Marquess of Londonderry denied that any offensive language had been used by the Lord Chief Baron. The Marquess of Clanricarde insisted that the Chief Baron's language and manner justified the motion for reading the standing order. [*Cries of Order, order. Shame, shame. The King, the King.*] At last his Majesty entered, and, having mounted the throne, thus began : ' My lords and gentlemen, I have come to meet you for the purpose of proroguing this Parliament, with a view to its immediate dissolution.' "[1]

Lord Lyndhurst, although generally possessing great presence of mind and showing a bold front, if suddenly disconcerted looked very *wooden*, and he is said to have done so on this occasion; but he soon recovered his composure, saying to a friend with whom he left the House, " All is not lost."

The turn which the elections took was rather appalling to anti-reformers, but the Lord Chief Baron had " courage never to submit or yield."

On the meeting of the new Parliament, while the Reform Bill was passing through the House of Commons, he attended private conferences to consider the best mode of obstructing it; but he took no part in the preliminary skirmishes which arose on the presenting of petitions for or against it, reserving himself for the grand conflict on the second reading. When this arrived he displayed extraordinary ability and extraordinary hardihood, which mainly contributed to the temporary victory then won

[1] 3 Hansard, 1806.

He spoke on the fifth night of the debate, immediately after Lord Chancellor Brougham.

Thus did he modestly begin :—

"After the splendid declamation, my lords, which you have just heard from my noble and learned friend, which has never been surpassed on any occasion even by the noble and learned lord himself, it is no matter of surprise that I should present myself to your lordships with great hesitation and anxiety; but feeling the situation in which I now stand, and recollecting the position which I formerly had the honor of holding in this House, I presume it would be considered a shrinking from an imperious duty if I satisfied myself by giving a silent vote on an occasion so momentous."

After throwing out some general observations indicating an inclination in favor of well-considered reform, he said,—

"But I feel it my duty to oppose this measure, because it appears to me not calculated to support the just prerogatives of the Crown, but to destroy them—not of a nature to establish the authority of this house, but to undermine and overthrow that authority—not to promote the rights and liberties of the people, but to destroy them."

He then resorted to his favorite manœvre; he accused his antagonists of political inconsistency, bringing forward passages from speeches and writings of Lord Grey, Lord John Russell, Lord Melbourne, nay, of Lord Brougham himself, expressing a favorable opinion of the existing House of Commons, and pointing out the danger of rashly changing the constituent bodies by which it is returned, suppressing the fact that these opinions were brought forward to combat universal suffrage, or some such chimera. He then proceeded to point out the fatal effects of the proposed reform upon all classes, beginning with the lawyers :—

"Among certain persons I know that gentlemen connected with the profession of the law are not considered of much importance; but, my lords, in times of trouble and danger this opinion becomes doubly erroneous. There are few men in such times who are so important—active agitators—keen and intelligent—prepared for a stirring life by previous education and habits. By what means have you secured for them an entrance into the House of Commons? None! But they will become agitators,—

they will excite public feeling, and make extravagant promises, in order to secure themselves a share in the representation. These active, intelligent, and ambitious men will necessarily therefore throw themselves into the democratic scale, and give it a fearful preponderance. The House of Commons, in which I have served a long apprenticeship, I know will become an unmanageable democratic body. *To the monarchical institutions of the country I have been attached both by habit and education.* I do not wish for a change which may affect the rights and privileges of the Crown, nor for one which will bring about a professed republic, or a republic in the shape of a limited monarchy. Republics are tyrannical, capricious, and cruel. I do not charge the ministers with having introduced the bill for the purpose of subverting our form of government; but such will be its certain effect. You are called upon to open the flood-gates which will admit the torrent of democratic power. That torrent will rush in and overpower us. The noble and learned lord on the woolsack, with his buoyancy and nimbleness, may for a time float upon the tide, and play his gambols on the surface, but the least check will submerge him, and he will sink to rise no more."

In his peroration the orator made a magnanimous allusion to his origin:—

"I cannot boast an illustrious descent. I have sprung from the people. I owe the situation I have the honor to hold in this House to the generous kindness of my late sovereign,—a monarch largely endowed with great and princely qualities. I am proud of being thus associated with the descendants of those illustrious names which have shed lustre upon the history of our country. But if I thought that your Lordships were capable of being influenced by the threats which have been audaciously held out to you, and that you should be so induced to swerve from the discharge of your duty when everything valuable in our institutions is at stake, I should be ashamed of this dignity, and take refuge from it in the comparative obscurity of private life, rather than mix with men so unmindful of the obligations imposed upon them by their high station and illustrious birth. Perilous as is the situation in which we are placed, it is, at the same time, a proud one,—the eyes of the country are anxiously turned upon us, and, if we decide as becomes us, we shall merit the eternal gratitude of every friend of the constitution, and of the British empire."

Earl Grey, in an admirable reply, touched very cuttingly on Lord Lyndhurst's charges of inconsistency, taunted him with his sudden conversion to Catholic emancipation, and hinted very intelligibly at his former democratic opinions. When he had concluded, a memorable scene took place, which I myself witnessed, standing on the steps of the throne.

Lord Lyndhurst.—" The noble Earl has been pleased in the course of his speech to allude to me, and he seemed to consider that at one period of my life I entertained opinions opposed to those I now avow and act upon. But, if the noble Earl entertains any such impressions, I beg to assure him that he is grossly misinformed, and utterly mistaken."

Earl Grey.—" My Lords, I did understand that the noble and learned lord at one period of his life entertained opinions favorable to the consideration of the question of parliamentary reform."

Lord Lyndhurst.—" NEVER!"

Lord Denman, who had gone the circuit with Lyndhurst, and full well knew what those opinions had been, was then standing by me. Shaking his fist in a manner which made me afraid that he would draw upon himself the notice of the House, he exclaimed, " Villain! lying villain!" But, in reality, what the noble and learned Lord said was literally true, for at the period of his life alluded to he was not favorable to parliamentary reform, but wished Parliament to be abolished, that a National Convention might be established in its place.

Upon a division, the second reading of the bill was negatived by a majority of forty-one peers.

Lord Lyndhurst was in hopes that ministers would resign, and that the Great Seal would again be in his possession; but this event, though decreed by fate, was delayed for several stormy and anxious years.

The session was speedily closed, that, according to parliamentary usage, the Reform Bill might be again introduced into Parliament; and upon the two Houses reassembling, after a recess of a few weeks, his Majesty, in his speech from the throne, began with saying, " I feel it to be my duty, in the first place, to recommend to your most careful consideration the measures which will be proposed to you for a reform in the Commons House of Parliament; a speedy and satisfactory settlement of this question becomes daily of more pressing importance to the security of the state, and to the content and welfare of my people." The new Bill was forthwith launched in the House of Commons, but it did not reach the Lords till the month of April in the following year. Lyndhurst's hostility to it remained unabated, and, notwithstanding the strong feeling in favor of reform then manifested by the great bulk of the nation, he was resolved again to reject it on the second reading. He spoke against it on the fourth night of the debate, and, in allusion to Lord Grey's pledge that it should be as efficient as the former bill, he said, "It is as efficient, and, according to my interpretation of its provisions, as mischievous and as flagrant. I have considered with great care, whether I was right in the decision at which I formerly arrived, and all my meditations and inquiries have satisfied me that it is impossible for me to pursue any other course."

The grand question now being whether, if necessary, there should be a large creation of new peers to carry the bill, Lyndhurst said, "I do not impute to the noble Earl the intention of resorting to such a rash, and desperate, and wicked measure, which would overwhelm him with disgrace, and the country with ruin." He then entered into a very invidious classification of the supporters of the bill. First, came the whole body of Dissenters, whom he severely stigmatised. Then the numerous band of persons without property or virtue, quoting the words of the Roman historian, "*Nam semper in civitate quibus opes nullæ sint, bonis invident, malos extollunt, vetera odere, nova exoptant; odio suarum rerum mutari omnia student.*" Next he specified the conductors of the daily press,— whether as a subdivision of the last class was left doubtful. "Of these," said he, "a great proportion support this measure because they prosper by agitation. Besides, they see that, in proportion as the principle of democracy is advanced, they rise in their condition. Their personal ambition has encouragements which in no other state of society could be offered to them."[1] He concluded by con-

[1] Lyndhurst afterwards felt that he had committed a great blunder by this

juring their Lordships " to lay aside all temporizing policy, which must assuredly, if they should be weak enough to entertain it, prove their destruction." [1]

The peers were as hostile as ever; but they quailed when they considered the consequences of the entire rejection of the bill on the second reading, which would have amounted to a declaration that they never would agree to any disfranchisement, or enfranchisement, or extension of the suffrage; and a section of them thought that the more expedient course would be to mutilate the bill in Committee, so that its authors might be placed in circumstances of great embarrassment, between the choice of being discredited with the public by submission, or, by resistance, of quarreling with the King, who had become much more cool in the cause of reform than when he had proposed to jump into a hackney coach, that he might hurry off to dissolve Parliament. Accordingly, the second reading was carried by a majority of nine.

The enemies of the bill might now substantially have defeated it, or greatly modified it by rescuing a number of condemned boroughs from Schedule A, by raising the qualification of the metropolitan constituencies, and by adding to the number of the county members, so as to have preserved to a considerable degree the ascendency of the aristocracy in parliamentary representation. But Lord Lyndhust's indiscretion gave a complete triumph to those who shouted out, "The bill, the whole bill, and nothing but the bill."

When the peers were to discuss the bill clause by clause in Committee, he resorted to a manœuvre which he thought very clever, but which was not only transparent, but clumsily executed. He moved that the disfranchising clauses with which the bill began should be postponed till the enfranchising clauses were disposed of; this he did in a speech against all disfranchisement, clearly betraying his purpose to defeat the measure altogether. The Duke of Wellington and the whole Tory party, confiding in his prudence, although wishing that he had taken a more straightforward course, rallied round him,

onslaught on the *genus irritabile* of "Gentlemen of the Press;" and to appease them he presided at an anniversary dinner of their society, when he extolled their abilities and accomplishments, and asserted that literature, science, and good government rested mainly on their exertions.

[1] 12 Hansard, 428.

and his amendment was carried by a large majority.
When the division was announced, he chuckled exceedingly, and in a stage whisper exclaimed, "Grey is checkmated!"

There had been no such crisis in England since the expulsion of James II. It is impossible to deny that the Reform Bill was a revolution, by suddenly transferring supreme power from one body in the state to another,—from an oligarchy to the middle orders,—although it was intended that the transfer should be made without physical force, and according to constitutional forms. There was now serious danger of civil war, for a probability appeared that the executive government would be speedily in the hands of men prepared to defend the existing order of things to the last extremity, and there were hundreds of thousands in the great provincial towns ready to march to the metropolis for the Bill, and to sacrifice their lives in its defense.

Lord Grey determining, without hesitation, that he would not submit to the amendment which had been carried, and thinking that it did not become him to leave the country without a government, while such a misfortune could possibly be warded off, immediately waited upon the King, and represented to him that the only mode of avoiding a public convulsion was for his Majesty to consent to the creation of a sufficient number of new peers to constitute a majority in favor of the Reform Bill. The King firmly refused; and he cannot be blamed for refusing, as such a step could be considered only a *coup d'état* and he had been told by persons about him that there was no necessity for it as a majority of the peers were now ready to yield a large measure of reform, although they would not agree to the ruin of their order. Lord Grey and his colleagues thereupon tendered their resignation, which was graciously accepted.

Now was the most splendid moment of Lyndhurst's career. On fine morning, while he was sitting in the Court of Exchequer, listening to the argument on a special demurrer, and asking Bayley which way he should give judgment, a letter was delivered to him from Sir Herbert Taylor, the King's private Secretary, requiring his immediate attendance at St. James's Palace. From a King's messenger being the bearer of the letter, the fact was immediately known all over Westminster Hall, and I well remember the sensation excited in the Court of King's Bench by the loud whisper—"The Chief Baron has been sent for." He immediately unrobed, and in a few minutes he was in the royal presence.

I never heard him relate the particulars of this audience, and the accounts of it circulated at the time were probably founded rather on conjecture than authentic information. The King, after the ceremonial salutation had taken place, was supposed to have said to him:—"I have great confidence in you, my lord, and I consider you a very honest man. I wish you to be my adviser in this conjuncture; but there is only one preliminary difficulty to be got over. You must know that my royal word is pledged to granting a liberal measure of parliamentary reform, and this nothing shall induce me to break, although my late ministers are for going farther than is necessary, or perhaps safe. But I have heard that your lordship is conscientiously persuaded that all reform would be mischievous, and that the representation ought to remain as it is, without any innovation. Now, if these are your sentiments, I fear I cannot have your aid in this emergency." *Chief Baron.*—"Sir,—Your Majesty has been entirely misinformed on this subject. True, I have been always opposed to the wild, democratical, Jacobinical principles which generated the horrors of the French Revolution; but I have long seen the necessity for temperate, well-considered reform in our representative system, to bring it back to what it was in the reign of your royal ancestor, Edward I. Your Majesty, I hope, will pardon me for saying that the Reform Bill of your late ministers as it now stands would, in my opinion, be fatal to the monarchy, and for that reason I have been driven very reluctantly to oppose it. But it no doubt contains enactments which may be salutary, and, if it could be reasonably modified, it might strengthen the Crown, while it gives contentment to your Majesty's subjects." *King.*—"My Lord Chief Baron, my Lord Chief Baron, you are the very man for me: you have hit upon the basis I wish for my new administration. If a majority of the Lords would have accepted the Bill as it is, I should not have withheld the royal assent, although my private opinion is that it may injuriously interfere with the efficiency of the Executive Government; but I find that it can not be constitutionally carried through both Houses of Parliament." *Chief Baron.*—" If your Majesty's late advisers refuse all compromise, I should think that your Majesty's patriotic intentions might be fully carried into effect by calling to your councils those who may approve of a measure of reform such as the Lords may agree to, and such as will accord with the royal pledge which your Majesty is so anxious to fulfill." After a good deal of further discussion in the same strain, it was agreed that Lord Lyndhurst should sound the leaders of the Tory party, as to the formation of a new administration to carry a modified Reform Bill.

He first went to Sir Robert Peel, who treated the proposal with scorn. But, to his great delight and surprise after this rebuff, he found the Duke of Wellington ready to make the attempt. This illustrious man had very peculiar notions of his duty to the Crown; and, although, in November, 1830, he had pronounced our representative system to be an absolute piece of perfection, yet as King William, both in speeches from the throne prepared for him, and by voluntary private declarations, had expressed an opinion that some change in the system was necessary, the monarchical patriot was willing to make a sacrifice of his own consistency to extricate the government of the country from the seemingly inextricable difficulty in which it was involved. He therefore professed his readiness to serve in the new cabinet, in any capacity in which his services might be deemed most available.

Lyndhurst seemed now to have the premiership within his grasp, although it turned out to be a phantom. Instead of trying to clutch it, however, he thought the more discreet course would be to content himself with the resumption of the Great Seal.

Therefore, having by appointment gone down to Windsor in the evening of the following day, he explained to the King the Duke of Wellington's willingness to comply with his Majesty's wishes, and tendered the advice that his Grace should immediately be sent for, and commissioned to submit a list of a new administration, with the Duke himself at the head of it.

This was accordingly done, and the Duke gallantly undertook the task, although fully aware of the troubles in which it must involve him. He first received an alarming check from an address of the House of Commons to the King, carried by a large majority, expressing deep regret at the resignation of the late ministers, and praying that his Majesty would not call to his counsels any others who were not prepared to support the Reform Bill in its integrity. Nevertheless, he persevered, and he had obtained the consent of respectable though second-rate men, to fill the most important offices of the new government, of which it was understood that Lord Chancellor Lyndhurst was to be the soul. But there was soon an appalling explosion of public opinion against it; and it was condemned, not only by Whigs and Radicals, who were Reformers, but by a considerable section of the Tory party, headed by Sir Robert Inglis, the consistent and popular representative for the University of Oxford. Still, the general opinion was that the Lyndhurst administration would, at least, be installed, till the embryo was extinguished during a discussion which took place in the House of Commons on the presentation of a petition in favor of the Reform Bill from the City of London. Such weakness was then displayed by the defenders of the new government, and such strong censure was poured upon its originator from all quarters, that, although the House came to no vote upon the subject, everyone felt that Lord Grey and his colleagues must be recalled.

With the concurrence of Lyndhurst, the Duke of Wellington had waited on the King, and announced to him that the formation of a new government was impossible, and Sir Herbert Taylor had written a letter to Lord Grey, requiring his presence in the royal closet. When the minister and his Majesty met, the condition of the Whigs resuming office was speedily conceded as a matter of necessity,—both parties still entertaining a hope that the power to create new peers would be sufficient, without the threatened wound to the constitution being actually inflicted.

When explanations of these proceedings were given in the House of Lords, the Duke of Wellington said:—

"His Majesty was graciously pleased, on that very day when he was left entirely alone by his ministers, to send for a noble and learned friend of mine, who had held a high place as well in the service as in the confidence of

his Majesty, to inquire if, in his opinion, there were any
means, and, if so, what means of forming a government
for his Majesty on the principle of carrying an extensive
reform in the representation of the people. My noble
and learned friend informed me of his Majesty's situation,
and I considered it my duty to inquire from others, for I
was as unprepared as his Majesty for the consideration of
such a question. I then found that a large number of
friends of mine were not unwilling to give their support
to a government formed upon such a principle, and with
the positive view of resistance to that advice which had
been tendered to his Majesty respecting the means of
carrying the Reform Bill in its present shape. I did not
look to any objects of ambition, I advised him to seek the
assistance of other persons to fill the high situations in
the State, expressing myself willing to give his Majesty
all assistance, whether in office or out of office, to enable
his Majesty to resist the advice to which I have referred."

After pointing out at considerable length, the unconstitutional character and the mischievous consequences
of the proposed creation of peers, he thus concluded :—

"Under these circumstances, I believe your Lordships will not think it unnatural, when I considered his
Majesty's situation, that I should endeavor to assist his
Majesty. But, my Lords, when I found that in consequence of the discussions in another place it was impossible to form a government on the proposed principle
which would secure the confidence of the country, I felt
it my duty to inform his Majesty that I could not fulfill
the commission with which he was pleased to honor me,
and his Majesty informed me that he would renew his
communications with his former ministry."

Lord Lyndhurst, immediately following, said,—

"My Lords, I am anxious to explain my part in these
transactions. I feel it a duty I owe to my Sovereign—a
duty I owe to the country—a duty I owe to your Lordships' House, and, if your Lordships allow me to say so,
a duty which I owe to myself. On the day when his
Majesty accepted the resignations of the late ministers,
he was graciously pleased to desire me to attend him at
St. James's. I had had no previous communication with
his Majesty for a long period."

Having stated, in vague terms, the commission he received from the King, who sent for him as his former Chancellor, to consult him in the extraordinary crisis which had arisen, he thus proceeded:—

"I, of course (as it was my bounden duty to do), obeyed his Majesty. I should have basely shrunk from my duty if I had declined. In consequence of this interview I waited upon my noble friend the illustrious Duke, and communicated to him the task which had been imposed upon me by my Sovereign, and the distressing position in which his Majesty was placed."

He relates his conversation with the Duke of Wellington, but is silent as to what passed between him and Sir Robert Peel, and thus continues:—

"I communicated the result of my inquiry to his Majesty at the time appointed; all that was best calculated to afford him assistance—all that I had heard, all that I had learned—the result of my own meditations, I frankly communicated to my sovereign. His Majesty requested me to invite my noble and gallant friend to call upon him; I did so, and thus my mission terminated. It is for this, my Lords, of which I have now given you a full and faithful narrative, that I have been traduced, maligned, caluminated."

Having mentioned calumnies upon him in the press, he thus replied to a speech made against him in the House of Commons by Sir Francis Burdett:—

"He is reported to have affirmed that I acted inconsistently with my duty as a Judge of the land. I say that if he asserted this, he must, taking it at the best, be ignorant of the constitution of the country. He ought to know that, as a member of the Privy Council, I am bound by virtue of my office to give advice to my sovereign if he requires it. More than this, he ought to know, if he knows anything of the Constitution, that I have taken an oath to this effect; and more, he ought to know *that as a Judge I am bound to volunteer my advice to his Majesty if I consider any proposed course of proceeding inimical to the safety of the crown.* My Lords, excuse me if I go one step farther; he has charged me, as a Judge, with being the leader of a violent and virulent party in this House. Whether there is or is not such a faction in this House I will not stay to inquire; I wish to have no motives imputed to me; I impute none to other men. I will only say that I never aspired to such a position as leader of a party; it is alike foreign to my inclination and my habits. After the noble Earl opposite became minister, I never engaged in political discussions till the Reform Bill was brought forward. Thinking that the tendency of this measure was to destroy the monarchy and the constitution, was it not my duty as a Judge of the land, as a Privy Councillor, as a Member of your Lordships' House, with all my power to oppose it? If this measure had originated with, and been supported by my earliest and most valued friends—by the very friends of my bosom—I would have acted in the same way. So much for my conduct and the attacks upon me. For the rest, the Reformers are triumphant—the barriers are broken down, the waters are out—who can predict their course, or tell the devastation they will occasion?"[1]

With a very ample exercise of the *suppressio veri*, and a little of the *suggestio falsi*, he made a favorable impression on the House, and for a brief space he was rather considered an ill-used man. He had calculated confidently (and as it turned out successfully) on the ignorance of the assembly he was addressing, while he denounced the ignorance of his assailant in the House of Commons; for, neither Lord Grey nor the Chancellor, nor any other Peer, questioned the doctrine which he laid down *ex cathedra*, —that it is the duty of the Judges, *qua* Judges, to volunteer advice to the Crown, if they consider any proceeding of the King's ministers, in or out of Parliament, unconstitutional or mischievous. I presume he did not mean to include all County-Court Judges and inferior Magistrates. But, supposing his doctrine to extend only to the Judges of the superior courts. who take a special oath of office, I must be allowed to doubt whether *Puisnes* or *Chiefs* are guilty of any breach of duty, if disapproving of the policy of the Government, with respect to parliamentary reform, or to peace or war, or any other important question involving the safety of the State, they omit to volunteer their advice to the Crown as Judges; and if they were to demand an audience for this purpose, the application would be treated with just ridicule. The Judges can only advise the Crown upon such a subject as the power of the reign-

[1] 12 Hansard, 993.

ing sovereign to direct and control the education and the marriages of members of the Royal Family; and this only when they are called upon to do so by the advice of the Lord Chancellor.

Lyndhurst never again appeared in the House of Lords during any of the subsequent proceedings on the Reform Bill. He acquiesced in the recommendation of the Duke of Wellington that, "to avoid forcing the creation of Peers, all opposition to the Bill should be withdrawn;" and it passed without modification or amendment. Such was the result of the indiscreet attempt to "postpone the disfranchising clauses;" and the noble and learned author of it was pointed to by the finger of scorn as "the engineer hoist with his own petard." Although his party seemed irrevocably crushed, he himself by no means lost hope, justly trusting to the reaction which must inevitably follow such a popular movement, and to the blunders likely to be committed by the Liberals, who now foolishly believed themselves in possession of permanent power. Instead of following the example of Lord Tenterden, who vowed that he would never again enter the House of Lords after the Reform Bill passed,[1] Lyndhurst sagaciously predicted that he should ere long be again presiding on the woolsack. I was appointed Solicitor-General shortly after the dissolution of Parliament which followed, and he blamed me for giving up my circuit to accept this office, as he assured me I could not possibly hold it more than a few weeks.

At first it looked as if the Tories as a party were annihilated. When the new elections took place they could hardly show themselves on the hustings, and when the House of Commons met, the small number returned hardly filled the opposition bench. Sir Robert Peel wisely *reformed* the party, laying aside its ancient name, and calling his supporters to rally round him under the designation of "Conservatives." He declared that he acquiesced in the Reform Bill now that it was law, although he had opposed it in its progress, but his policy should be to check the further efforts of the Radical party, who not contented with what had been achieved, were desirous of completely subverting our institutions. He determined

[1] This vow of Lord Tenterden was fulfilled; for he died before Parliament met again.

that he would not factiously oppose any good measure which the Government might introduce, but that if goaded by their radical allies to propose any dangerous innovation, he would try to rouse an anti-revolutionary spirit in the nation. He therefore constantly attended in his place, while the Speaker was in the chair, shouldered by Mr. O'Connell and Mr. Henry Hunt, the most egregious of demagogues, who often sat down on the opposition bench by his side. Dexterously availing himself of the extravagances and errors of his antagonists, he ere long appeared to the discerning to be on the road to victory.

Lyndhurst at this time did not at all act in concert with Peel, and was actuated by totally different feelings. His object was to harass and discredit the Government by all means, without considering whether they were fair or factious, and without foresight as to their effect upon the country, or upon the permanent success of his own party.

His first effort in the new Parliament was against myself,—not from malice, I believe, but rather from a love of mischievous fun. I had represented Stafford in two Parliaments, and had complied with the well-known custom, which had prevailed in the borough at least ever since Sheridan first represented it, of paying them "head money." This could not properly be called *bribery*, for the voter received the same sum on which ever side he voted, but it might be treated as bribery in a court of law. For the Parliament after my appointment as Solicitor-General I had been returned for the newly enfranchised borough of Dudley, where the most absolute purity prevailed. But there had been a petition against the new return for Stafford, and a bill had been passed by the House of Commons to indemnify all witnesses who should be examined to prove that bribery had been committed at the last or any former election for the borough. I had nothing to do with any of these proceedings; but when the bill came up to the lords, Lyndhurst represented that it was a job of the Solicitor-General, and that the bill had been so framed as to indemnify him without his being examined as a witness. In the debate on the second reading, he said:—

"It appeared that bribery to a great extent had existed at Stafford, both on former occasions and at the late election. The evidence showed that not only the electors but the candidates were deeply implicated in these transactions, and he considered it necessary that their lordships should take some effectual measure to check such flagrant corruption. But this was a Bill to indemnify all persons examined as witnesses, all candidates, and all others who had violated the law and been guilty of bribery."

In the meantime a whisper was circulated through the House that the Solicitor-General was standing below the bar, and all eyes were turned upon him. A noble lord present proposed to introduce a clause by which all who had been candidates for Stafford should be exempted from the indemnity; but Lyndhurst, satisfied with having had a laugh at an old friend, afterwards suffered the bill to pass quickly through the House. In truth it extended only to those who should be examined under it as witnesses.[1]

Lyndhurst was in downright earnest the next time he came forward, which was to oppose a bill introduced by Lord Brougham, for the establishment of the County Court jurisdiction, which, when at last carried, proved so beneficial. He prudently abstained from objecting to the second reading, but before allowing it to be considered in the committee, he delivered a very long and elaborate speech against it, giving a very favorable specimen of his powers of reasoning and misrepresentation. He said:—

" He would freely admit that with the multitude this was a popular measure. Well it might be so. It promised cheap—it promised expeditious law. These were plausible topics—topics well calculated to catch the breath of popular opinion. But it should be borne in mind—and he trusted the country and their lordships would think well upon it—that cheap law did not always mean cheap justice, nor expeditious law expeditious justice. To what," he asked, " is to be ascribed the admirable administration of real justice in the country? To the central system by which it is administered. Twelve or fifteen judges, educated in the same manner, sitting together at one time and in one place, consulting each other daily, and, if need be, hourly, subject to the criticism of their compeers, subject also to the examination of an acute and vigilant bar, kept constantly alive to the justice of the decision of the judges by their regard for the interests of the judges and their own credit,—ensure for the suitors a certainty, a precision,

[1] 17 Hansard, 1071.

a purity, and even a freedom from the suspicion of corruption, such as no other country in the world could ever boast of."

He then went over the several enactments of the bill, considerably perverting their meaning, and after representing that it was only a device to snatch at popularity and to extend the patronage of the Lord Chancellor, concluded by disclaiming any personal feeling on this occasion, or any party bias, and assuring their Lordships that he was "reluctantly compelled to try to arrest a measure so mischievous in discharge of the duty he owed to his country, to Westminster Hall, and to himself."[1]

On the third reading there was a fair trial of the strength of political parties, and the whippers-in on both sides exerted themselves to the utmost in the muster of peers and proxies from remote parts of Europe. Lyndhust again made a very clever speech, and, I really believe, even influenced some votes—particularly by his argument, that the bill was " an enormous job." Said he, with an ostentatious sneer:—

"I am well aware that personally my noble and learned friend on the woolsack has no wish for this unlimited power; my noble and learned friend does not desire this last patronage, and while exercised by him it would be safe; but the Great Seal may be transferred to another who may be ambitious and desirous of gratifying puffing and sycophantish dependents. My noble and learned friend has candidly told us that he had looked about to see where this formidable patronage could be lodged with less peril, and that, not being successful in his search elsewhere, he had been compelled as a *dernier ressort* to retain it for himself. I am ready and willing to give my noble and learned friend credit for the most patriotic views and the most disinterested intentions; but we must not legislate for individuals; we must contemplate the possibility of a Lord Chancellor, with the commanding eloquence and transcendent abilities of my noble and learned friend, yet not possessed of his moderation and disinterestedness,—on the contrary, anxious to devote the whole of his energies to the purposes of personal aggrandizement, and indisposed to those institutions which may appear to him calculated to check him in his

[1] 18 Hansard, 868.

career. Such a person, conscious of the fleeting nature of popular applause, might wish to establish his power on some more substantial foundation, and might find it convenient to surround himself with a band of gladiators arrayed as judges, ready to obey his commands and to deal destruction among his adversaries."[1]

Upon a division, the Peers present were equally divided, but, proxies being called, the bill was rejected by a majority of five,[2] and the measure was delayed above twelve years.

In 1834 Lyndhurst took very little part in parliamentary proceedings. Various bills for the reform of the Common Law had been prepared, but they could not be introduced by reason of my no longer being a member of the House of Commons. At the beginning of the Session, I vacated my seat on my promotion to the office of Attorney-General, and losing my election for Dudley, on account of the growing unpopularity of the Government, I was not returned for Edinburgh till within a few weeks of the prorogation. Pepys, although afterwards Chancellor was then of so little mark or likelihood that nothing was intrusted to him. The bill which chiefly occupied the two Houses was that for the Amendment of the Poor Law; and this Lyndhurst could not very well oppose, as it was warmly supported by the Duke of Wellington. But active assaults on the Whig Ministers were less necessary, as they seemed doomed to destruction by internal discord. The Radicals not giving the Reform Bill a fair trial, and still unreasonably urging on further concessions, the Cabinet was divided as to how far these demands should be complied with, and four of the then most Conservative members seceded. An arrangement followed which rather made the Government more popular—but this had scarcely been completed when a foolish dispute arose about some Irish job, which induced Lord Grey to "descend from power." Lyndhurst thought the Great Seal already his,—when, to the astonishment of all mankind, it was announced that the Whigs were to go on under Lord Melbourne as Premier. Many were astonished at

---

[1] It is a curious fact, that at this time Brougham had contrived to have all the journalists in London writing in his praise; some from real admiration—some from favors actually conferred, but more from expectations lavishly excited.
[2] 19 Hansard, 372.

Lyndhurst's inactivity for the remainder of the session. Brougham, still Chancellor,—boasting that he might have been First Lord of the Treasury himself, and that he put in Lamb as his subordinate,—played most fantastic tricks, which made his colleagues weep. These might have been turned to excellent account for the public amusement,— but Lyndhurst, who continued Chief Baron, was obliged to be out of town upon the circuit. He comforted himself by thinking that the best policy for the time probably was to abstain from the danger of resuscitating the popularity of the Whigs by any Tory assault upon them.

Had the Whig Ministers been allowed again to meet Parliament, Brougham holding the Great Seal, they must have been regularly and permanently turned out in a few weeks by a vote of want of confidence. But William IV., by an act of folly which was deplored by those whom he wished to serve, prolonged Whig rule for six years, with the interval of "the hundred days"[1] during which Lyndhurst was tantalized by holding the Great Seal in his slippery grasp.

No one heard the news of the dismissal of the Whigs with more astonishment than the Lord Chief Baron. It was then term time, and he was sitting in the Court of Exchequer, when a note was brought to him from the Duke of Wellington announcing that his grace had been summoned to attend the King at Brighton with a view to the formation of a new administration, and requesting the Chief Baron to call upon him at night when he expected to be again back in London. The manner of the noble and learned Judge, on this occasion, betrayed some excitement; but, without any communication to his brethren on the bench, he soon seemed to resume the consideration of the case under discussion, and he continued to attend to the arguments of counsel for the rest of the day as if nothing extraordinary had occurred. He was in a state of great anxiety from the time of his leaving the Court till the moment arrived for knowing his fate at Apsley House. The Duke at once told him that Sir Robert Peel, who was then at Rome, was to be Prime Minister; but there could be no doubt that he

---

[1] Sir Robert Peel's administration of 1835 was called " The hundred days," in reference to the designation given to Napoleon's reign after his return from Elba, which lasted exactly so long.

would concur in recommending that Lord Lyndhurst should again be Chancellor, and that the King wished the transfer of this, and all the other offices of the Government, to take place as speedily as possible. It was then agreed between them that, to gratify His Majesty's impatience to be rid of his Reform Ministers, a sort of interim Government should be arranged till Sir Robert Peel's return home; that the seals of all the Secretaries of State should be demanded from them, and held by the Duke of Wellington; but that the Great Seal, as was usual, should be allowed to remain in the hands of the present Chancellor for a short time, to allow him to give judgment in cases which had been argued before him.

Lord Brougham having, in a manner rather unusual and uncourteous, returned the Great Seal to the King on the 22nd of November, it was the same day delivered to Lord Lyndhurst; but he continued to preside as Chief Baron till the end of Michaelmas Term.

CHAPTER CCXIX.

LORD CHANCELLOR DURING THE 100 DAYS, AND EX-CHANCELLOR DURING THE ADMINISTRATION OF LORD MELBOURNE.

WHEN Lord Lyndhurst appeared as Chancellor at the sittings after term, there was a divided feeling among those whose personal interests were not touched by political changes. The eccentricities of his predecessor weighed in his favor as well as his own clear intellect and agreeable manners; but a recollection of his dislike of business and recklessness as to the fate of the suitors, caused some even to long for the conscientious *cunctating* and doubting Eldon.

Sir Robert Peel, on returning from Italy, although he acquiesced in Lyndhurst's appointment as Chancellor, reposed little confidence in him, and without consulting him wrote the "Tamworth Manifesto," laying down the liberal principles on which the new Government was to be conducted. As he chose to dissolve Parliament, I was obliged to go down to Edinburgh, and to stand a formi-

dable contest against the now Marquis of Dalhousie and
Governor-General of India, then Lord Ramsay, the Peelite
candidate. When I was going to the Court of King's
Bench the morning after my return to London, I encountered the Lord Chancellor stepping out of his coach at
Westminster. He took me into his private room, and
said, "Well! private friendship is more powerful than party
feeling. I can hardly be sorry that you have won, and,
behold! as a pledge of peace (so far as it can be permitted
between an ex-Attorney-General and the Lord Chancellor
he wishes to turn out) take that splendid nosegay and
carry it to the King's Bench, telling that I gave it you."
With proper acknowledgments, and a reciprocation of
good-will *equally sincere*, I took the nosegay which had
been prepared for the Lord Chancellor after ancient custom, in the fashion of that used by Lord Keeper Guild-
ford in the reign of Charles II., to conceal his dying lineaments from the gazing crowd. Entering the Court of
King's Bench in my robes, I exhibited the nosegay in
testimony of my Edinburgh triumph and of the magnanimity of the Lord Chancellor.

Upon the meeting of the new Parliament, the Lord
Chancellor had a very distasteful task to perform, which
was to express the King's approbation of the Speaker
elected by the Commons contrary to the wishes of his Ministers—a bitter foretaste of what was to follow. Nevertheless, said his Lordship, with a serene countenance:—
"Mr. Abercromby, his Majesty is fully satisfied of your
zeal for the public service, and his Majesty therefore does
most readily and fully approve of the choice of his faithful
Commons, and confirms you as their speaker." [1]

The King's Speech was most conciliatory to the Liberal
party, recommending the reform of the ecclesiastical courts,
a marriage bill for the relief of Dissenters, the reform of
municipal corporations, and almost all the other measures
which the late Government had promised. But this
attempt seemed only to inflame party animosity, and the
debate upon the address was carried on with extreme
rancor. The late Chancellor and his successor, although
afterwards on terms of the closest intimacy and cordial
co-operation, assailed each other in language which, had
they not presided on the woolsack—supposed to consti-

[1] 26 Hansard, 62.

tute a status of *non-combatancy* or *pugnacious incapacity*—would have rendered a hostile meeting on Wimbledon Common next morning indispensable. Lord Brougham began the affray by denouncing as unconstitutional the dismissal of the late Ministers while they fully enjoyed the confidence of the House of Commons. He contended that the present ministers, by accepting office, were answerable for it, whether they had previously advised it or not; and he particularly taunted the Chancellor with his sudden apparent conversion (manifested by the King's Speech) to liberal measures, which he had been in the habit of violently opposing. He at the same time insinuated that this conversion could not be sincere, and referred in a very galling manner to his miraculous change of opinion on the question of Catholic emancipation.

Lord Lyndhurst rose in a real passion, and after complaining that the noble and learned lord had maligned him, thus continued:

"The noble and learned lord has dared to say that I pursued the course I took for the purpose of retaining my possession of office. I deny peremptorily the statement of the noble and learned lord. I say, if I may make use of the expression, *he has uttered an untruth* in so expressing himself. So far from that measure being brought forward and supported by us with a view to preserve our places, it must be well known that we hazarded our places by pursuing that course. What right, then, has the noble and learned lord in his fluent, and, I may say *flippant* manner, to attack me as he has dared to do?"

He then referred to what Lord Brougham had said about the Duke of Wellington's explanation of the manner in which the change of Government had been brought about:—

"The view given of that statement was a misrepresentation by the noble and learned lord. His quickness and his sagacity must have caused him to understand the noble Duke, and I can ascribe what he affirmed only to an intention to misrepresent."—(Cries of *Order! order!*)

Lord Brougham.—" I will just use the same language to the noble and learned lord that he uses to me, if he chooses to make this an arena of indecency."

Lord Lyndhurst.—" Perhaps I had no right, in strictness, to say that the noble and learned lord intended to pervert, but I have stated my reasons for the conclusion to which I have come; those reasons are satisfsctory to my own mind, and the noble and learned lord has not denied the correctness of my statement."

Lord Brougham.—" Every word of it is incorrect."

Lord Lyndhurst then vindicated the manner in which the late ministers had been dismissed :—

"I should have acted exactly as his Majesty has acted. I consider myself, as one of the ministers, responsible for what has been done, and I should have been ashamed of myself if I had been called upon to advise his Majesty and I had not advised him to dismiss the late ministers."

Lord Brougham.—" The present is the first occasion on which I ever heard any one—beyond the merest wrangling clown—use language so confounding the difference between erroneous opinion and misstated fact. I deny positively having accused the noble and learned lord on the woolsack of having sacrificed his principles to retain office."

Lord Lyndhurst.—" Understanding that the noble and learned lord has withdrawn his offensive imputation, I feel bound to apologize for the warmth I have evinced."

Lord Brougham.—" I retract nothing."

It seems to me that Lyndhurst is to be blamed severely for his share in this squabble. The charge of having suddenly supported Catholic emancipation that he might keep his office was not an affirmation of a fact upon which the *lie* could properly be given; and secondly, he gave no answer to the charge actually made against him, when he said that the Duke of Wellington and Sir Robert Peel brought forward the measure of Catholic emancipation from good motives, as they were not inculpated, and although they might have acted patriotically, he might have acted from motives the most opposite.¹

During the fierce struggle which ensued in the House of Commons to determine the fate of the new Government, almost uninterrupted tranquillity prevailed in the House of Lords. There the opposition, having no strength, originated nothing; and Peel thought there would be no use in carrying bills through one chamber of the legislature unless he could command a majority in the other. Mean-

¹ 26 Hansard, 63-151.

while Lyndhurst and Brougham continued at mortal enmity, even renouncing, when referring to each other in debate, the nominal *friendship* which generally is preserved in the fiercest conflicts of hostile lawyers. As Lyndhurst declared the commission issued by the late Government to inquire into the abuses of municipal corporations to be illegal, Brougham moved that a copy of it should be laid before the House, saying that "the innocent public imagined that something was to be done under it for the reform of corporations, but they learned from the statement of the noble and learned lord on the woolsack that it was to be the foundation of an impeachment." Lyndhurst now denied that he had pronounced the whole of the commission to be illegal, and intimated that when the Report of the Commissioners was presented, it might be acted upon by the present Government.

Lord Brougham.—" My Lords, I am lost in astonishment at what has now occurred. In the memory of man never was there such a scene as we have now witnessed, taken in connection with what passed the other night, when I was charged with having put the Great Seal to an illegal commission. And now this illegal commission is to be adopted by his Majesty's present ministers, and it is to prop up their popularity."

"The noble and learned Lord who had lately held the Great Seal" proceeded bitterly to reproach "the noble and learned Lord on the woolsack" with his inconsistencies. Lyndhurst attempted to vindicate himself; but, for once, lost his presence of mind or effrontery,—stammered, was confused, and evidently quailed under the chastisement which Brougham inflicted upon him. Lord Wharncliffe, trying to rescue him, represented this as an attack upon the new cabinet, as a body, and said that they had all been described as "apostates and sham reformers."

Lord Brougham.—" I have never called any one *an apostate.* It is a hard word to use, and I have not used it, although, certainly, I might have called noble Lords opposite 'sham reformers,' 'half-and-half reformers,' or 'milk-and-water reformers.' But if they intend to yield to the wishes of the people, they will not deserve those titles; and I hope that the noble and learned Lord on the woolsack may feel it for his interest to persevere in the intentions he has expressed, with a view to municipal reform."[1]

Who would then have supposed that the two noble and learned enemies would, before the lapse of many months, not only be cordially reconciled, but zealously united in opposing a Whig Government?

Peel, considering the division in the House of Commons on the Irish Church question tantamount to a vote of *want of confidence*, and having resigned, it was thought as a matter of course that Lyndhurst and Brougham would exchange positions, the latter being restored to the woolsack on the morrow; but a prophetic voice had uttered the fatal words, "O never shall sun that morrow see."

Lyndhurst declared that Brougham was ill-used by his exclusion from office, and I fully agreed in this sentiment. For the present the seals were put into commission, and I was restored to my old office of Attorney-General. I was the first to be installed in office, that I might sign the patents of my colleagues, and I was sworn in before Lord Chancellor Lyndhurst at his house in George Street, Hanover Square. He received me in a green silk dressing-gown, and when the ceremony was over, we took a jocular retrospect and prospect of political affairs. He at first said, "You must not expect ever to be Chancellor, for Brougham, as he can not be the man, is resolved to destroy the office, and I am the last of the race." He afterwards added, "If there is still to be a Great Seal, I strongly advise you to stand out for it; Brougham, being *civiliter mortuus*, it is yours by right."

Lyndhurst thus began a course of policy which he long earnestly pursued—to stir up strife between Brougham and me—being prepared to tell Brougham, as soon as they were on speaking terms again, that "Campbell was intriguing against him, and was his destined successor."

By this fleeting tenure of the Chancellorship, Lyndhurst had lost his office of Chief Baron of the Exchequer; but he was not dissatisfied with his present position, compared with that which he had before occupied; for as ex-Chancellor he now had the increased retired allowance of £5,000 a-year, without the expense and bore of going

[1] 26 Hansard, 304.

circuits, and he had nothing to think of, day or night, except the best means of annoying the Government.

He began his new career by introducing a very important bill,—which was not a party measure. The Duke of Beaufort having no male issue by his first wife, upon her death married her half-sister, by whom he had a son, who bore the second title of the family, "Marquis of Worcester." By the existing law this marriage was voidable, though not void: and, if set aside in the life-time of the parents, their children would have been considered illegitimate. The Duke's younger brother, Lord Granville Somerset, was married, and had a son, who in that case would have been entitled to succeed to the Dukedom. Lyndhurst, an intimate friend of the Duke and Duchess, being informed by them of the apprehensions they entertained, although the younger branch of the family had taken no steps to annul their marriage, boldly undertook to alter the law retrospectively in their favor. In an admirable speech, he pointed out the inconvenience and injustice arising from voidable marriages, and, as a remedy, proposed that no marriage hitherto contracted should be set aside on the ground of *affinity*, no proceeding for that purpose having been commenced before the passing of the Act, and that hereafter all marriages within the forbidden degrees either of affinity or consanguinity should be null and void *ab initio*. The bill was right in principle. I myself supported it when it came down to the House of Commons, and I cannot regret that it passed, although it was used afterwards to spread a false belief that till Lord Lyndhurst's Act a marriage between a man and the sister of his deceased wife was perfectly legal: whereas it always was, and I hope ever will be, deemed incestuous; and the only defect to be remedied was the imperfect procedure for declaring its illegality. The general law being improved, we may give Lyndhurst credit for what he did in this affair, without inquiring into his motives. But in the next matter in which he took an active part, no defence can be made for him.

There is nothing on which the prosperity and happiness of a country depend more than on a good system of municipalities. Self-government is the true principle on which human affairs ought to be conducted; and every city, every town, and almost every villiage, may, for the management of its local affairs, be a separate republic, under the control of a superintending power, which ought not to interfere with its free will, but to see that it keeps within its just jurisdiction, and conforms to the general law of the land. In early times when municipal corporations in England arose by royal grant, they tolerably well answered the purpose of their creation, the defined area to which the charter applied comprehending the whole of the existing town, and provision being made for the good management of the local affairs of the community by functionaries in the election of whom all the inhabitant householders had a voice. But, in the course of centuries, towns spread far beyond their original limits, having a large urban population not within the municipal jurisdiction; by-laws were passed, to which the courts of law very improperly gave effect, limiting the right of electing mayors, aldermen, and common-councilmen to a select body; the distinction was established between *inhabitants* and *freemen*, whereby respectable traders, domiciled in the borough, might be deprived of all municipal rights, while strangers, residing in a distant part of the kingdom, had a right to vote at all elections, if descended from freemen of the borough; there was no control over the expenditure of the funds of the borough arising from lands or tolls, and a system prevailed among almost all the boroughs of the kingdom of the most profligate waste, jobbing, corruption, oppression, and misrule. Again, towns had sprung up, more populous than London in the times of the Plantagenets, which were left without incorporation or municipal institutions of any kind, and in which *paving, cleansing, lighting, supplying with water, watching* and *preserving the peace* were either entirely neglected, or left to conflicting and absurd Acts of Parliament. To investigate and suggest a remedy for these multiplied mischiefs, commissioners had been appointed under Lord Grey's Government. They had prepared a very able Report upon which a bill was about to be drawn at the time of the sudden dismissal of the Whigs by William IV. in November, 1834. No one was more sensible of the crying necessity for municipal reform than Sir Robert Peel, or more sincerely desirous to see it accomplished. Accordingly he introduced a paragraph into the King's speech, referring to the report of the commissioners, and there can be no doubt that if he had continued in office, a bill very much the same with that which we proposed would have been introduced by him, and would have been supported with warm zeal as well as signal ability by his Chancellor Lord Lyndhurst.

Lord Melbourne being again at the head of the Government, notice was given in the House of Commons that municipal reform was to be his first measure, and the bill for this purpose was framed under my superintendence. With a view to correct proved abuses, and to introduce a uniform, simple and efficient plan for the government of municipalities throughout the kingdom, it certainly dealt very freely with existing charters and usages; but I can conscientiously and solemnly say that it was framed without any party bias,—purely with a view to the public good. It passed through the House of Commons by large majorities, Peel very fairly criticising some of its details, but giving it his general support.

When it reached the House of Lords, Lyndhurst vowed its destruction. Having a large majority at his back, the systematic policy he adopted was to throw out or damage every Government Bill, whatever might be its object or merits, as far as he could do so without exciting a loud burst of public reprobation against him, and at the end of the session to reproach the ministers for not being able to carry their measures, and for retaining office without power. The Municipal Reform Bill was particularly obnoxious to him, for, if carried, it would confer considerable credit upon the Whigs, and consolidate the existing coalition between them and the Radicals, who were much pleased with it, although they said it was in some of its enactments too aristocratic. Lyndhurst, by holding up his finger as a signal to the Lords, might have had it utterly rejected on the second reading; but he foresaw that this would have been quite as serious an affair in its consequences as the rejection of the Parliamentary Reform Bill, and he resorted to another mode of defeating it, by allowing it to be read a second time, and moving that counsel should be heard, and witnesses examined against it, on going into committee. These proceedings, he calculated, might be interminably prolonged, so as to take away all chance of the bill passing,—at least during the then pending session of Parliament.

In support of this course he argued that,—

"As charges of *abuse* formed the chief foundation for the measure, the petitioners against it had a right to be heard, and to prove that those charges were unfounded. The only objection to this course was the length of time which it might occupy. But can that delay be called long which justice requires? By this sweeping measure 240 corporations were to be swept away,—and, as nobody could deny that, if it had been directed against one accused corporation, a full hearing must have been given, would the House precipitately proceed to condemnation because delinquency was charged against many? Were it for a party object that the reform of corporations was to be effected before a dissolution of Parliament, he and their Lordships would understand how delay might be dangerous; but investigation must be courted, instead of being resisted, where disclosure was not dreaded. The measure was Whig,—Whig in its principle,—Whig in its character,—and Whig in its object."

He then went over the names of the twenty Commissioners, and asserted that, with the exception of Sir Francis Palgrave—a Tory, who had recommended himself by publishing something against corporations—each of them was either "a Whig," or "a Whig and something more." He again ventured to question the validity of the Commission, saying that—

"The noble and learned Lord, who had issued and defended it, administered justice admirably in that House; but that no reliance could be placed upon his judgment respecting a question of law which assumed a political shape. It was impossible that their Lordships could proceed on this Report, sent out to the public by a packed Commission, such as he had described. They were asked, on this evidence, to rob men of their franchise, and of their property, without a hearing, and without the form of a trial. He would remind their Lordships that these corporations were copies—imperfect copies, he allowed—of the three estates of the realm, and yet they were to be annihilated, for what purpose he could not tell, unless the new corporations were to serve as models for a change of constitution in their Lordships' House, abolishing the invidious distinction between peer and commoner. There would be no defense for the Church,—no defense for their own privileges, if they surrendered the corporations to condemnation unheard. Pause, my Lords; consider. At all events, observe the forms of justice. I know the *civium ardor prava jubentium* will not operate here."

Lord Lansdowne, after expressing astonishment that this bill should be now described as detestable in its object, and unconstitutional in its enactments, although it had passed through all its stages in the other House, and had been read a second time in this House without a word being said against its principle, proceeded to defend the Commissioners who had been so vehemently assailed, and to allude to the noble and learned lord's supposed early liberal tendencies:—

"I can assure the noble and learned lord, that with the politics of the Commissioners I am myself unacquainted; they may be what the noble and learned lord described them; but, supposing that the noble and learned lord is quite right in that respect, I do not know that the circumstance of a man being or having been 'a Whig and something more than a Whig,' disqualifies him for the exercise of any sort of judicial functions. I am afraid that if the circumstance of an individual having been 'a Whig and something more,' were to be a disqualification, it would reach to much higher and more eminent characters than those who have been the subject of the noble and learned lord's insinuations. I must, in justice to individuals, both in this House and out of it, express my humble opinion that neither Whiggism nor ultra-Whiggism necessarily infers infamy."

Lord Lyndhurst.—"I beg to say in explanation, that I made no charge against the Commissioners; my charge was against those who appointed them. Further, I feel that the noble Marquis in what he has said of those who were *Whigs and something more than Whigs*, has conveyed an insinuation against me. I never belonged to any political party till I came into Parliament. I never belonged to any political society. I have been in Parliament sixteen years, and I wish the noble Marquis to point out any speech or act of mine which can justify my being described as *a Whig, or something more than a Whig.*"

This must be confessed to be a very lame defense of his political consistency, ignoring all that he had said or done before he entered Parliament at an age nearly equal to that of William Pitt, when that statesman closed his illustrious career. However, the motion against the Government was carried by a majority of seventy.[1]

The speeches of counsel and the evidence against the bill having lasted many days, the Tory Peers themselves became so tired and nauseated, that Lyndhurst could not persuade them to attend longer, and they seemed ready to give up Church and State to Whigs, or the devil himself, rather than submit longer to such infliction. Besides, there was a terrible cry raised out of doors against this outrageous attempt to strangle a popular measure. The evidence was therefore closed, and the bill was allowed to go into committee.

Here Lyndhurst, according to his preconceived purpose, mutilated it; and by adding as well as striking out clauses, reduced it to such a deplorable state, that in practice it could not be *worked*. The only hope of its friends was that, by sending it back to the House of Commons, there might be such an expression of opinion there as might induce the lords not to insist upon their amendments.

After carrying the *amendment*, by which aldermen were to hold their office for life, Lyndhurst came down to me, while I was sitting at the bar in Black Rod's box, and said, with the grin upon his countenance which makes him so like Mephistophiles, "Well, I suppose you think we are mad?" I only shook my head. "What! not a smile?" I said, "It now becomes too serious;" and he walked off.

When the Report of the Committee was discussed in the House of Lords, Lord Denman, as head of the Common Law, considered it his duty to defend the Commissioners, who were all barristers, from the aspersions cast upon them :—

"They have been described as entertaining extreme opinions on political subjects. Such an imputation is more applicable to the noble and learned person by whom it has been made. For that noble lord I have a great respect. I am indebted to him personally for a long succession of kindnesses: but if it be a calumny to declare that he has changed his opinions, I am bound to say that I make this statement with the most perfect good faith,

[1] 29 Hansard, 1379-1425.

and I believe that such is the conviction of all who have known the noble and learned lord. I must say it is rather hard that members of the bar should be thus attacked, in a quarter where they have a right to expect protection and favor. The Commissioners are men of learning; they are men of science; they are men of consistent opinions; they are men of honorable principles, who have undertaken an important duty with the purpose of performing it honestly to their king and to their country. In spite of the insinuations of the noble and learned lord, I do, in my conscience, believe that they have so performed it."

Lord Lyndhurst.—" When my noble and learned friend the Chief Justice throws his arrows in the dark, I know not how to combat him. When a fact is stated, I know how to deny it; when a particular opinion is imputed to me, I know how to repel the imputation. I have been on terms of intimacy with my noble and learned friend for a long period; I went the same circuit with him; I have been engaged in conversation with him at different times; and if he speaks of a period of twenty years past, I can only say I am unable to call to my recollection all the opinions I may have then entertained, or all the words I may have then uttered; but I am sure that I *never belonged to any party or political society whatever.* I was attached to no party, neither to the Whigs nor to the Tories, nor (as my noble and learned friend would insinuate) to the Radicals."

Lord Denman.—" The supposed calumny, which has been so often repeated, I stated, believing it to be true; and I should now believe it to be true were it not for the assertion of my noble and learned friend. And really I feel somewhat astonished that when we are considering what really were the opinions of my noble and learned friend on political questions of the greatest importance and interest, which divided his contemporaries into keenly conflicting parties, he should plead forgetfulness as to the opinions which he entertained on these questions—twenty years ago undoubtedly—but when he had reached mature years. If those opinions are forgotten by himself, they are not forgotten, and can not be forgotten, by others. They were not uttered merely in the presence of those who were on terms of close intimacy with him, or in the course of private conversation, but they were openly avowed rather as if my noble and learned friend felt a pride in entertaining and avowing them."[1]

When the bill came back to the Commons "amended," or *mutilated* by the Lords, Lord John Russell, to save the dignity of their Lordships, yielded to some of their alterations of smaller importance, protesting that he did not agree with them, but strenuously resisted those which would have completely obstructed its operation; and Sir Robert Peel, to his immortal honor, throwing his Chancellor overboard, took part with the Government. But what was to become of the bill when the Commons in conference informed the Lords that the Commons disagreed with these amendments?

Lyndhurst was alarmed lest there should be a public disturbance if the bill were lost, and began to consider that if he came to a downright quarrel with Peel, his chance of resuming the Great Seal, when the country should get tired of the Whigs, was gone. He therefore advised the Lords not to insist on the amendments to which the Commons dissented. Thus he concluded a very shuffling speech:—

"Your Lordships must be aware how much I have been assailed during these discussions, both in and out of Parliament, on account of the course which I have felt it my duty to pursue with regard to this Bill. Allow me to say, that I should not be ashamed to have been a volunteer in my attacks upon it; but the fact is, that I have been no volunteer. Many noble Lords with whom I have been in the habit of acting for years, and who thought that from my professional habits I was calculated to lead their efforts, requested me to take the management of the opposition to it. I yielded to their solicitations: and, having done so, I have endeavored to discharge my duty to them, and to my country, firmly, strenuously, and to the best of my ability. I have been charged with having some party views to accomplish, some indirect ambition to gratify by this opposition. I deny it once and for ever; all my ambition has long been satisfied. I have twice, to borrow a phrase from these municipal proceedings, *passed that chair* [pointing to the woolsack], under two successive sovereigns. I have had, to borrow a phrase from a successful revolutionary usurper, that

[1] 30 Hansard, 1042.

splendid bauble [pointing to the mace¹ which lay on the woolsack] carried before me. Whatever ambitious views I may have had in early life have all been fulfilled."²

Notwithstanding these asseverations of satiated ambition, the Great Seal was an object as near his heart as when he first made his famous speech against Catholic emancipation, and his famous speech for Catholic emancipation. Power and patronage were sweeter to him from having tasted them, and the emoluments of office were more than ever necessary to him, on account of the expensive establishment he had to support. But his head had been turned by the unlimited sway which he had established in the Upper House; and he appears actually to have had thoughts of turning off Peel, and setting up for himself as leader of the Tory party. When the Municipal Reform Bill was in the Committee, I took him aside and reproached him with striking out clauses which Peel had approved of, and supported in the Commons. His only answer was, " Peel ! what is Peel to me ? D——n Peel ! ! !" This, however, might be only *badinage*, intimating that he would not be slavishly led by Peel, although he might still consider him head of the party.

The bill received the Royal Assent, and Parliament was prorogued on the 10th of September.

Before the session closed Brougham and Lyndhurst were so far reconciled that they spoke to each other in private on a familiar footing, and Lyndhurst embraced the opportunity of trying to incense Brougham more keenly against Lord Melbourne and his former colleagues for excluding him from office, and against me, upon the alleged ground that I was plotting to obtain possession of the Great Seal. I remember once, after arguing a case at the bar of the House of Lords, coming upon the steps of the throne in my silk gown and full-bottom wig (such as the Chancellor wears), wishing to have an opportunity of speaking to Lord Melbourne. I then heard Lord Lyndhurst halloo out to Lord Brougham, so as almost to be heard distinctly in the gallery, " Brougham, here is Campbell come to take his seat as Chancellor upon the woolsack." The Duke of Cumberland (afterwards King of

¹ The Great Seal, being then in commission, was in the custody of Sir Charles Pepys, Master of the Rolls, the first Commissioner ; and Lord Denman officiated as Speaker. ² 30 Hansard, 1351.

Hanover) was standing close by, and Lyndhurst said to him, in Brougham's hearing, "Sir, this is Sir John Campbell, now Attorney-General, who is very soon to be our Chancellor." As yet Brougham had been hushed into a sort of feverish repose by the tale that his reappointment to his former office was deferred on account of some personal pique of the King, which they hoped ere long to overcome.

A calm prevailed till the beginning of another year; but before Parliament again met it was indispensably necessary that a new arrangement should be made with respect to the Great Seal, and that some one should be fixed upon for Chancellor, as the business of the Court of Chancery had been disposed of in a very unsatisfactory manner by the Lords Commissioners, and the judicial business in the House of Lords had, during the preceding session, been almost entirely neglected between the two ex-Chancellors, Lyndhurst and Brougham. The newspaper press was loud in its complaints, and Sir Edward Sugden (afterwards Lord St. Leonards) had published a pamphlet, to show the necessity for a change.

Lord Melbourne now announced to me that Brougham could not be reappointed, saying with deep emphasis—"It is impossible to act with him;" and stated the plan proposed to be, that Pepys should be Chancellor, and that Bickersteth should succeed him as Master of the Rolls, with a peerage. He tried to smooth me by a declaration, that he and all his collegues set so high a value on my services in the House of Commons, that they could not spare me from that field in which the real battle was to be fought. In truth, the battle most dreaded was in the House of Lords; for it was well foreseen, that Brougham's exclusion from office would drive him into furious opposition; and, Pepys being known to be very feeble in debate, the object was to select an assistant champion for the defense of the Government. A most unfortunate choice was made, and it was very speedily repented of.

The consequence was, that in the ensuing session of Parliament Lyndhurst was compared to "a bull in a china shop." Brougham took his exclusion so much to heart and was so much depressed. that his health suffered, his reason was in danger, and he remained in seclusion at his house in Westmorland. The new Chancellor, although an excellent Equity Judge, could hardly put two sentences together in the House of Lords; and the new Master of the Rolls, under the title of Lord Langdale, according to his own confesssion—" when he rose to speak, did not know whether his head or his heels were uppermost," and, intending to support ministers, unintentionally inflicted a mortal wound on a Chancery Reform Bill, which they had introduced. Lyndhurst, under these circumstances, took advantage of his position, laying down for law what suited his purpose, and making very unfair attacks upon members of the Government who belonged to the other House of Parliament.

A bill for disfranchising the borough of Stafford offered him irresistible temptation to assail the Attorney-General, under pretense of defending him. Although the fact was well known that every member who had sat for Stafford during the last hundred years had paid "headmoney" to the voters as regularly as he paid fees to the officers of the House of Commons when he was sworn in, and it had been proved before the committee that Sir John Campbell had conformed to the usage, yet Lyndhurst pretended to disbelieve this evidence, and opposed the further progress of the bill, unless the preamble were proved by witnesses examined on oath at the bar.

"Why, my Lords," said he, with affected solemnity, while there was a broad grin upon the face of every other peer present, " in the evidence on which you are asked to pass this bill, a case of the grossest bribery and corruption is made out against his Majesty's Attorney-General. Will your Lordships assume that charge to be established without affording to Mr. Attorney the opportunity of appearing at your bar to defend himself against an accusation so grave? I am making no rash or unfounded assertion. I will read to your Lordships that part of the evidence which must induce your Lordships unanimously to invite him to refute the calumny:—

" *Q*. 'Have you any knowledge of any bribery or corrupt practices having taken place at the last election, or any previous election for Stafford?—*A*. Not at the last; but at Sir John Campbell's in 1831.

" *Q*. 'What are you?—*A*. I am a solicitor by profession.

"*Q.* 'Do you know of voters being paid?—*A.* I paid them myself at Sir John Campbell's election.

"*Q.* 'In what interest were you?—*A.* In Sir John Campbell's.

"*Q.* 'How many did you pay?—*A.* 531 out of 556.

"*Q.* 'What was the sum of money paid?—*A.* £3 10*s.* for a single vote, and £6 for a plumper.

"*Q.* 'Did you pay every voter?—*A.* There were 556 voters, and 531 I paid.'[1]

"That solicitor there clearly imputes to the Attorney-General the infamous crime of bribery and corruption. A Stafford banker follows, who says, that 'Sir John Campbell, while a candidate, had drawn upon their bank to the amount of thousands of pounds.' But it is impossible for your Lordships, upon such an improbable tale, to proceed to the disfranchisement of this borough."[2]

As the session advanced—Lyndhurst, finding that he had supreme sway in the House of Lords, and that, by reason of the growing unpopularity of the ministry, the obstruction of their measures, even the most salutary, caused little public indignation,—hardly any Government bills were allowed to pass. Some were pusillanimously surrendered as soon as an intimation was given by the "Obstructer-General" that they were not approved. But several, which I had introduced, and carried through the House of Commons, I insisted that Lord Melbourne should struggle for to the last. The object of these was to remedy the mutilations which the Municipal Reform Bill had suffered in the last session, and to supply defects which experience had proved to lessen its utility. Lyndhurst smashed them all, without discrimination and without remorse. Peel still supporting us upon this subject, we persisted to carry our Bill, the necessity for which was most pressing and most palpable, till there was a collision between the two Houses such as had not occurred since the time of the Revolution in 1689. Each refusing to

---

[1] This witness had betrayed me, and gone over to the enemy. This part of his evidence, however, was quite true.

[2] 32 Hansard, 1005.

Extract from a letter to my brother, dated 12th July, 1836 :—

"I was in the House of Lords in a peerage case to-day. I asked Lyndhurst if he thought it a magnanimous warfare which the House of Lords was carrying on against me. He protested ignorance of any bad design, and swore that all he had said was in fun."

give way, and no effect being produced by reasons assigned in writing at *close conferences*, we at last came to an *open conference* in the Painted Chamber, which was conducted according to the ancient forms. One peer being considered equal to two commoners, we, the managers for the Lower House, were twice as numerous as the managers for the Upper House; but, considered little better than a mob, we stood bareheaded, while their Lordships sat covered. The debate was a sharp one, although conducted with decorum, and we certainly had the best of the argument. As might easily have been forseen, no converts were made, and on our return to our own House we soon had a message from the Lords that "their Lordships still insisted on their amendments," which nullified the bill. It was then abandoned, amidst bitter complaints against their Lordships and their factious adviser. These at last found sympathy with the public, and Lyndhurst was severely blamed by the press and at public meetings.

In the hope of palliating his conduct, a few days before the conclusion of the Session, he delivered one of his ablest and most memorable speeches. A few specimens will show sufficiently its tone and character:—

"It is with extreme reluctance that I rise to address you on this occasion; but I am charged with having 'mutilated' bills laid on your Lordships' table by his Majesty's Government. A noble Lord has stated in distinct terms that the course which I have individually pursued has been calculated to alienate from your Lordships' House the regard and the respect of the country. It is obvious that these charges are to take a wider range than the circle in which I move, and to make a lasting impression against me in the minds of all whom my name has ever reached. Therefore have I felt myself called upon to rise for the purpose of entering on a vindication of my character, which has been so unjustly assailed."

He proceeds to contend generally that he, and those with whom he acted, constituted the mildest, the most forbearing, the most disinterested, and the most constitutional opposition ever known since Parliaments began, and thus prepares for an illustration of his merits on particular occasions:—

"My Lords, it is impossible to take a view, however

slight, of the discussion in which we have been engaged, without referring to his Majesty's speech at the commencement of the session, and without contrasting the brilliant anticipations with which we began, with the sad reality which we have since had to deplore. The result has been as disproportioned in execution to the expectations which were held out, as the *lofty position* of the noble Viscount at that period with what he will allow me to style his *humble condition* at the present moment. Gazing on these two pictures, one is tempted to apply to the noble Viscount that which was said of a predecessor of the noble Viscount in the high office of first Minister of the Crown, who, in the careless confidence of his character, I can not help thinking, bore some resemblance to his noble successor:—

> ' His promises were as he then was—mighty;
> But his performance as he is now—nothing.' "

Lyndhurst then goes over *seriatim* the various measures recommended in the King's Speech, and shows that, notwithstanding his desire to support them as far as he could conscientiously, they had either entirely miscarried in Parliament, or had been partially adopted in an altered form. Thus he perorates:—

"In former times, my Lords, amid such defeats and disasters, and unable to carry those measures which he considered essential and necessary, a minister would have thought that he had only one course to pursue. These are antiquated notions—everything has changed. This fastidious delicacy forms no part of the character of the noble Viscount. He has told us, and his acts correspond with his assertions, that, notwithstanding the insubordination which prevails around him, in spite of the sullen and mutinous temper of his crew, he will stick to the vessel while a single plank remains afloat. Let me, however, as a friendly adviser of the noble Viscount, recommend him to get her as speedily as possible into still water.

> ' Fortiter occupa
> Portum.'

"Let the noble Viscount look to the empty benches around him.

> ' . . . nonne vides, ut
> Nudum remigio latus,
> . . . . ac sine funibus
> Vix durare carinæ
>   Possint imperiosius
> Aequor?'

After all, there is something in the efforts and exertions of the noble Viscount not altogether unamusing. It is impossible, under any circumstances, not to respect

> ' A brave man struggling in the storms of fate.'

May a part, at least, of what follows, be averted:—

> ' And greatly falling with a falling state.'

"My consolation is, that whatever be the disposition of the noble Viscount, he has not sufficient strength, though his locks, I believe, are yet unshorn, to pull down the pillars of the building, and involve the whole in his ruin. I trust it will long survive his fall."

It was supposed that he would conclude by moving an address to the King "to remove his present Ministers from his presence and councils forever;" but the actual motion (which caused considerable merriment) was for "a return of the public bills which had been introduced into Parliament during the present session, with the dates of their being rejected or abandoned, or receiving the royal assent."

Lord Holland expressed some astonishment that the noble Lord, instead of being ashamed of the devastation he had committed in the Parliamentary campaign, seemed to glory in his exploits, and to have made this motion that he might have an opportunity of recapitulating them, like Alexander at the famous " feast for Persia won":—

> Soothed with the sound the King grew vain,
> Fought all his battles o'er again,
> And thrice he routed all his foes, and thrice he slew the slain."

Lord Melbourne.—" I readily admit the great powers and eloquence possessed by the noble and learned Lord opposite—his clearness in argument and his dexterity in sarcasm can not be denied; and if the noble and learned Lord will be satisfied with a compliment confined strictly to ability, I am ready to render that homage to him. But, my Lords, ability is not everything—propriety of conduct —the *verecundia*—should be combined with the *ingenium*, to make a great man and a statesman. It is not enough to be *duræ frontis, perditæ audaciæ*. The noble and learned Lord has referred to various historical characters, to whom he has been pleased to say that I bear some resemblance. I beg in return to refer him to what was once said by the Earl of Bristol of another great statesman of former times (the Earl of Strafford), to whom, I think, the noble and learned Lord might not inapplicably be compared. 'The malignity of his practices was hugely aggravated by his vast talents, whereof God had given him the use, but the devil the application.' What must the House think of the noble and learned Lord when he concludes his speech with a miserable motion for returns, which, from the numerous minute details entered upon by him in the course of his address, he seems to be familiarly acquainted with, and to have been long conning over?"

Lord Melbourne then, in what was considered the best speech he ever delivered, went through the bills which Lyndhurst had factiously defeated, showing that several of the most important of them had been supported by the great bulk of the Conservative party in the other House, and thus concluded:—

"The noble and learned Lord kindly advises me to resign, notwithstanding his own great horror of taking office after his ambition is already so fully satisfied. But I will tell the noble and learned Lord that I will not be accessory to the sacrifice of himself which he would be ready to make if the duties of the Great Seal were again forced upon him. I conscientiously believe that the well-being of the country requires that I should hold my present office—and hold it I will—till I am constitutionally removed from it."[1]

The debate being over, the *desperate audacity* of the noble and learned Lord was converted into a good-humored smile, and, going over to Lord Melbourne, they laughed and joked together, both pleased with themselves, thinking that in this rencontre each had tilted to the admiration of the bystanders.

I ought to have mentioned that, during this session, Lyndhurst did support one good measure, which he had formerly violently opposed—the bill for allowing prisoners the benefit of counsel on all criminal trials. Fortunately, this time it was not brought in by the Government, and Lyndhurst now said that "withholding from prisoners in any case the aid of counsel was a disgraceful remnant of our barbarous criminal code;" and, without ever alluding to the fact that he had before opposed the Bill *totis viribus*, he gave an admirable answer to all his former arguments against it.

[1] 35 Hansard, 1282.

In 1837 the House of Lords assumed a new aspect, and Lyndhurst gained a most formidable ally, of whose assistance he unsparingly availed himself, if he had anything to say or to do of which he was ashamed. Brougham was, at last, convinced that what had been hinted to him about "superable objections" in the royal mind was pure fiction, and that the Whig leaders were determined never again to sit with him in the Cabinet. After a very narrow escape from insanity, having recovered both his physical and intellectual vigor, he returned to London, breathing revenge against his former associates. Lyndhurst not only incensed him still more by an exaggerated statement of his wrongs, but ambiguously held out to him vague hopes of being taken up by the Conservatives. Said he, "We are no longer to be considered Tories; we are actually more inclined to reform than the Whig party when you first joined it,—so that you may now coalesce with us without inconsistency,—leaving the apostate Whigs under the bondage of O'Connell and the ultra-Radicals." What other arguments were used, I know not, and it would be idle to conjecture; but certain it is that Lyndhurst soon acquired a complete ascendancy over Brougham's mind, which he has preserved, in a great degree, down to the present time. One art has been used, very palpably, by Lyndhurst,—to make Brougham believe that he influences Lyndhurst, and that Lyndhurst, whether in office or not, in point of consideration in the House of Lords, is contented to be second to him, but at a long interval. Lyndhurst pretended to abdicate the lead of the House of Lords in his favor, and, urging him to do what would be annoying to the Government, himself remained silent. When they were both standing together at the bar, I asked Lyndhurst what he now meant to do about the Irish Municipal Reform Bill, which he had contrived to defeat in the two preceding sessions. "Me!" exclaimed he, "what I mean to do! I never open my mouth now, and I oppose nothing. Ask Brougham, there, what he means to do. He is the man now. Brougham, lend me your majority—and 'I'll do, I'll do, and I'll do.'"

Assuredly he did long preserve a most wonderful reticence; but upon the motion for going into committee on this very bill, he again broke out, delivering a long and furious speech against it, or rather against its authors:—

"If the bill deserved all the praises bestowed upon it, what is the situation in which his Majesty's ministers stand? In no former period of our history has the government of this country been placed in such a position. To whom do they look for support? To the enemies of the Protestant Establishment. In Ireland their supporters are composed of the declared enemies of the Protestant Church in that country. In England the Dissenters are their chief friends and patrons. Deprive them of such supporters, and what becomes of the Government? They feel that they are gone, and that they can not float or draw breath a minute longer. My Lords, where is this to stop? Concession leads to concession. When will the noble Viscount stop in his downward career? The Ministerialists themselves say, 'We will receive all you offer, but we will take it only as an installment, and we will never cease agitating till the Protestant Church is laid prostrate. And this, the noble Viscount tells us, is the only mode of governing Ireland. It seems, my lords, that we Protestant Englishmen are to be governed by those who are *aliens in blood, in language, in religion.*"[1]

However, the friends of Sir Robert Peel, guided by his example, and alarmed for the consequences if the bill were again rejected, refused to stand by Lyndhurst any longer, and the bill was allowed to pass with a few slight mutilations.

Lyndhurst was about this time much alarmed by a bill I had introduced to abolish imprisonment for debt, and to provide a more efficient remedy for creditors, by the personal examination of the debtor as to his property and his past expenditure. As the bill originally stood, there was no limit to this power of inquiry, and every one was subject to it against whom a judgment was recovered. The stories about executions in Lyndhurst's house, I believe, were unfounded; but he was still needy from inconsiderate expenditure, and it was by no means clear that a judgment for a debt might not have been suddenly obtained against him. He came privately to me, and pointed out the oppression and extortion which might be practiced by the power proposed to be given to

[1] 38 Hansard, 1308.

judgment creditors, and insisted that, as the members of the two Houses were not subject to imprisonment for debt, they ought not to be subject to the inquisition substituted for it. There seemed to me to be reason in what he said, and I agreed to have the obnoxious clause amended; but, as expressly to exempt peers and members of the House of Commons from the pressure intended to compel the payment of just debts, as far as means existed, might have appeared invidious, we altered the enactment so as to gain our object, and finally the bill passed.

William IV. was now dying, and the Tories sanguinely looked forward to the commencement of a new reign. The power of the Crown in choosing ministers has been so much reduced that the Sovereign of England may be aptly compared to the marker in a billiard-room, who looks on and declares which competitor has won the game. Still, on rare occasions, when parties are nearly balanced, the royal will for a time prevails. The Whigs, retaining a considerable majority in the House of Commons, had, by resisting the unreasonable zeal of the ultra-Radicals for reforms inconsistent with our balanced constitution, lost popularity, and now a strong government might have been formed under Sir Robert Peel, who would have coerced the ultra-Tories led by Lord Lyndhurst. The Princess Victoria had cautiously abstained from indicating any political bias, and the Tories, hoping that she would prove to be theirs, extravagantly praised her nascent virtues. Terrible was their disappointment when it was announced that Lord Melbourne was to continue Prime Minister; and that, moreover, personally she felt a filial regard for him which, now that she was on the throne, she took no pains to conceal. A storm of vilification arose against her which was very discreditable to the Tory party. The practice was to contrast her invidiously with Adelaide, the Queen Dowager, and at public dinners to receive the Queen's health with solemn silence, while the succeeding toast of the Queen Dowager was the signal for long-continued cheers. Some writers went so far as to praise the Salic law, by which females are excluded from the throne, pointing out the happiness we should have enjoyed under the rule of the Duke of Cumberland, now King of Hanover, but consoling the nation by the assurance that his line would soon succeed, as the new Queen, from physical defects, could never bear children.[1]

I must do Lyndhurst the justice to say, that he not only did not encourage, but that he sincerely lamented all these foolish outrages, confining himself to what may be considered fair parliamentary warfare. Before the impending dissolution he took his annual review of the session, saying:—

"They were now at the close of the fifth month of the session of Parliament, and not a single important bill had been yet passed into law. They literally had done nothing during the five months they had been assembled. As far as legislation was concerned—and it was one of the most important duties of government—they had done nothing."

Then, *more suo*, having gone over the measures recommended from the Throne, the bills brought in, and the miserable fate which they experienced, he thus concluded:—

"The noble Viscount and his colleagues are utterly powerless. They are utterly inefficient and incompetent as servants to the Crown, and I must add also they are equally inefficient and incompetent as regards the people. Being now compelled to say so much respecting legislation, I abstain for the present from considering the foreign policy of the noble lord and his colleagues, and I will only say that all reasonable men have but one opinion of them—one idea is entertained respecting their conduct. It elicits the pity of their friends, and excites the scorn and derision of the enemies of our country. Such being the past and the present, what hope is there for the future? From the noble Viscount and his party there is no hope. But I do not entirely despair. A ray of hope breaks in upon us from another quarter, and I trust that at no distant period the alarm and apprehension on account of the danger to which the Church establishment in this country is exposed will be dissipated, and that perfect security will be given to the Protestant faith to which the great bulk of her Majesty's subjects are so warmly attached."[2]

Lord Lyndhurst had for some time been a gay widower, but being at Paris in the autumn of 1837, he fell in love

---

[1] Croker, in the "Quarterly Review," distinctly eulogized the Salic law, leaving the personal vituperation of the Queen to inferior hands.
[2] 38 Hansard, 1568.

with a beautiful Jewess. He gave her his hand, and spent the honeymoon with her at Fontainebleau. He used to give a glowing description of his happiness there, and she continued to make him a most excellent wife. She was the daughter of Lewis Goldsmith, a Portuguese Jew, once famous as the author of a Jacobinical, or rather regicidal, book—'The Crimes of Cabinets'—and who had been employed privately by all the great governments of Europe. Although the new Lady Lyndhurst, like her predecessor, tried to become a leader of fashion, she preserved an unsuspected reputation, and took devoted care of her husband, who, notwithstanding the juvenility of his mind and of his habits, was now sinking into the vale of years.

During the following year the ray of hope, alluded to by Lord Lyndhurst in his last speech, shone very faintly. The Queen continued to support Lord Melbourne, and he, by his very agreeable manners and excellent good sense, with the powerful help of Lord John Russell, tided over the session pretty smoothly. To be sure, the House of Lords was in a state of sad insubordination, and there we were at the mercy of our antagonists. The Chancellor (Lord Cottenham), with rising reputation as an Equity Judge, showed no improvement as a debater, and avoided any conflict with Brougham as with an evil spirit. Set on by Lyndhurst, Brougham now only considered how he could annoy and embarrass the Government most effectually. He did not profess to join the Tories, and was sometimes *ultra-Radical* in the principles he professed; but, whatever the Whigs did, his object was to show that, since they ceased to be guided by him, they were the most weak, ignorant, blundering, unconstitutional, wretched, and contemptible set of men on whom chance had ever conferred power. The rebellion in Canada having broken out, there were frequent discussions upon colonial and international law, in which Brougham, as suited the purpose of the moment, would lay down the most extravagant juridical doctrines. These Lyndhurst, I believe, secretly prompted; but although he never questioned them, he never openly corroborated them, for he was very chary of his reputation as a lawyer, and would always keep within the boundary which he encouraged others to transgress. Brougham was now by far the more conspicuous ex-Chancellor of the two, and

Lyndhurst, delighted by observing how perseveringly the Government was disparaged, remaining silent. Satisfied with what he had done by proxy, he did not even, this year, finish with "a review of the session."

"In the following year Lyndhurst was cruelly tantalized, for the Great Seal was not only visibly approaching him, but he had almost grasped it, when it was suddenly withdrawn from him, and he despondingly thought that it could never more be his. Lord Melbourne's Government was now becoming very weak. His alleged league with O'Connell, called the "Lichfield House Compact," was very unpopular. In his heart much more Conservative than Sir Robert Peel, he seemed occasionally to be ultra-Radical; and he did not proceed on any settled policy, but shaped his measures so as best to preserve a majority in the House of Commons. Contented with his own position and duties, he left the heads of departments to do as they liked. Dining almost constantly with the Queen, he neglected a most important duty of a prime minister—to give dinners to his supporters. Peel, on the contrary, by his assiduous attendance in the House of Commons, by avoiding grossly factious opposition, by the liberal indications he disclosed, and by the admirable dinners which he gave to all men of any eminence who were inclined towards him, stood very high in public opinion, and might be expected soon to command a majority in both Houses.

Lyndhurst opened the campaign in the Lords by bringing a charge against the Government for the appointment of the Earl of Fortescue as Lord-Lieutenant of Ireland, the ground being that he was unfit for this or any office under the Crown, because, when a member of the House of Commons (under the title of Lord Ebrington), in speaking upon a bill for the better collection of tithes in Ireland, he was reported to have said, "I do not approve of the bill itself, but I support it because I am satisfied that the effect of it will be to render the war now raging against the Protestant Church in Ireland more formidable." The first move was by putting a question to Lord Melbourne—" Whether, when he recommended that noble lord to fill the situation of Lord-Lieutenant of Ireland, he was aware of the noble lord having used such language." Lord Fortescue was absent, but Lord Lansdowne defended him, and concluded with the observation that, "if there was a noble lord in that House who was eminently interested in not having a particular expression which was used in one of the Houses of Parliament treated as a disqualification for office, that individual was the noble and learned lord himself."

Lord Lyndhurst,—" I beg, with all deference and submission to the noble Marquess, to state that I am not ashamed of any expression ever used by me in any debate either in this or the other House of Parliament. I am aware of the expression to which the noble Lord alludes, and I have over and over again explained the sense in which I used it. If the expression used by the new Lord-Lieutenant of Ireland was known to those who recommended him to the office, I am justified in saying that his appointment is a declaration of war on the part of the Government against the Protestant Church of Ireland."

Lord Brougham.—" Allusion is made to a speech made by my noble and learned friend three years ago; but there is this difference between the two cases, that my noble and learned friend has denied that speech."

Lord Lansdowne.—" He has not denied a word of it."

Lord Lyndhurst.—" The sense in which I used the expression referred to I have already fully explained. I had the choice of two expressions; I might have made use of the word '*race*,' but I spoke of '*aliens*,' and in what signification I have repeatedly stated."

On a subsequent day Lord Fortescue, having taken his seat in the House of Lords, fully explained the words he had used on the occasion referred to, and showed that they had been entirely misrepresented. Lyndhurst being again taunted with his denunciation of the Irish as "aliens in blood, language, and religion," he very candidly said :—

"My lords, considering the impression which that language has created in Ireland—considering the use that has been made of it—considering the odium that has been cast upon me in consequence of it, I say, in answer to the question put to me, that I should consider it a decided disqualification to me for holding that appointment."[1]

[1] 45 Hansard, 950, 1144. Lyndhurst made a poor excuse for his indiscretion by saying that although he called the Irish *aliens*, he did not mean

There was a suspension of hostilities in the House of Lords; but in the House of Commons there were keen struggles every evening, the Ministerialists becoming constantly weaker and at last they suffered what they considered an entire defeat on the Jamaica Bill. As we had still a majority of *five*, I said to Lord Melbourne, on accidentally meeting him next morning, "We must celebrate our victory of last night in pentameters." *Lord Melbourne.*—"We are all out, and you are again plain John Campbell." He had been with the Queen, and had tendered the resignation of all the members of the Cabinet, which had been accepted. Not the smallest difficulty was anticipated in any quarter in the formation of the new government.

Peel returned his distrust of Lyndhurst, but, considering his ascendancy in the House of Lords, could not possibly throw him aside. So it was at once arranged that he should resume the Great Seal, and his name was put second in the list of members, of the new Cabinet submitted to her Majesty, to which she made no objection. Lyndhurst was very much elated, and through a common friend entered into a negotiation with Lord Cottenham for fixing the day when the transfer of the Great Seal should take place, a complimentary hint being thrown out that an early day would probably not be inconvenient to Lord Cottenhan, *as he had so few judgments in arrear.* Two days after, I called on Lord Cottenham to arrange some matters with him upon our retirement. On entering I said, "I had just heard a rumor, that there was a *screw loose* in the new Government." "A screw loose," said he [the only time in all my life I ever knew him to be excited—now he flourished his hand over his head]—"a screw loose in the new Government! It has all fallen to pieces, and we are in again stronger than ever." Next evening came explanations in the two Houses of Parliament about the removal of the Ladies of the Bedchamber, the Queen's letter to Sir Robert Peel,

to use "aliens" in its usual sense. He should boldly have justified himself by the well-known passage from Sir John Davies, "The mere Irish were not only accounted *aliens*, but *enemies*, so as it was no capital offense to kill them." In Sir John Davies' Reports may be seen a plea of justification to an indictment for murder in Ireland, that the deceased was a mere Irishman, *meré Hibernicus.* The plea being allowed to be good in law, issue is joined upon the fact whether the deceased was one of the *Aborigines*, so as to make his death a case of "killing no murder."

written by the advice of her former servants, stating that "she could not consent to a course which she conceived to be contrary to usage, and which was repugnant to her feelings," and the famous *Cabinet minute* that "the principle of removing the household on a change of Government ought not to be applied or extended to the offices held by ladies in her Majesty's household."

There had been no actual surrender of the emblems of office, nor formal appointment of successors; so the march of government was resumed as if it had met with no interruption. I happened to be standing below the bar of the House of Lords on the first day that Lyndhurst showed himself after his disappointment. He was approaching me on his way to his seat, not on the woolsack, but on one of the back benches, which he usually occupied, and which I used to tell him was called "the Castle of Obstruction." He was afraid to meet my eye, and he tried to pass me as if I had been a stranger. I merely whispered in his ear, "How sadly Peel bungled it!—when we next resign you must take the construction of the new Government (all the ladies of the household included) into your own hands." He silently shook his head, and passing within the bar, again took the command of his stronghold.

However, he fired very few shots from it for the remainder of this campaign, till he finished off with his *grand review*.

To me he intimated an opinion that we could not last through the session, and that Peel would immediately have everything so completely his own way, that, in forming a new Government, he could not again "bungle it." Nevertheless these hopes were frustrated for two long years.

The English Radicals, whom I have often been obliged to censure, on the present occasion behaved well, for they agreed to support the Whigs, on one condition, that the "uniform penny postage" should be adopted. To this—the greatest social improvement of modern times—Mr. Spring Rice, the Chancellor of the Exchequer, was opposed, and there was great difficulty in prevailing upon the Cabinet to agree to it. As member for the City of Edinburgh I headed a deputation upon the subject to Lord Melbourne, and we expressly told him that "if he would persist in cramping commerce and preventing relations who were separated from carrying on an affectionate correspondence,—he charging one shilling and two pence for carrying a letter between London and Edinburgh, the expense of which might be covered by one halfpenny,—we were resolved that his Government should not stand." Strange to say, the measure was condemned by all Tories, and disrelished by many Whigs, and the merit of it is due to the Radicals. Its success has been great, beyond my most sanguine calculations, for it has been adopted by foreign nations, and has proved a blessing to the human race.

Lyndhurst was much surprised and mortified by observing how smoothly we went on, by quietly sacrificing the bills which he was resolved to smother when they came within his grasp.

However, before the prorogation, he again emptied upon us the vials of his wrath. He began a very elaborate harangue by saying, "*More meo*, I will compare the promises of the noble Viscount with his performances." He then went over the measures recommended in the Queen's speech, and showed how none of them had been carried. Thus he moralized:—

"What is the conclusion to be drawn from such a state of things? Obviously this: her Majesty's Ministers, at the commencement of the session, stated in this document deliberately the opinion they themselves entertained as to the measures of legislation which the interests of the country required; they stated what in their judgment, the country had a right to expect from a vigorous, an able, and an effective administration. Not one of these objects has been accomplished. They have thus enabled us to contrast their own opinion of what their duty required with their subsequent performance. They have thus pronounced their own condemnation. The ministry has passed judgment on itself—*habemus confitentem reum.* And yet, my Lords, these men still continue to hold the reins, without being able to direct the course of government.

'—— versate diu, quid ferre recusent,
Quid valeant humeri'

is applicable not to poetry alone; it extends equally and emphatically to those who undertake to conduct the affairs of a great empire. To undertake the conduct of such affairs without possessing the vigor, or the capacity, or the

Parliamentary confidence and support necessary to carry such measures as are essential to the interests of the country, is considered, and justly, by the constitution of these realms as a high misdemeanor, as subjecting the parties to impeachment."

He next commented on the dispute about the ladies of the bed-chamber:—

"Her Majesty's Ministers tendered their resignation. That resignation was accepted, and they stated that they only held office till their successors were appointed. Then commenced the negotiation for forming another administration. While these were still in progress, the Ministers, who only held office till their successors were appointed, interposed individually and collectively with their counsel —advised the letter addressed by her Majesty to Sir Robert Peel, and were thus the negotiators with their political opponents. In the result they advised her Majesty to break off the negotiation and to restore themselves to the position they formerly occupied,—for that was the constitutional effect of the whole proceeding, Such a course of conduct never before occurred in the history of this country, and I trust in God it never will occur again. And what, my lords, was the first act of the restored Government? to draw up their celebrated Cabinet minute—a document historically false, argumentatively false, legally false—and the unconstitutional character of which was only equalled by its folly, its extravagance, and its absurdity."

He then finished with the following attack on Lord John Russell:—

"We all remember the period when the noble lord, now at the head of the Home Department, received an address from 150,000 persons assembled in the neighborhood of Birmingham, ready at the word of command to march upon London. With affected humility, for

'lowliness is young ambition's latter,'

he received the address—'he was utterly unworthy of the great honor conferred upon him:'—'he was deeply grateful for it;'—and then it was that the noble lord drew a comparison between the conduct of that meeting and the proceedings of your Lordships' House; designating the one as the *voice of the nation,* and the other as the *whisper of a faction.* It is for the country to say whether it will longer submit to be ruled by such men. I have done my duty by exposing their misconduct."

Lord Melbourne.—" The real object of the observations of the noble and learned lord (although not avowed by him) is to foster any discontent that may exist in the country, to increase any unpopularity which he conceives we may labor under; and the noble and learned lord has undertaken the more hopeless, and, as I apprehend, the impossible task of raising himself in the estimation of his fellow-citizens. The noble and learned lord may possibly prove that we are unfit to conduct the affairs of the country; he may possibly show that we are unfit for the difficult position in which we are placed; but as to gaining for himself anything of credit, as to gaining for himself anything of character, as to conciliating any confidence towards himself and towards those who would have to administer the government of this country if it had the misfortune to be placed in his hands, the noble and learned lord may depend upon it that if his powers were 10,000 times what they are, he would be utterly unable to effect any such Herculean labor."[1]

During the whole session of 1840 Lyndhurst was very inactive. The question of parliamentary privilege between the House of Commons and the Court of Queen's Bench was now raging, and it placed him in a disagreeable predicament. For the sake of annoying the Government, he was strongly inclined to attack the proceedings of the House of Commons; but Peel had honestly and gallantly taken the other side, although he thereby displeased a large section of his party. Till this matter was adjusted, Lyndhurst saw that the Whigs were safe; for the Conservatives, while divided, could not form an administration. He therefore agreed to Lord John Russell's proposal that the Gordian knot should be cut by legislation, and he supported the bill, declaring that, as the right of the two Houses of Parliament to publish whatever they think it material that the people should know is essential to the due exercise of their functions, no action shall be maintained for any publication authorized by either House. So sincere was he that, by dextrous management, he gained over the Duke of Wellington, who had been captivated by sophism that " the legislature cannot morally justify the publication of a libel." Appealing to the ex-

[1] 50 Hansard, 496.

cellent discrimination of the illustrious warrior on all subjects he at last made him understand that a writing which charges another with misconduct is not necessarily a libel; otherwise the criminal justice of the country could not be administered; and that, to make it a libel, it must be published with a malicious motive, and without any laudable purpose being served by the publication. According to this definition of libel, neither the printer of the House of Commons nor those by whose orders he acts could be charged with the guilt of libeling.

Lyndhurst likewise persuaded Lord Denman to agree to the bill, although it amounted to a reversal of his own judgment in *Stockdale* v. *Hansard*, by reciting that the power recognized and protected was essentially necessary for the exercise of the inquisitorial and legislative functions of Parliament. So the bill received the Royal Assent, the Sheriffs of London were discharged out of custody, the publication of Parliamentary papers has since been free, and no question of privilege has subsequently arisen between the Houses of Parliament and the Courts of Law.

Lyndhurst was now so strongly convinced that it was his policy not to deal in factious assaults upon the Government, but to see it quietly sinking in public estimation, that he this session allowed an Irish Municipal Reform Bill, which he had hitherto strenuously opposed, to pass as if it had been a private bill for inclosing a common. He was, no doubt, partly actuated by the consideration that his return to office was certainly near at hand, and that then he would be obliged to undergo once more the damaging, if not painful, operation of sudden conversion; for Peel had supported this Irish bill, and if not previously passed, it would have been one of the first measures of his new administration.

I now come to the year when the long-looked-for change actually did take place, and Lyndhurst was Chancellor for the fourth time.

At the meeting of Parliament the public was amused with the farce of Lord Cardigan's trial; and then began the struggle in the House of Commons which terminated in the complete overthrow of the Whig Government. Lyndhurst anxiously, but silently, looked on. He now felt himself much more dependent upon Peel than he had been when there could be no Conservative competitor for the Great Seal. Pemberton Leigh, an eminent equity lawyer, who had refused the office of Solicitor-General, had distinguished himself in the House of Commons on the Conservative side, and would have made a most excellent Chancellor,[1]—and Sir William Follett, who had been Solicitor-General during "the hundred days," had displayed great debating powers, possessed Peel's entire confidence, and was looked forward to as the future Chancellor. Lyndhurst, therefore could no longer set up for himself, or venture to do anything to offend Peel, who was now recognized as the sole master of the destinies of Conservatism.

Lord Melbourne, although while minister he had declared that "to propose a repeal of the Corn Laws would be madness," as a last resort consented that a fixed duty—which amounted in effect to a repeal of the Corn Laws—should be proposed as a measure of his Government. But this alienated many Whig supporters, and gave fresh energy to Tory opposition. In consequence, the leading proposals of the ministerial budget were rejected by the House of Commons. A hope was fostered that Free Trade was more popular in the country, and a dissolution was determined upon. Peel then moved a direct vote of want of confidence, which was carried by a majority of *one.* Still many friends of the Government thought that an appeal to the people would be successful, and Parliament was dissolved.

I can not speak from my own observation of what was now going on in England, for I had been sent to Ireland to succeed Lord Plunket as Lord Chancellor there; but I was told that Lyndhurst watched the elections with very great solicitude, and that when the returns were decidedly on the Conservative side, free-trade professions as yet meeting with little favor, Peel intimated to him that he should wish for his assistance in the new Government, which he must be commissioned to form on the meeting of the new Parliament.

When I came over from Ireland to take my seat in the

---

[1] August 15th, 1858. The "London Gazette" announces that Pemberton Leigh is raised to the Peerage by the title of "Baron Kingsdown, of Kingsdown in the county of Kent." He will greatly strengthen the appellate jurisdiction of the House of Lords.

House of Lords, I was like a convict led out to execution. We full well knew our fate; but we resolved to put a good face upon it, to meet Parliament, and to make the Queen deliver a speech in favor of Free Trade. Then came the Amendment in both Houses,—"to assure her Majesty that no measures could be properly considered while her Majesty had advisers who did not enjoy the confidence of Parliament." This was carried by large majorities in both Houses, and of course led to a resignation of the Whig ministers.

CHAPTER CCXX.

LORD CHANCELLOR UNDER SIR ROBERT PEEL.

AFTER a short adjournment during the construction of the new Cabinet, which had been long foreseen and pre-arranged, Lyndhurst re-entered the House of Lords, preceded by his mace-bearer and his purse-bearer with the Great Seal, and took his place on the woolsack. He was excessively nervous, and, looking bewildered, did not seem at all to recollect the forms with which he had so long been familiar. Lord Melbourne, in a loud whisper, said to me, "Who would think that this is the same impudent dog who bullied us so unconscionably in his 'Reviews of the Session'?". But Lyndhurst was soon himself again, laughing at everybody and everything, and especially delighting in a jest against any of his colleagues.

During this brief session the new Chancellor only spoke once—which was respecting an amendment (my *coup d'essai* in the House of Lords) upon a bill for the creation of two additional Vice-Chancellors. I proposed to provide "that Irish as well as English barristers should be considered qualified for the appointment." He consented to the amendment; but slyly insinuated that the only object of the Irish ex-Chancellor was to make himself less unpopular in Ireland; that Irish barristers might give him a more cordial reception than he had experienced when he first visited that country to supersede Lord Plunket.

Sir Robert Peel now preserved the most profound silence respecting his future measures. The late Government having dissolved Parliament and gone to the country upon their Free-Trade budget, "Protection" was the cry of their opponents, and this cry had produced the overwhelming majority by which the Whigs were crushed. The new Premier was a "free-trader" in his heart, and already meditated the commercial reform which he afterwards accomplished. But as yet neither friend nor foe could extort from him any avowal of his intentions; and, having carried a few unimportant bills, he hurried on the prorogation. In the evening before the day of this ceremony—entering the House of Lords a few minutes past five—I found Lyndhurst returning to his private room, after an adjournment had been moved and carried, there appearing no business to be brought forward. I complained to him of this sudden adjournment as a trick—saying that, being now in opposition, I was coming down, after his example, to take "a review of the session," that I might contrast the *promises* of the Conservative party with their *performance* since they had been in office. *Lyndhurst.*—" If you had been as wise as we have been, and not brought forward measures to be rejected, I might still have been taking 'a review of the session,' and you might have been enjoying the sweets of power."

I ought to mention that in a very obliging and good-natured manner he now gave me a small place for my clerk, who had been with me when I was Chancellor in Ireland, and who was cast away along with me in the recent wreck. To excite me to discontent and desertion, he pretended to say that the Whigs were much to blame in leaving me without any retired allowance or provision of any sort. But I was quite content to remain five years working for the public in the judicial business of the House of Lords, and in the judicial Committee of the Privy Council. I had voluntarily waived my claim to the retired allowance of Irish Chancellor, and I had no right to complain.

On the first day of Michaelmas term, Lord Chancellor Lyndhurst again received the Judges and Queen's Counsel at his levee, and led the grand procession to Westminster Hall. He was now in his fourth Chancellorship,—the first having been under George IV.; the second under William IV., from the accession of that monarch till the formation of Lord Grey's Government, in November,

1830; the third again under William IV., during the hundred days from November, 1834, to April, 1835 ; and, lastly, under Queen Victoria, of whose conscience he was the keeper for five years. No Chancellor had received the Great Seal so often from different sovereigns since the Plantagenet reigns.

In the Court of Chancery he was now exposed to a very disagreeable comparison ; for Lord Cottenham, his immediate predecessor, although very inferior to him in grasp of intellect and general acquirements, was a consummate Equity Judge; and had given entire satisfaction to the Bar and the suitors in the Court of Chancery.

Some supposed that Lord Lyndhurst would not show himself (as he might have done) one of the greatest of Chancellors. Between five and six years he had enjoyed entire leisure, and as during the whole of that period he seemed to be in the near prospect of resuming his high office, and eager again to possess it, those who were not well acquainted with his habits conjectured that he was preparing himself for his duties, with which, when he before held it, he had been of necessity imperfectly acquainted. But, in truth, he had been absorbed in political intrigue. He hardly ever attended to the judicial business of the House of Lords; with one exception, he never sat in the Judicial Committee of the Privy Council, and he did not trouble himself with reading the periodical reports of the decisions of any of the Equity Judges.[1]

No improvement was discoverable. He took no bribes, and he never was influenced by any improper motive in deciding for one party rather than the other—further than taking the course which was likely to give himself least trouble, and which least exposed him to unpleasant criticism. His excellent good sense and admirable tact kept him out of scrapes. Avoiding danger, he was careless about glory; and not by any means over-anxious or

[1] The instance in which he did sit in the Privy Council was an appeal from the Arches on the will of *Jemmy Wood*, the banker at Gloucester, a case involving property to an immense amount, and attended with great difficulty. I was counsel for the appellant, and I thought Lyndhurst a Daniel ; for the Court, by his advice, decided for my client. But such was Lyndhurst's disinclination to judicial work, that I could not prevail upon him to attend the hearing of the appeal in the House of Lords on which the disruption of the Church of Scotland depended ; and this was disposed of exclusively by two peers, Lord Brougham and Lord Cottenham. His presence might have saved a great national calamity.

scrupulous about the business of his Court being disposed of satisfactorily. He sat in the Court of Chancery as little as he possibly could, and his great object was to shirk the decision of perplexed and difficult questions. Upon appeals from the Master of the Rolls and the Vice-Chancellors, he almost always *affirmed;* by which he had the treble advantage of lessening the number of appeals, of having the good word of the Judge appealed from, and of shunning the necessity for giving reasoned judgments.[1]

It is quite marvelous to find how few and how unimportant are Lyndhurst's recorded decisions in his last *quinquennium*. They are all comprised in a portion of the first volume of Phillips's Reports,[2] hardly exceeding in number, and certainly not in weight, the decisions of the Court of Queen's Bench in a single term.

After looking over all the Chancery cases *Tempore Lyndhurst*, the following is the only one I can discover likely to be interesting to the general reader,—" Viscount Canterbury *v.* the Attorney-General," which was commenced when I had the honor to be first law officer of the Crown.

On the 16th of October, 1834, the two Houses of Parliament were burnt down, with the Speaker's house and adjoining buildings, constituting the ancient Royal Palace of Westminister.[3] The conflagration was occasioned by the negligence of workmen in the employment of the Commissioners of Woods and Forests, who had made a bonfire of an immense quantity of " wooden tallies,"—implements by which the accounts of the Exchequer had been kept, as in the reign of Edward the Confessor. The Right Hon.

---

[1] Lord Lyndhurst's propensity to *affirm* was the more striking from Lord Cottenham's propensity to *reverse*. This distinguished Judge did not even acknowledge that there is a presumption in favor of the decree appealed against, and that it ought to stand until the appellate Judge is convinced that it was wrong. He treated every appeal as an original hearing, being governed by the smallest inclination in his own mind in favor of the appellant's side. This was his avowed principle; but the wags in the Court of Chancery went so far as to say that he always presumed the decree to be wrong till the contrary was clearly proved, the odds being *two to one* against Vice-Chancellor Shadwell, and *three to one* against Vice-Chancellor Knight Bruce.

[2] From p. 50 to p. 778.

[3] The apartments called " The Speaker's House " were first appropriated to the use of the Speaker in the year 1790, by warrant of George III., and George IV. at the time of his coronation occupied them for two days as part of the palace. The crypt of the ancient chapel of St. Stephen, till the fire, had been used as the Speaker's dining-room.

X.—

Charles Manners Sutton (afterwards created Viscount Canterbury) was then Speaker of the House of Commons, and this fire destroyed his furniture and plate to the value of 7,000*l*., and damaged other property of his to the amount of 3,000*l*. He took no steps with a view to obtain compensation during the reign of William IV.; but in the year of 1840 he presented a Petition of Right addressed to her Majesty Queen Victoria, setting forth the above facts, and alleging that as this loss had arisen in a royal palace, from the negligence of the servants of the Crown, the petitioner, as of right, was entitled to compensation from the Crown.

The Queen gave the answer "*Let Right be done*," and referred the case to her Lord Chancellor. The allegations of fact in the petition being substantially true, but affording no foundation in point of law for the claim, the Attorney-General confessed the truth of them, and "*demurred.*" After I was out of office, the case was very learnedly argued before Lord Lyndhurst—on one side by my successor, Sir Frederick Pollock, now Chief Baron of the Exchequer; and on the other side by Sergeant Wilde, afterwards Lord Chancellor Truro.

Lord Lyndhurst, having taken time to consider, delivered a very learned and excellent written judgment. He began with considering the true construction of the statute of Anne respecting liability for the consequences of accidental fire, as between subject and subject. He then proceeded to consider how far the claim could be supported against the Crown:—

"It is admitted that for the personal negligence of the Sovereign neither this nor any other proceeding can be maintained. Upon what ground, then, can it be supported for the acts of the agent or servant? If the master or employer is answerable upon the principle *qui facit per alium facit per se*, this would not apply to the Sovereign, who can not be required to answer for his own personal acts. If it be said that the master is answerable for the negligence of his servant, because it may be considered to have arisen from his own misconduct or negligence in selecting or retaining a careless servant, that principle can not apply to the Sovereign, to whom negligence or misconduct can not be imputed, and for which, if they occur in fact, the law affords no remedy. If the principle now contended for

were correct, the negligence of the seamen in the service
of the Crown would raise a liability in the Crown to make
good the damage, and which might be enforced by a Petition of Right. Though cases of this nature have happened
at different periods, it seems never to have occurred to the
parties injured or to their advisers that redress could be
obtained by means of a Petition of Right.

"Another objection urged is. that the petitioner's cause
of action arose in the time of the late King; and it is
clear that had this been a case between subject and subject, an action could not have been supported—*actio per-
sonalis moritur cum personâ*. We are told that a different
rule prevails when the Sovereign is a party; but some
authority should be adduced for such a distinction. It is
true, indeed, that the King never dies; the demise is
immediately followed by the succession; there is no interval. The Sovereign always exists; the person only is
changed. But if there is a change of person, why is the
personal responsibility arising from the negligence of
servants (if, indeed, such responsibility exists) to be
changed upon the successor, ceasing as it does altogeher
in the case of a private individual? In the case of a
subject, the liability does not continue in respect of the
estate; it devolves neither upon the heir nor the personal
representative; it is extinct."

Having then alluded to the objections arising from the
duty cast by Acts of Parliaments upon the Commissioners
of Woods and Forests respecting the Palace at Westminster, he asked:—

"Assuming that the fire had been caused by the personal
negligence of the Commissioners, would the Cown have
been liable to make good the loss? They are, indeed,
styled 'Servants of the Crown;' but they are, in truth,
public officers appointed to perform certain duties assigned
to them by the legislature, and for any negligence in the
discharge of such duties and any injury thereby sustained,
they alone, I conceive, are liable. These officers are
appointed by the Crown, and are removable at the
pleasure of the Crown; but that circumstance alone will
not create any such liability. The Keeper of the Great
Seal, and other persons holding high situations in the
State, have authority to appoint to many offices, and also
to remove the persons so appointed at pleasure. But they

are not on that account subject to make compensation for injury occasioned by the neglect or misconduct of the persons so appointed. The mere selection of the officers does not create a liability. But if the Crown would not be responsible for the act done, had it been done by the superiors, it follows that the Crown can not be held liable for the negligence of their subordinate agents, whom they appoint and remove, and with the selection and control of whom the Crown has no concern."

His Lordship then referred to the cases of *Robert de Clifton*, in the reign of Edward II., and of *Gervais de Clifton*, in the reign of Edward III., in which claims had been made on the Crown for damage done by the King's servants to the lands of the petitioners in improving the defenses of Nottingham Castle; and showing that they did not apply to the case now to be determined, he said.—

"I am compelled to come to the conclusion that this proceeding can not be maintained, and that the demurrer of the Attorney-General must be allowed. It is a great satisfaction to me to know that in this singular and novel case, involving much that is obscure and almost obsolete, if I am wrong in the opinion I have given, it is open to revision by writ of error, should the petitioner be advised that there are sufficient grounds to question its correctness."

No writ of error was brought, and the wonder is that men of eminence at the bar should have ever advised a proceeding so preposterous and hopeless.

For the judicial business of the House of Lords there was now the largest staff of law lords ever known,—Lord Lyndhurst, Chancellor of Great Britain, Lord Brougham, ex-Chancellor of Great Britain, Lord Cottenham, ex-Chancellor of Great Britain, and Lord Campbell, ex-Chancellor of Ireland. There was a considerable arrear of cases which stood for hearing, and we resolved to sit four days every week—the Chancellor being present two days, and the other law lords presiding by turns in his absence. The business certainly was done in a very satisfactory manner. Laying aside all party and personal feelings, we labored conscientiously to arrive at the right conclusion. Lyndhurst himself showed wonderful quickness of apprehension and power of ratiocination, again proving that, doing justice to himself, he might have left behind him a splendid reputation as a great magistrate. But although when necessary, he could make himself master of the most abstruse points in the law of Scotland, which he had never systematically studied, he was generally better pleased to lean upon others, and to be guided by faith rather than by reason. The eccentric Brougham occasionally discomposed our proceedings by coming in when the case was half heard, and putting questions without having listened to the argument; but he was docile and manageable, and when necessary, he could prepare himself and give judgment very creditably. Cottenham was pretty regular in his attendance, and displayed great aptitude for judicial business; but we could not always induce him to come to town from his villa, near Wimbledon. I was in my apprenticeship as a judge: and I may at least give myself the character of being attentive and industrious. In the absence of the Chancellor, the law lord who presided spoke first. Lyndhurst never betrayed the smallest degree of jealousy or envy. In truth, being indifferent about judicial fame himself, it gave him no uneasiness to see it acquired by others.

In the case of Johnston *v.* Beattie [1] a great difficulty arose from our being equally divided, and a fifth law lord, who did not usually attend the hearing in appeals, was called in to make a majority. A domiciled Scotchman, of large landed estate in Scotland, without any property in England, married to a Scotchwoman, had by her an only child, a daughter, for whom, before his death, he duly appointed tutors and curators, domiciled in Scotland, who were confirmed by the Supreme Court of Scotland, and who by the law of Scotland were entitled to the guardianship of her person and the management of her property. Some years after the death of both parents, she, while still an infant, happened casually to be in England; whereupon certain parties, wishing to obtain possession of her and to supersede the Scotch tutors and curators, who had acted unexceptionably in the guardianship of her person and her property since her father's death, filed a Bill in Chancery alleging falsely (as was admitted) that she had property in England, and praying that one of them might be appointed her guardian, and that the Scotch tutors and

[1] 10 Clark and Finelly, 42.

curators should account to the English guardian for all the rents and profits of the Scotch estates. The Vice-Chancellor, the facts being laid before him, made an order to that effect, and this was affirmed by Lord Chancellor Lyndhurst. Upon an appeal to the House of Lords, the order appeared to Lord Brougham and to myself not only absurd, but contrary to the law of England; while Lords Lyndhurst and Cottenham considered the proceeding as a matter quite of course and highly laudable, although they allowed that the person and property of the infant would henceforth be under the control of the English guardian, and that during her minority she would not without his consent be allowed to marry or to return to her native country. Lord Langdale, Master of the Rolls, being called in, after an argument in his hearing. declared himself the same of opinion. This was a most lamentable, but by no means singular, instance of the narrow-mindedness of English lawyers. Here three very able men, competent to form a sound conclusion upon any subject to which logical reasoning and common sense are to be applied, were satisfied with this order, because it is laid down in the books of practice that as soon as a bill is filed to make an infant a ward of the Court, the infant is a ward of the Court, and a guardian ought to be appointed—so that any foreign child, male or female, brought to England for a few weeks or days with a view to health, or education, or amusement, may be made a ward of Chancery and imprisoned in England till twenty-one, I did not much wonder at Cottenham and Langdale countenancing such nonsense, as they had never been freed from the trammels of the Equity draughtsman's office in which they learned to draw Bills and Answers; but when I found that the masculine and enlightened mind of Lyndhurst did not revolt at it, I was filled with astonishment as well as dismay. The truth, I believe, was, that he had committed himself by "affirming" as Chancellor, *more suo*, without much considering whether the order appealed from was right or wrong.

Soon after this, all the law lords were definitely divided equally upon a much more important question—indeed I may say, the most important question which ever came before the House of Lords as the Supreme Court of Appeal. Unfortunately such a question was decided on the technical maxim by which the House of Lords alone, of all the tribunals I ever read of, is governed,—*semper præsumitur contra negantem*, making the result often depend upon the language in which the question is framed.

In Ireland a man who was a member of the established Church was married to a woman who was a Presbyterian by a regularly officiating Presbyterian clergyman, both parties intended to contract a valid marriage, and believing that they had done so. They lived together some years as man and wife and had several children, who were acknowledged as legitimate. The husband then married another wife, the former wife being still alive, and was indicted for bigamy. His defense was that the first marriage was a nullity, and therefore that he committed no crime when he married the second wife. It was admitted that there was no statute law in Ireland applicable to a marriage between a member of the established Church and a Dissenter, and that the case was to be governed by the common law of England. Thus arose the fearful question —whether by the common law of England there might be a valid marriage by the consent of the parties without the presence of a priest episcopally ordained. It was admitted that a marriage celebrated by a Roman Catholic priest, although both parties were Protestants, would be valid; but a Presbyterian pastor, although he might have officiated in a parish for fifty years, and might have acted as Moderator of the General Assembly of the established Church of Scotland, was for this purpose a mere layman, because he had not been admitted to holy orders by a Bishop. Within the realm of England, marriage is entirely regulated by Lord Hardwicke's Act, passed in 1753, and by subsequent statutes, but the validity of marriages contracted by millions of British subjects in Ireland and in other dominions under the British Crown and upon the high seas depended upon the solution of this question. For half a century, ever since the decision of Lord Stowell in the famous case of *Dalrymple* v. *Dalrymple*, it had been considered established doctrine that the presence of an episcopally ordained priest was unnecessary, as the necessity for his presence in Roman Catholic countries was introduced only by the Council of Trent, and marriage, although a sacrament, like baptism, may effectually take place without a priest. This doctrine had been expressly approved of by Lord Kenyon, Lord Ellenborough, Lord Tenterden, and all our most eminent Judges; and upon the strength of it there had been repeated convictions for bigamy. But in an obscure book, lately published professing to state "the Law of Husband and Wife," the doctrine was controverted; and upon such authority proceeded this prisoner's defense. The Irish Judges were equally divided; and, strange to say, the English Judges, being consulted by the House of Lords, declared themselves unanimously of opinion that the first marriage was null, although they admitted that this was contrary to the Canon law which prevailed in every other country of Europe before the Council of Trent. They relied chiefly on a supposed Anglo-Saxon law, that, to make nuptials prosperous, "there must be present a *mass priest.*" Yet they admitted that a marriage celebrated by one in deacon's orders always was and is valid, notwithstanding that a deacon is not a *mass priest.* Six law lords had been present at the argument—the Lord Chancellor, Lord Abinger, Lord Cottenham, Lord Brougham, Lord Denman, and Lord Campbell. Of these, the first three voted for reversing the conviction, and the last three for confirming it. Lord Lyndhurst's judgment was very learned and able. He seemed most puzzled to give a definition of a priest to be recognized as having power lawfully to celebrate marriage. I had asked, " Is a priest of the Greek Church sufficient? or of the Church of Abyssinia, or of the Lutheran Church, which in some countries maintain episcopacy and in others looks only to a consistory by whom orders are conferred? Mr. John Morrison, who never had any ordination except by the imposition of hands of some Presbyterian ministers in Scotland, was licensed by Archbishop Grindal to preach and administer the sacraments all over the province of Canterbury; would a marriage by him have been held valid or void?" Thus answer Lord Lyndhurst:—

" Holy orders, according to the law of England, are orders conferred by episcopal ordination. This was the law of the Catholic Church in this country, and the same law continued after the Reformation as the law of the Episcopal Reformed Church. A marriage celebrated by a Roman Catholic priest, as in Fielding's case, and other instances, has been considered valid. A priest of the Romish church is a priest by episcopal ordination, and his orders are accounted holy orders by our Church."

This is all the answer I could get to my queries.

If the motion had been that the judgment be affirmed, we, the contents, should have succeeded in establishing the old common law as laid down by Lord Stowell, the *presumption* being against the *negative;* but the Chancellor, according to a standing order of the House, put the question that "the judgment be reversed," and we being obliged to say "*Not Content*," the presumption was against us, and a judgment passed by which hundreds of marriages, the validity of which had not been doubted, were nullified, and thousands of children were bastardized.

Legislation has since interfered to mitigate the evil by ratifying past marriages *bond fide* contracted without a mass priest, and providing that in Ireland and in the colonies marriages may in future be constituted by prescribed formalities without a mass priest: but such a place as Pitcairn's Island is left altogether unprovided for, and there the descendants of the crew of the 'Bounty,' who for fifty years in their domestic unions followed the purest precepts of the Gospel, are still to be considered as living in concubinage, with offspring incapable of inheriting their property.[1]

The most important political case which came before the House of Lords judicially while Lord Lyndhurst presided there, was *O'Connell* v. *the Queen*—a writ of error by the great Irish agitator upon a conviction arising out of his "monster meetings" held in various parts of Ireland for a repeal of the Union. The eyes of all Europe were turned upon this proceeding. Foreign nations had for some years thought it very probable that O'Connell, conducting a successful revolution, would become president of the Hibernian republic; and their opinion was that although he had been convicted and imprisoned, if liberated by a reversal of his sentence, he might still accomplish his great design. There had been various debates in the House of Lords, sitting politically, in which the Government had been loudly blamed for so long tolerating the "monster meetings," and then includ-

[1] Regina *v.* Millis, 10 Clark and Finelly, 534.

ing in one indictment against the leader and his associates all their supposed offenses committed for several years by acts, writings, and speeches. On the other hand, we of the opposition, who brought forward these accusations, were charged with factiously abetting treason and rebellion. To the honor of the Peerage the hearing of the appeal was conducted with the utmost calmness and seeming conscientiousness and impartiality. The demeanor of the Chancellor, who had hitherto been the most violent against O'Connell, was now that of a dignified magistrate whose only object was to arrive at a right conclusion, and to do justice between the Crown and the subject.

The Judges who were summoned to assist were divided in opinion, two thinking that the judgment was wrong and all the rest that it was right. A great number of Peers had attended the hearing at different times, but only five were present during the whole of the argument,—the Chancellor, Lord Brougham, Lord Denman, Lord Cottenham, and Lord Campbell. By all of them elaborate opinions were delivered,—the first two being for affirming, and the last three for reversing. According to the authorized report of the House of Lords,[1] "The Lord Chancellor, from his place on the woolsack, then put the question—'Is it your Lordships' pleasure that the judgment of the Court below be reversed? As many of your Lordships as are of that opinion will say *Content*.' Lords Denman, Cottenham, and Campbell answered *Content*. *The Lord Chancellor.*—'As many as are of an opposite opinion will say *Not Content*.' Lord Brougham and other Peers said *Not Content*." Lord Wharncliffe, the President of the Council, according to usage on such occasions when discussions arise after the question is put, remaining seated with his hat on, said:—

"My Lords,—In this state of things I can not help suggesting that your Lordships should not divide the House upon a question of this kind, when the opinions of the law Lords have been already given upon it, and the majority is in favor of reversing the judgment. In point of fact, my Lords, they constitute the Court of Appeal; and if noble Lords unlearned in the law should interfere to de-

---

[1] 11 Clark and Finelly, 421.

cide such questions by their votes, instead of leaving them to the decision of the law Lords, I very much fear that the authority of this House as a Court of Justice would be greatly impaired."

Lord Brougham.—" Deeply lamenting the decision about to be pronounced—a decision which will go forth without authority, and come back without respect,—nevertheless, I highly approve of the view of this matter taken by my noble friend, and implore your Lordships who have not heard all the arguments—who have not made yourselves perfectly acquainted with the subject, and whose habits do not lead you to take part usually in the discussion of such questions,—not to take any part in this decision. In justice to myself I ought to say that I do think it is very wrong to go against the opinion of a majority of the Judges in this case, although I did wish to go against the opinion of all the Judges in the Irish Marriage case, because that opinion differed from the eminent and venerable authority of Lord Stowell, and other learned persons well capable of forming a correct opinion upon the subject."

Lord Campbell.—" I concurred with my noble and learned friend in opposing the unanimous opinion of all the Judges in the case of the Irish Marriages, because I thought it contrary to the law of England; and I now oppose the opinion of a majority of the Judges because I believe it to be contrary to the law of England. With reference to what has been said of the distinction between *Law Lords* and *Lay Lords*, and leaving the decision of this case with the *Law Lords*, it is unnecessary for me to say more than that the distinction is unknown to the Constitution, and that there is no order of *Law Lords* in the formation of your Lordships' House. But there is a distinction in reason and the fitness of things between members of a court who have heard a case argued, and members of that court who have not heard it argued; and those only who have heard the argument should take part in the decision. I believe that none but those who are called *Law Lords* have constantly attended while this case has been debated at your Lordships' bar."

Lord Chancellor.—" I think those noble Lords who have not heard the arguments will decline voting if I put the question again."

All the lay Lords then withdrew, when, the question

being again put, "That the judgment be reversed," it was carried in the affirmative.[1]

The Government might easily have had the judgment affirmed, but acted wisely in deputing the President of the Council to advise the lay Peers to withdraw; for an affirmance so obtained would have made O'Connell more than ever the idol of his countrymen, and it is an un-undoubted fact that from the time of his liberation his influence steadily declined.

The general reader will probably think he has had enough of law, and would be glad to return to topics of a more popular character. Lord Lyndhurst had now little weight in the Cabinet; Peel placed no confidence in him, and would have been well pleased to have got rid of him altogether. Sugden was still more disliked, and he was promptly sent to succeed me as Chancellor in Ireland. But the Premier would have been highly delighted to give the Great Seal of Great Britain to Pemberton Leigh or Sir William Follett, both of whom were admirably well qualified for all its duties. Lyndhurst, however, had such a position in the House of Lords, and stood so well in the estimation of the Duke of Wellington, that his re-appointment to his former office was indispensable to the formation of the new Government. Peel was at no pains to conceal how little he cared for his Chancellor. To illustrate this, an anecdote was afterwards related for which I can vouch no authority, but which was generally circulated and (although very improbable) generally believed. Peel having, early in 1842, resolved in his own mind how he meant to modify the tariff, explained his plan to the Cabinet, without as yet hinting at the repeal of the Corn Laws. His colleagues all nodded assent, except the Chancellor, who began a speech of objections. Peel thereupon took up a newspaper and read it till, after a long interval, silence was restored. He then threw it down, exclaiming, "Well, I suppose we are all agreed!" and broke up the meeting. Even upon questions of law reform (as we shall see) the Chancellor was not always consulted, and Sir James Graham, who filled the office of Home Secretary, acted as Chief Minister of Justice.

Still, in the House of Lords the Chancellor played osten-

[1] 11 Clark and Finelly.

sibly a very prominent part. The Duke of Wellington, without any civil office, was the leader on the Government side ; but he was then in a very feeble state of health, from which he aftewards rallied. At this time, as often as he rose to speak, both his supporters and his opponents were afraid that he would break down ; and his colleagues who sat on the ministerial bench along with him were exceedingly incompetent to resist an onslaught, if any had been made upon them. The prostrate Whigs pretended that their opponents practiced the device of a beseiged city, according to which the aged and infirm are placed on the walls, that the enemy, out of compassion, may cease to fire. Nevertheless, there were occasional little debates upon the improper appointment or the improper dismissal of magistrates, and similar subordinate matters, in which the Chancellor stood forth as the defender of the Government with much vigor and effect.

The law lords gave him very little trouble. Cottenham seldom attended the meetings of the House in the evening for legislation or political discussion, and, when he did come, he took hardly any part in the proceedings. Langdale could not be prevailed upon to assist even in discussions respecting the reformation of the Court of Chancery. Brougham was always present, and sat on the Opposition side of the House ; but, in truth, from a rankling desire to be revenged upon the Whigs, who had discarded him, he had become the slave of the Tories. Lyndhurst managed him with admirable dexterity by persuading him that he himself meant ere long to resign the Great Seal, and that Peel would then eagerly offer it to the man whose extraordinary talents, eloquence, and reputation would so powerfully strengthen the Goverment. I alone ventured on anything approaching to opposition, and I appeared in the House of Lords not under very auspicious circumstances, having held the Great Seal of Ireland for a few weeks only when I was forced to abandon power and place. Lyndhurst, notwithstanding our long and familiar intimacy, was disposed to treat me very cavalierly, and with Brougham's help, to crush me as speedily as possible.

Early in the Session of 1842 I laid on the table three bills, the object of which was to make a permanent Chief Judge in the Court of Chancery ; to abolish the Judicial Committee of the Privy Council ; and to constitute the

House of Lords, presided over by the Chancellor, the only Court in the last resort for appeals from England, Scotland, Ireland, or the colonies, civil, criminal, and ecclesiastical. Upon this occasion, in a very modest and deferential manner, I explained the necessity for altering the constitution of the Court of Chancery, pointed out the inconvenience of having two co-equal Courts of Appeal—the House of Lords and the Privy Council—before which the same question of law might arise and be decided differently, and tried to show that the House of Lords, with the assistance of the Common Law, Equity, and Ecclesiastical Judges, might efficiently and satisfactorily dispose of all the appeals in the empire; sitting, if necessary, for judicial business when the other House of Parliament might be adjourned.

Lyndhurst, with a very sneering countenance and mock-heroic tone, said:—

"He was not surprised that his noble and learned friend, the ex-Chancellor of Ireland, should have come down to the House with this proposition; he had led a life of continuous activity, and having now little occupation he appeared desirous to devote himself to the introduction of alterations in the laws of his country—

'Quod petiit, spernit; repetit quod nuper omisit;
Æstuat, et vitæ disconvenit ordine toto :
Diruit, ædificat, mutat quadrata rotundis.'"

In my reply I alluded to the remark of my noble and learned friend on the woolsack that I had prepared and brought in these Bills merely *pour écarter l'ennui*, and said:—

"I assure him that, when out of office, I will not follow the example of those who, by reckless factiousness, show only their eagerness to return to it. I beg leave to remind your Lordships that law reform scoffed at by my noble and learned friend, is not new to me; and that in my busiest time I sent up from the House of Commons various important bills for the improvement of the law, which met with the approbation of your Lordships and are now to be found on the Statute Book."

So wanton was Lyndhurst's attack that even Lord Brougham thought himself bound to come to the rescue, and to bear testimony to my services in reforming the law when at the head of the Real Property Commission and a member of the House of Commons.¹

The bills coming on for a second reading, Lord Lyndhurst opposed them most violently, and was particularly severe upon the proposal that the House of Lords might sit as a Court of Appeal for judicial business exclusively, at times when the House of Commons was not sitting:—

" My noble and learned friend," said he, " expects to be able so to tie up your Lordships' tongues as that they shall not be able to speak except upon judicial matters. How is this to be accomplished? How force men to be silent? If prevented one way, another will be discovered. Your Lordships have seen a little of the recklessness of my noble and learned friend since he came into this House. During the hearing of an appeal, he would like to get up and taunt a political opponent; he would be met by his own clause imposing silence; but I am afraid the result would prove that nature or habit would prevail—thus verifying the line—

' Naturam expellas furcâ, tamen usque recurret.' "

Lord Campbell.—" My noble and learned friend is afraid that, notwithstanding any law to the contrary, there might be political discussions during these judicial sittings in the autumn. What is my noble and learned friend's own practice at present, during our morning sittings for judicial business? As yet he has not, while hearing a Scotch appeal, broke out with a speech in favor of the Corn Laws or against Whiggish opinions, which nowadays he is ever so eager to assail, although there be no positive law to forbid such unseasonable haranguing. He may surely give others credit for being able to curb their desire to mix politics with judicial proceedings, in obedience to an Act of Parliament. For the present, my Lords, the measure is defeated; but I do not despair of seeing it carried before long with the powerful support of my noble and learned friend. Although strong in the profession of his opinions at the moment, he can not be accused of obstinacy. I could mention more than one important measure which, having warmly opposed, he has supported with equal warmth—making the best speech that has been made either against it or for it. Having

¹ Hansard, vol. lx., 1248, 1266.

to-night made a very able speech, denouncing these Bills as mischievous, I may yet hear him make a still better, recommending them as safe and beneficial; and, my Lords, when passed under his auspices, I am convinced that they will be found to have introduced a substantial improvement into the administration of justice in this country; and that his apparent inconsistency will only give him a new claim to the admiration of prosperity."[1]

In the Session of 1843 Lyndhurst behaved very laudably in assisting to amend the law of libel. He at once agreed to the Select Committee to consider the subject, and he very handsomely supported the bill framed upon the report of the Committee for allowing (among various other improvements) that, upon a criminal prosecution for libel, the truth of the charge in the alleged libel may be pleaded and given in evidence and shall amount to a defense, if the jury think that the alleged libel was published for the public good. I knew that Peel very much approved of the bill, and wished it to be carried; for from the beginning of his career, he was inclined to liberal opinions as far as his situation would permit. He had now openly hoisted the liberal flag, and, both with respect to trade and the internal rule of the country, he wished it to be understood that his government was quite as liberal as Lord Melbourne's. But I have no reason to suppose that Lyndhurst's support of this measure did not spontaneously flow from his own conviction; for, when without an interested motive to the contrary, he was himself always for progress.

A great Chancellor ought to have directed the resolutions of the Government on the subject which occupied public attention during a considerable part of this session, the controversy between the civil and the ecclesiastical Courts of Scotland; but, unfortunately, Lyndhurst listlessly left the subject to Lord Aberdeen, who, by his temporizing and vacillation, brought about the "Disruption." He led both parties by turns to believe that the Government sided with them; and by hopes of concessions held out to them, the *ultra-montane* Presbyterian clergy were induced to commit themselves by declarations respecting the inalienable rights of the Church, exceeding in extravagance anything ever claimed by the most violent

[1] Hansard, lxxii., 175.

of the Popes of Rome. He then suddenly drew back, and proclaimed himself the champion of spiritual subordination to the civil magistrate. The disruption which followed might certainly have been prevented by a display of firmness and decision when the struggle began. The whimsical conclusion of the whole was that, after the mischief was irremediable, Lord Aberdeen granted to the clergy who remained in the Church powers which, if granted in time, would have amply satisfied those who went forth to found the hostile Free Kirk.

Lyndhurst having, against his early opinions, conformed to the ultra-Tory policy of Lord Castlereagh, and, by supporting the Six Acts, done his best to establish tyranny in England, now very zealously supported the policy of Sir Robert Peel, which had become as liberal as any friend to monarchial and aristocratical, combined with democratical, institutions could desire. The Premier did not, according to the prophecy of Lord Eldon, put himself at the head of the mob and try to overturn the Church; but he wished that he might govern by enlightened public opinion, and that civil rights should be equally enjoyed by all classes in the community without regard to their religious belief. According to his instructions, the Chancellor, in the Session of 1844, introduced three very excellent bills, which the Whigs could not have ventured upon, and which caused great alarm to the Bishops, even when coming from a quarter once supposed so orthodox and so well affected to the Church. The first was to allow all persons in Ireland to be united in marriage by their own pastors, so that the validity of the marriage, when duly registered, could not afterwards be questioned; the second was to do away with *Præmunire*, and other terrible penalties imposed upon Roman Catholics; and the third was to entitle Unitarian congregations in Ireland and England to enjoy the endowments attached to their places of religious wordship after a prescription of twenty-five years, although those endowments had been granted by Trinitarian or Calvanistic founders with a view to the support and propagation of their own sect. Lyndhurst, taking care to announce that all the three bills emanated from Government, explained and defended them with admirable perspicuity and force. The Marriage Bill passed pretty smoothly, as it did little more than extend to Ireland, the

English Dissenters' Marriage Bill, passed under the government of Lord Melbourne; and so did the Præmunire Repeal Bill, for practically these penalties were never enforced; but the Unitarian Bill was denounced by Philpotts of Exeter as a repeal of the Athanasian Creed, and was severely censured even by the mild and wary Bloomfield of London.

I had now great satisfaction in fighting under the Lyndhurst banner, to which I had so often been opposed—

" —in this glorious and well fought field
We kept together in our chivalry."

The three bills being placed on the Statute Book,¹ he thanked me very handsomely, both in private and in public, for the aid I had afforded him. The cry raised on this occasion by the Intolerants was very absurd; for, as might have been foreseen, the Church of England has never flourished so much as since all real grievances of Dissenters and Roman Catholics have been removed.

Lyndhurst, however, would not coalesce with me in my attempts at legislation. Having established the point by the Libel Bill of 1843, that upon a private prosecution for libel, the truth might be given in evidence, I now wished this to be extended to public prosecutions for libel by the Attorney-General, instancing the case of the criminal information against the *Morning Post* newspaper for alleging that transports in which troops had been embarked were not seaworthy,—a fact which might have been distinctly proved, and which, for the public good, ought to have been made known. But most unaccountably, I was now opposed by Lord Denman, who delivered a violent speech against allowing the truth to be given in evidence in any libel for truth whatever. He pointed out the hardship lately imposed on the refugee Duke of Brunswick, against whom, while residing in England, very serious charges had been made by the press. It so happened that those charges were proved to be true; and his Serene Highness soon after was obliged to fly the country,—an indictment being found against him for sobornation of perjury. All were astonished and grieved to hear the Chief Justice of England, so long a steady and rational supporter of liberty, thus bitterly condemn the Bill which had passed with his entire approbation the year before,

¹ 7 and 8 Vic., c. 45, c. 81, c. 102.

and which had already operated most beneficially. Lyndhurst in a much more moderate tone tried to draw a distinction between prosecutions by individuals and by the government, and made a great impression by hinting at the possibility of a prospect for a libel imputing crimes or vices to the sovereign on the throne, with the privilege conferred upon the libeler of bringing forward witnesses to establish the truth of his charge—the issue perhaps whether the king had married a Roman Catholic, thus making our allegiance to depend upon the verdict of the jury.

I expressed my readiness to introduce an exception as to libels on the King and Queen or the heir to the throne; but my bill was thrown out on the second reading by a majority of 33 to 3.[1]

Lyndhurst likewise, with equal success, opposed another bill which I introduced to allow persons who, having been convicted of misdemeanor, and sentenced to imprisonment, have, upon the *fiat* of the Attorney-General, sued out a writ of error, to be admitted to bail while the writ of error is pending, This appeal may be decided in their favor when the period of imprisonment has expired—the established practice being, according to the procedure of the Court of Rhadamanthus, "Castigatque auditque dolos" —first to punish, and then to consider whether the punishment was lawful. The Chancellor, who had always at this period an overwhelming majority at his beck, not only objected to the bill on the ground that it might be supposed to favor O'Connell, whose writ of error was then pending, but likewise contended that it would generally be extremely mischievous, by enabling persons justly convicted of misdemeanors to escape punishment altogether.

In the Session of 1845 Sir Robert Peel's Government was immensely strong, and many supposed that it would be as durable as Sir Robert Walpole's. His income-tax, instead of proving his ruin as had been foretold, made him popular; he had restored our financial credit; his free-trade measures had all succeeded, and, as he had hinted no change of opinion respecting the Corn Laws, he was

---

[1] Hansard, vol. lxxvi., pp. 395, 417. There had been a whip on the Ministerial side, and our benches were empty. Lord Brougham made a strong speech for the Bill, but being engaged out to dinner, went away without voting or pairing.

still warmly supported by the landed aristocracy. A rumor was industriously spread that he was about to transfer the Great Seal to some one for whom he had more respect. This, I believe, was without foundation. Follertt had been prematurely cut off by disease; Pemberton Leigh having succeeded to a large fortune, had retired into the country and taken to fox-hunting; and Lyndhurst, giving no trouble in the Cabinet, disposed of his judicial business, if not without criticism, at all events without any open scandal. The Chancellor, however, was certainly treated with undisguised neglect by his colleagues. For example, a government Irish Bill being in the House of Lords, one clause of which was to vest in the Lord-Lieutenant the patronage of appointing all the officers in all the superior courts in Dublin, an amendment was moved that this should, as in England, be exercised by the chiefs of the several courts; and the Chancellor supporting the amendment, it was carried. But in the next stage of the bill this decision was reversed by a ministerial majority, notwithstanding the taunts uttered against those who preferred the power of doing jobs at the Castle to the advice of the Keeper of the Queen's conscience and the pure administration of justice.

Whether spontaneously, or by command, I know not, but to my great astonishment, without any communication on the subject to me, he early in the session introduced the Bail in Error Bill which he had treated so contumeliously, and, without any allusion to what had before passed on the subject, represented it as a new and beneficial measure, although it remained almost exactly as I had framed it. There was a prodigious laugh against him for his forgetfulness and versatility, but this he took in very good part.[1] The Bill now passed both Houses *nemine dissentiente*.

He introduced, in a most beautiful speech, a bill for the regulation of Charitable Trusts,—taking occasion to describe with much humor the guzzling propensities of corporate trustees of charities, whereby the will of the donor is often sadly disappointed. He was particularly happy upon the *lunch* of the Lord Mayor and Aldermen of London when going to visit some almshouses, showing how light and delicate the dishes then tasted were, lest they

[1] Hansard, lxxviii., 123.

should spoil the solid dinner looming in the distance.¹ I may here observe that in making an introductory statement of any measure he ever displayed powers unrivalled in either House of Parliament. Whatever the subject might be, no one could be within sound of his voice without earnestly listening, and warmly admiring, although he might remain unconvinced.²

He next brought in a bill which went a great way towards the emancipation of the Jews. When Attorney-General I had passed an act to allow a Jew to be sheriff of a corporate town—not then venturing to go farther, from the dread of entire failure—but now Jews were to be permitted to fill all corporate offices, and almost everything was to be open to them except a seat in Parliament. I privately advised him to go all lengths, but he said " he was afraid of the Bishops and Sir Robert Inglis." In public I congratulated him upon his growing liberality, and expressed a hope that, in another session of Parliament, we should find him pointing out the inconsistency of the clamor that the country would be " unchristianized " by allowing a few Jews to sit in the House of Commons while we are willing to allow the Lord Mayor and Aldermen of London all to be Jews,—when Jews may be sheriffs and justices of the peace, when a Jew may preside in the Central Criminal Court over all the Queen's Judges, when Jews holding India stock join in governing India, and when Jews, having the same right to the elective franchise as Christians, by their representatives legislate for the empire.³

In return Lyndhurst supported bills which I introduced for the Abolition of *Deodands*, for giving compensation to the families of persons killed by negligence, and for allowing suits to be brought against British subjects resident abroad for causes of action which had accrued within the realm. These bills were all sent down to the Commons; but there the Goverement refused to support them, and they were lost. In great wrath I moved for a Committee in the House of Lords to search the Commons' Journals,

¹ He might have mentioned one Lord Mayor who, although famous for his gastronomy, denounced luncheon altogether, saying, "I consider luncheon as an insult to breakfast and an injury to dinner."
² Hansard, vol. lxxx., pp. 766, 782.
³ Hansard, vol. lxxviii., pp. 515, 775, 885.

and to report how these bills had been disposed of after reaching the Lower House,—intimating what the probable result of the search would be, complaining of the disrespectful usage of the Lord Chancellor by his colleagues, and denouncing the mischievous discord which seemed to prevail between the members of the Government in the two Houses; for the Duke of Wellington, as well as the Lord Chancellor, had voted for the bills, and had expressed particular satisfaction with the bill intended to meet fatal accidents by railways. Brougham followed, and was much more severe than I had ventured to be,—charging Sir James Graham, the Home Secretary, with the crime of *usurping the woolsack*. Lyndhurst remained silent, but looked unhappy, as if struck with a presentiment of his official death. This was at no great distance, but it came about in a manner which no one then anticipated, and which gave him little pain; for the ministerial vessel went to the bottom, and instead of the Chancellor being thrown overboard, as he dreaded, the rest of the crew perished with him.

There were several cases of breach of privilege this session which by the advice of the Chancellor, were treated very properly. Actions for defamation were brought without leave of the House for evidence given upon oath before select committees. According to Lord Denman's doctrine in *Stockdale* v. *Hansard*, the Peers ought not to have interposed,—leaving it to the courts in which the actions were brought to determine whether the actions were fitly commenced or not. But, by order of the House, the plaintiffs were brought to the bar in custody of the Sergeant-at-Arms, and, being ordered to remain in custody till the actions were discontinued, were afterwards, on a humble petition stating that the actions had been discontinued, set at liberty, with a suitable reprimand by the Lord Chancellor. To my great surprise, Lord Denman did not oppose or protest against this proceeding.[1]

The only point on which I differed from my noble and learned friend, the Lord Chancellor, this session, was respecting the Queen's proposed visit to Germany without appointing Lords Justices to represent her during her absence. Such an appointment had invariably taken

[1] Hansard, vol. lxxxii., pp. 303, 384, 526, 1678.

place on the sovereign going beyond the sea ever since the time of the Norman Conquest; and, it was quite certain that the Great Seal could not be carried out of the realm without an impeachable offense being committed, there was strong reason for arguing that it could not be used within the realm by warrant from the sovereign signed out of the realm,—the facility of communication between Vienna and Dover by means of steamboats and railways not altering the ancient law. However, the Chancellor laid down, and the House agreed, that although the Great Seal could not be used out of the realm, the mandates of the sovereign by sign manual out of the realm are valid, and that it is in the breast of the sovereign, on going abroad, to appoint a representative or not, as may be deemed for the public good. I rather think that this was a stretch of authority, and that it would have been better to have had the matter settled by Act of Parliament—but little practical inconvenience is likely to arise from the innovation. No minister will advise a proclamation by the sovereign for summoning or dissolving Parliament to be signed at Calais, and the validity of proper acts of state done abroad in the common administration of the government will never be questioned.

The autumn of 1845 witnessed the most sudden and unexpected turn in domestic politics recorded in our party annals. When Parliament was prorogued all was calm and prosperous and the most calculating and clear-sighted lover of place would have been delighted to declare himself an adherent of the existing administration. Before Parliament met again that administration expired, and, although it was apparently brought to life again, it then rather resembled a dead body moved by galvanism. I have never heard, from any authentic source, what part Lyndhurst took when, famine approaching by reason of the *potato blight*, and Lord John Russell having written his famous Edinburgh letter recommending an immediate abolition of the Corn Laws, Peel himself proposed this measure to his Cabinet, and resigned that it might be carried by his successor. Certain it is that the Chancellor expressed great joy when, from the opposition of Lord Grey to the appointment of Lord Palmerston as Foreign Minister, Lord John Russell failed in forming a government. This failure, nevertheless, was a most fortunate occurrence for the Whig party and for the country. Lord John Russell could not have carried the repeal of the Corn Laws, and if by any chance he had succeeded in the attempt, his immediate and permanent exclusion from power must have followed.

I saw Lyndhurst several times in the beginning of 1846, but he preserved a deep silence respecting the measures of the ensuing session, perhaps (among other reasons) because he did not know them.

At last, on the memorable 27th day of January, 1846, I was present in the House of Commons when Peel made his famous speech recommending the repeal of the Corn Laws. Next morning, at 10 o'clock, I went into the House of Lords to hear the argument upon a Writ of Error. As I entered, Lyndhurst beckoned to me, and when I approached him, he exclaimed in a loud voice, "Campbell! I find the Corn Laws are all a humbug. I used to suppose that the prosperity of our agriculture and of our commerce all depend upon *Protection;* but I tell you *Protection* is a *humbug*. There is nothing for it now but Free Trade." He then informed me that "although Stanley had gone out because he was so prejudiced as to stick up for Protection, he himself, and all the other members of the Cabinet, had resolved to sacrifice themselves for the good of their country. The truth I believe to be that calculating upon the strength of the Government, the temporary aid of the Whigs, the favor of the Court and the *prestige* of Peel's name, they all expected to carry the abolition of the Corn Laws and still to retain office. And so they probably would if Lord George Bentinck and Benjamin Disraeli had not been raised up, miraculously, as it were, for their destruction. Once on a time an intimate familiarity had subsisted between Lyndhurst and Disraeli, and it was believed that they used jointly to write articles in *The Times* against Lord Melbourne. Lyndhurst thus took a peculiar interest in Disraeli's new career, and as I went frequently to the House of Commons to hear him abuse Peel, which the Chancellor could not decently do, he curiously interrogated me about Disraeli's salient points and the effect which they produced. When I told him, according to the truth, that the House seemed to relish very much the jokes upon Peel's alleged hypocrisy, pedantry, and inconsistency, Lyndhurst could hardly conceal his satisfaction, although he might have seen that this feeling in the House of Commons must speedily work his own downfall.

An unmistakable forewarning followed. This was the rejection by the Lords of the Chancellor's "Charitable Trusts Bill," which in the preceding year he had carried through the Upper House without difficulty, although from the lateness of the season when it reached the Commons it had been dropped there. Now it was considerably improved in its details, and several clauses to which I had most objected had been omitted or modified. But the Protectionist Peers, headed by the Duke of Richmond—to show their spite—offered to coalesce with us in throwing it out, and we, alas! had not the virtue to withstand the temptation. Accordingly it was thrown out on the second reading, and I must, with shame confess, very factiously. I can only say that the Protectionists were more to blame than the Whigs; for we had always expressed a dislike of the Bill, whereas in the preceding session they had cordially supported it. Lyndhurst and Brougham have often taunted us all bitterly, both in public and private, with this coalition, and I have never been able to do more than plead in mitigation the force of bad example and pray privilege for a "first fault."

The loss of the "Charitable Trusts Bill" was the death-warrant of Sir Robert Peel's administration; but it did not receive the *coup de grace* till the division in the House of Commons upon the "Irish Coercion Bill," when there was a similar coalition with a similar result, and this proved instantly fatal.

In the mean time business had gone on in the House of Lords, as if nothing extraordinary were to happen. I again pushed through the "Deodand Abolition Bill," and the "Death by Negligence Compensation Bill." The latter was now a good deal discussed, and Lyndhurst showed some disposition to cavil at it. He pretended rather to stand up for the old common law-maxim, that "the life of man is too valuable to allow of any estimate of the damages to be given for the loss of it." I said:

"If a Lord Chancellor were killed by an accident on a railway there might, certainly, be a difficulty in estimating the sum his family should receive by way of compensation for the pecuniary loss; this would depend much upon the probable tenure of his office, if he had survived; for he might be likely to retain it for twenty years, or he might be on the point of being ejected from it by an inevitable change of ministry."

Lord Lyndhurst.—" There is a much more difficult case which may arise than that which my noble and learned friend has had the kindness to suggest. If my noble and learned friend should unfortunately, himself, fall a sacrifice to railway negligence, being at present without office and without retired allowance, how would a jury be able to estimate the value of his hopes?"[1]

The Bill, however, did pass both Houses, notwithstanding a powerful exertion of railway interest to crush it, and it has been the most popular of all my efforts at legislation.

I ought here gratefully to notice the very handsome compliment which Lord Lyndhurst this session publicly paid me as an author. Shortly before the commencement of the session I had published the first three volumes of the " Lives of the Chancellors." He took occasion in the course of a debate to praise the work in very high terms, and his remarks being received with loud cheers from all parts of the House, I rose in my place and bowed my thanks.

When the Corn Laws Abolition Act came to the House of Lords, I said to Lyndhurst that he was bound to defend it. "No," answered he, "this is unnecessary, for the Duke of Wellington has secured a majority in its favor, although he thinks as badly of it as I should have done seven years ago. Thus he addressed a Protectionist Peer, who came to lament to him that he must on this occasion vote against the Government, having such a bad opinion of the bill. 'Bad opinion of the bill, my Lord! You can't have a worse opinion of it than I have; but it was recommended from the Throne, it has passed the Commons by a large majority, and we must all vote for it. The Queen's Government must be supported.'"[1] The argument arising out of *opinion* being thus silenced, the Protectionists were helpless and the bill passed. How-

---

[1] Hansard, vol. lxxxvi., p. 174.
[2] In truth this is pretty much the substance of the Duke's speech in moving the second reading.

ever, they vowed vengeance against the author of it, and Peel was soon ejected, with all his colleagues, as well those who approved as those who abhorred it.

CHAPTER CCXXI.

OUT OF OFFICE.

LYNDHURST viewed his final descent from power very calmly. I really believe that from growing infirmities (for he was lame of one leg and his eyesight was much impaired) he was not sorry to retire into private life, so that he shared the fate of the rest of his party, and did not appear to be ignominiously discarded by them.

It was on the 6th of July that the government was transferred. The outgoing and incoming Ministers met at Buckingham Palace, and Lyndhurst having resigned the Great Seal into Her Majesty's hands, it was delivered to Lord Cottenham. Lyndhurst, again an ex-Chancellor, very cordially congratulated me on becoming a member of the Cabinet and Chancellor of the Duchy of Lancaster. On this very day the Benchers of the Inner Temple were to give a grand banquet, to which the heads of the law had been invited some weeks before. Lyndhurst, Brougham, and myself meeting in the House of Lords at five o'clock, we agreed to go together, and Lady Lyndhurst took us in her coach.

Being set down at the Temple, we had a sumptuous dinner from the Benchers, drank their wine copiously, and passed a very merry evening. The chair was filled by Sir Charles Wetherell. He was extravagantly ultra-Tory and ultra-High Church, but a most honorable and excellent man, who had resigned the office of Attorney-General in 1829 rather than agree to the Roman Catholic Emancipation Bill. He gave successively the healths of all the distinguished guests, nor concealing his own principles, but saying nothing to hurt the feelings of any one.

Lyndhurst made an exceedingly good-humored and beautiful speech, alluding to the alacrity with which he had that morning, for the last time, resigned the Great

Seal, and the pleasure with which he found himself among his old associates, whose company and good opinion must be the chief solace of his remaining days.

Brougham delivered a very warm panegyric upon the ex-Chancellor, and expressed a hope that he would make a good end, "although to an expiring Chancellor, Death was now armed with a new terror."

The Chairman, in proposing my health, called me his "noble and biographical friend," and expressed great confidence in my discrimination and impartiality if I should live to delineate the virtues of Lyndhurst and Brougham.

I said that my great hope was yet to see Wetherell himself in the "Marble Chair;" and then, although I might not agree in all his opinions, I should be delighted to celebrate his honorable career, and to hold up for the imitation of posterity his chivalrous devotion to principle, at whatever sacrifice. Some said that I then maliciously looked askance at Lyndhurst; but this is untrue, for I then had forgotten that his path had ever been otherwise than straightforward, or that he had not through life been disinterested and consistent.

We were afterwards much shocked by learning that during this merriment Lord Chief Justice Tindal, whom we all knew and much esteemed, had been in his last agony. We had known of his being unwell, but were not aware that his life was in any danger.

Lyndhurst now talked very freely—I may say licentiously—of all parties and all public men; but he retained a hearty grudge against the Whigs, and although I believe he had no longer any notion of again coming into office, he would have been delighted to have done a mischief to Lord John Russell's government. With this view he entered into an intrigue to bring about a reconciliation between Sir Robert Peel and the Protectionists, urging that their cause of quarrel was gone, and that they ought to combine against the common enemy.

The rather unpopular Bill for allowing the free importation of foreign sugar, whether produced by free or slave labor was then before the House of Commons, and he suggested that by a coalition between Protectionists and Peelites, under the title of the "New Conservatives," the Bill and its authors might be at once crushed. This was not a very happy thought, considering that the Sugar Bill

really was a free-trade measure—upon which Protectionists
and Peelites were not very likely to unite—so that the attempt was better calculated to widen than to close the
breach between them.

Never was any scheme more unfortunate, for it not only
utterly failed, but it drew down upon its projector the violent resentment of those for whose benefit it was intended.
Lord Stanley happened to be in the country and knew
nothing of it till it had blown up. He then, using a favorite expression of his, declared that "he would not have
touched it with the tongs." Being now the acknowledged
head of the Conservatives, he considered himself the future
Prime Minister, and he had no notion of again playing
second fiddle to Peel. Lord George Bentinck, who was
in London, on receiving the proposal from Lyndhurst, was
thrown into a frenzy of passion. He immediately went
down to the House of Commons and denounced it. From
a mere man of the turf he had been suddenly constituted
the leader of a great party, and he was shocked not only
with the notion of coalescing with the faithless Peel, but
of being again reduced to insignificance. He therefore
used some very strong language against "the meddling ex-
Chancellor." This Lyndhurst replied to in the House of
Lords, referring in a very cutting manner to Lord George's
former pursuits. Lord George rejoined in the House of
Commons, and after giving a very circumstantial account
of the intrigue to throw out the Sugar Bill—about which
the ex-Chancellor was so impatiently hot as to send
a messenger to rouse him out of bed at night—thus proceeded:—

"Sir, I will not say of Lord Lyndhurst as he has said of
me, that his calumnies are coarse or that his weapons are
of the same description. I will not deny that his sarcasms
are dressed in more classical language than mine; I admire the sharp edge and polish of his weapons. I admit
that, while I wield the broadsword and the bayonet, he
has skill to use the rapier, and uses it with the power of a
giant. But *I* am an *honest* man, and my past career will
bear a scrutiny perhaps better than that of the meddling
ex-Chancellor."[1]

Peel, although more guarded in his demeanor, was

[1] A common joke against Lord George Bentinck was that he was "a man
of a *stable* mind," but he was, in truth, one of the most honorable of mankind.

equally indignant. Lyndhurst had been so infatuated as to ask an interview with him, that he might explain to him and gain his consent to the coalition. Confident in the success of his free-trade policy, and forseeing that the Protectionists would soon be brought to shame, Peel shrunk from their contact. The particulars of the interview we know from a letter which Peel wrote to Lyndhurst, and insisted on his reading in the House of Lords:—

"You wrote to me a note expressing a wish for an interview which took place on the same day. At that interview you informed me of a fact of which I was not previously aware—that you had been in communication with some members of the late Government and of the party which supported it, with a view to the healing of animosities and the reconstruction of the Conservative party; that before you went farther you had resolved to speak to me; that the part you were taking was a disinterested one, for that your own return to office was out of the question. My answer was that I must decline being any party to the proceeding to which you preferred. I said that the return to office was as little in my contemplation as it was in yours, and that as I was not prepared to enter into any party combination with that view, I felt it incumbent upon me under such circumstances, to leave to those with whom I had been previously connected in political life the entire liberty to judge for themselves with regard to the formation of any new party connection."

This letter Lyndhurst did read in the House of Lords, in the midst of a long explanation vindicating his conduct and dwelling upon the purity of his motives, which he thus concluded:—

"Everyone knows that I am no longer a candidate for office; that in consequence of a severe illness the holding of office during the last session has been a painful and irksome task for me; and that I am desirous of passing the short remainder of my days among my family and my friends; and nothing, even on this occasion, should have drawn me forth, but the virulent personal attack made upon me."[1]

Lyndhurst never forgave Peel the cruel rebuff which he now received instead of expected thanks, with perhaps an

[1] 88 Hansard, 974.

offer of becoming Chancellor *quinto*. Peel relented as
little, and the estrangement continued down to the prema-
ture death of that distinguished statesman. In reality
there never had been much love lost between them. Peel,
having soon discovered Lyndhurst to be pretty much
devoid of principle and very unscrupulous as to the performance of the duties of his office, had never acted with
him cordially, and always regarded him with suspicion.[1]
Lyndhurst, on the other hand, was in the habit of laughing at Peel's official pedantry, affectation of secrecy, constrained manners, and incapacity to pronounce his
" h's."[2]

Lyndhurst was so much disgusted with the bad success
of his attempt to upset Lord John Russell's government
and to re-construct the Conservative party, that he resolved never again to speak in Parliament or to meddle
with politics. He said to me, " I have as little respect for
the Whigs as ever; but you have nothing more to fear
from me—my career is run." He really was quite sincere,
and he had then no *arrière pensée*. At another time,
soon after, he observed to me, " I may vegetate five or
six years longer; but I am politically dead."

He long adhered to his resolution. He continued to
attend the House of Lords as an evening lounge, but for
three whole years he never opened his mouth, unless once
to say a few words on a Railway bill, nor did he ever
vote in any party division.

I urged him to attend the hearing of appeals in the
House of Lords and in the Privy Council, reminding him
that the retired allowance of 5,000*l.* a year to ex-Chancellors was upon the understanding that they were thus to
assist in the administration of justice; but he said his
sight was so much impaired that he could not read the
appeal papers properly, or safely take part in any decision.
Unfortunately there was too much ground for this excuse.

[1] This I discovered so far back as the year 1828, when not yet having
entered Parliament, I was serving on the Real Property Commission, Lyndhurst being Chancellor and Peel Home Secretary. They nearly quarrelled
about appointing the secretary to the commission, and Peel took the whole
management of the commission into his own hands.

[2] By hard labor, Peel had acquired the faculty of pronouncing *H* when it
occurred at the beginning of a word. Thus, he would say "*House*" and
"*Hustings*," not, in Lancashire fashion, " *'ouse*," or " *'ustings ;*" but *h* in the
middle of a word he would still omit. Thus he would say, " the man *be-aves*
well who always *ad-eres* to his friends."

He was twice couched by an eminent oculist, and then only imperfectly recovered his power of vision. His lameness likewise increased upon him so that he could hardly walk without assistance. All his mental powers, however, remained in full vigor, and his conversation was as sprightly and reckless as ever.

In 1847 I had the honor of entertaining him at a dinner which I gave as Chancellor of the Duchy of Lancaster, and which made a considerable noise at the time. Lord Stanley had brought forward a charge against me in the House of Lords about the formation of the Council of the Duchy, and this gave rise to a good deal of angry as well as jocular discussion. To make matters smooth, there being no real hostility intended on either side, I asked if he had any objection to meet the Council of the Duchy at dinner at Stratheden House; to which he very good humoredly assented. I invited Lord Lyndhurst, Lord Brougham, Lord Melbourne, Lord John Russell, Lord Clarendon, Lord Lincoln, Sir James Graham, and Edward Ellice, to assist. And a most jovial day we had of it. Strange to say, Lyndhurst declared that although he had abused Lord John so long, and plotted so much against him, now was the first time that he ever dined in his company. At this "Love-feast" Whig and Tory, Protectionist and Free-trader, occupant of office and expectant of office—all drank wine with each other, and instead of politics being banished, the doctrines and faults of all parties were freely made the subject of ridiculous comment. This license of talk was highly to Lyndhurst's taste, and he was so delighted and genial, that in going away with Brougham he left a message for me with my butler that "he hoped the dinner would be annual while his Lordship remained Chancellor of the Duchy."

During the recess of Parliament Lyndhurst spent the whole of his time at Turville, a very nice country-house, with beautiful gardens and a moderate-sized farm, which he had hired in Oxfordshire; and here he pretended to devote himself to improved methods for the raising of flowers, corn, and cattle; but his time was spent in reading the newspapers, in sauntering about his grounds, in corresponding with Lord Brougham, from whom he almost daily received a letter, and in quiet chat with a few friends who paid short visits to him. Although so well grounded at the University both in classics and mathematics, he had no real pleasure in literary or scientific pursuits, and his reading did not extend beyond the volumes supplied by a circulating library. When living in London in his father's old house, George street, Hanover square, he had a daily call from Lord Brougham, who brought him the gossip of the clubs. All rivalry having ceased, there was now equal cordiality between the two—with this difference, that Brougham generally spoke rather respectfully of Lyndhurst behind his back, while Lyndhurst, behind Brougham's back, was always ready to join in exaggerating his faults and in laughing at his eccentricities. During the rest of the day till it was time to take an airing in his carriage, Lyndhurst was ready to receive all visitors who might drop in—and a great many came, chiefly lawyers and members of the *corps diplomatique*. On these occasions it was expedient to go late and stay the last; for I observed the practice to be that each visitor, on departing, furnished a subject of satirical remark for the master of the house and those who remained.

But such tranquil pleasures began to pall upon the jaded appetite of the ex-Chancellor. He really had no more any desire for office. Being nearly blind, the Great Seal was out of the question; and as Lord Privy Seal, or President of the Council, he could have had no increase of pay beyond his pension, the dignity being no compensation for the trouble. What he did long for was the excitement of again belonging to a party with whom he was to attack and be attacked. He had his choice—Whig, Peelite, or Protectionist. The Whigs he still hated, as they had been twitting him with apostacy ever since he first took office. The Peelites would have been his natural allies; for, with his own single exception, all the members of Peel's Cabinet who, after carrying the repeal of the Corn Laws, resigned with him in 1846, had stuck together—a serried band—neither amalgamating with Whigs nor Protectionists. But he knew that they looked upon him as little better than a traitor ever since his clumsy and calamitous intrigue about the Sugar Duty Bill. He therefore made advances to the Protectionists, and they were delighted to enroll him in their ranks. As the event afterwards proved, they dreadfully needed men of reputation and experience as partisans, insomuch that it seemed impossible to form a government out of them, if by any chance such a task should ever be assigned to their chief. Damaged as Lyndhurst was, they hailed him "*Deus ex machinâ*"! He was much flattered with a reception which would have been impossible had Lord George Bentinck survived, but which was facilitated by the ancient liaison between Lyndhurst and Benjamin Disraeli, who was now acknowledged, though most reluctantly, by the country squires, as their leader in the House of Commons.

We of the Government had not heard of the new recruit to the Protectionists, when one evening—Lord Stanley having made a very mischievous motion for the purpose of compelling the Crown to disallow an Act passed by the Canadian Legislature for granting compensation to those who had suffered losses in the suppression of the rebellion, and having been well answered by Lord Grey, the Colonial Secretary,—to the astonishment of the whole House, slowly rose Lord Lyndhurst

> "With grave
> Aspect he rose, and in his rising seemed
> A pillar of state; deep on his front engraven
> Deliberation sat, and public care;
> And princely counsel in his face yet shone,
> Majestic though in ruin."

And thus he spoke:—

"My Lords, it is several years since I intruded myself on your notice, and I thought I never should have addressed you again; but seeing the peril to which this great empire is exposed, and recollecting the important part which I have had to take in guiding its counsels under successive monarchs, I have thought I should ill discharge my duty to the Crown and to the people if I longer remained silent. This may be the last time that my voice may be ever heard within these walls, but I could not descend to the tomb with peace of mind if I did not make a dying effort to save my country."

Such was the proœmium to the most factious, the most democratical, and the most sophistical speech I ever heard in Parliament. He declared that the Act of the Canadian Legislature ought to be disregarded, because, as he said, it was passed against the will of the people; and that under these circumstances the people had a right to say how the prerogative of the Crown was to be exercised, as this prerogative had been created by them for their own benefit. He then reviewed various acts of the Canadian as well as the Imperial Legislature, misconstruing and perverting them, and pretty plainly indicated that the Canadians ought again to hoist the standard of rebellion rather than submit to such misrule.

I was called upon by Lord Lansdowne to answer him which I am sorry to say I did with considerable intemperance, and in a tone which might have been very successful in the House of Commons, but was unsuited to the "ears polite" of their Lordships. Amongst other things supposed to be unjustifiably personal and offensive, although resting on the undoubted basis of truth, I said:

"My Lords, I ought not to be surprised at the extraordinary speech which has just been delivered, having been well acquainted with my noble and learned friend for a vast many years. He reminds you of the time when he held office under the Crown. The sentiments we have heard from him to-night are very different from those which he then uttered, for your Lordships must be aware that he then generally took the side of arbitrary power and expressed great horror of *insurrectionary and tumultuary rule*, I might almost say of *popular privileges*. But, my Lords, I am old enough to have known my noble and learned friend in an earlier part of his career, when, as he has often truly said, he was not a Whig—when he held pure democracy in high respect, and when he strongly sympathized with those who contended for the holy right of insurrection. Naturally enough, such are again his principles—now when, as he has told you with so much solemnity, his career is drawing to its close—

'On revient toujours
A ses premières amours.'"

I then followed him through his misrepresentations and sophisms, but by no means so efficiently as I might have done, for I perceived that the House thought I had transgressed the bounds of propriety. Lord Stanley answered me, and handled me unmercifully, dwelling particularly on the bad taste of assailing so bitterly a venerable peer who had declared that this was probably the last time his voice would ever be heard within these walls, although Lord Stanley himself well knew that this was a mere figure of rhetoric, and that the speech was meant as a first contribution of the "venerable peer," under an alliance for carrying on an active campaign against the Government. Lord Lansdowne followed, but said hardly a word in my defense, illustrating a remark I have often heard made, that the Whigs never stand up for each other, while the Tories will not allow even the dead body of a slain comrade to fall into the hands of the enemy.'

Next morning, meeting Lyndhurst in a Select Committee of the House of Lords on a Law Bill, he came up and spoke to me, as if nothing had happened. He continued thenceforth to vote steadily with Lord Stanley; and, forgetting that he had discovered *Protection to be a humbug*, he professed a desire to see the Protectionists in power, although they still expressed a determined resolution to restore the "sliding scale" as soon as they could, by an appeal to the people upon a dissolution of Parliament.

He did not again speak for a twelvemonth, nor until I had been removed from the arena of party politics by being appointed Chief Justice of England. He then invited me to dinner, and desiring me to fill a bumper of *still champagne*, he said to me, "Here, Campbell, in this loving cup let us drown forever all our animosities." From that time to the present there has been between us in public as well as in private, a cordial good understanding, and a reciprocation of civilities.

In the Session of 1851 Lyndhurst seemed to have renewed his youth, and to be starting on a fresh career. No aspiring youth, returned for the first time to the House of Commons and desiring to make himself a name, could be more solicitous or more persevering in seeking opportunities to come forward as an orator and an agitator. Till Lord John Russell was forced to resign, Lyndhurst was always putting questions and making motions, with a view to harass the Government; and when Stanley, now Lord Derby, became Minister (utterly renouncing the Peelites, who joined the Whigs in opposition), he took the new Government under his special guardianship, ready at all times to support it by praising its measures and the

---

¹ The motion on the Canada Rebellion Compensation Bill had been well imagined, and had almost proved successful. On the division there was a majority against us of Peers present; and by calling proxies we had only upon the whole a majority of three.

men who composed it, including Sugden, the new Chancellor, hitherto an object of his special aversion.

In the beginning of the Session of 1851, when the Whigs still clung to office, although in a "staggering state," Lyndhurst tried to bring fresh obloquy upon them by a motion respecting Mazzini and the Italian refugees, representing that they were countenanced and encouraged in their plots for stirring up insurrection on the Continent by the government of England, and that Austria in particular had great reason to complain of this breach of the law of nations.[1] He was abetted on this occasion by Lord Aberdeen, who as yet had shown no tendency towards the Whigs, and seemed ready to join Lord Derby if the stumbling-block of Protection, which alone divided them, could in any way be got rid of. Now Lyndhurst began to hope that his plan for a reconstruction of the Conservative party, which had failed so signally in 1846, might yet succeed. But, for reasons incomprehensible to me, every attempt at this sort was still steadily opposed by Lord Derby. Although without recruits from the Peelites he could not expect to form a permanent administration, he would make no concession to them, and he recklessly irritated them by ridicule.

Lord Truro, who had become Chancellor, had incurred the ill-will of Lord Brougham by very properly refusing to make a brother of his a Vice-Chancellor; and there was now a combination between Lord Brougham and Lord Lyndhurst to drive him from the woolsack. They took a dexterous advantage of his antipathy to law reform, which he had not the prudence to disguise.

Lyndhurst attacked him violently for allowing Lord John Russell to bring in a bill in the House of Commons for reforming the Court of Chancery, instead of introducing it himself in the House of Lords. This bill Lyndhurst laughed at with great felicity, and, I must admit, with some justice. Alluding to several ministerial defeats which Lord John had recently experienced, he said:—

"One of the enactments of the bill was to transfer, by a sort of sleight-of-hand movement, all the patronage of his noble and learned friend on the woolsack into the lap of the First Lord of the Treasury, already sufficiently laden with patronage of this description. The noble lord at the

[1] 115 Hansard, 621.

head of the Government had of late been worsted in contests with his foes, and now, turning round upon his friends, he sought to obtain a victory and to indemnify himself by the plunder of a colleague—

'So much 'tis safer thro' the camp to go
And rob a comrade than despoil a foe.'

It was gravely urged that the Lord Chancellor was overwhelmed by the weight of judicial business, and that he ought to be relieved of his ecclesiastical patronage. This would be like relieving by the removal of a feather the horse whose back is nearly broken by his heavy load of lead."[1]

A few days after, again goading Lord Truro about Chancery Reform, which he represented to be very urgent and very easy, he received the following unexpected retort:

"The urgency I do not deny; but can hardly think the remedy is so easy, or the noble and learned lord, who has been four times Chancellor, would not have been so often and so long in office without proposing one, instead of leaving the task entirely to his successors."[2]

Lyndhurst next complained of a breach of the privileges of the Lords by the Commons, who had inserted a clause in a bill originating in the Lower House, whereby it was enacted that the Equity Judges should attend in the House of Lords to assist in the hearing of Equity appeals. He contended that such legislation could properly originate only in the House whose constitution and proceedings were to be affected by it, and further urged that in this instance legislation was wholly unnecessary, as the Equity Judges are usually Privy Councillors, and all Privy Councillors are bound, when summoned by the House of Lords, to attend to give their advice upon any point of law which may be submitted to them.[3]

Till the very end of the session Lyndhurst continued equally active, charging Ministers with misconduct in the government of the colonies, and almost in every other department. The design was now imputed to him even of forming a party of his own, and himself becoming Prime Minister, that he might rival the fame of the octogenarian Ximenes.

Whatever his ulterior views might be, on the meeting of Parliament in the beginning of 1852 he was more than

[1] 115 Hansard, 770. [2] 116 Hansard, 989. [3] 117 Hansard, 1069.

commonly factious. Every evening in the House of Lords
he spoke at least once—frequently several times, so as to
outdo the loquacity of Brougham—not making formal harangues, but putting questions, supporting or opposing petitions, and moving for returns, always seeking to discredit
and to hasten the fall of the Whig Government. Although
during the whole of his Parliamentary career he had hitherto professed himself an *optimist* as to our law and jurisprudence, saying, "Whatever is, is right," he seemed suddenly
to have become a *pessimist*, being ready to denounce as
narrow-minded bigots those who would allow any rag of
what he had before venerated to remain untouched. A
bill had been brought forward by the Government founded
upon the Report of Commissioners for improving the
procedure of the Common-Law Courts. This introduced
greater changes than had been proposed or thought of
since the reign of Edward I.; but it was denounced as a
mere *evasion* by the recently reform-hating Lyndhurst—
who expressed a desire to do away with all legal forms,
who in a suit of great complication, difficulty, and value,
was for following the course in which a milk-score is settled
in the County Court, and who even appeared to sanction the
absurd notion that in England all suits may be summarily
decided by a Judge sitting like a Turkish Cadi, and instantly giving judgment when he has heard the verbal
statement of the disputants.

It was lucky for the cause of rational and practicable law
reform, that in three weeks from the commencement of
this session the Whigs were obliged to resign; for while
they remained languishing in office all their measures
would have been effectually obstructed. Lyndhurst
showed that he had no object of personal ambition to
gain, further than the glory of being the unofficial protector of the new Government. Refusing to become President of the Council, he crossed over to the ministerial side
of the House, and was at all times prepared to extend his
ægis over the head of the Premier, saying by his looks,—" I
am content he shall reign : but I'll be Protector over him."

He now joined most cordially and most usefully in carrying through and improving the Whig reforms which he
had before opposed. Both parties were aiming at popularity by law reform, and Lyndhurst's object was to gain
for the Protectionists the credit of all that was done in

this department. A few trifling alterations being made in the Common-Law Procedure Bill, which had before called forth his reprobation, he now eulogized it extravagantly, and he paid a very just tribute of applause to the Bill for abolishing Masters in Chancery, prepared according to the report of a Whig commission, and presented by Lord St. Leonards, the Protectionist Chancellor. Lyndhurst's zeal carried him so far as to pronounce this functionary the model of every cancellarian good quality, accomplishment, and virtue,—declaring that "no government ever was more fortunate in a Chancellor, and that the present occupant of the woolsack, besides being the greatest of lawyers, was distinguished by his placid temper and his mild and gentlemanly manners."

During the session he himself originated only one bill, which arose out of the action against Mr. Salomons, the Jew, for sitting and voting in the House of Commons without having in due form taken the Abjuration Oath, leaving out the words "Upon the true faith of a Christian." This offense not only subjected him to a pecuniary penalty of £500 recovered against him, but made him liable to the pains of a *præmunire*, according to which he might anciently have been put to death by any one who met him, as having *Caput Lupinum*. The proposed bill to meet this and all similar cases left the law untouched as to the necessity for taking the oath in the prescribed form, and preserved the pecuniary penalty, but it swept away all other punishments and disabilities as remnants of a barbarous age.

Lyndhurst now spoke upon Legal Education, Chancery amendment, the County Courts Jurisdiction, the Consolidation of the Criminal Law, the Law of Evidence in Scotland, Lunacy, the Law of Marriage and Divorce, the Law of Libel, Copyhold Tenure, the Kafir War, the State of Ireland, and the Convention with France for the Extradition of Criminals, always taking care, whatever the subject might be, to give his observations a ministerial tincture, and to have a fling at the Whigs.

By one motion which he made, wholly unconnected with party, he acquired immense *éclat*. This was for the appointment of a Select Committee to inquire into the claims of Baron de Bode under the treaty with France in 1815, which gave compensation to British subjects for the loss they had sustained by French decrees of confiscation.

He was now turned of eighty; he was obliged to support himself on a walking-stick while he spoke, and he was nearly blind. But his voice was strong, articulate, and musical, his arrangement lucid, his reasoning ingenius and plausible, and he displayed a power of memory which at any age would have appeared almost miraculous. He had to narrate very complicated proceedings, extending over a very long period of time, and to specify numerous dates and sums of money forming items in voluminous accounts, and the names of many foreign places and persons—yet in a speech of two hours he never was at fault, he never hesitated, he never looked at a note, and he never made a mistake. This was the most wonderful effort of a public speaker I ever witnessed in all my time. He had a very bad case, yet he not only riveted the attention of all who heard him, but enlisted their sympathies on his side, and made all who had not before studied the facts convinced that he was pleading for a much injured and oppressed individual. But the Duke of Wellington was too knowing and too shrewd to be taken in. As we were leaving the House he said to me, " Well, I admire Lord Lyndhurst, but I was not convinced. What do you say to it, Lord Chief Justice?" I stated the truth—that it was all delusion; that the Baron de Bode was not substantially a British subject, although he happened by accident to be born in England; that we should not have had a right to shoot or hang him (as Lyndhurst had fallaciously stated), if we had found him carrying arms against us for the Czar of Russia, to whom he owed allegiance; that the loss for which he sought compensation had not occurred to him as a British subject, and that as we should have had no right to claim this loss from France, it did not come within the spirit or letter of the treaty which his Grace had dictated at Paris. *Duke of Wellington.*—" Chief Justice, you are right; you are right! you are quite right!" Nevertheless Lord Derby, to please Lyndhurst, granted the committee, and the members were so selected that they made a unanimous report in favor of Baron de Bode's claim, to the amount of about a million sterling, although every tribunal in the country, including the Houes of Lords, as a court of appeal, had, without hesitation, decided against him.[1]

[1] I had prepared myself to speak against granting the committee ; but after

No advantage, after all, was gained by Baron de Bode, or the holders of "de Bode stock," from this daring attempt, for Lord Derby left office without providing any fund to answer the claim, and it being repudiated by his successor, Lord Aberdeen, only five could be mustered to vote for it when Lyndhurst, in 1853, again brought it before the House.

At the general election, in 1852, Protection was in little favor, but so many who called themselves "free-trade Derbyites" were returned, that the permanent stability of Lord Derby's government appeared by no means improbable. If he had managed well he might have remained a long while in office, and, at any rate, he might have retired from it with dignity, remaining the respected head of a great party. But, to the deep grief of Lyndhurst, he committed a series of blunders. In the first place he yielded to "free-trade" too easily, so as to make the squires doubt his sincerity. But the fatal mistake was in bringing forward the budget three months sooner than was necessary or expedient for the public good, in the belief that it would be highly popular, and put to silence the leaders of the Opposition,—Peelites, Whigs, and Radicals. The vote condemning "Protection" being carried in the House of Commons, the ministers had only to say, "We acquiesce, though unwillingly, and we adjourn the two Houses till the spring of the next year, when, having had a fair hearing, we will tell you what our measures are to be, and you will deliberately exercise your judgment upon them." But, instead of this, with a flourish of trumpets they called upon the public to come and see them "their quietus make with a bare *Budget*." What could any reasonable man expect from wantonly and capriciously shifting the burden of taxation, relieving those who would be thankless, and laying new imposts on classes the most sensitive, the most clamorous, and the most influential.

While the struggle was going on in the House of Commons we were very tranquil in the House of Lords, and nothing occurred to call forth the eloquence of Lyndhurst. However, he came every evening the Lords met, to hear the news, being as anxious as if his own fame and fortune

Lyndhurst's brilliant oration, and the enthusiasm it created, I had not courage to rise.

had depended upon the result. He would ask me to go to the Commons and bring him word what they were doing, as from his lameness and blindness he could not well make his way through the lobbies and corridors; but on the evening when the budget was actually to be opened, he was conducted into a snug seat in the gallery of the House of Commons, for the use of the Peers, and there he remained during Disraeli's speech of five and a-half hours, the whole of which I likewise heard. With melancholy secret forebodings, Lyndhurst still held confident language, till, at last, suspense was put an end to by Gladstone's reply, and the fatal decision which followed.

I must say that he then talked very rationally, and even patriotically, observing that "as nothing could save the Derbyites from destruction, Jupiter having *demented* them, his only wish now was, for the good of the country, to see a strong government established, and, although he had hated the Whigs and had hated the Peelites as separate parties, he might endure the amalgamation of both, cemented by a slight infusion of Radicals." Accordingly, when Lord Aberdeen's government was announced, he said "Things might have been worse, and I am disposed to give it a fair trial."

He was as good as his word, and his conduct through the whole of the long session of 1853 was unexceptionable. He returned to his old position in the House of Lords—a back row on the Opposition side—which I used to call "the Castle of Obstruction," but which might now be called "the Bulwark of the Constitution." He continued to be exceedingly active—attending select Committees on law bills in the morning, and the regular meetings of the House in the evening—still avoiding the appeals, except when the great Bridgewater case came on, in which he took a leading part.

Without quarreling with Lord Derby, he ceased to be a Derbyite; but he would not join the Coalitionists, and, remaining entirely unconnected and independent, he really took the part which the welfare of the empire seemed to require. The great dread he had entertained of a French invasion subsided on the augmentation of our fleet, and the embodying of the militia, and it now entirely gave way to his abhorrence of the outrages of the Czar Nicholas. He had been exceedingly intimate with Baron Brunnow, the Russian Ambassador at our court, and had been induced by him several times to favor the *absolutist* autocrats who were anxious to put down constitutional governments all over the world. But when he saw that Nicholas, under pretense of protecting the Greek Christians in the Turkish dominions, meditated the dismemberment of the Turkish empire, and the planting of the Russian Eagle on the dome of St. Sophia, he came forward as the champion of European independence. Standing up for the faith of treaties, and urging the obligation on this country to enforce them for our interest, as well as for our honor, he denounced "Count Nesselrode's note" which set forth the pretensions of Nicholas, as "the most false, sophistical, and insolent state paper ever issued by any Government pretending to be civilized." This declaration of Lyndhurst made a great sensation all over Europe, and called forth a flattering anathema from the Russian ambassador, concluding with the awful declaration, "I will never again sit down in company with the man who could speak so disrespectfully of my august Master." Lyndhurst thought (with most sensible men) that Lord Aberdeen treated the outrage of Nicholas in passing the Pruth and invading the Turkish provinces, without pretending to have a cause of war, with far too much forbearance; but, considering that there might be some undisclosed reason for the seemingly timid and vacillating policy pursued, he forbore till the conclusion of the session to express any censure of the Government, or to make any observation which could embarrass the pacific negotiations said to be pending.

During the session of 1853, Lord Lyndhurst really did strive to gain the title of "Emancipator of the Jews." In his heart he had been inclined in their favor, but while in office he had always felt himself restrained from voting for any of the bills passed by the Commons for allowing them to sit in Parliament. After he had resigned the Great Seal he promised actively to take the other side, but as yet he had not been able to pluck up sufficient courage to speak or vote for any of the Jew bills which came up annually during Lord John Russell's administration, from 1846 to 1851, although he absented himself from the division when the bills were thrown out by the influence of Lord Derby. At length, however, he was determined to follow his own inclinations on this important subject, and, waving his sword, he cried aloud, "To your tents, O Israel!" He at first meditated the direct and bold course of laying on the table of the House of Lords a bill enacting that Jews might sit in Parliament on taking the usual oaths in the manner most binding on the conscience,— omitting the words "on the true faith of a Christian," which the judges had held in Salomons' case to be part of the Oath of Abjuration, and not merely to indicate the manner in which it was to be administered to Christians. But he deemed it more discreet, after recent growing majorities in the House of Lords against the Jews, to propose by his bill to enact a consolidation of the existing oaths of allegiance, abjuration, and supremacy, into one short, simple, and sensible oath, which might be taken by all loyal subjects, whatever their religious persuasion,— omitting from it such absurdities as a renunciation of all allegiance to the descendants of James II., who have ceased to exist for nearly a century, and allowing the words "on the true faith of a Christian" to remain as part of the oath. To such a bill he thought the Lords could not decently object. Then his anticipation was that these words would be struck out by the House of Commons, and that when the bill came back amended, the Lords would not venture to reject it by reason of such a slender and reasonable amendment. He introduced it in a very admirable speech, in which, after quoting passages from opinions of Judges showing that the Abjuration Oath was not passed with the view of excluding the Jews, he thus proceeded :—

"I go farther, and I say that it is utterly against the principles of the Constitution to exclude the Jews from Parliament on any such ground. I say it is the mainspring of our glorious constitution that no British subject —no natural-born subject of the Queen—ought to be deprived of the rights enjoyed by his fellow-subjects, unless he has committed some crime, or unless he is excluded by some positive enactment of the Legislature directed against him or against the class to which he belongs. None can be rightfully excluded unless by the concurrent voice of the two Houses of Parliament, and with the assent of the Crown. If you exclude them by the casual operation of a clause which was never directed against them or the class to which they belong, you unjustly deprive them of their birthright. I say then, my Lords, that if I retain these words 'on the true faith of a Christian' in my Bill, I retain them entirely *ex necessitate* and entirely against my own deliberate conviction."[1]

The second reading of the bill was allowed to pass without a division; but, at the next stage, Lord Derby strongly objected to the tortuous course now attempted with a view to reverse the repeated decisions of their Lordships; and the bill was thrown out by a large majority.

During this session of Parliament there were several Select Committees on bills for the amendment of the law. I attended them as often as I was not kept away by my judicial duties in the Queen's Bench, and I almost always found Lyndhurst at his post, rendering valuable service. This was very laudable conduct; for here he had no party or personal bias to follow, and there was no *éclat* to be obtained, for we sat *foribus clausis*. I sometimes wished to have reporters present, so that the *dicta* might be recorded, like "*Consultations*" in framing the *Code Napoléon*. Lyndhurst always showed admirable good sense, as well as acuteness and logical discrimination. He took particular pains with a bill which was intended to be the first part of a Codification of the Criminal Law of England, and which was confined to "offenses against the person." After the Committee had sat upon it eleven days, it seemed to me to be still very crude, no definition even of "murder" or "manslaughter" being devised which would not raise new questions, and a clause being inserted—that, as far as concerned "offenses against the person," the common law should be considered as repealed. Brougham was for immediately passing it as it stood; but, with Lyndhurst's concurrence, I stopped it when it came back to the House, with a protestation that, although I by no means despaired of codifying the criminal law, I should strenuously resist any attempt to put a part upon the Statute Book till the whole code was before us in a perfect form. All my brother judges have since concurred in the opinion that the bill, if passed, would have thrown the administration of the criminal law into utter confusion.

Lyndhurst was likewise very useful this session in sup-

[1] 127 Hansard, 7833.

porting and improving the bill for the Registration of Deeds respecting real property. But, although it passed the House of Lords, Lord St. Leonards alone dissenting, it was lost in the Commons through the opposition of Sir Richard Bethell, the Solicitor-General, who was allowed to defeat a measure which the Chancellor himself had introduced, and on which the credit of the Government materially depended.

Although since Lyndhurst's last resignation he had declined to take any part in the judicial business of the House, there was one appeal this session of such great importance—estates of the value of £80,000 a year being at stake, and the principles on which it was to be decided touching all the rights and duties of peers,—that he thought himself bound to assist in hearing and determining it. This was the great "Bridgewater case."

The seventh Earl of Bridgewater by his will left his lands in the counties of Salop and Chester in tail male to his nephew, Lord Alford, eldest son and heir apparent of the Earl of Brownlow, provided that if Lord Alford should die without having acquired the title and dignity of Duke or Marquis of Bridgewater, the lands should go over to other devisees, named in the will, as if Lord Alford had died without issue male. Lord Alford died leaving a son, without having acquired the title of Duke or Marquis of Bridgewater, and the question was whether this son should take the lands, or whether they should go over to the devisees who would have been entitled to them under the will if he had died without leaving a son; and this depended upon the validity of the condition or proviso for *cesser* if the Crown should not confer upon Lord Alford the title of Duke or Marquis of Bridgewater.[1] On the part of these devisees it was argued that the condition was not tainted with illegality, for it could not be presumed that the Crown would create a peerage from any improper motive; that the proviso must be taken to have been meant as an incentive to earn the peerage by eminent services to the State, and that it was to be considered in the same way as if the lands had been limited to go over

[1] The testator's great object was, that the existing title of Bridgewater becoming extinct, the Bridgewater estates and name should not be absorbed in the Earldom of Brownlow, and that a new title of Duke or Marquis of Bridgewater should be created, to be borne by those who were to inherit the Bridgewater estates.

if the first devisee did not obtain at the University of Cambridge the degree of Senior Wrangler.

Of this opinion was Lord Cranworth, sitting as Vice-Chancellor; and of this opinion were all the Judges except two, when consulted by the House of Lords. But Lord Lyndhurst thought that the son of Lord Alford was entitled to the estates, on the ground that this was an illegal condition subsequent, and therefore utterly void, so that the will would operate as if no such condition were contained in it.

"This," said he, "is not a technical question, but must be considered on general principles, with reference to the practical effect of the condition; and we must bring our observation and experience to bear in determining it. It is a well-established rule of law, that a condition against the public good or public policy, as it is usually called, is illegal and void. Shepherd's Touchstone and Coke are direct authorities on this point. In more modern times, we find Lord Hardwicke stating that 'political arguments, in the fullest sense of the word, as they concern the government of a nation, must be, and always have been, of great weight in the consideration of the Court; and though there may be no *dolus malus* in contracts as to other persons, yet if the rest of mankind are concerned as well as the parties, it may properly be said that it regards the public utility. These reasons of public benefit and utility weigh greatly with me, and are a principal ingredient in my present opinion.' It is unnecessary to cite other authorities in support of this well-established rule of law. What cases come within the rule must be decided as they successively occur. Each case must be determined according to its own circumstances. When the case of a trustee dealing with his *cestui que trust* was first considered, it must, in the absence of precedent, have been determined upon weighing the public mischief that would arise from giving a sanction to such dealing. So as to transactions between attorneys and their clients; also as to seamen insuring their wages, and other similar cases referred to in the course of the argument. The inquiry must, in each instance where no former precedent occurred, have been into the tendency of the act to interfere with the general interest. The rule then is clear. Whether the particular case comes within the rule is the province of the Court in each instance, acting with due caution, to determine. My Lords, the duties incident to the peerage (and Lord Alford might at any moment, by the death of Lord Brownlow, have become a peer) are of the gravest and highest character, and in the proper discharge of which the interests of the Crown and the public are deeply concerned. These duties are both legislative and judicial; in addition to which, a peer of the realm has a right, when he deems it necessary, to demand an audience of the Sovereign, and to tender his advice respecting public affairs. In the framing of laws, it is his duty to act according to the deliberate result of his judgment and conscience, uninfluenced, as far as possible, by other considerations, and least of all by those of a pecuniary nature. He acts judicially, not merely in the appellate jurisdiction of the House, but also in the various matters usually referred to committees, in which the strictest independence is to be observed, and all foreign influence of every description to be carefully avoided. Such is the position, and such the duties of a peer of the realm; and it follows that any application or disposition of property, that has a tendency to interfere with the proper and faithful discharge of these duties, must be at variance with public good, and consequently illegal and void. It is true that creations of peers and promotions in the peerage emanate from the Crown; and the respect we entertain for the Sovereign will not allow us to suppose that, in the exercise of this or any other prerogative, he can act otherwise than according to the best and purest motives. But we all know that, practically, this power is exercised according to the advice of the Minister—that the Crown rarely exercises it except at his suggestion, and on his recommendation; and, further, that these honors are usually granted, except in cases of extraordinary merit or distinguished public services, to the partisans and supporters of the administration for the time being, and seldom to its opponents. This is obvious to all, and confirmed by every day's experience. What, then, would be the practical result of this state of things with reference to the proviso now under consideration? If an estate, in this case of great extent and value, is made to depend upon a creation or promotion in the peerage, is it reasonable to suppose—speaking generally (for we must so consider the subject), and without reference to particular individuals—that such a state of things would not have at least a tendency to lead the party thus interested to act, and without much inquiry, in accordance with those who could insure the permanence of the estate to his descendants, to induce him to support their views and measures, without any scrutinizing regard as to their effect or propriety, and thus to affect that free agency which it is a duty as far as possible, to keep unimpaired? That there may be exceptions—honorable exceptions—to such an influence I do not mean to doubt. There may also be individuals who, from the dread of being supposed to be swayed by such motives, might adopt the opposite course, which would also be liable to objection. But, taking mankind as we find them, we could not, without willfully closing our eyes and discarding all the results of our observation and experience, come to the conclusion that such a position would not have a tendency, and, in some cases at least, a strong tendency, to produce the result which I have stated, viz., to fetter the free agency of the party in the performance of the important duties incident to his position as a member of the peerage; and it follows, I think, that a proviso or condition which has a tendency to produce such results must be at variance with the public good and general welfare. It is admitted that any contract or engagement having a tendency, however slight, to affect the administration of justice, is illegal and void. The character of the Judge, however upright and pure, does not vary the case. No less strong must be the principle where applied to the important duties of legislation and to those judicial duties of the peerage upon which so many and vast interests depend. In the decision already adverted to, as to the insurance of the wages of a seaman, the only principle upon which it proceeded was that such a practice, if permitted, would tend to relax his exertions for the safety of the ship, and thus affect the proper performance of his duty, in the faithful and active discharge of which the public interest is concerned; and so in other instances which have been mentioned, and to which it is not necessary more particularly to refer. Each case must, as I have already mentioned, be decided upon its own circumstances, as applied to the established rule of law regarding the public interest and welfare; or, to use the words already quoted of Lord Hardwicke, 'upon political arguments in the fullest sense of the word, as they concern the government of a nation.' It is true, and can not be disguised, that other motives, such as love of power, eagerness for office, &c., may, and undoubtedly do, more or less influence the conduct of men in the performance of these various and important duties. But if cases exist which are beyond the reach of the law, they afford no reason why, when a further influence is attempted to be created by an unusual disposition of property, and courts of justice are called upon to give effect to such disposition, they should not refuse to give it their sanction. The question then, is whether a proviso, such as we are considering, would have, if acted upon, a tendency to influence improperly the performance of those duties to which I have referred. I think it would have such an influence, and I consider it, therefore, to be against the public good, and, consequently, illegal and void."

Lord Brougham, Lord Truro, and Lord St. Leonards concurred, and the decree was reversed,—Lord Cranworth retaining his former opinion. Not being able to attend during the argument, I took no part in the decision, but I can not help thinking that those who pronounced it were legislating rather than administering the existing law. In this country the power of disposing of property by will is carried to a useless and mischievous length, and such a fantastical shifting of property on contingencies from one family to another, as the Earl of Bridgewater proposed, ought not to be permitted; but I can see no illegality in the condition, and it would be vesting a very dangerous power in Courts of Justice if they were allowed to adjudge illegal and void all contracts and all dispositions of property by will which, as they fancy, are inexperienced and ought to be forbidden.[1]

[1] Perhaps I can not consider the question impartially, having given the same opinion when at the bar in the lifetime of Lord Alford; but in this opinion Pemberton Leigh, now Lord Kingsdown, and several very eminent lawyers then consulted, unanimously joined.

CHAPTER CCXXII.

IN the Session of 1854 Lyndhurst detached himself from the Derbyite party, who declined to express any opinion upon the policy of our protracted negotiation with Russia, till the result could be more distinctly known, and he resolutely urged the Aberdeen Government to act with more vigor and decision. Speaking of the papers which had been laid before the House relating to this subject, he said:—"They will be found to afford a lively picture of the shuffling, evasive, and (if I might apply such terms to persons in such exalted stations, I would say) *truckling*, and *mendacious* diplomacy of the Court of St. Petersburgh."

Ministers having declared that a change of territorial boundary should be no object of the war, he admonished them that the *status quo* would not content the nation. He said:—"It has become absolutely necessary that a change should take place at the mouth of the Danube—a cession of territory there is required for securing that most important, and I may add necessary object, on which so much reliance is placed by Austria and Germany, namely, the free and uninterrupted navigation of this great river."[1] To this warning Europe may be indebted for the important cession of territory on the left bank of the Danube, which was insisted upon and obtained by the Peace of Paris in 1856.

In the course of this session I had a little specimen of the incurable lubricity of my octogenarian friend, and his readiness to make any sacrifice of consistency for the purpose of gaining his end,—whatever that end may be. He cared no longer about place or preferment, but he was now as eager to gain applause for oratory, as he had once been to secure the Great Seal. On account of a very foolish address, carried over by the Lord Mayor and merchants of London to Louis Napoleon, after the *coup d'état* which made him Emperor, and a mischievous, as well as ludicrous deputation of Quakers, who, under pretense of being peacemongers, went to pay homage to the Emperor Nicholas at St. Petersburgh, and to persuade him that he might do what he liked with Turkey, without any danger

[1] 136 Hansard, 311

of English interference, I laid a Bill on the table of the House of Lords, to prohibit the subjects of this country from having any intercourse with foreign governments on public affairs, unless with the sanction of the Crown, I had as a *precedent* an Act of the American Congress, and for the *principle* I had the high authority of Mr. Burke, in denouncing as treasonable the mission by Mr. Fox of Mr. Adair to the Empress Catherine, at the time of the Russian armament. Lyndhurst gave me to understand that he would warmly support me, and I make no doubt that he sincerely intended to do so. But a strong opposition to the Bill springing up from Lord Shaftesbury, Lord Roden, and others, who contended that it would prevent them from protecting converts to Protestantism in Roman Catholic countries, "the old man eloquent" could not resist the temptation of gaining popularity by leading the attack.

"Everybody knows," said he, "that my noble and learned friend himself is such an avowed and unflinching advocate for freedom of discussion in religious matters, that there is no danger of his intentions being misinterpreted; otherwise I have no doubt it would be supposed that the author of such a bill entertained some insidious design hostile to the religious liberty of the Roman Catholics. Again, an act of injustice and cruelty has lately been committed by the Tuscan Government on two of its own subjects, found guilty of reading a translation of the Holy Gospels. Deputations from different Protestant States appeared at Florence for the purpose of remonstrating against this oppression; one deputation, headed by a noble Earl, a member of this House, distinguished for his strong Protestant feeling, joined in the pious effort" (Hear, hear). Lyndhurst continued, turning up his eyers to heaven, "Does my noble and learned friend really mean to restrain acts of this sort, prompted by a regard for our Christian brethren, united to us by a common faith, and equally our brethren, although being under a foreign sky? My noble and learned friend coldly proposed that such matters should be left to our diplomatic agents; but the consequence would only be a correspondence extending through many pages of Blue Books, and barren of any beneficial result."[1]

[1] 133 Hansard, 25.

The bill, although read a second time, was ultimately lost, when Lyndhurst once more laughed, as he had been accustomed to do, at what he called the absurdities of Shaftesbury and Roden.

For a great many years Lyndhurst had occupied a hired country-house at Turville, near Henley, in the county of Oxford, but—the lease having expired, and the landlord having refused to renew it, except for a long term of years,—this summer, after the prorogation, he made a tour in France, and he there received very marked attention from the Emperor Louis Napoleon,—the third great foreign ruler with whom he had been very familiarly acquainted—the last of the three being destined to leave behind him a name as distinguished as that of Washington or Louis Philippe—although some parts of his career had given so little promise. Lyndhurst used to contemn the exile living in a garret in London; but now, dazzled by his success, or softened by his civilities, he had learned to speak of him with respect and with kindness.

On his return to London, Lyndhurst summoned me to a conference in George street, and he expressed his impatience to denounce the Aberdeen Government for their unskillful conduct of the war. Ere long a ministerial crisis was brought on by the sudden secession of Lord John Russell, which was followed by the dissolution of Lord Aberdeen's Cabinet, and the promotion of Lord Palmerston to the Premiership.

Lyndhurst took an active part in the parliamentary campaign which followed; but he chiefly distinguished himself by a great speech (which he published) against the crooked policy of Prussia. Going back to the treacherous part played by that state after the battle of Austerlitz, he showed how she abandoned her character of mediator, entered into an alliance offensive and defensive with Napoleon, and accepted as a bribe for so doing the cession of Hanover—the immemorial family inheritance of the King of England, her ally. Said he:—

"I well remember the stream of indignant eloquence poured forth on that occasion by Mr. Fox, so characteristic of his generous and noble spirit. The utter selfishness and vacillation of Prussia at that period, professing one thing and doing another, playing the game of *fast and loose*, corresponds in principle, is in accordance with the conduct which she has pursued throughout the whole of these recent nogotiations. My lords, I have no faith in the Prussian Government, and if my noble friend should be tempted to enter into any engagement with that Power I should be disposed to address him with words of caution—*Hunc tu, Romane, caveto.*"

He concluded with sarcastic observations on Lord John Russell, who, having become President of the Council and Colonial Secretary, was suddenly sent as our negotiator to Vienna·—

"It requires but little of a prophetic spirit to foresee that he is destined at no distant period to occupy a still more elevated and commanding position in her Majesty's councils. These things fill me with wonder, and when I contrast the noble lord's present situation and future brilliant prospects with his modest, retired, and anxious appearance a few weeks since, on the fourth row behind the Treasury bench, I almost insensibly murmur to myself a well-known poetical description,—

> ' Parva metu primo, mox sese attollit in auras,
> Ingrediturque solo, et caput inter nubila condit.'

I rely on the sagacity of the noble lord, on his firmness, his vigor, his decision, and on the strong language which he held not long since in the other House of Parliament as a sure pledge that he will not consent to any terms of peace short of those which shall fully secure the great objects for which the war was undertaken."[1]

However, the prediction was not then destined to be fulfilled, and soon after, the once popular Whig leader was forced to retire from office.

At the conclusion of the session of 1855 Lyndhurst caused a great sensation by proclaiming, as the champion of the Jews, their complete and immediate emancipation, and he certainly exerted himself for the Israelites as sincerely as he could have done had he himself been a descendant of Abraham.

His device (about which at the close of the session he confidentially consulted me) still was to bring in a bill to repeal or alter the Abjuration Oath,—the only obstacle to Jews sitting in Parliament,—to allow the words " on **the true faith of a Christian**" to stand in the bill as passed

[1] 137 Hansard, 871.

by the lords, to have these words struck out in the Commons, and then to try to get a vote in the Lords agreeing to this amendment.

But Lord Derby warned him of a commanding Conservative majority, by which the bill would have been crushed upon a division, and it was withdrawn professedly on account of the lateness of the session.

Upon the prorogation, Lyndhurst again went to France, and he remained in Paris till the beginning of the year 1856, charming all classes there by his reckless conversation and his *bonhomie*.

He returned to London in a few days before Parliament met, and I had various consultations with him on the foolish Government scheme of creating peers for life. He was delighted to be put forward as the leader of the opposition to it, in which I cordially joined. He now showed marvelous energy and talent. His speech on the 7th of February, 1856, on the Committee of Privileges, in support of the resolution, " that Baron Wensleydale, under the grant of a peerage to him for life, had no right to sit in Parliament as a peer," was, I really believe, the most wonderful ever delivered in a deliberative assembly. Sergeant Maynard spoke several times in the House of Commons when as old, but only briefly and dryly, in arguing points of law. Lyndhurst on this occasion, if a man of thirty-five, would have excited unbounded astonishment by his retentive memory, his deep research, his powers of reasoning, and his strokes of sarcasm. Without ever referring to a note, he went over all the instances of peerages for life—from that of Guiscard de l'Angle, in the reign of Richard II., to Lady Yarmouth's in the reign of George II. —showing that not one of them was a precedent for a peer for life, as such, sitting in Parliament; he turned into ridicule Lord Coke's dictum that the grant of a peerage for life would be good, although for a term of years it would be bad, because it would go to executors; he was very droll upon the grants of peerages for life to the royal mistresses, who had never claimed a right to sit in the House or to vote by proxy; he even ventured, with an air of triumph, to rely on Lord Chancellor Shaftesbury, because this profligate statesman had thrown out something against life peerages, as a great legal authority, quoting Dryden's well-known lines,—

> "In Israel's courts ne'er sat an Abethdin
> With more discerning eyes, or hands more clean,
> Unbrib'd, unsought, the wretched to redress;
> Swift of dispatch, and easy of access."

Coming to constitutional considerations, he pointed out with irresistible force the fatal consequences of the attempted innovation, illustrating his argument with the contempt and insignificance into which Louis Philippe's Assembly of Peers for Life fell, followed by the extinction of freedom in France, and he bitterly reproached the Government for their ignorant precipitation in bringing forward such a revolutionizing measure, admitted to be of doubtful legality, without ever consulting their Attorney or Solicitor-General upon it, or even deliberately discussing it in the Cabinet.

After the victory had been achieved by the rejection of Lord Wensleydale, Lyndhurst very properly gave notice of moving for a Select Committee, to consider the means of improving the appellate jurisdiction of the House, which had fallen into sad disrepute.[1] His proposal was that the Master of the Rolls and the Vice-Chancellors should be summoned to advise the House in equity appeals, as the Common Law Judges are summoned in writs of error from the courts of common law. But Lord Derby strangely and unfortunately took the subject out of his hands, delivered a very indiscreet harangue, in which, although sincerely desirous of retaining the appellate jurisdiction in the House, he furnished many plausible topics to those who wished to deprive us of it. To the Committee then appointed I am much afraid will hereafter be justly attributed the permanent discredit of our appellate jurisdiction, which had been held in reverence for so many generations. The bill which emanated from this Committee was concocted between Lord Derby and Lord Granville, to sanction the appointment of a limited number of life peers for assisting in the judicial business of the House. Lyndhurst neither supported nor opposed this bill in its passage through the Lords, but he expressed great pleasure to me when it was rejected by the Commons,—not sparing

---

[1] It was notorious that Cranworth and St. Leonards, who often sat without a third law Lord frequently differed, and sometimes left the decision to depend on the maxim *praesumitur pro negante*. If Brougham happened to be present, he was occupied with various matters which interested him more than the appeal.

what he described as "the presumption of Derby, for rashly meddling with matters which he ought to have left in more competent hands."

During this session Lyndhurst made speeches which attracted considerable notice, on the future government of the Danubian provinces, as arranged by the treaty of Paris, and upon the oppression exercised by Austria and France over the once free states of Italy.

But, the Russian War being over, foreign affairs had lost much of their interest, and Lyndhurst thought that he should gain more distinction by devoting himself to social questions which were now agitating the public. So he proclaimed himself "Champion of the Rights of Women." To this course he was impelled partly by the fascination of the accomplished, witty, and still beautiful Mrs. Norton, who had acquired no small literary fame by her poems, as well as by several pamphlets she had written on the wrongs of her sex.

A bill was pending in the House of Lords which originated from the report of a royal commission, over which I had the honor to preside, appointed to consider the subject of divorce. We had recommended that that the law should remain as it had practically existed for near 200 years,—according to which a husband whose wife had been unfaithful to him, without any fault on his part, could obtain a dissolution of the marriage, but the corresponding right was only given to the wife if the husband had been unfaithful under circumstances of aggravation which rendered it impossible that they should afterwards live together as man and wife. The proposed change was chiefly in the manner of obtaining the dissolution of the marriage,—viz., by the decree of a regularly constituted judicial tribunal, instead of an act of the legislature, passed in each individual case, after an action at law for criminal conversation and a divorce *a mensa et thoro* in an ecclesiastical court. The first session in which the bill framed on this principle was introduced, Lyndhurst did not object to it, but now he denounced it as shamefully inadequate. In the first place, he denied that adultery was the only ground on which marriage ought to be dissolved, and he insisted that cruelty, desertion, conviction upon a charge of felony, and other causes which rendered cohabitation of husband and wife *inexpedient*, should be added. Then he contended that whatever was good cause of divorce for the husband should equally be good cause of divorce for the wife, so that the two sexes should be placed on a footing of perfect equality. He next exposed very forcibly, and very truly, the injustice of the common law of England, which gives absolutely to the husband all the personal property of the wife, so as to enable him, after he has deserted her, to seize the earnings of her honest industry, that he may supply the extravagant wants of his mistress. But not contenting himself with providing the means of enabling the wife to obtain a judicial separation, and thenceforth protecting her property and her person against the husband, he proposed that the personal as well as the real property of the wife should always remain exclusively hers, and that, as far as property is concerned, husband and wife should always be two distinct persons, who may contract together, specially, how their property is to be enjoyed during the coverture, and in what proportion they shall respectively contribute to the maintenance of their household and the rearing of their common offspring. He likewise dwelt very pathetically, and with very sound reason, on the reproach to our jurisprudence caused by the action for criminal conversation, and the monstrous hardship which this throws upon the wife, who, although innocent, can not be heard in defense of her innocence.

On Lyndhurst's motion, this bill was referred to a Select Committee, that he might there have an opportunity of adding clauses to meet these multiplied grievances. The Committee sat several weeks, during which all these subjects were deliberately considered, and were ably treated by the venerable domestic Regenerator. He did not succeed in altering the principle upon which the dissolution of marriage was to rest,—the tremendous danger being pointed out of giving facility of divorce, and the rule of allowing the dissolution of the marriage only where cohabitation is no longer morally possible, being shown to apply very differently to the adultery of the wife and the adultery of the husband.[1]

---

[1] Afterwards, in a subsequent stage of the Bill, a Right Rev Prelate, the Bishop of Salisbury, who holds that Scripture forbids the dissolution of marriage, even for the adultery of the wife, denied that our principle would lead to divorce *a vinculo;* for, said he,—" It is always the duty of the Christian husband to forgive, and he is bound to do so *toties quoties*, and the

Lyndhurst succeeded in making some useful additions to the bill, for which he was rapturously praised by the press, while we, who would not acknowledge the entire equality and homogeneity of the sexes, were scurrilously abused as "cruel tyrants," and sometimes as "ignorant monks." The bill was so long delayed in the Committee, that it did not reach the Lower House in time to be considered there.

In this session Lyndhurst again strenuously advocated the Jew Bill; but he made no converts, and it was again rejected by a large majority. He deeply deplored the blindness of Lord Derby, who, he said, "for the sake of Disraeli, and the good of the Conservative party, should have dismissed his scruples about *unchristianizing the Legislature*, if he had any.

I took leave of him in his house in George street, Hanover Square, where I found him deeply engaged in studying the writings of St. Augustine, with a view to the next Session of Parliament, that he might be able to prove (contrary to the assertion of the Bishop of Oxford) that this distinguished Father of the Latin Church does not consider marriage indissoluble, and does not think that it is adultery to marry a divorced woman, if she was really divorced for adultery. He told me that he was going to spend the autumn at Dieppe, where a month later I heard he was assisting his great friend Baron Alderson to fly paper kites—and amusing himself, by turns, with the writings of the Greek and Latin Fathers on divorce and the amorous novels of Eugene Sue.

During the short Session in 1857 which preceded the abrupt dissolution of Parliament, Lyndhurst and I coalesced in lamenting the course taken by Lord Chancellor Cranworth, who again, without having consulted us, had introduced the two great annual measures, (1) "for the abolition of the ecclesiastical courts, and the establishment of a civil court of probate," and (2) " for regulating the law of divorce." These he introduced in a

---

more frequently and the more grievously the wife sins the more the husband is bound to forgive and cherish her, having taken her *for better for worse.*"

I remember when I first came to London, Kotzebue's play of the "Stranger" was very popular, and was thought to be very demoralizing, on account of the hero having taking back to his bosom his erring wife. But the Bishop of Salisbury would have applauded and pronounced his blessing on the re-union.

shape which needlessly excited opposition to them, as he proposed to make the will of every man who dies the subject of a suit in Chancery, and to give to all married people a power of voluntary divorce *a mensa et thoro*, whenever they have a temporary quarrel, or grow tired of one another. I was extremely sorry to be obliged to show hostility to the Government, as I considered the country safer under Lord Palmerston than it could then be under any other minister; but Lyndhurst, no longer with any view to office himself, and merely from a love of excitement, eagerly wished to bring about a change of government, and he had again allied himself with Lord Derby. Accordingly, when the motion was brought forward about the rupture with China, he delivered a very long and able speech in defense of Mandarin YEH and the Cantonese, and against the ministry at home, for supporting the aggressive proceedings of Sir John Bowring and Admiral Seymour. He distorted the facts considerably, and laid down a good deal of questionable law. I was strongly urged by Lord Granville to answer him; but I refused to interfere, as I was not quite master of all the complicated facts, and my law would certainly have been questioned. I therefore merely paired against the vote of censure, and went home. Next day I had the pleasure of twitting Lyndhurst with the majority of thirty-six against him, notwithstanding the liberties he had used with fact and with law. But he told me triumphantly that the result would be very different in the Commons, where the motion was to be made by Cobden, and was to be supported by all the Radicals, by all the Conservatives, by all the Peelites, and by a pretty sprinkling of the Whigs. I called in George street on Sunday, March 1st, to take leave of him previous to my departure on the Spring Circuit. He was in high glee. The China debate, after two adjournments, was still pending in the Commons, and several hot Tories came in, assuring him of victory, and ascribing the coming change of ministry mainly to his efforts. He told me there would have been no doubt as to the result, if the House had divided on Thursday or Friday, but that on Sunday, Hayter, the Whig whipper-in had been very profuse of bribes and promises, and that a number of shabby fellows were afraid of losing their seats upon a dissolution.

In spite of these bribes, promises, and fears, ministers were beaten, and a dissolution followed. But Lyndhurst was cruelly disappointed by finding that there was a general feeling in the country against his boasted coalition of Radicals, Conservatives, Peelites, and disappointed Whigs, and that the result of the election made Palmerston much stronger than ever. He was in hopes that the promised parliamentary reform might have caused a mutiny in the Liberal camp, but this measure being by universal consent adjourned for a year, the Government was safe for the session, and Lyndhurst only considered how he could gain most *éclat* by the exertion of his oratorical powers. He had become feebler in his body, not being able to walk into the House without assistance from a friend, nor to stand without support from his staff; but his wonderful memory, and all his mental powers, remained in full vigor. Having brought Mrs. Newton to hear and applaud him, he was more enthusiastic and determined in advocating the rights of women. He now produced the fruit of his researches in the writings of St. Augustine and the Fathers, Latin and Greek, and showed that, till Romish tyranny was established, the absolute and perpetual indissolubility of marriage was a doctrine unknown to the Church. Not contented with the just interpretation of the texts in the Gospels which permit divorce for adultery, he still insisted on the right to divorce for desertion, cruelty, and other causes which might render the continued cohabitation of a woman with her husband unhappy for her; and he bitterly inveighed against those who, tyrannizing over the weaker sex, did not give them the same right which men arrogate to themselves of getting rid of an unworthy yoke-fellow. He paid, I believe, a just compliment to wives, in saying that instead of seeking to take advantage of a casual infidelity of their husbands to avail themselves of their right to dissolve the marriage, they would be disposed to condonation: but he could not answer the objection that if the infidelity of the husband were constituted a just cause of divorce, it would be made an instrument of fraud and collusion, and husbands and wives would often wish to change partners if this could be done without any of the parties concerned losing caste, or suffering materially in the estimation of the world. The result of this facility

of divorce in moral Scotland, with which he tauntingly
complimented me, affords no inference as to its result in
England; and we ought rather to look to Prussia, where
in a moderately sized fashionable assembly, a married
lady is almost sure to meet with two or three gentlemen
to whom she has been before married, and where, if she
feels a new change of her affections, she may, without
scandal, make another transference of her conjugal
duties.

Lyndhurst was now in hopes that he was about to earn
the permanent enjoyment of the title of "Liberator of
the Jews," conferred upon him when he passed the bill
permitting Jews to hold all offices in municipal corporations. The bill for permitting them to sit in Parliament
had passed the Commons by an immense majority, being
supported by Lord Derby's own son, by his Colonial
Secretary Sir John Pakington, and by his leader in the
House of Commons, a Jew by birth and warmly attached
to his race. There was a notion that Lord Derby himself
from policy, if not from conviction, would be desirous to
see the final settlement of a question which divided his
adherents, and must greatly embarrass him if he should
again have an opportunity of obtaining the premiership.
But he was inflexibly obstinate. and, with one or two
unimportant exceptions, all the Lords spiritual and temporal who had before voted against the Jews, after hearing an admirable speech from Lyndhurst in favor of toler-
ation, voted against them once more, so that the legislature
was not yet "unchristianized."

. . . .
. . . .

Having observed from several trials before me the
frightful extent to which the circulation of obscene books
and prints was carried, and the insufficiency of the remedy
by indictment against the publishers, I had introduced a
bill giving a power to search for, carry away, and destroy
such abominations, under a warrant to be obtained from a
magistrate. For some unaccountable reason, Lyndhurst
violently opposed this measure, and on the second reading
he delivered a most elaborate, witty, unfair, and, I must
add, profligate speech against the bill, and moved that it
be read a second time that day three months. His

motion was rejected, and on the third reading we had such a rough passage of arms that the *entente cordiale* which had subsisted between us for nearly ten years was for a while suspended, and diplomatic relations were not restored between my noble and learned friend and myself till the beginning of the following year.

He did not appear at the short meeting of Parliament which took place in the end of the year 1857, to indemnify the Government for having authorized an issue of notes by the Bank of England beyond what they were justified in doing under Peel's Act, in relation to the gold bullion in their coffers. Palmerston at this time appeared to be stronger than any English minister since the time of the younger Pitt, and Lyndhurst despaired of further political excitement from ministerial changes.

But before Parliament again met, there were visible symptoms of an approaching convulsion. Palmerston's head appeared to be turned by his elevation. He became careless about the opinion of his colleagues, or of his supporters in the House of Commons, or of the public, and gave great offense to many of his well-wishers. Nevertheless, he would have weathered another session but for the manner in which he met the crisis caused by the attempt to assassinate the Emperor Louis Napoleon. Orsini and the other conspirators had hatched their plot in England, and here had manufactured the hand-grenades by which their object was to be executed. The cry arose in France that the English harbored and encouraged the conspirators; and the French Government, by the speeches of its functionaries, and by a diplomatic despatch, very improperly called upon us immediately to alter our laws with respect to aliens resident in the United Kingdom. The right answer clearly would have been, that aliens resident in the United Kingdom were bound by the same laws as native-born subjects, so as to be liable to punishment if they conspired to disturb the tranquillity of a foreign state in amity with her Majesty, or to assassinate any one, of whatever degree, living abroad; that we were still resolved to afford an asylum to all political exiles while they conducted themselves peaceably among us, and that, being satisfied with our laws, and no others having just cause to complain of them, we must decline the invitation to alter them. Unfortunately, without returning

any written answer, the Government resolved to bring in
a Bill to amend the law respecting conspiracies by foreigners, and to make the punishment of a conspiracy to murder the same in all parts of the United Kingdom. Hearing a rumor of this intention, and highly disapproving of
it, a few days before Parliament was to reassemble I wrote
a note to Lyndhurst, announcing my intention to put a
question to the Government upon it in the House of
Lords unless he would, and strongly urging him to do so.
The same day he called at Stratheden House when I was
not at home, and, along with his card, left a very civil
answer to my note, saying that he entirely agreed with me
respecting the course which our Government ought to
adopt, but that Lord Derby himself meant to mention
the subject the first night that the House sat.

Sir George Grey, the Home Secretary, learning at
Brookes's what I contemplated, called upon me and assured
me that the Government had no intention to ask for
power to send aliens out of the country, and that Lord
Derby had undertaken to support the alteration of the law
which was to be proposed. I took the earliest opportunity
in debate to lay down the law as it actually stands, and to
express my strong opinion that it required no alteration.
Lyndhurst concurred. The Bill, however, passed the
Lords, and if it had not been demanded by the French
Government, it would have been harmless enough. But
it was strongly opposed in the Commons, and, to smooth
its way there, the Attorney-General misrepresented the
existing state of the law, saying that acts offensive to
foreign governments might be done with impunity by
aliens residing in England, although the same acts would
be punishable if done by native-born British subjects.
Next evening Lyndhurst, without any previous concert
with me, asked me in his place if my attention had been
directed to the law alleged to have been laid down "elsewhere" by her Majesty's Attorney-General, and if I approved of it. I then, "in defense of our jurisprudence,
and to quiet the alarm which might be excited among
neighboring nations," denounced the law imputed to Mr.
Attorney as erroneous, and explained how aliens resident
here owe a temporary allegiance to the Crown of England,
and are liable to be prosecuted and punished for any acts
in violation of the law of England done by them in this

country, in the same manner as if they had been born within the sound of Bow bells. Lyndhurst and all the law lords *seriatim* expressed their concurrence. Nevertheless, Mr. Attorney renewed the attack in the Commons, asserting that this scene in the Lords had been got up by concert between the venerable ex-Chancellor and the Lord Chief Justice.

Without giving me any notice of his intention, Lyndhurst soon after made a violent speech against a bill I introduced according to the reeommendation of a select committee, to legalize reports of the proceedings of the two Houses of Parliament, and of discussions at public meetings on subjects in which the public have an interest. He professed a wish that the bill might be read a second time, "in the hope that it might be amended in committee;" but he most unfairly misrepresented the mode in which it would operate if passed as it was originally drawn, and, having concluded his speech in the midst of "cheers and laughter," he immediately left the House, that I might not retaliate upon him in my reply.

However, we cordially co-operated in the emancipation of the Jews, which in a strange manner was this session finally and unexpectedly accomplished. According to his early liberal creed he was rather disposed to be on their side, but a slight hope of advantage to his position or his fame from taking the other side would have brought from him a seemingly earnest representation of the terrible dangers to be produced by "unchristianizing the Legislature." When the bill for reforming the University of Cambridge was lately before Parliament, as High Steward of that corporation still devoted to exclusiveness, he had as zealously combated all concession to the Dissenters as when he first fought under Lord Castlereagh. But he had no private motive for opposing the *Israelitish cause*, and he easily discovered that there would be much more distinction in being the leader in the House of Lords of the advocates for religious liberty, than in playing a subordinate part under Lord Derby, who seemed determined at all hazards to secure to himself the title of "the last of the bigots." I had incurred considerable obloquy with extreme and foolish Liberals by denouncing Lord John Russell's scheme for introducing Jews into the House of Commons by Resolution, but I had always sought to gain this object by constitutional means. Soon after the commencement of the session I had a consultation with Lyndhurst as to the course now to be pursued ; and acknowledging him as my chief, I advised that we should originate nothing in the Lords, but wait till the annual Jew Bill should come up from the Commons, when we should do our best to support it. He showed a great desire to reintroduce his " Oaths Bill," but he agreed to allow the contest to take place as I suggested.

When the Bill, introduced into the Commons by Lord John Russell, reached us, we were in great spirits, being told that the Government intended to support the second reading ; and as three of Lord Derby's cabinet (including his own son) had voted for it, the general expectation was that, yielding to public opinion, and extricating his party from a great embarrassment, he now intended to let it pass.

When the second reading came on, Lyndhurst once more delivered an excellent speech in support of religious liberty—unnecessarily shocking some more temperate friends of the cause by professing his readiness to admit into Parliament Mahometans and Deists, if they were good citizens. But Lord Derby, although he consented to the Bill passing this stage without a division, expressed a firm determination in Committee to strike out the clause which admitted Jews to take the new oath without saying, " on the true faith of a Christian." In the Committee, Lord Chelmsford, the Chancellor, after an uncompromising speech against the Jews, moved to omit the obnoxious clause, and the motion was carried by an immense majority. We thought that the theme would be heard of no more during this Session, unless the *coup d'état* should be again attempted in the Commons of proceeding by Resolution. But when the bill came back from the Commons with their reasons for insisting upon the negatived clause, Lord Lucan gave notice of a bill to authorize either House of Parliament to admit Jews by Resolution, and Lord Derby expressed his willingness to agree to what he called *a compromise* on this principle. Lyndhurst was much hurt by the notion of a cavalry officer carrying off the glory of being " Liberator of the Jews," and on the same evening that Lord Lucan's bill was produced, laid on the table a new bill of his own as a substitute for the Commons' bill

—introducing into it an enabling clause, which would have extended to all who disbelieve the Christian religion. Both bills stood for a second reading the same evening. Lord Derby declaring that he preferred Lord Lucan's bill, Lyndhurst, with a mortified air, withdrew his own, but still made a good fight in exposing the course which Lord Derby was pursuing,—viz., with Lord Lucan's Bill, to send back to the Commons the Oaths Bill—to insist on striking out from it the clause in favor of the Jews, and to assign to them as a reason for this, that it would be impious to admit a Jew to sit in a Christian assembly. At Lyndhurst's instigation I several times pointed out the incongruity and absurdity of this proceeding, which was as much as to say to the Commons, "We know that we should be damned if we agreed to admit a Jew to sit among us, but we give you authority to allow Jews to sit among you, and if you please you may do so, and be damned to you."

In a few days after, Baron Rothschild duly took his seat as one of the representatives for the City of London, and the object for which Lyndhurst had struggled was gained; but he was sadly mortified that the glory of the victory was divided between Lord John Russell and Lord Lucan. I had the satisfaction of telling him that he had been exceedingly ill-used by Lord Derby, and that, leaving the Tory ranks forever, he ought again to be a Liberal *in omnibus*.

He went to the House of Lords on the day of the Prorogation, to hear in what terms Jewish emancipation, the most important event of the Session, would be noticed in the Royal speech. To his great disgust it was not even alluded to; while her Majesty was made to rejoice in the benefits to be derived by her subjects, from the Bill for uniting King's College and Mareschal College in the University of Aberdeen.

Heaven knows whether Lyndhurst and I shall both survive, so as that I may narrate his career in the year 1859; and, if we do, Heaven only knows what party he may then belong to, and what opinions he may then profess. Meanwhile I must conclude this Memoir. The extraordinary man who is the subject of it may live to do and to say things as remarkable as any I have related of him : but lest my own career should be suddenly closed, and I should not be able to make an examination of his character after his death, I add a few comments, as if he belonged entirely to the past.

I do not think that those who have known him thoroughly will say that I have treated him unjustly or harshly. Having passed so many merry hours in his company, I bear him only good-will, and I am ever pleased when, with a safe conscience, I can write anything in his praise. But truth would be violated, and pernicious consequences would follow from his example, if his errors were not pointed out—if it were considered that brilliant qualities may supply the place of sound principles, and that a man utterly disregarding the means by which he seeks advancement, may calculate on enjoying, along with splendid success in public life, the esteem and respect of his contemporaries and of posterity.

I am bound, therefore, sternly to pronounce, that although Lyndhurst had opinions, inclinations, and propensities which were generally right, so that he was not indifferent to human happiness,—and still less could he be justly compared (as he sometimes was) to an evil spirit who delights in mischief,—yet, from his entrance into public life, he has shown himself to be devoid of public principle, and to be actuated too often by a sense of interest. He has been consciously contented with "a wounded name," the only limit to his aberration from rectitude being that he should not lose his social position, trusting to dexterity and good luck to escape the perils he encountered, and occasionally venturing on the very brink of destruction. He justly placed great reliance on his manners, which were most agreeable, and which often saved him; for they were accepted as a substitute for virtue. His chief resource was recklessness in conversation. He used unmeasured freedoms with himself, as well as his colleagues and opponents, and, representing his own character to be worse than it really was, he often induced a belief that all that himself and others said against him must be taken as mere *mystification* and *badinage*. But the painful recollection recurs that he was a professed Jacobin, while he thought there might be a revolution in this country, after the fashion of France; that he suddenly became the tool of an arbitrary government, and zealously assisted in undermining our free in stitutions; that within one short year he ardently opposed, and as ardently supported Catholic emancipation, first that he might mount, and then that he might remain upon, the woolsack; and that he was Protectionist, Free-trader, and Protectionist again, merely as it suited his convenience.

He must have had many uneasy moments, notwithstanding the gay looks which he always assumed; and surely it would have been more for his happiness to have preserved his self-esteem, even if he had never risen higher than a puisne judge or a well-employed barrister. I make no doubt that a more splendid eminence than he ever attained was actually within his reach, if he had always kept in the path of honor and consistency. At one time there was a scheme seriously entertained of making him leader of the Conservatives in the House of Commons, with a view to his succeeding Lord Liverpool as Prime Minister; but, for want of confidence in his character, it was soon abandoned. While he held the Great Seal he might have enjoyed the power and influence of Lord Hardwicke under the Pelhams; but he was distrusted by Sir Robert Peel, and he was obliged to obey the orders he received from his chief, as if he had been a junior Lord of the Admiralty.

His abilities certainly were of the highest order. For the *genus demonstrativum dicendi* he was by far the best performer I have known in my time, yet he had not much fancy, and he never rose to impassioned eloquence. Along with a most vigorous understanding, he was gifted with a wonderful memory, which has remained unimpaired down to the present time.

I never heard of his being engaged in any literary undertaking, except writing some letters in "The Times" newspaper along with Benjamin Disraeli, under the signature "Runnymede." He was fond in his speeches of introducing quotations, but they were supplied by his early reading, and some favorite ones (as Burke's on "American Taxation," touching the happy effects of a conciliatory policy) had often received the meed of Parliamentary approbation.

He might have risen to celebrity as a "diner-out." Without being epigrammatic or positively witty, his talk was always sparkling and always pleasing. He possessed to a high degree the invaluable art of making those with whom he conversed *dearer to themselves*. He never condescended to anything like direct flattery; but he felicitously hit upon the topic which he knew would tickle the *amour propre* of those whom he wished to dulcify. His grand resource was to abuse or to ridicule the absent. He relied, with undoubting faith, upon the implied confidence among gentlemen, that conversational sallies are sacred, and he would, without scruple or apprehension, say things which if repeated must immediately bring about a quarrel if not a duel. He was accustomed, when conversing with political opponents, to abuse and laugh at his own colleagues and associates, and above all to abuse and laugh at the rivals of those whom he was addressing. Yet such was his tact, that I never knew him brought into any scrape by this lingual license.

In his person he was tall, erect, and gracefully proportioned. His features were strongly marked, and his whole countenanced well-chiselled—with some fine lines of thought in it—nevertheless, occasionally with a sinister smile of great cunning, and some malignity, which obtained for him the *sobriquet* of Mephistophiles. The best portrait of him is by Shee, the President of the Royal Academy, among the Judges in Sergeant's Inn Hall.

He used to affect to be a *roué*, and after he was married he would say, what a charming thing it was to visit Paris *en garçon ;* but he has long laid aside such puerilities, and he has affectionately lived with the present Lady Lyndhurst in a state of uninterrupted harmony. To his great mortification he has no son to inherit his title. If the peerage had been transmitted, it would have been poorly endowed; for although now relieved from pecuniary embarrassment, he is only able to live comfortably on his retired allowance as ex-Chancellor, and to make a decent provision for his daughters. But he has always given away money very liberally in charity, and has behaved very kindly to all his relations, both in England and in America.

Postscript by the Editor.

This memoir is carried down to the month of August, 1858. My father might have continued the narrative through nearly three years more before his own life was suddenly closed, but having meanwhile become Lord Chancellor, he lost the scanty leisure that he had previously devoted to biographical labors, and no further entry was made.

Little, however, remained for him to record. In the year 1859 Lord Lyndhurst made but one great speech, that on National Defenses, when he roused himself to all his former energy; but my father would doubtless have also gratefully mentioned how gallantly the ex-Chancellor came to his defense when he was much abused for a judicial appointment which he had recently made.

The following is Lord Lyndhurst's characteristic speech :—

"My Lords, I wish to call your Lordships' attention to a recent appointment to the judicial bench—the appointment of Mr. Blackburn to a puisne judgeship in the Court of Queen's Bench. I have been asked, Who is Mr. Blackburn? And a journal which takes us all to task by turns has asked, somewhat indignantly, 'Who is Mr. Blackburn? who is Mr. Blackburn?' I take leave to answer that he is a very learned person, a very sound lawyer, an admirable arguer of a law case, and from his general acquirements eminently fitted for a seat on the bench. These appointments are exclusively in the hands of the Lord Chancellor; he is solely responsible for them, but of this I am sure that if the distinguished Judge who now presides in the Queen's Bench,—a Judge remarkable for his knowledge of law, and for the admirable manner in which he applies it,—had been consulted, he would have cordially concurred in the judgment of my noble and learned friend on the woolsack. I owe this explanation to the learned Judge, Mr. Justice Blackburn, and I owe it also to my noble and learned friend, though I know he can always take good care of himself. I am one of those who think it of great importance that the public should not entertain any doubt or any jealousy with respect to appointments to the judicial bench. I hope my noble and learned friend will allow me to take this opportunity of congratulating him on his elevation—on his having attained everything that he has ever looked forward to. We may say of him, in the words of the poet—

> 'Thou hast it now, King, Cawdor, Glamis, all
> As the weird women promised.'

Without being a countryman of my noble and learned friend, I may take credit to myself for a species of foresight, having on a former occasion predicted the advancement of my noble and learned friend."

In the following year (1860) his strength seemed rather to increase than to diminish. On the 1st of May he spoke for nearly an hour on the subject of the Naval Reserve, and on the 21st of May, the day on which he completed his 88th year, he poured forth eloquent strains on the danger of repealing the Paper Duty.

The last time he came to Stratheden House was on June 20th, when he joined a dinner-party at which my father had gathered together the greatest lawyers of the day. Lord Lyndhurst was too infirm to walk upstairs; but going straight into the dining-room the rest of the company joined him there, and he delighted them all with his wit and good-humor. One of those who were present on that occasion writes thus of it, more than eight years afterwards:—"It was a very remarkable party, from the distinction and age of many of those present, and the vivacity and interest of the conversation. I remember well that Lord Lyndhurst was unusually lively and agreeable. That which dwells on my memory is his leave-taking. He rose to leave the room before the rest of the party—but all the rest rose too—and there was something like a cheer from the others as he went out. I thought that the old man was fatigued and was retiring early, but it turned out he was going on to a party at Apsley House. The scene and the events of the evening generally made a strong impression on me, even before they received an additional although sad interest by subsequent events. There was something almost affecting in the deference and respect, as to one entitled to the reverence due to age, paid by men like Lord Campbell, Lord Wensleydale, and Lord Cranworth—all of whom were far advanced in life,

I wish I could paint the scene as vividly as it impressed me."[1]

In the Session of 1861, Lord Lyndhurst again appeared in the House of Lords, and on the 7th of May spoke on the law of domicile at considerable length, and with much of his wonted brilliancy and vigor. But this was his last speech. His name does not appear in the debates again.

He lived for two years longer, seeing his friends and retaining his cheerfulness and composure. But his public life was over, and his strength gradually decaying, he breathed his last on the 13th of October, 1863, in the 92nd year of his age.

CHAPTER CCXXIII.

LORD BROUGHAM'S EARLY LIFE.

HAVING lived familiarly with the subject of this Memoir for more than forty years, and having had ample opportunities of observing all his merits and defects, I may be supposed to be peculiarly well qualified to be his biographer.[2] On the other hand, as we have often been in collision, and as keen rivalry has produced private as well as public quarrels betwixt us, I must have misgivings with respect to my impartiality, and the reader may reasonably regard my narrative with suspicion. I am quieted, however, by the consideration that we are now on a friendly footing, and that, from our respective positions, nothing is likely to occur which can again embroil us. I am sure that I entertain no resentment against him for past injuries, and while mindful of kindness occasionally received from him, I trust that I am not in danger of proving too encomiastic, from the dread of being suspected of an inclination to disparage or to censure him.

The chief difficulty to be encountered in this undertaking is to determine the scale upon which the "Life of

---

[1] Letter from the Right Honorable James Moncreiff (then Lord Advocate). Amongst my father's papers I find a memorandum showing that he intended to give an account of this dinner, as well as of Lord Lyndhurst's speech of the 1st of July, 1859, quoted in the preceding pages.

[2] This memoir was begun in April, 1853, when the author had for two years been Lord Chief Justice of England.—*Ed.*

Lord Brougham" is to be composed. Volumes to load many camels might be filled with detailed accounts of all the doings, writings, and speeches, by which he has excited the passing interest of his contemporaries. If these were read posterity might consider him a *myth*, like the Grecian Hercules, to whom the exaggerated exploits of many different individuals are ascribed. But notwithstanding the very large space which, while living, he has occupied in the public eye, a considerate man may doubt whether his permanent fame will be great in proportion. By seeking distinction in almost every department of genius, he has failed to establish a great name in any. He accomplished nothing as a statesman; he can not be said to have extended the bounds of human knowledge by philosophical discovery; his writings, although displaying marvelous fertility, are already falling into neglect; his speeches, which when delivered nearly set the world on fire, when in print cause disappointment and weariness; and he must chiefly be remembered by the professional and party struggles in which he was engaged, and by the juridical improvements which he assisted to introduce. The narrative of his biographer ought to be proportioned to the curiosity respecting him which is likely to be felt in after times. Let me crave indulgence proportioned to the difficulty of the task.

I should much displease Lord Brougham if I did not begin with some account of his descent. He was very desirous of being considered a distinguished statesman, philosopher, orator, fine writer, and lawyer, but much more desirous of being believed to be "Brougham of that ilk,"—the representative of a great family, who derived their name from the name of the landed estate of which they had immemorially been in possession. His weakness upon this point was almost incredible, and I am afraid to repeat what I have heard him gravely state respecting the antiquity and splendor of his race. He asserts that *Broacum*, in the *Itinerary of Antoninus*, is the identical spot which he calls *Brougham*, and where he now lives, that it was the property of his ancestors when this ancient Handbook for Roman travelers was compiled; and that there they have lived in splendor ever since, except when campaigning in Palestine against the Saracens. He has told me that "Jockey of Norfolk," the democratic and proud Duke who flourished in the reign of George III., used to say when he came to the North of England, "You talk of Percys and Greys in this country, but the only true gentleman among you is Mr. Brougham of Brougham. We Howards have sprung up only recently; but the Broughams were at Brougham in the time of Antoninus. They distinguished themselves in the Holy Wars, and in some of the most important events of early English History."

Lord Brougham was likewise in the habit of insisting that he was entitled to the Barony in fee of VAUX or DE VAULX, as heir-general of Ranulph de Vaulx, and William de Vaulx, who were summoned to sit in Parliament in the reign of Henry II. Nay, he has gone so far as to say in my hearing, that this barony formerly gave him great uneasiness, as he was afraid that, at the death of an old lady, who stood before him in the pedigree, it would devolve upon him, and disqualify him for practising at the Bar or sitting in the House of Commons. He alleged that it had come into his family by an ancestor of his having married the heiress of the De Vaulxes of Tremayne and Caterlin. The pedigree of the Chancellor in the popular peerages, of which he must be aware, takes no notice of the De Vaulxes, but represents that his ancestors were seated at Brougham in the time of Edward the Confessor, and that "John Brougham, of Scales Hall, came into possession of the ancient family demesne in the beginning of the last century." Let us come to History from Romance.

There certainly is a parish and manor called *Brougham* or *Burgham*, near Penrith, in the county of Westmorland, and, for anything I know, this may be the Broacum of Antoninus. Here, but at a distance from the Brougham of Lord Brougham, there stood in very ancient times, and still stands in ruins, a magnificent Norman castle, frowning over the River Eamont, with machicolated gateway, donjon, and towers, called Brougham Castle, the undoubted residence of the knightly family of *Brougham* or *de Burgham*. Walter de Burgham flourished here in the reign of Edward the Confessor, and his descendant, Odoard de Burgham, was heavily fined by Henry II. for having surrendered it, with Appleby Castle, to the Scots. In subsequent reigns the De Burghams recovered their reputation by fighting valiantly for the Cross of Christ in the Holy

Land; and one of these gallant crusaders reposed in the parish church of Brougham with his effigy on his tombstone, representing him in full armor, and a greyhound at his feet.

But in the fourteenth century the Lord of the Manor and Castle of Brougham died without male issue, leaving three daughters. Thenceforth Brougham Castle has been entirely dissevered from the name of *Brougham*, as in the division of the property among the co-heiresses it fell to the portion of the eldest, and by marriage came to the *De Cliffords*, Earls of Cumberland. Here Francis, Earl of Cumberland, entertained James I., in the year 1617. Afterwards the castle was inherited by the famous Anne, Countess of Pembroke, who repaired it, and placed the following inscription in capital letters over the principal gate:—

"This Brougham Castle was repaired by the Ladie Anne Clifford, Countesse Dowager of Pembroke, Dorsett, and Montgomery, Baronesse Clifford, Westmorland, and Vescie, Lady of the Honor of Skipton in Craven, and High Sheriffesse by inheritance of the countie of Westmorland in the years 1651 and 1652, after it had layen ruinous ever since August, 1617, when King James lay in it for a time in his journie out of Skotland towards London, until this time.

"Isa. Chap. 58 Verse 12
God's name be praised."

As sheriffess, carrying her white wand, and attended by her javelin men, she here received the Judges of Assize, and conducted them to Appleby Castle, where their successors continued to be lodged and splendidly entertained by the hereditary sheriffs of Westmorland, till the death of the last Earl of Thanet a few years ago, when the office was abolished by Act of Parliament. Brougham Castle is now the property of Sir Richard Tufton, his natural son and devisee.

Another of the co-heiresses of the last "Brougham of Brougham Castle" was married to a collateral relation of the same name, and in their descendants one-third of the property remained till the fifth year of James I., when the last male of the old family of Brougham died without issue. A family of the name of *Bird*, who had inherited a portion of the manor as early as the reign of Henry VI., now acquired this third also. Upon a wooded eminence, several miles from the castle, Mr. Bird built a small, quaint dwelling-house in a castellated style, with little turrets at the corners of it, which was familiarly called "The Bird's Nest."[1]

This is the *Brougham* from which "Henry, Baron Brougham and Vaux, of Brougham in the county of Westmorland," takes his title, and where he has persuaded himself his forefathers have lived in baronical grandeur since the time of Antoninus.

In sober truth his ancestors, who, during the few generations for which they could be traced, really were called Brougham (a name not rare in Westmorland and Cumberland), where *statesmen* or small freeholders, being owners of a farm in Cumberland called "SCALES HALL." This farm they cultivated as respectable yeomen, and, by their industry and fugality, became well-to-do in the world. Aspiring to absolute gentility, the Chancellor's real ancestor, at an heraldic visitation by Sir William Dugdale, Garter King-at-Arms, for the county of Cumberland in 1665, not yet venturing to assume the addition of "Esquire," and calling himself only "Henry Brougham, of Scales Hall, *Gentleman*," presented a claim to be entitled to bear arms—"but it was respited for exhibiting the arms and proofs "—and it does not seem to have been renewed.[2]

John Brougham, the next owner of Scales, called "the Commissioner," great grand-uncle of the Chancellor, having accumulated a considerable sum of money by skilful farming and cattle dealing, and by acting as commissioner, or steward, to several large landed proprietors in the neighborhood, purchased from James Bird Brougham

---

[1] "The hall, when he came to reside there, obtained the name of Birdnest, which he called it partly on account of his name, and partly from the appearance of the house at the time, which was almost hid by trees, the chimneys only being in view; and even to this day many old people in the neighborhood know it by no other name."—Hutchinson's Hist. of Westmorland, vol. i. p. 303. It would seem, however, that there had before been some sort of house there called *Brougham Hall*.

[2] Nicolson and Barn's "History of Westmorland and Cumberland," vol. i. p. 395. The authors of this work, who were very laborious antiquarians, in speaking of the "Scales Broughams," say: "We have met with no authentic account of the pedigree of this family of Brougham." The pedigree presented to Sir William Dugdale did not go higher than the claimant's grandfather, and did not affect to derive him from Walter, or Odoard, or any of the Broughams, or De Burghams, of Brougham Castle. It was likewise entirely silent about the descent from De Vaulxes, which, if known, might have encouraged the claimant to style himself *Esquire*.

Hall, or the "Bird's Nest," which, although a domain of
small extent, had been much improved, and could now
boast of great beauty and amenity. Having no children
of his own he left the Westmorland property to his
nephew, the Chancellor's grandfather, the noted attorney,
steward to the Duke of Norfolk. This "Mr. Brougham,
of Brougham," was a very active, bustling gentleman, and
is said to have taken a conspicuous part in the politics
of the city of London during the disputes between Wilkes
and the House of Commons. He resided chiefly at the
Bird's Nest, taking, however, great pains to drop this appellation and to restore the more aristocratic name of
Brougham Hall. But the rejection of the word Hall was
reserved for his illustrious descendant, and I do not find
that he himself or his son claimed to be chief of the
Broughams of Brougham Castle, or represented Brougham
Hall as Broacum, or the seat of the ancient crusaders.'

These pretensions on the part of Lord Brougham had
the effect of raising doubts as to his right to the house
and land, and certain persons of the name of Bird, who
claimed to be the heirs of the former owners of the
"Bird's Nest," in the year 1846, actually attempted to
seize the mansion *munu forti*. This gave rise to a trial at
the Westmorland Assizes when Sir Thomas Wilde (afterwards Lord Chancellor Truro) attended as counsel for the
ex-Chancellor, and proving a clear title by occupation for
more than sixty years, obtained a verdict. The continuous possession since the time of Antoninus was hinted
at, but the counsel truly said that "to go farther would
be to overload the case with unnecessary proof."

This sketch of the history of "Brougham," a place made
historical by its present possessor, may not be devoid of
interest, but I msut now hasten to relate what further I
have learned of the Chancellor's grandfather, the first of
his ancestors of whom we have any authentic information.
He married Mary, daughter of the Rev. William Freeman, a respectable clergyman, and had by her a numerous

¹ In Hutchinson's "History of Cumberland," vol. i. p. 300, there is a sort
of pedigree of the Broughams, attempting to connect the Scales family with
the ancient De Burghams through a *Peter*, supposed to be a younger son of
Thomas De Burgham, temp. Phil. and Mary. But this is wholly unau-
thenticated; and the author himself says, " the table may more properly be
called an account of this ancient family than a regular descent, the family
papers affording us little light as to the point of succession in the right line."

family, who were well educated and settled respectably in the world.

Henry, the eldest son (as I have been several times told by the Chancellor), was sent to Eton, and there had the Duke of Buccleuch for his fag. As he grew up he displayed much cleverness, but still more eccentricity. Coming while still quite a young man, by his father's death, into the small patrimony of Brougham Hall, he did not embrace any profession or devote himself to farming or rural sports, but spent his time in reading and in roaming about the country. In the summer of 1777 he set out upon a tour in Scotland, meaning to pass only a few weeks there, but *there* he spent the whole remainder of his days, and there he died without having recrossed the border.

While walking round the ramparts of the Castle of Edinburgh he was so much struck with the beauties of this "romantic town" that he resolved to take up his abode there for a time, and he was recommended to the lodging-house of Mrs. Syme, the widow of a clergyman, and the sister of Dr. Robertson, the historian. Although reduced in circumstances she was of very ladylike manners, and Mr. Brougham being much struck by her agreeable conversation, was glad to become an inmate in her establishment. The same evening he found that she had an only child—a most beautiful and accomplished daughter in the fresh bloom of youth. At first sight he was in love, and as soon as propriety would allow he solicited her hand in marriage. The young lady expressed great reluctance to leave her widowed parent, whereupon he offered to give up his pursuits in England and for her sake to fix himself in Edinburgh, where by strict economy they might decently live upon the revenue derived from his small property in Westmorland. Such proofs of devoted attachment overcame all obstacles. The marriage was arranged, and in due time was solemnized by Dr. Robertson, uncle of the bride.[1]

[1] Thus Dr. Robertson was the grand uncle of the children of this marriage, and it is bare justice to our Lord Chancellor to say that he was as proud of his real relationship to the celebrated historian as he pretended to be of his imaginary descent from the crusader. I have frequently heard him allude to it publicly in the House of Lords as well as in private conversation; and he added that through the Robertsons he had in his veins the blood of all the most distinguished Presbyterian reformers. He would not even patiently allow any one to criticise Dr. Robertson's writings, or to say that his kinsman did not speak as well as write English better than native Englishmen.

The young couple having prudently determined to live within their means, took an upper flat or floor in the house No. 19 on the north side of St. Andrew's Square, the south windows looking upon St. Giles's spire and the old town, and those opposite commanding an extensive view across the Firth of Forth into the fertile county of Fife.[1]

Here, on the 19th day of September, 1778, was born their eldest son HENRY, the future LORD CHANCELLOR OF GREAT BRITAIN.

Like many other great men, he tried to make a mystery both with respect to the place and time of his birth. He seems to have wished that the well-known couplet might be applied to him:—

"Smyrna, Chios, Colophon, Salamis, Rhodos, Argos, Athenæ.
Orbis de patriâ certat, Homere, tuâ."

Accordingly, of the printed memoirs of his life now lying before me, one makes him born in London,[2] another in Cumberland, and a third in Westmorland. His latest biographer boasts of superior accuracy, and declares that *he* can not be mistaken, as he proceeds upon the authority

[1] In this account of the marriage of the Chancellor's father and mother, I had closely followed the authentic information I had received from persons intimately connected with the family; but I have since found the following statement, headed "The House in which Lord Chancellor Brougham was born," in Chambers's "Recollections of Edinburgh," and I think it ought to be submitted to the reader: "He was about to be married to a lady in his own neighborhood to whom he was passionately attached, and every preparation had been made for their nuptials, when, to Mr. Brougham's great grief, his mistress died. To beguile himself of his sorrows, he determined on traveling and came to Edinburgh, where wandering about on the Castle Hill to view the city, he happened to inquire of a fellow-idler where he could find respectable and convenient lodgings. He was directed to Mrs. Syme, sister of Principal Robertson, widow of the Rev. Mr. Syme, minister of Alloa, who then kept the largest and most genteel boarding and lodging establishment in town in the second flat of McLellan's land, head of the Cowgate, the front windows of which look straight up the Candlemaker Row. Here Mr. Brougham forthwith proceeded to settle himself, and though he did not at first contemplate a permanent residence in this city, he soon found occasion to make that resolution; for, falling in love with Miss Eleanor Syme, who was a young lady of great merit and beauty, he abandoned his early sorrows, and espousing her, lived all the rest of his life in Edinburgh. He resided for some time after his marriage in Mrs. Syme's house, and thereafter removed to No. 19 St. Andrew's Square, where Henry Brougham, who has since risen by the pure force of genius to a distinction equally honorable to himself and the country which gave him birth, first saw the light."—*Chambers's Recollections of Edinburgh*, vol. i. p. 191.

[2] "Biographie nouvelle des Contemporains," tom. iii., p. 519: "Brougham, [Henri] est né à Londres vers 1779."

of the noble biographee. "The place of his nativity was long ago settled satisfactorily by his Lordship himself, who, during the contest for the representation of Yorkshire in 1830, while addressing the electors at Leeds on July 26th, met the objection urged against him on the score of his having no interest in the county by declaring that he spent one week more in Yorkshire than he did in Westmorland annually, 'although,' continued he, 'I am a Westmorland man by birth and possessions.'"[1]

Accounts sanctioned by him likewise varied as to the time when he first saw the light—the day in the Peerages being the 19th of September, 1779—but if this was accurate he must very rapidly have acquired the full use of his limbs; for in the authentic "Life of Francis Horner," by his brother Leonard, we find this statement:—"His earliest friend was Henry Brougham; before we left St. David Street in May, 1780, they used to run together on the pavement before our door."

But in truth the place and time of his birth as I have given them are as capable of authentication as those of Albert Prince of Wales, the heir apparent to the throne.[2]

I do not hear that any dreams, omens, or extraordinary appearances in the heavens prognosticated his future greatness; but it is quite certain that from earliest infancy he gave indications of being something quite extraordinary. Before he could walk he ran about on all fours with wonderful energy, and he was constantly in motion. He spoke much earlier and more distinctly than children usually do, and he improved his articulation by incessant exercise. He would imprudently climb upon chairs and tables and fall flat to the ground amidst the laughter of his playmates; but he sprung suddenly on his legs and became a successful candidate for applause by some new feat of agility. His nurse, Barbara or *Bawby* Dempster, found great difficulty in hushing him to sleep at night. On one occasion she had prevailed upon him to lie down,

[1] "Law Magazine," vol. lii., August, 1854, p. 2.
[2] Extract from the Register of Births of the City of Edinburgh:—
"30th Sept., 1778. Henry Brougham, Esq., Parish of St. Giles, and Eleanor Syme, his spouse, a son, born the 19th current, named Henry Peter: Witnesses, Mr. Archibald Hope, Royal Bank, and the Reverend Principal Robertson."
I can not say that he ever mentioned in my hearing the time of his birth, but he has told me the number of the house in St. Andrew's Square, Edinburgh, in which he was born.

and although still awake, to shut his eyes while she hummed him a lullaby; but he suddenly started up, saying, "Naw, naw, Bawby, it wunna' *du.*"[1] In his childhood he lisped the broadest Scotch, and indeed he has spoken English with a genuine Caledonian accent and pronunciation all his life.

I have not been able to learn anything with certainty respecting his education till he went to the High School. It is said, and with great probability, that he was taught ro read at home by his mother. She was a most remarkable woman for intellect, for acquirements, for engaging manners, and for devoted attention to her maternal duties. Mr. Brougham, her husband, although irreproachable in his moral conduct, and very affectionate both as a husband and a father, interfered little with the management of the family, and was almost entirely absorbed in his own literary pursuits, which had nothing for their object beyond his own amusement. Henry traced to his mother both his genius and its early cultivation. She thoroughly understood his disposition, and was ever on the watch to encourage his laudable aspirations and to repress his irregularities. In all the vicissitudes of his life she continued to show her discernment and disinterestedness, insomuch that when she first heard of her boy being Lord Chancellor and a Peer, instead of exulting, as most mothers would have done, she exclaimed, "Well, if he is pleased I must not complain; but it would have suited our Henry better to have continued member for the county of York and a leader of the Liberals in the House of Commons."[2]

[1] This vowel must be pronounced like the French *u,*—very difficult to English, but very natural to Scotch organs.

[2] Since writing the above, I have received from Lord Murray, the Scottish Judge, who was much attached to Mrs. Brougham, the following beautiful little sketch of her and of her son Henry:—"The memory of Mrs. Brougham is dear to all who were well acquainted with her. She was kind, considerate, calm, and intelligent; and ready without a shadow of pretension to assist every person who stood in need of her unobtrusive aid. She was fully able to appreciate the great talent of her eldest son, and much devoted to him, but. I doubt whether any person, however intimately acquainted with her, could have observed any partial measure of affection bestowed upon one of her children more than the other. Their welfare was her constant object, but so imperceptibly and steadily pursued, as not to attract the notice of any but intimate friends. Henry Brougham was a most affectionate son, though he was in no way disposed to display that or any other of his tender feelings. He thought that she would be much amused with seeing Paris, and he took her there at a time when I happened to be there. She became unwell, and

Lord Brougham never spoke irreverently of his father, but evidently did not consider himself under any peculiar obligations to him. The following sketch of the old gentleman is by my late friend Sir Thomas Dick Lauder, who was very intimate with the whole family :—

"I have the old gentleman's figure perfectly before me at this moment when taking his walk in George Street, confining his turns entirely to the short space between his own door and the bend of Hanover Street. He wore his hair powdered and tied, a stock, and ruffled shirt like the driven snow, a peagreen coat cut away in front and confined by a single button over an ample white waistcoat, nankeen short breeches, large silver or gold buckles in his shoes, and a tall gold-headed cane in his hand, which he grasped at some distance from the head, and the point of which he put to the ground with a mathematical exactness as regarded his steps."

Lord Brougham's education was essentially and exclusively Scotch, and his brilliant career reflects great credit upon our system, which certainly does, with all its deficiencies, well answer the grand end of education by cultivating and invigorating the intellectual faculties. When he entered the High School, Adam, to whom so many owe a taste for classical literature, was head-master; but he began with an under-master, named Fraser, who, though a very zealous teacher, was not supposed to be much of a scholar. As his pupil, young Henry Brougham made wonderful proficiency in spite of occasionally taking delight in teazing him and playing tricks upon him. The Scotch Judge, Lord Cockburn, who was at the High School at the same time, has related to me the following anecdote:—"An exercise being given out—to translate a paper of the 'Spectator' into Latin—Brougham set to work upon it, with a view to mystify Fraser, and introduced several expressions for which he had classical authority, but which had the aspect of bald and barbarous Latinity. At first he had to repent of the joke, for Fraser called him up, and actually punished him with the '*taws*,'

nothing could exceed his attention to her. I recollect ransacking all Paris with him to get calf's-foot jelly, which invalids in Scotland and most parts of England are accustomed to have; but strange to say it was not to be found or even known in that city of cooks, and we got M. Beauvilliers, a great restaurateur, and also, as he said, ' un peu médecin,' to make a jelly of ' pied de poulet,' which was the nearest approach we could get."

or ferula, partly for his alleged bad Latin, and partly for his impertinence in maintaining that it was good. Next morning, however, Henry Brougham entered the school with a load of books upon his back, and out of these he demonstrated that all his alleged Anglicisms or solecisms had been used by Roman writers of the Augustan age. Fraser had the magnanimity to listen to him, and to compliment him on his industry and taste; and from that time the flogged boy was hailed as the king of the school."[1]

An insatiable thirst after knowledge, a singular aptitude for acquiring it, unbounded self-confidence, and an utter contempt for the ordinary rules of life, appear to have characterized him from early boyhood. While at the High School he not only diligently attended to the tasks set him, but voluntarily made considerable proficency in modern languages and in mathematics. Mr. Richardson, a valued friend of mine and a far-away cousin of Brougham, writes to me:—

"The first time I was introduced to him he was about twelve years old, and was on one of the bridges at Edinburgh, with a huge quarto under his arm, which proved to be a volume of the work of La Place, in the original. I wondered what sort of a lad this must be who not only studied mathematics for pleasure, but through the medium of a foreign tongue."

It would appear that at the same time he partook of theatrical amusements, and that he acquired some reputation as a critic in the dramatic art. The following anecdote is in the words of Professor Pillans, a distinguished classical scholar, who was born the same year with Brougham, was in the same class with him at the High School, was for some years head-master of that school, and now worth-

[1] I believe these are substantially the words of Lord Cockburn as spoken to me. Since I wrote them his "Memorials of his Time" have been published, from which I copy the following extract :—" Brougham made his first public explosion while at Fraser's class. He dared to differ from Fraser, a hot but good-natured old fellow, on some small bit of Latinity. The master, like other men in power, maintained his own infallibility, punished the rebel, and flattered himself that the affair was over. But Brougham reappeared next day, loaded with books, returned to the charge before the whole class, and compelled honest Luke to acknowledge that he had been wrong. This made Brougham famous throughout the whole school." In a critique on Lord Cockburn's book in the "Law Review," evidently from the pen of Lord Brougham, he throws discredit on this anecdote without expressly contradicting it.

ily fills the Humanity Chair in the University at Edinburgh, having been a public teacher above forty-six years. By way of explanation I must state—what Professor Pillans reminded me of, and what I myself perfectly well recollect,—that in the end of the last and the beginning of the present century, whenever there was a dinner-party, after the ladies had withdrawn, the gentlemen continued giving toasts at every round of the bottle, till at last the toast of "Good-afternoon" was given, upon which the party broke up and left the room:—" While we were under Fraser together a new play was to be brought out at the Edinburgh Theater, written by Robert Herron, a very foolish fellow. It was called, I think, *The Jolly Toper*. I went by myself to the shilling gallery, where I met very good company. I hope you know that we modern Athenians consider that we have a very delicate taste in the drama, but are very tolerant to a new piece till we can fully judge of its merits, and then we are very decisive. This piece was exceedingly absurd and dreadfully dull, though intended to be witty. The first four acts were heard out, though with a few groans and hisses. When the curtain drew up for the fifth act, the stage was occupied by a large party at table, with bottles and glasses before them. The gentleman in the chair then flourishing his glass, said, '*All charged! Give us a toast!*' when a tall stripling in the pit stood up and exclaimed, 'I humbly propose GOOD-AFTERNOON.' He then made for the door, waving his hat for the rest of the audience to follow him; and the cry of *Good-Afternoon* being repeated by boxes, pit, and galleries, there was a general dispersion, and the piece was damned. This stripling was Henry Brougham, the future Lord Chancellor."[1]

In the end of the year 1789 Brougham was promoted to the class of Dr. Adam, the Rector; but he had barely impressed this enthusiastic teacher with a notion of his extraordinary powers, when the poor boy was seized with an illness which kept him at home near a twelvemonth. His love of reading did not forsake him, and, stretched on a couch, he still constantly had a book in his hand. When he returned to school in October, 1790, the Rector said to Lord Murray[2] (who told me), "That boy, although he has

---

[1] Told to me at Hartrigge, 12th October, 1855.
[2] Francis Horner and Lord Murray entered the High School in 1787, a year later than Brougham.

been absent so long, will beat you all." Ere long he was *Dux*, and he so continued till August, 1791, when he left the school with the dangerous reputation of a "Prodigy." This might have been his ruin, but he was endowed with unexampled and inexhaustible energy to carry him with distinction through every stage of his long career.

In 1792 he became an *alumnus* of the University of Edinburgh, then in its glorious zenith. Here (every one knows) the mode of teaching is by lectures from professors who permanently devote themselves to one branch of literature or science, as in the foreign universities, instead of the students being, as in England, under the tuition of a single individual, who only plies his task till he gets a living in the Church, and who is supposed to instruct his pupils *de omni scibili*.[1]

During a curriculum of four years, Brougham attended almost all the classes, including that of Church History,[2] and acquired a store of information, which, if not always profound and exact, was prodigiously extensive, and over which, with the assistance of a powerful memory, he ever had a ready command; insomuch that if shut up in a tower without books, at the end of a year he would have produced (barring a few ludicrous blunders) a very tolerable "Encyclopædia."

When only eighteen he wrote and sent to the Royal Society of London a paper entitled "Experiments and Observations on the Inflection, Reflection, and Colors of Light;" which was read before that learned body and published by them among their "Transactions."[3]

Thus he commences with characteristic boldness and confidence:—

"It has always appeared wonderful to me, since Nature seems to delight in those close analogies which enable her to preserve simplicity and even uniformity in variety, that

---

[1] I had forgotten the English bisection of knowledge, and that there are two tutors, one said to be for *mathematics*, and one for *classics*. It is, indeed, marvelous that such a system should turn out men so accomplished, although it must still be confessed that a *senior wrangler* and *double-first class man* may be ignorant of much which a well-educated person ought to know.

[2] "1792. Brougham. Litt. Hum. 2. Litt. Gr. 2. Math.
1793. Brougham. Litt. Gr. 2. Log. Phys. Math. 2.
1794. Brougham. Rhet. Eth.
1795. Brougham. Jur. Civ. Inst."
Extracted from Matriculation Book of University of Edinburgh.

[3] Vol. lxxxvi., pp. 227–277. Read January 28th, 1796.

there should be no dispositions in the parts of light, with respect to inflection and reflection, analogous or similar to their different refrangibility. In order to ascertain the existence of such properties, I began a course of experiments and observations, a short account of which forms the substance of this paper."

He then takes great credit to himself for the care and patience with which he had made and repeated his experiments, guarding against any preconceived theory, the danger of which he illustrated by the saying of a Brahmin, that it will make a man believe "a piece of sandal-wood to be a flame of fire."

The following year he presented another paper to the Royal Society of London, containing "Further Experiments and Observations on the Applications and Properties of Light."[1]

The young philosopher does not seem then to have caused much sensation in this island, but he was criticised by Professor Prevost of Geneva, in a paper read before the Royal Society the following year.[2] This antagonist, although courteous in phrase, was very severe upon him, complaining particularly of the indistinctness of his propositions; "il semble qu'il ne parle pas d'une manière précise—"

But Brougham himself, at this time, seems sincerely to have believed that he was another Newton. He spoke respectfully of him who

"Untwisted all the shining robe of day,"

but he does not conceal the conviction that the prism in his own hand was about to disclose greater wonders than had hitherto been told to mankind. And having accomplished so much in Optics, he proceeded in due course to "the higher parts of geometry," anticipating the discovery of a new *calculus* which would supersede *Fluxions*. In 1798 he presented to the Royal Society of London a paper "On Porisms," which he thus modestly eulogises :—[3]

"As a collection of curious general truths of a nature, so far as I know, hitherto quite unknown, I am persuaded this paper, with all its defects, may not be unacceptable

---

[1] "Transactions," vol. lxxxvii., pp. 352–382. Read June 15th, 1797.
[2] "Transactions," vol. lxxxviii., p. 311.   [3] Ib. pp. 378–396.

to those who feel pleasure in contemplating the varied and beautiful relations between abstract quantities, the wonderful and extensive analogies which every step of our progress in the higher parts of geometry opens to our view."

Unfortunately, never having myself advanced in geometry much beyond the first six books of Euclid, and having a very imperfect notion of a *porism*, even after reading that, "it is a proposition affirming the possibility of finding such conditions as will render a certain problem indeterminate, or capable of innumerable solutions," I can not presume to offer any opinion upon Brougham's *poristic* propositions on the *conic hyperbola*. I have heard it flippantly observed by persons who pretended to be competent judges of the propositions in this and his other Papers presented to the Royal Society, that "such as are true are not new, and such as are new are not true." Nevertheless, from my intimate knowledge of him, I should say that he has a very good head for mathematics, and that if he had devoted himself to abstract science he might have been a discoverer, although his *perfervidum ingenium* carried him off to other pursuits before he had fairly entered into rivalry with the great philosopher whose fame he hoped to eclipse. He deserves no small praise for having shown such high aspirations at such an early age; and it is creditable to the land of his birth and education that he was qualified to engage the attention of the first scientific body in Europe by such speculations at an age when in England the sixth-form boy wastes all his energies on *longs and shorts*.

These scientific exercitations of Brougham, while at college, were viewed by him rather as extravagances for the purpose of amusing himself and astonishing his contemporaries. He believed his real business to be in Debating Societies, which have long been the grand stimulus to mental effort in the Scottish universities. On the 21st of November, 1797, he was admitted a member of "the Speculative," along with Francis Horner, and they were soon joined by Lord Henry Petty, afterwards Marquis of Lansdowne. This was a school for literary composition, as well as for oratory; the first proceeding of the evening being the reading of an essay. The following subjects are said to have been written upon very ably by Brougham:—

"The Effect on Scotland of the Union with England;" "The Balance of Power;" "Indirect Influence of the People;" "Influence of National Opinion on External Relations."

But it was in the oral discussions on some grave question of morals, history or political economy, that he chiefly distinguished himself; and here he gave full earnest of the pugnacious powers which he afterwards displayed in both Houses of Parliament. He was then considered the readiest and most energetic speaker that had appeared among the Edinburgh students, and it was truly prophesied that he would maintain his reputation for readiness and energy when removed to a much wider sphere.

Meanwhile he was almost equally distinguished for his irregularities, which, however, were all of a venial description, and were to be accounted for by his early passion for *universality*.

"Brougham's companions consisted of two sorts, viz., intellectual men, such as Jeffrey, Cockburn and Murray,—and fellows of dissipation, fun and frolic, such as Sandie Finlay, Jack Gordon, and Frank Drummond. Perhaps these two sorts of associates might have occasionally blended themselves together. But after having been found discussing literary and philosophical questions with the first set, he was sure soon after to be found rollicking in taverns, ringing bells in the streets, twisting off bell-pulls and knockers, or smashing lamps, with the second."[1]

On one occasion, when there seems to have been a coalition of the two sets—for Jeffrey, Cockburn, Moncrieff, afterwards Lord Moncrieff, and Cunninghame, afterwards Lord Cunninghame, were present—Brougham, after having himself twisted off divers knockers and smashed divers lamps, suddenly disappeared; and the result showed that, for the sake of having a wicked laugh against his companions, he had gone and given information against them to the police, that they might be shut up all night in the *tolbooth* and carried next morning before the Lord Provost. However, they took to their heels on the police appearing, and they all escaped except one, who likewise got off by a bribe of five shillings to his captor.[2]

While at college, Brougham never went to Edinburgh

---

[1] Letter to me from Sir Thomas Dick Lauder, Bart.
[2] This anecdote I had from Lord Cunninghame.

balls or assemblies, although they were much frequented by other students; but he was a member of several convivial clubs, and took the lead in them whenever he appeared. One autumn, by way of seeing a little of what was in Scotland considered "fashionable life," he went to the meeting of the Caledonian Hunt, which was held at Dumfries. According to the prevailing custom, all orders and degrees dined at a *table d'hote*, and after dinner all sorts of bets were laid. Brougham offered a wager against the whole company that none of them would write down in a sealed packet the manner in which he meant to travel to the races which were to take place a few miles from Dumfries the next day. As many as chose to accept his challenge wrote down their conjectures, which were sealed up along with his actual purpose. When the packets were opened, it was found that he would go in a sedan-chair, which none of them had thought of. Accordingly, he made his progress to the races carried in that way, and accompanied by an immense crowd. After dinner he renewed the bet against all who chose to take it, and when the packets were opened he was equally successful. He had written down that he would go in a post-chase and pair, all the persons who had accepted the bet having written down the strangest and most absurd modes of conveyance they could devise. In whatever company he was, he betrayed a resolution to make himself prominent and to be talked of, which pleased him nearly at much as unmixed admiration.[1]

At the Scotch universities there is a curriculum of four years for "Humanity and Philosophy," by which we understand general unprofessional academical training, supposed to be adapted for all who are to appear in the world as men of education, whether divines, lawyers, physicians, soldiers, sailors, or country squires,—embracing the learned languages, rhetoric, logic and moral philosophy, mathematics, natural philosophy, astronomy, and political economy. This Brougham finished in the year 1795. He had no opportunity of gaining academical honors. At Edinburgh scholastic disputations were abandoned, and even the granting of degrees, except in medicine, had ceased. He had a prodigious general reputation for talent and acquirements, and perhaps it was rather lucky

[1] Ex relatione Sir Thomas Dick Lauder.

for him that no *tripos* had been established, requiring written examinations; for his knowledge was rather multifarious than exact, and if called upon categorically to give written answers to nice questions and actually to solve difficult problems proposed to him at the instant, I am afraid that Professor Prevost's remark might have been repeated, that he was "wanting in precision;" so that men reckoned dull might have been placed far above him. But if the trial had been to give an impromptu lecture for a given number of days upon any subject that might be proposed, I verily believe that he would have beaten all the "Wranglers" and "Double-firsts" who had taken honors at Cambridge and Oxford for seven years.

He had now to choose a profession. He was heir-apparent to Brougham Hall, but this property produced annually only a few hundred pounds—an income barely sufficient decently to support the family, the numbers being increased by the arrival of several brothers and sisters. He did not hesitate long. The French War was raging; but he never had much inclination for fighting unless with words, wherein he was the most combative of men. If the endowments of the Church of Scotland had not been so poor, he might have devoted himself to pulpit eloquence; and in that case I doubt not he would have acquired fame as a preacher not inferior to that of Knox, Melville, and Chalmers. He had most admirable qualities, physical and mental, for this exercitation. The danger would have been that he might have tired his congregation by dwelling too long on the same topic, whether severe or pathetic, and that he might unconsciously have preached rank heresy from not having accurately studied the Confession of Faith. Without really meaning "to wag his head in the pulpit," as he had a taste for genuine eloquence wherever displayed, he used to follow the popular Presbyterian preachers, particularly Sir Henry Moncrieff and Mr. Greenfield; and many years afterwards he, with wonderful success, occasionally modelled his own tones and gestures after theirs.[1]

---

[1] This he has himself told me, and I might have observed :—*e. g.*, his attitude in his peroration in the Queen's case, with both arms equally uplifted above his head, was exactly that of a Scotch Presbyterian minister in blessing the congregation.

He had a great relish for medical books; he would occasionally attend Dr. Monroe's lectures on anatomy, and he would even be present when some remarkable surgical operation was to take place in the infirmary; but to spend his life in feeling pulses and writing prescriptions was wholly at variance with all his notions of dignity and enjoyment.

Law alone remained; and although he was alarmed by what he heard of its dry technicalities, he felt that he had resolution to master them. He was delighted by scenes in the Parliament House, which appeared in vision before him, and in which he himself was to play the principal part. He thought he might yet be Lord President of the Court of Session, and it is said that even at this early period the elevation of Wedderburn to the woolsack had given him a glimpse of the future glory which awaited him in a wider sphere. He expressed a strong desire to be an advocate, and his father and mother concurred in this choice.

According to ancient usage, he ought to have been sent to prosecute his legal studies at the University of Leyden; but since the time of Boswell, the celebrated biographer, the tuition of foreign jurists had been considered unnecessary to qualify for the Scottish bar, and after the *curriculum* through which he had gone, nothing more was demanded than attendance for two years upon the lectures of the Professor of Civil Law in the University of Edinburgh, to be followed up by examinations and a juridical thesis as tests of proficiency. In truth, great laxity in the required preparations for the *forum* had been introduced both in Scotland and in England,—candidates being left almost entirely to the freedom of their own will whether or not they were initiated even in the rudiments of their profession, and being allowed to assume the robe on going through certain ceremonies, for which the most idle might be competent.

Brougham was ever earnest in what he undertook, and for a time devoting himself to the Pandects and to Craig, he gained a considerable insight into both Roman and Feudal jurisprudence. By this discipline he so far *legalised* his mind, that ever after, *pro re natâ*, he could understand, get up, and plausibly discuss any question of law which came in his way, however abstruse and however strange to him. But for want of continued and steady application he never approached the reputation of a " sound lawyer," and he used rashly to blurt out *dicta* which caused a general stare, and which would have ruined any other Advocate or Judge.

During the period when he was attending the law classes he availed himself (probably with more relish) of the lectures of some of the other professors, who then rendered Edinburgh so illustrious—particularly of Dr. Black, Professor of Chemistry, the discoverer of the true doctrine of *latent heat*, of whose inimitable skill in experimenting his pupil has given us a graphic description in a life of that philosopher.

Continuing to act as leader of the " Speculative," he founded a new Society, which he named the " Academy of Physics," the professed object being " the investigation of Nature, the laws by which her phenomena are regulated, and the history of opinions concerning these laws." He declined the honor of being President, but he moved a special resolution defining the duties and powers of this great functionary: " To keep order, as he pleases, without limiting the freedom of discussion ; to ask all the members present their opinion, and not to allow a few to engross the conversation ; to keep the speakers from wandering from the subject ; to direct attention, *at intervals of silence*, to what he thinks the most interesting points of the question under discussion ; to declare at the end of the meeting on what side he conceives the opinions of the majority to be ; and upon his election to the office to make himself master immediately of the laws, customs, and history of the Academy." The " Speculative " flourishes to this day, but the " Academy of Physics," from which so much was expected, perished prematurely,—the cause of its early dissolution (as was asserted by the wicked wags of Edinburgh) being that the founder engrossed the whole conversation to himself ; that no " interval of silence " was ever known to occur ; that the President, finding his authority set at naught, abruptly left the chair ; and that no one would agree to be his successor. As no Transactions or Annals of the Academy were ever published, and no inquest sat upon the body, I can quote no written authority for this statement, and it may be unfounded or exaggerated ; but from what I myself have seen *elsewhere*, I may not, as a conscientious biographer reject it on the ground that *it can not possibly be true.*

Meanwhile he was admitted into a Society in which silence and secrecy are expected. In the summer of 1799, along with a roistering party of fellow-students, he hired a vessel at Glasgow to visit the Hebrides. From their pranks she acquired the name of the " Mad Brig." At Stornoway, in the Isle of Lewis, Brougham almost frightened to death the master of the hotel where they lodged by entering his bedroom during the night with loaded pistols, shooting a cat and pretending that he was a messenger from the infernal regions.[1] Nevertheless here he became a free and accepted Mason, as appears from the following entry in the Records of the Society:—

> "*Fortrose Lodge, Stornoway,* 20th of August, 1799.
> " Admitted as true and accepted Mason,
> Brother Henry Peter Brougham."

On his return to Edinburgh after this *spree*, he applied himself diligently to his studies, and he flattered himself by thinking that his fame was spreading in foreign lands. He carried on a correspondence with some continental philosophers respecting his experiments on Light; and Horner, when *grinding* for his examination to pass advocate, thus complains in his journal:—
" Brougham came to show me a mathematical communication that had been anonymously sent from London, in which some criticisms were contained upon his last Paper on Porisms."

Before commencing his forensic career he had a great desire to follow the example of Lord Bacon and Lord Mansfield by having the advantage of foreign travel; but the French war then raged, and all the middle and southern states of Europe were closed to him. Under these circumstances he gladly accepted an offer from Mr. Stuart, afterwards Lord Stuart de Rothesay, to accompany him on a hyperborean tour, and crossing over to Hamburg they visited the capitals and the most interesting provinces of Sweden, Norway, and Denmark. But although well acquainted with French and Italian, he never made any progress in Gothic or Scandinavian dialects.

On his return he did again dally a little with *Porisms;*

---

[1] This was made the subject of a caricature published at Edinburgh, of which a copy lies before me.

but he found that the time was now come when he must descend from "high geometry," and stoop to a little *grinding*, however small the chance might be of his being "plucked." What distinction he gained by his examinations I know not,—all the information I have been able to obtain on the subject being comprised in the following extracts from the 'Minutes of the Faculty of Advocates':—

"Edinburgh, 23rd May, 1800.

"Mr. Henry Peter[1] Brougham, eldest son of Henry Brougham, Esq., of Brougham Hall, was examined on the Scots law, and found sufficiently qualified. The Examinators recommended him to the Dean to assign him a subject for his public examination."

"Edinburgh, 7th June, 1800.

"Mr. Henry Peter Brougham, eldest son of Henry Brougham, Esq., of Brougham Hall, was publicly examined on *Tit. V., Lib.* 3. *Digest. De Negotiis Gestis*, and found sufficiently qualified, &c.

(Signed) "R. DUNDAS, D. F."

The call of an advocate to the Scotch bar is nominally the act of the Lord President and other Senators of the College of Justice sitting in open court; but it rests practically with the Dean and Faculty of Advocates, according to rules and regulations which they lay down from time to time. Formerly the candidate wrote a Latin Thesis on some title of the Civil Law, and engaged in a Latin disputation with all who came forward to combat any of his propositions. These tests of proficiency, however, had now fallen into neglect, and at the sitting of the Court on the 10th of June, 1800, Henry Peter Brougham appeared at the bar in the Parliament House, with a cocked hat under his arm, and, when the Judges took their seats, he began an oration according to a well-settled cantilena— "Domine Præses, ingens hujus Curiæ decus et ornamentum, et cæteri Senatores doctissimi, illustrissimi, honoratissimi,"—Here he was stopped by a nod and a smile from the President, giving him to understand that his prayer to be admitted was granted. He then put on his cocked hat, took it off again, bowed to the Bench, retired, and was an advocate.

[1] He appears to have been baptised, and still to have called himself, Henry *Peter*, but the Peter he afterwards dropped when he settled in England.

I have repeatedly attempted in vain to learn from his
Edinburgh contemporaries with whom I was intimate,
something of his first appearance as counsel in a cause :
and the Scotch Law Reports, which I have diligently
searched, do not mention his name. I suspect that at this
time, although his talents and acquirements had gained
him a certain sort of celebrity, he was considered a man
of science rather than a lawyer, and that no writer to the
signet would trust him with a brief.

A common mode for a Scotch advocate to obtain an
opportnuity for oratorical display without pecuniary profit
was to be ordained a Ruling Elder in some Kirk Session,
and to be returned as a lay member of the General Assembly of the Church of Scotland, which meets yearly in
the month of May, when very interesting debates take
place respecting the induction and deposition of ministers
and the putting down of heresy; greater power lawfully
belonging to this tribunal than has ever been claimed by
the English Convocation. Principal Robertson had been
the leader of the governing party in the General Assembly
many years, and it was thought that under his auspices
his grand-nephew would commence public life by a speech
in support of the right of lay patronage as established in
the reign of Queen Anne, or by the prosecution or defense
of some popular preacher, like Adam Blair, against whom
there was a charge of immorality,—a theme justly thought
to be peculiarly adapted to Brougham's powers, as was
afterwards verified by his defense of Queen Caroline.
But from this ready road to distinction he turned away
with aversion—why I know not—for he could then have
had no objection to conform in all things to the Established Presbyterian Church in which he was baptized, and
with which he was in communion; and there would have
been no loss of dignity in taking this course, as he would
have found among his colleagues James Moncrieff, afterwards Lord Moncrieff; the Hon. Henry Erskine, afterwards Dean of Faculty ; and Charles Hope, afterwards
Lord President of the Court of Session, together with
several Scottish Peers. Some said that he had conscientious scruples about becoming (as it were) " a shred of
the linen garment of Aaron," so soon after the notoriety
he had acquired by wringing off brass knockers and by
other such levities, but his versatility and his power of

acting a part were too considerable to allow such misgivings to have place in his own breast.

Whatever might be his motive, it is certain that he said he had a surer way to get forward, which was to go a circuit, and act gratuitously as counsel for the pauper prisoners. According to Scottish procedure in the criminal courts a full defense by counsel was always allowed to all prisoners, whatever might be the nature of the charge against them, and such as were too poor to retain counsel had counsel assigned to them by the Court. Brougham said he would go the Southern Circuit as a Brother of Mercy—"all his pleasure praise"—a young advocate who had officiated in this capacity having been promoted to be one of the Lord Advocate's *Deputes* or (as we say in England) *Devils*, and being now to prosecute the prisoners. The Judge of Assize was a foolish old gentleman, called Lord Eskgrove, of whom ludicrous stories had been told, and upon whom tricks had been played for near half a century. Brougham never much liked to grapple with a strong Judge, but had a natural delight in taking liberties with a feeble one. He seems to have laid down a systematic plan of making game of Lord Eskgrove. On this occasion he traveled from Edinburgh in a one-horse chaise, and as he entered Jedburgh, where the Assizes were to be held for the counties of Roxburgh, Selkirk, Peebles, and Berwick, he found that the Judge's procession attended by the Sheriffs of the four counties, the magnates of Jedburgh, and other functionaries, with halbert men called "the Crailing Guard" was, according to ancient custom, marching across the High Street from the Spread Eagle Inn, where it had been formed, to the Town Hall in the Market Place, where the Court was to be held. The procession was advancing at a very slow pace, all the population of the town having turned out to have a peep at my Lord Judge, who was arrayed in his full pontificals. Brougham approaching at a hard trot, the Crailing Guard presented their halberts and ordered him to stop. He thereupon whipped his horse, put to flight the Crailing Guard, charged the procession, broke the line a little ahead of the Judge, and the mob making way for him, drove on to his inn. There was great apprehensions that the Judge would be upset in the kennel;

but his Lordship escaped with a few splashes of mud, and took his seat on the bench.

An extempore prayer was said by the clergyman of the parish, the sheriffs of counties were called over, and other preliminary forms were gone through, when Brougham entered the court, made a respectful bow to my lord, and took his seat at the bar, as if nothing extraordinary had happened.

Lord Eskgrove was in great perplexity, feeling that he ought to have ordered the assailant to be committed for a *contempt*, but not having the courage to do so, and not knowing what other course to adopt. While his lordship was evidently in a great fuss, Brougham rose and said very composedly: "My Lord, the court is very close—I am afraid your Lordship may suffer from the heat; perhaps your Lordship will be pleased to order a window to be opened." A window was opened, and no further notice was ever taken of the *fracas*.

Brougham was the only advocate present besides those who attended to conduct the prosecutions on behalf of the Crown; thus as a matter of course he was called upon to defend all the prisoners.[1]

The first trial was for sheep stealing, and Brougham objected to the relevancy of the libel, on the ground that it did not specify the sex of the animal stolen, without saying whether tup, ewe, or wether, which he contended was necessary for the purpose of informing the panel exactly of the offense with which he was charged; for to say that the offense was the same, whether tup, ewe, or wether was to say that tup, ewe, and wether were all one—a proposition which could be disproved by Bankton, Sir George Mackenzie, and Hume, and by all naturalists as well as jurists. It might be said truly, he would candidly admit, that every tup was a sheep, but he strenuously denied that every sheep was a tup, and so of ewes and wethers. Would it have been sufficient if the libel had said that a certain *quadruped* or a certain *animal?* No! the living thing alleged to have been stolen must be individualized (as the

[1] I presume the whole number was very small. In the year 1853, having sat as Chief Justice at Liverpool for a portion of the county of Lancaster, I tried 170 prisoners; and a few weeks after I attended this very court at Jedburgh as an *amateur*, when the Lord Justice Clerk held the assizes here. For the four entire counties there were only five prisoners.

best Crown writers call it) by a *condescendence* upon genus, species, and sex. Could you indict a man for stealing an ox, and convict him on evidence that he stole a cow? or for stealing a goose, and show that he stole a gander, although there be a well-known maxim that " what is sauce for the goose is sauce for the gander?"

Lord Eskgrove took a full note of this argument, and was greatly shaken by it, but the Crown counsel brought him back by showing that "sheep" is the word used in the Act of Parliament, and that the libel was drawn in the form which had been constantly used since the Act passed.

In the next case the learned counsel allowed that the libel was sufficient *ex facie* in charging the *pannel* with stealing " a pair of boots," but when it was referred to an assize, *i. e.* was submitted to the jury, he strenuously contended that his client was entitled to be acquitted, "for the articles stolen, when produced, appeared to be *half boots*, and he argued that *half boots* were not *boots* any more than a half guinea is a guinea. So half a loaf is surely not equal to a whole loaf, although it is better than no bread."

There was here a general laugh, and Lord Eskgrove was much annoyed, for the truth suddenly darted into his mind that he was played upon. So he resolved to be firm and dignified, and, without calling upon the opposite counsel for an answer, he at once overruled the objection, saying, with much self-complacency, "I am of opinion that *boot* is a *nomen generale*, comprehending a half boot. The distinction is between a *half boot* and *half a boot*. The moon is always the moon, although sometimes she is the half moon." His lordship was dearer to himself by this display of logical acuteness, and looked round for applause.

The only other trial at this assize, of which any authentic account has reached me, was that of a man indicted for a violent assault upon his wife. Brougham set up as a defense that when the blows were inflicted the husband and wife were both drunk with whisky, which the wife had purchased by pawning her clothes, and had administered between them in equal shares, till they were both much excited, when she provoked him by challenging him to dance a *twasome reel* with her, and taunting him that he could no longer keep on his legs, while she could exhibit all the graces of the "highland fling." The learned counsel *arguendo* admitted that, "generally speaking ebriety is no defense in point of law against a criminal charge," but he took the distinction that "here the wife, the party alleged to be injured, was the *causa causans*—ipsa doli fabricatrix, artifex et particeps, or in the language of the Scottish law *art and part*, so that the maxim applied 'volenti non fit injuria.'" This point was urged by Brougham in a speech nearly an hour long, delivered with much vehemence and seeming sincerity.

Lord Eskgrove at first suspected that this was another attempt to play upon him, but gradually felt misgivings lest there should be something in it, and called upon the Advocate Depute, who conducted the prosecution, for an answer. He was soon emboldened to overrule the defense, when reminded that the "*pannel*" was indicted for a breach of the public peace, that the King—by the Lord Advocate, the public prosecutor—and not the wife, was the true party complaining, and that the circumstances relied upon could not amount to a plea in bar, although they might operate in mitigation of punishment.

Sir Thomas Dick Lauder, from whom I have the memorabilia of this assize at Jedburgh, gives me no further particulars of the trials, but says:—

"Brougham continued to persecute my poor old relative Lord Eskgrove, whom he nearly tormented to death; about this time his conduct was so eccentric that he was supposed to have shown a slight tendency to insanity, and his friends were very uneasy about him."

The worthy baronet then mentions some instances of his eccentricity during the circuit, such as taking to wear spectacles, on the suggestion that he had suddenly become short-sighted; of his riding away from the circuit town upon the horse of a friend, *invito domino*, and of his having thrown some tea over a young lady, for which he was called personally to account; but I forbear to enter into the details of such stories, which rest only on rumor, and which might probably be explained by an exuberance of animal spirits and a love of frolic.

When Brougham returned to Edinburgh from the circuit he fell ill, and was for some weeks confined to the house, suffering from a great depression of spirits, supposed to be brought on by over-excitement: but he soon re-appeared, as cheerful, elastic, vigorous, enterprising and indefatigable as ever.

He was now appointed by the Faculty to the annual office of "Civil Law Examiner" of candidates to be admitted to the degree of advocate. But these examinations seem to have become merely farcical. It was the duty of the Examinator to assign to each candidate a Title in the Digest in which he was to be publicly examined, and that which Brougham uniformly chose was, Dig. Lib. xxv. Tit. 4, "De Ventre Inspiciendo."[1]

Without finally abandoning the profession of the law as a refuge, and feeling confident that he could safely retreat upon it if necessary, he now chiefly devoted himself to literature, and sought renown by writing a book to rival Adam Smith's great treatise on political economy. The Scotch advocates united law and literature with brilliant success;[2] whereas in England a barrister who writes a play, a novel, or a history, renounces all hope of professional advancement.

Brougham took for his subject, "The Colonial Policy of the European Nations," and he worked upon it with great earnestness for several months. The labor of a life might have been expended in doing it justice, but he had not the patience and perseverance which produced the "Wealth of Nations." He wrote *currente calamo*, and although probably no other man could have written so large and so good a book in so short a time, it was destined to a rather obscure career, and but for the fame subsequently acquired by the author, which reflects some interest upon it, long ere now it would have fallen into complete oblivion.

Never at a loss for materials, or stopping long to digest those which he had collected, and not very anxious about

[1] This appears from a newspaper controversy carried on in the year 1828, in consequence of Brougham, while commenting in the House of Commons on a trial at Lancaster, in which the now President Mac Neill was examined as a witness, having reflected on Scotch Advocates as being ignorant of the Civil Law. Professor Brown took up the cause of his countrymen, and severely, retaliated upon their accuser. See "Remarks on the Study of the Civil Law, occasioned by Mr. Brougham's late attack on the Scottish Bar," by James Brown, LL.D., Advocate. Edinburgh, Adam Black, 1828.

[2] Lord Jeffrey and Sir Walter Scott may be cited as examples. The latter continued in the legal profession all his life, and while writing "Marmion" and the "Waverley Novels," held the office of Clerk of Session, and was Sheriff or Judge for the county of Selkirk.

succinctness or perspicuity, his great difficulty in composing his work was, whether he should make it wear a Whig or a Tory aspect. In Scotland party politics now ran very high, and no man wrote a sermon, or a treatise upon algebra, without showing whether he approved or condemned the French Revolution—whether he was a Pittite or a Foxite. Brougham had imbibed highly conservative principles from his uncle, Principal Robertson, but these had been much shaken by some of his companions in the Speculative Society, who were inclined to the extremes of democracy. He himself wavered much, and from time to time took the opposite sides with equal violence. In his first appearance before the public as an author, he resolved to assume the rare character of political neutrality. Nevertheless, I think a slight leaning to the Tory side is disclosed by him. I have heard it stated that at this time he was (as any person might well be) an enthusiastic admirer of the eloquence and heroic spirit of Pitt the younger, and that he would have been extremely happy, on proper encouragement, to have enlisted under the banner of the "Heaven-born Minister." There certainly is nothing in the book which could have marred such prospects, if he entertained them, while it expressed no sentiment which might not be adopted by a good conservative Liberal.

Many of the Colonial questions which he discusses have ceased to retain any interest, and the principle of *self-government*, upon which almost all our relations with the Colonies now turn, had not then been dreamed of. The author declares himself a decided enemy to the African slave-trade, both for the sake of the slaves and their masters; but in no part of this work do we discover the burning indignation against negro slavery as a *status* which he afterwards evinced, and several passages in it were quoted against him, during the struggle for slave emancipation in the West Indies, as evidence of his opinion of the natural inferiority and subjection of the colored race to the white. Touching on general politics, he not only justifies the war which we were then carrying on against the French Republic and the First Consul, but,—in alluding to the horrors which had taken place in Paris and in the provinces under the name of liberty, to the atheistical professions of the Jacobin leaders, to the aggressive principles acted upon by the revolutionary governments, and to the anarchy and oppression which revolution had produced in France, and which threatened to overturn all Europe,—he concealed not his opinion that the very fact of the existence of so great a political nuisance gave the "vicinage" a right to interfere to have it *abated*.

If he was at this time a little dazzled by the brilliant chivalry of Burke, or if from interested motives he vacillated between rival factions, circumstances soon occurred which decidedly carried him over to the Liberal side, and kept him there above thirty years.

In the end of the year 1801, Sydney Smith, along with Jeffrey, Horner, John Murray, and several other young and enthusiastic Whigs, formed the bold design of reforming the age by a new Review, to be published quarterly, and to contain more lengthy, weighty, witty, and pungent articles than had ever appeared in any periodical publication. The scheme was first concocted in a room on the eighth or ninth story or flat of a house in Buccleuch Place, then the residence of Jeffrey, and instead of the motto ultimately adopted from Publius Syrus, "Judex damnatur cum nocens absolvitur," it was proposed to take the line from Virgil's first "Eclogue," "Tenui musam meditamur avena." "We cultivate the Muse, living on a little *oatmeal*."

The arrangement for this celebrated periodical had been originally made without the privity of Brougham. A proposal that he should be invited to join the association was long resisted by Sydney Smith, from "a strong impression of Brougham's indiscretion and rashness." At last there was a vote in his favor, partly from the hope of advantage from his vigorous co-operation, and partly from dread of his enmity if he should be excluded. He joyfully accepted the offer, and vowed obedience. But he soon caused regrets and misgivings by his waywardness. In a letter dated the 9th of April, 1802, Jeffrey writes to Horner respecting the new Associate:—

"I proposed two or three books that I thought would suit him; he answered with perfect good-humor that he had changed his view of our plan a little, and rather thought now that he should decline to have any connection with it."

Nevertheless he soon again changed his mind, and

Horner, in a letter dated the 1st of September, 1802, respecting the expected appearance of the first number, says:—

"Jeffrey has written three or four excellent papers, and Brougham is now an efficient and zealous member of the party. Brougham has selected from the 'Philosophical Transactions' Herschell's discovery of the sympathy between the spots of the sun and the prices of wheat in Reading market."

On the 10th of October, 1802, the first number of the "Blue and Buff" actually appeared, with three articles from Brougham's pen: Art. 23, on "Wood's Optics"; Art. 24, on "Acerbi's Travels"; and Art. 27, on the "Crisis of the Sugar Colonies."[1]

I need not mention the prodigious success of the publication. Brougham, ascribing this to his own contributions, was so much pleased that he almost overwhelmed the editor with his help, and, like Bottom the Weaver, he wished himself to play all the parts,—criticising, one after another, works on chemistry, surgery, divinity and strategy. Each number contained an article discussing the most exciting political question of the day, zealously taking the Whig side. This Brougham avoided till, in 1803, he had published his "Colonial Policy."[2] After the appearance of this work he frankly cast in his lot with the Liberals, although well aware how dreary their prospects then were under the despotism of Henry Dundas. Thenceforth he courted opportunities for political discussion, and was of essential service in enlightening the public mind. In this department he was moderate and constitutional, displaying that dislike of *radicalism* which has always honorably distinguished him.

In criticising books, however, seeing that the *tranchant* or "slashing" style was so much relished, he indulged in it to an excess which not only tortured his victims but alarmed his colleagues. Hence Lord Byron's onslaught—

---

[1] It had been said, on the authority of a pretended letter from Lord Jeffrey to Mr. Chambers, that Brougham did not contribute to the first three numbers; but my information must be correct, as I have it in a letter under the hand of Lord Murrry, one of the founders, which now lies before me.

[2] Jeffrey, in a letter to an American, dated 2nd July, 1803, shows the light in which Brougham was then beheld in Edinburgh: "Mr. Brougham, *a great mathematician*, has published a book on the Colonial Policy of Europe, which all you Americans should read."

his "English Bards and Scotch Reviewers" being produced by Brougham's contemptuous notice of "Hours of Idleness." The poor editor bore the brunt, as when obliged to fight Tom Moore at Chalk Farm :—

> " Health to great Jeffrey ; Heaven preserve his life,
> To flourish on the fertile shores of Fife," &c.

The only blame that could truly be imputed to Jeffrey was that he had granted his *imprimatur* for the censure of Lord Byron's first poetical efforts, and this censure, although very bitter, may well be justified. The noble poet does not illustrate the maxim that "the boy is father of the man ;" for "Childe Harold" has none of the lineaments of the vain, petulant, presumptuous stripling portrayed in "The Hours of Idleness." Though the chief onslaught was on Jeffrey, Brougham was not spared in the satire :—

> " Yet mark one caution, ere thy next Review
> Spread its light wings of saffron and of blue,
> Beware lest blundering Brougham destroy the sale,
> Turn beef to bannocks, cauliflowers to kail."

Lord Byron's wrath is said to have been chiefly inflamed by the grave judicial sentence overruling his plea of *infancy*.

"The law upon this point we hold to be perfectly clear. It is a plea available only to the defendant ; no plaintiff can offer it as a supplementary ground of action. Thus, if any suit could be brought against Lord Byron for the purpose of compelling him to pay into Court a certain quantity of poetry, and judgment were given against him, it is highly probable that an exception would be taken were he to deliver for poetry the contents of this volume. To this he might plead *minority;* but as he now makes a voluntary tender of the article, he has no right to sue on that ground for the price in good current praise, should the goods be unmarketable."

But although Byron had little cause to complain of the critique on the "Hours of Idleness," and he successfully retaliated upon the assailant, there were other instances in which Brougham as a reviewer recklessly pronounced undeserved censure, and fatally crushed rising merit. His most distinguished victim was Professor Young, who had in a very able publication explained the phenomena of light on the theory of *Undulation*, in opposition to that of *material rays*. Among other experiments, he had described one of stopping the rays which passed on one side of a thin card or wire exposed to a sunbeam admitted into a dark chamber, and which was found to obliterate the internal bands formed in its shadow whenever the light passed freely on both sides of it. Brougham, unable to explain away the result, if the experiment were truly made, in a very rash and flippant manner denied the accuracy of the experiment without repeating it :—

"The fact is, we believe, the experiment was inaccurately made; and we have not the least doubt that if carefully repeated, it will be found either that the rays when inflected cross each other and thus form fringes, each portion on the side opposite to the point of its flection, or that in stopping one portion Dr. Young in fact stopped both portions, a thing extremely likely, where the hand had only one-thirtieth of an inch to move in, and quite sufficient to account for all the fringes disappearing at once from the shadow."

The article was hailed as a complete refutation of the Undulatory Theory, and Dr. Young was covered with ridicule. He published a pamphlet in reply, in which, when he came to the experiment gratuitously explained away by awkward manipulation, he says :—

"The Reviewer has here afforded me an opportunity for a triumph as gratifying as any triumph can be where an enemy is so contemptible. Conscious of inability to explain the experiment, too ungenerous to confess that inability, and too idle to repeat the experiment, he is compelled to advance the supposition that it was incorrect, and to insinuate that my hand may easily have erred through a space so narrow as one-thirtieth of an inch. But the truth is, that my hand was not concerned; the screen was placed on a table and moved mechanically forward with the utmost caution. The experiment succeeded in some circumstances when the breadth of the object was doubled and tripled. Let him make the experiment, and then deny the result if he can."

If this pamphlet had been read, it must have vindicated the philosopher, and covered the critic with shame. But such was then the supposed infallibility of the "Edinburgh Review," that there was no appeal from its decision ; and Peacock, in his "Life of Dr. Young," asserts that of the

Reply one copy, and one copy only, was sold.[1] The fact undoubtedly is that for many years Dr. Young was considered a sciolist and a charlatan. At last he was taken up by the French *savans*, and his theory of undulation is now almost universally adopted.

CHAPTER CCXXIV.

LIFE OF LORD BROUGHAM FROM HIS REMOVAL TO ENGLAND TO THE DEATH OF GEORGE III.

IF Brougham had continued to reside in Scotland, and had devoted himself to his profession there, he no doubt would ere long have been in good practice, and he probably would have been in due time Dean of Faculty, Lord Advocate, and Lord President of the Court of Session. He had existed near a quarter of a century before his ambition soared to official distinctions, although it must be borne in mind that he had always high aspirations in literature and science. But the favorable impression which he had made as often as he had enjoyed an opportunity of speaking in public, created real discontent in his mind, and he thought he was fitter to succeed Lord Chancellor Loughborough than Lord President Sir Islay Campbell. Horner was now studying for the English bar, and Brougham could not brook the idea of a schoolfellow, a brother advocate and brother Edinburgh Reviewer, having in prospect such a noble career, while he himself was limited to comparative obscurity. He never had any misgivings as to his own powers to enter into competition with English lawyers; and his confidence in himself was considerably increased by a view he had of their performances when engaged at the bar of the House of Lords as counsel for Lady Essex Kerr, in an appeal from the Court of Sessions. Measuring himself by the standard of English excellence then presented to him, his dimensions were greatly expanded in his own estimate.

Before bidding adieu to Edinburgh he entered himself of Lincoln's Inn, attracted as well by the superior lustre of that Society as by a liberal regulation of the benchers,

[1] Vol. i. p. 182.

whereby members of the Faculty of Advocates in Scotland were placed on the same footing as graduates of the English Universities, in not being required to make any pecuniary deposit, and being entitled to be called to the bar at the end of three years from their admission.[1]

For two years longer he continued to make Edinburgh his usual residence, taking care to be in London five days each term that he might eat dinners in the hall,—the only requisite training for the English bar. At last he transferred his domicile to the southern metropolis, and thenceforth he wished it to be forgotten that he had been born and bred in Scotland, and that to Scotland he owed the education which enabled him to excel so many senior wranglers and double-classmen of Cambridge and Oxford. Although the Scottish accent has continued to stick closely to him, and to betray his origin, he now began to sneer at Scotland and Scotchmen, unable to resist the temptation of raising a laugh by repeating some trite jest at their expense. Yet in his heart he had a warm affection for what must be considered his native country, and when he speaks his sincere sentiments he is always loud in upholding the superiority of the law and literature of Scotland.

He supplied himself with a copy of "Coke upon Littleton," but found himself unable to apply to it with energy, as he had formerly done to "Craig de Feudis." Hence it was only *pro re nata* that he was ever at all acquainted with the subtleties of the law of real property in England, although he really was a very respectable Scotch feudalist, and he had a good notion of *a me vel de me*, and of the "fettering clauses." He now spent the greatest part of his mornings in writing articles for the "Edinburgh Review,"[2] and of his evenings in attending the gallery of the House of

---

[1] "Lincoln's Inn, 1803.—Henry Brougham, of the Faculty of Advocates in Scotland, Esquire, Eldest Son of Henry Brougham of Brougham Hall, in the County of Westmorland, Esquire, is admitted into the Society of this Inn, the 14th day of November, in the 44th year of the Reign of our Sovereign Lord George the 3rd, by the Grace of God, of the United Kingdom of Great Britain and Ireland King, Defender of the Faith, and in the year of our Lord 1803, and hath thereupon paid to the use of this Society the sum of three pounds three shillings and four pence.

"Admitted by
"Sp. Perceval, *Treasurer.*"

[2] "Glad in his vacant moments to renew
His old acquaintance with the Great Review."

But it afforded to him at this time subsistence as well as amusement.

Commons, dining with Whig peers, and lounging at Brookes's Club. Lord Cockburn, the biographer of Jeffrey, told me the following anecdote, for the truth of which he said he could vouch:—"Brougham, after he came to reside in London, wrote to Jeffrey, saying that he had immediate occasion for £1,000 which must be remitted to him by return of post, and for which there should be value delivered for the *blue and bluff*. The £1,000 was duly remitted, and in the course of six weeks Brougham sent down articles on a vast variety of subjects, which made up an entire number of the 'Edinburgh Review,' one of these being on a 'New Mode of Performing the Operation of Lithotomy,' another upon 'The Dispute as to Light between the Emissionists and the Undulationists,' and a third on the 'Music of the Chinese.'"[1]

He calculated with absolute certainty on getting almost immediately into Parliament, and he wished to become familiar with the aspect and the ways of the lower House. Among givers of good dinners there was a competition to have Brougham at their tables. Contriving to make it appear a favor conferred on them to accept their invitations, he joined the Whig symposia with little reluctance. Although he frequented Brookes's he strictly abstained from the deep gaming which still prevailed there; but he would freely partake of the hot suppers which nightly smoked for those who had previouly partaken of a luxurious dinner, and after large potations of mulled claret he would walk home to his chambers by daylight. At no period of his life was he justly liable to the charge sometimes brought against him of habitual intemperance.

Soon after he settled in London he was made free of Holland House, which then, and for many years after, presented the most agreeable society in Europe.[2] By a

[1] I afterwards asked Jeffrey if this was true?—His answer was, "I will not vouch for its literal truth, but Brougham certainly was wonderful for his vigor and variety." In a letter of Horner to Jeffrey, dated 11th of January, 1805 (Life of Horner, vol. i. p. 278), he writes:—"You were relieved, I trust, from all difficulties by the arrival of Brougham's packet. It would be new indeed, if anything connected with Brougham were to fail in dispatch. He is the surest and most voluminous among the sons of men."

[2] See Macaulay's eloquent and accurate description of this in the "Edinburgh Review," for July, 1841:—" The time is coming when perhaps a few old men, the last survivors of our generation, will in vain seek amidst new streets and squares and railway stations for the site of that dwelling which

natural instinct which taught him his own relative value he seemed, from his first introduction to men of the highest birth and the most distinguished position, to feel himself on an entire equality with them, and, without any approach to vulgarity or impertinence, he treated them with the utmost familiarity. While he could address himself with much dexterity to the *amour propre* of those with whom he conversed, he betrayed occasionally his power of sarcasm, and he was courted both on account of what was pleasant about him and what was formidable. As he advanced, in consequence, he ruled more by fear than by love; but when envy and rivalry did not interfere, his amiable qualities again shone out; he was almost always obliging, and sometimes he was actually friendly.

In spite of a secret distrust of him, which was generated in the minds of almost all who knew him by his occasional forgetfulness of promises, and incorrectness in his statement of facts, he was rapidly rising from the ground, and flying through the mouths of men.

Nothing had helped him more in his ascent than his connection with a party called "The Saints," having William Wilberforce at their head. Their war cry was, "Abolition of the slave trade, and *of slavery*." They

---

was in their youth the favorite resort of wits and beauties, of painters and poets, of scholars, philosophers, and statesmen. They will then remember with strange tenderness many objects once familiar to them, the avenue and the terrace, the busts and the paintings, the carvings, the grotesque gilding, and the enigmatical mottoes. With peculiar fondness they will recall that venerable chamber, in which all the antique gravity of a college library was so singularly blended with all that female grace and wit could devise to embellish a drawing-room. They will recollect, not unmoved, those shelves loaded with the varied learning of many lands and many ages, and those portraits in which were preserved the features of the best and wisest Englishmen of two generations. They will recollect how many men who have guided the politics of Europe, who have moved great assemblies by reason and eloquence, who have put life into bronze and canvas, or who have left to posterity things so written as it shall not willingly let them die, were there mixed with all that was loveliest and gayest in the society of the most splendid of capitals. They will remember the peculiar character which belonged to that circle, in which every talent and accomplishment, every art and science, had its place. They will remember how the last debate was discussed in one corner, and the last comedy of Scribe in another; while Wilkie gazed with modest admiration on Sir Joshua's Baretti; while Mackintosh turned over Thomas Aquinas to verify a quotation; while Talleyrand narrated his conversations with Barras at the Luxembourg, or his ride with Lannes over the field of Austerlitz. They will remember, above all, the grace and the kindness, far more admirable than grace, with which the princely hospitality of that ancient mansion was dispensed."

held that the negro race were fellow Christians and fellow men, all descended from Adam and Eve, and quite equal to the whites in faculties as well as destiny. By embracing this doctrine, and by unremitted homage, Brougham gained the entire good-will of the Negro Liberator, and was proclaimed by him a gifted coadjutor in the holy cause.

At this stage of his career it seemed as if Brougham's lofty ambition were to have very early gratification. The death of Mr. Pitt was followed by the sudden advent of the Whigs to power, and the new Government was to comprehend "All the Talents." Brougham naturally supposed that it could not deserve the title conferred upon it while he was excluded, and he considered his claim to an appointment strengthened by a pamphlet which he published, entitled "The State of the Nation," in which he pointed out very forcibly the blessings to be expected from the auspicious change. He received in return fair words and the hope of future advancement, but neither place nor seat in Parliament; and the only mark of favor he obtained was to be sent as a sort of secretary to Lord St. Vincent and Lord Rosslyn, on a short mission which they undertook to Portugal. He ever after spoke with great admiration of Lord St. Vincent's abilities as a politician, and he remained on the most friendly terms with Lord Rosslyn, even when the current of party politics carried them in different directions.

Soon after Brougham's return to England the Whigs were banished from office, the party being destined for many long years to languish in the ungenial regions of opposition without Court favor and without popular support. Their speedy restoration, however, was then expected, as they had been most unjustly turned out for attempting to procure a very harmless relaxation of the penal code against the Roman Catholics, and Brougham unhesitatingly and zealously remained true to his colors.

The gigantic and incredible (unless miraculous) efforts which he then made to influence the public mind through the press are thus described by Lord Holland in his "Memoirs of the Whig party":—

"We raised a subscription, the very day of the dissolution, for the management of the press and the distribution of hand-bills. In the meanwhile the elections went much against us. The management of our press fell into the hands of Mr. Brougham. With that active and able man I had become acquainted, through Mr. Allen, in 1805. At the formation of Lord Grenville's ministry he had written, at my suggestion, a pamphlet, called "The State of the Nation." He subsequently accompanied Lord Rosslyn and Lord St. Vincent to Lisbon. His early connection with the Abolitionists had familiarized him with the means of circulating political papers, and given him some weight with those best qualified to co-operate in such an undertaking. His extensive knowledge and extraordinary readiness, his assiduity and habits of composition enabled him to correct some articles and to furnish a prodigious number himself. With partial and scanty assistance from Mr. Allen, myself, and two or three more, he, in the course of ten days, filled every bookseller's shop with pamphlets: most London newspapers and all country ones without exception, with paragraphs; and supplied a large portion of the boroughs throughout the kingdom with handbills, adapted to the local interests of the candidates: and all tending to enforce the principles, vindicate the conduct, elucidate the measures, or expose the adversaries of the Whigs."

If all this be literally true, he must have exceeded all the exploits of "Wallace Wight" or "Jack the Giant Killer." His fertility, copiousness, energy, and perseverance in completing a particular effort, certainly were most stupendous; and he doubtless did more in these ten days than any other human being would have attempted. But he had probably persuaded Lord Holland, who was very good-natured and a little credulous, that he had worked impossibilities.

The crisis being over, Brougham saw that he must for a time become a professional man, and fit himself for practice by becoming possessed of at least a smattering of English law. Accordingly he submitted to the necessary drudgery of a special pleader s office, and he became a pupil of Mr. Tindal, then practicing under the bar—afterwards Chief Justice of the Court of Common Pleas. Here he formed an intimacy with a brother pupil, James Parke, subsequently so famous for technical lore and love of antiquated forms.[1] Following his example for a short

---

[1] Afterwards created Lord Wensleydale.

time, Brougham condescended to copy the "money counts," and from his wonderful quickness of perception he got a tolerable insight into the mysteries of special pleading.

On the 22nd day of November, 1808, he was called to the English bar.

Owing to his great reputation in society, it was supposed by many that he would exceed Erskine in the rapidity of his rise, while the more judicious foresaw that the effect of his brilliant parts would be seriously obstructed by want of steadiness and discretion.

Alas! for a long while the favorable anticipations were in no degree verified. Neither brief nor retainer came in, and the world seemed quite unconscious of the great epoch which was supposed to have arrived in our forensic history. Term and sittings ended, and the voice of the modern Cicero, who was to unite law, philosophy, statesmanship, and eloquence, had not once been heard in Westminster Hall. He chose the Northern Circuit, where it might have been expected that a great sensation would have been created by the descendant of the *De Burghams*, those mailed knights who had fought so bravely in Palestine, appearing in a wig and gown, ready to attack the oppressor, to defend the innocent, and to obtain redress for the wrongs of man, woman, and child. But he proceeded from York to Durham, from Durham to Newcastle, from Newcastle to Carlisle, from Carlisle to Appleby, and from Appleby to Lancaster, without receiving a guinea or even being called upon to defend a prisoner without a fee. Occasionally he must have had misgivings as to the step he had taken in leaving the Scottish bar, and he may have wished that he were again making wretched the life of Lord Eskgrove, or raising a laugh against "the Fifteen" in the Parliament House. His demeanor, however, was extremely amiable, and he made himself very popular with his brother barristers. They received him the more cordially when they found that the alarming apprehensions entertained of his making a terrible foray upon them and carrying off all the business, proved groundless. He was duly admitted at the Grand Court, drank every toast with the usual solemnities, sang an appropriate song when required, and showed that in future he might be looked to as a valuable contributor to the "High Jinks" festivities of the meeting.

Not until he had become a member of the House of Commons, and had acquired fame there as a debater, did he gain anything approaching to regular practice in courts of law. Occasionally he was employed where a splashing speech was wanted in an assault case or an action for slander, but it was soon remarked that he was more solicitous to gain distinction for himself than to succeed for his client; he could not resist the temptation to make a joke at his client's expense; he showed no *tact* in conducting a difficult case, and if he was a "vigorous" he never was a "verdict-getting counsel."[1]

His professional income at this time arose almost exclusively from Scotch appeals, in which he was employed at the bar of the House of Lords. It is a curious fact that he then drew the appeal case and argued for the appellant in *Shedden* v. *Patrick*, which he is now, after the lapse of half a century, with other ex-Chancellors, assisting Lord Chancellor Cranworth, who was then in petticoats, to rehear on the ground of fraud and collusion.

Lord Eldon, who was almost uniformly courteous and kind to counsel, had at first a strong prejudice against Brougham, and used to annoy him (it was supposed designedly) by always calling him Mr. *Bruffam*. "De Burgham" might have sounded sweetly in his ear; but amidst the winks and smiles of malicious bystanders who enjoyed his mortification, to be repeatedly addressed by a sound which, although the spelling of his name might phonetically justify it, was vulgar and obscure—this was not to be borne by a man of spirit. He therefore sent a message to the Lord Chancellor by Mr. Cowper, the assistant clerk, in rather angry terms, as if he had to notice a premedi-

---

[1] This panegyric of being "a vigorous verdict-getting counsel" was applied to Mr. Clarke, leader of the Midland Circuit, and was long well known in Westminster Hall.

We have an account of Brougham's manner in *banc*, in a letter from Horner, written in 1812. After giving an exaggerated statement of Brougham's success at the bar, he says:—" I have been present at several arguments of his in *banc*, of which I should not, to say the truth, make a very high report, that is, in comparison of his powers and his reputation. Great reach and compass of mind he must ever display; and he shows much industry, too, in collecting information; but his arguments are not in the best style of legal reasoning. Precision and clearness in the details, symmetry in the putting of them together, an air of finish and unity in the whole, are the merits of that style, and there is not one of these qualities in which he is not very defective. But his desultory reasoning has much force in some parts, and much ingenuity in others."

tated insult; and, that there might be no mistake, wrote down in large round text the letters B R O O M, to mark the monosyllabic pronunciation, for he is nearly as much offended with " Bro—am " or "Broo—am " as with *Bruffam* itself. The Chancellor took the remonstrance in good part, and at the conclusion of the argument observed " every authority upon the question has been brought before us: New BROOMS sweep clean."

Now it was that I first came into professional rivalry with Brougham, and at this stage of our career he greatly eclipsed me. Hitherto, since I was called to the bar, I had been creeping on very slowly but steadily—justifying or opposing bail—moving for judgment as in case of a nonsuit, or arguing a special demurrer turning upon whether a venure had not been improperly omitted in alleging a traversable fact. Suddenly I was called upon to appear as counsel at the bar of the House of Lords on behalf of Firmin De Tastet, a wealthy Spanish merchant, to oppose a bill, introduced by the Government as a great war measure against Napoleon, by preventing the exportation of Jesuits' bark from England to the continent for the supply of his armies then suffering from intermittent fever. My client had several cargoes of this medicine stored in England which, if this bill passed, would become a *useless drug* upon his hands.

Brougham at the same time was retained as counsel at the bar of both Houses for the Liverpool merchants who had petitioned against the Orders in Council, framed by way of retaliation for Napoleon's Berlin and Milan decrees, which declared the British Isles in a state of blockade.

My affair was soon over, as I had only one evening given me to examine my witnesses and to make my speeches; and I returned to my bail, my motions of course, and my special demurrers. Brougham's lasted six weeks, during which he may be said to have made his fortune. For many successive days, in both Houses, he examined a vast crowd of witnesses, and he delivered many most admirable speeches showing great knowledge of political economy and the details of trade, and inveighing in unmeasured terms against the false policy of the English government, by which not only neutral nations were grossly injured, but our own commerce and manu-

factures were nearly ruined. The speeches of counsel at
the bar of either House are generally delivered to empty
benches, but Brougham spoke to crowded audiences, and
hundreds were turned away every evening who could
not gain access even to hear the broken murmurs of
his eloquence. The petitioners were defeated and did
not gain their object till 1812, when Brougham himself
was a member of the House of Commons; but from his
efforts in this case he acquired brilliant fame as an orator,
and the certainty was established that he would make a
figure in public life.

Nevertheless, the next two years were very disheartening to him, and he complained that "he was going down
in the world." He made little progress on his circuit, and
he never had been employed in any great trial in Westminster Hall. He became discontented with the Whig
leaders, and very clamorous against them, by reason that
he had not yet been brought into the House of Commons.
Under the unreformed system, an aspiring young man who
attached himself to either of the great parties in the State,
who made himself useful, and was likely to do credit to it
by his oratorical powers, counted upon a seat in Parliament with as much confidence as upon an invitation to a
political dinner from a Whig or Tory Lord, or a card to
her Ladyship's assembly. Borough-mongers on each side
had as many as eight or ten Members in the House of
Commons. Those whose ambition it was to maintain and
increase their importance and influence in their respective
parties, were on the watch to pick up as recruits adventurous youths of the greatest talent and promise. Brougham's chagrin was much exasperated by the circumstance
that a class-fellow, who had been both at school and
college with him, who had been called to the Scotch bar
at the same time with him, who had been his fellow-laborer in the "Edinburgh Review," who had left Edinburgh about the same time to enter the profession of the
law in England, and who had likewise devoted himself
to the Whigs, had been placed by them in the House of
Commons four years ago, and at two successive general
elections had, by aristocratic influence, been returned for
a Whig borough. Francis Horner,—who though very inferior to Brougham in energy of character, had much more
of prudence and of principle,—had been warmly befriended

by the leaders of the Liberal party, and, if he had lived, would in all probability have been Prime Minister of England. Brougham looked on his success with jealousy and envy, and, without any fault of Horner, all intimacy between them had ceased. Unfortunately, little confidence was reposed in the sincerity of Brougham's professed attachment to the Whig cause, and serious apprehensions were entertained that if he should acquire distinction in the House of Commons, he might turn his power and influence to some purpose of his own at variance with the policy of the party. Being thus fed only by civility, promises, and hopes, he at last threatened abruptly to leave the Whigs, and they, after due deliberation, came to the conclusion that he would be less formidable as a friend than as a foe. It luckily happened that at this time a Whig seat became vacant by the accession of Lord Henry Petty to the peerage on the death of his brother, the second Marquis of Lansdowne; and it was determined that Brougham should be the new Member for the rotten borough of Camelford. The news being communicated to Horner by Allen, who lived with Lord and Lady Holland as their companion and secretary, the following answer was returned, disclosing much generosity on the part of Horner; but at the same time a just sense of the failings of his former school-fellow:

"Lincoln's Inn, 6th January, 1810.

"DEAR ALLEN,

"I rejoice exceedingly at the news you give me of Brougham coming into Parliament; and I am particularly glad that Lord Holland has had so great a share in effecting it. Brougham never could have found a more fortunate moment for setting out upon his career, which, though it may appear less brilliant at first, on account of the expectations which are formed of him, will be very speedily distinguished; and upon the whole I would predict that, though he may very often cause irritation and uncertainty about him to be felt by those with whom he is politically connected, his course will prove, in the main, serviceable to the true faith of liberty and liberal principles. For him personally it will be very fortunate if he has some probationary years to pass on the Opposition side of the House."

Parliament meeting on the 23rd of January, a new writ

was issued for the election of a burgess for the borough of Camelford, and in a few days afterwards "Henry Brougham, Esq., of Brougham Hall, in the County of Westmorland,"[1] was returned as duly elected. He had gone down to solicit the votes of the electors, but, unfortunately, we have no account of his canvass or of any of his hustings speeches on this occasion. He no doubt played his part of candidate for the first time very ably, as well as successfully, for he had the faculty of making himself agreeable in all situations, and he could dexterously address himself to the sympathies of persons in every situation of life. The twenty paid electors of Camelford, when acting under the *congé d'élire* issued by the Lord of the Borough, were probably told, and nearly made to believe, that they were the most important, independent, and patriotic constituency in the kingdom.

There was now keen speculation in the clubs and coteries of London respecting the maiden speech of the new Member. From his impetuous and impatient temperament, it was expected that he would burst out with a flaming oration the very night he took his seat. But, to astonish his friends, and to prove to the world his forbearance and self-control, he had made a vow that he would be silent for a month. Having actually kept this vow in the midst of many temptations to break it, he thought he had acquired a sufficient character for taciturnity to last him during the rest of his life, and it was remarked that for the future he never was in his place a whole evening in either House of Parliament without regularly or irregularly more than once taking part in the discussions.

His first effort was considered a failure. The subject of debate was the Narrative of the Expedition to the Scheldt written by the Earl of Chatham, then a member of the Cabinet, and delivered by him to the King with a request that it might be kept secret.

On the second night of the debate, Mr. Brougham rose to support the resolution moved by Mr. Whitbread, " that this proceeding on the part of the Earl of Chatham was unconstitutional." To the surprise of the House, to whom the propensities of the *débutant* were pretty generally known, his tone was mild, and not a single sarcastic obser-

[1] "London Gazette," 5th Feb. 1810.

vation dropped from his lips. Instead of dwelling upon the disastrous incidents of the Walcheren campaign, and denouncing the listless and supine disposition of the Commander-in-Chief, he strictly confined himself to the question, and tried logically to prove that this communication to the Sovereign by one of his ministers, without the knowledge of the others, was contrary to the spirit of the constitution, which now makes all the members of the Cabinet jointly liable for the advice given by any of them. The following was the most elevated passage in the oration:—

"What constitutes the breach of the constitution is the privacy with which the affair was conducted, coupled as it was with a request of secrecy. Now it may be, and, indeed, it undoubtedly is difficult for me to point out any particular Act of Parliament making this unanticipated course of conduct a breach of the privileges or the practice of Parliament; but I confidently appeal to the sound and established principles of which the constitution is made up, or rather which themselves form the constitution. Is it not necessary that the constitutional Ministers of the Crown shall communicate with each other constitutionally and confidentially on all public affairs? Is it not absolutely requisite for the harmony and completeness of all ministerial acts that they conduct the business of Government with united counsels, and mutual advice and co-operation? In the present case, however, we find Lord Chatham separating himself from his colleagues, and tendering a statement merely to his Majesty, that is, giving his advice to his Sovereign, without consulting the other members of the administration. How can we consider his Majesty's Ministers as responsible for this private communication made by Lord Chatham? If an expedition be determined upon by a Cabinet, one Minister, under the influence of such a system, might suppose that the object in view was to be best attained by artillery, and give advice to that effect to his Sovereign; another by infantry; another, as in a late case, by a *coup de main;* whilst another might give the preference to a troop of light-horse. Every one might have a different opinion, while the only point on which all would agree, would be that their advice should be kept snug in the possession of his Majesty. Can we suppose any state of confusion worse confounded, and, as it might be, more disastrous or absurd, than that which must result from such a state of ministerial separation?"[1]

The honorable and learned member resumed his seat without a single cheer, to the disappointment of his friends, and the great relief of a considerable number of members of rising or established reputation, who had dreaded the approach of a comet to set the world on fire. But he very speedily restored the confidence of friends, and the consternation of rivals, by renouncing forever affected mildness, and indulging without restraint his taste for vituperation. Before the end of his first session he had conquered a commanding position in the House of Commons, and had presented himself as a candidate for the leadership of the Liberal party. George Ponsonby was acknowledged by the regularly disciplined Whigs as their chief; but he had not much brilliancy as an orator to counterbalance the disadvantages of being an Irishman and a lawyer, and, although he had been Lord Chancellor of Ireland, Brougham vilipended his authority, and was pleased with an opportunity of sneering at him. Richard Brinsley Sheridan was still a member of the House, but "the flaming patriot who scorched in the meridian was sinking *in*temperately to the West." He was no longer capable of addressing the House till he had swallowed a quart of brandy, and then his oratory consisted of a mixture of nauseous sentimentality and stale jests. Samuel Whitbread, nicknamed "Fermentation Sam" partly from his profession of a brewer, and partly from the ferment in his brains, though gravely pronounced "the pride of the democracy," was deficient in common sense and tact, and showed occasionally that want of self-control which drove him to a voluntary death. Sir Francis Burdett, long in the mouths of men, had never any higher ambition than to receive the plaudits of the mob, and to enjoy the distinction of being sent to the Tower of London. Henry Grattan, notwithstanding his prodigious Irish reputation and considerable success in the Imperial House of Commons, had never thoroughly taken root there, and was now withering away. Tierney had seriously damaged his reputation by taking office under Lord Sidmouth, and, although he had considerable influence from his excellent good sense and perspicuous elocution, he was considered by very few fit to

[1] 16 Hansard, 7.

be a party leader."[1] Horner was getting on, being the first man who ever made the doctrines of political economy intelligible to the House of Commons.[2] Although very speedily surpassed by Brougham as a debater, had he survived I make no doubt that he would have regained his ascendency. The only other distinguished Member on the Liberal side was Romilly, who was much esteemed for his pure principles and high sense of honor, but was looked upon as somewhat impracticable, and his Genevese notions on religion and politics were always unpalatable in England.

The leading men on the other side were Castlereagh, Canning, Perceval, and Gibbs the Attorney-General. With any or all of these Brougham was ever ready to enter the lists as occasion required. His keenest contests were with Canning, but, notwithstanding great sharpness of language, there was always a friendly feeling between them, and when Canning was at last Prime Minister, Brougham, without office, proved his warmest supporter.

The subject to which the member for Camelford first showed his devotion was Negro Slavery; and by the successful treatment of this he suddenly raised himself to a high position. Wilberforce, satisfied with his share in the glory of the act for abolishing the English slave trade with Africa, and now declining in physical vigor, was willing to surrender to his new coadjutor the task of commencing and carrying through the further measures which were deemed necessary for giving full effect to the views of the abolitionists. During the present century there has not been any instance of the rank of leading member of the House of Commons being attained so rapidly as by Brougham. Within four months from the day when he took his seat, without being supposed to be guilty of any presumption, he brought forward a motion for an address to the Crown on the subject of slavery as if he had long been the acknowledged chief of a party. This he pro-

[1] I have often heard him deeply regret that he had left the bar, and he used to tell me that no lawyer ought to come into the House of Commons till he has fair pretension to be Solicitor-General.

[2] Pitt, the younger, had a considerable smattering of that science; but Fox and Sheridan and Whitbread and Grey knew as little of it as Lord Chatham himself, who swore that "he never would allow the colonies even to manufacture a hob-nail for themselves."

posed in an admirable speech, of which I can only give a few detached passages:

"The question was, whether any, and what, measures could be adopted in order to watch over the execution of the sentence of condemnation which Parliament had, with a singular unanimity, pronounced upon the African slave trade? It was then four years since Mr. Fox had made his last motion upon the subject, pledging the House to the abolition of the traffic, and beseeching his Majesty to use all his endeavors for obtaining the concurrence of foreign Powers. Early in the next year Lord Grenville and Lord Grey, inferior only to Mr. Wilberforce (unfortunately now absent from severe indisposition) in their services to the cause, gave the Parliament an opportunity of redeeming its pledge, by introducing the Abolition Bill. That measure, which had formerly met so many obstacles, whether, as some were willing to believe, from the slowness with which truth works its way, or, as others were prone to suspect, from the want of zeal in its official supporters, now experienced none of the impediments that had hitherto retarded its progress; far from encountering any formidable difficulties, it passed through Parliament almost without opposition ; and one of the greatest and most disputed measures was at length carried by larger majorities perhaps than were ever known to divide upon any contested question. The friends of the abolition, however, never expected that any legislative effort would at once destroy the slave trade; they were aware how obstinately such a noxious weed would cling to the soil where it had taken root. Still they had underrated the difficulties to be encountered. They had not made sufficient allowance for the resistance which the real interests of those actually engaged in the traffic, and the supposed interests of the colonists, would oppose; they had not formed an adequate estimate of the wickedness of the slave trader, or of the infatuation of the planter. While nothing has been done to circumscribe the foreign slave trade, this abominable traffic is still carried on by British subjects."

He then proceeded at great length and with masterly ability to prove these assertions from papers before the House. With respect to our own countrymen, he said:

"For accomplishing this detestable purpose, all the various expedients have been adopted which the perverse ingenuity of unprincipled avarice could suggest. Vessels were fitted out at Liverpool as if for innocent commerce with Africa. The goods peculiarly used in the slave trade were carefully concealed, so as to elude the reach of the port officers. The platforms and bulkheads, which distinguish slave ships, were not fitted and fixed until the vessel got to sea and cleared the Channel,—when the carpenters set to work, and adapted her for the reception of slaves. Lurking in some dark corner of the ship, was almost always to be found a hoary slave trader—an experienced captain, who, having been trained up in the slave business from his early years, now prowled about as a super-cargo, helping the gang of man-stealers by his wiles, both to escape detection, and to push their iniquitous adventure. But a few months ago, in the very river which washed the walls of that House, not two miles from the spot where they now sat, persons, daring to call themselves English merchants, had been detected in the act of fitting out a vessel of great burthen for the purpose of tearing seven or eight hundred wretched beings from Africa, and carrying them through the unspeakable horrors of the middle passage to endless bondage and misery in the sands and swamps of Brazil. At one port of this country six vessels had only just been fitted out by a similar course of base frauds for the same trade—or rather the same series of detestable crimes. Three years having elapsed since this abominable traffic had ceased to be sanctioned by the law of the land, he thanked God he might now indulge in expressing feelings, which deference to that law might before have rendered it proper to suppress. Our indignation might now be hurled against those who still dared to trade in human flesh—not only practicing the frauds of common smugglers, but committing crimes of the deepest dye. It was not commerce, but crime, that they were driving. Of commerce, that most honorable and useful pursuit, whose object is to humanize and pacify the world—so inseparably connected with freedom, and good-will, and fair dealing—he deemed too highly to endure that its name should, by a strange perversion, be prostituted to the use of men who live by treachery, rapine, torture, and murder! When he said *murder*, he spoke literally and advisedly. He meant to use no figurative phrase;

and he knew that he was guilty of no exaggeration. He
was speaking of the worst form of that crime. For ordinary murders there might be some excuse. Revenge
might have arisen from excess of feelings, honorable in
themselves. A murder of hatred or cruelty, or mere
bloodthirstiness, could only be imputed to a deprivation
of reason. But here we have to do with cool, deliberate,
mercenary murder—nay, worse than this, for the ruffians
who go upon the highway, or the pirates who infest the
seas, at least expose their persons, and by their courage
throw a kind of false glare over their crimes. But these
wretches dare not do this; they employ others as base, but
less cowardly than themselves; they set on men to rob
and kill, in whose spoils they are willing to share, though
not in their dangers. Traders and merchants do they presume to call themselves? and in cities like London and
Liverpool, the very creations of honest trade! Give them
their right name at length, and call them cowardly subor-
ners of piracy and mercenary murder. Deprive these mis-
creants of the means of safe criminality, and society may
be purified and avenged. Some of them will naturally go
on the highway; others will betake themselves to open
piracy, and we may see them hanging in chains along with
other malefactors, as we descend the river Thames,—a fit
retribution for their crimes!"

Mr. Brougham was highly complimented, not only by
his own side but by Mr. Perceval and Mr. Canning, and
his address was carried *nem. con.*[1]

In the following Session of Parliament, with unrelaxed
zeal he pursued the object of effectually suppressing the
slave trade, and he carried a bill by which persons engaged
in it were declared to be guilty of felony.[2]

In the Session of 1812, which closed the first period of
his parliamentary career, he applied himself with ultimate
success to the abolition of the Orders in Council respecting neutral commerce. These in the year 1808 he had
impugned as counsel for the mercantile body at the bar of
both Houses of Parliament, but the injury they inflicted
on their own commerce was not then sufficiently severe to
counterbalance the blind resentment created in the English nation by the outrageous violence of Napoleon's Berlin and Milan decrees, by which he presumed to declare

[1] 17 Hansard, 689.   [2] 19 Hansard, 233

the whole of the British Isles in a state of blockade, without a ship-of-war which durst approach our shores. It was supposed that the extraordinary zeal which Brougham then displayed as counsel was stimulated by the heavy fees which he received from wealthy clients; but now that he was acting as a representative of the people from pure patriotism or love of fame, his zeal was still more ardent, and to gain his object he sacrificed much time which he might profitably have employed in his profession. To his honor be it spoken, that if he was liable to be misled by an inordinate love of notoriety, he was ever above the sordid influence of pecuniary gain, which has darkened the reputation of very eminent advocates. From covetousness he was entirely free, and he was always ready to spend with liberality what he had legitimately earned.

After several debates, in which Mr. Brougham took the lead, the House agreed to hear evidence in support of the innumerable petitions presented for the recall of the Orders in Council. "The case was conducted seven weeks by Mr. Brougham and Mr. Alexander Baring, afterwards Lord Ashburton, than whom it would not have been possible to find a more powerful coadjutor. . . . The inquiry on the side of the petitions was wholly conducted by these two members, and each night presented new objections and new defeats to the Orders in Council, and new advantages to the opposition—by incidental debates on petitions presented, by discussions arising from evidence tendered, by other matters broached occasionally in connection with the main subject. The Government at first, conceiving that there was a clamor raised out of doors against their policy, and hoping that this would of itself subside, endeavored to gain time and put off the hearing of the evidence, But Messrs. Brougham and Baring kept steadily to their purpose, and insisted on calling in their witnesses at the earliest possible hour. They at length prevailed so far as to have it understood that the hearing should proceed daily at half-past four o'clock, and continue at the least till ten, by which means they generally kept it on foot till a much later hour. On the 11th of May Mr. Brougham was examining a witness when he thought he heard a noise as if a pistol had gone off in some one's pocket—such at least was the idea which instantaneously passed through his mind, but did not interrupt his interrogation. Presently there were seen several persons in the gallery running towards the doors, and before a minute more had passed General Gascoigne rushed up the House and announced that the Minister had been shot, and had fallen on the spot dead. The House instantly adjourned. . . . . The opponents of the Orders in Council refused to suspend their proceedings in consequence of this lamentable event. Indeed, the suspension of all other business which it occasioned was exceedingly favorable to the object of those who were anxious for an opportunity to produce their proof and obtain a decision. A vast mass of evidence was thus brought forward, showing incontestably the distressed state of trade and manufactures all over the country, and connecting this by clear indications, with the operation of the impolitic system which had been resorted to for *protecting our commerce and retorting on the enemy the evils of his own injustice.*" [1]

At length Mr. Brougham brought forward his motion for an address to the Crown to recall the obnoxious Orders. On this occasion he delivered a speech which he himself considered a *chef-d'œuvre*. The details of the controversy have lost their interest, but the peroration advocating conciliation with America, and deprecating the impending war between the two countries, which soon proved most injurious to our commerce, and which in some degree tarnished our naval fame, refers to immutable principles, and is remarkable both for soundness of thought and brilliancy of language :—

"I am told that these counsels proceed from fear, and that I am endeavoring to instil a dread of American manufactures as the ground of our measures. Not so, sir. I am inculcating another fear—the wholesome fear of utter impolicy mixed with injustice—of acting unfairly to others for the purpose of ruining ourselves. And after all, from what quarter does this taunt proceed? Who are they by whom I am upbraided for preaching up a dread of rival American manufactures? The very men whose whole defense of the system is founded upon a fear of competition from European manufactures—who refuse to abandon the blockade of France from an apprehension (most ridiculous as the evidence shows) of European manufactures rivaling us through American commerce—who

[1] "Introduction" in "Lord Brougham's Speeches," vol. i. 410.

blockade the continent from a dread that the manufactures of France, by means of the shipping of America, will undersell our own—the men whose whole principle is a fear of the capital, industry, and skill of England being outdone by the trumpery wares of France as soon as her market is equally open to both countries! Sir, little as I may think such alarms worthy of an Englishman, there *is* a kind of fear which I would fain urge—a fear, too, of France—but it is her arms, and not of her arts. We have in that quarter some ground for apprehension, and I would have our policy directed solely with a view of removing it. A great effort is to be made, and though of its result others are far more sanguine than I am able to feel, I can have little hesitation in thinking that we had better risk some such attempt once for all, and either gain the end in view, or, convinced that it is unattainable, retire from the contest. If this is our policy, for God's sake let the grand effort be made, single and undivided—undisturbed by a new quarrel, foreign to the purpose, and fatally interfering with its fulfillment. Let us not, for the hundreth time, commit the ancient error, which has so often betrayed us, of frittering down our strength—of scattering our forces in numerous and unavailing plans. We have no longer the same excuse for this folly which we once had to urge. All the colonies in the world are our own—Sugar Islands and Spice Islands there are none from Martinico to Java to conquer—we have every species of unsaleable produce in the gross, and all noxious climates without stint. Then let us not add a new leaf to the worst chapter of our book, and make for ourselves new occasions when we can find none, for persisting in the most childish of all systems. While engaged heartily on our front in opposing France, and trying the best chance of saving Europe, let us not secure to ourselves a new enemy, America, on our flank. Surely language wants a name for the folly which would, at a moment like the present, on the eve of this grand, and decisive, and last battle, reduce us to the necessity of feeding Canada with troops from Portugal—and Portugal with bread from England. I am asked whether I would recommend any sacrifice for the mere purpose of conciliating America. I recommend no sacrifice of honor for that, or for any purpose; but I will tell you that I think we can well, and safely for our honor, afford to conciliate

America. Never did we stand so high since we were a nation in point of military character. We have it in abundance, and even to spare. This unhappy, and seemingly interminable war, lavish as it has been in treasure, still more profuse of blood, and barren of real advantage, has at least been equally lavish of glory. Use this glory—use this proud height on which we now stand, for the purpose of peace and conciliation with America. Let this, and its incalculable benefits, be the advantage which we reap from the war in Europe; for the fame of that war enables us safely to take it. And who, I demand, give the most disgraceful counsels—they who tell you we are of military character but of yesterday—we have yet a name to win—we stand on doubtful ground—we dare not do as we list for fear of being thought afraid—we can not, without loss of name, stoop to pacify our American kinsmen; or I, who say we are a great, a proud, a warlike people—we have fought everywhere, and conquered wherever we fought—our character is eternally fixed—it stands too firm to be shaken—and on the faith of it we may do towards America, safely for our honor, that which we know our interests require? This perpetual jealousy of America! Good God! I can not with temper ask on what it rests! It drives me to a passion to think of it. Jealousy of America! I should as soon think of being jealous of the tradesmen who supply me with necessaries, or the clients who entrust their suits to my patronage. Jealousy of America! whose armies are still at the plough, or making, since your policy has willed it so, awkward (though improving) attempts at the loom—whose assembled navies could not lay siege to an English sloop of war! Jealousy of a Power which is necessarily peaceful as well as weak, but which, if it had all the ambition of France and her armies to back it, and all the navy of England to boot, nay, had it the lust of conquest which marks your enemy, and your own armies as well as navy, to gratify it, is placed at so vast a distance as to be perfectly harmless! And this is the nation of which, for our honor's sake, we are desired to cherish a perpetual jealousy for the ruin of our best interests.[1] I trust, sir, that no such phantom of

[1] Brougham was taunted with his "usual indiscretion" in talking so contemptuously of the Americans, whom he wished to conciliate, and it was afterwards said that such a disparaging representation of their prowess de-

the brain will scare us from the path of our duty. The advice which I tender is not the same which has at all times been offered to our country. By the treaty of Utrecht, which the execrations of ages have left inadequately censured, we were content to obtain, as the whole price of Blenheim and Ramillies, an additional share of the accursed slave trade. I would have you employ the glory which you have won at Talavera and Corunna in restoring your commerce to its lawful, open, honest course, and rescue it from the mean and hateful channels in which it has been lately confined. And if any thoughtless boaster in America, or elsewhere, should vaunt that you had yielded through fear, I would not bid him wait until some new achievement of our arms put him to silence; but I would counsel you in silence to disregard him."[1]

Such an impression was made by this speech, that after Mr. Rose, the Secretary to the Treasury, had in vain attempted to answer it, Lord Castlereagh, on the part of the Government, announced "that the question need not be pressed to a division, because the Crown had been advised immediately to rescind the Orders in Council."

For a few moments there seemed a prospect of Brougham being speedily in office—although it soon vanished, and was not realized till after the expiration of twenty years. George III. was now insane beyond hope of recovery, and the heir apparent occupied the throne under the title of Regent. He had been for many years at the head of the Whig party, who counted with undoubting confidence on their advent to power when George III., their inveterate enemy, should cease to reign. The Regent, although by no means so much devoted to Whig principles as in the life-time of Mr. Fox, still bore a grudge against his father's Tory Ministers, by whom he thought he had been long persecuted, and he would have been willing on his own terms, to have formed a Liberal Government, with Lords Grey and Grenville at the head of it. For this purpose a negotiation was opened, which at first wore a promising aspect, and it was expected that Brougham,

termined them or a rupture to show the result of a fight between one English and one American frigate, yard-arm and yard-arm. Wonderful to think that Brougham, still in the full possession of his bodily and mental vigor, and of his eloquence, survives to see the United States with the greatest commercial navy of any nation in the world, the conquerors of Mexico, and with ships of war on every sea! [April 7th, 1854.]   [1] 28 Hansard, 486.

abandoning the law as a profession, would hold a high political office, that of President of the Board of Trade being said to be the one with which he would be contented. But through the bad faith or indiscretion of Mr. Sheridan, and the foolish conduct of all concerned in the new arrangement, it went off, and the Tories continued in power till the accession of William IV. A dissolution of Parliament immediately followed this transient glimpse of office to the Whigs. Camelford, in the meantime, had been transferred to a new owner *who knew not Brougham*, and to Brougham's great indignation, no other seat had been provided for him. Instead of being President of the Board of Trade, with the prospect of the premiership, his political career seemed closed forever.

While brooding over his disappointed hopes, a deputation arrived from a large class of Liverpool merchants, who, grateful for his exertions against the Orders in Council, solicited him to become a candidate to represent them. He accepted the invitation, along with Mr. Creevey, another Whig candidate; but the Tories were too strong for them. To no purpose Brougham made many eloquent speeches, setting forth his services to the men of Liverpool. The following was the most stirring appeal :—

" Brace your nerves! I bid you all be prepared to hear what touches you all equally. We are, by this day's intelligence, at war with America in good earnest—our Government has at last issued letters of marque and reprisals against the United States. [*Universal cries of God help us! God help us!*] Aye, God help us! God of his infinite compassion take pity upon us! God help and protect this poor town, and this whole trading country! Now, I ask whether you will be represented in Parliament by those who have brought this grievous calamity upon your heads, or by us, who have constantly opposed the mad career which was plunging you into it? Whether will you trust the revival of your trade—the restoration of your livelihood—to them who have destroyed it, or to me, whose counsels, if followed in time, would have averted this unnatural war, and left Liverpool flourishing in opulence and peace? Make your choice—for it lies with yourselves which of us shall be commissioned to bring back commerce and plenty—they, whose stubborn infatuation has chased those blessings away, or we, who are only known to you as the strenuous enemies of their miserable policy, the fast friends of your best interests."[1]

Nevertheless, from *golden* arguments addressed to the freemen, which outweighed all this eloquence, Mr. Canning and General Gascoigne were returned by a large majority, and poor Brougham was obliged to leave the town, with the intelligence which added much to the poignancy of his mortification, that the Whigs had provided another seat for Creevey, whose claims on the party were so much less considerable.

Though filled with resentment, he concealed his feelings at the time, even from those who were most intimate with him. Lord Murray in a letter to me says:

"After his defeat at Liverpool I passed a day with him at Lord Sefton's, and traveled with him to Brougham Hall. He was invariably good-humored— I may say exactly as he would have been if nothing untoward had happened."

When left alone, however, he became very moody, and in his dispair he rode down to Scotland, and made a dash at the Inverkeithing district of burghs; but, notwithstanding reiterated expositions of his public services, he was again defeated, and he found himself excluded from Parliament.

His resentment against the Whig party for thus deserting him sunk so deep in his mind that, many years afterwards, he thus described a "discontented, but discerning Whig," as making a just estimate of their demerits:—

"He despised the timidity which so often paralyzed their movements; he disliked the jealousies, the personal predilections, and prejudices which so frequently distracted their councils; he abhorred the spirit of intrigue, which not rarely gave some inferior man, or some busy, meddling woman, probably unprincipled, a sway in the destiny of the party, fatal to its success, and all but fatal to its character; he held in utter ridicule, the squeamishness, both as to persons and things, which emasculated so many of the genuine regular Whigs; and no consideration of interest, no relations of friendship, no regard for party discipline, could prevail with him to pursue that

[1] "Lord Brougham's Speeches," vol. i. 485.

course so ruinous to the Whig opposition, of half-and half
resistance to the Government, marching to the attack with
one eye turned to the court, and one askance to the
country, nor ever making war upon the Ministry without
regarding the time when themselves might occupy the
position now the object of assault. The patrician leaders
of the party never could learn the difference between
1810 and 1780—still fancied they lived 'in times before
the flood' of the French revolution, when the heads of a
few great families could dispose of all matters according
to their own good pleasure—and never could be made to
understand how a feeble motion, prefaced by a feeble
speech, if made by an elderly lord, and seconded by a
younger one, could fail to satisfy the country, and shake
the Ministry."[1]

Brougham remained out of Parliament nearly four years,
and we must now go back to trace his career at the bar.

He first obtained a commanding position there by his
speech on "Military Flogging." The "Examiner" newspaper had published an article containing an account of a
sentence of 1,000 lashes being pronounced by a courtmartial, of which 750 were inflicted, when the unfortunate
soldier was carried senseless from the field, with the following comment:—

"Bonaparte does not treat his refractory troops in this
manner; there is not a man in his ranks whose back is
seamed with the lacerating cat-o'-nine-tails; his soldiers
have never yet been brought up to view one of their comrades stripped naked; his limbs tied with ropes to a
triangular machine; his back torn to the bone by the
merciless cutting whip-cord, applied by persons who
relieved each other at short intervals, that they may bring
the full unexhausted strength of a man to the work of
scourging. Bonaparte's soldiers have never yet with
tingling ears listened to the piercing screams of a human
creature so tortured; they have never seen the blood
oozing from his rent flesh; they have never beheld a
surgeon, with dubious look, pressing the agonized victim's
pulse, and calmly calculating to an odd blow, how far
suffering may be extended, until, in its extremity, it encroached upon life. In short Bonaparte's soldiers
can not form any notion of that most heart-rending of

[1] "Lord Brougham's Speeches," vol. i. 473.

all exhibitions on this side hell—an English military flogging."

For this Sir Vicary Gibbs, then Attorney-General (who may be considered the liberator of the press, by bringing prosecutions for libel into such odium, that they were almost discontinued after his time), filed an *ex officio* information against John Hunt and Leigh Hunt, and Brougham was their advocate. His speech was extremely temperate and judicious as well as forcible. After a few introductory observations upon the address of the Attorney-General, he thus proceeded :—

"Gentlemen,—If you are not convinced—if, upon reading the composition attentively, you are not every one of you fully and thoroughly convinced—that the author had a blamable, a guilty intention in writing it, that he wrote it for a wicked purpose, you must find the defendants NOT GUILTY. But I will not disguise from you, that you are trying a more general and important question than this. You are now to determine whether an Englishman still enjoys the privilege of freely discussing public measures; whether an Englishman still enjoys the privilege of impeaching, not one individual character, not one or two public men, not a single error in policy, not any particular abuse of an established system; the question for you to try is, whether an Englishman shall any longer have the power of making comments on a system of policy, of discussing a general, I had almost said an abstract, political proposition, of communicating to his countrymen his opinion upon the merits, not of a particular measure, or even a line of conduct pursued by this or that administration—but of a general system of policy, which it has pleased the Government to adopt at all times;—whether a person devoted to the interests of his country, warm in his attachment to its cause, vehemently impelled by a love of its happiness and glory, has a right to endeavor, by his own individual exertions, to make that perfect which he so greatly admires, by pointing out those little defects in its constitution which are the only spots whereupon his partial eyes can rest for blame? Whether an Englishman, anxious for the honor and renown of the army, and deeply feeling how much the safety of his country depends upon the perfection of its military system, has a right to endeavor to promote the good of the service, by showing wherein the present system is detrimental to it, by marking for correction those imperfections which bear indeed no proportion to the general excellence of the establishment, those flaws which, he is convinced, alone prevent it from attaining absolute perfection? Whether a person anxious for the welfare of the individual soldier, intimately persuaded that on the feelings and the honor of the soldier depend the honor and glory of our arms, sensible that upon those feelings and that honor hinges the safety of the country at all times, but never so closely as at present,—whether imbued with such sentiments, and urged by these motives, a man has not a right to make his opinions as public as is necessary to give them effect? Whether he may not innocently, nay, laudably, seek to make converts to his own views, by giving them publicity, and endeavor to realize his wishes for the good of the State and the honor of its arms, by proving, in the face of his fellow-citizens, the truth of the doctrines to which he is himself conscientiously attached? These, gentlemen, are the questions put to you by this record ; and your verdict, when entered upon it, will decide such questions as these."

The staple of his subsequent address, consisted of extracts from pamphlets, written by officers of undoubted gallantry and loyalty, censuring in severe terms the established system of excessive military punishments and other grievances to which our soldiers are subjected. Having read with particular emphasis a description by Sir Robert Wilson of the frightful sickness and mortality among our troops in the West Indies, he thus continued :—

"The gallant officer even goes so far as to wish those colonies were abandoned, rather than they should be an inglorious cemetery for our soldiers. I am not disposed to follow him in this opinion ; I can not go so far. But God forbid I should blame him for holding it ; or that for making his sentiments public, I should accuse him of having written a libel on that service, of which he is at once the distinguished ornament and valued friend. Far from imputing blame to him, I respect him the more for publishing a bold and downright opinion,—for expressing his feelings strongly, and thus affording the best proof of his sincerity. He proposes no less than that the West India Islands should be given up, in order to improve our means of defense at home. He says—'It is to be hoped, that the day is not remote, when our colonies shall cease to be such a drain upon the active population of this country; that charnel-house must be closed forever against British troops. The soldier who dies in the field, is wrapped in the mantle of honor, and a ray of glory is reflected upon his surviving relatives; but in a warfare against climate, the energy of the man is destroyed before life is extinguished; he wastes into an inglorious grave, and the calamitous termination of his existence offers no cheering recollections to relieve the affliction of his loss.' Did Sir Robert Wilson mean to excite the brave and ill-fated regiments to mutiny and revolt, who were already enclosed in those charnel-houses? Or did he mean to deter persons from enlisting in those regiments, who might otherwise have been inclined to go there? Did he mean to address any of the regiments under actual orders for the West India service, and excite revolt among them, by telling every one who read the passage I have cited, that which it so forcibly puts to all soldiers under such orders: '*Where are you going? You are rushing into a charnel-house!*' Far be it from me to impute such motives. It is impossible! The words I have read are uttered in the discussion of a general question—a question on which he speaks warmly, because he feels strongly."

He concluded by thus exposing the absurd inconsistency of the argument for the prosecution:—

"The men, therefore, are to see their comrades tied up, and to behold the flesh stripped off from their bodies, aye, bared to the bone, without any emotion but that of tranquil satisfaction! And all this the bystanders are also to witness, without the smallest risk of thinking twice, after such a scene, whether they shall enter into such a service! But have a care how, at a distance from the scene, and long after its horrors have closed, you say one word on the general question of the policy of the system; because, if you should attempt to express your opinions upon that subject, a single word of argument, one accidental remark, will rouse the whole army into open revolt! Take no precautions for concealing such sights from those whom you would entice into the service; do not stop up their ears while the air rings with the lash; let them read the horrors of the spectacle in the faces of those who have endured it. Such things can not move a man; but description, remark, commentary, argument, who can hear without instantaneous rebellion?"

Lord Ellenborough, in summing up the case to the jury, characterized this as "a speech of great ability, eloquence, and manliness," but observed :—

"You (the Jury) are to say whether this is a fair discussion of a public question, or whether it is calculated to inflame the passions, to induce the soldiers to believe they are worse dealt with than the soldiers of France, to blunt their resistance to the efforts of Bonaparte for our destruction. In the presence of one of the officers (Sir Robert Wilson) whose publications have been quoted, I have no difficulty in saying that he would have done better if he had imposed more of a guard upon his observations. The purity of his purpose no man can doubt. He addressed his observations to the Minister of the country, but I think he would have done better if he had discussed the subject privately with Mr. Pitt. Although you are entitled to find a verdict according to your own opinion, it is generally expected that I should, under the suggestion of the Act of Parliament, tell you mine. I have no doubt that this libel has been published with the intention imputed to it, and that it is entitled to the character which is given to it in the information." [1]

The jury retired, and after a consultation of two hours returned a verdict of NOT GUILTY, which was received with loud acclamations.[2]

As a proof of the unsatisfactory manner in which the criminal law was put in force by the Crown in those days, it is melancholy to relate that exactly three weeks from this acquittal another information for the same libel was tried at the assizes for the county of Lincoln against the proprietor of a country newspaper, in which it had appeared, and this jury finding the defendant GUILTY, he was sentenced to eighteen months' imprisonment. Brougham attended on a special retainer, but he might as well have wasted his eloquence on the desert air, as to try to make any impression on the old-fashioned ultra-Tory, fox-

[1] This was a flagrant perversion of Mr. Fox's Libel Act, under which the Judge ought to tell the Jury what intention on the part of the writer will make the writing a libel, but should leave it exclusively to the jury to say whether they believe that such was the intention of the writer.
[2] 31 State Trials, 367.

hunting squire he had to address. The judge was Baron Wood, who for twenty years, while at the bar, had been "devil to the Attorney-General," and, much less liberal than Lord Ellenborough, thought every man ought to be severely punished who writes anything to question the Acts of the Government for the time being:—

"If," said he, "the learned counsel for the defendant really entertains the opinion he expresses on military flogging, I wish he would make use of that eloquence of which he is so eminently possessed, in that House of which he is a member. The House of Parliament is the proper place for the discussion of subjects of this nature. There it should appear, and not in pamphlets or newspapers. The right to discuss the acts of our Legislature would be a large permission indeed. Is the libeler to come and make the people dissatisfied with the Government under which they live? This is not to be permitted to any man. It is unconstitutional and seditious. Of this publication I have no difficuly in asserting that it has a tendency to produce the mischief ascribed to it, and that it is a libel." [1]

Brougham was exceedingly mortified by this defeat after his recent victory, and he threatened to move for the impeachment of Judge Wood, but he wisely abstained from the attempt, knowing that in the House of Commons, as then constituted, he could have met with no sympathy.

In again defending the Hunts for a libel in the "Examiner," upon the Prince Regent, Brougham had an opportuuity of which he amply availed himself, of pouring out sarcasms upon the vices of the royal prosecutor. A letter of Horner, who, sitting by my side, heard this speech, gives its just character, with an unexaggerated account of the demeanor of the judge:—" Brougham made a powerful speech—unequal and wanting that unity which is so effective with a jury; some parts were eloquent, particularly in the conclusion, where he had the address, without giving any advantage, to fasten the words *effeminacy* and *cowardice* where everybody could apply them. One very difficult part of the case, the conduct of the Regent to the Princess, he managed with skill and great effect; and his transition from that subject to the

[1] 31 State Trials, 535.

next part of his case was a moment of real eloquence. Lord Ellenborough was more than usually impatient, and indecently violent. He said that the counsel was inoculated with all the poison of the libel."[1] The defendants were found guilty, and sentenced to a long imprisonment.

Although Brougham had gained brilliant reputation as an advocate in what used to be called technically "the sedition line,"[2] after ceasing to represent Camelford, and failing in his attempts upon Liverpool and Inverkeithing, he greatly missed the House of Commons, which had not only procured him agreeable excitement, and strengthened his claim to political promotion, but assisted him materially in his profession. Generally with us, a lawyer's practice at the bar leads to Parliament; but in Brougham's case Parliament led to practice at the bar. His forensic performances, unaided, never would have given him any considerable position. His habit was immediately before setting off upon the circuit to make a long "splashing" speech about jurisprudential reform, copiously introducing black-letter lore, got up for the nonce, which persuaded the northern attorneys and their clerks that he was profoundly versed in the common law of this realm. *Præsentia minuit famam;* they were a little disappointed when he came down among them and showed that he was not quite up to the distinction between actions *ex contractu* and actions *ex delicto.* But when in a few months, they read another speech of the same sort, which he had delivered to an admiring senate, they thought he must be able to obtain ample damages for non-payment of a bill of exchange or for an assault. Excluded from Parliament, there was nothing to counteract the unfavorable impression he made when a brief in any ordinary matter was intrusted to him. Accordingly, his business fell off, and he began to despond. He might have got on in the Crown Court, where a knowledge of law may be dispensed with, but here also he failed; for when engaged for the prisoner he was singularly indiscreet

---

[1] Life of Horner, vol. ii. 137.
[2] *I. e.*, defending persons prosecuted by the Attorney-General for political offenses—a highway to fame which has long been closed. A more obscure avenue still subsists called "The Rope Walk," that is, being counsel for prisoners at the Old Bailey or the Assizes, and receiving briefs from the jail attorneys or the prisoners themselves. It took the name, which it still retains, when almost every conviction for felony was followed up by *hanging*

in the questions he put. Seemingly he acted upon the supposition that his client was really innocent (a presumption of law which, nine times out of ten, was contrary to the fact), and as at that time the prisoner's counsel could not address the jury, he made but a poor hand of it when employed to get off a burglar or a highwayman. He even contracted a distaste for the circuit, and till he wore a silk gown as Attorney-General to Queen Caroline, he was glad of an excuse for staying away from an assize town.

But about this time he began to form the connection which finally led to that distinction. At first, this extraordinary and ill-fated woman had looked upon him with suspicion and dislike, as belonging to the Whigs, who, when in office, had instituted the "delicate investigation" against her, and she placed all her confidence in Lord Eldon and the Tories, who had warmly espoused her cause; but George III. becoming permanently insane, and the Prince of Wales as Regent having renounced his Whiggish propensities and confirmed in office his father's Tory Ministers, and they having suddenly not only abandoned her, but entered into a combination with him to destroy her, she was obliged to throw herself for protection on the Whigs, and Brougham became her chief adviser. He was first casually introduced to her by Mr. Canning, who was under the ungrounded suspicion of being too intimate with her, and had even excited jealousy in the mind of her profligate husband. She was highly pleased with Brougham's conversation, and she invited him to visit her at Blackheath. He cultivated her acquaintance with much assiduity, as it gave him consequence in the meantime, and offered the prospect of substantial advantages hereafter, whatever turn her conjugal disputes might take, before or after the time of her reaching the dignity of Queen. She was likewise an instrument of high interest and importance, as mother of the Princess Charlotte, the heir presumptive to the Crown, who was much attached to her, and over whom she was likely to exercise permanent influence. Brougham, by his agreeable manners, by expressing deep sympathy in the wrongs of the injured Caroline, and above all by denouncing with indignation the treachery and baseness of Eldon and Perceval in abandoning her cause when they were taken into favor and continued in office by the Regent, gained her confidence, and received a promise for her that, when Queen, he should be her Attorney-General.

This prospect was consoling to him, and did not seem distant, for George III. had reached a very advanced age, and with his infirmities of mind and body, could not be expected to last much longer. But entire faith was not to be placed in Princesses more than in Princes, and Brougham was by no means satisfied with his position as Caroline's prime minister. He became more and more impatient to be again in the House of Commons, which he justly considered the true arena for a display of the peculiar powers with which he was gifted. Various plans were talked of for gaining his object; but to no purpose. From the successful conclusion of the war against Napoleon, the Tory Government had gained unbounded popularity, and there was no open constituency before whom a professed Whig, trusting merely to his principles, could appear with much chance of success. The nomination seats belonging to the Whig aristocracy were all filled up, and there was little sincere desire to create a vacancy for one in whose steady attachment to the party no safe reliance could be reposed.

Considering that this was the most eventful crisis in the modern history of Europe, we may conceive Brougham's mortification in being excluded from taking any part in the debates of Parliament—more particularly when Horner, who had started in the race of public life with him, had not only distinguished himself by discussing questions of political economy, but had acquired considerable reputation by speeches respecting the new distribution of territory in Europe, on the fall of Napoleon, and his banishment first to Elba, and afterwards to St. Helena.

At last the object was accomplished through female influence. The Earl of Darlington was then the greatest borough proprietor in England. For a second wife he had married his mistress, and the great ambition of the two was that, although she was not "visited," she might become a duchess. His fortune was immense, and he would freely, at any reasonable price, buy seats for the session, the Parliament, or in fee-simple. These he generally distributed among men on whose steady voting according to his orders he could implicitly rely; but one or two seats he would trust to aspiring youths of extraordinary talents, who professed to be of the same side in politics which he took, and, although, somewhat unsteady, and presuming to have an opinion of their own, would add to his credit, from being called his Members. The privilege of selecting these, was generally exercised by the Countess, and in the beginning of the year 1816, she returned Henry Brougham for the borough of Winchelsea —once a flourishing Cinque Port, now deserted by the sea and become a depopulated village. Brougham never did anything mean to gain her favor, and never, in any degree, sacrificed his independence while representing a peer or peeress. He continued to act for Winchelsea during the most brilliant portion of his career, and when his politics differed from those of his patron, he transferred himself to the Duke of Devonshire, who surrendered him to the county of York.

It may be conceived in what a state of repletion Brougham was after a retention which had endured nearly four consecutive years. Writing frequent pamphlets and countless articles for reviews, magazines, and newspapers, had brought him some occasional relief, aided by after-dinner speeches, and copious ebullitions of rhetoric at public meetings; but there remained an immense conglomeration of ideas in his mind, which could only be vomited forth in the House of Commons. Accordingly he made a long speech against the address to the Crown, the night when he first took his seat for Winchelsea, and subsequently he spoke as much during the single session, as would be a sufficient contribution to debate from an ordinary man during a long parliamentary life.

Supporting the amendment to the address in answer to the speech from the throne, he drew a melancholy picture of the condition of the country at the conclusion of the war, and shadowed forth the various alterations in our laws and institutions by which we might be rescued from the distress which all classes, and more particularly landed proprietors, were suffering, by the sudden fall of prices. He concluded by urging—

"That our expenses should be reduced to the smallest amount possible, consistently with our safety. For it was a robbery of the people, it was a cruel mockery of their sufferings to tell them, after twenty-five years of misery,

and when the looked-for peace was at last arrived, that
they were still to be loaded with the expenses of war without the benefits of peace,—and for what purpose? For
the purpose of securing the cession of new islands, of appointing new governors, new secretaries, new clerks; of
establishing new sources of patronage, new causes of alarm
to the people, and new dangers to public liberty." [1]

In a few days he made an attack upon the *Holy Alliance*,
by moving for a copy of the treaty between Russia, Austria, and Prussia. Alas! upon a division, it was found
that his energetic speech upon this combination of despots
against the liberties of mankind, influenced only a minority of thirty! [2] His grand object was at once to seize upon
the leadership of the Opposition; but his bold pretension was by no means acquiesced in; for the aristocratic
tendency of the Whigs pointed to Lord Althrop, the representative of the Spencers, and, if a new man must be chosen,
the election would have fallen upon the steady Horner
much sooner than upon the reckless Brougham. This accounts for the small numbers that voted with him in support of Opposition motions.

Besides taking part in every debate originated by others,
he himself brought forward motions of great importance
about finance, Spain, excise prosecutions, the education of
the people, the law of libel, and the general distress
arising from the low price of corn. His treatment of this
last subject shows the crude notions still prevailing among
well-educated men on vital questions of political economy.
Assuming, with the applause of both sides of the House,
that the low price of corn was an evil to be deplored and
remedied if possible, he ascribed it mainly to excess of cultivation, adding,—

"This, however, is not the only cause of the evil I complain of, although I am entirely disposed to rank the great
extension of cultivation among the principal causes, or at
least to regard it as lying near the foundation of the mischief." [3]

His chief effort during the session was a proposed bill
for reforming the law of libel, and particularly for depriving the Attorney-General of the power of filing criminal
informations, which had been brought into great odium
by Sir Vicary Gibbs; but having obtained leave to lay the

[1] 32 Hansard, 37. [2] Ib. 363. [3] 9th April, 1816.

bill on the table and having read it a first time, he allowed it to drop and never resumed it, although it contained other valuable enactments which were afterwards adopted by the legislature.

In the following year there was severe manufacturing distress, which gave rise to the "Battle of Peterloo," or the "Manchester Massacre," and dangerous riots in other parts of England. Brougham very forcibly assailed the Government for the unconstitutional means employed to restore the public tranquillity, and afterwards yielded powerful aid in opposing Lord Castlereagh's "Six Acts," by which, for a season, arbitrary government superseded the English constitution. Such times are never likely again to recur in this country.

Brougham had no peculiar connection with this struggle beyond the other leaders of the Liberal party then in Parliament. I hasten therefore to scenes in which he played the sole or the most distinguished part.

From his many lengthy parliamentary speeches in the years 1817, 1818, and 1819, I can find nothing grave to select which would not repay perusal, but the reader may be pleased with specimens of the pleasantry with which he indemnified the House for his somewhat tiresome attempts to persuade them by much speaking, importunity, and repetition.

He was now usually pitted against Canning, and in answer to a motion for an address to the Prince Regent enumerating the grievances of which the nation was then entitled to complain, his opponent had expressed surprise that "the necessity for Parliamentary Reform" was omitted, and had then gone on to prove that none was wanted. Brougham in his reply observed,—

"The right honorable gentleman has charged this address principally with omissions, and above all, leaving out the subject of Parliament Reform. Now, for my part, I can hardly regret this, as it has afforded the right honorable gentleman an occasion for letting off his long meditated speech on that question; and I must say the right honorable gentleman himself was rather ungrateful in making such invectives against an omission which he has turned to so much account; to be sure, had it been otherwise, I do not at all know that he would not have contrived to bring in the speech which he had ready for use—

such is his versatility in debate. The right honorable gentleman has honored me by comparing me to a commander, and has given a very distorted account of my operations; and it is said that chiefs, accustomed to be opposed, get to know one another's tactics very precisely. Now, I can not have the presumption to say it of myself; but we have all learned pretty accurately his course of conducting the parliamentary campaign. He takes care to have magazines well stored with ready-made cut-and-dry speeches, prepared for future occasions, and adapted as *impromptu* replies to the topics he supposes may be used. He deems it more convenient, better suited to the importance of the subject, and more becoming the dignity of the place, to weigh well what his adversaries are to say, and be ready with an elaborate—answer, may not always be the fit word, but, *harangue*, or *merriment*, perhaps—than rashly trust to the inspiration of the moment. The plan, no doubt, has great advantages; but it has its inconveniences also. While the expected topics are used, for which the answers are ready, all goes well. But if, as will now and then crossly happen, they never are used at all, then comes the difficulty how to get in all the fine things prepared with so much labor to meet them. That all this work should be thrown away, all hours of day, and the midnight oil, consumed in vain—in common humanity, this can not be expected. The passages got up must at all events be introduced. The right honorable gentleman fancies his adversary has used the arguments he himself is prepared to meet; he puts them into his mouth and answers them; or he supposes something left out which would really have been out of place, and he amuses himself and the House by being very droll upon the omission."[1]

In one of his speeches on the benefits of general education he pointed out the advantages of the Scotch parochial schools, thus slyly sneering at the land of his birth and breeding:—

"Go where you will over the world, the name of a Scotchman is still found—*combined in the minds of all men, perhaps with some qualities which sincere regard for that good people restrains me from mentioning*—but certainly with the reputation of a 'well-educated man.' To

[1] 36 Hansard, 1439.

the possession of this enviable characteristic, and not, I trust, to the other qualities imputed to them, we may fairly ascribe the high credit, the great ease and what is usually termed the success in life, which generally attend Scotchmen settled abroad. The countries where they have settled partially followed their example—as, indeed, into what part of the world have they not immigrated? and sir, let me ask, where have they gone without conferring benefits on the place of their adoption?"[1]

Charles Williams Wynn, for many years the father of the House of Commons, from his youth upwards had been the great oracle of parliamentary law, and would himself have been elected to the chair had it not been for his unfortunate voice, which it was feared would have procured for him the appellation of Mr. Squeaker, instead of "Mr. Speaker." Upon a question of privilege, this venerable senator having delivered an opinion contrary to Brougham's, and fortified it with many precedents and references to the Journals, Brougham thus complimented him amidst the "cheers and laughter" of all Members present:—

"I am particularly grieved by the sentiments expressed by my right honorable and learned friend, the member for Montgomeryshire—a man learned beyond all others in the history of the assembly whose privileges I am endeavoring to support—skilled beyond all men, deeper than all the children of men, in the knowledge of the voluminous records of parliamentary precedents—a man who is even supposed by most people to know the whole of the Journals of the House by heart, who devotes to their study the light of day and the midnight oil, whose attention to everything connected with Parliament is so rigid that many persons suppose he really comes down to the House every morning at ten o'clock, the hour at which the House ought to assemble according to the strict letter of the adjournment; in short, a man whose devotion in this respect, can only be equaled by that of a learned ancestor of his,[2] who having fainted from excessive toil and fatigue, a smelling-bottle was called for, when one who knew much better the remedy adapted to the case, exclaimed—' For God's sake bring him an old black-letter Act of Parliament, and let him smell at that.' I can not help thinking, that in like manner, if my right

[1] 38 Hansard, 585.   [2] Speaker Williams, temp. Car. II.

honorable and learned friend should ever be attacked in a similar way, the mere smelling of a volume of the Journals could not fail instantly to revive him."

These specimens, the most favorable I can select, seem rather to justify the remark that in debate he dwelt too long upon the same topic whether grave or gay, and that he weakened both his logic and his wit by excessive elongation.

CHAPTER CCXXV.

ATTORNEY-GENERAL TO QUEEN CAROLINE.

AT the death of George III., Brougham certainly filled a large space in the public eye; but his position was not very comfortable for himself. His own party never conceded the lead to him in the House of Commons, and still regarded him with some degree of jealousy and distrust. If he had been so inclined, it would have been impossible for him to have coalesced with the Tories; for they unreasonably considered that he was an enemy to the monarchy. As yet, the Radicals could hardly be considered a party, and Brougham could not join them without lowering himself to the level of Cobbett and Hunt. But what discouraged him more, he was by no means flourishing in his profession. He made no progress on the circuit. In London his House of Lords business had left him from his neglecting it, and he only expected to be employed on extraordinary occasions in the courts of law. In common suits I myself was sometimes opposed to him, which I thought a luxury; for his name gave a sort of celebrity to every trial he was engaged in, and if the verdict could by indiscreet management go against him he was sure to confer the splendor of victory on his opponent. Reports were circulated that he was about to leave the bar in despair, and to devote himself exclusively to politics. A most marvelous revolution was at hand. In the course of a few months his parliamentary was merged in his forensic reputation, and for a time he held a higher position at the bar than any man in England ever did before, or probably ever will again. Caroline of Brunswick was now Queen of Great Britain, and Brougham was about to defend her upon a charge which affected her honor and her life—the profligate, styled " our most religious and gracious King," being her prosecutor, the Imperial Parliament being her Judges, and all Europe looking on as spectators of the trial.

Whatever may have been the failings or the faults of the unhappy Caroline, it is impossible not to pity her for the adverse circumstances in her career over which she had no control, and which had a powerful tendency to involve her in difficulties and disgrace. Although her father was one of the bravest of men, and her mother one of the most virtuous of women, she had been educated in a Court where purity was little regarded, and vice was doubly mischievous from the grossness by which it was accompanied. The match with the heir to the British Crown seemed splendid, but she found herself united to a heartless voluptuary, who had already gone through the religious ceremony of marriage with another lady, and who treated his lawful wife with contumely,—till at last he renounced all right over her as a husband, and gave her a license to follow his example in forgetting that the conjugal relation had ever subsisted between them. Driven into doubtful society, she became wholly indifferent to public opinion, and if imputations were cast upon her which were unjust, she was guilty at all events of levity and indecorum which seriously compromised her fair fame. As she certainly had experienced harsh usage in England, justified by nothing which she had done here, contending parties in the State, and selfish individuals, under pretense of vindicating her wrongs, seized upon them as property which they could convert to their own purposes, caring little for her honor or her welfare. While the belief prevailed that the heir-apparent still fostered his long professed attachment to the Whigs, the Tories, with the view of disparaging his character and lowering his influence, declared themselves her champions, and were loud in her praise. Even grave and decent men, like Lord Eldon and Mr. Perceval, wrote and printed a book to establish her innocence, and to hold up her accusers to public execration. But when, from the permanent insanity of George III., the Prince of Wales had become Regent without restrictions, and when, imbibing from a lady of high rank, who was considered to be his mistress, a new zeal for the Protestant faith, he had renounced Lord Grey and the friends to Catholic emancipation, and had manifested an intention to retain in office his father's Ministers, this "Book" was suppressed, and all intercourse between the Princess and the Tory leaders was put an end to forever. Till the commencement of the new reign, however, they did not become her active persecutors. On the contrary, they were secretly disposed still to do her a good turn, and they discountenanced the proposal of bringing her to trial which was urged by her husband, and was strongly supported by Sir John Leach, who hoped thereby to become Lord Chancellor, instead of dying Master of the Rolls.

The Princess, when abandoned by her Tory advisers, fell, as I have before explained, into the hands of Mr. Brougham, the most enterprising, the most insinuating. the most accomplished, and the most unscrupulous of the Liberal party. She tried to form a political connection with Lord Grey and Lord Grenville, who, being now discarded by her husband, she thought would eagerly embrace her cause; but from the "Delicate Investigation" directed by them during the administration of "All the Talents," they had become aware of the perils to which any intimacy with her might lead, and they kept themselves at a dignified distance from all her intrigues. Brougham, who had still his fortune to make, could hardly be expected to be so squeamish. He put forth all his great powers of pleasing, and soon firmly established himself in her confidence; and for the present he was perfectly contented with the distinction which he enjoyed as first law-adviser to the Princess of Wales, and the certainty that ere long he must be Attorney-General to the Queen of England, the reign of George III. being already the longest in our annals, and, from the enfeebled state of his bodily as well as of his mental health, being likely very soon to close.

Court favor no adherent of Caroline could hope for under George IV., but from the irregular life which His Majesty had led, the general expectation (afterwards verified) was that the space of time he would occupy the throne in his own right would be brief, and Brougham had the brilliant prospect of another reign looming in the distance; for he had won the confidence of the youthful Charlotte of Wales, next heir to the monarchy. This hopeful Princess was then residing with a separate establishment under a governess, in Warwick House, having leave rarely, and with severe restrictions, to visit her mother, who occupied a mansion in Connaught Place. On these occasions opportunity was taken to praise Mr. Brougham in her hearing as one of the greatest of lawyers as well as of orators, and she was taught to look upon him with kindness as the adviser, friend, and protector of her mother. The sad differences between her parents it had been impossible to conceal from her, and although she spoke and tried to think respectfully of her father, she was naturally inclined to take her mother's side, and she complained bitterly of the restraints under which she lived, making Warwick House little better than imprisonment in the Tower of London. However, all went on without any public disclosure till the proposal was made, and, notwithstanding her declared antipathy, pressed upon her, that she should marry the Prince of Orange.

At last in the month of July, 1814, all her attendants being suddenly changed, she became alarmed lest there should be an intention to force her inclinations; and one fine evening, as twilight was thickening, she made her escape all alone from Warwick House, ran along the pavement unnoticed, amidst a crowd of foot-passengers, to Charing Cross, then jumped into a hackney coach, and, with the aid of a promised bribe, drove rapidly to Connaught Place. Her mother was from home, having gone to pass the day at Blackheath. The princess sent a messenger for Miss Elphinstone, who had been her playmate, and for Mr. Brougham, whose advice she intended to solicit. When Mr. Brougham arrived he found her with Miss Elphinstone. He implored her to return immediately to Warwick House, so that her flight might not be publicly known. She expressed a determined resolution that she would not voluntarily again submit to captivity. While this discussion was going on her mother returned, accompanied by Lady Charlotte Lindsay. The debate was resumed, and Caroline (to her honor) concurred in the recommendation of immediate return to Warwick House, but Charlotte became more violent in her refusal. Brougham laid down the law to her, explaining how, in the reign of George II., all the judges had signed an opinion that, by virtue of the prerogative, the reigning sovereign has a right to control the custody and education of all the branches of the royal family during their minority. While he was yet speaking, in came Lord Chancellor Eldon, the Duke of York, and the Duke of Sussex, who had all arrived at the same moment, in different hackney coaches, from distant parts of the town. The Princess Charlotte's escape being discovered, she had been traced to Connaught Place, and messengers had been sent off in all directions to those who, it was supposed, had authority or influence over her. She at last yielded to the reiterated remonstrances and entreaties of those who now surrounded her. But before she would consent to return she directed the following declaration to be drawn up, which she dictated, and which was signed by all present :—

"I am resolved never to marry the Prince of Orange. If it shall be seen that such a match is announced, I wish this my declaration to be borne in mind, that it will be a marriage against my will. And I desire that my uncle, the Duke of Sussex, and Mr. Brougham, will particularly take notice of this."

Day now began to dawn. It so happened that an election for the city of Westminster was going forward, so that the mob were beginning to collect, and to shout out the names of the popular candidates. Brougham, according to his own account,[1] then led his youthful princess into a balcony, from which could be seen streets, and a square, and the parks at a distance, and thus addressed her :—

"I have only to show your Royal Highness a few hours later, on the spot where you now stand, and all the people of this vast metropolis would be gathered together on that place with one common feeling in your behalf; but the triumph of one hour must be dearly purchased by the consequences which must assuredly follow in the next— when the troops would pour in, and quell all resistance to the clear and undoubted law of the land with the certain effusion of blood; nay, your Royal Highness should know that through the rest of your life, you never would escape the odium, which in this country always attends those who, by breaking the law, occasion such calamities."

"This consideration," says Lord Brougham, in conclud-

[1] Edinburgh Review, vol. lxvii., 35.

ing his narrative of the royal elopement, "much more than any quailing of her dauntless spirit, or faltering of her filial affection, is believed to have weighed upon her mind, and induced her to return home."

Between four and five she reached Warwick House, in the care of her governess. All the inhabitants of the metropolis were informed at breakfast, by the morning journals, of her nocturnal ramble; but the part which Mr. Brougham acted in it remained unknown till after the death of both mother and daughter, when he published it to the world.

The Regent ought now to have been one of the most applauded princes who ever sat upon the throne. After the overthrow of Napoleon he received a visit from the Emperors of Austria and Russia, the King of Prussia, and many other foreign potentates; and Louis XVIII. returning to France declared that he owed his restoration to the Regent. But all this profited him nothing while Caroline was in England ready at any moment to cross his path, like his evil genius. His great object was to drive her abroad, and this he accomplished by refusing to receive at court any one who associated with her, and by resorting to every expedient by which he could annoy her. Caroline declared that she was afraid if she further opposed his wishes upon this point her life would not be safe, and that she even trembled for the life of her child. Brougham tells us that he considered this a device of the Regent to induce her to leave the protection of the English nation, and to live in foreign countries where she might commit some indiscretion, and where at any rate there would be no difficulty in procuring witnesses to convict her of offenses which might lead to her degradation. "Therefore it was," said Brougham, in a speech delivered in 1820 during the parliamentary inquiry into her conduct, "that foreseeing all these fatal consequences of a foreign residence, years ago I told her and her illustrious daughter, in a letter yet extant, how willingly I would answer with my head for the safety of both in this country; but how impossible it was to feel safe for an hour if either should go abroad, abandoning the protection which the character of the people, still more than the justice of the law in England, throws around all its inhabitants."

It is well known that in 1814 she did leave England for

her travels in Germany, Italy, and the Holy Land, which afterwards became so disgustingly notorious. Brougham still corresponded with her, and was regarded as her representative. The rumors of her misconduct reached him, and seem to have made a very deep impression upon his mind. In 1819 it was known that a commission, sent to Milan under Mr. Cooke, the Chancery Barrister, had been diligently employed in collecting evidence against her; and it was stoutly asserted that proofs were forthcoming which would effectually bar her claim to mount the throne. A proposal was then made to Lord Liverpool by Mr. Brougham, on her behalf (but, as he always asserted, without her authority), that her then income of £35,000 a year should be secured to her for her life, instead of terminating on the demise of George III., as provided by the Act of Parliament by which it was conferred, and that she should undertake, upon that arrangement being made, to reside permanently abroad, and never to assume the rank or title of Queen of England. The government only replied that there would be no indisposition at the proper time to entertain the principle on which the proposal was grounded, if it met with the approbation of Her Royal Highness. The negotiation, however, went no farther while George III. survived. Enemies of Brougham suggested that he wished to gain favor with the Regent by bringing about such a treaty; but my sincere and firm conviction is that he would at no time have advised her to accept any terms that he did not consider for her advantage. From his conduct I infer that he then concluded, giving faith to statements which he had heard, that it would be more prudent to compromise her rights than to insist upon them, and that it was better to submit to violent suspicion than to clear proof of guilt. Her subsequent indignant refusal of more favorable terms corroborates his assertion that the proposal was made without her authority, and only leaves him liable to the charge of rashness and presumption in offering, without her authority, for £35,000 a year to surrender her throne and her character. The proposal gave great satisfaction and confidence to the Regent and his Ministers, who, armed with the supposed discoveries of the Milan Commission, thought that when the time for action arrived they must be able to dictate their own terms of degradation.

At last, on the 29th of January, 1820, died George III., and Caroline was *de jure* Queen of Great Britain. It is curious that while, by the law and constitution of this country, the status of the consort of a Queen Regnant is entirely *ignored*, the rights and privileges of the Consort of a King Regnant are most elaborately and minutely defined. If he is a foreigner, the Consort of a Queen Regnant, instead of wearing the crown matrimonial, lives amongst us merely as a naturalized alien, with such precedence as the Queen may think fit to give him; but still a commoner, liable to serve in the House of Commons and to perform the duties of a parish constable, or any other office which may devolve upon a commoner. But the moment George IV. was King, Caroline, although still a subject, was the first subject in the realm, to be addressed as "Her Majesty the Queen," with power of appointing her Attorney and Solicitor-General to represent her in all the King's courts, being entitled to *Queen's silver* towards her maintenance, and all her wants being foreseen and provided for, down to her royal stays, which, by the law and constitution of England, were to be stiffened by the bones of any whale wrecked or caught on the English shore.

One of these rights, according to the best authorities, was that the Queen Consort should have the prayers of the Church, her name being introduced into the liturgy for that purpose along with that of her royal husband. This, however, was denied by George IV. and his Ministers, and the first act of the new reign was to direct, very properly, that Caroline should no longer be prayed for as Princess of Wales, and very improperly that a new form of prayer for the Royal Family should be used, from which her name was entirely excluded. The ultimate consequence of this rash proceeding was the "Queen's Trial," which brought such disgrace upon King and Queen, which disgusted the whole world, and which nearly brought about a revolution in this country.

Caroline was sojourning in Italy, when she accidentally learned from the public journals that she had become Queen, and that her name was excluded from the liturgy. She complained loudly, not only of the Government, but of her representative, Mr. Brougham, who had declined the preceding autumn to meet her on the Continent, and had omitted to send dispatches to inform her of her new position. Nevertheless, she soon renewed her correspondence with him, and exercised her prerogative as Queen, by appointing him her Attorney-General. On his recommendation, she likewise appointed his friend, Mr. Denman, her Solicitor-General.

On the first day of Easter Term following, Lord Chief Justice Ellenborough, who had conducted the Delicate Investigation, in 1806, and who had a very great dislike to Caroline and all connected with her, was obliged to say to them in open court, according to the ancient formula:—

"Her Majesty the Queen, having been pleased to appoint you her Attorney and Solicitor-General, you will take your places within the bar, with the rank belonging to your offices."[1]

An unaccountable delay arose in taking any further proceedings to determine the Queen's position, each side thinking it prudent to wait till the other should make a new move. At last, on the 15th of April, Lord Liverpool transmitted to Mr. Brougham a proposal to be communicated to Her Majesty, which, after reciting that the allowance of £35,000. a year to her had ceased by the demise of the Crown, stated that the King was willing to recommend to Parliament to settle upon her an annuity of £50,000 a year for life, provided she would engage not to come into any part of the British dominions, and provided she engaged to take some other name or title than that of Queen, and not to exercise any of the rights or privileges of Queen, *other than with respect to the appointment of law officers.*

A mystery now arose, which never has been and never will be cleared up: Mr. Brougham having received this proposal, did not communicate it to the Queen, and left the Government in the belief, that he would obtain an answer to it with all convenient speed. When questioned upon the subject in Parliament, he declared that his parliamentary and professional avocations at that season of the year rendered it impossible for him to carry it in person to Rome, where the Queen then was, that he could not safely trust it to other hands, and that he considered that the Government could be in no hurry for an answer,

[1] I well remember the sarcastic smile with which this speech was accompanied.

or they would have resorted to some other channel of communication with her Majesty. She wrote a letter to Lord Liverpool, as first Minister of the Crown, complaining of her name being left out of the liturgy, and of the neglect and ill-usage she experienced, and announced her intention of speedily arriving in England to assert her rights. This dreadfully alarmed her husband, who insisted that if she persevered in her threat, she should, as soon as she set foot on English ground, be arrested, committed to the Tower, and brought to trial for high treason. He further urged upon his Ministers that, if she should prevent this prosecution by remaining on the Continent, a bill should immediately be introduced into Parliament to degrade her from her royal state and dignity, and to dissolve the marriage between him and the object of his detestation. They pointed out to him, that the precedents of Anne Boleyn and Katharine Howard did not apply; for their lovers were guilty of high treason, their offense having been committed within the Statute of Treasons (25 Edw. III.), were guilty, as *accomplices* in that treason; but that Bergami, an alien, and owing no allegiance to the English Crown, could not be guilty of any crime against the law of England, by any act committed by him in a foreign land, and, therefore, that the Queen could not be guilty as an accomplice with him. With respect to the proposed bill, his Majesty was reminded of the great difficulty of proving satisfactorily by foreign witnesses, the alleged adulterous intercourse; to his utter horror, he was told that she would certainly attempt to recriminate, and that if she succeeded, the divorce might be withheld; in very delicate terms, allusion was made to the manner in which she had been first received by her husband, and of the manner in which she had been turned adrift by him; the scandal which the investigation would create, was strongly dwelt upon by the decorous Lord Liverpool; and Lord Castlereagh, though one of the most stout-hearted of men, declared that he looked forward with fear and trembling to the sympathy which might be expressed in her favor, notwithstanding the clearest evidence of her guilt. The King was in a fury, and talked of changing his Ministers; but Sir John Leach stood alone in advising him to pursue violent measures. Lord Wellesley and the leading Tories out of office, spoke the same language as his cabinet.

Pride precluded him from applying to the Whigs whom
he had deserted; and he said he knew, that out of spite
to him they were all ready to rally round the Queen. He
was obliged reluctantly to yield, and to consent to this
compromise, that, all notion of a prosecution for high
treason being dropped, there should be no parliamentary
proceeding against her, provided she would agree to reside
abroad on the terms proposed to her; but that if she
should come to England to demand her rights, a bill
should be introduced at any risk, to dissolve the marriage,
and to degrade her from her *status* as Queen. From the
tardiness of her proceedings hitherto since her legal rights
accrued, and from the proposal which had been previously
made by her chief law adviser (supposed not to have been
without her privity), Ministers were sanguine in the expectation that when the crisis arrived, she would shrink
from the threatened investigation. But they did not
sufficiently calculate upon her indomitable spirit, which,
whether arising from conscious innocence or not, was
ready to disregard all consequences in asserting her right
to be the crowned Queen of England.

By a letter of hers from Rome, detailing her wrongs,
which was published in all the journals, a strong sympathy
in her favor had been excited in the public mind; and she
now believed that, availing herself of this sympathy, she
might come and dictate her own terms. Accordingly, she
began her journey from Italy, with the avowed purpose of
confronting her husband at St. James's. She made a stop
at Geneva, and invited Mr. Brougham to meet her there;
but he suggested that some place nearer England would
be more convenient, and St. Omer was fixed upon. It
was arranged, that here there should be a conference, with
a view to an amicable arrangement. Accordingly, Lord
Hutchinson on the part of the King, and Mr. Brougham
on the part of the Queen, left London, and traveled together to St. Omer,—where, on the 3rd of June, they
found Queen Caroline. Mr. Brougham immediately
waited upon her Majesty, and informed her that Lord
Hutchinson had come in the spirit of sincere friendship,
to make some proposals to her in his Majesty's name.
She replied that she would be happy to see him; and
Lord Hutchinson was accordingly introduced to her.
But at this interview nothing occurred beyond conver-

sation on indifferent subjects. The King's negotiator, it seems, expected that an overture was to come from the other side, or that an answer was at last to be given to Lord Liverpool's proposal, which had been communicated to the Queen's Attorney-General. In the course of the same day, the following note was transmitted to Lord Hutchinson:—

"Mr. Brougham having humbly submitted to the Queen, that he had reason to believe that Lord Hutchinson had brought over a proposition from the King to her Majesty,—the Queen has been pleased to command Mr. Brougham to request Lord Hutchinson to communicate any such proposition as soon as possible, in writing. June 4, 1820."

Lord Hutchinson's answer, after stating that he was not authorized to make an offer in any specific form of words, went on to say:—

"His Majesty's Ministers propose that £50,000 per annum should be settled on the Queen for life, subject to such conditions as the King may impose. I have also reason to know that the conditions likely to be imposed by His Majesty are, that the Queen is not to assume the style and title of Queen of England, or any title belonging to the Royal Family. A condition is also to be attached to this grant, that she is not to reside in any part of the United Kingdom, or even to visit England. The consequence of such a visit will be an immediate message to Parliament and an entire end to all compromise and negotiation. The decision, I may say, is taken to proceed against her as soon as she sets foot on the British shores."

The very instant the Queen had read this epistle she ordered post horses, and she drove off for Calais with the utmost possible speed. Mr. Brougham was not answerable for the determined resolution she had formed, and he was not conscious that she was gone till he saw from a window in the hotel her carriage hastening away. The moment that she reached Calais she hurried on board an English packet boat in the harbor, from an apprehension that if she remained on shore difficulties might he thrown in the way of her embarkation. The following day she landed at Dover, amidst the plaudits of an immense multitude, who had assembled on the beach to welcome her, and she pursued her journey in a triumphal procession to London.

Brougham was severely but inconsistently blamed for the result of this negotiation. He was charged by the King's friends with causing the rupture that he might take advantage of the popularity which now attended the Queen's cause. On the other hand, the enthusiastic partisans of the Queen not only accused him of lukewarmness but of treachery, asserting that he wished to have brought about a compromise dishonorable to the Queen, with a view to "curry favor with the King." Such suspicions actually entered the mind of the Queen herself. She now put herself entirely under the guidance of Alderman Wood, who went by the *sobriquet* of Absolute Wisdom. Apartments in a royal palace being denied to her, she lodged in his house in South Audley-street, and he stood by her as her Lord Chamberlain when she received deputations and addresses, which poured in upon her from all parts of the kingdom. By his advice she made an attempt to supersede Brougham as her chief legal adviser, and Mr. Scarlett (afterwards Lord Abinger), then the most eminent advocate at the English bar, was applied to; but he declined the honor, and the Aldermanic council resolved that Brougham should continue as her Attorney-General, ostensibly to conduct her affairs, but that Mr. Wilde (afterwards Lord Chancellor Truro), then rising into practice at the common-law bar, should be associated with him. In this gentleman Alderman Wood very properly placed implicit confidence, for he was strictly honorable, sincere, and disinterested. It was vulgarly said that he was a spy upon Brougham, but I believe that they, along with Mr. Denman, the Queen's Solicitor-General, always acted cordially and harmoniously, with the undivided object of doing what they considered most for the advantage of their royal mistress.

They were speedily called into action, for the very day of the Queen's arrival in London a message was brought down from the King to both Houses of Parliament, communicating certain papers sealed up in a green bag, respecting the conduct of her Majesty, which he recommended to their immediate and serious attention, observing:—"That he felt the most anxious desire to avert the necessity of disclosures and discussions which must be as painful to his people as to himself: but that the step now taken by the Queen left him no alternative."

A lively debate arose in the House of Commons upon the negotiations of St. Omer, and the terms offered to the Queen were denounced as unjust, cruel, and insulting. Brougham was in his place, but he contented himself with complaining of an imperfect statement which had appeared in the newspapers, professing to narrate the transactions in which he had borne a part, and of the publication of Lord Hutchinson's letter, attributing this to "a breach of confidence which he was at a loss to account for." The common opinion had been that he himself had communicated the letter to the newspapers. From its harsh and unguarded phraseology it had deeply roused the public indignation, and operated powerfully in the Queen's favor. At that time the fact was not known that Brougham himself had spontaneously proposed nearly the same terms on her behalf when Princess of Wales.

It is impossible to deny that hitherto his conduct in this affair had been wavering, mysterious, and suspicious. Henceforth he proceeded in an open, bold, and skillful manner, so as to rescue the Queen from the destruction to which she seemed to be doomed, to make the King tremble on his throne, and to gain for himself immortal renown.

The plan of the Government was to hurry on the prosecution as rapidly as possible, and to stun the nation by the immediate explosion of the green bag. The following day was fixed for moving, in the House of Commons, an address to the King, thanking him for his gracious message; but before the debate began Mr. Brougham read to the House of Commons the following communication which he had composed:—

"The Queen thinks it necessary to inform the House of Commons, that she has been induced to return to England in consequence of the measures pursued against her honor and her peace for some time past by secret agents abroad, and lately sanctioned by the conduct of the Government at home; and that in adopting this course, her Majesty has had no other purpose whatsoever, but the defense of her character, and the maintenance of those just rights, which have devolved upon her by the death of that revered monarch, in whose high honor and unshaken affection she had always found her surest support.

"Upon her arrival, the Queen is surprised to find that a message has been sent down to Parliament, requiring its attention to written documents; and she learns with still greater astonishment that there is an intention of proposing that these should be referred to a secret committee. It is this day fourteen years since the first charges were brought forward against her Majesty. Then, and upon every occasion during that long period, she has shown the utmost readiness to meet her accusers, and to court the fullest inquiry into her conduct. She now also desires an open investigation, in which she may see both the charges and the witnesses against her—a privilege not denied to the meanest subject of the realm.

"In the face of the sovereign, the Parliament, and the country, she solemnly protests against the formation of a secret tribunal to examine documents privately prepared by her adversaries, as a proceeding unknown to the law of the land, and a flagrant violation of all the principles of justice; she relies with full confidence upon the integrity of the House of Commons for defeating the only attempt she has any reason to fear.

"The Queen can not forbear to add, that, even before any proceedings were resolved upon, she has been treated in a manner too well calculated to prejudge her cause. The omission of her name in the Liturgy, the withholding the means of conveyance usually afforded to all the branches of the Royal Family, the refusal even of an answer to her application for a place of residence in the royal mansions, and the studied slights, both of English ministers abroad, and of the agents of all foreign powers over whom the English Government has any influence, must be viewed as measures designed to prejudice the world against her, and could only have been justified by trial and conviction."

Lord Castlereagh having then moved that the papers in the green bag should be referred to a Select Committee to report their observations thereupon to the House, Mr. Brougham delivered a very able and dexterous speech, evidently betraying apprehension of the evidence which might be adduced against the Queen, and having for its object, by alarming the opposite side, to obtain delay and a compromise on advantageous terms. Having pointed out the unfairness of prejudicing the case by the report of a committee which the prosecutor had named, to be founded upon garbled documents which the prosecutor might think fit to lay before them, he thus glanced at the nature of the inquiry on which the Government proposed to enter:—

"Not merely was the Queen's character at stake—not merely must the treatment she had received be investigated, but all the private history of all those exalted individuals to whom she was related, might be forced into the conflict. He must be a sagacious man who could pretend to describe the course which the inquiry might take—who could assert what steps men bound by professional ties to regard nothing but the safety of their client, might think it necessary to recommend. He must be a bold man who would say, that if he were in the situation of a professional adviser of the Queen, he would hesitate one moment in securing his client at any desperate expense. The advocate has only one point to look to. He is ruined, disgraced, degraded—he may render himself fit to be at the head of a Milan Commission—if he regards the fatal consequences to others which may arise from obtaining '*a good deliverance*' for the accused party he has undertaken to defend. He must be a bolder man still who would rashly plunge this country into a state of irritation and confusion, while there remains a possibility of amicable adjustment. For God's sake—for the sake of all who are honorable and just—for the sake of those whose memories may deceive them, whose wishes may mislead, whose blindness may beguile them—for the sake of the wives and daughters of all who love decency and morality, and who recollect when but a few years since, the opening of a newspaper was regarded with fear and disgust by the father of every modest and well-conducted family'—I call upon the House to pause, only to pause, to ascertain if it be not yet possible to escape from this threatened calamity. The Queen thinks it necessary for the clearing of her own honor, that the inquiry should be persisted in to the end; she shrinks not from it; she courts it; she is prepared to meet it; she comes from safety into—I will not say *jeopardy*, because the innocent in this land of law and liberty can know no jeopardy—but trouble, vexation, and anxiety—to go through this painful, and in my view, odious and frightful

[1] Alluding, I presume, to the parliamentary inquiry respecting the Duke of York and Mrs. Clarke.

investigation. I have the honor of being a servant of her Majesty; I have also the honor of being a member of this House. As her Majesty's servant, I would not disobey her commands, and where her honor is at stake, I would do my best to defend it; but, in the upright performance of my duty in this House, I feel called upon even to thwart her Majesty's inclination, and I would tell her—'Madam, if negotiation yet be possible, rather go too far, and throw yourself upon your country, and upon Parliament for your vindication, than not go far enough: if yet it be possible to avert the ruin which threatens the nation, your honor being safe, be ready to sacrifice all besides.' If I might advise those who stand in a similar situation with respect to the King, I would say to them—'act like honest men, and disregard all consequences—tender that counsel to your sovereign which the case demands, and do not fear that Parliament will betray you, or the country desert you. Do not apprehend that even political calamity will attend you; for if successors must be appointed to your places, be sure that they will not be found within these walls.'"

This speech made a deep impression, which was strengthened by Mr. Canning's chivalrous declaration in favor of the Queen; and Mr. Wilberforce, observing that nothing but the absolute despair of any reconciliation or adjustment would induce him to abandon the course which he now felt it his duty to adopt, moved, with a view to renewed negotiation, an adjournment of the debate. This was carried by acclamation.

Two days were spent in waiting to see from which side the overture was to come, the King and Queen having respectively declared that each must first know what the other offered. At last her Majesty's resolution yielded to the strong remonstrances of her legal advisers, and the following note was transmitted on her behalf to Lord Liverpool:—

"The Queen commands Mr. Brougham to inform Lord Liverpool that she has directed her most serious attention to the declared sense of Parliament, as to the propriety of some amicable adjustment of existing differences being attempted; and submitting to that high authority with the gratitude due to the protection she has always received from it, her Majesty no longer waits for a communication from the Ministers of the Crown, but commands

Mr. Brougham to announce her own readiness to consider any arrangement that can be suggested, consistent with her dignity and honor. 9th June, 1820."

An answer was immediately received, referring the Queen to the memorandum delivered to Mr. Brougham by Lord Liverpool on the 15th of April. The Queen's reply by Mr. Brougham stated the extraordinary fact that this proposal was only then for the first time communicated to her, the reason assigned being that it appeared to have been superseded by the mission of Lord Hutchinson to St. Omer. After some further correspondence, in which it was laid down on the behalf of the Queen that the recognition of her rank and privileges as Queen must be the basis of any admissible arrangement, it was agreed that two of his Majesty's confidential servants, in concert with the like number of persons to be named by the Queen, should frame an arrangement to be submitted to his Majesty, for settling the necessary particulars of her Majesty's future situation. Accordingly, the Duke of Wellington and Lord Castlereagh on behalf of the King, and Mr. Brougham and Mr. Denman on behalf of the Queen, met at the Foreign Office and held five conferences, of which formal protocols were made and signed by the plenipotentiaries.

Little progress was ever made in the negotiation, and it finally broke off on the refusal to restore the Queen's name to the liturgy,—a condition demanded as a *sine qua non* to her consenting to reside abroad. The truth was that ministers had gone too far now to concede this point without a confession of wrongful conduct to her, and this confession would have been very injurious to themselves, as well as to the dignity of their master. At the same time the public voice had become so strong in support of the Queen, that she and her advisers concluded that she was safe, whatever evidence might be adduced against her.

"All men said, if blame there was, a far larger share of it fell on her royal husband than on herself. When it was found that he, the wrong-doer, was resolved to visit upon his victim the consequences of his own offenses—when it was known that he whose whole life since his marriage, had been a violation of his marriage vows, was determined to destroy his consort after deserting and ill-using her—and when it was announced that his design was to obtain a release from the nuptial ties which had never for an hour held him fast, on the pretense of the party so deeply injured by his inconstancy and his oppression having at length fallen into the snares set for her,—the public indignation knew no bounds, and all the people with one voice exclaimed against a proceeding so indecently outraging every principle of humanity and of justice. Whether the facts alleged were true or false, the people never gave themselves a moment's trouble to inquire; and if the whole case should be confessed, or should be proved, it was quite the same thing; he who had done the wrong had no right to take advantage of it, and if any one title of the charges made had been admitted by the party accused, the people were resolved to stand between her and her persecutor's injustice." [1]

The Select Committee of the Lords to whom the green bag was referred, having reported that the charges against the Queen ought to become the subject of solemn inquiry, which might best be effected in the course of a legislative proceeding, Lord Liverpool introduced "A Bill to deprive her Majesty Queen Caroline Amelia Elizabeth of the title, prerogatives, rights, and privileges of Queen Consort of this realm, and to dissolve the marriage between his Majesty and the said Caroline Amelia Elizabeth." The bill was immediately read a first time, and a copy of it ordered to be sent to her Majesty. Next day she presented a petition that her counsel should forthwith be heard against the principle of the bill, and the mode of proceeding adopted. An order was accordingly made that counsel should be called on, and Mr. Brougham appeared at the bar.

Being informed by the Lord Chancellor in pursuance of a previous resolution of the House that he must now confine himself to "the mode and manner of proceeding to be had on the bill, and the time when those proceedings should take place," he addressed the peers in a tone of defiance, and poured out sarcasms against them, to which they had been previously little accustomed, but with which, before the trial was over, he rendered them familiar. A little specimen must suffice for the present:—

"It has been argued, I am informed, by the promoters

[1] Introduction to Lord Brougham's Speeches, published by him, 1838. Vol. i., p. 88.

of this bill, that my illustrious client is to be dealt with as if she were the lowest, not the highest, subject in the realm. God grant that she were in the situation of the lowest subject in the realm. God grant that she had never risen to a higher rank than the humblest individual who owed allegiance to his Majesty. She would then have been fenced round by the triple fence whereby the law of England guards the life and honor of the poorest female. Before such a bill could have been introduced against any other individual, there must have been a sentence of divorce in the Consistory Court, there must have been a verdict of a jury who might have sympathized with her feelings, who, being taken from the same rank of life as herself, and knowing that the evidence produced against her might under similar circumstances be produced against their wives and daughters, would have been influenced by a desire to guard against a common danger. There would then have been among her judges none who were the servants of her husband, for her counsel would have had the right of challenging all such—none who were hired by him during his pleasure—none who were placed in a situation to feel gratitude for the past or expectation for the future favors which he had it in his power to bestow. She would have been tried by twelve honest, impartial, and disinterested Englishmen,—at whose doors the influence which may act upon her present judges might agitate for years, without making the slightest impression either upon the hopes or the fears which it was calculated to excite. She has, therefore, good cause to lament that she is not the lowest subject of his Majesty, and I can assure your Lordships that she would willingly sacrifice everything, except her honor, which is dearer to her than her life, to obtain the poorest cottage which has ever sheltered an Englishwoman from injustice."

He was several times called to order for exceeding the limits prescribed to him, but only to give him a fresh advantage, and at last he thus concluded :—

" With the confidence of injured innocence she flings herself upon the House, and trusts that no mixture of party—no presence of interested persons—no adventitious influence exercised out of doors—no supposed want of sympathy with the feelings of the country—no alleged, though falsely alleged, tendency on the part of your Lordships to truckle to royal favor, will stand between the Queen and justice, or prevent her case from receiving a fair, impartial, and unprejudiced decision."

The House having refused a very reasonable request that the Queen might be furnished with a list of the witnesses to be produced against her, and a specification of the times and places where the offense charged against her was supposed to have been committed, proceeded to the second reading of the bill; but, before receiving evidence, admitted an argument against the principle of the bill, which raised the question whether, even if the preamble could be proved alleging her guilt, this was the fit mode of proceeding against her.

Mr. Brougham attempted to distinguish the present from all other bills of pains and penalties that had ever been introduced into Parliament, and contended that the fit course, if there were to be any proceedings, would have been by suit in the Consistorial Court, or by indictment or by impeachment; but the weapon to which he chiefly trusted was the threat of going into evidence of the King's marriage with Mrs. Fitzherbert before he led Caroline of Brunswick to the altar, and of the profligate life which he had subsequently led, so as to show that according to established principles and uniform practice he was disentitled to ask a divorce:—

"The right of recrimination," said he, "I could not exercise without directly violating the express injunctions of her Majesty; nor is it my purpose to resort to that right, unless driven to it by absolute and overruling necessity. In obedience to the same high command, I lay out of view, as equally inconsistent with my own feelings and those of my client, all other questions respecting the conduct or connections of any parties previous to marriage. These are dangerous and tremendous topics, the consequences of discussing which, at the present moment, I will not even trust myself to describe; but when the necessity arrives an advocate knows but one duty, and, cost what it may, that duty he must discharge. Be the consequences what they may to any other persons, powers, principalities, dominions, or nations, an advocate is bound to do his duty, and I shall not fail to exert every means in my power to put a stop to the progress of this bill. I will appeal to the spirit of holiness, and to the heads of the

Church now ranged before me, whether adultery is to be considered only a crime in woman. Whether all of us, nearer to the object, do or do not see through the flimsy pretext—be assured that the good sense of the nation can not be deceived, and that those at a distance will be both shocked and astonished. In their homely language, they will assert that it is an attempt to accomplish one purpose under the color of another. 'Here is a man,' they will say, 'who wishes to get rid of his wife; he talks of the honor and safety of the country, yet its dearest interests, its peace, its morals, and its happiness are to be sacrificed to gratify his desires.' I shall think it likewise fit to remind your Lordships that it is provided by your Lordships' Standing Orders that the husband who applies for a divorce shall personally attend the House, in order that he may be examined before the divorce is granted, in order to show that there is no collusion, that he himself stands *rectus in curia*, and that he himself, having always acted as a kind and faithful husband, is entitled to a dissolution of the marriage by reason of the infidelity of his wife."

The Attorney and Solicitor-General having spoken on the other side, it was plain from the undisguised favor with which they were listened to that a large majority of the Lords were still ready to support the bill, and that the trial must proceed. Mr. Brougham, in his reply, therefore chiefly applied himself to discredit, by anticipation, the witnesses who were to be examined. It was known that they were chiefly Italians; that they had been brought over to this country by agents of the Government; that many of them were in a low condition of life; that several of them had been newly clothed at the public expense; that they were kept together in one large dormitory, and fed at a common table. Said Mr. Brougham:—

"If the prosecution is to proceed, we must suppose that the charges are to be substantiated by witnesses above all suspicion. My impression is, that they must be persons of exalted station, or at least looking in their exterior like those persons with whom your Lordships are accustomed to associate. This respectable external appearance they rejoice in, I doubt not, *proprio marte*. They must be seized in fee simple of those decent habiliments in which it will be fitting that they should appear before your Lordships, and those, too, purchased out of their own ample revenues. I suppose they must be persons who can regale themselves at their own expense—who can live in separate apartments, and can fare sumptuously every day. They surely can not be persons who are called together by the ringing of a bell, or the beating of a drum to a common meal, provided at the expense of others. At least, they must have full liberty of locomotion, and when they go abroad no other individual will be seen attending them, or watching their motions, but their own *lacquais de place*. To meet a cloud of such witnesses must be enough to appal any man."

The trial proceeded and the first witness was Teodoro Majocchi, postilion to General Pino. If his evidence in chief was believed, he proved abundantly enough to establish the guilt of the Queen, but he entirely broke down when cross-examined by Mr. Brougham; and to a long succession of questions respecting matters of which he must have had a lively recollection, the only answer to be obtained from him was "*Non mi ricordo,*" which passed into, and still continue, " household words," in England for denoting *mendacity*.

The case for the prosecution was not closed till the 9th of September. The Queen's Attorney-General all the while preserved his ascendency, causing dismay by what he did, and still more by what he threatened to do. In alluding to the King, his object was to say what should be most cutting and alarming, without giving an opportunity, decently, to call him to order on the ground that he was transgressing the limits to be allowed to an advocate, and wantonly insulting his sovereign. He claimed the right of considering this as a *divorce suit*, the promoter of which was the husband. To deprive counsel of the license which this view of the proceeding might be supposed to give, the other side contended that the bill was a public measure of the Government for the safety of the State. On one occasion, in replying to an argument of the Attorney-General to this effect, he said:—

"After the assertion of my learned friend, I am bound to believe that this measure is not to gratify the wishes of the King, and that his Majesty looks on with indifference, solicitous only that 'right be done.' But who, then, is the prosecutor? What is this mysterious being—

> '———that shape hath none
> Distinguishable in member, joint, or limb;
> Or substance may be called which shadow seems.
> ——— what seems his head
> The likeness of a kingly crown has on.' "[1]

Brougham had a prodigious advantage in the inefficiency of Gifford the Attorney-General, who, although an acute lawyer, had received an imperfect education, was ignorant of foreign languages, customs, and manners, and from a sense of his defects was diffident, timorous, and easily cowed. Copley, the Solicitor-General, on the other hand, whose University education had been followed by foreign travel, and who was by nature bold and pugnatious, supported the royal cause with such energy as sometimes to give his client confident hope of ultimate success. His speech in summing up the evidence for the prosecution, was so masterly and made such a deep impression, that Brougham was thrown into sad perplexity as to the course now to be adopted. Afraid to allow this speech to remain unanswered during the interval to be assigned for preparing the Queen's defense, he proposed that he should be allowed forthwith to open his evidence, an adjournment of some weeks following to enable him to adduce it, or that he should be permitted to divide his speech, one half of it commenting upon the evidence already given for the prosecution, to be fired off at once, and the other half, explaining the evidence for the Queen, to be reserved till after the adjournment. But the Lords fairly enough offered him the alternative, to adjourn at the close of the case for the prosecution for as long a period as he should require to prepare fully for the Queen's defense, or to go on continuously without any adjournment till her defense should be closed.

In spite of all the evidence and all the eloquence directed against the Queen, the public voice was declaring itself more and more loudly in her favor, and it was hoped that the increasing agitation would shake the nerves of the King and his Ministers, and induce them, under some decent pretense, to abandon the bill. An adjournment was therefore prayed till the 3rd of October.

[1] This quotation was suggested at the moment by a friend who stood near him. It produced a great sensation. Some Lords afterwards said that he ought to have been committed to Newgate or to the Tower; but the better opinion was that such a step would only have gratified the offender.

Brougham employed a great part of this time in getting up his oration by daylight and by the midnight oil. He boasted much of the pains he had bestowed upon it. The peroration, he says, he wrote over with his own hand seventeen times. He himself considered, and I believe still considers, his performance the most wonderful effort of genius recorded in the annals of oratory; and when listened to in the excitement and suspense which then prevailed, it had very brilliant success; but I must confess that when now read in print, as published by the author, it appears by turns stiff and affected, tame and vapid, turgid and declamatory, swarming with palpable and bad imitations of ancient orators, and altogether much inferior to the unpremeditated ebullitions of invective and sarcasm which he had poured forth in discussions which had arisen in previous stages of the proceedings. Thus he began, and the labored composition might well be mistaken for a schoolboy's translation of the prœmium to an oration of Cicero:—

"The time is now come, my Lords, when I feel I shall truly stand in need of all your indulgence. It is not merely the august presence of this assembly which embarrasses me, for I have oftentimes had experience of its condescension; nor the novelty of this proceeding that perplexes me, for the mind gradually gets reconciled to the strangest things; nor is it the magnitude of this cause that oppresses me, for I am borne up and cheered by that conviction of its justice which I share with all mankind; but, my Lords, it is the very force of that conviction, the knowledge that it operates universally, the feeling that it operates rightly, which now dismays me with the apprehension that my unworthy mode of handling it may for the first time injure it; and while others have trembled for a guilty client, or been anxious in a doubtful case, or crippled with the consciousness of some hidden weakness, or chilled by the influence, or dismayed by the hostility, of public opinion, I, knowing that here there is no guiltiness to conceal, nor anything save the resource of perjury to dread, am haunted with the apprehension, that my feeble discharge of this duty may for the first time cast that cause into doubts, and may turn against me for condemnation those millions of your Lordships' countrymen whose jealous eyes are now watching us, and who will not fail to impute it to me if your Lordships should reverse the judgment which the case for the charge has extorted from them. And I feel, my Lords, under this weight, so troubled, that I can hardly at this moment, with all the reflection which the indulgence of your Lordships has accorded to me, compose my spirits to the discharge of my professional duty, under the weight of that grave responsibility which accompanies it."

Having glanced at the arrival of Caroline of Brunswick in England, in 1795, and her departure for the continent in 1814, he apologizes for not dwelling upon intervening events:—

"I rejoice that for the present at least the most faithful discharge of my duty permits me to draw this veil; but I can not do so without pausing for an instant to guard myself against a misrepresentation to which I know this course may not unnaturally be exposed, and to assure your Lordships most solemnly, that if I did not think that the cause of the Queen, as attempted to be established by the evidence against her, not only does not require recrimination at present, not only requires no duty of even uttering one whisper by way of attack, by way of insinuation, against the conduct of her illustrious husband—but that it prescribes to me, for the present, silence upon this great and painful topic—I solemnly assure your Lordships that, but for this conviction, my lips would freely and boldly, unscrupulously and remorselessly, pour forth all I know respecting it, and all that I should be prepared to prove. In postponing the statement of that case, of which I am possessed, I feel confident that I am waiving a right which I have, and abstaining from the use of materials which are mine. But I feel that if I were now to approach the great subject of recrimination I should seem to give up the higher ground of innocence, on which I rest my cause. I should seem to be *Justifying* when I plead *Not Guilty*. I should seem to argue in extenuation and in palliation of offenses, or levities, or improprieties, the least and the lightest of which I stand here utterly to deny."

The following is the most pathetic part of the speech, describing the ill-usage of the Queen on the occasion of the marriage and the death of her daughter:—

"An event now took place which, of all others, most

excites the feelings of a parent: that daughter was about
to form a union upon which the happiness—upon which,
alas! the Queen knew too well how much the happiness,
or the misery of her future life must depend. No announcement was made to her Majesty of the projected
alliance. All England occupied with the subject—Europe
looking on with an interest which it certainly had in so
great an event; England had it announced to her; Europe
had it announced to her; each petty German prince had
it announced to him; but the one person to whom no
notice of it was given, was the mother of the bride who
was to be espoused. She heard it accidentally by a courier
who was going to announce the intelligence to the Pope—
that ancient, intimate, much-valued ally of the Protestant
Crown of these realms, and with whose close friendship the
title of the Brunswicks to our Crown is so interwoven. A
prospect grateful to the whole nation, interesting to all
Europe, was now afforded, that the marriage would be a
fruitful source of stability to the Royal Family of these
realms. The whole of that period, painfully interesting
to a parent as well as to a husband, was passed without the
slightest communication; and if the Princess Charlotte's
own feelings had prompted her to open one, she was in a
state of anxiety of mind and of delicacy of frame, in consequence of that her first pregnancy, which made it dangerous to have maintained a struggle between power and
authority on the one hand, and affection and duty on the
other. An event most fatal followed, which plunged the
whole of England into grief: one in which all our foreign
neighbors sympathized; and while, with a due regard to
the feelings of those foreign allies, and even of strange
powers and princes with whom we had no alliance, that
event was speedily communicated by particular messengers to each, the person in all the world who had the
deepest interest in the event—the person whose feelings,
above those of all the rest of mankind, were most overwhelmed and stunned by it,—was left to be stunned and
overwhelmed by it accidentally; as she had, by accident,
heard of the marriage. But if she had not heard of the
dreadful event by accident, she would, ere long, have felt
it; for the decease of the Princess Charlotte was communicated to her mother by the issuing of the Milan
Commission, and the commencement of the proceed-

ings, for the third time, against her character and her life."

Occupying two days, during the whole of which he fixed the unflagging attention of his audience, he went over all the instances in which the Queen was supposed to have misconducted herself, analyzing the evidence in support of each, and trying to show either that no unfavorable inference was fairly to be drawn from it, or that the witnesses who gave it were wholly unworthy of credit. He thus powerfully assailed the leader of the band:—

"*Teodoro Majocchi*, of happy memory, will be long known in this country and everywhere else, much after the manner in which ancient sages have reached our day, whose names are lost in the celebrity of the little saying by which each is now distinguished by mankind, and in which they were known to have embodied the practical result of their own experience and wisdom ; and, as long as those words which he so often used in the practice of that art and skill which he had acquired, by long experience and much care—as long as these words should be known among men, the image of Majocchi, without naming him, will arise in their remembrance. My Lords, this person is a witness of great importance ; he was the first called and the latest examined ; continuing by the case and accompanying it throughout. His evidence almost extended over the whole of the period through which the case and the charge itself extends; in fact, only dismissed, or rather retiring, from the Queen's service, and refusing to be taken back, about the time when the charge closed. He and Demont stand aloof from the rest of the witnesses, and resemble each other in this particular, that they go through the whole case. They are, indeed, the great witnesses to prove it ; they are the witnesses for the bill ; the others being confirmatory only of them ; but, as willing witnesses are wont to do—as those who have received much and been promised more—they were zealous on behalf of their employers, and did not stop short of the two main witnesses, but they each carried the case a great deal further. This is, generally, with a view to their relative importance, the character of all the witnesses. . . . I have often heard it remarked, that the great prevailing feature of Majocchi's evidence—his want of recollection—signifies, in truth, but

little; because a man may forget—memories differ. I
grant they do. Memories differ, as well as honesty, in
man. I do not deny that. But I think I shall succeed in
showing your Lordships, that there is a sort of memory
that is utterly inconsistent with any degree of honesty in
any man, which I can figure to myself. But why do I talk
of fancy? for I have only to recollect Majocchi; and
I know cases, in which I defy the wit of man to conceive
stronger or more palpable instances of false swearing, than
may be conveyed to the hearers and to the court, in the
remarkable words, '*Non mi ricordo*'—I do not remember.
I will not detain your Lordships by pointing out cases
where the answer, 'I do not remember,' would be innocent,
where it might be meritorious, where it might be confirmatory of his evidence, and a support to his credit. Neither
need I adduce cases where such an answer would be the
reverse of this—where it would be destructive to his credit,
and the utter demolition of his testimony. I will not quote
any of these cases. I shall content myself with taking the
evidence of Mojocchi as it stands: for if I had been lectur-
ing on evidence, I should have said—as the innocent forgetfulness is familiar to every man, so is the guilty forgetfulness; and in giving an instance, I should have just found it
all in Majocchi's actual evidence. Now, at once, to give
your Lordships proof positive that this man is perjured—
proof I shall show to be positive, from his mode of forgetting. In the first place, I beg your Lordships' attention to
the way in which this witness swore hardily in chief, eke as
hardily in cross-examination, to the position of the rooms
of her Majesty and Bergami. The great object of the
Attorney-General, as shown by his opening, was that for
which the previous concoction of this plan by these witnesses had prepared him; viz., to prove the position of
the Queen's and Bergami's rooms always to have been
favorable to the commission of adultery, by showing that
they were near and had a mutual communication, whereas
the rooms of all the rest of the suite were distant and cut
off; and the second part of that statement was just as essential as the first, to make it the foundation of the inference
of guilt which it was meant to support. Accordingly,
the first witness who was to go over their whole case appears to have been better prepared on this point than any
ten that followed—more inferences—more forgetfulness in

detail—perfect recollection to attack the Queen—utter forgetfulness to protect himself from the sifting of a cross-examination 'Where did the Queen and Bergami sleep?' 'Her Majesty slept in an apartment near that of Bergami.' 'Were those apartments near or remote?' for it was often so good a thing to get them near and communicating with each other, that it was pressed again and again. 'Where were the rest of the suite; were they distant or near?' says the Solicitor-General. This was at Naples; and this is a specimen of the rest—for more was made of that proximity at Naples than anywhere else—'Were they near or distant?' 'They were apart.' The word in Italian was *lontano*, which was interpreted 'apart;' I remarked, however, at the time, that it meant 'distant;' and 'distant' it means, or it means nothing. Here, then, the witness had sworn distinctly from his positive recollection, and had staked his credit on the truth of a fact, and also of his recollection of it—upon this fact, whether or not the Queen's room was near Bergami's, with a communication. But no less had he put his credit upon this other branch of his statement, essential to the first, in order to make both combined the foundation of a charge of criminal intercourse, 'that the rest of the suite were lodged apart and distant.' There is an end, then, of innocent forgetfulness, if, when I come to ask where the rest slept, he either tells me, 'I do not know,' or 'I do not recollect;' because he had known, and must have recollected, that, when he presumed to say to my learned friends, 'these two rooms were alone near and connected, the others were distant and apart;' when he said that, he affirmed his recollection of the proximity of those rooms, and the remoteness of the others. He swore that at first, and afterwards said, 'I know not,' 'I recollect not,' and perjured himself as plainly as if he had told your Lordships one day that he saw a person, and the next day said he never saw him in his life; the one is not a more gross or diametrical contradiction than the other. Trace him, my Lords, in his recollection and forgetfulness—observe where he remembers and were he forgets —and you will find the same conclusion following you everywhere, and forcing the same conviction."

Having commented upon Mademoiselle Demont and several prominent witnesses, male and female, with equal severity, he said:

"My Lords, I take this filthy cargo by sample purposely. Let those who will, delve into the bulk—I will not heave it more. That it is damaged enough the sample tells sufficiently, and with a single remark I dismiss it. I recollect, my Lords, these foolish stories, not only about the hand and about the bracelet-chains being put round her neck, with I know not what other trumpery, got up for the purpose of variegating the thrice-told tale. And your Lordships will, I think, agree with me, that the Italians who coined the fiction are pretty much the same now that they were known to our ancestors to be a few centuries ago. Whether Iachimo be the legitimate offspring of our great Shakespeare's mind or not, may be doubted; but your Lordships will readily recognize more than one of the witnesses, but one especially, as the own brother of Iachimo. How has he represented himself?—

> ——— I have belied a lady,
> The princess of this country, and the air o'nt
> Revengingly enfeebles me—
> ——— mine Italian brain
> 'Gan in your duller Britain operate
> Most vilely; for my vantage excellent;
> And, to be brief, my practice so prevailed,
> That I returned with similar proof, enough
> To make the noble Leonatus mad.'

My Lords, the cases are the same. We have the same evidence, from the same country, and for the same purpose, almost with the same effects; and by the same signs, marks, and tokens, by an extraordinary coincidence, the two cases are sought to be substantiated."

Having touched upon every topic which could be pressed forward in defense of the party accused, and cited with great effect the case of Susannah and the elders, he at last came to the seventeen times rewritten peroration:

"Such, my Lords, is the case now before you! Such is the evidence in support of this measure—evidence inadequate to prove a debt—impotent to deprive of a civil right—ridiculous to convict of the lowest offense—scandalous if brought forward to support a charge of the highest nature which the law knows—monstrous to ruin the honor, to blast the name of an English Queen! What shall I say, then, if this is the proof by which an act of judicial legislation, a parliamentary sentence, an *ex post facto* law, is sought to be passed against this defenseless woman? My

Lords, I pray you to pause. I do earnestly beseech you to take heed! You are standing upon the brink of a precipice—then beware! It will go forth your judgment, if sentence shall go against the Queen. But it will be the only judgment you ever pronounced, which, instead of reaching its object, will return and bound back upon those who give it. Save the country, my Lords, from the horrors of this catastrophe—save yourselves from this peril—rescue that country, of which you are the ornaments, but in which you can flourish no longer, when severed from the people, than the blossom when cut off from the roots and the stem of the tree. Save that country, that you may continue to adorn it—save the Crown, which is in jeopardy—the Aristocracy, which is shaken—save the Altar, which must stagger with the blow that rends its kindred Throne! You have said, my Lords, you have willed—the Church and the King have willed—that the Queen should be deprived of its solemn service. She has instead of that solemnity, the heartfelt prayers of the people. She wants no prayers of mine. But I do here pour forth my humble supplications at the Throne of Mercy, that that mercy may be poured down upon the people, in a larger measure than the merits of its rulers may deserve, and that your hearts may be turned to justice."

He delivered the concluding prayer very solemnly and impressively in the well-remembered attitude of the Presbyterian clergy in Scotland, when they bless the congregation at the conclusion of public worship—raising both his opened palms above his head at the same height, and holding them motionless till his voice ceased.[1]

He tells us that he himself was so satisfied with the effect he had produced on the minds of the judges, that when he had finished he resolved not to permit further addresses on the Queen's behalf, nor to call witnesses to prove her innocence, but at once to demand judgment; nevertheless, by some misunderstanding, Mr. Williams followed on the same side, which rendered it necessary to give evidence, and the proceedings did not terminate till nearly six weeks after.

[1] I have heard him say that the Scotch clergy had been his instructors in oratory, and particularly that he had learned from Dr. Greenfield suddenly to lower his voice when he wished to be distinctly heard, as thereby he arrested attention and procured stillness.

Brougham was greatly oversanguine in his calculation. There can be no doubt that a large majority of the Lords were still prepared to support the bill, and that the Queen's cause gained much from subsequent discussion and from the still rising indignation of the people.

The Bill of Pains and Penalties was finally ruined by a split among its supporters. The Episcopal bench had almost unanimously voted for the second reading; but one half of them had strong scruples about the clause for dissolving the marriage, although they were willing to degrade the Queen from her royal state and dignity—and a considerable number of temporal peers took the same view of the subject—considering marriage as a *quasi* sacrament, and that, at all events, it could not be dissolved for the adultery of the wife, the husband being *in pari delicto*, which without formal evidence adduced by way of recrimination they thought, as conscientious men, they were obliged to take notice of from the notoriety of the fact. The only chance of carrying the bill now was by omitting the divorce clause, and accordingly the Government peers voted for omitting it; but the opposers of the bill voted for retaining the divorce clause, saying that it would be monstrous to condemn the King to remain forever the husband of a wife solemnly convicted of adultery. The divorce clause thus remained part of the bill, and upon the third reading the *anti-divorcians* going over and saying *not content*, the majority was reduced to nine. Lord Liverpool thereupon declared that he could not push such a bill after the opinions of their Lordships upon it seemed to be so equally divided, and he moved, instead of "that this bill do pass," that the further consideration of the bill should be adjourned for six months.

This was clearly the dictate of prudence, for there was not the remotest possibility of being able to carry the measure through the Commons, and the country was on the brink of rebellion.

Brougham, who continued to be present in the House of Lords during all the discussions on the Queen's case, although he was no longer privileged to attend at the bar as her counsel, hurried off to her with the news of the victory, being afraid to break it to her suddenly, lest her emotions should be too powerful. But whether she had anticipated the event, or whether she really never had believed that she was in serious danger, she received the announcement with indifference. Her gratitude to her legal advisers, however, immediately burst out. She said she had £4,000 at her banker's, and she directed her Attorney-General immediately to divide the whole sum between himself and her other counsel, over and above any fees that might be paid to them by the public, on whom all the expenses of the trial, King's and Queen's, were thrown. He respectfully declined her bounty, expressing the high gratification he had enjoyed in assisting to defeat the improper attempt that had been made against her, and assured her Majesty that the same sentiments must be entertained by all the gentlemen with whom he had had the honor to be associated in the glorious task. He adds, as an illustration of the eccentric and incongruous disposition which she sometimes showed, that notwithstanding this trait of munificence she would never pay the salaries of her Attorney or Solicitor-General, and at her death the whole of the arrears were discharged by the Treasury.

In the debate which subsequently took place in the House of Commons respecting the Queen's trial, Brougham made the following declaration :—

"If, instead of an advocate, I had been sitting as a Judge, I should have been found among the number of those who, laying their hands upon their hearts, conscientiously pronounced her NOT GUILTY. For the truth of this assertion I desire to tender every pledge that may be most valued and most sacred. I wish to make it in every form which may be deemed most solemn and most binding; and if I believe it not as I now advance it, I here imprecate on myself every curse which is most horrid and most penal." [1]

This, it will be observed, applies only to the *vote he should have given*, which might well have proceeded on "*not proven,*" the evidence being such as could not with safety be judicially acted upon. But as to his private opinion on her guilt or innocence he remained silent. Although he has talked to me with unbounded license on almost all other subjects, and of almost all other persons, he has never volunteered to tell me what he really thought of the truth of the charge against his royal client, and I could not with any decency ask him his conscientious be-

[1] 4 Hansard, N. S. 503.

lief. Denman, who had about him more enthusiasm than discrimination, used to profess, and I doubt not sincerely, that he considered her "pure as unsunned snow." Brougham's conduct before the trial began can only be justified upon the supposition that he thought there was satisfactory evidence to convict her.[1]

During the trial, although there was no doubt much false swearing against her, there were facts proved by witnesses of credit from which, had she been a woman of sober sense and ordinary regard for the opinions of others, the inference of guilt was almost inevitable. Her chance of a favorable verdict from posterity must depend upon the weight given to the *bizarrerie* (as she called it) which she affected, and to her culpable contempt for appearances. She sometimes talked and acted as if with a view to excite suspicion, when no actual guilt had been incurred. This might be from a love of mystification, without ulterior object, or it might be designedly to take off the effect of evidence which she might apprehend of her being seen in situations which *primâ facie* would prove her guilt. She certainly conferred no credit on her station, and her conduct can only be palliated by the unfortunate circumstances in which she was placed, and the ill-usage which she experienced from her worthless husband. He has been severely punished. Considering the glories of the Regency from Wellington's Peninsular campaigns, the battle of Waterloo, and the transportation of Napoleon to St. Helena, his name might have shone forth with the most distinguished of the Edwards and Henrys; but he is detested as the worst of the Georges—as a selfish voluptuary, whose flagrant vices were unredeemed by a single public or private virtue.

Brougham acquired immense glory and popularity from his defense of the Queen. Denman was said to have stood by her with more sincerity and disinterestedness; but his fame was tarnished by his *go and sin no more*

[1] The attempts that he made to reconcile with her innocence the proposal which he made in 1819, that in consideration of £35,000 a year for life she would always reside abroad and never assume the title of Queen, by pointing out that she then was only Princess of Wales, and might never be Queen, were most futile; and his assertion that he made the offer entirely without her authority, knowledge, or privity, is almost incredible; while, if believed, it convicts him of unexampled temerity. See 4 Hansard, N. S., 495. His conduct as her adviser from the time she went abroad in 1814, till the trial began in 1820, is the most equivocal part of his whole career.

peroration, and Brougham was celebrated as her great deliverer. The freedoms of corporations in gold boxes poured in upon him from all quarters; a splendid candelabra was presented to him, paid by a penny subscription of peasants and mechanics; his bust was carried about for sale in the streets by Italian boys, along with Queen Caroline's; and the *Brougham's Head* became a common sign for beershops.

What was of more importance, his practice at the bar was suddenly increased fivefold. When he next appeared on the Northern Circuit the attorneys crowded round him with briefs, that they might be privileged to converse with Queen Caroline's illustrious advocate. During one whole round of the assizes at York, Durham, Newcastle, Carlisle, Appleby, and Lancaster, crowds came from distant parts to see and listen to him, and the Civil Court and the Crown Court were respectively overflowing or deserted as he appeared in the one or in the other. Here he did not long maintain his ascendency, for Scarlett (afterwards Lord Abinger) and even Pollock (afterwards Lord Chief Baron of the Exchequer) when opposed to him by their superior knowledge of law and *nisi prius* tact easily got the verdict, unless from the overpowering strength of his case there was an impossibility that he should lose it; but ever after, both on the circuit and in London, whenever there was a cause to be tried exciting great popular interest, he was sure to be retained in it. Nevertheless he did not get into regular enployment in the ordinary routine business of the courts; and it used still to be said that whereas Erskine never spoke a word except with a view to the verdict, Brougham, chiefly solicitous about himself, having made a brilliant speech, was rather apathetic as to the event of the trial.

His fame as an advocate, however, now added considerably to his ascendency in the House of Commons. Debates arose, after the Queen's trial, about restoring her name to the liturgy, and about making a provision for her support, in which he took a leading part and successfully assailed the proceedings of the government. He was often taunted about the mysterious part he had acted in the negotiations for the *status* of the unhappy Caroline at the close of the last reign and the beginning of the present; but so bold had he become that he considered it enough

to assert, with an air of defiance and of triumph, that
without her authority he had made the offer, when she
was Princess of Wales, for her to remain abroad for life,
without assuming the title of Queen, in consideration of
an allowance of £35,000 a year; that he had not communicated to her Lord Liverpool's proposal, after she became
Queen, to allow her £50,000 a year on the same conditions; that his reason for this omission was because it was
not convenient to him to go to Geneva in person; that
there was no medium through which the proposal could
be transmitted to her before the interview at St. Omer,
and that he then considered himself superseded as a
negotiator by Lord Hutchinson. In spite of the suspicions secretly entertained or whispered against him, he
was now listened to in public with attention, deference,
and admiration, and he held a position in the House of
Commons equal to that of any Member of it either in
office or in opposition.

The session of 1821 having been brought to a close, the
agitation in favor of Queen Caroline was continued by
her claim to be crowned along with her husband. An
intimation being given that no preparations were to be
made for her to take a part in the ceremony, she petitioned that she might be heard by her Attorney-General
before the Privy Council in support of her right, and he
argued at great length that, although the King must give
the order for the Queen's coronation, he was as much
bound by law to do so as to issue a writ to an hereditary
peer to sit in Parliament. He succeeded in showing that
in a great majority of cases the Queens Consort of England had been crowned along with the King; but, unfortunately, it turned out that in five instances the King had
been crowned alone, with a wife living and then in England. Brougham was so hard pressed as to be obliged to
argue that although there was no proof that Henrietta
Maria was crowned along with Charles I., the event might
have happened without being noticed by heralds or his-
torians, and that the explanations of her absence given by
contemporary writers—from the difficulty of conducting
the ceremony, she being a Roman Catholic—were wholly
to be disregarded. Uniform usage failing, he was driven
to such arguments as these:—

"Doubts may exist as to the validity of a King's

marriage, and as celebrating the coronation of the Consort tends to make the testimony of it public and perpetual, so omitting it, and, still more, the withholding that solemnity, has a tendency to raise suspicions against the marriage, and to cast imputations upon the legitimacy of the issue, contrary to the genius and policy of the law. The Queen Consort's coronation is not so much a right in herself as in the realm; or rather it is a right given to her for the benefit of the realm, in like manner as the King's rights are conferred upon him for the common weal; and hence is derived an answer to the objection that the Queen has always enjoyed it by favor of her Consort, who directs her to be crowned as a matter of grace. The law and constitution of this country are utterly repugnant to any such doctrine as grace or favor from the crown regulating the enjoyment of public rights. The people of these realms hold their privileges and immunities by the same title of law whereby the King holds his crown, with this difference, that the crown itself is only holden for the better maintaining those privileges and immunities."

The claim was unanimously rejected by the Privy Council, and the manner in which it was urged rather turned public opinion against the Queen, for although it might be very fit that she should be prayed for, whatever her character and conduct might have been, the notion of her being exhibited before the people in Westminster Hall by the side of her husband, and that they should be jointly consecrated by the Archbishop of Canterbury with the holy oil, shocked the common sense and right feeling of all.

In making the claim she acted by the indiscreet advice of her Attorney-General; but she injured herself still more by attempting, contrary to his earnest remonstrances, to force her way into Westminster Abbey on the day of the Coronation. She was repulsed amidst the hisses, instead of the plaudits, of the mob, and the mortification she suffered was supposed to have brought on the disorder which, very soon afterwards, suddenly put an end to her melancholy career.—(See Appendix.)

CHAPTER CCXXVI.

FROM THE DEATH OF QUEEN CAROLINE TILL HE BECAME LORD CHANCELLOR.

THE death of Queen Caroline was a heavy blow to Brougham. He not only was lowered in political consequence by losing an instrument of annoyance which he could wield with effect, but it touched him very closely in his profession; for, losing his office of Attorney-General to the Queen, he was obliged to doff his silk gown and full-bottomed wig, and attiring himself again in bombazin and a common tie, to "take his place in court *without* the bar accordingly." George IV. had the pusillanimity to make a personal affair between himself and Brougham and Denman of what had passed during the Queen's trial. Out of revenge for having been compared by them to Nero, he expressed a determined resolution that neither of them should be admitted into the number of his " counsel learned in the law," and that they should be depressed as long and as much as it was in his power to depress them. This resolution, to which he long adhered, till it was finally overcome by the manly representations of the Duke of Wellington, at first annoyed Brougham very much; but the ex-Attorney soon found that, for a time at least, his consequence was rather enhanced by being considered the victim of royal animosity because he had courageously done his duty.

Now he conducted to a successful termination two prosecutions connected with the late Queen, which had been commenced in her lifetime. The first was a criminal information granted by the Court of King's Bench against the Rev. Mr. Blacow for a libelous sermon delivered by him from the pulpit the Sunday after the Queen's procession to St. Paul's to return thanks for her victory over all her enemies. The defendant addressed his congregation in the following terms:—

"After compassing sea and land with her guilty paramour to gratify to the full her impure desires, and even polluting the Holy Sepulchre itself with her presence—to which she was carried in mock majesty astride upon an ass

—she returned to this hallowed soil so hardened with sin, so bronzed with infamy, so callous to every feeling of decency or shame, as to go on Sunday last, clothed in the mantle of adultery, to kneel down at the altar of that God who is 'of purer eyes than to behold iniquity,' when she ought rather to have stood barefooted in the aisle, covered with a shirt as white as the 'unsunned snow,' doing penance for her sins. Till this had been done, I would never have defiled my hands by placing the sacred symbols in hers; and this she would have been compelled to do in those good old days when Church discipline was in pristine vigor and activity."

The rule for the criminal information was granted in the Queen's lifetime on the application of her Attorney-General, without an affidavit (as is usually required) denying the truth of the imputations. He says she was eager to make such an affidavit, but that he would not permit her to do so, because upon searching for precedents, it was found that a Queen, on account of her dignity and supposed impeccability was entitled to the protection of the Court against calumny, without any declaration of innocence, and it was thought that to make an affidavit in this instance would have been to derogate from the Reginal prerogative :—

"During the interval between the information being obtained and tried," said Lord Brougham, "an event happened which gave a peculiarly mournful interest to the proceeding—the death of this grand Princess, who fell a sacrifice to the unwearied and unrelenting persecution of her enemies. A circumstance well-fitted to disarm any malignity merely human seemed only to inspire fresh bitterness and new fury in the breast of the ferocious priest."[1]

The trial came on before Mr. Justice Holyrood at Lancaster, when the defendant, as his own counsel, reiterated and aggravated all the criminality charges in the libel.

The late Queen's Attorney-General, now a simple *outer barrister*, conducted the prosecution with great good taste. Having read the above passage from the sermon, and made a few simple comments upon it, he thus concluded :—

"Of the illustrious and ill-fated individual who was the object of this unprovoked attack, I forbear to speak. She is now removed from such low strife, and there is an

[1] "Lord Brougham's Speeches," vol. i., p. 296.

end,—I can not say of her checkered life, for her existence was one continued scene of suffering, of disquiet, of torment from injustice, oppression, and animosity by all who either held or looked up to emolument or aggrandizement, all who either possessed or courted them; but the grave has closed over her unrelenting persecutions. Unrelenting I may call them, for they have not spared her ashes. The evil passions which beset her steps in life, have not ceased to pursue her memory with a resentment more relentless, more implacable than death. But it is yours to vindicate the broken laws of your country. If your verdict shall have no effect on the defendant—if he still go on unrepenting and unabashed—it will at least teach others, or it will warn them and deter them from violating the decency of private life, betraying sacred public duties, and insulting the majesty of the Law."

The defendant was found guilty, and sentenced to three months' imprisonment.[1]

Brougham's next speech was, in my opinion, by far the best he ever delivered either at the bar or in Parliament, and I would almost say that it is worthy to be bound up in a collection of English oratory with Erskine's and Burke's. The news of the death of Queen Caroline was received all over the kingdom with the usual mark of respect to the Royal family, of solemnly tolling the bells of all cathedrals and churches, except in the city of Durham. This omission was commented upon with great severity in a newspaper called the "*Durham Chronicle*," which contained the following strictures on the Durham clergy:—

"In this episcopal city, containing six churches independently of the cathedral, not a single bell announced the departure of the magnanimous spirit of the most injured of Queens—the most persecuted of women. Thus the brutal enmity of those who embittered her mortal exist-

---

[1] Brougham was extremely indignant at the mildness of the punishment, but had his revenge by inserting in an introduction which he wrote to a printed account of the trial, the following extract from Dr. King's "History of the Rebellion in 1745," a favorite Jacobite production, the following extract: "Blacones apud Anglos sunt infames delatores, gigantum filii; quos naturâ malevolos spes præmii induxit in summum scelus: qui quum castos et integerrimos viros accusare soleant, omnia confingunt, et non modô perjuria sua vendunt, verum etiam alios impellunt ad pejerandum. Nomen sumunt a Blacow quodam sacerdote, qui ob nefarias suas delationes donatus est canonicatu Vindsoriensi a regni præfecto."

ence pursues her in her shroud. We know not whether any actual orders were issued to prevent this customary sign of mourning; but the omission plainly indicates the kind of spirit which predominates among our clergy. Yet these men profess to be followers of Jesus Christ, to walk in His footsteps, to teach His precepts, to inculcate His spirit, to promote harmony, charity, and Christian love! Out upon such hypocrisy! It is such conduct which renders the very name of our established clergy odious till it stinks in the nostrils."

The Court of King's Bench having granted a rule to show cause why a criminal information should not be filed against Mr. Williams, the proprietor of the newspaper, for a libel upon the clergy of Durham, Mr. Brougham in vain tried to show that the rule should be discharged, on the ground that the alleged libel was a fair comment upon the conduct of the public functionaries, and that the Durham clergy themselves had been in the habit of using much stronger language even as applied to one another. As an example he read an extract from the writings of Bishop Barnes, who says of Durham, in the reign of Elizabeth, that "it is Augeæ Stabulum;" and of the Durham clergy, that "they do stink in the nose of God and his people." He further observed that the same freedom of tone was preserved by the Durham clergy of the present day, "for Mr. Philpotts,[1] one of the number, publishes a pamphlet in which he describes Mr. Williams, the defendant, of whom he and his brethren now complain, as 'a miserable mercenary, who eats the bread of prostitution and panders to the low appetites of those who can not, or dare not, cater for their own malignity.'" The rule was nevertheless made absolute, and the trial came on at the Durham Summer Assizes, 1822.

Coltman, an intimate friend of mine (afterward a Judge of the Common Pleas), then a barrister on the Northern circuit, told me that the night before the trial he saw Brougham in a sequestered spot by the river-side pacing backs and forwards with folded arms, and that as he approached, Brougham suddenly turned round, held up both hands, and exclaimed in a hollow voice, "Avaunt! depart! I am distilling venom for the Durham clergy!"

I can only give two specimens of what he poured out

[1] Afterwards Bishop of Exeter.

next day. Thus he commented upon the English hierarchy and that portion of it who were the prosecutors on this occasion—alluding to the visit which George IV. was then making to his Presbyterian kingdom of Scotland:—

"If any hierarchy in all the world is bound on every principle of consistency—if any Church should be forward not only to suffer but to provoke discussion, to stand upon that title and challenge the most unreserved inquiry—it is the Protestant Church of England; first, because she has nothing to dread from it; secondly, because she is the very creature of free inquiry—the offspring of repeated revolutions—and the most reformed of the reformed Churches of Europe. But surely if there is any one corner of Protestant Europe where men ought not to be rigorously judged in ecclesiastical controversy—where a large allowance should be made for the conflict of irreconcilable opinions—where the harshness of jarring tenets should be patiently borne, and strong, or even violent language, be not too narrowly watched—it is this very realm, in which we live under three different ecclesiastical orders, and owe allegiance to a sovereign, who, in one of his kingdoms, is the head of the Church, acknowledged as such by all men; while, in another, neither he nor any earthly being is allowed to assume that name—a realm composed of three great divisions, in one of which Prelacy is favored by law and approved in practice by an Episcopalian people; while, in another, it is protected indeed by law, but adjured in practice by a nation of sectaries, Catholic and Presbyterian; and, in a third, it is abhorred alike by law and in practice, repudiated by the whole institutions of the country, scorned and detested by the whole of its inhabitants. His Majesty, almost at the time in which I am speaking, is about to make a progress through the northern provinces of this island, accompanied by certain of his chosen counsellors, a portion of men who enjoy unenvied, and in an equal degree, the admiration of other countries, and the wonder of their own—and there the Prince will see much loyalty, great learning, some splendor, the remains of an ancient monarchy, and of the institutions which made it flourish. But one thing he will not see. Strange as it may seem, and to many who hear me incredible, from one end of the country to the other he will see no such thing as a Bishop; not such a thing is to be found

from the Tweed to John O'Groat's; not a mitre; no, nor
so much as a minor canon, or even a rural dean; and in
all the land not one single curate, so entirely rude and
barbarous are they in Scotland; in such outer darkness
do they sit, that they support no cathedrals, maintain no
pluralists, suffer no non-residence; nay, the poor be-
nighted creatures are ignorant even of tithes. Not a
sheaf, or a lamb, or a pig, or the value of a plough-penny
do the hapless mortals render from year's end to year's
end! Piteous as their lot is, what makes it infinitely
more touching, is to witness the return of good for evil in
the demeanor of this wretched race. Under all this cruel
neglect of their spiritual concerns, they are actually the
most loyal, contented, moral, and religious people anywhere, perhaps, to be found in the world. Let us hope
(many, indeed, there are, not afar off, who will with unfeigned devotion pray) that his Majesty may return safe
from the dangers of his excursion into such a country—
an excursion most perilous to a certain portion of the
Church, should his royal mind be infected with a taste for
cheap establishments, a working clergy, and a pious congregation! But compassion for our brethren in the north
has drawn me aside from my purpose, which was merely
to remind you how preposterous it is in a country of
which the ecclesiastical polity is framed upon plans so
discordant, and the religious tenets themselves are so
various, to require any very measured expressions of
men's opinions upon questions of Church government.
And if there is any part of England in which an ample
license ought more especially to be admitted in handling
such matters, I say without hesitation it is this very Bish-
opric, where, in the nineteenth century, you live under a
Palatine Prince, the Lord of Durham; where the endow-
ment of the hierarchy—I may not call it enormous, but I
trust I shall be permitted without offense to term it
splendid; where the establishment I dare not whisper
proves grinding to the people, but I will rather say is an
incalculable, an inscrutable blessing—only it *is* prodig-
ously large; showered down in a profusion somewhat
overpowering; and laying the inhabitants under a load of
obligation overwhelming by its weight. It is in Durham
where the Church is endowed with a splendor and a
power unknown in monkish times and popish countries,

and the clergy swarm in every corner, an' it were the patrimony of St. Peter—it is here where all manner of conflicts are at each moment inevitable between the people and the priests, that I feel myself warranted on *their* behalf, and for *their* protection—for the sake of the Establishment, and as the discreet advocate of that Church and that clergy—for the defense of their very existence,—to demand the most unrestrained discussion for their title and their actings under it. For them, in this age, to screen their conduct from investigation, is to stand self-convicted; to shrink from the discussion of their title, is to confess a flaw; he must be the most shallow, the most blind of mortals, who does not at once perceive that if that title is protected only by the strong arm of the law, it becomes not worth the parchment on which it is engrossed, or the wax that dangles to it for a seal. I have hitherto all along assumed, that there is nothing impure in the practice under the system; I am admitting that every person engaged in its administration does every one act which he ought, and which the law expects him to do; I am supposing that up to this hour not one unworthy member has entered within its pale; I am even presuming that up to this moment not one of those individuals has stepped beyond the strict line of his sacred functions, or given the slightest offense or annoyance to any human being. I am taking it for granted that they all act the part of good shepherds, making the welfare of their flock their first care, and only occasionally bethinking them of shearing, in order to prevent the two luxuriant growth of the fleece proving an encumbrance, or to eradicate disease. If, however, those operations be so constant that the flock actually live under the knife; if the shepherds are so numerous, and employ so large a troop of the watchful and eager animals that attend them (some of them, too, with a cross of the fox, or even the wolf, in their breed), can it be wondered at, if the poor creatures thus fleeced, and hunted, and barked at, and snapped at, and from time to time worried, should now and then bleat, dream of preferring the rot to the shears, and draw invidious, possibly disadvantageous comparisons between the wolf without, and the shepherd within the fold? It can not be helped; it is the nature of things that suffering should beget complaint; but for those who have caused the pain to complain of the outcry and seek to punish it—for those who have goaded to scourge and to gag, is the meanest of all injustice. It is, moreover, the most pitiful folly for the clergy to think of retaining their power, privileges, and enormous wealth, without allowing free vent for complaints against abuses in the Establishment and delinquency in its members; and in this prosecution they have displayed that folly in its supreme degree."

He then went over the parts of the alleged libel most complained of, insisting that its language was mild compared with that of Milton and other writers eminent for their piety as well as genius, and contended that the heartless and disloyal conduct of the prosecutors in insulting the memory of the Queen would have justified strictures much more severe. Thus he concluded by drawing the eyes of all upon Dr. Philpotts, the supposed instigator of the prosecution, who was sitting on the bench near the Judge:—

"My learned friend Mr. Scarlett, has sympathized with the priesthood, and innocently enough lamented that they possess not the power of defending themselves through the public press. Let him be consoled—they are not so entirely destitute of the aid of the press, as through him they have represented themselves to be. They have largely used that press (I wish I could say '*as not abusing it*'), and against some persons very near me; I mean especially against my client, the defendant, whom they prosecute, having scurrilously and foully libeled him through the great vehicle of public instruction, over which, for the first time, among the other novelties of the day, I now hear they have no control. Not that they wound deeply or injure much; but that is no fault of theirs—without hurting, they give trouble and discomfort. The insect brought into life by corruption, and nestled in filth, though its flight be lowly and its sting puny, can swarm and buzz, and irritate the skin and offend the nostril, and altogether give nearly as much annoyance as the wasp, whose nobler nature it aspires to emulate. These reverend slanderers —these pious backbiters—devoid of force to wield the sword, snatch the dagger, and, destitute of wit to point or to barb it and make it rankle in the wound, steep it in venom to make it fester in the scratch. The much venerated personages whose harmless and unprotected state is now deplored, have been the wholesale dealers in calumny, as well as largest consumers of the base article—the especial promoters of that vile traffic, of late the disgrace of the country—both furnishing a constant demand for the slanders by which the press is polluted, and prostituting themselves to pander for the appetites of others : and now they come to demand protection from retaliation, and shelter from just exposure ; and to screen themselves, would have you prohibit all scrutiny of the abuses by which they exist, and the mal-practices by which they disgrace their calling. After abusing and well nigh dismantling, for their own despicable purposes, the great engine of instruction, they would have you annihilate all that they have left of it, to secure their escape. They have the incredible assurance to expect that an English jury will conspire with them in this wicked design. They expect in vain ! If all existing institutions and all public functionaries must henceforth be sacred from question among the people; if, at length, the free press of this country, and with it the freedom itself, is to be destroyed—at least let not the heavy blow fall from your hands. Leave it to some profligate tyrant ; leave it to a mercenary and effeminate Parliament—a hireling army, degraded by the lash, and the readier instrument for enslaving its country; leave it to a pampered House of Lords—a venal House of Commons—some vulger minion, servant-of-all-work to an insolent Court—some unprincipled soldier, unknown, thank God! in our times, combining the talents of a usurper with the fame of a captain ; leave to such desperate hands, and such fit tools, so horrid a work ! But you, an English jury, parent of the press, yet supported by it, and doomed to perish the instant its health and strength are gone—lift not you against it an unnatural hand. Prove to us that our rights are safe in your keeping ; but maintain, above all things, the stability of our institutions by well guarding their corner-stone. Defend the Church from her worst enemies, who, to hide their own misdeeds, would veil her solid foundations in darkness; and proclaim to them by your verdict of acquittal, that henceforward, as heretofore, all the recesses of the sanctuary must be visited by continual light of day, and by that light all its abuses be explored."

The jury found a verdict of " Guilty of publishing a libel

against the clergy residing in and near the city of Durham and the suburbs thereof." Next term a rule was granted to show cause why judgment should not be arrested, on the ground that this finding did not agree with the information, and that the offense found was too vague to justify any prosecution. Cause was not shown, and the prosecution was allowed to drop.

In truth it ought never to have been instituted, and the Judges were justly punished for having improperly granted the information by the difficulties in which they were involved, and the ridicule which they incurred. One of them, Mr. Justice Best, showed such zeal and ignorance in trying to answer the objection that no one could tell what class of clergymen was meant by "the clergy residing in and near Durham," that he asked, "Are the Dissenters ever called *clergy?*"—when he was truly told that not only are the Roman Catholic priests allowed to be "clergy" by the Church of England herself, but that Presbyterian ministers are denominated "clergy" in many Acts of Parliament.

This prosecution closed the public proceedings respecting the character and conduct of Caroline of Brunswick, in which Brougham had made a very conspicuous figure.

During the five following years and until the formation of Mr. Canning's administration nothing occurred materially to alter his position either professionally or politically. The King's resentment against him not having cooled, he continued to wear a stuff gown. His practice at the bar rather declined; nevertheless, from the notoriety of the cases in which he was retained he was a good deal before the public as an advocate, and the splendor of his career in the House of Commons was of steady use to him professionally by inspiring clients with the natural desire of having for their counsel a gentleman so much talked of, and so much praised as well as abused in the newspapers. I do not find any other case of permanent celebrity which he patronized while he continued at the bar; and as a mere barrister-at-law he would soon have been forgotten, being much inferior to Follett and others, of whom the next generation will know nothing.

In the House of Commons he maintained and extended his reputation. His great subjects were Slavery, Education, Public Charities, and Law Reform. The slave-trade had been abolished before he entered Parliament; but he gave new efficiency to that measure by passing an Act by which it was made felony for any British subject to be engaged in the slave-trade in any part of the world.

In education he had great designs, for he vowed the reformation of our Universities and public schools, and the introduction of a new system of instruction for the whole mass of the lower orders. At first he caused much consternation by summoning some of the Dons from Oxford and the Masters from Eton, and catechising them about their antiquated processes. Wearing his hat as Chairman, they complained (I make no doubt without cause) of his treating them rudely, and they said the Committee-room resembled the Court—

"Where England's Monarch once uncovered sat,
While Bradshaw bullied in a broad-brimmed hat."

But these inquiries produced no practical effect, as the Universities and public schools could not be touched without sacrilege, and the divisions between Churchmen and Dissenters effectually prevented the establishment of any general system of education. But Brougham had the reputation of being the founder of London University College, open to all religions, although Thomas Campbell, author of the "Pleasures of Hope," complained to me (and I believe justly) that the ostensible founder had stolen the plan from him,—the poet concluding his narrative by exclaiming, "Greatest, brightest, *meanest* of mankind!"

His efforts to remedy the abuses in public charities cost the nation several hundred thousand pounds distributed among various sets of Commissioners, but as yet no real benefit has been derived from their labors.

In Law Reform he was more successful; and I shall hereafter have much to say of his services in this department.

The first great speech which he made in Parliament, after the *Carolinian* agitation had subsided, was on "Agricultural Distress," and here he again showed a sad ignorance or forgetfulness of the first principles of political economy; he earnestly advocated the protection of native industry against free trade in corn :—

"It is well," said he, "to talk in honeyed accents of suiting the supply to the demand, and throwing bad land out of cultivation. These words, however smoothly they may sound upon the tongue, will be found, if interpreted, full of serious and dangerous meaning. They suppose the laying waste of a fair proportion of England, the breaking up of all endearing connections, the destruction of all local attachments, the most frightful agonies to which the human mind can be subjected. To this conclusion the thing must, after all, come. Persons talk of the ruin of the landed interest; but it is not meant to say that the land will become sterile, or that the houses will be leveled and the owners exterminated. No; what is understood by the ruin of a great class, and by the destruction of one of the most commanding interests in the country, is shortly this: —a great change of property, much individual misery. Such is what is called the destruction of a class, and when it happens to a community it becomes the destruction of the State."

He has lived to see free trade in corn not only giving a new impetus to manufactures, but greatly improving agriculture, raising the rent of the landlord, improving the condition of the tenant farmer, adding immensely to the comforts of the laborer, making employment and contentment universal, and rendering the British Empire more powerful than at any former period of our history. But no one can be much blamed for being deluded by erroneous dogmas in which he has been educated, and which continue to be considered axioms by the great bulk of his contemporaries. English legislation had proceeded for five centuries upon the principle that the free importation of foreign corn would be ruinous to the State, and this was still undoubtingly believed by statesmen and politicians of all parties and classes, with the exception of a few individuals whose hallucinations were considered rather fitter for being cured by medicine than refuted by philosophy. So late as the year of grace 1838, Lord Melbourne, at the head of a Whig Government, said, in his place in Parliament, that "the Minister who should propose the abolition of the corn laws would only be fit for a lunatic asylum." And Lord John Russell, in 1841, by proposing that the importation of foreign corn should be permitted on payment of a fixed duty, lost the support of a large portion of the Whigs and paved the way for the return to power of Sir Robert Peel, then believed to be the devoted friend of Protection.

The leading subject of debate in the following Session of Parliament was the relief of the Irish Roman Catholics. Canning, when about to proceed to India as Governor-General, had been appointed Secretary of State and leader of the House of Commons on the sudden death of Lord Castlereagh—the condition of his appointment (as was generally supposed) being, that, although he was still to be at liberty to profess himself in favor of Catholic emancipation, he was not seriously to press this measure upon the legislature. Brougham, during a debate upon a motion for taking the Roman Catholic claims into consideration, animadverted with great severity upon a speech made by Canning, who had hitherto been hot and impatient in the cause, but now, though pretending to befriend it, recommended delay, and was cooled down almost to the freezing point:—

"When," asked Brougham, "did this change come upon him? Was it when the question arose whether he should go to India into honorable exile, or take office in England, and not submit to his sentence of transportation, but be condemned to hard labor in his own country—doomed to the disquiet of a divided council—sitting with his enemies and pitied by his friends—what he most desired having become the *forbidden fruit* which he must not touch without being ejected from Paradise! His fate then depended upon his sentiments, or rather the part he was to take respecting Emancipation. He has said to-night that he would not truckle to a noble lord,[1] who in truth required no such sacrifice; but on the occasion I refer to, when truckling was necessary, he exhibited a specimen—the most incredible specimen—of monstrous truckling for the purpose of obtaining office that the whole history of political tergiversation could furnish—"

Mr. Secretary Canning: "I rise to say that that is false."

The Speaker interposed, but the right honorable gentleman declared that although he was sorry to have used any word which was a violation of the decorum of the House, nothing—no consideration on earth—should induce him to retract the sentiment. Mr. Tierney and several other members attempted in vain to bring about an explanation, and at last a motion was made, "That the

[1] Lord Folkestone, afterwards Earl of Radnor.

Right Honorable George Canning, and Henry Brougham, Esq., be committed to the custody of the Sergeant-at-Arms."

After a good deal of discussion, in which it was suggested that Mr. Canning had misunderstood Mr. Brougham's meaning in supposing that any personal dishonor was inputed to him, and that there ought to be a conditional retraction of the offensive language, Mr. Brougham, who long remained obstinately silent, at last said :—

"If I were to consult my own feelings alone I should wish to finish the sentence in which I was interrupted, and the right honorable gentleman would see whether, in his own opinion, that interruption could be justified. But the question is whether the right honorable gentleman who has used the disorderly expression and myself shall be taken into custody. That he has been guilty of a breach of the rules of the House has been declared by the highest authority, and no dissent on this point has been expressed. The question is whether not only the right honorable gentlemen who has been unanimously pronounced GUILTY shall be taken into custody, but also myself, against whom no charge has been made. I know that the power of the House in this respect is absolute; but if such an order is made, it will be a flagrant violation of the principles of justice. I beg the House to understand that I oppose the first part of the motion no less than the last. I would by no means hold up my hand for passing a censure upon the right honorable gentleman, or for committing him to custody for the expression he used on hearing one half of the sentence which I was about to deliver. I feel it extremely difficult to speak with the accuracy which has now become necessary of the language I used. I will, however, tell the House what I meant to say, the facts on which I reasoned, and the inference which I have drawn from these facts. I believed them to be true; but if not, and the conclusion I have drawn be erroneous, I shall rejoice. I used the words, 'political tergiversation.' I described the conduct of the right honorable gentleman as something which stood prominent in the history of parliamentary tergiversation. The expression, I admit, was strong, but I thought it an expression which I had heard used over and over again without giving offense. I am sure I have never heard of any occasion on which it was more accurately applied. I entertained a strong feeling, and I meant to express it, with respect to the right honorable member's public and political life. As a private individual I never knew aught of him but what did him the highest honor. But having had the high honor of being connected with him heretofore in advocating the Catholic cause, I understood that in a speech delivered by him at Liverpool he had said, for the first time in the history of the Catholic question, that '*he did not wish that question to be discussed again in Parliament.*' If the right honorable gentleman did not say so, I heartily beg his pardon. But I read it in what professed to be a corrected copy of his speech. At that moment it was known that the right honorable gentleman was about to become a Minister at home, or to go out as Governor-General of India. And it was a matter of perfect notoriety that the all-powerful Lord Chancellor was in direct hostility not only to the Catholic question, but to the right honorable gentleman as its most powerful supporter. When, therefore, I connected that Liverpool declaration with that hostility, and the subsequent appointment of the right honorable gentleman to the office he now holds, I could not repel the conclusion I stated in the objectionable expression. It was under that impression, and with a view of transfering it to the House, that I spoke. If the expression was too strong for the orders of the House, I most readily apologize, although it be not too strong for my feelings. I conceive that I had a right to form an opinion of the right honorable gentleman's motives from the outward and visible sign of his actions. All these things seemed to me to show a truckling to the Lord Chancellor. His appointment as Minister and Manager of the House of Commons (as it is unconstitutionally called) confirmed the opinion I had formed. I am aware that it is wrong to impute motives to the conduct of any one, and I gather from the right honorable gentleman that I have been mistaken in doing so in this instance. But I had a right to speak of his conduct as a statesman, which I deplored; and this is all that I have done. I am actuated by no party, still less by any personal, considerations. I lamented only a death-blow to that cause in which we had both been ardently engaged."

Peel, then the great anti-Catholic leader, not sorry to see his rival damaged, suggested that the explanation should be considered satisfactory, and, with affected magnanimity, declared that the facts must have been grossly misrepresented to the honorable and learned gentleman, for that nothing could by possibility be more free from *truckling* than the manner in which his right honorable friend had accepted office. The motion for committing the two members was then withdrawn, and Canning declared that " he should think no more of it."

This scene laid the foundation for one of Charles Dicken's most amusing chapters in " Pickwick," where a similar quarrel was adjusted among the *Pickwickians* by a declaration that certain offensive expressions had not been used in their *usual* and *natural*, but in their *Pickwickian* sense.

Then, and for about ten years longer, such scenes were not rare in the House of Commons, this being the transition state between the period when political duels were frequent and creditable, and the fashion of the present day, when, political duels bringing odium or ridicule upon the combatants, they may be considered extinct. I remember the time when almost all the parliamentary leaders on both sides had "been out "—Fox, Pitt, Tierney, Castlereagh, Canning, O'Connell, and, last of all, Wellington himself— but I can not call to mind a single surviving leader who has ever actually exchanged balls as well as words with a rival. We could hardly conceive such a thing now as an encounter on Wimbledon Common between the solemn Aberdeen and the sprightly Derby, or between Lord John Russell, the impersonation of Whiggery, and Mr. Cobden, the apostle of Free Trade. Indeed one of the most prominent leaders in the House of Commons is a Quaker—and the scene would be too amusing if he should be taken into the custody of the Sergeant-at-Arms to prevent bloodshed! This change is certainly to be applauded, as it not only puts an end to deadly strife but to ostentatious displays of mock valor. We used to be told that without dueling there would be intolerable scurrility in debate, but no such consequence has followed its abolition. Looking at home, and casting a glance across the Atlantic, we may see that decorum in deliberative assemblies is more effectually preserved by good taste and enlightened public opinion, than by the use of rifles, revolvers, or bowie knives.

In the following Session of Parliament the House of Commons showed a new expedient for preventing members from fighting duels, by treating every outrage which might provoke a challenge as proof of insanity. A gentleman of the name of Gourlay, whom I well knew, having been at College with him, was very much offended by some observations which Mr. Brougham had made upon him in presenting a petition, and, an apology being refused, assaulted him with a horse-whip in the lobby of the House. The offender was immediately taken into custody by the Sergeant-at-Arms, and some members declaring that although he was very clever and had written an excellent book, he was very eccentric, and had been supposed to be out of his mind, he was ordered to be kept in prison till the end of the Session as a lunatic. The matter was thus adjusted to the entire satisfaction of all parties. Mr. Brougham's honor was untarnished, and Mr. Gourlay, when discharged, conducted himself ever after peaceably and properly.

In the course of this Session, Brougham delivered a speech which he frankly declared he considered his *chef d'œuvre*. In the introduction to it, as it appeared in his printed Speeches, published by him in 1838, he ascribes to it mainly the abolition of slavery in the English Colonies:—

"All men now saw that the warning given in the peroration, though sounded in vain across the Atlantic Ocean, was echoing with a loudness redoubled at each repetition through the British Isles; that had rung the knell of the system; and that at the fetters of the slave a blow was at length struck which must, if followed up, make them fall off his limbs forever."

Smith, a missionary minister in Demerara, had exerted himself very zealously in the conversation of the negroes to Christianity—teaching them to read and to pray, and inculcating upon them the sacredness of marriage and the duties of wedded life. For such enormities he was brought to trial before a court-martial on pretense that he had encouraged a revolt, and he was sentenced to be shot. Brougham's treatment of the subject might be good for a mixed popular assembly, but the speech, though much applauded at the time, now that all accidental interest is gone, can hardly be read through by the most indulgent of critics. There is no simplicity or pathos in any of its passages that are intended to be touching, and the air of exaggeration which pervades his vehemence sadly detracts from its effect. But I must introduce the peroration which uttered forth the prophetic warning, which rung the knell of slavery, and which struck off the fetters of the negro :—

"This lesson must now be taught by the voice of Parliament—that the mother country will at length make her authority respected; that the rights of property are sacred, but the rules of justice paramount aud inviolable; that the claims of the slave owner are admitted, but the dominion of Parliament indisputable; that we are sovereign alike over the white and the black; and though we may for a season, and out of regard for the interests of both, suffer men to hold property in their fellow-creatures, we never, for even an instant of time, forget that they are men, and the fellow-subjects of their masters; that, if those masters shall still hold the same perverse course, if, taught by no experience, warned by no arguries, scared by no menaces from Parliament, or from the Crown administering those powers which Parliament invoked it to put forth, but, blind alike to the duties, the interests, and the perils of their situation, they rushed headlong through infamy to destruction; breaking promise after promise made to delude us; leaving pledge after pledge unredeemed, extorted by the pressure of the passing occasion; or only, by laws passed to be a dead letter forever, giving such an illusory performance as adds mockery to breach of faith;—yet a little delay; yet a little longer of this, unbearable trifling with the commands of the parent State, and she will stretch out her arm, in mercy, not in anger, to those deluded men themselves: exert at last her undeniable authority; vindicate the just rights, and restore the tarnished honor of the English name."

The Session of 1825 was chiefly distinguished by attacks on Lord Eldon and the delays of Chancery. Eldon was considered the key-stone of the great Tory arch; and, if this could be dislodged, an expectation arose that the whole fabric would tumble down in ruins. Not only when motions directly aimed at him were debated, but whatever the professed subject of discussion might be, Brougham neglected no opportunity of assailing him. For example, in treating Catholic emancipation, he represented the Lord Chancellor as the only real obstacle to the measure, and thus exhorted the pro-Catholic members of the Cabinet fearlessly to proceed in spite of him :—

"Of what are they afraid? What is their ground of alarm? Do they think he would resign his office? that he would quit the great seal? Prince Hohenloe, the modern miracle-worker, is nothing to the man who could work such a miracle. (Cheers and laughter.) A more chimerical apprehension never entered the brain of a distempered poet—anything but that. Many things may surprise me; but nothing would so much surprise me as that the noble and learned individual to whom I allude should quit his hold of office while life remains. A more superfluous fear than such an event never crossed the wildest visionary in his dreams. Indeed, sir, I can not refrain from saying that I think the right honorable gentlemen opposite greatly underrate the steadiness of mind of the noble and learned individual in question. I think they greatly underrate the firmness and courage which he bears, and will continue to bear, the burdens of his high and important station. In these qualities the noble and learned lord has never been excelled—has never, perhaps, been paralleled; nothing can equal the forbearance which he has manifested. Nothing can equal the constancy with which he has borne the thwarts that he has lately received on the questions of trade. His patience under such painful circumstances can be rivaled only by the fortitude with which he bears the prolonged distress of the suitors in his own court; but to apprehend that any defeat would induce him to quit office is one of the vainest fears—one of the most fantastic apprehensions—that was ever entertained by man. Let him be tried. In his generous mind, expanded as it has been by his long official character, there is no propensity so strong as a love of the service of his country. He is, no doubt, convinced that the higher an office, the more unjustifiable it is to abandon it. The more splendid the emoluments of a situation—the more extensive its patronage—the more he is persuaded that it is not allowed to a wise and good man to tear himself from it. His present station the noble and learned lord holds as an estate for life. That is universally admitted. The only question is, whether he is to appoint his successor. By some it is supposed that he has actually appointed him. If it be so, I warn that successor that he will be exceedingly disappointed if he expects to step into the office a single moment before the decease of its present holder. However, I do entreat that the perseverance of this eminent person may be put to the test. Let the right honorable gentleman say he will resign, if the Catholic question be not carried in the Cabinet: let the noble and learned lord say that he will resign if it be carried. I am quite sure of the result. The Catholic question would be carried, but the noble and learned lord would retain his place. He would behave with the fortitude which has distinguished him in the other instances in which he has been defeated; and the country would not be deprived, for a single hour, of the inestimable benefit of his services."

Next morning, after reading the report of this debate in the newspapers, Lord Eldon, in a letter to his daughter, thus commented upon it:—

"You will see that Brougham has had no mercy upon the Chancellor. Laughs and cheers he produced from the company repeatedly with his jokes, which, however, he meant to play off in bitter malignity; and yet I could not help laughing at some of his jokes pretty heartily myself. No young lady was ever so unforgiving for being refused a silk gown, when silk gowns adorn female forms, as Brougham is with me, because, having insulted my master, the insulted don't like to clothe him with distinction, and honor, and silk. In the straightforward discharge of my public duty I shall defy all my opponents; their wit, their sarcasms, their calumnies, I regard not, whilst conscious I have a great duty to perform, and *that* I have now in the support of the constitution in Church and State. I shall do what I think right—a maxim I have endeavored in past life to make the rule of my conduct—and trust the consequences to God."

Notwithstanding such language, the consummate hypocrite, who tried at times to deceive his own daughter and himself, was in the habit of sending messages to Brougham, lamenting that no impression could be made upon the King's prejudices; otherwise that the professional rank to which he was justly entitled would immediately be conferred upon him.

Brougham was more exasperated by the wrong done to himself from observing a job of the Chancellor's, by which—that there might be some one in the House of Lords who would do the Chancellor's duty in disposing of appeals, the arrears of which had become quite overwhelm-

ing, and at the same time who would not in any degree
rival him in reputation or in influence—Gifford had been
put over the heads of hundreds at the bar, his superiors
in learning and talent as well as in standing. Here is a
rapid sketch by Brougham of his career:—

"Lord Gifford who has just been elevated to the peerage, owes his advancement to the favor of the Lord Chancellor. I never saw any man raised to eminence in a manner so extraordinary. He is seen practicing at the Eexter Sessions, and three weeks after he was Solicitor-General. The man so raised certainly owes a great deal to the architect of his fortunes, being in no respect that architect himself. He has been raised to his present eminence upon the credit of possessing abilities which he never exhibited —he has got everything upon tick. I have not spoken to an individual in the profession who does not consider this noble lord's rise the most extraordinary flight upwards of anything, except a balloon, that has ever been witnessed. After the noble lord had been raised to the highest point, not of royal, but of chancellarian favor—after having sat for a short time in the Common Pleas (and I believe he is the youngest judge who ever sat on that bench)— he is, by a sort of ledgerdemain known only to the Lord Chancellor, advanced to the office of Master of the Rolls, the most lucrative and the easiest of the law appointments. Then, as if to make assurance doubly sure, and that no latent seed of partiality should lurk in the noble lord's mind, which might bias his judgment in favor of his patron, he is made a sort of deputy Chancellor to the House of Lords, to do the Chancellor's journeywork. In order, if possible, to make this person the victim of what Sir Robert Walpole called political ingratitude, he is pointed out as the individual to whom the Lord Chancellor means to leave his office by way of legacy. It is understood that the learned lord means to make him his heir and legatee, by devising to him the Great Seal for the term of his natural life— that being the term for which it appears the office in future is to be held."

Still when the division came, the small Whig minorities knew no increase, and Brougham might have remained in stuff for many more years to come, fruitlessly uttering sarcasms against Tory Ministers and their favorites, had it not been for Lord Liverpool's apoplexy. This event brought about a contest for the succession to his office which entirely changed the aspect of party politics, and clothed in silk the ex-Attorney-General of Queen Caroline. Canning had for some years been at the head of a liberal party in the Cabinet—not only advocating the cause of the Irish Romanists, but proposing relaxations of the old monopolist commercial system, and in foreign politics swerving from the absolutism of the Holy Alliance, which, since the peace of Vienna, had warred against free institutions all over the world. The contest was between Canning and Peel, who although in his heart inclined to the liberal side, at this time presented himself as the champion of ultra-Toryism. After long intrigues, the King, caring little about the public questions by which rival factions were divided, but influenced chiefly by the Marchioness of Conyngham, who then ostensibly held the station at Court of his mistress, commissioned Canning to submit to him the list of a new Administration. This proceeding being made known, almost all his colleagues, by the advice of Lord Eldon, refused to serve under him, thinking that he must fail in his enterprise, and that a Government would be formed under Peel purged from all taint of liberality. In this extremity Canning opened a negotiation with the Whigs. Although with splendid historical recollections to support them, they could still boast of leaders belonging to the first class of orators and statesmen, their position as a party was then very hopeless. The King, according to the maxim "we hate whom we have injured," had held them in utter aversion since he betrayed them on becoming Regent, and his abhorrence of them was increased by the part they took in the affair of the Queen's trial, to which he imputed the cruel disappointment and the lamentable humiliation he had then experienced. The Whigs had not the consolation of being popular in the country, and the phrase of "storming the King's closet" had become obsolete. They were believed to be wrongheaded in their movements, and to be unfit for office; and the sentence of perpetual banishment supposed to be passed upon them, made them to be shunned by adventurous aspirants to office.

All that was held out to Whigs at this time was that a few of the more moderate might be admitted into the new arrangement, with the hope that, by degrees, there might

be a complete coalition between them and the Liberal
Tories, headed by Canning. This proposal was extremely
distasteful to Earl Grey, who felt that he could not be
included; and that, losing his position as undisputed
leader of a formidable and undivided party, he might soon
be left without followers and reduced to insignificance.
Brougham took a totally different view of the projected
coalition, and, from Canning's liberal principles, had a
very decent pretext for joining him. He declared that he
would not take office himself, but he advised Lord Lansdowne and other staunch Whigs to do so, and, with his
usual energy, declared his readiness to cast in his lot with
the new Government. Thus Canning was started as
Prime Minister; and, when he took his place on the
Treasury Bench, Brougham walked over from the Opposition side of the House, sat down behind him, and stuck
his knees into the back of his former opponent.

As a reward for his good services, the offer was made
to him of the dignity of Lord Chief Baron of the Exchequer: but this, unaccompanied by a peerage, he unhesitatingly declined, as it would have disqualified him to
sit in the House of Commons, and (as he said) "it would
have amounted to *shelving*, for which he was not yet quite
prepared." His cherished ambition was to be appointed
Master of the Rolls, so that he might have held a high
judicial office, which would have prepared him for the
highest, and, still remaining a representative of the people,
he might preserve and extend his political importance.
This arrangement might easily have been made, as Lord
Lyndhurst, who had been Master of the Rolls, was the
new Chancellor, having declared himself for the nonce a
violent anti-Catholic, to suit the religious whim of George
IV.: but, upon consideration, it was thought that it would
not be safe to give Brougham any judicial promotion
which should not entirely remove him from politics.
However, the King's scruples were overcome as to his
having a silk gown, although Lord Elden had often declared that they were insurmountable. He received a
patent of precedence, which gave him the same rank as if
he had been a King's Counsel; and, once more rustling in
silk, "he took his place within the bar accordingly." No
step in his career of advancement probably ever gave him
so much pleasure, considering the difficulty with which he

had obtained it, and that at last he owed it to a great political move, of which he truly said that he was *pars magna*. He delighted much in the new and prominent *role* he now acted as "Protector of the Fusion." He complained to me, but with evident complacency, of the trouble he had in answering the innumerable applications poured in upon him for favors from the Government, which it was supposed that his interest could command. All his correspondents, he said, concluded with these words: "You have only to say the word, and the thing is done." He assured me that at last he found it necessary to have a lithographed form of answer, leaving blanks for name and office, asseverating that "he had no influence whatever with the present Ministers, although he wished them well, and that he could not, with any propriety or hope of success, ask any favor from them."

Being attacked in the House of Commons for "going over," he boldly asserted that in now supporting Mr. Canning he acted with perfect consistency; and he tried to prove to an astonished audience that for years past he had entirely concurred in the sentiments expressed by this "liberal statesman." Thus, in ironical strain, he attempted to show that on all great questions of policy there had been entire harmony between them:—

"Because I support this Government, though I go no further, I am to be charged with having acceded to an unnatural coalition. I am to be told there has been a monstrous and unnatural alliance formed between the right honorable gentleman below me and those friends with whom I have had, and still have, the happiness and honor of acting. An unnatural alliance — because there are points of difference which should have eternally forbade the junction! an unnatural alliance — because we have differed, and particularly of late years, on the most material questions of internal and foreign policy; an unnatural alliance — because, since the death of Lord Londonderry, we have been striving to rivet fast to the chariot-wheel of the Holy Alliance the triumphant fortunes of Great Britain; an unnatural coalition — because we have been amongst those who have been the staunchest friends to the liberal system of commercial policy adopted by that Ministry; because, amongst others, I myself have been the constant supporter of those free doctrines in trade which were afterwards received, sanctioned, and carried into practice, by men more enlightened and of far more political weight than myself! An unnatural coalition, undoubtedly, because we have constantly differed from the right honorable gentleman, as to the internal policy of the empire; because we, forsooth, have ever disputed with him, as to that great corner-stone, the mode fitting to be adopted for the government of the sister kingdom of Ireland. Look over all the great political questions that divide some men and approximate others at the present day. Travel with your eyes over the affairs of Europe, or even across the Atlantic, and see the dawn of liberty in South America, where millions are blessing the grateful light, while the hearts of millions in this country are beating in unison with theirs, yet rejoicing in their new-born freedom. Whether we look, I say, to the east or the west, to America or to Europe, to our domestic policy, or questions of trade, or improvement or our mercantile system, or to the agricultural interests of the country,— surveying all those great questions which divide men in their opinions, and animate conflicting parties and rival statesmen, I can conscientiously declare that, passing them all in review, I can not discover one single tenet or sentiment, nay, one solitary feeling, which, practically speaking, has influenced the councils of his Majesty's Government during the last three or four years, and which did not find in my opinion a firm support, and in my feelings a faithful echo."

A few days after, he was again attacked with more bitterness, and accused of having, from selfish motives, deserted the cause of Catholic Emancipation. He again defended his consistency, and added:—

"As it is the custom to talk of sacrifices, I may mention mine. I have quitted a situation in this House which, considering the influence of opinion and feeling, was in the highest degree grateful to me; and in which I was surrounded and (if it may be permitted me to say so) supported by one of the largest, most important, the most honorable, and — now I may say it, for I was privy to all their councils, and my motives can not be suspected — the most disinterested Opposition that ever sat within the walls of this House, men who supported what they deemed right, though it kept them out of power, and con-

firmed their adversaries in office; and who persevered in
that course year after year, without a possible hope of
benefit ever accruing to themselves. I have quitted that
honorable and eminent situation, even to gratify the ambition of the proudest of men, on an express stipulation
which utterly excludes the possibility of my taking office.
I have done so deliberately and advisedly. I shall be
sufficiently gratified in watching the progress of those
opinions to which I am attached, both as to our foreign
and domestic policy; including with the rest the Irish
question, but not giving it a prominence which would
render it exclusive, and impede its success by making it
unpopular in this country, by arousing the religious
jealousy of the people. The right honorable gentleman
has successfully established a system of liberal foreign
policy. Upon these grounds I gave him my best assistance. Guided by these principles, and founding his
measures on such grounds, in the course of his adminstra-
tion the right honorable gentleman shall have from me
that which he has a right, in point of consistency to demand, a cordial, zealous, and disinterested support."

With Brougham's support, and his own brilliant eloquence, Canning got on pretty well in the House of Commons; but in the Lords he was "done to death." There
a most formidable coalition was formed against him, led
by the Duke of Wellington and Lord Grey. The Duke,
long distrustful of his own "civil wisdom,"[1] had acquired
new confidence, and was actually prepared to take upon
himself the office of Prime Minister. He considered that
it was usurped by Canning, and he was determined to
expel him from it as soon as possible. Lord Grey was
still more impatient to extinguish the present Government, which if it succeeded, would leave him a leader
without followers. Therefore a well-understood, although
not regularly-formed, concert arose between them to
thwart all ministerial measures. Canning sometimes
swore that he would go into the House of Lords and defend himself there, and the King was said to have offered
him a peerage for this purpose; but, if thus transferred,
he was afraid that in his absence Brougham might gain a
great ascendency in the Commons, and, under pretense of

---

[1] His brother, Marquis Wellesley, once said to me, "Arthur is a great commander, but he has no civil wisdom."

serving him, might become his master. He tided over the
session of Parliament amidst shallows, rocks, and breakers,
often in danger of running aground or of going to the
bottom; and he reached the shore in a condition so shattered that he could hardly hope to be able again to put to
sea.

Soon after the prorogation, Brougham hurried off to
the Northern circuit, where, with his new silk gown, he
expected to be *facile princeps.* Scarlett, the " cock of the
walk," although a staunch Whig had become Canning's
Attorney-General, and thus, according to etiquette, was
disqualified for assize business, except on special retainers.
This step he had taken with the strong recommendation
of Brougham, whose zeal was supposed to have been
heightened by the splendid opening which it would make
for him. You when they afterwards quarreled, the same
Brougham accused Scarlett of having deserted the Whig
party and strove to prevent him from again being reconciled to it, that there might be no man belonging to it of
superior reputation to himself as a lawyer.

For a short time Brougham's sanguine hopes were
realized. He had a brief in every cause, and his brilliant
speeches were listened to with loud plaudits. From his
very agreeable manners and power of amusement, he was
wonderfully popular with his brother barristers, and, by
way of "high jinks," they agreed to raise him to the royal
dignity under the title of Henry IX. Accordingly, at
the Grand Court, held at Lancaster, he was crowned with
all due pomp and solemnity. He instituted an Order of
Merit, with an appropriate decoration, which he distributed among those whom he dubbed with his sword
Knights of St. Henry. An ode, composed for the occasion, was recited, and the principal ceremonies of a royal
coronation were mimicked with much burlesque humor
and fun.

Nevertheless, his Majesty's reign as Northern Autocrat
was not of long continuance. Great as was the admiration excited by his eloquence and his wit, it was found
that neither juries nor judges yielded obedience to him.
The statistics at the end of the circuit showed that, in a
considerable majority of the causes tried, where the new
leader had been for the plaintiff the verdict was for the
defendant; and *vice versa,* where the new leader had been

for the defendant the verdict was for the plaintiff. The points of law which he made and most earnestly insisted upon were almost all overruled. Whereupon a joke (ascribed to Tindal, afterwards Chief Justice of the Common Pleas) was widely circulated and created much mirth in legal circles, viz.: "whereas Scarlett had contrived a machine, by using which while he argued he could make the judges' heads nod at his pleasure, Brougham had got hold of it, but, not knowing how to manage it, when *he* argued, the judges, instead of nodding shook their heads."

Truth to tell, notwithstanding his splendid abilities, Brougham was unaccountably deficient in *nisi prius* tact; and, Scarlett having left the circuit, Pollock was now discovered to have a far better chance of the verdict than Brougham, and on all common occasions was decidedly preferred to him. In practice at the bar Brougham continued to decline till, as we shall see, he was unexpectedly raised to the woolsack.

His political career received a violent shock, and took an entirely new turn from the alarming failure of Canning's health. Hopes had been entertained that the Liberal Prime Minister would rally when relieved from the anxiety of parliamentary business and when he saw that the aristocratic combination against him rather endeared him to the people. If his health had been re-established, I am inclined to think that he would have triumphed over all difficulties and long ruled the State. In that case, how different would have been the history of England in the nineteenth century! But the deadly dart stuck in Canning's side; within a few weeks from the prorogation of Parliament preparations were making for his funeral, and a subscription had been begun for raising a bronze statue to his memory.

Brougham heard the fatal news with sincere regret. He was absent from London when the new arrangement was made by which Lord Goderich was placed at the head of the Treasury. I believe that Brougham was not even consulted about this arrangement by any of the parties concerned. If his opinion had been asked by his old friends, the Whigs who had joined Canning, he would have warned them against continuing in office, unless indeed from private motives of his own he had wished their destruction. Goderich's Government was so distasteful both to the

Duke of Wellington and to Lord Grey as Canning's had
been, and it met with no favor in any class of the community.

When Brougham returned to London after the long
vacation, he found that the Government was sure to be
crushed before the approaching Session was a week old,
and Lord Goderich anticipated the blow by a voluntary
death.

Now was formed the Duke of Wellington's government
—Peel being the leader of the House of Commons,—without any Whig admixture. Brougham was again reconciled
to Lord Grey, and, co-operating with him, materially contributed to the advent to power of the Whigs as a party,
which ushered in the Reform Bill.

In the House of Commons the lead on the opposition
side was still contested, The steady aristocratic Whigs
wished to be considered as under Lord Althorp, bearing
the illustrious historical name of Spencer, and being the
most honorable, amiable, kindhearted, straightforward,
and excellent of men, but destitute of eloquence, of very
limited powers of reasoning, and of acquirements not superior to those of an ordinary country squire. The Whig
party never took cordially to Brougham, nor Brougham to
the Whig party. They had no confidence in his steadiness, nor much in his sincerity; and he was constantly
alarming them by coqueting with the Radicals, and starting schemes of his own. Retaliating, he complained that
they were exclusive and narrow-minded; that resting on
their traditions they did not keep pace with the march of
intellect, and that they were disposed to depress all Liberals who would not abjectly serve in their clique. Still
he kept on good terms with them all, and treated the bulk
of them as his subordinates. He stood somewhat in awe
of Lord Grey; and Lord Lansdowne's perpetual polished
courtesy protected him from *sobriquet* or any very familiar
appellation; but he called the Marquis of Tavistock
"Tavy," Lord John Russell "John," the old earl of Lauderdale "Jack," the present Earl of Derby "Ned," and
the Right Honorable Edward Ellice "the Bear." He
supported his social position by following the admonition
of Rochefoucauld, which I have observed to have uniformly governed both Lyndhurst and Brougham ever since I
first knew them, and which they seem to have thus trans-

lated:—"In private conversation flatter those who are present and abuse and ridicule the absent, although closely connected in office or friendship with those who are present—for you may safely trust to the law of confidence which forbids a betrayal of such communications, and you may be certain that the witty censure of others is always agreeable to the *amour propre* of the listener, so that it creates an impression in favor of the amusing detractor."[1]

At the commencement of the new administration Brougham censured as unconstitutional the union of civil and military power in the prime minister, and, professing to allay, he thus tried to excite the apprehensions of his hearers:

"Let it not be supposed that I am inclined to exaggerate. I entertain no fear of slavery being introduced by the power of the sword. It would demand a more powerful man, even, than the Duke of Wellington to effect such an object. The noble duke may take the army, he may take the navy, he may take the mitre, he may take the Great Seal. I will make the noble duke a present of them all. Let him come on with his whole force, sword in hand, against the Constitution, and the energies of the people of this country will defeat his utmost efforts. Therefore, I am perfectly convinced that there will be no unconstitutional attack on the liberties of the people. These are not the times for such an attempt. There have been periods when the country heard with dismay that 'the soldier was abroad.' That is not the case now. Let the soldier be abroad; in the present age he can do nothing. There is another person abroad—a less important person in the eyes of some, an insignificant person, whose labors have tended to produce this state of things. The schoolmaster is abroad! And I trust more to him, armed with his primer, than I do to the soldier in full military array, for upholding and extending the liberties of his country. I think the appointment of the Duke of Wellington is bad in a constitutional point of view; but as to

---

[1] I am ashamed when I consider how much I am myself the dupe of this system, as practiced among the Law Lords down to the present time. Lyndhurst, in conversing with me, abuses and laughs at Brougham; Brougham abuses and laughs at Lyndhurst. I am morally certain that Brougham and Lyndhurst when talking together abuse and laugh at Campbell. Yet, instead of checking them, I am afraid that I join with them in this wicked propensity. 5*th Sept.*, 1855.

any violence being in consequence directed against the liberties of the country, the fear of such an event I look upon to be futile and groundless."

Brougham's great exploit during the present session was his memorable speech on 'Law Reform,' which may now be glanced at with wonder, although I can not say that it would be justifiable to condemn any one actually to read it through unless as a punishment for some grave delict. It lasted above six hours, during which long period of time, notwithstanding the dryness of the subject, there was seldom any serious danger of the House being counted out. In his details and illustrations he did fall into a few blunders; but he displayed marvelous power of memory—and stores of legal knowledge, multifarious if not exact. Over the whole field of our jurisprudence did he travel,—civil, criminal, and ecclesiastical—common law, equity, and conveyancing—taking a survey of all our tribunals from the House of Lords to the Court of *pied poudre*—pointing out defects and suggesting remedies. Having paid a graceful compliment to Peel, who had already shown a liberal spirit by his consolidation of the statutes on several branches of the criminal law, he thus nobly concluded:—

"In pursuing the course which I now invite you to enter upon, I avow that I look for the co-operation of the King's Government; and on what are my hopes founded? Men gather not grapes from thorns, nor figs from thistles. But that the vine should no longer yield its wonted fruit—that the fig-tree should refuse its natural increase—required a miracle to strike it with barrenness. There are those in the present Ministry whose known liberal opinions have lately been proclaimed anew to the world, and pledges have been avouched for their influence upon the policy of the state. With them, others may not, upon all subjects, agree; upon this, I would fain hope, there will be found little difference. But be that as it may, whether I have the support of the Ministers or no—to the House I look with confident expectation that it will control them, and assist me; if I go too far, checking my progress; if too fast, abating my speed; but heartily and honestly helping me in the best and greatest work which the hands of the lawgiver can undertake. The course is clear before us; the race is glorious to run. You have the power of sending your name down through all times, illustrated by deeds of higher fame, and more useful import, than ever were done within these walls. You saw the greatest warrior of the age—conqueror of Italy—humbler of Germany—terror of the North—saw him account all his matchless victories poor compared with the triumph you are now in a condition to win—saw him contemn the fickleness of Fortune, while, in spite of her, he could pronounce his memorable boast, "I shall go down to posterity with the Code in my hand!" You have vanquished him in the the field; strive now to rival him in the sacred arts of peace! Outstrip him as a lawgiver, whom in arms you overcome! The luster of the Regency will be eclipsed by the more solid and enduring splendor of the Reign. The praise which false courtiers feigned for our Edwards and Harrys, the Justinians of their day, will be the just tribute of the wise and the good to that monarch under whose sway so mighty an undertaking shall be accomplished. Of a truth, the holders of sceptres are most chiefly to be envied for that they bestow the power of thus conquering, and ruling thus. It was the boast of Augustus—it formed part of the glare in which the perfidies of his earlier years were lost—that he found Rome of brick, and left it of marble; a praise not unworthy a great prince, and to which the present reign also has its claims. But how much nobler will be the Sovereign's boast, when he shall have it to say that he found law dear, and left it cheap; found it a sealed book—left it a living letter; found it the patrimony of the rich—left it the inheritance of the poor; found it the two-edged sword of craft and oppression—left it the staff of honesty and the shield of innocence! To me, much reflecting on these things, it has always seemed a worthier honor to be the instrument of making you bestir yourselves in this high matter, than to enjoy all that office can bestow—office, of which the patronage would be an irksome incumbrance, the emoluments superfluous to one content, with the rest of his industrious fellow-citizens, that his own hands minister to his wants. And as for the power supposed to follow it—I have lived nearly half a century, and I have learned that power and place may be severed. But one power I do prize, that of being the advocate of my countrymen here, and their fellow-laborer elsewhere, in those things which concern the best interests of mankind. That power, I know full well, no government can give—no change take away!"

In consequence, two royal commissions were issued, one for the proceedings in the common-law courts; and another for the law of real property. The reports of these commissions were followed by various Acts of Parliament, which have most materially improved the juridical institutions of this country. Brougham showed himself enamored of some *crotchets*, such as "Courts of Reconciliation," in which parties were always to meet, face to face, before they engaged in adverse litigation; but his suggestions, generally speaking, were rational and practicable. He himself has not the most distant notion of drawing an Act of Parliament. The hundreds that he has laid on the table of the House of Lords are always drawn by others, and he does not scruple to move a first and a second reading of them without his own perusal of them having gone further than the title, or perhaps the preamble, and a few of the marginal notes.[1] Yet without his exertions the *optimism* of our legal procedure might have long continned to be preached up, and *Fines and Recoveries* might still have been regarded with veneration.

About this time Brougham changed the constituents whom he represented in the House of Commons. For a good many years he had continued the nominee of the Earl of Darlington, who, having eight or ten seats at his disposal, intended to barter them against a dukedom. The aspirant Duke had professed liberal principles; but he now thought the great object of his ambition was more likely to be obtained by adhering to the present Government, and he defended his consistency by saying that the Duke of Wellington had come over to the liberal side. But this reasoning not being quite satisfactory to Brougham, he resigned Winchelsea by taking the Chiltern Hundreds, and he was immediately returned for Knaresborough by the Duke of Devonshire, who still sturdily adhered to the old Whig standard.

I ought to have mentioned that Brougham felt very much mortified that he had not been returned by any pop-

[1] If it would not appear malicious, I should like to move for a return of all the Bills introduced into the House of Lords by the Lord Brougham and Vaux since the month of November, 1830, with the number of them that have passed into Acts of Parliament, the stages in which the others have died, and the estimated expense of printing them.

ular constituency, notwithstanding the great reputation he had acquired for oratory and for patriotism. Twice had he stood for what he called his "native county." Brougham Hall, it may be recollected, stands in Westmorland. Although his ancestors were said by him to have lived there since the time of Antoninus, he himself had never seen the spot till his education was completed and he was of mature years. But after his father's death, which happened some time after he himself had come to reside in London, he transferred his mother from Edinburgh to Brougham Hall, and there he set up an establishment.[1] The Lowthers, who had migrated into Westmorland in comparatively modern times, having been there only a few centuries, had usurped complete dominion over it, and returned both members for the county as well as those for several boroughs in that region. Brougham with Winchelsea in his pocket, very gallantly offered himself for the county of Westmorland, and each time stood a lengthened poll. He was an excellent canvasser, made capital speeches, and had all the non-electors on his side. But though supported by the Earl of Thanet, the hereditary sheriff of the county, and although a good many sham freeholds were created in favor of his personal friends, who were willing to take a long journey for the purpose of obliging him, he never had a chance of success, and he was obliged to complain that from bribery and intimidation the real wishes of the electors were cruelly disappointed. Still, while sitting for a rotten borough, he was rather shy of declaiming against our corrupt representative system, and it was not till he was returned for Yorkshire that he came out with his plan for parliamentary reform.

The Session of 1829 was entirely occupied with carrying the measure of Catholic emancipation, brought forward by its strenuous opponents, the Duke of Wellington and Sir Robert Peel. Brougham and the other Whig leaders gave their cordial aid against the bigots, who would willingly have seen a civil war raging in the country rather than a Roman Catholic sitting in Parliament. It must be confessed, however, that the "Eldonites" had more reason for their apprehensions from the never-dying aggressiveness of Romanism than we then supposed. The

[1] His father died February 19, 1810. His mother continued to live till December 31, 1839.

fashionable belief (of which I was one of the many dupes) then prevailed that the Roman Catholics when they were no longer persecuted would no longer be intolerant, and that being relieved from all civil disabilities they would live quietly and contentedly, like the members of other religious persuasions which differ from the established church. We ought to have known them better, and to have provided against their incurable propensity to prefer the power of the Pope of Rome to that of the King and Parliament of their native land. In granting emancipation we ought either to have insisted on conditions (which might easily have been obtained) for repressing papal aggression in this kingdom, or by endowing the popish clergy in Ireland, we should have brought them into a state of dependence on the Government, which would have secured their loyalty and peaceable demeanor. If either course had been adopted, no bulls would have been published to repeal Acts of Parliament, and no attempt would have been made by the Vatican to parcel England into new bishoprics against the will of the Crown. Brougham, with others more far-seeing than himself, praised the inconsiderate manner in which the measure was framed, misapplying the maxim "Confidence is better than coercion." He afterwards expressed a wiser opinion upon the subject, and regretted that the precaution had not been taken, which is common in Roman Catholic countries, to stipulate with the Pope that no bull should be published in the British dominions till first examined by the civil authority at home, and that the Jesuits and other regular orders, if tolerated, should be under effectual legal control. Educated in Presbyterian Scotland, he had a very reasonable and salutary horror of the "idolatry of the Mass," of indulgences, and above all of the power and rapacity of the Roman Catholic priesthood.

During the Session of Parliament which began in February, 1830, there was a suspension of party struggles. The declining state of the health of George IV. indicated that his reign was drawing to a close, and there was an understanding among the three great sections into which politicians were then divided, — ministerial Tories, discontented ultra-Tories, and Whigs, — that, as Parliament must ere long be dissolved, they should wait for an appeal to the people before entering into any new combinations or making any onslaught upon each other. The subject of Parliamentary Reform being brought forward, Brougham not only uttered a violent tirade against universal suffrage and the ballot, but intimated an opinion that, although the representation of the people in Parliament was not in a satisfactory state, any alteration of the system should be undertaken with much caution. The utmost extent of change which he then seemed to meditate was that the great unrepresented towns in England should have members, and that in Scotland the abuse should be corrected of voting for fictitious superiorities, whereby the counties in that part of the United Kingdom were not better than English rotten boroughs. It is a curious fact that although the storm of the Reform Bill was impending, and in a few months the whole empire was convulsed by it, at this moment Parliamentary Reform excited little interest, hardly a petition for it was presented during the Session to either house of the legislature, and the opinion of those who considered themselves far-sighted politicians was that for years to come it would only continue to be talked of by eccentric enthusiasts.

The *entente cordiale* established between Lord Grey and the Duke of Wellington in opposing the administration of Mr. Canning, although lessening, had not entirely subsided, and there were still speculations about their forming a regular coalition in the new reign. It was quite clear that the Duke of Wellington must either attempt this or reconcile himself with the ultra-Tories, whom he had outraged by carrying the emancipation of the Catholics.

Brougham was rather fearful of Lord Grey's supposed inclination to become less liberal, and he strenuously tried to draw off the Whig party from the danger of Tory contact. With this view he embraced any favorable opportunity of throwing out sarcasms against the Government, and when accused by Sir Robert Peel of speaking disrespectfully of the Duke of Wellington, he expressed high admiration for the character of this great warrior, but added "I despise his fawning parasites and sycophants." This caused a great tumult in the House, which was appeased in the usual way by an explanation that the words were spoken in a "Parliamentary sense," and were not meant to convey any imputation on the personal honor of individuals.

Bulletins had been for some time issued respecting his Majesty's illness, which attempted to represent it as slight, and always assured his faithful subjects that he was "better." But at last came a royal message to both Houses stating that "His Majesty was laboring under a severe indisposition, which rendered it inconvenient and painful to sign with his own hand public instruments requiring the sign manual." A bill was speedily passed, allowing, under certain precautions, the use of a stamp for this purpose; and in a few weeks it was announced that "it had pleased Almighty God to take to his mercy our late most gracious Sovereign Lord George IV., of blessed memory."

A message from the new Sovereign recommended that the existing business in both Houses should be wound up as expeditiously as possible, to prepare for the calling of a new Parliament. The immediate consequence was the dispersion of members, with a view to the general election.

Before the hustings were erected, suddenly there arose all over the kingdom, in the place of apathy and indifference, a state of almost unexampled excitement. This was caused by the great Revolution in Paris, which exiled the elder branch of the Bourbons, and placed Louis Philippe, the "citizen King," upon the throne. Englishmen seemed to awake from torpor to the sudden belief that they were slaves. No imported plague ever produced such rapid effects, or spread so widely. In the year 1848 a similar epidemic traveled all over Europe except Great Britain, which on this occasion remained unscathed; but in 1830 Great Britain was more severely visited by the malady than any other country in Europe.[1]

The proclamation for a new Parliament strikingly exhibited the state of the public mind. Now the great object of the electors was to find out champions on whom they thought they could rely in fighting for popular rights.

Hitherto, from the earliest times, although towns had elected as their representatives strangers distinguished by their talents and public services, counties, without a single exception, had confined their choice to the great land-

---

[1] Phenomena explained by the theory that the corrupt state of our representation exposed us to the contagion at the former era, and the purified state of our representation saved us from the latter.

holders, or the members of ancient families residing and having property within their limits. Nevertheless the proud county of York, abounding in such candidates indigenous to the soil, sent a deputation to Henry Brougham, who had not an acre of land in either of the three ridings, and had no connection with the locality, except that twice a year he plied for business at the York assizes. The freeholders, so eager to be represented by him, did not even know that he had a patch of ground in Westmorland, and they had never heard of him as the representative of the De Burghams. But they regarded him as a man who, by brilliant talents, had raised himself from obscurity; who upon all important questions had taken the liberal side with zeal and energy, and who at the present crisis seemed to them the fittest interpreter of their principles and their wishes. This innovation was rather a shock to Whig traditions and prejudices, and many of the party, thinking it *unconstitutional* that a man locally unconnected with a county should represent it in Parliament, would have been better pleased that a Tory, if a true Yorkshireman, should have beaten the Liberal intruder. Brougham himself, however, entertained no such silly scruples, and at once consented to be started as a candidate.

No man ever went through such fatigue of body and mind as he did for the three following weeks. The assizes at York were about to begin, and he chanced to have a good many retainers. Instead of giving these up, he appeared in court and exerted himself as an advocate with more than wonted spirit. Having finished an address to the jury, he would throw off his wig and gown and make a speech to the electors in the Castle-yard on "the three glorious days of Paris," and the way in which the people of England might peaceably obtain still greater advantages. He would then return to court and reply in a cause respecting right of common of turbary, having in the twinkling of an eye picked up from his junior a notion of all that had passed in his absence. But what is much more extraordinary, before the nomination day arrived he had held public meetings and delivered stirring speeches in every town and large village within the county—still day by day addressing juries, and winning or losing verdicts. By these means, from the time when polling began, his election, which neither he nor his sober-minded supporters had seriously considered possible, appeared absolutely certain. Lord Morpeth, from great personal popularity as well as from hereditary love for his race, took the lead; but Brougham was far higher on the poll than Stuart Wortley, who had extraordinary advantages both personal and family,—counterbalanced at this moment by the heavy drawback that he was against progress, and was willing that Old Sarum, without inhabitants, should send as many members to represent the people in Parliament as the whole of Yorkshire. County elections at that time lasting fifteen days, excited prodigious interest. All England looked with eagerness on this contest, and, when Brougham's return was actually proclaimed, the triumph was said to form a grand epoch in the history of parliamentary representation.

An ancient ceremony remained, of which Brougham was rather afraid. He had to buckle on a sword, to cover his head with a cocked hat, to wear a pair of long spurs, to mount a charger, and, with his colleague, to ride round the castle of York, and through some of the principal streets of the city. He was not much of a horseman, and several times he was in danger of the fate which befell Mr. Justice Twisden in Lord Chancellor Shaftesbury's famous equestrian procession to Westminister Hall. But the ceremony concluded without his meeting with any disgrace, and the Yorkshiremen declared that he was every way worthy to be their representative.

This may be considered the proudest passage of Brougham's life. His return for Yorkshire was the spontaneous declaration of the most numerous, wealthy, and intelligent constituency in England that he was the fittest man to guide the destinies of his country. And he really may be said to have gained this elevation by good, without any mixture of evil, arts. The honor was wholly unsolicited, and he had carried his election not only without any *scintilla* of corruption in the way of bribery or treating, but he never had resorted to the tricks or cajolery of a demagogue, and to please the multitude he had not advanced any doctrines which were not recognized by our constitution. A little envy and jealousy may have been felt by a few of the Whig leaders, and danger was predicted to our representative system from such a violation of established usage; but the event was regarded with general satisfaction and good-will.

The new member for Yorkshire, when riding round the castle girt with his sword, might fairly be considered the foremost man in England by himself as well as by others. I do not think he can be taxed with inordinate vanity in the speech which he then made, and I dare say he was sincere at the moment in the resolutions which he then announced, although he afterwards saw good reasons for breaking them. Said he:—

"I have denounced the Duke of Wellington the *'general officer at the head of the government,'* and in spite of him your liberties are safe. I am now possessed of a power (having such a constituency to support me) that will enable me to compel the execution of measures which I have only hitherto been ventilating. *Nothing on earth shall ever tempt me to accept place.* I have more pride in representing Yorkshire, than I could derive from any office the King can bestow, because I have more effectual means of being useful to my fellow-citizens, and of gaining for myself an honest fame."

Till Parliament actually met it remained a mystery what part the Duke of Wellington was to play. He had it in his power long to remain Minister. He stood well in the opinion of the Liberals from the repeal of the Corporation and Test Act, and from the emancipation of the Catholics; and had he gone on to consent that Birmingham, Manchester, and the unrepresented great towns, should immediately have members—with a promise that the rotten part of the representation should gradually be examined and repaired—at the same time explaining his views of foreign policy, so as to relieve us from the dread of Absolutism, and the Holy Alliance—he would have had sufficient support to enable him to defy the ultra-Tories on the one hand, and the ultra-Radicals on the other. But he was now found wanting in "civil wisdom." He sadly undervalued the desire which had suddenly sprung up in the public mind for parliamentary reform; he not only believed himself, but was convinced that all sensible men believed, our representative system, with all its anomalies, to be perfect; he was deeply grieved by his separation from that section of the Tories who condemned his ecclesiastical policy; he thought that, reciprocally, they were willing to be reconciled to him; and he was resolved to bring about this reconciliation, disregarding the Whigs, who, for a while, had served his turn.

Accordingly he now took a decided part, which speedily brought on a crisis. Whereas the whole of the Liberal party approved of the expulsion of Charles X., and thought that the Belgians were fully justified in throwing off the Dutch yoke, he made the King say in his speech from the throne, ' The enlightened administration of the King of the Netherlands has not preserved his dominions from revolt;" and in his own speech in the debate on the Address he pronounced our representative system, as then existing, to be a piece of absolute perfection, liable to no censure, and capable of no improvement.

Unwittingly he had doomed his Government to destruction. The whole Liberal party felt that they were insulted, and impartial discerning men declared that he had committed an irretrievable error.

The very same night Brougham had given notice in the House of Commons of a motion for leave to bring in a bill to amend the representation of the people in Parliament, and had thus spoken of the French Revolution of July:—

"That revolution, which in my conscience I believe to be the most glorious in the annals of mankind, whether we regard the promptitude with which the acts of lawless despotism were repelled, or the yet more glorious temperance which distinguished the combatants after the battle was gained; for it is far more glorious for a people to gain a conquest over their passions when roused to vengeance than to overcome a tyrant in the field of battle."

Strange to say, the ultra-Tories were not in any degree propitiated by the Duke's concessions to their prejudices. They exclaimed, "*Nusquam tuta fides!*" His vow against parliamentary reform is like his vow against Catholic emancipation, and before the end of the session he may propose a bill for universal suffrage, annual parliaments, and vote by ballot." They swore that they would no longer delay the gratification of their vengeance.

The fall of the Duke of Wellington's Government was now inevitable, and it was hastened by the very ill-judged step of preventing the King from going to dine with the Lord Mayor and Corporation of London according to his engagement, under the pretense that from the alleged spread of disaffection it would be dangerous for his Majesty to trust himself among the citizens. A display of weakness and infatuation so striking indicated preordained perdition. Thus Brougham professed to lament what he now beheld:—

"I wish to Heaven that I had not lived to see the day when the forgetfulness of the people to the merits of the SOLDIER, and the forgetfulness of the SOLDIER to his own proper sphere of greatness, display to England, to Europe, and to the world an occasion when he can not accompany the Sovereign on his journey into the heart of an attached and loyal population."[1]

In the midst of these proceedings of national interest Brougham drew the notice of the public to a combination against himself of the attorneys and solicitors, in consequence, as he said, of a bill he had introduced for the establishment of local jurisdiction, which they thought would lessen their profits. The learned gentleman read a letter addressed to him containing this threat, which he complained of as a breach of privilege. He exclaimed:—

"Let them not lay the flattering unction to their souls that I can be prevented by a combination of all the attorneys in Christendom, or any apprehensions of injury to myself, from endeavoring to make justice pure and cheap. These gentlemen are much mistaken if they think I will die without defending myself. The question may be whether barristers or attorneys shall prevail; and I see no reason why barristers should not open their doors to clients without the intervention of attorneys and their long bills of costs. If I discover that there is a combination against me, I will decidedly throw myself upon my clients—upon the country gentlemen, the merchants and manufactuers —and if I do not, with the help of this House, beat those leagued against me, I shall be more surprised at it than at any misadventure of my life."

But all interest was absorbed in the anticipated ministerial crisis, and before long a question was brought forward on which Liberals and ultra-Tories could unite in a vote against the Government—when its doom was sealed. This was on Sir Henry Parnell's motion to inquire into the expenditure of the Civil List. Ministers were relieved that death should come to them in so gentle a shape.

[1] Speech in the House of Commons, 8th November, 1830.

They were well pleased to find themselves in a minority, and next day they announced their resignation, saying that " they only held their offices till their successors were appointed."

Earl Grey was sent for to submit to the King the list of a new administration. And now began his difficulties, the greatest of which was—*what was to be done with Brougham?* He dreaded the member for Yorkshire in the Cabinet, and the danger was appalling of entirely excluding him from the new arrangement; for in that case he might head a Radical opposition, and Whig rule would be very brief. Lord Grey said to Lord Althorp :—" May he not belong to the Government, and be obliged to support us, without being in the Cabinet? He may like to be Attorney-General. It is a high and a very lucrative office. He does not care much for money, to be sure, but he professes a great liking to his profession as an advocate, and he may not be contented to sacrifice it for a political office which he might not long hold. Let us see whether he will not be our Attorney-General." Lord Althorp, who, from sitting so long with Brougham in the House of Commons, better knew his insubordinate nature, shook his head, but said there could be little harm in the offer if Lord Grey had the courage to make it. Brougham was accordingly asked to call on Lord Grey, and the offer was made, but was rejected with scorn and indignation.

What Brougham's views and wishes originally were with respect to the office he should fill on the advent of the Whigs to power, I never could rightly learn. I hardly think that he had long aimed at the Great Seal, for this necessarily involved the loss of his dignity as member for the county of York, and forever excluded him from the House of Commons,—the only scene for which, as an orator, his powers were well adapted. He positively refused on this occasion to make any counter proposal, or to give a hint of the sort of place he desired, saying that " he was resolved not to be included in the arrangement, although he should be disposed to support the new government, *in as far as he conscientiously could*." These portentous words caused great dismay, but the conference broke up, and the hour of the two Houses assembling arrived, without anything being settled respecting his appointment.

It so happened that this was the very day for which his notice stood on the great question of Parliamentary Reform; and he entered the House evidently in a very perturbed state, having resolved to bring it on, whatever confusion might arise from such a discussion in the existing distracted state of the Government. Lord Althorp, representing the Whig *nucleus*, suggested that it would be improper to undertake any important debate after the communication from Sir Robert Peel that he and his colleagues only held office till their successors were appointed, and no appointment of successors had yet taken place.

"I trust, therefore," added he, "that for this reason, as well as for the advantage of the question itself, my honorable and learned friend will comply with the suggestion I make, and postpone his motion till we can enter upon the subject more coolly and deliberately." [*Hear, hear, hear.*]

Mr. *Brougham:* "I do feel the greatest repugnance to putting off the motion which stands for this evening. I admit that no question of so much importance has ever been brought forward when there was such a deficiency in the executive Government; but my difficulty is this—that no question of so much importance—no question involving such mighty and extensive interests—has ever been discussed at all within the walls of this House. Sensible, therefore, of the deep responsibility which I have incurred in undertaking to bring forward a question of such vast importance, I can not help feeling the difficulty in which I am placed in being called upon by my noble friend to defer it,—especially as his suggestion has been backed in some degree by the apparent concurrence of others. I am anxious, both from my sincere respect for the House and out of regard to the interests of the question itself, to defer to the opinion of those by whom it must ultimately be decided. I throw myself, therefore, fully, freely, and respectfully, upon the House. If the motion be put off, I own it will be contrary to my opinion and to my wishes. And further, *as no change that may take place in the administration can by any possibility affect me, I beg it to be understood that in putting off the motion I will put it off until the 25th of this month, and no longer. I will then, and at no more distant period, bring forward* the question of *Parliamentary Reform*, whatever may be the then state of affairs, and whosoever may then be his Majesty's Ministers."

As soon as he had finished, he cast a glance of defiance behind him, stalked off to the bar, and disappeared.

At the distance of a quarter of a century I retain a lively recollection of the sensation which this scene produced. He concluded his speech in a low and hollow voice, indicating suppressed wrath and purposed vengeance. The bravest held their breath for a time, and in the long pauses which he allowed to intervene between his sentences a feather might have been heard to drop. It was evident to all present that there was a mutiny in the Whig camp, and the Tories were in hopes that the new Government would prove to be an abortion.

The following day Brougham showed in the House, by his words as well as his looks, that no accommodation had taken place. A proposal being made that the consideration of election petitions should be put off till the crisis was over, he said, in a very sulky and sarcastic tone:—

"I am decidedly opposed to this motion. I think it a matter of the utmost necessity that you should fill up your numbers; and entertaining that opinion, I can not but be astonished both at the proposition itself and still more at the reason given in its favor. What do we want with the presence of the Ministers on election petitions? What do we want with Ministers? We can do as well (I speak with all possible respect of any future Ministry) —we can do as well without them as with them. I have nothing to do with them, except in the respect I bear them, and except as a member of this House. I state this for the information of those whom it may concern."

When he came next morning among his brother barristers in the robing-room, he declared that "he should take no office whatever, and that when he was returned for Yorkshire he made his election between power and the service of the people."

I do not certainly know the exact turn which the negotiation then took, but I have heard, and I believe, that the Whig leaders still expressing a strong desire that Brougham should join them on his own terms, he caused a verbal intimation to be given to them that he expected an offer of the Great Seal. Lord Grey, although well stricken in years, was supposed at this time to be *platonically* under the fascination of the beautiful Lady Lyndhurst, and to have had a strong desire to retain her husband as his Chancellor. It is said that he expressed considerable doubts whether Brougham, whose stock of Common Law was slender, and who knew nothing about Equity whatever, was well qualified to preside in the Court of Chancery. The general feeling of those present at the conference, however, was that Brougham's adhesion was indispensably necessary to the formation of the Government, and that he must have a *carte blânche*. Whether this be fact or fiction, certain it is that on Saturday, the 20th of November, it was announced from authority that Brougham was to be Chancellor, and coming into the Court of King's Bench on that day he accepted the congratulations of his friends on his elevation. He had no misgivings as to his sufficiency for the office, and I believe that he was more delighted than he had been a few months before, when girt with a sword, and wearing long spurs, he rode round the castle of York as knight of the shire. I ventured to give him some good advice, which he repaid twenty years after, when I was myself made a judge; and all that was said to him seriously or jocularly he took in good part. It was expected that he would have made a flaming oration in taking leave of us, in the King's Bench, and a great crowd had assembled to hear it, but as the Court was rising, he contented himself with making a silent bow to the bench and another to the bar.

CHAPTER CCXXVII.

LORD CHANCELLOR.

ON Monday, the 22nd of November, 1830, the Great Seal was delivered to him by the King, at St. James's Palace, and he took his place on the woolsack; but being still a commoner, and plain Henry Brougham, he acted only as Speaker of the House of Lords. His patent of nobility was in preparation, but had not been completed. I believe that, although he saw an immense crowd below the bar, on the steps of the throne, and in the galleries, who had come to see him inaugurated, he regretted, for a time at least, the elevation he had reached; for an animated discussion immediately arose in the House respecting the formation of the new ministry and parliamentary reform, in which he was pointedly alluded to; and, as yet having no right to open his mouth in the assembly, unless to put the question, he was condemned to silence, and by the impatience he manifested he seemed to signify that he could have vindicated himself and his colleagues much better than Lord Grey or Lord Lansdowne had done.

Next morning, without yet having been sworn in or installed in the Court of Chancery, he took his place on the woolsack to hear a Scotch appeal. The counsel were surprised to find that, according to a form which had been long disused, they were compelled by the Yeoman Usher of the Black Rod to make three *congées* as they were marched up to the bar, when the Chancellor, who had been covered, took off his cocked hat with much solemnity, and signalled to them to begin. Notwithstanding the contempt which he expressed for the "trappings of his office," he was by no means without a taste for scenic representation, when he had to play the principal character.

The appeal heard was *Grieve* v. *Wilson*, respecting the right *hypothec* of Scotch landlords on the produce of the *located land*. He laughed a good deal at this law, and said that it must immediately be altered, as the doctrines "ventilated" in the appeal would, if known, excite great alarm in Mark Lane. He was very pleasant and jocose, but his humor was more agreeable to the bystanders than to the objects of it—the Lord Ordinary and the Lord Justice Clerk Boyle, the latter of whom was said to have made a grave remonstrance against the ridicule cast upon him.

But the same day there was much laughing at the expense of the Lord Chancellor himself, when it was announced that his patent of nobility was completed, and that he was now a Baron, by the title of "Lord Brougham AND VAUX." To some private friends he had formerly stated in confidence that he was entitled to a Barony of Vaux by descent through the female line, but no one imagined that he would do so unusual a thing as to add this word to a new created peerage; for all the instances (such as Hamilton and Brandon, Buccleuch and Queensberry, Leven and Melville, Say and Sele, or Dudley and Ward) of the copulative being so used are where two titles of the same grade, having been separately created, are united by descent in one individual. Among the innumerable jokes against this new title, the most cutting, if not the best, was that "Henry Brougham had destroyed himself, and was now *Vaux et præterea nihil.*" To meet these jokes, and to show how little he cared about titles, he had always, with real or affected humility, refused to sign his name as peers usually do, but signed H Brougham, or more commonly H. B.[1]

The following is the entry in the journals of his taking his seat as a peer:—

"The Duke of Gloucester informed their Lordships that his Majesty had been pleased to elevate Henry Brougham, Esq., Lord Chancellor of Great Britian, to the dignity of a peer of the realm by the title of Baron BROUGHAM AND VAUX. The Lord Chancellor, on hearing this intimation, quitted the Woolsack, and left the House to robe. He speedily returned, and was introduced as a Baron by the Marquess Wellesley and Lord Durham. His Lordship took the oaths, resumed his seat on the woolsack, and received the congratulations of his friends."[2]

The same day he laid on the table, in a very strange and irregular manner, a copy of a petition he had presented to the Crown, claiming a right to be summoned to Parliament as representative of an ancient barony of Vaux, which he alleged had descended upon him through the female line. The House had no jurisdiction to take cognizance of such a claim, except on a reference by the Crown, and such a reference is only made upon the report of the Attorney-General that a *primâ facie* case is made out by the claimant. Brougham never ventured to take any step to substantiate his claim, and it must be considered a mere dream

---

[1] In former times English peers used always to sign their christian name as well as name of dignity, merely substituting this for their surname; but if Brougham was aware of the old fashion, I believe that he had no thought of reviving it, and was only desirous of doing something out of the common course.

[2] On inspecting the Journal I find:—"Friday, 19th November, Ds. Lyndhurst, Cancellarius; Monday, 22nd November, Henricus Brougham, Cancellarius; Tuesday, 23rd November, Ds. Brougham and Vaux, Cancellarius.

or fiction. He uttered nothing on this occasion, and, to the astonishment of all present, the House rose without the sound of his voice being heard, except in putting the question, "That this House do now adjourn."

On this very day on which he took his seat as a peer, a motion being made in the House of Commons for the issuing of a writ to elect a new member in his stead, he was violently assailed by Mr. Croker, who recapitulating the protestations he had made there and elsewhere against accepting any place in the new Government, and his repeated vows never to exchange the representation of Yorkshire for any honors which the Crown could confer, called for "an explanation of his having suddenly vacated his seat in that House by becoming Lord High Chancellor and Baron Brougham and Vaux; which either showed a successful grasping at office by false pretenses, or a sudden change of purpose unexplained and inexplicable."

"*Mr. Duncombe* deeply lamented the time and the circumstances in which that distinguished person had allowed himself to be seduced from the commanding eminence which he occupied in that House. This was the place in which his transcendant abilities were wanted. The noble and learned lord had often told them of 'another place from which they had little to expect,' and yet he had gone to that place—never to return. If he had remained member for Yorkshire until he had redeemed his pledges and fulfilled his promises by carrying his important measures respecting negro slavery and parliamentary reform, he might have gracefully retired to *elsewhere*. His appointment would then have been hailed with the acclamations of his friends; whereas it is now only satisfactory to those who hate him, and take a malignant pleasure in seeing his fair fame forever tarnished."

"*Sir James Mackintosh* pointed out the unfairness of such attacks, when, though unfounded, they could not be repelled without disclosures which could not possibly be then made."

"*Mr. Macaulay.*—I owe the noble and learned lord no political allegiance, but as a member of this House I can not banish from my memory the extraordinary eloquence with which he has made these walls resound—an eloquence which, being gone, has left nothing equal to it behind; and when I behold the departure of that great man from amongst us, and when I see the place in which he usually sat, and from which he has so often astonished us by the mighty powers of his mind, occupied so very differently this evening by the honorable member who commenced this assault, I can not express the emotions to which such a contrast gives rise. An opponent who would sooner have burnt his tongue than used such language in his presence, now thinks he may rail at him with impunity!"

The defense was interrupted by a cry of *Order*, and after explanations and apologies, the vote passed for issuing the writ.[1]

The new Lord Chancellor, after deliberating for three days whether he should take any public notice of the attack, asked Lord Grosvenor, when presenting a petition in favor of parliamentary reform, to allude to what had lately passed in the House of Commons. Accordingly the noble Earl said that—

"Seeing his noble and learned friend on the woolsack, after having been so long the ornament of the other House, and now likely to be the ornament of this, he was anxious to give him an opportunity—if he chose to avail himself of it—of correcting some misrepresentations and replying to some charges made against him in another place."

"*Lord Chancellor.*—' My Lords, I am obliged to my noble friend for the opportunity he has afforded me of stating my opinions upon the subject of his petition, but many opportunities will soon occur when I may do so with more regularity. That my opinions may be already known to your Lordships in common with the great mass of my fellow-citizens is not improbable, and I hope may not be to my disadvantage. It is painful to me, and the more so from the unexpected appeal of my noble friend, that now, when for the first time I have the honor of addressing your Lordships, I should be called upon to speak of a subject in every way of such inferior importance as myself. Nevertheless, as misrepresentations have gone abroad, and

---

[1] 1 Hansard, N. S., 649. When Macaulay first came forward Brougham professed to patronize him; but as the client's fame flourished the patron's jealousy was excited, and gradually an unfriendly feeling grew up between them, till at last Macaulay spoke of Brougham as "a turbid rhetorician," and Brougham designated Macaulay "a tolerably good writer of romances." Brougham thought that nothing had appeared during the present generation deserving the name of history, except his own "History of the House of Lancaster."

remarks of an unfriendly nature touching the consistency of my public conduct have been uttered *elsewhere*, should I now shrink—or rather let me say, should I decline offering a few words in deference to your Lordships, and I may add, out of respect to myself,—after the call which has been made on me, it might wear the appearance of shrinking from attack. It will be sufficient, however, to say very briefly, that I bear, and shall continue to bear, with perfect equality of mind, everything that may be said of me in any quarter whatsoever; that I am not at all surprised, but the contrary, that a person respectable for his knowledge and talent (meaning Croker [1]), has been led into errors concerning me, from ignorance of my character; and that I bear, with an equal mind, what has been said by that individual under the influence of mistake. I am not astonished at the observations which have been made by persons in another place expressing their astonishment at my present position; they can not feel greater astonishment than I myself do at my consenting to my elevation to the distinguished place which I now hold in his Majesty's councils. I share their astonishment, for they can not be more stricken with wonder than I am, that at this late period, at this eleventh hour, I should have overcome my repugnance to resign my high station as representative for Yorkshire. Up to that time when I am reported to have stated my intention of not severing myself from the representation of Yorkshire, I no more contemplated the possibility of my being prevailed upon to quit the station I held for that which I now hold, than I at the present moment fancy I shall ever go back to that House from which the favor of his Majesty has raised me.[2] I need not add, that in changing my station in Parliament, the principles which have ever guided me remain unchanged. When I accepted the high office to which I have been called, I did so in the full and perfect conviction that far from disabling me to discharge my duty to my country--far from render-

[1] At this time there was enmity between Brougham and Croker which seemed implacable; but when Brougham, as a discarded ex-Chancellor, was assailing the Whig Government, they became fast friends, and warmly complimented each other both in public and private.

[2] It is a curious fact, while almost all the members of the House of Peers are in the habit of going into the Peers' gallery in the House of Commons, Brougham, whether under a vow or from want of curiosity, has never bodily been under the roof of the House of Commons since he ceased to be a member of it.

ing my services less efficient, it would but enlarge the sphere of my utility. The thing which dazzled me most in the prospect opening to my view, was not the gewgaw splendor of the place, but that it seemed to afford me, if I were honest—on which I could rely; if I were consistent —which I knew to be matter of absolute necessity in my nature; if I were as able as I was honest and consistent— a field of more extended exertion. That by which the Great Seal did dazzle my eyes, and induce me to quit a station which till this time I deemed the most proud an Englishman could enjoy, was that it seemed to hold out to me the gratifying prospect that in serving my King I should be better able to serve my country.' "[1]

"The lady protests too much, methinks." Although born in Scotland, he had not been endowed with the " second sight," or, coming events casting their shadows before, he might have seen visions of himself in battle array against his former associates and his former principles. His acceptance of the Great Seal, if fairly offered to him, required no justification, and by excusing he accused himself. Regard being had to the various functions of the office of Chancellor, he was, upon the whole, by no means unqualified for it. His acquaintance with the practice of the Equity Courts was necessarily slender; but he was well imbued with a general knowledge of jurisprudence, and conscious of his unrivalled industry and energy, he might well hope to perform in this department better than if he had been reared as a mere " conveyancer and equity draughtsman." To carry into effect his great plan for reforming our jurisprudence, his position as Lord Chancellor would give him influence which he could not possess in any other; and he might, at the same time, still promote the cause of education, the effectual suppression of the slave trade, and all other such salutary measures, more effectually than if he had remained in the House of Commons, the representative of Yorkshire. Therefore for the simple fact of his being in possession of the Great Seal, I do not see that any apology was required. Others were astonished merely because he had so peremptorily and solemnly declared, while the new Government was in the process of formation, he would take no office whatever under Lord Grey—at the same time

[1] 1 Hansard, 674.

showing strong symptoms of disappointment and irritation. Whence his own astonishment arose it is more difficult to conjecture. Burke, in his treatise, "On the Sublime and Beautiful," says—"Astonishment is that state of the soul, in which all its motions are suspended, with some degree of horror." Why should this state of Lord Brougham's soul have been produced by the Whig leaders offering him the only office which he would accept, knowing that he could not be left out without imminent peril to their stability, or by his accepting an office which he desired, and in which he reasonably thought that he might usefully serve his country?

Being indifferent as to the pecuniary emoluments of this office, he was much pleased with the immense patronage which belonged to it—partly from the pleasure which he sincerely felt at being able disinterestedly to oblige a friend, but partly also, perhaps, from considering what a high price he could now pay for praise, and how lavishly it would be bestowed upon him. At the same time, I believe that he did form very high and noble designs—overrating, I fear, his powers of performance. Of the ancients, his great model was Cicero, whom he hoped to rival as an orator and a fine writer. Of the moderns, he thought Lord Bacon's fame was most to be envied, and there was no department of genius in which he did not hope that he might fairly enter into competition with this "brightest of mankind." As a judge he boldly and openly said he should excel him, intending that the decisions "*Tempore Brougham*," should be received with as much reverence as Lord Hardwicke's; and in philosophy he had treatises part begun, and part conceived in his own mind, which would excel the *Novum Organum*.[1]

It was not till Thursday, the 25th of November, that he was regularly installed in the Court of Chancery and sworn,—"the Master of the Rolls holding the book." He wished to make this ceremony as imposing as possible, and it was deferred that he might have as much of royalty and nobility about him as he could muster. He was attended by three royal highnesses, the Duke of Sussex, the Duke of Gloucester, and Prince Leopold, and by various noblemen, of whom the Duke of Devonshire was

---

[1] Some of these he afterwards gave to the world.

highest in rank. It was thought, that after the fashion of Cardinal Wolsey, Sir Thomas More, Lord Bacon and the old Chancellors, he would, on being placed in the "marble chair," have delivered an oration upon the duties of Chancellor, and the manner in which he proposed to perform them; but he followed the more modern precept, by bowing out the grandees who attended him as soon as the oath was recorded on the motion of the Attorney-General, and then proceeding with the common business of the Court.

The new Ministers were to stand or fall by their promised bill for parliamentary reform, and at the first Cabinet which they held after their installation the subject was discussed. The Chancellor proposed that this bill, which he was impatient to introduce on the memorable 16th of November (when he declared that no change in the construction of the ministry could possibly affect *him*) should be adopted as the basis of the government measure, but his explanation of it, and the answers to a few questions put to him, showed his scheme to be so defective and so crude that reference to it could only perplex and mislead. It contained some startling clauses for lowering and extending the franchise beyond what was considered prudent, but hardly any disfranchisement, all the nomination boroughs being allowed to retain at least one member.[1] I know not whether at this time he favored the doctrine that the privilege of sending members to Parliament, once granted to a place, could not be taken away constitutionally, except on clear proof of corruption; or thought that the small boroughs should be protected for the good service they had rendered to the Liberal side

[1] Mr. Roebuck asserts, in his "History of the Whig Administration," that on the 18th of November Brougham called a meeting of his House of Commons friends, and fully explained to them his measure—of which eight heads are given—making it very like Lord Grey's Bill. This statement I can most positively contradict. I was then one of Brougham's "House of Commons friends," and had sent in my adhesion to him as far as parliamentary reform was concerned, when he gave his notice at the commencement of the Session; and I am certain that he never called any such meeting of friends as is here supposed, and that he never explained to me or to any of them the particulars of his plan; on the contrary, he said he wished it to remain secret till he detailed it in the House of Commons. On the 18th of November, he was entirely absorbed in the negotiation about the Great Seal, and so remained till he had obtained it. But then and during discussions which followed, Brougham's most intimate friends not in the Cabinet professed entire ignorance of the proposed enactments of his bill.

ever since the revolution of 1688; or felt that having himself sat in the House of Commons as the representative of a peer, till he had very recently been elected for Yorkshire, it would have been very ungracious to prevent others from entering the House of Commons by the same honorable means—but he has always shown a rooted antipathy to disfranchisement, and he subsequently threw out in the Lords bills passed by the Commons to disfranchise Stafford, Warwick, and Sudbury, for corruption very clearly proved.

Lord Durham, the member of the Cabinet most eager for a thorough reform, and particularly zealous against the rotten boroughs, was much alarmed by the views which the Chancellor disclosed, and suggested that the subject should be referred to the committee of the Cabinet. This being agreed to, he contrived that the Chancellor, on account of his multiplied engagements, should be excused from serving upon it. The members selected, who really acted, were Lord Althorp, Lord Durham, and Sir James Graham; Lord John Russell, although not then of the Cabinet, being associated with them. Brougham did not trouble himself further with the subject till the committee, in the beginning of the new year, made their report, accompanying a draft of their proposed bill. On account of the importance and difficulty of the measure, Ministers claimed ample time to prepare it, and both Houses stood adjourned from the 23d of December to the 3d of February following.

Before the adjournment, Brougham made no further demonstration in the House of Lords, and confined himself to laying two bills on the table, one to take away the *lien* or *hypothec* which landlords have in Scotland on the produce of the land for the payment of rent, and the other for the establishment of local courts to try small causes in England. The first turned out an inauspicious failure—for it raised such a tempest of opposition that the author was obliged to withdraw it before it had been read a second time. The other would have passed if the friendly feeling towards the Government still entertained by Lord Lyndhurst, now become Lord Chief Baron of the Exchequer, had continued. This judicial appointment was a contrivance of the Lord Chancellor, who entertained the vain hope that Lyndhurst, in consideration of this *sup* would steadily support the Whig Government. The Premier declared this to be a masterly move, and as soon as Chief Baron Alexander could be prevailed upon to resign, the arrangement was completed. Lyndhurst had cautiously avoided giving any pledge, or making use of any expression which could be quoted as even a faint promise to adhere to the Whigs. Lord Grey, however, had asked him to carry the Regency Bill through the Lords after the change of Government, and there seemed a very friendly understanding between them. But the new Chief Baron having been sworn in on the 18th of January, he immediately after gave the most unequivocal signs of a determination to lead the Opposition in the House of Lords, and as soon as possible to storm the Treasury Bench.

The Chancellor, when adjourning his court on December 24th for the Christmas holidays, delivered a short address to the bar, in which he indulged pretty freely in self-laudation while reviewing his exploits since he had presided there—and I must say, very excusably, although it might have been better if the task had been left to others. However new to the situation and to the business in hand, he had, upon the whole, disposed very reputably of most of the cases which came before him; and, notwithstanding some few mistakes and eccentricities which caused momentary mirth, he commanded the respect of the bar and of the public. It might have been feared that his *judicial* performance might resemble Jean Jacques Rousseau's *musical* performance in the concert given by that wonderful man before he had been initiated in the rudiments of music; but, on the contrary, Brougham's natural genius, assisted by slender cultivation, carried him through with *éclat*. He was by no means timid in offering an opinion upon points which were quite strange to him; and when he found, by observing the faces of those who were listening, that he was quite wrong, instead of being abashed and submitting to any continued triumph over him, he rallied in a most marvelous manner, and preserved his ascendancy after misadventures which would have ruined seven ordinary mortals. His habit which caused him the greatest peril was writing letters while he was sitting on the bench and supposed to be listening to arguments from the bar. He did not resort to the art of the wily Eldon, who, when writing letters in court to his private friends, folded the paper as if he had been taking notes of the argument. Lord Chancellor Brougham, above all disguise, many times in the course of a morning would openly receive letters on the bench, read them, and write, seal and despatch answers, meanwhile listening to the counsel and asking them questions.

This habit was particularly distasteful to that very petulant, though very learned and able counsel, Sir Edward Sugden (now Lord St. Leonards), who tried to correct it, but was unlucky in the occasion which he took and the method he employed for that purpose. As the most marked and effectual intimation of his displeasure, he suddenly stopped in the middle of a sentence while the Chancellor was writing. After a considerable pause the Chancellor, without raising his eyes from the paper, said, "Go on, Sir Edward; I am listening to you." *Sugden.*—"I observe that your Lordship is engaged in writing, and not favoring me with your attention." *Chancellor.*—"I am signing papers of mere form. You may as well say that I am not to blow my nose or take snuff while you speak." Sir Edward sat down in a huff; but on this occasion he was laughed at, and the Chancellor was applauded.

The court being adjourned, Brougham like a pious son (as he ever showed himself), took a journey to Brougham Hall, to visit his venerable mother, and, kneeling before her, to ask her blessing on a Lord Chancellor. The good old lady still preserved her fine faculties quite entire; but, while she reciprocated her boy's affection for her, and was proud of his abilities and the distinction he had acquired, she said with excellent good sense and feeling, "My dear Harry, I would rather have embraced the member for Yorkshire; but God Almighty bless you!"

When Parliament re-assembled, the Chancellor brought forward his scheme for reforming the Court of Chancery, thus humorously apologizing for not taking further time to mature it:—

"I, who have little or no experience, whose knowledge of the practice of the Court must necessarily be limited— I, a mere novice in the law of that Court, nevertheless begin with attempting what others, to the very close of their career, have not attempted—a change, an innovation; and, to sum up all in one expression so hateful, so alien to long-established habits, so sore, so agonizing to the experienced practitioner,—in one hateful word, the head and front of my offending—A CHANCERY REFORM. Reform, odious and reprobated in all places, is especially odious and especially reprobated there, when it appears as it were a monster, composed of two parts so utterly irreconcilable and incongruous as CHANCERY and REFORM. Short as my experience has been in that Court, I almost already begin to feel those difficulties and those incumbrances which have overpowered and mastered the good intentions of all my illustrious predecessors. I feel afraid that I am already, as it were, becoming attached to the soil; I am already in the course of seduction; I am getting involved in the integuments and entanglements which I have been describing as forming the excuse of those who succumbed. I, who came into the Court pouring out prayers for reform, am almost already incapacitated for attempting it.

"'Vix prece finitâ, torpor gravis alligat artus,
Mollia cinguntur tenui præcordia libro:
In frondem crines, in ramos brachia crescunt;
Pes, modo tam velox pigris radicibus hæret,
Ora cacumen obit; remanet nitor unus in illâ.'

"I feel that I am on the point, if I delay but an instant, of fleeing altogether from the day, of becoming fixed and rooted in the ground; and that I shall flourish only like the laurel in the fable, a monument of her escape from the embraces of the God of Light."[1]

He then went on, at very great length, to propose the abolition of a vast number of sinecures in the Court of Chancery, and various improvements in its procedure; but he did not touch the radical grievance—the system of *Masters in Chancery*, to whom every cause was referred after any point in it had been decided by the Equity Judge, with a power of appealing to him again and again upon every question of law or fact which the Master had decided; so that the cause used to go to sleep for years in the Master's office, and the suitors being kept oscillating between the Master and the Equity Judge by a sort of *perpetuum mobile* no suit was ever terminated. But the time for such a change had not yet arrived. Although the

[1] 2 Hansard, 850.

abolition of the Masters in Chancery was carried in little more than twenty years after, such a purpose at this time would have been considered as preposterous as a bill to abolish the satellites of Jupiter.

The attention of both Houses of Parliament and of the nation was soon entirely absorbed by the question of Parliamentary Reform. The Committee of the Cabinet had recommended a very sweeping scheme, entirely disfranchising a large number or boroughs, limiting the right of a great many others to one representative, creating a considerable number of new constituencies, extending the right of voting to copyholders and leaseholders in counties and to all householders in boroughs paying £15 a year rent, and introducing vote by ballot. The Chancellor was rather shocked to find the projected measure going so far beyond that which he himself had contemplated; but, to avoid disunion, he consented to adopt the whole, except vote by ballot, to which he expressed an insuperable antipathy. Upon this point he was supported by Lord Grey and several other members of the Cabinet. Lord Durham and Sir James Graham long held out for the ballot, alleging that without it the measure would give no satisfaction. At last a compromise was entered into: the ballot was given up, and, by way of compensation, the town franchise was to be reduced from £15 to £10, whereby several hundred thousand more voters would be created. The bill so framed the Chancellor agreed to, and very gallantly and with perfect good faith supported, although he several times in debate hinted that it was not entirely to his mind, that it was rather too sweeping, and that if its principle were adopted its details might be materially modified.

The bill being launched in the House of Commons, while it was proceeding there almost daily discussion took place upon it in the House of Lords, brought on by the presentation of petitions. In these the Chancellor bore the principal part, attacking with much violence the anti-reforming Lords. He was particularly sarcastic upon the poor Marquis of Londonderry, who had exposed himself by several unfortunate mistakes in his references to history.

The victimized peer now sought revenge by bringing before the House a matter which had made a great noise in the clubs and in the newspapers. The Lord Chancellor,

attended by his officers, driving in his coach from the
Court of Chancery at Westminster to assist at the Queen's
Drawing-room, when he reached the Horse Guards and
wished to pass into St. James's Park, was stopped by the
military stationed there, and told that orders had been
given by the King to allow no carriage to be admitted,
except that of the Speaker of the House of Commons.
Nevertheless, the Chancellor's coachman whipped his
horses and the carriage passed through, the military giving
way on both sides.

A few days after, the Marquis of Londonderry, in pursuance of a notice he had given, rose to put certain questions on the subject to the Commander-in-Chief. He
said :—

" Their Lordships must see how necessary it was that
military orders should be upheld, and that no individual,
however high his station, should be permitted to contra-
vene them ; and he was sure that when it was alleged that
the first law officer of the country had defied that authority,
some explanation was due. The Lord Chancellor had
been charged with breaking through the King's Guard on
the day of the last drawing-room. There might be some
exaggeration; and in order that their Lordships might be
in possession of the facts, he would ask his noble and gallant friend three questions. First, Whether the King's
Guard had been forced by the Lord Chancellor? Secondly,
Whether this arose from mistake or from a misconception
of the orders given to the Guard? Thirdly, Whether the
officer whose Guard was forced had been put under arrest,
or had satisfactorily explained his conduct?"

Lord Hill, the Commander-in-chief, said that after the
fullest investigation, he came to the conclusion that the
officer was not to blame, and that the soldiers under him
had done their duty ; and he was quite satisfied, from his
communication with the noble and learned lord himself,
that he had no idea whatever of forcing the Guard.

"*Lord Chancellor.*—I can assure your Lordships that no
one in the world thinks less of the state and pomp of the
office which I hold than I do. The observances of that
state and pomp are to me certainly the most irksome and
the most oppressive parts of my public duty ; and it was
not from any foolish wish of passing through the Horse
Guards, instead of going round by Piccadilly and down

Constitution Hill, that I ordered my carriage to the Horse
Guards. I had been detained late in the House of Lords
to determine an appeal of great urgency, and I had only
time by the shortest route to pay my duty to their Majesties. When suddenly stopped by my horses' reins being
seized, I thought there must be some mistake, which was
strengthened by the remark of the officer, that it was
only the Speaker of the House of Commons who had permission to pass, as I could not imagine that the same
privilege should not be extended to the Speaker of the
Upper House. The officer, however, having satisfied me
that there was no mistake, and that his orders were peremptory, I said, 'Then I must turn back.' But I suppose
the footman had not communicated to the coachman the
order to turn back. I certainly was never more surprised
in my life than when I found that my coachman had taken
me through, and I was in St. James's Park before I could
pull the check-string. I certainly then thought that it would
have been ridiculous to have turned back as the mischief
had been done by the mistaken zeal of my coachman, who
had acted on his former orders, to make as much haste as
possible. In conversation, to save the man I have taken
the whole blame upon myself; but I can assure your Lordships that I am the last person to furnish an example of
setting military discipline at defiance, and that I was far
from entertaining the idea of forcing the King's Guard.
I do not well see how I could have accomplished this exploit single-handed, even with the aid of the mace and the
purse. Nothing could be further from my intentions than
to sanction any breach of the orders of his late or his present Majesty."[1]

King William IV., who thought that this was little short
of a "levying of war," publicly professed himself satisfied
with the Chancellor's explanation; but privately expressed
a doubt whether the order given to the coachman, when
he whipped his horses, had not been "*Forward!*" And
ever after, when anything occurred to alarm him by Lord
Chancellor Brougham's vagaries, this incident of *forcing
the Guard* came back to his recollection. For a while it
made a great sensation, and was the subject of many songs
and caricatures.

The "*Times*" had an elaborate leader upon it, supposed

[1] 3 Hansard, 493.

to smack of the Chancellor's own touch, and saying that "the coachman had done it all." But as yet there was a close fraternity between him and Barnes, the editor; insomuch that this journal, which was hereafter to vilify him grievously, swarmed with puffs on Lord Brougham so gross that he could not have penned them himself; extolling to the skies his genius, his acquirements, and his Herculean application to all his labors.[1] And, such was the effect of iteration, that before he had said a word in Parliament upon the bill, Reformers deemed him the hope of the nation. County meetings, and other popular assemblies, passed resolutions expressing their confidence in him; and several corporations, as prepayment for his services, voted him their freedom. On receiving this honor from the citizens of York, to increase their enthusiasm he already expressed his regret that he had accepted the Great Seal and was no longer their servant.

The grand crisis of the Reform Bill was now at hand. Although popular with the nation, it was distasteful to the existing House of Commons. If the votes upon it had been taken by ballot, it would have been rejected by an immense majority; and, with all the terrors of open voting before the eyes of members, they passed the second reading by a majority of *one* only. Subsequently, on General Gascoigne's motion against reducing the number of representatives for England, they plainly showed a determination to mutilate the bill; and, with small majorities in favor of any part of it in the Lower House, there seemed a certainty that it would be at once crushed by the Lords. The following evening a very hostile disposition to the Government was shown in a committee on the Ordnance Estimates, and what was done was said to amount to a *stopping of the supplies.*

The following day a Cabinet was held, and a resolution was unanimously passed to advise the King immediately to dissolve the Parliament. At the rising of the Cabinet this resolution was communicated by Lord Grey and the Lord Chancellor to his Majesty, who very readily assented to it; and the usual manner for the ceremony of a prorogation to take place next day.

Yet, to shake all faith even in contemporary history,

---

[1] *E. g.*, "Parliamentary Reform is safe from the gigantic powers of its champion on the woolsack."—"*Times,*" 1st February, 1831.

within twenty years from the event a publication appeared, professing to be a "History of the Whig Administration : by John Arthur Roebuck, Esq., M.P. for Sheffield." This gentleman was a particularly intimate, private friend of Lord Brougham, and professed that he obtained from Lord Brougham authentic information of all the secret proceedings of the Government while Lord Brougham remained in office. The author gives a totally different account of the interview between the King and his two Ministers;[1] yet, with such claims to authenticity, it is utterly fabulous.[2]

Mr. Roebuck's narration being every way so closely connected with the subject of this memoir, I copy it *in extenso*, and it will at all events amuse the reader, although I fear that it violates probability too much to be considered artistically good :—

"On the morning of the 22d, Lord Grey and the Lord Chancellor waited on the King in order to request that he would instantly and on that day dissolve the House. The whole scene of this interview of the King and his Ministers, as related by those who could alone describe it, is a curious illustration of the way in which the great interests of mankind often seem to depend on petty incidents, and in which ludicrous puerilities often mix themselves up with events most important to the welfare of whole nations. The necessity of a dissolution had long been foreseen and decided on by the Ministers, but the King had not yet been persuaded to consent to so bold a measure; and now the two chiefs of the administration were about to introduce themselves into the royal closet, not only to advise and ask for a dissolution, but to request the King on the sudden, on this very day, and within a few hours, to go down and put an end to his Parliament in the midst of the session, and with all the ordinary business of the session, yet unfinished. The bolder mind of the Lord Chancellor took the lead, and Lord Grey anxiously solicited him to *manage* the King on the oc-

[1] Vol. ii., 148.
[2] See " Correspondence of the late Earl Grey with King William IV.," published in 1867, where it appears that the King had given his consent to a dissolution, in a letter to Lord Grey early on the 21st of April ; and the subsequent interview of Lord Grey and the Chancellor with the King on the 22nd, before the Council met at 12 o'clock, was to request the King to prorogue Parliament in person, which he at once agreed to do.—ED.

casion. So soon as they were admitted the Chancellor, with some care and circumlocution, propounded to the King the object of the interview they had sought. The startled monarch no sooner understood the drift of the Chancellor's somewhat paraphrastic statement, than he exclaimed in wonder and anger against the very idea of such a proceeding. 'How is it possible, my Lords, that I can after this fashion repay the kindness of Parliament to the Queen and myself? They have granted me a most liberal civil list, and to the Queen a splendid annuity in case she survives me.' The Chancellor confessed that they had, as regarded his Majesty, been a liberal and wise Parliament, but said that, nevertheless, their further existence was incompatible with the peace and safety of the kingdom. Both he and Lord Grey then strenuously insisted upon the absolute necessity of their request, and gave his Majesty to understand that this advice was by his Ministers unanimously resolved on, and that they felt themselves unable to conduct the affairs of the country in the present condition of the Parliament. This last statement made the King feel that a general resignation would be the consequence of a further refusal; of this, in spite of his secret wishes, he was at the moment really afraid; and therefore he, by employing petty excuses, and suggesting small and temporary difficulties, soon began to show that he was about to yield. 'But, my Lords, nothing is prepared; the great officers of State are not summoned.' 'Pardon me, Sir,' said the Chancellor, bowing with profound apparent humility, 'we have taken the great liberty of giving them to understand that your Majesty commanded their attendance at the proper hour.' 'But, my Lords, the crowns and the robes, and other things needed, are not prepared.' 'Again I most humbly entreat your Majesty's pardon for my boldness,' said the Chancellor; 'they are all prepared and ready, the proper officers being desired to attend in proper form and time.' 'But, my Lords,' said the King, reiterating the form in which he put his objection, 'you know the thing is wholly impossible; the guards, the troops, have had no orders, and can not be ready in time.' This objection was in reality the most formidable one. The orders to the troops on such occasions emanate always directly from the King, and no person but the King can in truth command them for such service; and as the Prime Minister and daring Chancellor well knew the nature of royal susceptibility on such matters, they were in no small degree doubtful and anxious as to the result. The Chancellor therefore, with some real hesitation, began as before: 'Pardon me, Sir; we know how bold the step is, that, presuming on your goodness and your anxious desire for the safety of your kingdom and happiness of your people, we have presumed to take—I have given orders, and the troops are ready.' The King started in serious anger, flamed red in the face, and burst forth with 'What, my Lords, have you dared to act thus? Such a thing was never heard of. You, my Lord Chancellor, ought to know that such an act is treason, high treason, my Lord.' 'Yes, Sir,' said the Chancellor, 'I do know it; and nothing but my thorough knowledge of your Majesty's goodness, of your paternal anxiety for the good of your people, and my own solemn belief that the safety of the State depends upon this day's proceedings, could have emboldened me to the performance of so unusual, and, in ordinary circumstances, so improper a proceeding. In all humility I submit myself to your Majesty, and am ready in my own person to bear all the blame, and receive all the punishment which your Majesty may deem needful; but I again entreat your Majesty to listen to us and to follow our counsel; and as you value the security of your crown and the peace of your realms, yield to our most earnest solicitations.' After some further expostulations by both his Ministers, the King cooled down and consented. Having consented, he became anxious that everything should be done in the proper manner, and gave minute directions respecting the ceremonial. The speech to be spoken by him at the prorogation was ready prepared, and in the Chancellor's pocket. To this he agreed; desired that everybody might punctually attend, and dismissed his Ministers for the moment with something between a menace and a joke, upon the audacity of their proceeding."

Although the King subsequently became very much alarmed by the "Reform mania" which burst out upon the dissolution of Parliament, and he then took a keen dislike to the measure and to the Ministers who introduced it, at this time he was a hearty reformer, and he enjoyed much the popularity which this character conferred upon

him. In truth, he was chagrined by the opposition to
the bill which had sprung up in the Commons,—being
then persuaded that it arose from a combination of
borough-mongers, who wished to control the Crown
and to center all power in an odious oligarchy. He therefore sincerely approved of an appeal to the people. It
was reported that there being some delay in the arrival of
the royal carriage with the eight cream-colored horses to
carry him to Westminster, he exclaimed, "Never mind;
I am ready to go in a hackney-coach." This, though much
less improbable, I dare say is not more true than that the
Chancellor, before the King had been consulted about a
prorogation, had ordered the great officers of State, the
crown, the royal robes, and the military, to be in readiness
for the ceremonial at a given hour. But, after diligent
inquiry, I can take upon myself to say, that all who had
an opportunity of knowing or ascertaining the fact, with
the exception of Lord Brougham's *protégé*, concur in testifying that his Majesty, instead of being constrained upon
this occasion, most joyously adopted the advice which was
tendered to him.

The prorogation scene, which I myself witnessed, strongly corroborates this supposition. It greatly resembled the
termination of some of the refractory Parliaments in the
reign of Charles I.,—when the Gentleman Usher of the
black rod, coming to summon the Commons, was *barred
out*, tumultuary resolutions were moved, and at last the
Sovereign addressed the representatives of the people in
the tone of a Judge passing sentence of death on a
criminal.

As the Earl of Mansfield had given notice for this day of
a hostile motion concerning the Reform Bill, the Chancellor manœuvred to deprive him of the opportunity of
bringing it forward. He continued hearing an appeal till
a late hour, and then withdrew, not meaning to return till
he should enter in the procession with the King. But, as
soon as he was gone, Lord Mansfield, according to the
privilege of the Peers, moved that the Earl of Shaftesbury
should take the chair as Speaker—which was done immediately. Lord Wharncliffe then rose to move an address
to the King, praying that he would not dissolve the present Parliament. He was interrupted by ministerialists,
and at least five Peers were on their legs at one time trying

to gain a hearing, and looking as if resolved to come to
blows. At last Lord Wharncliffe was permitted to make
his motion, and there seemed great danger that it might
be carried by acclamation, when Lord Shaftesbury was
dislodged from the woolsack by the appearance of the
Lord Chancellor in a state of great distraction, and scream-
ing out in the most passionate tone of voice:—

"I never yet heard that the Crown ought not to dissolve
Parliament whenever it thought fit, particularly at a moment when the House of Commons had resorted to the
extreme step of refusing the supplies."

There were loud cries of "*Hear, hear. The King, the
King!*" and (according to Hansard) "altogether immense
confusion."

The Lord Chancellor thought he had effectually prevented any further attempt at discussion, and again withdrew. But no sooner was he gone than Lord Shaftesbury
was again placed on the woolsack, and Lord Mansfield was
declaiming furiously against the dissolution and against
the Reform Bill, when cries were heard of "*The King!
The King! God save the King!*" At that instant the
large doors were thrown open on the right of the throne,
and his Majesty, accompanied by the Chancellor and other
great officers, entered the House with a firm though rather
hasty step, and having seated himself upon the throne,
looked round to the quarter from which the disturbance
had come with evident signs of anger. The Commons
were then summoned, and when they had arrived his
Majesty began: "My Lords and Gentlemen, I have come
to meet you for the purpose of proroguing the Parliament,
with a view to its immediate DISSOLUTION"—pronouncing
the word with deep emphasis and evident exultation.[1]
We do not follow the fashion of the French, who on these
occasions holloa out "*Vive le Roi!*" or "*Vive l'Empereur!*"
(as it may be) while his French Majesty is still sitting on
his throne; but when our Sailor King was returning to
his Palace he was saluted with loud cries of "Well done,
old boy!—*sarved* them right! Three cheers for the King
and Reform. Hip, hip, hurra!" And he seemed much
delighted with the applause which he received.

The dissolution was attended with the most splendid
success. At the elections the anti-reformers were scat-

[1] 3 Hansard, 1810.

tered like chaff before the wind, and an overwhelming majority was returned to the House of Commons for " the bill, the whole bill, and nothing but the bill."

Still the Lords resolutely stood up in opposition, and at the opening of the new session the Lord Chancellor was severely called to account for his conduct on the day of the prorogation. After appealing to his general character and the uniform respect and courtesy with which he had ever treated the House and every individual member of it, he came to the particular charge :—

"It has been asserted, my Lords, that I threw my hat on the woolsack and flounced out of the House in an unbecoming manner, at a time when I knew that the King was not nearer to the House than the Horse Guards. I did not leave the House, however, until I received a positive order from the King, communicated to me by the Gentleman Usher of the Black Rod in these words: ' *The King doth command the Lord Chancellor instantly to give his attendance upon his Majesty, who waits at the bottom of the staircase.*' The person who had a right to be offended with me on that occasion was the Gentleman Usher of the Black Rod ; and he, finding me slow to obey his summons, pulled me, with his usual courtesy, by the sleeve, and added, ' Did you hear what I said ? The King has arrived, and is at the bottom of the staircase.' So far from the King being then at the Horse Guards, I can assure your Lordships that upon this remonstrance I went as fast as I could to the bottom of the staircase, and found his Majesty there waiting for me. I hope it is perfectly unnecessary for me to assure your Lordships that I would not have quitted my post in this House upon any fictitious pretense whatever. It might have been *impar congressus*, but I would rather have stayed and broken a lance with the noble Earl if imperative duty had not called me away."[1]

The bill now proceeded through all its stages in the House of Commons, supported by steady majorities. On the fifth night of the debate, on the second reading in the House of Lords, Brougham delivered his great speech in defense of it, which by many was considered his *chef-d'œuvre*. It certainly was a wonderful performance to witness. He showed a most stupendous memory and extraordinary dexterity in handling the weapons both of

[1] 4 Hansard, 153.

ridicule and of reason. Without a note to refer to he went through all the speeches of his opponents delivered during the five nights' debate, analyzing them successively, and, with a little aid from perversion, giving them all a seemingly triumphant answer. But in looking through the printed speech, as reported by himself, I find great difficulty in selecting any passages which would give any idea of its excellence; and I must confine myself to the peroration. This was partly inspired by draughts of mulled port imbibed by him very copiously towards the conclusion of the four hours during which he was on his legs or on his knees:—

"Among the awful considerations that now bow down my mind, there is one which stands pre-eminent above the rest. You are the highest judicature in the realm; you sit here as judges, and decide all causes, civil and criminal, without appeal. It is a judge's first duty never to pronounce sentence, in the most trifling case, without hearing. Will you make this the exception? Are you really prepared to determine, but not to hear, the mighty cause upon which a nation's hopes and fears hang? You are. Then beware of your decision! Rouse not, I beseech you, a peace-loving, but a resolute people; do not alienate from your body the affections of a whole empire. As your friend, as the friend of my order, as the friend of my country, as the faithful servant of my sovereign, I counsel you to assist with your uttermost efforts in preserving the peace, and upholding and perpetuating the constitution. Therefore I pray and I exhort you not to reject this measure. By all you hold most dear—by all the ties that bind every one of us to our common order and our common country, I solemnly adjure you—I warn you—I implore you—yea, on my bended knees (*he kneels*), I supplicate you—reject not this bill!"[1]

He continued for some time as if in prayer; but his friends, alarmed for him lest he should be suffering from the effects of the mulled port, picked him up and placed him safely on the woolsack.

Like Burke's famous dagger scene in the House of Commons, this prostration was a failure. So unsuited was it to the spectators and to the actor, that it produced a sensation of ridicule, and considerably impaired the effect of

[1] Lord Brougham's Speeches, vol. ii., p. 629–630.

a speech displaying wonderful powers of memory and of intellect, although hardly deserving the epithets bestowed upon it by the 'Times'—" overpowering, matchless, and immortal."

Lord Lyndhurst answered the Chancellor with great ability; but, to neutralize his panegyric on Schedule A, by which so many boroughs were disfranchised, he very unfairly quoted a letter on Reform, written by Brougham in 1810, in which he deprecated disfranchisement, declaring that "healing is better than amputation." In explanation, the Chancellor said that the letter had been stolen from him by a servant and improperly published, and that he had that very day granted an injunction against its further publication. With candor and dignity he admitted "a change in his opinions" on this subject.

The injunction caused the letter to be published in all the newspapers in the kingdom. In truth, the writer had no reason to be ashamed of it. Soberly it advocates reform, but preaches moderation, preserving the tone of the 'Edinburgh Review' upon the subject,—then considered the exponent of orthodox Whig doctrine.

Notwithstanding the Chancellor's prayer and his "overpowering, matchless, and immortal speech," at half-past six in the morning the bill was rejected by a majority of forty-one Peers.

The country now seemed to be on the eve of a revolution. The people and one House of Parliament representing them were resolutely determined to have reform; the other House of Parliament had shown a fixed resolution to resist it, and the King, now heartily repenting that he had ever encouraged it, wished most earnestly that he might hear of it no more.

The Whig leaders felt that they could not possibly remain in office without again bringing forward the measure, and they sincerely and patriotically felt that no efficient Government could be formed by their adversaries on anti-reform principles. Therefore, instead of resigning, they came to the resolution that it was their duty still to try to carry the measure by the aid of the King, however plainly he might now show his dislike to it, and Brougham, with his usual boldness proposed that they should ask him to consent to the creation of the requsite number of Peers for accomplishing the object in view. This was allowed to be an unconstitutional proceeding, a sort of *coup d'état*, a disguised revolution ; but a hope was expressed that the power to do the deed would be sufficient, without the deed being actually done—and that at all events public convulsion and civil war might thus be avoided. The King at first declared that the proposal was to rob him of a great prerogative for the purpose of employing it against the Crown; but when he was told that his present servants must all resign unless his Majesty should be graciously pleased to take their advice upon this point, and that they all conscientiously and strongly believed that the advice was, under the present unprecedented circumstances, for the honor of the Crown and the benefit of the people, he said he could hold out no longer, and gave them to understand that, if necessary, he was ready to agree to the creation of Peers to carry the Reform Bill, but did not give any absolute pledge, and did not sign anything on paper, upon the subject. Upon this verbal understanding Parliament was prorogued with an intimation from the Throne that the subject of Reform would speedily be again brought forward.

Although during the late Session of Parliament Reform absorbed all attention, there was a bill introduced by the Chancellor which deserves to be noticed, as showing the reckless manner in which he proceeded, with the view of mortifying and degrading a political opponent. Lord Wynford, late Chief Justice of the Common Pleas, had been entrusted to preside in the House of Lords on the hearing of Scotch Appeals, and had, in a case, *McGavin v. Stewart*, rightly enough reversed a decree of the Court of Session, and ordered a new trial, but inadvertently had directed that the second trial should be before a *Special Jury*, and that on this occasion *both parties should be examined viva voce*. Unfortunately special juries were then unknown in Scotland, and both parties were dead. Subsequently, Brougham holding the Great Seal, Lord Wynford had given him much offense, not only by opposing the Reform Bill but by petulantly objecting to all the measures of the Government.

To be revenged, my Lord Chancellor one evening, shortly before the prorogation, laid on the table "A Bill to reverse the Judgment of the House of Lords on the Appeal of McGavin *v.* Stewart," saying :—

"The judgment, my Lords, is utterly inconsistent with the law of Scotland. It must have been pronounced by some of your Lordships unacquainted with the Scotch law. The natural consequence is that it is contrary to that law. The thing must have arisen in the pressure of business—owing to that *inopia consilii* which you have had to lament in this House. The judgment was pronounced some months before I had the honor of a seat here. I shall move that the Standing Orders be suspended, as it is very desirable that the bill should pass without delay."

The bill was accordingly read a first time, and an article appeared in the "Times" next morning showing "how the Chancellor had been compelled to do all this, and that the defaulting Appellate Judge was Lord Wynford." But the impropriety of the proceeding was so great, and it caused such an outcry among considerate persons, that on the day fixed for the second reading of the bill and carrying it through all its other stages, the Chancellor said "he found that no material inconvenience would arise from postponing it." Lord Wynford denied that the judgment was wrong. Lord Lyndhurst, Chief Baron, was of opinion that "it was quite right; but that at all events this House, like any other Court, might amend its own judgments." *Lord Chancellor :* " That power only belongs to inferior Courts, and the most serious consequences would follow if it were assumed by this the Court of *dernier ressort.*"

In truth a power of reversing its judgments after they have been solemnly recorded does not belong to any Court, high or low ; and a solemn judgment of the House of Lords, after the termination of the Session in which it has been pronounced, could only be reversed by Act of Parliament. But the judgment in question was right in point of law, and required no reversal, but a mere correction of what might be considered a *misprision*, or clerical mistake. Accordingly it was rectified by omitting the the word *special* and the direction as to the examination of the parties, and the bill for reversing it was withdrawn amidst symptoms of a universal opinion that it ought never to have been presented. However, the Chancellor, though feeling some annoyance at the moment, very soon got over it, and was able to exercise a complete ascendancy over Lord Wynford.

I ought now to mention that during the whole period

when the Reform Bill seemed entirely to absorb the attention of mankind, and the Lord Chancellor's share in it seemed occupation enough for the most vigorous mind, he was devoting himself to his judicial duties with an assiduity and perseverance hardly ever manifested by Judges who did not mix in politics and thought of nothing but their cause papers. He sat later into the autumn, and later into the night, than he had ever been before known, notwithstanding the remonstrances of counsel, solicitors, and officers of the Court.

From the address which he delivered on taking leave of the bar for the long vacation, his head seems actually to have been turned by the whirl of violent excitement in which he lived. I can not suspect him of willfully misstating the truth, or of proposing to do what he himself knew to be impossible. Yet he did make statements entirely at variance with fact, and he promised a feat as difficult for him as to jump into a pint bottle. Although Sir John Leach, one of the most expeditious Judges who ever sat, was then Master of the Rolls, and Sir Lancelot Shadwell filled the office of Vice-Chancellor (necessarily created for the assistance of the Lord Chancellor), and, though not a profound lawyer, was well acquainted with the routine of Chancery business and dispatched it very rapidly, and the Lord Chancellor himself had worked very hard and got through a long list of appeals; in point of fact, there were large arrears in the Court of Chancery still remaining to be wiped off; and instead of the Chancellor doing the whole of his own work and the Vice-Chancellor's too, it was ere long found necessary to create two new and additional Vice-Chancellors. Yet thus spoke Lord Chancellor Brougham on the 2d day of September, A. D. 1831, before an immense audience, many of whom he might have been aware perfectly well knew the accuracy or inaccuracy, the reasonableness or the folly, of what he uttered :—

"It is a great satisfaction to me, in taking my leave of the bar and of the suitors, to know that I have been able to dispose of all the arrears of the business of this Court, and that there are no appeals undisposed of, no petitions unanswered, and no causes unheard except such as are not ready, and which have been put upon the files of the Court subsequent to last June. It is a very great relief to

the Court; it will be a very great relief to the bar; it will
be a very great relief to all professional men; above all, it
will be a very great relief to the suitors to feel that they
shall have their business henceforward regularly going on,
not encumbered by arrears, and not have their minds
oppressed with the harassing prospect of never getting
through their business. In the course of next term the
benefit of this will be perceived, and it will be allowed
that our time has been well spent. It has pressed hard
on the Court, but I have been willing to bear that pressure, knowing well that the public will feel the full benefit
of the more than ordinary exertions that have been made.
It was said of a great man, the most illustrious of all my
predecessors, that he allowed the pressure of business
upon him to be more than he could bear; to which he
replied ' the duties of life are more than life'—memorable
words, to be had in everlasting remembrance by all men
who serve their country. . . . I beg to add that I
have now the most sanguine hopes of being able for the
future to relieve his Honor the Vice-Chancellor from
hearing the greater part of the causes which have been,
since the year 1813, ordinarily heard in his Court. . . .
When I came into the Court I found that every cause
which was of great importance in point of value, or of
difficulty in point of law or of fact, and which in the first
instance came before their Honors the Master of the
Rolls and the Vice-Chancellor, almost inevitably found
its way here by appeal, and generally, certainly in the
majority of cases, only led to great expense, great delay,
and great inconvenience, whether there should be an
ultimate affimance or reversal of the decree pronounced
in the first insance. I proposed, therefore, that all such
cases of difficulty and importance in point or value, or
from the law as applying to them, should be at once
transferred here and heard by me, as thereby the, otherwise inevitable, appeal would be avoided. The event has
justified my prospective conjecture, and leads me now to
form the plan which I shall certainly adopt, namely, that
of transferring at once the bulk of that business into this
Court. . . . I admit that though I have sat only
two days later than Lord Eldon ever did, yet I have sat
many more hours in the course of the day; and I am
aware of the embarrassments and inconveniences which

this may have caused. I am not, however, aware that its tendency has been to abridge arguments in any case; for I am sure I have endeavored to show as much patience as any man could possess, that I might not indicate the slightest indisposition to hear the longest argument. Even where I have thought argument superfluous, I have hardly ever stopped the reply in cases where I have been in favor of the side on which the reply was to be made; and still more rarely have I disposed of cases on hearing one side only. I therefore can not charge myself with having got rid of this arrear, and accomplishing this dispatch, at the expense of curtailing the hearing of causes."

Although the judicious grieved, I have been told that the great mass of by-standers who heard this address were thrown into such transports of enthusiasm by it that they could scarcely be restrained from violating the decorum of the place by loudly applauding the Judge, and when it was read in the daily newspapers, the public really believed that a new era had arrived, and that, as far as the administration of justice was concerned, there was now to be a golden age.

"The Chanceller is determined," said the *Times*, "that nothing of a personal nature shall interfere with the discharge of his public duty. He has cleared the Court of Chancery. He is resolved to do the same with the judicial proceedings of the House of Lords, by sitting seven hours each day. No one but himself would have ventured on the task. Relaxation he will have none. His carping assailants ought to know how immeasurably he is above their reach."

The Coronation of William IV. now took place, and afforded an excellent test of the popularity of the respective members of the peerage. As they came successively, according to their precedence, to pay homage to the crowned Sovereign seated on his throne in Westminister Abbey before the assembled nation, silence prevailed, or plaudits, according to the general opinion of the merits and services of each particular Peer. "Lord Brougham, at the Coronation, received every testimony of the warmest and most eager approbation." So said the *Times*—and (on this occasion) *truly*. Having been present myself as a member of the House of Commons, I can testify that when the Lord Chancellor, the first of the lay Peers after the Royal Dukes, presented himself on the steps of the throne, knelt and went through the antique ceremony of doing homage to his liege lord, the plaudits were so loud and general as not only to make the vaulted roofs of the sacred edifice to resound, but almost to shake its massive walls. Sad example of the fleeting nature of popular applause!—but instructive lesson as to the arts by which popular applause should be sought!

After a short recess a new Reform Bill, with some alterations, but no improvements, was introduced into the Commons, and passed that House with comparatively little opposition.

When brought up to the Lords there was a firm purpose entertained by a decided majority that it should not finally pass, but a certain section of their Lordships who were irreconcilably adverse to it, influenced partly by the odium they had incurred from the hasty step of throwing out the former bill on the second reading, and partly by the vague rumor of a contemplated creation of Peers upon a similar occurrence, determined to reserve themselves for the committee, and then and there to wreak their vengeance by tearing every clause of it into shreds. Still so large was the number of those who thought any seeming concession treason, that the second reading was considered doubtful, and the Chancellor was again obliged to put forth his strength. On this occasion, however, he reasoned more soberly, and the kneeling scene was entirely omitted. He concluded by thus forcibly meeting the observation that the anxiety of the people as to the success of the bill had subsided :—

" Do not, my Lords, let any man among you deceive himself with this belief. I tell you that the anxiety of the people has not gone by, that it exists as strongly and as intensely as ever, with this only difference, that it has stood the test of disappointment and long delay—of the hope deferred that maketh the heart sick. Rely on it that from one end of this land to the other, the people—the intelligent, the thinking, the rational, the honest people—not merely of this metropolis, but of every town, village, and hamlet in England, and, if possible, still more in Scotland—hang with breathless suspense upon your decision this night. I hope, I confidently believe, indeed I expect with certainty, that the decision will diffuse universal joy throughout the empire; that it will terminate the painful suspense with which this bill has been so long regarded, and above all, that it will greatly increase towards your Lordships the affections of your fellow-citizens." [1]

The second reading was carried by a majority of nine. [2]

I have explained in my "Life of Lyndhurst" [3] how that unscrupulous chief might now easily have won a victory for the anti-reforming Peers by moving in the Committee amendments which would not have given the Whig leaders plausible grounds for throwing up their offices and appealing from the King to the people, but which would have so damaged the bill that the Whig leaders could not have agreed to them without being liable to the charge of pusillanimity and tergiversation. Brougham has often told me with glee the fatal mistake which Lyndhurst committed by his sweeping motion in the Committee that the consideration of Schedules A and B should be postponed, supporting it by a speech against all disfranchisement. Happily for the cause of reform this motion was carried by a considerable majority. Lord Grey might have exclaimed, "The Lord' hath delivered them into my hand!"

Brougham, by the general consent of the Cabinet, now dictated the course to be pursued. Although always

"Pleased with the danger when the waves run high,"

I can not say that he is always

"A skillful pilot in extremity."

But on this occasion he acted boldly, prudently, and successfully.

A respectful representation was made to the King that the time was now come when, without an absolute power of creating Peers, the Reform Bill could not pass. His Majesty had been led to believe by the Queen and others with whom he lived, that the people really had become indifferent about reform, and that at any rate they would be contented with a much smaller measure of reform than that to which his present Ministers were pledged. He had likewise a notion which seemed very absurd when first mentioned, but which the event proved to be true, that Lord Lyudhurst and his coadjutors, who strenuously argued against all reform, and who had insisted that the House of Commons as then constitued was the *beau ideal*

[1] 12 Hansard, 428.   [2] 184 to 175, Ib. 454.   [3] See p. 80.

of a representative body in a free country, might be induced to become his Ministers for the purpose of adopting the bill with amendments and carrying it, so that the royal word given in favor of the Reform Bill might be saved. His Majesty, therefore, courteously but firmly refused the demand made upon him by his Ministers; they resigned in a body, and he sent for Lord Lyndhurst.

Brougham immediately took leave of the bar in the Court of Chancery, and on this occasion in a very temperate and becoming tone. After saying that he trusted the time would ere long come when the highest judicial duties of our civil tribunals would be unmixed with political functions, he thus concluded:—

"And now, upon quitting this Court, I should, in ordinary circumstances, feel nothing but the pain of parting with those to whom my kind and respectful thanks are so justly due, for the unvaried respect and kindness which I have experienced from them. But in my voluntary retirement from hence, which is only painful as it causes this separation, I am supported by the principles which have dictated the course I pursue. I am more than supported; the personal feelings to which I have adverted are lost in those which now compel me, I trust without any undue sense of pride, to regard the abandonment of power at the command of public duty, not as misfortune, but as glory."

He then set to work in good earnest in his political capacity, and while an attempt was making to quicken into life the feeble embryo of the new Government, speedily about to be annihilated, he raised a storm all over the island as if by magical *cantrips*. In truth, he was more busy than Lord Holland describes him on the breaking up of the Government of "All the Talents," writing pamphlets and paragraphs for newspapers, framing petitions to the King and the two Houses of Parliament, directing public meetings to be called, furnishing topics for the speakers, and cautioning against tumults or any open breach of public tranquillity.

One stratagem resorted to for the purpose of enhancing his popularity and his influence, was to spread a report that he had been strongly solicited to retain his office under the new Government. Said the *Times:*

"The Lord Chancellor was pressed again and again to

continue in his high office, but peremtorily refused. Surely his Majesty must have forgotten that bloody record in the house of Brunswick, when the too seductive persuasions of his father induced the amiable Charles Yorke to abandon his principles and his colleagues."

But it is quite certain that such a preposterous conception never entered the royal mind. The King was acting entirely under the advice of Lyndhurst, who was himself impatient again to possess the Great Seal.

Brougham's occupation now was to regulate the proceedings of the political unions, and to restrain their impetuosity. The Birmingham Union had a band of 100,000 men ready to march upon London, and he had great difficulty in prevailing upon them to wait for further orders.

His favorite brother, William, the Master in Chancery, was then member for the borough of Southwark, and thus (primed, I presume, by the Chancellor) exploded at a meeting of his constituents, assembled to petition for the recall of the Whigs:—

"A report has been very prevalent that the Lord Chancellor is to continue in office, and form part of a Government—but not Earl Grey's Government. This report I have authority to contradict. My brother will ever continue to support the cause of the people, and with no other cause will he identify himself. Something has been said about the people not paying taxes, and a resolution to that effect would be highly illegal. People might individually refuse without rendering themselves amenable to law. Now this is an affair easily arranged. If a tax-gatherer calls upon me, and asks me to settle his little bill for taxes, I may say to him in reply, 'I have got a little bill of my own, sir, which I should like to have settled by the gentlemen down in Westminster who owe it me, and unless that little bill of mine be satisfactorily settled, you must never expect me to settle yours.' Before I conclude, I beg to state to this meeting that my brother the Lord Chancellor is at this moment in better health than ever; he is in good fighting order, as the sham reformers will discover to their cost. [*Thunders of applause.*] He will prove a sharp thorn in their sides; he will never desert the cause of the people."[1]

[1] "Roebuck's History of the Whig Ministry," vol. ii., p. 297. I presume revised by one of the brothers, if not by both. I have reason to remember

Lord Lyndhurst was not successful in his attempt to form a new Government to carry the modified Reform Bill, and although, to the astonishment of all mankind, the Duke of Wellington was willing to join him, he was obliged to throw up his commission, censured by Peel, and covered with ridicule.

The King was reduced to the sad necessity of submission, and having signed a formal promise to consent to create Peers for the purpose of carrying the Reform Bill when advised so to do by Lord Grey, the Whig Ministry was to be reinstated.

In the explanations which then took place, Brougham was very temperate and forbearing, leaving it to Lord Grey to state the motives of the Cabinet in retiring and returning, as if he himself had taken no part in it, uttering only these words:—

"I do not mean to occupy your Lordships' time by adding a word to what has dropped from my noble friend, except to state that which I am sure was passing across his mind when he addressed your Lordships—that considering the absolute necessity, in the present state of the country, of passing this measure, we shall not again return to office except upon the condition not only of our possessing the ability to carry the bill efficiently through the House, but also to carry it through with every reasonable despatch." [1]

This intimation was well understood, and had the desired effect of carrying the bill through the House with every reasonable despatch, without exercising the power which had been obtained. At the suggestion of the Duke of Wellington (it was said upon a hint from the King himself), a considerable number of Tory Peers absented themselves from the House during the subsequent stages of the bill, so that it went through the Committee without any material alteration, and finally passed the House by a majority of eighty-four. The sister bills for Scotland and Ireland soon followed, and the cause of Reform had a complete triumph.

---

this speech, for when Attorney-General I was much embarrassed by it when quoted against me, conducting an ex-officio prosecution begun by my predecessor, Sir W. Horne, for a libel in a newspaper exhorting a passive resistance to the payment of taxes.

[1] 12 Hansard, 1022.

Lord Brougham makes a question in his "Political Philosophy"[1]:—

"Whether or not, if no secession had taken place, and the Peers had persisted in really opposing the most important provisions of the bill, we should have had recourse to the perilous creation?"

And he adds:—

"I can not, with any confidence, answer it in the affirmative. I had a strong feeling of the necessity of the case in the very peculiar circumstances we were placed in. But such was my deep sense of the dreadful consequences of the act, that I much question whether I should not have preferred running the risk of confusion that attended the loss of the bill as it then stood; and I have a strong impression on my mind that my illustrious friend [Lord Grey] would have more than met me half-way in the determination to face that risk (and of course to face the clamors of the people, which would have cost us little) rather than expose the Constitution to so imminent a hazard of subversion."

But I can not doubt that if Lyndhurst had not quailed, the fact would have been accomplished. I have heard, and I believe, that a list of fifty new Peers was made out, and, consisting chiefly of Scotch Peers, eldest sons of British Peers, and respectable elderly gentlemen without any sons, it would not have made a larger permanent addition to the peerage than Pitt had made in a single batch. But there can be no doubt that it would have been a serious blow to the Constitution, and we must greatly rejoice that it was warded off.

At last, the royal assent having been given to the three Reform Bills, and his Majesty in his speech from the throne having expressed a hope that they would restore to the nation general confidence in the legislature, and give additional security to the settled institutions of the State, the Chancellor had the satisfaction of declaring it to be "his Majesty's royal will and pleasure that Parliament should be prorogued until the 16th day of October."[2]

This turned out to be the closing scene of the last unreformed Parliament, for it never met again. But this was not then by any means the intention of King William.

He now felt, not unnaturally, a grudge against his pres-

[1] Vol. iii., p. 308.   [2] 14 Hansard, 1416.

ent Ministers, and he resolved to get rid of them as speedily as possible—in the meantime thwarting them when he constitutionally could. They were desirous of dissolution, as soon as preparations could be made for a general election under the new *régime*. He wished to mortify them by deferring the time when the much-coveted fruits of reform were to be tasted, and he thought that the proposal was an uncalled-for interference with his prerogative.

I happened to be within hearing when, in the beginning of November, this controversy between them was brought to a conclusion. In consequence of the promotions occasioned by the death of Lord Tenterden, I had been appointed Solicitor-General; and as there was to be no public levee held soon, I was summoned to a private audience of his Majesty, that I might kiss his hands and be knighted. I found Lord Grey, Brougham, and several other Ministers, standing round the King in his closet. They all seemed, at first, to be in a state of great excitement; but this gradually subsided. I was presented, knelt, and rose " Sir John." His Majesty then put a few unmeaning questions to me without attending to my answers, and we *subjects* all withdrew. As we were going down the steps to our carriages, Brougham whispered to me, " Off for Dudley—Parliament dissolved."

He afterwards fully explained to me that they had just had a most stormy interview with the King, who had been more obstinate and wrong-headed than they had ever found him; that they had tried with all sincerity and respect to explain to him that, although he might have withheld his assent from the Reform Bill, now that it had, with his concurrence, become law, a dissolution was inevitable, as the existing Parliament stood condemned and sentenced, and the people were entitled to the exercise of their new franchises. " No! " he declared, " he could see no necessity for that." The new franchises were to be exercised when a new Parliament was called, but the present Parliament had sat a little more than a year, and although the two Houses had lately been at variance, he thought there would be perfect unanimity between them.

This being a sort of legal question, the argument on the side of the ministers was left almost entirely to the Chancellor, who tried to show that the Reform Bill in its spirit

really enacted immediate dissolution, and who assured his
Majesty that, if not fairly acted upon instead of being, as
his Majesty had in the conclusion of his speech from the
throne prayed that it might be--" fruitful in promoting
the security of the State, and the contentment and welfare
of the people "—it might lead to rebellion and civil war.
Still the King was not convinced, when Lord Grey, in a
low, respectful, but solemn tone, informed his Majesty that
his present servants, after due deliberation, were unanimously of opinion that the reassembling of the present
Parliament would be an unconstitutional and most inexpedient step, for which they could not be responsible, and
therefore that they must immediately, with all humility,
resign their offices into his Majesty's hands. " Well," said
the King, " I yield, but, my Lords and gentlemen, remember it is against my opinion and wishes."

Brougham now bore " his blushing honors thick upon
him," and may be considered as at his highest point of
greatness. Although he held the Great Seal for two
years more, ere long there were dissensions in the Cabinet,
there were discontents among the Radicals, there were
dangerous disturbances in Ireland, there were complaints
that the Reform Bill by no means produced the felicity
promised from it ; discoveries were made that the Chancellor's judgments were sometimes rather crude, and
heavy reproaches were leveled against him from many
quarters that he had utterly forgotten solemn promises
of promotion and patronage. But for a brief space, com-
prising the end of the year 1832 and the beginning of
1833, he enjoyed, I really believe, a greater supremacy and
popularity than any of his predecessors, Cardinal Wolsey
alone excepted. The nation was actually mad about the
Reform Bill, and the merit of carrying it through the Lords
was chiefly attributed to Lord Chancellor Brougham. He
boldly asserted, and people for a while believed, that he
had cleared off all arrears in the Court of Chancery—the
first instance of such an exploit since the time of Sir
Thomas More; he had promised reforms in every department of jurisprudence, which were to render the administration of justice in all courts, civil and criminal, common
law and equity, temporal and ecclesiastical, simple, speedy
certain, and cheap. He circulated reports that in the
midst of all his political and judicial labors he had re-

newed his experiments on light and colors, and that he
was preparing a new edition, with notes and illustrations,
of Paley's "Natural Theology"; and by the distribution of
his own patronage, and borrowing liberally from the patronage of his colleagues—and above all, by promising,
five or six deep, places which were in his own gift, and
many which were not—he had enlisted in his service a
corps of literary janissaries such as had never before existed or had been imagined in this country. He was
eulogized superlatively in all sorts of publications. The
Times newspaper was called his organ—even the Opposition journals[1] excepted him from the censure cast on the
other members of the Whig Cabinet, on the plea that,
although associated with them, he was exempt from their
odious aristocratic tendencies, while he eclipsed them all
by his talents and acquirements. Dedications, attempting
to describe his virtues, were showered down upon him by
all classes, particularly by the clergy; strangers flocked to
London from all parts of the kingdom to look at him; the
Court of Chancery, generally a desert from its dullness, as
often as he sat there was crowded to suffocation; when his
carriage drew up in the street a mob of admirers gathered
round to see him get into it, cheering him as he passed
by; and the Italian image-boys gave orders for grosses
of Lord Brougham in plaster of Paris faster than they
could be manufactured. In this palmy state he could not
be accused of " high-blown pride," for he was good-humored
and courteous and kind to everybody, and seemed to regret that he could not at all times enjoy social intercourse
with old acquaintances on a footing of perfect equality.[2]

But he was

" Like little wanton boys that swim on bladders,"

and before three fleeting summers were gone he had not
only fallen from power, but he was ungenerously deserted

[1] Particularly the *Morning Herald.* It was said that the brother-in-law
of the editor, a really very worthy divine, had received a good living from the
Chancellor, who declared that " in Church promotion party must be disregarded."

[2] I happened to have an interview with him in his private room in the
House of Lords on the 16th of August, 1832, the day of the prorogation after
William IV. had withdrawn, and vast multitudes continued still congregated
to have a peep at Henry IX. He recalled with regret the time when he
could walk away unobserved from the robing room of the King's Bench with
his great-coat on and his umbrella under his arm. " How I hate these
trappings," said he, pointing to his gold gown and the mace and purse.

by friends, while cruelly assaulted by foes; he was maligned by those to whom he had been a benefactor; all mankind seemed to be in a conspiracy against him; and his own mental faculties could hardly bear the shock which they had to sustain. From this depression he rallied. He was again held up to the public gaze, but rather resembling a target to be fired at than, as once, a Divinity to be worshipped.

I have now to describe some of his exploits while his prosperity continued, and painfully to accompany his downward career.

The elections for the first Reformed House of Commons went strongly in favor of the Whigs. Having myself, after a sharp contest, been returned for the newly-enfranchised borough of Dudley, I had the honor of being warmly congratulated by the Lord Chancellor as representative of "iron,"—the professed object of creating this constituency having been the protection of the "iron interest." His Lordship, however, waggishly observed, that the bill was defective in not providing a seat for the "*brassinte rest*," which Mr. Solicitor might more appropriately have filled. As long as he held the Great Seal we went on together most harmoniously and cordially, although I had reason to believe that he opposed my appointment as a law officer of the Crown. I did my best to support him in all that he brought forward, and he always treated me with consideration and kindness.

Whig rule now seemed permanently established in England, and the general expectation was that its march would be smooth and easy. But, in truth, however prudently the Whigs hereafter had behaved, they were sure to cause disappointment and to incur censure. The great mass of the people had imbibed the notion that political corruption was now at an end forever; and that in all time to come, the nation being wisely governed, all ranks would be prosperous and contented.

The evils which must necessarily be generated by the inherent vices of governors and governed, and the imperfection of all human institutions, were soon greatly aggravated by gross blunders which the Whig Government committed after being possessed of absolute power with popular applause. I do not know that Brougham was personally to be charged with any of these: for at this time, although a prominent member of the Cabinet, he was not allowed to originate important measures. But, as Chancellor, he was especially responsible for the bill which, at the first meeting of the Reformed Parliament, brought about a severance between the Whigs and a large section of the Liberal party.

Ireland was then under the administration of Mr. Stanley, heir to the house of Derby, who, as Chief Secretary to the Lord-Lieutenant, had made himself viceroy over him; and this very clever but very rash youth, by his irritating proceedings respecting the collection of tithes, operating upon a constant predisposition among the Irish to agrarian outrage, had brought about a general disregard of the laws intended for the protection of life and property. He saw no remedy except a suspension of the Constitution and the establishment of military despotism in that portion of the United Kingdom. This he proposed in the shape of his famous "Irish Coercion Bill;" and, unfortunately, it was not distasteful to Lord Grey, who, although at all times the champion of liberty in England, believed with the great body of English gentlemen, Whig and Tory, that our Hibernian brethren were only to be governed by force. If this maxim had been steadily acted upon, it would have produced tranquillity and material prosperity, as was seen under the Earl of Strafford and Oliver Cromwell; but the alternation of severity and license was long the bane of that unhappy country, keeping it both turbulent and enslaved.

When the subject came before the Cabinet, there was some difference of opinion. From the Chancellor's ultra-Liberalism, it might have been expected that he would have been shocked by the notion of the first act of the Reformed Parliament, instead of extending freedom and security over the empire, being to render all Irishmen liable to be transported beyond the seas, by the sentence of a court-martial, for merely alleged civil offenses. But he—forgetting the provocation of which Ireland had to complain in the anti-Catholic penal code, and the commercial restrictions forbidding her to import cattle or corn into England, or to trade with the English colonies—had, like Lord Grey, fostered a strong prejudice against the Irish people, and he gave it has his opinion that Stanley should be gratified. Accordingly, the Chancellor with his own hand composed the following sentences for the Royal speech : —

"It is my painful duty to observe that the disturbances in Ireland have greatly increased. A spirit of insubordination and violence has risen to the most fearful height, rendering life and property insecure, and threatening the most fatal consequences if not promptly and effectually repressed. I feel confident that to your loyalty and patriotism I shall not resort in vain for assistance in these afflicting circumstances."

The bill being introduced by Lord Grey to suspend the Habeas Corpus Act and to establish courts-martial in Ireland, the Chancellor, deploring the sad necessity for a measure of such severity, declared that "the time had arrived when it would be inhuman as well as unjust to hesitate about supporting it," and he readily took upon himself the full share of the responsibility which might attach to his Majesty's Government for having proposed it. He then resorted the ingenious argument that, as we had no right to expect the alleigance of the Irish people unless we afforded them protection, a refusal to pass the bill would justify them in separating from us and setting up an independent government of their own.[1]

This inauspicious bill easily passed the House of Lords, being hailed with joy by Lord Eldon and his Tory associates as outdoing their "Six Acts," passed after the "Manchester Massacre;" but it called forth execrations in the House of Commons against "the base and bloody Whigs." It seriously damaged the reputation of Lord Grey's Government, and in the following year it was the direct cause of his fall from power.

During this session Brougham was very assiduous in his efforts for improving the administration of justice in England. He passed a bill for the abolition of a great many sinecure offices in the gift of the Lord Chancellor; and for fixing the salary of this high functionary at £14,000 a year, with a retiring pension of £5,000 a year. He likewise succeeded in abolishing the Court of Delegates—a very inconvenient tribunal of appeal from the Ecclesiastical Courts, invented at the Reformation, when the appeal to Rome was taken away. He substituted for it a much better tribunal of appeal—"the Judicial Committee of the

[1] 15 Hansard, 718.

Privy Council," which still subsists and has worked very satisfactorily.

He was not so fortunate with a bill for establishing local Courts, which he had proposed in the House of Commons when member for Yorkshire, which he laid on the table of the House of Lords when, "to his own astonishment," he became Chancellor, and which then dropped amidst the tumults of Parliamentary reform. He now pressed it forward with the greatest earnestness. Although the principle of the bill was good, it was not by any means skillfully framed, and it was properly rejected. Several years afterwards a similar bill, much improved, was introduced into the House of Commons by Mr. Fitzroy, under the name of the "County Courts Act," and received the sanction of the legislature.

Before the session closed, the House of Lords was much scandalized by a very indecorous altercation between the Chancellor and another law lord. Chief Justice Best, who had been very improperly appointed to preside in the Court of Common Pleas by the personal interference of George IV. when Prince Regent, and had very improperly been created a peer on condition of resigning his office to favor a ministerial job, frequently took part in the discussion of the law bills, and never without displaying ignorance and incapacity. He was now enlisted in the Tory opposition, and laying himself so open to exposure, Brougham was in the habit of attacking him most unmercifully. On one occasion, having pointed out some mistake into which Lord Lyndhurst had fallen, he added—"and thus from over-indulging his fancy, my noble and learned friend, the Lord Chief Baron, has got into as gross an inaccuracy as would have done honor even to the late Chief Justice of the Common Pleas himself."

Lord Wynford.—"I have submitted to this for a long time, but I will not be held up to ridicule in this way any longer." [Cries of *order, order.*]

The Lord Chancellor.—"My noble and learned friend, the late Chief Justice, is most disorderly no doubt, but I do not complain. When I speak of his inaccuracy or forgetfulness, I merely mean that he has forgotten, or perhaps he has never read, the books he refers to. I was not holding up to ridicule my noble and learned friend the late Chief Justice. It was no holding up of mine, and I hope my noble and learned friend, the late Chief Justice, will bear in mind what Dean Swift said of persons who were laughed at—"

Lord Wynford.—" I will bear this no longer. The noble Lord has attacked me by name. He who is appointed to enforce the orders of your Lordships' house is ignorant of them or wantonly breaks them. I move that the Clerk do now read the 15th of your Standing Orders, which requires ' all personal, sharp, or taxing speeches to be forborne.' "

The Standing Order was read, which goes on to say— " and as nothing offensive is to be spoken, so nothing is to be ill-taken if the party that speaks it shall presently make a fair exposition of the words that might bear an ill-construction; and if any offense be given in that kind, the House will sharply censure the offender, and give the party offended a fit reparation."

Lord Chancellor.—" Well, my lords, if my words might bear any *ill-construction*, have not I presently made a *fair exposition* of them? This being so, my lords, I am the party *offended;* and my noble and learned friend, the late Chief Justice, being the *offender*, ought to be *sharply censured* by your lordships, and is bound to give me a *fit reparation.*"

Soon after, when the Warwick Disfranchisement Bill came up from the Commons, he gave great offense to the whole body of barristers by supposing that they were prowling about for a brief, as dogs for a bone. On his own motion, the usual order had been made for the hearing of counsel, and the common course would have been for the promoters and opposers of the bill themselves to have chosen their counsel respectively ; but the Chancellor wantonly observed,—

" It will be necessary for the House to *name* the counsel by whom it would be assisted ; if not, all Westminster Hall may be let in upon us [a laugh]. There is now an order generally that counsel may be heard, and any one gentleman, or score of gentlemen, *on the look out*, may come dropping in under the cover of that general order for the purpose of being engaged as counsel. A more absurd course could not be followed."

But, in truth, the order could have misled no one ; and no one would have taken advantage of it for a purpose so disgraceful as the imputation thrown out implied. But he had always great delight in laughing at briefless barristers.—a class to which at some periods of his life he was himself in great danger of belonging. He was very incautious in attacking bodies of men, and thus sometimes excited more ill-will than by a personal quarrel which might be soon appeased. Having flattered some of the Bishops by asking them to name incumbents for small livings in his gift, he offended them all by saying in their absence, when they had left the house to go to dinner, that "their god was their belly."

The memorable public legislative measures of this session were (1), The Irish Church Temporalities Act, by which ten bishoprics were suppressed, and the Church cess or rate was to be paid from the produce of Church lands: and (2), The Slavery Abolition Act, by which, after a short apprenticeship to freedom, all slaves in the British colonies were to be set free. The Lord Chancellor supported them usefully as they passed through the House of Lords; but they both originated with the Commons, and were both measures of Stanley, who, in spite of his Coercion Bill, was still considered the chief prop and ornament of the Whigs. Brougham, who now held himself out as the head of the anti-Slavery party, was desirous of taking to himself all the merit of the last bill; but he certainly had very little to do with it, and in the Cabinet he warmly opposed the pecuniary grant to the masters of the slaves, which turned out to be a poor compensation to them for what they had lost. The bill, in its results, can not be much boasted of or rejoiced in; for, while it has been seriously injurious to the cultivation of the soil in the West Indies, I fear it has not improved the condition of the negroes; and wiser plans might have been adopted for conferring upon them, along with freedom, the blessings of industry, knowledge, and religion.

The novelty of the Chancellorship being now over, Brougham found the duties of an equity Judge rather irksome, and he wished for some change in his situation, but could not make up his mind what it should be. He often talked of becoming "Minister of Justice," till the difficulties which obstructed the creation of such an office proved to be insurmountable. Its emoluments, patronage, precedence, and *prestige* likewise must have been much inferior to those enjoyed with the Great Seal. If he was believed to compose, or to suggest, or to rejoice in the daily paragraphs still puffing him in the *Times*, it might have been conjectured that he wished to be written up to the Premiership, for this journal, not praising Lord Grey or the other members of the Cabinet, and occasionally leveling severe sarcasms at some of them, held up the Chancellor to constant admiration, not only for his eloquence and his legal lore, and his literary and scientific acquirements, for his unrivaled talents as a statesman.

About this time he resented in a very marked manner what he considered a piece of impertinence in H.R.H. the Duke of Cumberland, afterwards King of Hanover. While the Chancellor was addressing the House very calmly and very much to the purpose, the Duke called out "Question, Question." Chancellor *in furore.*—" I ask your Lordships whether there is decency in that call?" Not contented with this expression of resentment, he lay by for an opportunity of still further punishing the royal delinquent, and soon after, speaking on the Slavery Abolition Bill, he said:—

"It would give the man of color as clear a right to sit in that house (if his Majesty should so please) as either of the illustrious Dukes now present [Wellington and Cumberland], whether the illustrious Duke who is illustrious by his deeds, or the illustrious Duke who is illustrious by the courtesy of the House."

Meanwhile he continued to work on very industriously in the judicial business of the House of Lords. His early training gave him a considerable advantage in dealing with Scotch appeals, and he was by no means in the bewildering position of his successors, Pepys, Truro, and Cranworth, who were suddenly called upon to review the decisions of the Supreme Court of Scotland, never in their lives having been concerned in a Scotch cause or read a word of Scotch law. They, as their safer course, were driven to *affirm*—but he, to show his skill, was rather pleased to *reverse ;* and he continued to give offense by sarcastic observations on the Lords of Session, so that in the Parliament House at Edinburgh there were serious complaints of his rashness.

In the Court of Chancery, where he was quite a novice, he had counted upon support and assistance from Horne, now Attorney-General, an equity counsel of some reputation, whom, with this view, he had appointed a law officer of the Crown; but that speculation turned out most unfortunate. Mr. Attorney was opposed by Sugden, a Tory lawyer infinitely superior to him in capacity and acquirement, and eager, for personal and political reasons, to expose the inexperience of the Whig Lord Chancellor. One contest between them, in which the learned counsel was compared by the Lord High Chancellor in plain terms to a *bug*, gave rise to many newspaper paragraphs and many caricatures, and is now sometimes alluded to when he has become an ex-Chancellor.[1]

Brougham was so eager for the glory of clearing off all arrears that he would sit at unjuridical times—on Good Friday or Easter Monday—and in the evenings, after the House of Lords had adjourned. On these occasions he was not supposed to make good speed, and while the counsel were arguing, the Judge's spirit was supposed, from his shut eyes and depending head, to be wandering in the land of *Nod*. I can not say that I ever saw him asleep in all my life; but, by way of secondary evidence, I have seen in the print-shops an engraving representing a strong likeness of him in the "marble chair" overpowered by slumber, with the words underneath, *quandoque dormitat.*

His labors, judicial and political, being closed for the season, he repaired to Brougham Hall, and an absurd paragraph having appeared in a London newspaper representing him as an opium-eater, to subdue certain pains from which he suffered, and stating that in traveling to Westmorland he had slept fifty successive hours, he thought it worth while to make his brother write a letter to be published, saying:—

"The Chancellor has no pains of any kind; he never took laudanum or opium in any way whatever in the whole course of his life; he is enjoying the very best health, and no man of his age is more likely to live thirty years. And as for the story of his sleeping fifty hours, I was with him, and he did not sleep five hours the whole way."

[1] The *Times* of 28th July, 1832, suggested another comparison not quite so contemptuous for this enemy of the Lord Chancellor: "Has Sir Edward Sugden no friend to tell him that the *cock-sparrow* can not contend with the *eagle?*"

The long vacation of this year he professed to devote to philosophy. During a sojourn at his *Tusculum* in Westmorland he did compose some dialogues in imitation of Cicero's, and he had some communication with Sir Charles Bell respecting a new edition of Paley's "National Philosophy," with *cuts* and illustrations. At this time he was most potently persuaded that while holding the Great Seal and discharging all the duties of Chancellor with unprecendented efficiency, he should be able to give to the world a new work which would eclipse the "Novum Organum." He not unreasonably expected that his tenure of office would be long, and he could reckon with absolute certainty on his own energy and perseverance.

It would appear from successive defenses of character and conduct which appeared in the *Times*, that he began to be considerably annoyed by attacks in the *Quarterly Review* and other periodicals. We find in the leading journal an article headed, "Unjust charges against the Chancellor triumphantly refuted," and such observations as this:—

"We really pity these Tory slanderers, who must be almost suffocated with baffled malice and overwhelming shame."

"The violent abuse of the Chancellor is said to be by two briefless barristers, who write negro-fashion, under the scourge of the whipper-in. The result is impotent rage and pointless slander. An eminent law authority superintends the operation."

This was supposed to mean Lord Lyndhurst. Notwithstanding their subsequent strict alliance, the two noble and learned friends were now at mortal enmity. I had about this time the honor to be counsel for the Chancellor in a frivolous action for false imprisonment brought against him by a pettifogging attorney of the name of Dicas, who had been regularly committed to the Fleet in the course of a Chancery suit. The trial came on before Lord Lyndhurst as Chief Baron, and he strove hard to obtain a verdict for the plaintiff, but could not contrive to do so. I must confess, however, that he seemed less actuated by malice than a love of fun, for he seemed to think that there would be much laughter if the great Lord Brougham, the Whig Lord Chancellor, should be found to have unlawfully deprived a freeman of his liberty, and a jury should award damages against him, were it only a farthing.

Brougham now suffered a heavy loss by the death of his brother James, who had, without any of the brilliancy of the Chancellor, possessed much more prudence and discretion. He had been called to the English bar, but did not regularly follow the profession of the law. For some years past he had acted as a sort of private secretary to the Chancellor, and had great influence over him. To his death many ascribed the fantastical acts and the misfortunes which soon after marked the Chancellor's career, but I doubt whether anything could have saved this misguided man from the promptings of the evil genius which he carried about with him in his own breast, and which was ever ready to lead him astray. He was blessed, however, with one counteracting influence, the love of kindred, which he ever strongly felt, and, guided by which, he was ever ready to be kind and generous. On this occasion he was deeply affected, and he paid to a very large amount all the debts of his deceased brother.

When Michaelmas term came round the Chancellor's great object was to get rid of Horne as Attorney-General. His incapacity to conduct some state trials for libel which were coming on was given as a pretext, but the true motive was to withdraw him from the Court of Chancery, and to substitute for him, as the equity law officer, Pepys, a consummate equity lawyer, and much better qualified to enter the lists against Sugden.

The transaction at first appeard to proceed very smoothly. I received a note from the Chancellor announcing that I was Attorney-General, Horne having agreed to become a puisne Baron of the Exchequer, on the resignation of Baron Bayley. But meeting Horne soon after, he thus addressed me:—"I have been shamefully deceived and ill-used. Brougham asked me to become a puisne Judge. I said, 'there is an insurmountable obstacle. I have conscientious scruples about pronouncing sentence of death, and therefore I can not go the circuit or sit in a criminal court.' 'Never mind that,' cried Brougham, 'you accept the appointment, and you shall never go the circuit or sit in a criminal court. We are going to remodel the Court of Exchequer. There will be a puisne Baron confined entirely to equity business, and you shall be

the man.' On these terms I could not refuse, for such a
Baron of the Exchequer would be the same as a Vice-
Chancellor. I went to take leave of Lord Grey—a proper
mark of respect as I thought—and I said to him, ' I was glad
that the Government had resolved to remodel the Court of
Exchequer, and to have an equity Baron, an office I was
glad to accept, although I never could have acted as a
criminal Judge.' ' Equity Baron!' exclaimed Lord Grey,
'it is the first time I have heard of such an arrangement,
and I can not say that the Cabinet, much less that Parliament, will sanction it. I understood from the Chancellor
that you wished to become a puisne Judge in the common
course, without any special stipulations; and I confess for
one, I do not understand a puisne not being ready to discharge all the duties of the office.' Then," continued
Horne, " I told him plainly and distinctly and literally all
that had passed between me and the Chancellor on the
subject. Lord Grey observed, ' This is wondrous strange,
but I think it my duty to warn you that you ought not to
accept the appointment upon a supposed pledge that the
Government will do what you say the Chancellor promised.' Now, my dear Campbell, you and I have always
acted cordially together. I can throw no blame upon you,
whatever may happen. Would you mind going to the
Chancellor and hearing what he says about it?" I went.
Brougham assured me that he had never given any pledge
upon the subject; that Horne was under an entire delusion; that having said something about disliking circuits,
he had merely been told that perhaps the other Judges
might make some arrangement to relieve him from this
duty; but that there never was any contemplation to
legislate upon the subject, and that Horne having agreed
to resign the office of Attorney-General, the good of the
service required that he should do so.

I refused to be the bearer of any such message to him,
and vowed that I would in no way further interfere in the
affair—a vow which I most rigidly observed, after I had
told Horne that he must settle the dispute with the Chancellor himself, or find another negotiator. The result was
that Brougham persuaded Lord Grey to concur in his
views, and an intimation was given to Horne that the
King's pleasure had been taken upon the point, and that
he must either resign the office of Attorney-General or be

superseded. Horne replied with great spirit that he was ready to resign, but that he would sooner suffer death himself than pronounce sentence of death upon a fellow-creature. His resignation was accepted, and, refusing the puisne Judgeship, he retreated on his private practice at the bar, which was very inconsiderable.

I knew nothing more of the affair till I received a note from Brougham desiring me to meet him at his private room in Lincoln's Inn Hall. I found Sir John Bayley with him, executing the resignation of his office of puisne Baron. He said to me:—"I could make nothing of that foolish fellow Horne. I am sorry for his hallucination, but the King has signed the warrant for your appointment as Attorney-General, and Pepys is your Solicitor."

Horne complained to every one that Brougham had swindled him out of his office. My only consolation was that while some blamed Brougham, and some blamed Horne, and some blamed both, I did not on this occasion incur even a suspicion of any intrigue to push out my predecessor.[1]

Before this affair was brought to a conclusion another Session of Parliament had begun; an eventful session, the conclusion of which saw Brougham presiding on the woolsack for the last time, notwithstanding all his manœvres to strengthen his position and to prolong his power.

It opened very inauspiciously in the House of Commons with discussions on the Pension List, which damaged the popularity of the Whig Government still more than the Irish Coercion Bill. A writ was ordered for the election of a new member for Dudley on the same evening, when, "amidst loud and general cheers," notice was given of a renewed motion on the abuses of the Pension List. I expressed to Brougham great apprehensions that I might be rejected at Dudley, although my constituents, when I had visited them in the preceding autumn, had come to a unanimous vote approving of my conduct as their representative. He laughed me to scorn, telling me to trust to the *prestige* which the Government had acquired. He added, "The electors are not to be blown about by every

[1] When Lord Cottenham became Chancellor, Horne willingly accepted from him the humble office of Master in Chancery. He was afterwards reconciled to Brougham, but what explanation passed between them I never learned.

wind of doctrine; but I advise you not to flatter them too much, lest your praises should be thought to be *iron*ical."

In my next interview with him, at the end of six days, I had to relate to him that I had been dreadfully beaten,— that the electors of Dudley were all exasperated against the "base and bloody Whigs," who, having surrendered Ireland to martial law, now, by defending the Pension List, showed a determination to devote the public revenue raised by the sweat of the people to the support of the poor relations of wealthy Peers, and to perpetuate all the corrupt practices which had prevailed before the *mock Reform Bill.* He behaved very magnanimously, saying:— " Well, Jack, it is a heavy blow. Who could have looked for this Dudley hallucination? But never mind, its no fault of yours. We shall, I hope, soon get you in for another place—where, I don't yet exactly see. Till you are restored, my law reforms are stopped, for no one else can carry them through the House of Commons for me. We already feel that Schedule A, from which such glory was acquired, is not without its inconveniences."[1]

The Lord Chancellor himself undertook the task of arranging a seat for Mr. Attorney, and we had several conferences on the subject with Charles Wood, now First Lord of the Admiralty—then Secretary to the Treasury and whipper-in for the House of Commons; but the difficulty was found greater than had been anticipated, for popular constituencies were perilous, and the scandal of showing that the Whigs had reserved a few nomination seats to themselves was to be avoided.

In the meantime great alarm was created by a bill of a very preposterous nature upon the Law of Libel, brought into the House of Commons by O'Connell. He was then very hostile to the Government, and his object was to propose enactments *ad captandum*, such as putting an end to all proceedings by "information," whether under the authority of the Attorney-General or the Court of King's Beech,—so that the " base and bloody Whigs " might be still further damaged by being driven to oppose what he

[1] He did not then tell me that he had opposed the wholesale disfranchisement of the small boroughs, but he afterwards made no secret of this; and I have repeatedly heard him in the House of Lords declare that "from the Attorney-General being thrown out of Parliament in 1834, legal reform was stopped for a whole session."

called "salutary reform." Brougham being then very unwell, a meeting of the Cabinet was held at his house in Berkeley Square, which was attended by the Attorney and Solicitor-General. The result of their deliberations was, that instead of attacking General O'Connell in front, there should be a flank movement which would effectually defeat him. A motion was to be made for a Committee to inquire into the "Law of Libel." The difficulty was that this motion could, under existing circumstances, only be made by Mr. Solicitor, and he having spent his life in drawing "bills and answers," professed an entire ignorance of the subject. Brougham then, in a very lucid manner, stated the topics to be treated, the manner of treating them, and the order in which they should be introduced, and—Mr. Solicitor still looking unhappy—he added: "Should you like to have a sketch upon paper of your speech?" This offer was gratefully accepted, and the Chancellor, though in a very weak state of health and with judgments in arrear which he was very desirous of writing, must have employed some hours in preparing a brief for Mr. Solicitor. This learned functionary, when the evening for his motion arrived, delivered a speech on the Law of Libel which called forth cheers and applauses from all sides of the House. But, the Committee being granted, the subject dropped for the Session; and, as he never again spoke in the House of Commons so as to attract notice, if he had not been destined to immortality as Lord High Chancellor and Earl of Cottenham, he might have gone down to future ages as "Single Speech Pepys."[1]

After some months had expired a vacancy at last occurred at Edinburgh by the elevation of Lord Advocate Jeffrey to the Scottish Bench, and Lord Grey said to me, "You must try your luck there; but first get the sanction of the Lord Chancellor, or *the fat will be in the fire.*" The Lord Chancellor approved, and condescended to give me some valuable advice for conducting my canvass.

When I had been about eight days in Edinburgh I was knocked out of bed at four in the morning and told that a King's messenger had arrived from London with a letter from the Lord Chancellor, which I must read immediately.

---

[1] See 22 Hansard, 410. I have always thought this speech one of Brougham's most wonderful exploits. No one else would have ventured to cram a law officer of the Crown, or could have done it so felicitously.

I have not preserved it, but I believe that it ran as follows:—

"DEAR JACK,—Ned Stanley, Graham, Richmond, and Rippy have left us. But be not alarmed. We shall go on better without them. This you must inculcate upon the modern Athenians. Persevere. I really believe that we are safe. You shall know all when we meet.

"Yours,   H. B."

The messenger likewise brought a letter from the Secretary to the Treasury stating that the Colonial Secretary, the First Lord of the Admiralty, the Postmaster-General, and the President of the Board of Trade, had resigned—that all the other members of the Cabinet remained steady, and that in this crisis everything might depend upon carrying Edinburgh. At dawn of day there was a handbill posted all over the city, congratulating the electors on the secession of the fugitive Ministers, and extolling those who remained true to the cause of freedom—particularly the Lord Chancellor, who, born and bred among them, reflected such credit upon his "own romantic town."

When I returned to London victorious, he complimented me on having served the State; but he did not enter into any particulars of the disruption of the Cabinet, and I have never heard from any authentic source what part he personally took upon this occasion. From the speech then delivered by him in the House of Lords, as reported in Hansard,[1] he appears to have been quite sound and rational on the vexed "Appropriation Clause."

"I agree," said he, "in thinking that not one shilling of any surplus fund arising from the revenues of the Protestant Church in Ireland should be appropriated to any other purpose, until the spiritual wants of the Protestant community have been fully provided for. That having been done on a liberal, even an extravagant scale, what man is there with audacity to state that the residue of the fund may not be fitly applied towards the moral and religious instruction of the rest of the people. In determining what is ample provision for religious worship, must the number of those to join in that worship be wholly kept out of view? Let me suppose that there should cease to be any members of the Established Church in Ireland, instead of there being, as at present, a small minority of the

[1] 24 Hansard, 298.

population attached to it. This you say is an extreme case, but it is by putting an extreme case that principles are best tried. If all the inhabitants of Ireland should be Roman Catholics or Presbyterians, must we still keep up the full Protestant Episcopalian Establishment? The leader of this secession from the Cabinet, by his own Irish Church Temporalities Bill, allows that you may make any redistribution of the property of the Protestant Church, according to the spiritual wants of different localities; and when all these have been amply satisfied, to deny the power of the State to apply any surplus which remains to the general education of the people, or to any other laudible national purpose, is rank superstition and mischievous folly."

The religious question being disposed of, and Lord Grey having filled up the vacancies in his Cabinet by subordinate adherents devoted to the policy he was pursuing, it was expected that his Government would now be famous for unity of action, and that he would long remain in office to enjoy his triumph over inveterate Tories and mutinous Whigs. But in a little month he finally fell, or in his own language "descended," from power.

Lord Grey himself suspected, and his family openly asserted, that he was betrayed by Brougham, who, wishing to be Prime Minister, originated and fostered the intrigues which produced this catastrophe. I believe this charge to be unfounded. That Brougham's ambition made him aspire to the "bad eminence" I do not doubt; and that his opinion of his own talents and acquirements led him into the delusion that he was as well qualified for it as Burleigh, Godolphin, Walpole, Pitt the father or Pitt the son, is not improbable; but he could not be unconscious of the truth that he was regarded with dislike by the King —what was worse, that the leaders of the Liberal party reposed no confidence in him and would not agree to serve under him,—and worst of all, that the popularity which had made him the representative for the county of York had been nearly destroyed by the strange course which on several occasions he had pursued. Therefore the notion of his being first Lord of the Treasury can hardly at this time have taken possession of his mind. But, although he had no wish forcibly to displace Lord Grey, or systematically to annoy him so as to induce him to retire in disgust, he certainly was a very troublesome and uncomfortable colleague—constantly grasping at power and patronage that did not legitimately belong to the office which he held.

Lord Grey had been much annoyed by the insatiable demands of the ultra-Radicals, who, instead of giving the Reform Bill a fair trial, were clamorous for vote by ballot, the shortening of parliaments, the further extension of the suffrage, and organic changes in the House of Lords. All this he could have combated: but the constant fretting caused by the insubordination and aggressive spirit of an ever-restless colleague he found unsupportable, and he had expressed and felt a desire to withdraw into private life almost from the assembling of the first Reformed Parliament in the spring of 1833. He was not then aware of what he afterwards experienced, that inaction, after violent political excitement, is still more distressing than official crosses, and that the transfer of party chieftainship to a former dependent causes a bitter pang in the breast of him who has longed for repose. Lord Grey's murmurs and threats had caused much uneasiness to the Whig party, who then had no hope of retaining office without him; and strong representations were made to him respecting his obligation to remain in office at whatever sacrifice, that he might guide the working of the new constitution which by a revolution he had achieved.[1] By such considerations he was long influenced; but any fresh annoyance made him wish that he were reclining under the shade of his trees at Howick, and made him again resolve that he would no longer submit to the miseries of Downing Street. In this vacillating frame of mind a little matter was enough to induce him to take the irrevocable step, and there is no occasion to invent treason or intrigue to account for his resignation.

But although Brougham was falsely charged with fradulent design, he may certainly be considered the immediate cause of this event. When the Irish Coercion Bill, which had been passed only for one year, was to be renewed, a question arose whether it might not be in some degree mitigated by omitting the court-martial clauses. The

[1] Among others, I myself, although never enjoying much of his private intimacy, was requested by some of his particular friends to write to him in the autumn of 1833, pointing out to him how the good of the country, as well as of the Whig party, required him to sacrifice his ease to his duty.

Lord-Lieutenant (Lord Wellesley) at first expressed a strong opinion against any change. Lord Grey and a majority of the Cabinet concurred. Lord Althorp and three others were for mitigation, but from deference for the opinion of the Lord-Lieutenant, who declared that he could not undertake to govern Ireland with impaired powers, they succumbed. Accordingly, a bill for simply continuing it was introduced in the House of Lords.

This raising a terrible outcry, Brougham without Lord Grey's privity, entered into a correspondence on the subject with the Lord-Lieutenant, and sanctioned a communication by Mr. Littleton, the Chief Secretary for Ireland, to Mr. O'Connell, with a view to obtain his consent to the Continuation Bill, if the court-martial clauses should be omitted. The Lord-Lieutenant relented, and then a proposal was abruptly made to the Cabinet to abandon what they had all agreed to, and what the House of Lords had been pravailed upon by Lord Grey to sanction as indispensably necessary for the tranquillity and safety of Ireland. Lord Althorp and his minority declared that they had been prevailed upon to consent to military tribunals being kept up for civil offenses solely on the opinion of the Lord-Lieutenant, and this being withdrawn, they could no longer support the bill in its present shape. Lord Grey declared that his own opinion remained unaltered, and that the Government, after being so pledged, could not recede. The Chancellor in vain tried to bring about a compromise, urging that on fresh information there might be a change of policy without inconsistency or dishonor.

As soon as the Cabinet broke up Lord Althorp sent in his resignation to Lord Grey, and Lord Grey sent it to the King with his own. William IV. very readily accepted them, for he had become tired of his Whig Ministers, and conceiving that he had effectually got rid of them, he was about to send for the Duke of Wellington or Sir Robert Peel.

A new Conservative Government would certainly then have been formed, but for the extraordinary promptitude, vigor, and daring exhibited by Brougham. He contrived to see all the members of the Cabinet privately and separately, and he persuaded them that there was no occasion for them to retire; that if Althorp would come back they could get on without Grey; that Althorp would come back for the public good if his original wish for the mitigation of the Coercion Bill were now complied with; that they ought not to send in their resignations, and that the King—while the House of Commons, elected in the fervor of reform, still subsisted—could not force them out, to bring in the borough-mongers. They all agreed to " stand by their guns."

Brougham has often told me that at this time he had himself the offer of being Prime Minister, but that he positively declined it, and named Melbourne. I strongly suspect that this only appeared to him in a dream, and that the story is now believed by him only because it has been so often narrated by him. But certain it is that, either without any such offer to Brougham or after it was rejected, the offer was made to Melbourne, and that he, despising all pretended modesty, at once agreed to become Prime Minister, if the King's sanction could be obtained. The King was cruelly disappointed; but he was told by sensible Conservatives that the time for his emancipation had not yet arrived, and he gave his consent.

A tragi-comical scene was acted in the House of Lords, when the ministerial crisis was first noticed there. Lord Grey, uninformed of what had been passing among his colleagues since his own resignation had been accepted by the King, considered that Whig rule was over for the present, and he gave a very pathetic account of the different events which had led to this catastrophe. He said:—

" It was the opinion of myself and all my colleagues, in consequence of previous communications, that it was indispensable the Act, with all its clauses, should be renewed. I myself instructed the Attorney-General to prepare a bill for its renewal, which is now on the table of your Lordships' house.[1] I will once more take upon myself the responsibility of declaring, that in the present condition of Ireland, the passing of that bill is, in my opinion, indispensably necessary. But I am deprived of the assistance of my noble friend the Chancellor of the Exchequer, the leading member of the Government in the Commons—the indi-

[1] I well remember receiving these instructions at the King's levee, and being told that all the members of the Government, both in Ireland and in England, were of opinion that the Act must be renewed without any mitigation.

vidual on whom my chief confidence rested—whom I considered as my right arm; and I feel it impossible for the Government to go on. I can no longer serve the Crown or the country to any useful purpose. On my receiving my noble friend's resignation, I saw no alternative, but felt impelled by irresistible necessity to tender my own to his Majesty at the same time. Those resignations have been accepted by his Majesty, and, I now stand here discharging the duties of office only till such time as his Majesty shall be enabled to supply my place."

He then took a valedictory review of his administration, showing that he had ever acted on the principles which on assuming office he had professed.

The Tory peers cheered him loudly, their generosity being warmed by the conviction that at the next meeting of the House they would walk across and take possession of the ministerial benches. But great was their consternation when up rose the Lord Chancellor, and, after a great deal of obscure periphrasis, thus distinctly spoke out:—

"Of all men who ever held office, the present ministry would be the most without excuse if they could think of leaving the service of their King and country unless through an unavoidable necessity. This has ever been my opinion since I came into office; it is my opinion to the present hour; and I feel that I should not discharge my duty if, at all sacrifice of my comfort—at all abandonment of my own ease—at the destruction, if so it may be, of my peace of mind, I do not stand by that gracious monarch and that country, whose cordial support I have received during the three years and a half I have had the honor to hold the Great Seal. After having said this, need I add that *I have not tendered my resignation.* [Loud laughter in the house below the bar and on the steps of the throne.] Do your Lordships, or do any who listen to me, think that there is anything peculiarly merry or amusing in being a minister at the present conjuncture? If they do, I invite them to take a part in the reconstruction of the Government. But they know better. If they are not aware of the annoyance which must attend such a situation, I am; and I will tell these noble and laughing Lords, that such is my feeling with respect to office, that nothing but a sense of imperative duty could have kept me in office one hour after the resignation of my noble friend." [1]

The following day, being interrogated by the Marquis of Londonderry and other peers, whether any person had yet been intrusted with the formation of a new ministry, the Chancellor said :—

"Neither interruptions, nor sneers, nor good-humored jokes shall compel me to answer a question which duty to my sovereign ought to make me refuse to answer. I should betray my duty to my sovereign if I were to answer it. If I knew nothing, I could answer it—easily answer it; but because I do know, I refuse to answer; and I trust that your lordships will think I am not guilty of taciturnity. [Repeated cheers of assent.] True, my lords, I am not always taciturn; I can defend myself when attacked, and I can defend my friends when my friends are attacked. But now silence is required, that I may not mar the public service and defeat the end which we all wish to see speedily accomplished, and prevent his Majesty from obtaining that assistance to which he is entitled from all his loyal subjects." [2]

In a few days Lord Melbourne appeared in the House as First Minister, and Lord Brougham nominally as his Chancellor, but showing a disposition to be "Viceroy over him." Upon the announcement that the Irish Coercion Renewal Bill depending in the Lords was to be dropped, and that a milder bill was to be introduced in the Commons, the Duke of Buckingham insisted that—

"The bill, abandoned when it stood for a third reading, was in accordance with the feelings of the country. Within a little week the noble Earl who had brought it in amidst the cheers of all his colleagues, had gone to his political sepulture; and the noble and learned lord on the woolsack was ready to bring in another bill of a totally different complexion. The country would require an explanation from the noble lord who thus acted in contradiction of his own speeches. The noble and learned lord might think he had buried the noble lord lately at the head of the Government, but he was also mistaken upon that point. The noble Earl's spirit would arise and scare some of the dignified occupants from their arm-chairs and interrupt the festivities of the noble and learned lord on

[1] 24 Hansard, 1312   [2] 25 Hansard, 5.

the woolsack when he may attempt to forget the history with *pottle-deep potations* to the health and prosperity of the new administration."

The Lord Chancellor.—"The noble Duke who has just addressed the House must be conversant with the dialect adopted in some alehouse, with which I am unacquainted. I have been in the habit of meeting the noble Duke elsewhere, but I have never had the honor of seeing him at the alehouse, where the noble Duke must have been so often in order to have picked up the terms of his slang dictionary."

Cries of "*Order*" resounded from all sides, and a scene followed, which for the dignity of their Lordships' House, and the credit of all concerned in it, I wish to be forgotten.[1]

The Session lasted only a month longer—during which Brougham dressed in his brief authority did play fantastic tricks, which if they did not make the angels weep, made the judicious grieve. Publicly pretending to regret, he privately showed that he was delighted by the retirement of Lord Grey. Lord Melbourne, whom he addressed and talked of by the name of "Lamb" or "William," he considered a mere subordinate, although in the House of Lords he called him "my noble friend at the head of the Government." All the other members of the Cabinet, as they owed their continuance in office to him, he thought owed him allegiance, and he was disposed to treat them, if not as subjects, as schoolboys.

---

[1] 25 Hansard, 49. In a publication of Lord Brougham, printed in the year 1838, he gives the following account of this ministerial crisis: "This unreasonable feeling of disappointment, and the unhappy necessity which existed for the Coercion Bill in Ireland, had excited a clamor against the Government of Lord Grey; and when that justly esteemed individual quitted office, the King had undoubtedly resolved to take advantage of this clamor, and would have at once changed his Ministers, had they given him an opening by hesitating whether or not they should continue to hold the Government after Lord Grey's secession. The declaration *first communicated by the Chancellor* in private to his Majesty, and then on the same day made by him in the House of Lords, that the Ministers were quite willing to remain, disconcerted all such designs; and the King could not take the step he so much wished until Lord Spencer's death in the following November gave, or seemed to give, a kind of ground (or rather a hollow pretext) for accomplishing the same purpose. This was the very worst step, as it was the most inconsiderate, and proved for his own comfort the most fatal that this excellent monarch ever took; and he had been beforehand warned distinctly of the inevitable consequences, but he disregarded the warning."—*Lord Brougham's Speeches*, vol. iv. p. 90.

To proclaim his complete "independence," when asked to give evidence before a Committee of the House of Commons appointed to inquire into the "Taxes on Knowledge," he eagerly expressed his willingness to attend, permission for this purpose being obtained from the House of Lords, and when examined he expressed opinions wholly at variance with those which had been advocated by his colleagues in debate, himself recommending the immediate and total repeal of the stamp duty on newspapers, of the tax upon advertisements, and of the duties upon paper of every description—which he denounced as impolitic, unjust, and oppressive—although he appeared before the Committee, not as a private individual but as Lord Chancellor. Indeed he came in his robes, attended by his mace bearer, purse bearer, and other officers, and in the presence of the members of the Committee he exercised his privilege of wearing his cocked hat, till after a little time he condescendingly uncovered. He likewise on this occasion blurted out some crude notions of his own about limiting the power of the Attorney-General to file criminal informations.[1]

But his greatest mistake was in behaving with *brusquerie* even to the King. Nothing could excuse the unceremonious and dictatorial tone which he now assumed in the royal presence—making the Lords of the Bed Chamber stare—and evidently exciting surprise and disgust in the mind of the King. Entertaining stories were circulated of deliberations in the Cabinet, in which he denounced the *hallucinations* of his colleagues in very unmeasured terms; but these rest on no authority and were probably pure invention. As far as his own proceedings were concerned he cared very little about the opinion of his colleagues, and he did not give himself the trouble to consult them. He laid upon the table of the House of Lords bills which he declared to be "Government bills"—some of very considerable importance, about which I certainly knew that no one member of the Government, in the Cabinet or out of the Cabinet, has been consulted. One of these was for entirely altering the appellate jurisdiction of the House of Lords, and introducing an organic change in the constitution.[2]

[1] I remember complaining of this to Lord Althorp and Lord John Russell They only laughed, and said "no harm followed from such extravagances."
[2] 25 Hansard, 1255. This bill he professed to lay on the table on the 14th

The business of the Session being over, we had the usual ministerial fish dinner at Blackwall, which was celebrated this year with peculiar hilarity on account of the dangers we had run. Brougham attended and entered into our " high jinks " with much good-humor. I thought of impeaching him for high treason by *accroching* upon the royal dignity; but this would have been considered too near the truth for a joke, and I contented myself with renewing a motion which had been several times made and refused in the Lords and in the Commons, "That there be laid before this House a copy of the correspondence between the Lord High Chancellor of Great Britain and the Lord-Lieutenant of Ireland, touching the renewal of the Irish Coercion Act." Brougham, in resisting the motion in the Upper House, had declared that his letters to Lord Wellesley, in which the topic had been alluded to, were entirely of a private nature, and contained as much verse as prose. I urged this as a reason for granting the papers, as I had no doubt it would convince the world that our Chancellor who equalled Cicero as an orator and a philosopher excelled him as a poet—dealing in no such lines as

"O fortunatam natam me consule Romam."

He made a good answer by denying that such *barbarous* critics were qualified to estimate the beauty of his performances.

On the 15th of August the prorogation actually took place, when Brougham sat for the last time on the woolsack as Chancellor. He then not only had the usual confidence of absolute safety till Parliament should again assemble, but he was sanguine enough to anticipate a Cancellarian career as long as Lord Eldon's, the Tories being defunct as a party, and he himself being worshiped as the impersonation of Liberalism.

In the King's Speech on this occasion prepared by Brougham, he justly took credit for two excellent bills which he had carried during the Session,—one for the

of August, 1134. The prorogation following next day, it never was printed; and I have been credibly informed that it never was drawn, a blank sheet of paper endorsed, "An Act to amend the Jurisdiction of the House of Lords in the hearing of Appeals and Writs of Error" representing it. But I myself with astonishment heard him detail the various clauses it was supposed to contain, and which, if it had proceeded, my duty would have required me to defend in the House of Commons.

Amendment of the Poor Laws, and the other for the Establishment of the Central Criminal Court.[1] The abuse of the fund intended by the 43d of Elizabeth for the support of the destitute had been carried to such an excess as to demoralize the great mass of the lower orders, and to bring such a burden on the land as to render it in some parishes of no value to the nominal owners, who abandoned the cultivation of it that they might escape the assessment. Upon the recommendation of a set of most intelligent commissioners to whom the subject was referred, a new system was devised, to be uniformly enforced all over England and Wales, under the superintendence of a Metropolitan Board, whereby provision was made for the really destitute, without pandering to idleness, or relaxing the springs of industry. This met with a vulgar opposition, and was denominated as cruel and unjust; when Brougham rendered essential service in explaining its principles, and showing that it was for the benefit of the poor as well as the rich. He indiscreetly went too far in blaming all compulsory provision for the poor, and contending that mischievous effects are produced by all public charities. These sentiments may perhaps be defended on abstract economical principles, but they are shocking to the vulgar, and they were afterwards very unscrupulously repeated and perverted for the purpose of casting obloquy upon the Whig party, from whom the bill originated.[2]

The other measure has had unmixed applause, and in fairness the merit of it ought to be almost exclusively imputed to Brougham.[3] From ancient times there was a Court, called the Old Bailey, which met frequently throughout the year for the trial of all offenses committed in the county of Middlesex and in the metropolis, which formerly did not extend beyond the ancient walls of the City of London. But large portions of the metropolis were now to be found in the counties of Surrey, Kent, and Essex, and persons charged with offenses in them might lie seven or eight months in prison before being

[1] 25 Hansard, 1207.
[2] See 25 Hansard, 435. The Duke of Wellington, and all the respectable Tory leaders, supported the bill, but it was afterwards by their subordinates shamefully converted into a weapon of offense at popular elections all over the kingdom, and down to 1841 materially added to Sir Robert Peel's strength in the House of Commons. [3] 25 Hansard, 240.

brought to trial. The evil had been frequently complained of, and plans had been proposed for extending the jurisdiction of the Old Bailey; but I believe that had it not been for Brougham's energy the evil would have remained unremedied to the present hour. Assisted by myself and others who were only his instruments, he prepared a bill by which a population of above two millions and a half are subjected to the jurisdiction of the new court, and a tribunal is established of which the Lord Chancellor[1] and all the Judges are members, and which has ten sessions in the year for the trial of all offenses within an area of about twenty miles from St. Paul's Cathedral.[2]

When Brougham, after the delivery of the King's speech, had in his Majesty's name declared Parliament to be prorogued, he would have returned home perfectly satisfied with himself and with all the world, had it not been for the war raging between him and the *Times* newspaper.

Till about Easter, 1834, Brougham had the full favor of the *Thunderer*,[3] and was supposed himself to be allowed to hurl thunderbolts under the guise of the dread Divinity. Such paragraphs as the following were still frequently to be read in the *Times:*

"The attack on the Chancellor respecting the late Mr. James Brougham's sinecure is one of the almost daily instances of the mode in which the enemies of the Chancellor conduct their opposition to that eminent man."

"The dullest fag does not work so hard as the man even his enemies acknowledge to be the most accomplished and brilliant intellect of his age and country."

"We present to our readers an abridgment of the return of the state of business in the Court of Chancery, moved for in the House of Lords by the Lord Chancellor, and no doubt authentic, being made under his superintendence. What an answer does this abridgment of a par-

---

[1] I believe that Lord Chancellor Brougham, to give dignity to the court, meant himself occasionally to preside in it, but *fata aspera* broke this purpose.

[2] This tribunal and the Judicial Committee of the Privy Council ought to perpetuate his fame. With his new Court of Bankruptcy he was not so lucky, for he created four Judges to sit all the year round for the purpose of doing business, which in experience it was found might easily be done by one Judge in a few days. So the Court of Bankruptcy fell with its founder.

[3] Then the designation of the *Times*.

liamentary paper delivered this morning make to the calumniators of the Lord Chancellor!"

But he had now a private quarrel with Barnes the editor, who thought himself slighted by him, and he was first attacked for his speech in support of the new Poor Law, against which Mr. Walter, the chief proprietor of the newspaper, had a strong prejudice, and which the newspaper continued for years systematically and vehemently to oppose.

But what completed the rupture and made it irreparable was Brougham's carelessness in allowing to come to the knowledge of the *Times*, the following "secret and confidential" letter he received one morning when sitting on the bench in the Court of Chancery in Lincoln's Inn Hall:

"DEAR BROUGHAM,

"What I want to see you about is the *Times*, whether we are to make war on it or come to terms.

"Yours ever

ALTHORP."

This Brougham read during the argument,—answered immediately and tore up—throwing away the fragments. These fragments were picked up by a shorthand writer, put together and carried next day to the office of the *Times*. It so happened that this very day some information which the editor asked from the Government was abruptly refused. The inference drawn was that by the Chancellor's advice a determination had been formed by the Government to make war on the *Times*, and the *Times* determined to make war upon Brougham, sparing for a while at least the main body of his colleagues. Accordingly, while a general support was given to Lord Melbourne's Government, a series of bitter attacks began upon the devoted Chancellor.

The disruption of the Cabinet by the retirement of Lord Stanley, Sir James Graham, Lord Ripon, and the Duke of Richmond, having taken place about this time, a party, headed by the *Times*, wished that Lord Durham should be introduced into the Cabinet, but were disappointed, and the blame was thrown on the Chancellor, who was known to look upon him with jealousy. Accordingly this sly paragraph appeared in the *Times*:—

"It is insinuated that the Lord Chancellor is at the

bottom of the exclusion of Lord Durham. Every friend of the noble and learned Lord must be impatient, as we are, to meet this with a flat denial."

The *Times* next tries in a long article to prove that the Chancellor has been guilty of inconsistency by agreeing to the " Appropriation Clause," having said within a year that "as to the Catholic Church receiving any of this possible surplus, he should as much oppose *that* as any of their Lordships." What is worse, they most groundlessly and falsely imputed to him the habit of intemperate drinking.

In a subsequent number the following question is put "Is it not melancholy that this noble and learned Lord, like a nisi prius advocate, exhibits an inconsistency so palpable, and a levity of political principle so all-but-præternatural?" And they ask him to compare his speech of July 4, and that of last Thursday, July 17, when the Duke of Wellington told him that it would take more than even the ingenuity of the noble and learned Lord himself to explain these contradictions.

On Lord Grey's resignation, the *Times* ridiculed the Chancellor's assertion that the Government still subsisted; "because cutting a man's head off involves the death of the body. Decapitation is death."

Thus they express their regret for the course they are now pursuing:—

"We have stood by him for fifteen years, but are now compelled to throw him over."

"Lord Durham ought to know the Chancellor by this time. He it was who excluded him from the Cabinet. Lord Melbourne will find him out. The honest men of the community are an overmatch for the knaves."

"The notion people have is, that the Lord Chancellor goes down to the House to have some fun with the old ladies. He appears like a young pickle turning the house out of window, quizzing his great grandmother and great aunts, making sport of their antique habits, upsetting their revered china, and roasting the parrot. And after he is tired, and the public somewhat scandalized at his amusing himself thus, out he comes with a sermon professing his duty and profound reverence and respect."

"It was Lord Brougham's correspondence with Lord Wellesley behind his back that destroyed Lord Grey's

Government. For confirmation we apply to Lord Grey's valedictory speech."

" For some months past Lord Brougham has been under a morbid excitement, seldom evinced by those of his Majesty's subjects who are suffered to remain masters of their own actions."

This was the beginning of a long leader continued in the same strain.

After being almost suffocated by newspaper praise, he could very ill brook these attacks. Meeting Lord Melbourne one day at the King's levee, I said to him :— " What is the matter with your Chancellor this morning? He seems very much disturbed." *Lord M.*—" Have you not seen this morning's *Times?*" *C.*—" No; not I." *Lord M.*—" Another *Broughamic*, hinting that he is out of his mind, exaggerating his peculiarities, vilipending his rhetoric, and, above all, asserting that there are heavy and increasing arrears in the Court of Chancery. He takes these attacks most seriously to heart, and I may really say that they drive him mad. I am very uneasy about him, and I am very glad that the session is so near its end."

While we were talking about him Brougham came up to us, and, after some little *persiflage* respecting another matter, took me aside and said that I must assist him that very night in the House of Commons, by showing that there were no arrears in the Court of Chancery, or in the House of Lords' appeals. I expressed my willingness, if he would furnish me with proper materials. He said, I will instantly send you a statistical statement on which you may rely."

I soon received a packet containing my instructions, and made a speech, of which I take the following specimen from Hansard :—

The Attorney-General.—" I rise for the purpose of moving for certain returns from the Court of Chancery, the result of which I am sure will give the greatest satisfaction to the House and to the country. It is of importance to the public that they should be truly informed of the manner in which judicial business is disposed of; and even to the Judges themselves it is but fair that a statement should be made, in order that where arrears exist a stimulus to exertion may be furnished; and where there are no arrears an estimate may be formed of the attention and energy which have produced this satisfactory result. It gives me much pleasure to announce that in the Court of Chancery there are now no arrears subsisting—which I believe could never be so effectually said since the time of Sir Thomas More. Nor does this arise from any falling off in the business of the Court, because in fact it has been progressively increasing."

Then follows a long tabular statement professing to come from the files of the Court of Chancery.

"With respect to the House of Lords, the account will be equally satisfactory; for, whatever honorable members here may think of the political proceedings of their Lordships during the present session, their judicial labors are worthy of all praise. In fact, although there have formerly been arrears in the House of Lords that it required years to clear off, there is at present no arrear whatever; and I trust that the example thus given by the Court of last resort, will have a salutary effect on all inferior tribunals in the realm."

The statement was received with prodigious applause, and the returns to verify it were immediately ordered.

But the following day a Chancery barrister rose, and complained of the Attorney-General—

"Who in moving for certain returns had made comparisons between the amount of business done by the present Lord Chancellor and his predecessors, which cast a reflection on great men now no more, and were calulated exceedingly to mislead the public. The fact was that there were upwards of 200 cases undisposed of in the Court of Chancery at the present moment, and in the House of Lords the arrear was still more considerable."

The Attorney-General could only say that—

"He had every reason to believe that the returns ordered would verify his statement, and that he had no intention of reflecting upon any one."

This conversation occurred just before the Black Rod appeared to summon the Commons for the prorogation, and, fortunately or unfortunately, the order for the returns dropped, so that I was never able to ascertain whether my instructions exactly correspond with the fact.[1]

Brougham himself certainly had a sincere conviction that he was fully competent not only to perform all the duties

[1] 25 Hansard, 1200, 1269.

of Lord Chancellor without assistance, in a manner which never had been accomplished before, but at the same time voluntarily to undertake extra-official labors in literature and science. To appease a class of reformers who were clamorous for the separation of the judicial and political functions of the Lord Chancellor, he had, at the commencement of the last session, laid on the table of the House of Lords a bill for that purpose; but he never took further notice of it till the very night when the Attorney-General was charged to eulogize him in the House of Commons. Having introduced his embyro bill for altering the appellate jurisdiction of the House, he concluded with this testimony in his own favor upon the vexed question whether there still remained any arrears in the Court of Chancery:—

"Before I sit down, my Lords, I wish to state my reason for not proceeding with my bill for separating the judicial and political functions of the Lord Chancellor. When I came to consider the subject at Easter, I found that I had no arrears of judicial business, and therefore I felt that, with respect to that bill, I had no ground to stand upon."[1]

On the day of the prorogation, the King, who had not the art of concealing his feelings, seemed to me to look rather sternly when receiving his speech from the kneeling Chancellor, and whispering to him the order to prorogue till the 25th of September; but this might only be my fancy. When his Majesty had set out on his return to the palace, I had the honor of an interview with the Chancellor in his private room, and I found him in the most exuberant spirits. He graciously condescended to thank me for what I had said of him in the House of Commons, and expressed a confident hope that the calumnies of the "rascally *Times*" were now effectually silenced. He then announced to me his approaching *tour* in Scotland. "Call it *Progress*," said I.

A royal Progress it certainly turned out to be. At this epoch Brougham's reputation in Scotland was much greater than ever had been Lord Mansfield's or Lord Loughborough's—the two Scotsmen who, having changed their domicile to England, had reflected the brightest splendor

[1] 25 Hansard, 1260.

on their native country. He was considered not only a
profound lawyer, who had accomplished judicial feats beyond example, but as the great regenerator of the age,
by his exertions for the abolition of slavery, for the spread
of education, for the reform of the law, and above all for
the emancipation of Scotland from political thraldom.
There can be no doubt that the situation of North Britons
with respect to parliamentary representation had been
most degrading; and they had given implicit credit to
pamphlets and articles in newspapers, imputing to the
Lord Chancellor the chief merit of destroying the corrupt
little self-elected *municipalities*, and the fraudulent *superiorities* in counties, which had made North Britain one
rotten borough, with the power of returning 45 members
to the House of Commons. Brougham's supposed ascendancy was viewed with pride and exultation by my countrymen, when they considered that he was born and bred
among them. Those admitted to familiar intimacy with
him might discover failings and weaknesses which prevented us from worshipping him; but to the distant
Caledonians, who judged him only by what they read, he
was a hero or a demigod.

Various supplications were offered up to him from private individuals and public bodies, praying that he would
revisit the scenes of his youth, and receive the homage of
a grateful nation. An objection was started by the Purse-
bearer and other officers to the emigration of the Great
Seal. The ancient law says that the *Clavis Regni* must
always be in the personal custody of the Lord Chancellor,
and that it must be kept and used within the realm of
England. One of the articles of impeachment against
Cardinal Wolsey was that he had carried it to Calais.
But this difficulty was surmounted by the consideration
that since the Union it is the Great Seal of Great Britain,
and that John o' Groat's House, should it even be carried
thither, is within the kingdom.

Brougham's inclination to show himself to admirers who
thus displayed their noted *perfervidum ingenium* was
quickened by intelligence that Lord Grey had actually
accepted an invitation to a public banquet to be given to
him at Edinburgh. The ruling passion immediately
operated upon him, and he was resolved to show that he
had more popularity there than the supposed father of

the Reform Bill, or, in common phrase, *to take the wind out of Lord Grey's sails.*

It was announced that the Lord Chancellor would visit both the Lowlands and the Highlands of Scotland, and take up his abode for some days in the northern metropolis. The news spread more rapidly than if carried from glen to glen by the fiery cross; and tar-barrels for beacon fires, devices for illuminations, worm-eaten muskets and rusty claymores were put in requisition to do him honor. Lord Provosts, Lord Rectors, and sheriffs principal, sheriffs depute, and sheriffs substitute, set their wits to work to pen addresses in his praise. As he had not yet acquired the faculty of ubiquity, the scheme adopted was that he should visit the castles of a few great chieftains; that he should there receive deputations from the surrounding counties and corporations; that in moving rapidly from one such castle to another, he should stop for a few hours at the populous towns between them; and that, partaking of a collation, he should then and there make suitable speeches in return for the compliments showered down upon him.

When he arrived at Lancaster, on his way to Scotland, he was pleased to find that the assizes were going on there, and that this was the night for holding the Grand Court, in which the Junior presided for the trial of all bar offenses. By rights, he ought to have dined with the Judges, but he expected much more fun with his old associates, and he sent them an intimation that he proposed to take his seat in the court as an ancient member of the circuit. This of course caused great joy, and a deputation immediately waited upon him to invite him to the honors of the sitting.

The carouse, as might have been expected, was the merriest ever known on the Northern Circuit. The Lord High Chancellor dropped all the proud trappings of office; himself sang two French *chansons à boire*, and was the life of the company. He declared (and perhaps for the moment believed in his own sincerity) how sorry he was that he had ever left the circuit, and wished that he might exchange the Great Seal for a nisi prius brief, and the drowsy Lords over whom he was condemned to preside for the choice spirits with whom he had now the happiness to fraternize. His demeanor was universally allowed to be most amiable and most becoming. While the barristers did whatever they could to humor him and to draw him out, they all showed a certain deference for him till a junior, hot with the Tuscan grape, proposed that his majesty should resume his royal title of Henry IX., and that they should, one by one, come and do homage to him as the peers did at the coronation to William IV. He thought it was time to be gone, so he exclaimed:—

"—— happy low, lie down,
Uneasy lies the head that wears a crown."

He then took leave, hurried to his hotel, and, the sun being up, he ordered his carriage and pursued his journey.

Having passed a day at Brougham Hall, that he might visit his beloved mother, whom in all states of mind he duly honored, he posted off for the North, and crossed the border at Gretna Green. His first resting-place was Hamilton Palace, in the county of Renfrew, where he was received by him who used to sign himself " H. B. and C." Hamilton, Brandon, and Chatelherault, Duke in three kingdoms, Scotland, England, and France. I have no authentic account of what passed on this occasion, except that the Chancellor was here made a burgess of the ancient burgh of Hamilton. No doubt there was a suitable speech by the Provost, followed by a suitable answer from the Chancellor, but they have perished. If I were to indulge in probable conjecture as to the speech of his host, I might say, with little risk of being wrong, that the old Duke, with the most high-bred politeness hinting at the royal blood in his veins, tried to convince his audience that the union between England and Scotland ought to be repealed, as degrading and injurious to the latter kingdom.[1]

The first authentic information I have obtained of the Chancellor's progress in Scotland, is his visit at Taymouth Castle, the seat of the Marquess of Breadalbane. When he approached Killin, at the head of Loch Tay, a salute of twenty-one guns announced that he had entered " the country of the Campbells." There was a gathering of the clan, and above a thousand men in tartan plaids and phili-

---

[1] I had the honor of his Grace's acquaintance, and have often heard him converse, but seldom on any other topics. He was the only Scotch Repealer I ever met with, but he was more sincere than Daniel O'Connell. His ancestor having been declared by the Scottish Parliament next heir to the Crown, failing Queen Mary and her issue, he had an indistinct notion that he had a better claim to it than the descendant of a Duke of Brunswick.

begs were drawn up in military array, carrying banners not only with the boar's head, the gyronny of eight, and the lymphad of Lorn, but likewise inscriptions celebrating the exploits of their illustrious guest. An aquatic procession then took place from one extremity of Loch Tay to the other, much grander than Roderick Dhu's as described in the *Lady of the Lake*, pipers from far and near playing favorite pibrochs. When they reached the Castle there was another royal salute from a battery at a little distance, and the Marquess, with his tail on, delivered an address, the burden of which was that all the glory conferred in former times on different branches of the Campbells by visits from Kings of Scotland, whether Macalpines, Bruces, or Stuarts, was elipsed by this visit from one of the greatest of lawyers, orators, and patriots, who, from his efforts in framing and carrying the Reform Bill, might well be called the " Liberator of Scotland." Brougham, in answer was eloquent upon what the Campbells had done in the field—still more in the cause of civil and religious liberty —exploits which all call to mind when they hear " The Campbells are coming;" and he dwelt particularly on the patriotism of the present chief of Breadalbane.

By referring to the newspapers of that time I might fill a volume with similar addresses and answers, as the Chancellor proceeded to different noblemen's houses, and visited Perth, Glasgow, Inverness, Aberdeen, and Dundee, on his way. At Rothiemurchus, then the residence of the Dowager Duchess of Bedford, he found a large party of English ladies, with whom he romped so familiarly that, to be revenged on him, they stole the Great Seal, and hid it where neither he nor his attendants could discover it. This was rather a serious practical joke, for without the Great Seal the government is at a stand-still; the Great Seal alone gives validity to the most important acts of the executive Government, and every grant in the Sovereign's name bearing the impression of it, is in point of law conclusively authentic. At last he was in such real distress about it that the ladies took compassion upon him, assured him it was in the drawing-room, and that he might find it blindfolded, one of them assisting him by playing loud on the piano when he approached it. He was blindfolded accordingly, and by the hints which the piano gave him, he, in due time, dragged the bauble from a tea-chest.

This was very harmless sport; but unfortunately exaggerated accounts of it were sent to a lady in waiting at Windsor Castle, and she exaggerating these accounts still further in relating them to the royal circle there, they did much mischief.

His speech on receiving the freedom of the city of Inverness excited most notice, and I shall therefore give a few extracts from it. After, as usual, modestly accounting for his enthusiastic reception from "the circumstance that he had the honor of serving a monarch who reigned in the hearts of his subjects," he said:—

"To find that he lives in the hearts of his loyal subjects inhabiting this ancient and important capital of the Highlands, as it has afforded me pure and unmixed satisfaction, will, I am confident, be so received by his Majesty when I tell him (as I will do by this night's post) of such a gratifying manifestation."

Then referring to the complaints against the Government for not "going ahead," he said:—

"My own opinion is that we have done too much rather than too little. By passing the new Poor-law, were the Government to do nothing more for ten years to come, they would have deserved well of the country. If we did little in the last session, I fear we shall do less in the next. But what we do will be done well, because it will be done carefully."

A loud clamor was raised by the expressions in this speech about the Government having done too much and being about to do less. Taken with the context, they were merely a just rebuke to the ultra-Radicals, who seemed to think that however much had been done, as much remained to be done as if nothing had been done, and that a Session without a revolution was a lost Session. But I fear that nothing can be said in excuse of the rhodomontade about the Invernessians showing their loyalty to the King by applauding the Keeper of his Conscience, and the assurance that he would by that night's post convey the happy tidings to his Majesty. The epistolary correspondence of the tourist with his Majesty, however, was not (as many suspected) a mere invention. The following communication to me is from a valued friend, on whose honor and accuracy entire reliance may be placed:—

"The Inverness letter to King William was written over a tumbler of whisky toddy, in the presence of a Mr. MacPherson, who told me the fact. The good-natured Chancellor had espied him (Lord Brougham, to this day, has wonderfully fine sight, and can distinguish faces quicker than most men), I say his Lordship detected the face of MacPherson, in the crowd of listeners, as that of an old College acquaintance at Edinburgh. He sent for him. In the evening MacPherson found the Chancellor alone in the best room, of course, of Wilson's Caledonian Hotel. The Great Seal was drinking punch, and forthwith commanded a tumbler to be brought for MacPherson. The two passed the evening, or a considerable part of it, together. Now MacPherson told me that, when the hour for the despatch of the South post was approaching, Lord Brougham said he had to write to the King about that day's proceedings; but that it would not take him long, and he desired MacPherson to go on with his toddy. The Chancellor accordingly went to a side-table, and there indited the fatal missive which was soon to prove the chief instrument of his downfall. From what MacPherson said, I fancy it could not have been a long epistle. But the notion of writing to the King at all on such a subject was an absurdity, into which Lord Brougham was drawn by his own argument in the morning, that the honors he had received belonged truly to the gracious Prince he had served for nearly four years, and consequently it followed logically enough that the King had a right to be exactly apprised of them."

By the time he reached Aberdeen the comments in the newspapers on his Inverness speech seemed to have excited him almost to fury, and he threatened the *printers*, as he derisively called the "gentlemen of the Press," with his utmost vengeance. In addressing the Aberdonians, he said:—

"You will be all well aware of the absurd and stupid and indefensible attacks which have been showered against me, not one word of which is true or deserved. But," said the Chancellor, in an impassioned manner, "a day of retribution is at hand; it approaches. I have allowed certain persons to go on. They have gone on. The net is enclosed around them, and they shall soon be held up to ridicule and to scorn, aye and perhaps to punishment."

"Perhaps," said the *Times*, "he is going to write to the King without the loss of a single post."[1]

These ebullitions certainly produced a very unfavorable effect upon the public mind, and I believe that O'Connell could get no one to take the wager which he thus publicly offered in a "Letter to the People of Ireland":—

"I pay very little attention to anything Lord Brougham says. He makes a greater number of foolish speeches than any other man of the present generation. There may be more nonsense in some one speech of another person; but in the number, the multitude of foolish speeches, Lord Brougham has it hollow. I would start him ten to one— ay, fifty to one—in talking nonsense and flatly contradicting himself, against any prattler now living."[2]

Whether Brougham continued to write to the King by every post, giving an account of his progress, or what specific effect these letters produced, I have not been able to learn, but, according to authentic information, King William, who had been much offended by the Chancellor's demeanor since the resignation of Lord Grey, had looked upon his journey to Scotland with amazement and consternation, and had complained to Lord Melbourne of some of his speeches as democratical. It was even said that his Majesty had declared to others with whom he conversed more freely, that "He could not account for the Chancellor clandestinely running away with the Great Seal beyond the jurisdiction of the Court of Chancery, except upon the supposition that he was out of his mind, of which there had for some time been strong symptoms."[3]

---

[1] His speeches after Inverness, however, were silent as to *Government having done too much*, and were more in the go-ahead strain, which induced the *Times* to remark, "The Lord Chancellor has bolted at Aberdeen and Dundee all that he had said at Inverness, without a single wry face."

[2] Soon after a public dinner was given at Glasgow to his rival, Lord Durham, who then assailed Brougham very bitterly, and (as was reported) with great approbation. In drawing a comparison between him and Lord Melbourne, the orator observed, laying his emphasis so as that he could not be misunderstood, "*Lord Melbourne* is incapable of treachery or intrigue." Here there was a general apprehension that the roof would come down from the shouts of applause.—See *Times*.

[3] I certainly know that William IV. had a strong opinion that no English Judge could lawfully go beyond the realm of England without the express personal permission of the King. He once caused Lord Abinger, when C. B. of the Exchequer, to be reprimanded for doing so; and this doctrine had been so traditionally established at Court that when I myself became a Judge, I did not venture upon a tour to Italy till I had first obtained the Queen's consent, although I hold it to be quite clear that there is no such prerogative. A

The day appointed for the Grey Festival was now at hand, and there were various speculations as to the course which Brougham would take respecting it. The general opinion was that he would feign some sudden call to London. Lord Grey was to be accompanied by Lady Grey and his daughters, who in loud terms accused Brougham of having treacherously caused the late change of Government, and had hitherto refused to see him since the event happened. Their theory was, that Brougham, wishing to get rid of Lord Grey as Prime Minister, purposely made the place irksome and annoying to him, and that having heard of Lord Grey's threats of resigning, he had designedly got up the intrigue about the renewal of the Coercion Bill, to induce him by a fresh disgust, to carry his threat into execution. Brougham knew that no proof could be adduced to support the charge, and he thought that his most politic plan would be to face it and so to put it down.

The whole Grey family were to be the guests of Sir John Dalrymple (afterwards Earl of Stair), at Oxenford Castle, near Edinburgh, and Brougham, who had been an old friend of Sir John, boldly wrote to him to say that, if it was convenient for him and Lady Adamina,[1] he should be glad to take up his quarters at Oxenford Castle during the approaching solemnity at Edinburgh, which he felt bound to attend from his profound respect for Lord Grey, whose retirement from office he so deeply deplored. Sir John, who, living in the country, was not aware of the actual relations between Brougham and the Greys, answered that he should be delighted with his company. The Greys did not at all know whom they were to meet at Oxenford till they had arrived there, and the arrangement which had been made could not be altered. Being then member for the city of Edinburgh, I had been invited to Oxenford to join Lord Grey's *cortége*. Well aware of the abhorrence in which Brougham was held by the Grey family, I never was so much astonished as when I heard that Brougham was to sit down at table with them there, and to pass the night under the same roof. He was very late in appearing, and we had all

Judge may go where he likes, either in or out of the realm, without any Royal consent, if he does not neglect his judicial duties; and if he does, the consent of the Crown would be no excuse for him.

[1] Lady Adamina Dalrymple, sister of the Earl of Camperdown.

been assembled in the drawing-room expecting him. My heart beat violently as often as any noise arose that might indicate his approach. At last a servant opened the door and announced " The Lord Chancellor." I must say that his demeanor was noble and grand. Without any approach to presumption or vulgar familiarity, in an easy, frank, natural manner, he laid hold of the hand of Lord Grey, who, though stiff and stately, could not draw it back or refuse to acknowledge his salutation. He then most respectfully, but without betraying any consciousness of there being any misunderstanding between them, paid his court to Lady Grey and actually engaged her in conversation, beginning with some complimentary expressions about the festival to be celebrated on the morrow. The two daughters, the Ladies Grey, long avoided him by every manœuvre they could resort to, but, before the evening was over, he had got them both to talk to him about the place where they were to be stationed next day so that they might best see and hear their papa. In his conversation he seemed anxiously desirous that the festival should be devoted exclusively to the honor of Lord Grey, and should be so conducted as most to gratify the feelings of all connected with him.

Next day, however, at the public dinner, his object evidently was to make himself the most conspicuous object —improving the opportunity to glorify himself and to assail his opponents. In responding to the toast of " his Majesty's Ministers," which was received with much applause, he began with the praise of his Royal Correspondent :—

" I owe this expression from you, not by any means so much to any personal deserts of my own, as to the accidental circumstance, but to me most honorable, of having the pride and gratification to serve that great and gracious Prince who lives in the hearts of his people, and who for all the services he has rendered his country, and for his honest, straightforward, and undeviating patronage of the best rights and interests of that country, has well earned the unparalleled praise bestowed on him so justly and without any exaggeration by your noble Chairman, ' that none of his predecessors ever more richly deserved the affections and gratitude of his subjects.' "

He next alluded to " the irreparable loss which his

Majesty's Ministers had lately sustained in the chief, to whose great services this most splendid and unparalleled national testimonial had been so appropriately given." Then he came to the more agreeable topic of *himself*, when he really grew sincere, earnest, eloquent, and impressive :—

"My fellow-citizens of Edinburgh, after having been four years a Minister, *these hands are clean.* In taking office, and holding it, and retaining it, I have sacrificed no feeling of a public nature; I have deserted no friend; I have forfeited no pledge; I have done no job; I have promoted no unworthy man to the best of my knowledge; I have stood in the way of no man's fair pretensions to promotion; I have not abused my patronage; I have not abused the ear of my master; and I have not deserted the people."

In this strain he went on for near half-an-hour, declaring his purpose never to be deterred by the clamor of the people, more than by the frown of the Prince, from doing his duty to the Prince and to the people. He then enumerated the great measures which the Government had carried through since the passing of the Reform Bill—particularly the abolition of slavery. "I am ready," said he, " to take on my head singly, if necessary, the undivided responsibility of making the slave free." Of the credit of reforming the Church Establishment in Ireland he only claimed a share—but he exclusively appropriated to himself the reform of "the great nest of abuse, the Court of Chancery." He next fell foul of the Earl of Durham and others who had censured some of his Conservative speeches on his " progress," and who, instead of thinking that the Whigs had gone too far, as Brougham had hinted, urged them still to advance till all grievances should be redressed :—

"We shall go on," said he, "heedless of the attacks of those hasty spirits. They are men of great honesty, of much zeal, and of no reflection at all. They would travel towards their object; but they are in such a hurry to set out, and to get there three minutes earlier than ourselves, that they will not wait to put the linch-pins into the wheels. They would go on a voyage of discovery to unknown regions, but would not tarry to look whether the compass is on board. When they see the port in view, they will not wait for five minutes to go round by the safe channel to it, but dash in among breakers, and run the vessel ashore."

He at last concluded with an account of his "progress," for the purpose of showing that there was no reaction in favor of Toryism:—

"I can say most conscientiously and most correctly that I have not seen one single specimen of reaction all over Scotland; and I have traversed it to within forty miles of John O'Groat's House, and in all directions, highland and lowland, agricultural, commercial, and manufacturing."[1]

The same night I sat by him at supper at Lord Jeffery's, where a large party of the most delightful companions I have ever associated with, the Edinburgh lawyers of a now by-gone generation, were assembled to meet him. We sat up till long after cock-crow, and Brougham was most good-natured and agreeable, making us all forget for a time his waywardness. He certainly engrossed by far the largest share of the talk, but every one by quickly watching an opportunity might put in a wise saw or a joke, and we all parted pleased with ourselves and with him. *Noctes cœnæque Deum!*

I am sorry to say that this was the last reciprocation of cordiality between Brougham and myself till more than ten long years had elapsed. He now began and long continued (without any fault of mine, as far as I am aware) to view me with jealousy, suspicion, and ill-will, and to do everything in his power to thwart my plans and to injure my prospects.

Immediately after the "Grey Festival" he set off for London, and he soon heard of the death of Sir John Leach, the Master of the Rolls. This event threw him into great perplexity. In the common course, I, as Attorney-General, ought to have had the offer of succeeding to the vacancy. But the notion of my becoming an Equity Judge was very distasteful to him. He told Melbourne that he himself being from the Common-Law bar, and Lyndhurst the Chief Baron, then an Equity Judge, being from the Common-Law bar, it would give great dissatisfaction if the third great Equity Judge were likewise taken from the Common-Law bar. So Pepys **was**

[1] Lord Brougham's Speeches, vol. iv. p. 77.

appointed Master of the Rolls. I contented myself with protesting against the precedent, knowing that plausible reasons might be given for it. Brougham felt that he had injured me, and he hated me accordingly. But ere long he found himself "the engineer hoist with his own petard."

On the first day of next Michaelmas Term he held his levee with great glee; but, alas! in little more than a week, when I was walking down to the Court of King's Bench and crossing Palace-yard, the Lord Chancellor's carriage drove by, carrying him who was then doomed to be an ex-Chancellor for the rest of his days. Seeing me he pulled the check-string, and when I stepped up he exclaimed, "How do you do, Sir John—Attorney-General no longer—we are all out. The Duke of Wellington is with the King concocting a new Government." And so he passed on to take leave of the Chancery bar, as he then believed for a short space, but, as it proved, forever.

In the robing-room I found the *Times* newspaper, containing an account of the dismissal of the Whigs, which it was asserted Brougham had furnished, concluding with the words "The Queen has done it all."

The charge against him of thus calumniating Queen Adelaide was frequently repeated both in the Press and in the House of Commons, and I believe it never received any contradiction. If he was the author of the article, he must have rashly proceeded on the supposed probability of the fact that the King on this occasion was acting under his wife's advice. She certainly was strongly Conservative and anti-Whiggish; but is was afterwards shown beyond all doubt that she was not in the remotest degree privy to this transaction till the day after Lord Melbourne's dismissal. Indeed any sane person would have dissuaded a step which must necessarily lead to disappointment and mortification, as, notwithstanding the removal of Lord Althorp from the House of Commons by his father's death, the reform mania had by no means as yet sufficiently subsided to tolerate the existence of a Conservative Government. It is even said that the Duke of Wellington, when sent for, refused to take office till the King showed him the manner in which the Queen had been insulted in the *Times* when he admitted that what had been done was irrevocable, and sent off for Sir Robert Peel, who was then in Italy.

I believe that the King's act in dismissing his Ministers was prompted by his general notion of the prostrate state of the Whig party, without any particular reference to the misconduct of the Lord Chancellor; but it suited the views of those who had a personal spite against this erratic functionary to lay the event entirely to him:—

"There could not indeed," said the *Times*, "be a more revolting spectacle than for the highest law officer of the empire to be traveling around like a quack doctor through the provinces, puffing himself and his little nostrums, and committing and degrading the government of which he had the honor to be a member. His Majesty could not but be indignant at such conduct. And it is a fact, notwithstanding all the fulsome adulation heaped on his 'gracious master' at Inverness, Aberdeen, Edinburgh, and elsewhere, that the peripatetic keeper of the King's conscience has not once been admitted since his return from his travels to the honor of an interview with royalty either at Winsdor or Brighton.'

Again:—

"It is in general admitted that the downfall of the Government is referable in a great measure to the unbecoming conduct of Lord Brougham as Chancellor."[1]

The Chancellor, in his parting address to the bar, rather indicated by his manner that he thought he was taking a short leave of them, and that he should shortly be back again to perfect the juridical system which he had established. What he chiefly rejoiced in was the appointment of "that consummate Judge," the Master of the Rolls (Pepys), the merit of which he justly took entirely to himself, although the patronage is supposed to be exclusively in the Prime Minister, and he congratulated future Chancellors in being able implicitly to rely on such an able assistant. He evidently considered this appointment his master-stroke of policy, as securing his return to his office on the restoration of his party.

Whatever may have brought about the change of Government, Brougham, after the crisis occurred, certainly misconducted himself, in two matters arising out of it, in a manner deserving severe reprehension. He had been

[1] *Times*, 19th November.

allowed to retain the Great Seal some time after his colleagues had been deprived of the insignia of their offices that he might deliver judgment in cases argued before him, and, according to established etiquette and propriety, he ought to have delivered it back into the King's own hands; but, having heard that the King talked of him very resentfully, and had even pettishly declared that "he never wished to see his ugly face again," he sent the *clavis regni* to the King in a bag, as a fishmonger might have sent a salmon for the King's dinner.[1]

But his solicitation of the office of Chief Baron of the Exchequer called forth graver censure. Lyndhurst being again Chancellor, this office was vacated by him, and was destined for Sir James Scarlett, who had been harshly used by the Whigs, and was now a warm adherent of the Conservative party. · Brougham, not ignorant of this fact, wrote a letter to Lyndhurst, which was shown to me within a few minutes after it was received, offering to accept the office of Chief Baron, without any salary beyond his pension as ex-Chancellor—pointing out the saving to the public which would arise from this arrangement—and undertaking that, if appointed, he would do all the equity business himself, so that no Vice-Chancellors or Vice-Chancellor, would be required. He probably supposed that the arrangement would not be unacceptable to Lyndhurst, as it might lead to an understanding that the two rival legal chiefs should exchange the offices of Chancellor and Chief Baron during their lives, as their parties were respectively in office or in opposition. But Lyndhurst laughed at the proposal as absurd, and returned for answer that no decision could be pronounced upon it till Sir Robert Peel should return back from Italy. Upon this proceeding being made known there was a burst of public disapprobation. "We can now understand," it was said, "what he meant when he described barristers as gentlemen who *ply* in Westminster Hall." "The offer to do the work cheap is spitefully to prevent Sir James Scarlett from having the office which is his due."

So pelted was he by the pitiless storm, that, to avoid it, he ran off to France and wrote the following letter of revocation to Lord Lyndhurst:—

[1] On the 21st November, 1834, exactly four years all but one day from the time he had received it.

"Paris, Saturday, Nov. 29.

" MY LORD,—I had the honor of receiving your lordship's letter, announcing the state in which the Government at present is, and that nothing of any kind can be settled either as to measures or anything else until the arrival of Sir Robert Peel.

"Although I felt extremely anxious to accomplish the two objects of saving a large sum of money and of completing the reform of the Court of Chancery, by abolishing the office of Vice-Chancellor (a subject on which I transmitted a full memorial to your lordship from Dover, and on which I had sent a memorial before I left the Great Seal), yet some communication which I have since received from persons in whose judgment I entirely confide, give me room to think that my accepting a judicial situation, though without any emolument, might appear to others to interfere with my parliamentary duties; I therefore feel myself under the necessity of desiring that the tender of gratuitous service formerly made should be considered as withdrawn.

" My own clear and unhesitating opinion is, that, following the example of Lord Loughborough and others, I could attend as much to parliamentary duties when on the Bench as when in a private station. But in these times, I have no right to take any step which has any tendency to discourage the efforts of those whose principles are my own, and whose confidence I am proud to enjoy.

" I have the honor, &c."

Many people supposed that Brougham was now extinguished. He had violated the rules of professional etiquette on a point of vital importance to the due administration of justice; he had tried to undermine a private friend; and (what might have been expected to be more fatal still) he had caused himself again to be compared to the " bottle conjurer," by promising to perform a feat which was physically impossible. But such is the elasticity of his powers, so inexhaustible are his resources, such sway does he possess by being both fascinating and formidable, so many more lives has his reputation than any of the feline race, that he speedily made the world overlook all his recent vagaries; and although he has never since enjoyed the confidence of any party or of any individual, he has been well received in private society, and has continued to play a very distinguished part in public life.

CHAPTER CCXXVIII.

"THE HUNDRED DAYS" TO THE FINAL RESIGNATION OF LORD MELBOURNE.

PEEL, being now Prime Minister, published a very skillful manifesto, acquiescing in the Reform Bill, and promising liberal policy in all departments of the State.[1]

If, without dissolving Parliament, he had brought forward his measures, keeping an appeal to the country as a resource in case of factious opposition to them, he would have copied Pitt's policy in 1784, and, like Pitt, he might have ruled for twenty years. But by immediate dissolution he recklessly threw away the trump card by which the game might perhaps have been won.

In spite of all the blundering and bad luck of the Whig leaders, there was no sufficient reaction to give stability to those who, within two years, had strenuously opposed the almost universal national impulse in favor of Parliamentary Reform. The elections were unfavorable to the Conservatives, and the rejection of the Ministerial nominee for the office of Speaker proved that in the House of Commons there was a decided majority against the Government.

Brougham was boyishly exhilarated by this occurrence, and expected to have the Great Seal again in his custody before a month was over. As yet he acted in concert with Melbourne and the rest of his late colleagues, and he assisted in preparing an amendment to the address to be moved in both Houses " lamenting that the progress of salutary reforms had been interrupted and endangered by the dissolution of a Parliament earnestly intent upon the vigorous prosecution of measures to which the wishes of the people were most anxiously and justly directed."

The amendment being moved by Melbourne, and opposed by the Duke of Wellington, Brougham instantly started up to support it, and delivered an elaborate speech of three hours, which he immediately published as a phamphlet, and he has included it among his Select Orations. But I must confess it is only as biographer that

---

[1] His address to the electors of Tamworth.

have been enabled to read it through. The whole drift of it may be learned from a few of the opening sentences:—

"I have risen, my Lords, thus immediately after the noble Duke, because I thought that he manifestly misunderstood the sound constitutional proposition of my noble friend (Lord Melbourne), and the consequences that flow from it—namely, that for the dismissal of the late Government, the noble Duke, by accepting office on our dismissal, incurred the whole responsibility. This proposition the noble Duke thought that he met, relieving himself from its consequences by solemnly protesting—and I, for one, my Lords, readily and perfectly believe in the sincerity of that protest—that he knew nothing previously of the circumstances of the dismissal; that he never had been consulted about the matter; that he was entirely ignorant of the intentions and motions of the Court with regard to it; and that he had no communication with any such quarter for above two months before the change took place. But he entirely misunderstood the doctrine of constitutional law on which my noble friend founded his argument that the noble Duke was responsible for the dismissal of the late Government. My noble friend never asserted that the noble Duke was *de facto* the adviser of that dismissal. No such thing. I repeat that the noble Duke is responsible in point of fact, as well as in point of law. Without the noble Duke's assistance, the act of dismissing the late Government could not have been accomplished. If indeed, instead of being dismissed, the members of the late Administration had resigned, or if asked to return they had declared that they would not come back to their places, that would have been another matter. But if, instead of resigning they were dismissed against their will, and were not asked to resume office, then those who took office after them became accessories after the fact to the dismissal—nay, before the fact, and actual accomplices in the fact itself; for, without their acquiescence, that act of dismissal could not have been perfected."

The same facts and reasonings are repeated with little variety of expression or illustration, and the tedium is only relieved by a personal attack upon Lyndhurst, with whom he was then at bitter enmity, and whom he accused of having consciously pursued an improper course in Parliament, for the purpose of retaining possession of office.'

Lord Lyndhurst said in answer—

"I deny peremptorily the statement of the noble and learned Lord. I say, if I may make use of the expression, *he has uttered an untruth* in so expressing himself. What right has the noble and learned Lord in his fluent, and I may say flippant manner, to attack me as he has dared to do? The view given by the noble and learned Lord of what was said by the noble Duke, was a misrepresentation by the noble and learned Lord. His quickness and his sagacity must have caused him to understand the noble Duke; and I can ascribe what he stated only to an intention to pervert the meaning of the noble Duke."

Lord Brougham.—" I will just use the same language to the noble and learned Lord that he uses to me, if he chooses to make this an arena of indecency." ²

With this " tu-quoque," and no explanation even that the word " untruth " was not meant to be used in an *unparliamentary sense*, it might have been expected that the two noble and learned vituperators would have met next morning with their seconds in Hyde Park; but no such encounter, as far as was publicly known, took place, and in little more than a twelvemonth, both of them strangely finding themselves opposed with equal eagerness to a Whig government, they swore an eternal friendship, which has remained inviolate to the present hour.

Although the amendment was carried by a considerable majority in the Commons, so weak were the Whigs in the Upper House that they did not venture to decide upon it—or indeed upon any other question during the existence of the present Government. But while the real work of overturning it was going on in the Commons, where Sir Robert Peel with a minority was making a gallant stand, Brougham in the house of Lords very zealously kept up a constant irregular fire of petitions, questions, and motions for papers, by which the ministerialists were constantly galled ; and, foreseeing that a decisive victory was at hand, he made no doubt of having his appropriate share of the spoil. At last came the fatal division on Lord

---

¹ Lord Brougham's Speeches, vol. iv. p. 97.   ² 25 Hansard, 127.

John Russell's motion respecting the Irish Church, when Peel surrendered and his ministry dissolved.

Brougham considered the Great Seal to be again his own property, and was turning in his mind on what day the transfer would take place, and whether he should make any special address to the bar on resuming his seat in the Court of Chancery.

Lord Melbourne was "sent for," and the King as a matter of necessity, conferred upon him unlimited power to arrange a new administration. But Lord Melbourne had resolved in his own mind that Brougham never should be Chancellor again, and that he himself never would sit in the same Cabinet with one so erratic, so troublesome, and so little trustworthy. No man ever was placed in a more embarrassing position than Lord Melbourne at this juncture. Brougham had a sort of vested right in the office on the restoration of his party to power. He had rendered brilliant service to that party, and to him the present ostensible head of it was mainly indebted for the function he was now performing of naming his colleagues. If a support with due regard to subordination could not be confidently reckoned upon from the late Whig Chancellor, the most fearful apprehensions were to be entertained from his hostility; for in the history of party men in England, an opposition assailant so active, so enterprising, so energetic, so adventurous, so persevering, so unscrupulous, was not recorded. But said Melbourne, "Although he will be dangerous as an enemy, he will be certain destruction as a friend. We may have small chance of going on without him, but to go on with him is impossible." What was felt and expressed on the occasion I well knew, for when I was told of the difficulty about Brougham, I put in my own claim. I then strongly advocated Brougham, as I was not yet aware of the full amount of his waywardness when he before held the Great Seal. Next to him I urged that from my position and my services the public would expect that I should be preferred. Melbourne observed to me:—"With Brougham I can not act, and I will not again make the attempt. We are sensible of your services, and have perfect reliance on your steadiness and your discretion, but there are circumstances which will render it impossible for us to give you the Great Seal at present, and we must think of some other arrangement."

He gave me no further explanation then, but in a little time I knew all. Brougham being absolutely and definitively excluded, the grand object was to give him as little offense as possible, and as long as possible to ward off his active hostility. To have made me Chancellor would have instantly thrown him into a paroxysm of fury. On the contrary, they resolved to keep the office vacant for an indefinite time, and diplomatically to hold out to him the hope of still filling it. They told him that from his proceedings in Scotland during the last autumn having been misrepresented to the King, his Majesty had contracted a strong, although groundless, prejudice against him, which would gradually wear away—that according to a French phrase, "Si vous avez un Roi, il faut un peu le ménager"—you must not fly into his face; if you insult him, the people may take part with him against you; therefore to give a little time for things to run smooth, the Great Seal would be put in commission. When I was told of this, and that the Commissioners were to be Shadwell, the Vice-Chancellor, Pepys, the Master of the Rolls, and Bosanquet, a Common-Law Judge, all of them having more business in their own courts than they could dispose of, I earnestly and honestly remonstrated, foreseeing that the plan could not possibly work well, and that the interests of justice would be sacrified by it to party expedience. But Brougham was duped, and acquiesced—nay more, undertook as " an independent peer " to patronize the new Government. Till the affair had been finally settled, he was rather sulky, and (as he had done in the House of Commons on the formation of Lord Grey's Government, in November, 1830) he insisted on bringing forward on a day he had named a motion on Education, of which he had given notice, saying, "it was of no conseqnence to him who was in or out of office."[1] But on the day when Melbourne announced himself minister and delivered an inauguration address, Brougham zealously took him under his protection.

Without any written convention or express bargain, an understanding had been entered into which was long acted upon, that O'Connell with his party should support the new Liberal Government, Roman Catholics in Ireland having their fair share of government appointments.

[1] 27 Hansard, 974.

There was no real harm in this arrangement, supposing that no objectionable measures were proposed, and no appointments of unfit men were made under it—as in the result really was the case. But there was much clamor about the alleged "Compact,"[1] and it was made use of successfully as a weapon by the flying Tories. On this occasion, when Melbourne had finished, Lord Alvanley, a Tory peer—after reading a letter lately written by O'Connell in which he declared that he was determined to bring about a repeal of the Union—desired to know,

"'Whether the new Prime Minister agreed with these sentiments, and whether he was to have Mr. O'Connell's support, and on what terms?'

"*Lord Brougham* rose to order, and entreated his noble friend to allow *him* to say a word before he gave any answer to the question put by the noble Lord opposite. (Loud cries of *order*.)

Lord Alvanley.—"I did not address the question to the noble and learned Lord."

Lord Brougham.—"No; and it is precisely for that very reason that I rise to answer it." (Cry of *order*, and that Lord Melbourne should answer.)

Lord Melbourne.—"I am asked how far I coincide in the opinions of Mr. O'Connell about the Union with Ireland? I answer, *not at all.* I am asked whether I am to have the aid of Mr. O'Connell? I answer, *I can not tell.* And, lastly, on what terms? I answer, *I have made no terms with him whatever.*"

This officious interference created a great deal of ridicule—and it was said that Brougham having lost his former office of *Lord Chancellor* now aspired to the higher office of *Lord Protector*. Melbourne, who when roused could display considerable spirit and resolution, disdained such humiliating *protection;* and by his impatient repudiation of it expressed the sentiment of Home's hero,—

"The blood of Douglas can protect itself."

Brougham was afterwards a little less presumptuous, but he continued to vote with ministers, and to do whatever he thought would be agreeable to them, in spite of the efforts of Lyndhurst to persuade him that he was duped

---

[1] It was sometimes called the Lichfield House Treaty, because a meeting attended jointly by Whigs and O'Connellites was held about this time at the house of the Earl of Lichfield, in St. James's Square.

by his old colleagues. His confidence in his speedy restoration continued, and he was the faithful slave of the ministers till the very end of the session. They stood much in need of his aid, for in the House of Lords they had to encounter the most factious and unprincipled opposition I have ever known. Peel in the House of Commons was very moderate and fair in not obstructing the measures of Government, except on just or plausible grounds; but Lyndhurst, who was supreme in the House of Lords, at the head of a large section of peers who implicitly obeyed him, laid down a rule that no Government Bill should pass which could be rejected without strong popular odium, being actuated by the premeditated purpose of afterwards taunting the Government with having accomplished nothing, and of triumphantly quoting the maxim of King William III., that "of all Governments that is the worst which has not the power to carry its own measures." Various salutary bills which passed the Commons with little objection he threw out on the second reading in the Lords, if they had not attracted much popular notice, and their rejection was not likely to give the Whigs a useful grievance.

Thus he could not treat the Bill for the Reform of Municipal Corporations—the great boast of this Session. Posterity will hardly believe the corruption and mischievous absurdities which distinguished the infinitely varied constitutions of the towns in England down to the year of grace 1835, all professing to have one object in view—the good government of the locality. A bill to give them an uniform constitution, based on representation and self-government, had been framed after a laborious investigation, by intelligent commissioners, into the abuses of the existing system. The principle of this bill Peel warmly applauded, and after some amendments to its details it had passed the Commons with his approbation. Lyndhurst, although he vowed its destruction, could not venture to execute his purpose sooner than in the Committee, but there he meant that it should be strangled. Had it not been for Brougham's strenuous and unwearied exertions, it could not have escaped. A motion was carried to hear witnesses and counsel against it at the bar. One counsel (Sir Charles Wetherell) in opening his objections to it occupied twelve hours and a half, and there was a list of town clerks and other witnesses whose examination against it would have lasted several months. Had the two rival Law Lords coalesced at the time, they must have succeeded, for there was no Law Lord to oppose them; but Brougham remained true, and, proclaiming that the bill was exclusively his, as he had been Chancellor when the Commission of Inquiry passed the Great Seal, he defended it with gallantry, perseverance, and success. It underwent several important mutilations under the name of *Amendments* in the Committee. These, however, although introduced by his own Chancellor, when sent back to the Commons, Peel would not agree to, and, after this almost unanimous dissent of the Commons, Lyndhurst did not venture to insist upon them. So the bill passed nearly in its integrity, and has been found to work most admirably for the public good.

Besides rendering effectual service in rescuing the Municipal Reform Bill from the fate to which Lyndhurst had destined it, Brougham wasted during this session an infinity of parliamentary labor upon an almost infinite variety of other subjects without any useful result. I thank Heaven that I was not then a member of the House of Peers, and I do not speak from the testimony of my senses; but, judging from Hansard, the expectant Chancellor must have been "upon the floor" several hours every evening the House met, and he must have spoken as much as would be enough for any other public orator during a long life. He was constantly introducing bills for important national objects, such as "General Education," "the Management of Charities," and the "Prevention of Bribery," or moving resolutions for the suppression of slavery, for the better administration of the Poor Laws, or for lessening the imposts on knowledge; or opposing or defending every other bill which was passing through the House, or presenting petitions himself, or commenting upon petitions presented by other peers. As I might well be suspected of exaggeration, I refer to the "record," and it will be found that of his speeches delivered in the session of 1835, Hansard immortalizes no fewer than two hundred and twenty-one. Many others must have perished for want of the *vates sacer*, for his habit was to make a long speech on giving a notice of motion, another in postponing it (which might happen several times), and another in withdrawing it. Then he would often make a speech in putting a question without having given any notice whatever. These interludes the fatigued reporters often listened to without taking a note. Hansard's Alphabetical Index to subjects of debate on which he made reported speeches in the session of 1835, I beg leave to copy for my own justification, the amusement of my reader, and the wonder of future ages:—

"BROUGHAM, Lord.—Address to the King. Administration of Justice in Ireland. Admission of Ladies. Agricultural Distress. Breach of Naval Discipline. Bribery at Elections. Borough Reform in Scotland. Business, delay of. Canada Central Criminal Court. Charities. Church of Ireland. Church of England. Church of Scotland. Church Property. Church-rates. Commissioners of Law Inquiry. Commissioners of Public Instruction. Committees of Privilege. Constabulary of Ireland. Corporation Commission. Corporation Reform. Corn Laws. Counsel for Prisoners. Dissenters' Marriages. Dissolution of the Ministry. Dublin Police. Duty on Paper. Ecclesiastical Courts. Education. Entails in Scotland. Houses of Parliament, new. Imprisonment for Debt. Indemnity to Witnesses. Islington Market. London University. Marriage Law. Music and Dancing. Newspaper Stamps. Oaths Abolition Bill. Patents. Poor Law, the new. Post Office. Prison Discipline. Processions in Ireland. Russia and Austria. Sheriffs' Accounts. Slavery. Spain. Stoke Pogis. Taxes on Knowledge. Tithes, recovery of. Tithes of Turnips Exemption Bill. University Oaths. Western, Great, Railway. Wills, execution of. Writ of Certiorari, abolition of."[1]

He thus appears to have been ready to speak and to have spoken *de omni scibili et quolibet ente;* and, considering the length of his parliamentary career, he must, during his life, have emitted a much greater number of words in public than any man that ever appeared in this world —at least since Noah's flood.

His popularity, notwithstanding all these efforts, seems now to have been rapidly declining, for he complains of being abused in all the newspapers—particularly in the Government newspapers,—

"Newspapers," growled he—"I will not say *having the*

[1] 30 Hansard, Index B.

patronage of the Government, nor will I say *under the protection of the Government*; certainly not the protection and patronage of my noble friend (Lord Melbourne)—but newspapers which have taken my noble friend under their protection. I do not think, if I were allowed to give an opinion on the subject, that the attacks are very judicious,—made on one like myself, unconnected with the Government, never saying one word against the Government—and I am happy to say that I have not had occasion to do so—but uniformly defending and supporting it. I am sure the attacks do not proceed from my noble friend; he can have no hand in them; he is a man of sense; his underlings are those who assail me. One man is disappointed by not getting anything while I was in office. Another is vexed for some similar reason. It is the underlings who do all this, instigated by the sort of motive I have described."[1]

He likewise complained of attacks made upon him in the House of Commons:—

"It is said there that I enjoy a pension of £15,000 a year. I wish I did; but it is only one-third of that amount. Then I am charged with enjoying this pension merely for having drawn a large salary as Chancellor during the term of four years. I should have been entitled to that pension if I had been Chancellor only five minutes. I am taunted with having given up nothing for it. I gave up for it a larger, a much larger income. If these excellent persons would send up a bill enabling me to have again what I have given up, my practice at the bar—I mean not offensively to your lordships, whose good-will and favor I am always anxious to conciliate, however unfortunate I may have been in the attempt—I shall zealously support the bill, and further its progress through this House.[2] These persons—these very persons who, when I made an offer to save the pension—these very persons were those who, by the clamor they raised, drove me, against my bet-

[1] 29 Hansard, 1234.

[2] During the fervor of the Reform Bill, I belonged to a club of Scotch members called the "Sheep's Head Club." Brougham and Melbourne dined with us one day. The chairman gave the health of the CHANCELLOR with a eulogistic speech. But he, having well drunk, talked with the utmost contempt of the bauble he had the misfortune to possess called the Great Seal, and expressed an eager wish to throw his patent of Peerage into the fire, that he might return to the House of Commons. But after all, I doubt his sincerity, particularly as I have heard him say that he has made better speeches in the House of Lords than he ever did in the House of Commons.

ter judgment, to retract the offer I had made. I said at
the time 'Now mark what will follow; these very persons
who raise this clamor will be the first to complain of me
for having a pension.'"[1]

On the prorogation of Parliament ex-Chancellor Brougham retired to his seat in Westmorland, neither satiated
nor fatigued by all the speaking he had indulged in during
the session. Flattered with the notion which he entertained and pretty freely expressed, that he had saved the
Government, and that it could not exist without his aid,
he was not much dissatisfied with his position, and he was
exuberantly gay. Without any promise from Melbourne,
or any further personal explanation with him since the
Government was first formed, he counted with confidence
on a speedy restoration to his former office, and he anticipated that, being again in the Cabinet, he must of necessity be the actual Prime Minister. This change seemed to
him to be natural and certain, being (as he conceived) for
the advantage of those who could easily bring it about.
He imagined it clear to all mankind that as the Government could not stand without him, much less against him,
and as he could not be expected (indeed it would not be
constitutional) that he should continue to direct the
measures of the Crown without being in office, he would
soon be called from his rustic retirement among the tombs
of the De Burghams to re-occupy the "marble chair," and
to form a plan for the next parliamentary campaign at
Westminster. The King's prejudices might still subsist,
as he was of a race obstinate in their personal dislikes; but
George II. had at last taken Pitt the elder into favor, and
George III. had been obliged to accept as his minister
Charles James Fox, whom he actually abhorred and had
denounced as a traitor. Nothing seemed so simple and
easy as the desired and expected arrangement; the King
had only to hold a council, and, receiving the Great Seal
from the Commissioners, to deliver it to Lord Brougham
with the title of Lord Chancellor, and then the Government
would be complete, no one would be aggrieved, and no
expectation, reasonable or unreasonable, would be disappointed.

But the Long Vacation passed away without any indication of change, and when the first day of Michaelmas

[1] 28 Hansard, 710.

Term arrived the three Lords' Commissioners resumed their sittings in the Court of Chancery. Truth to tell, Melbourne was so much pleased with the manner in which he had "tided over" the last session that he had resolved to start on another voyage without altering in any respect the manning or the trim of the vessel of the State.

Meanwhile a storm was rising for which he was not at all prepared. When reminded that what had been foretold about the Great Seal being in commission had come true, that there were serious discontents in Westminster Hall, and that the arrears in the Court of Chancery were rapidly accumulating to the enormous grievance of the suitors, he exclaimed, with his usual affectation of reckless *insouciance*, "the groans of the suitors do not disturb my rest."

But while he thought he should enjoy entire tranquillity for a long while to come his repose was most cruelly disturbed by a pamphlet of Sir Edward Sugden—then ex-Chancellor of Ireland (now Baron St. Leonards)—entitled "What has become of the Great Seal?" in which he depicted in glowing colors the sad state of affairs in the Court of Chancery, and complained that the administration of justice was sacrificed to Whig expediency. The sound of this explosion was reverberated far and near. All the newspapers—both Whig and Tory, both London and provincial—in the want of foreign news or of domestic topics more stirring, took up the delays and arrears arising out of the Commission, and either in the tone of threat or of recommendation pressed that it should be put an end to. The fact was that the Commissioners in their own several Courts had more causes than they could possibly determine; so that when the Chancellor's work was likewise thrown upon their hands, all was confusion. Again they acted most unsatisfactorily as a court of appeal, for the Master of the Rolls and the Vice-Chancellor sat to revise the decrees of each other, and it was observed that when the decree of one was reversed the balance of credit was preserved by the reversal of the next decree of the other appealed against. The judicial business of the House of Lords also, for want of a Chancellor during the last session, had been disposed of in a very unsatisfactory manner, Lyndhurst and Brougham presiding by turns, and the spite between them still being so bitter as visibly to disturb their equanimity.

A meeting of the Cabinet was called to consider what was to be done under these circumstances, and I afterwards had a minute and accurate account of the proceedings which took place.

After much deliberation as to whether they would again admit Brougham, or what better course they could pursue, they came to the very hasty, rash, and foolish resolution that the Commission should be put an end to; that Brougham should be abandoned; that Pepys, the Solicitor-General, should be Chancellor; and that Bickersteth, who had never been in office nor in Parliament should be Master of the Rolls, with a peerage. The foundation of the whole scheme was the supposed power of Bickersteth to quell Brougham, and this they believed on the authority of Sir John Cam Hobhous, who assured them that on one occasion when Brougham was Chancellor, Bickersteth was arguing a case in the Privy Council about a charter to the University of London, and Brougham being at first inclined to be impertinent, was completely put down by him, and had not another word to say for himself during the rest of the day. This anecdote made a deep impression on all present, and the hope of finding in Bickersteth an overmatch for Brougham, raised an irresistible desire to have the benefit of his championship.

No means were used to break or to soften the intelligence to Brougham. He first learned from the public newspapers that Sir Charles Pepys was Chancellor under the title of Lord Cottenham.

In my opinion, Brougham was atrociously ill-used on this occasion. Considering his distinguished reputation, considering what he had done for the Liberal cause, considering his relations with the Melbourne Government, I incline to think that at every risk they ought to have taken him back into the Cabinet, however difficult it might have been to make conditions or stipulations with him as to his future conduct and demeanor. But sure I am that in the manner in which they finally threw him off, they showed disingenuousness, cowardice, and ingratitude. I have myself heard him say, with tears in his eyes:—"If Melbourne had treated me openly and kindly, he might have done what he liked with the Great Seal, and we might have ever remained friends. The pretense about the King's dislike I found to be utterly false. William may have been angry at the moment, and perhaps justly, for things I had said and done; but in April, 1835, when he was obliged to dismiss his Tory ministers, he did not care a button what individuals succeeded; and I was not a bit more disagreeable to him than Melbourne himself."

I place no faith in the story circulated that a further attempt was made to mystify him by a communication that a bill was to be brought in to divide the functions of Lord Chancellor, and that he was to have the political half. It was part of the plan now adopted to bring in such a bill, but this half had been promised solemnly to me, and Brougham, even if he had believed such an offer to be sincere, would have condemned it.[1]

I have never learned on any authority the particulars of what Brougham said or did when he first heard that he had been betrayed, and that he was now an outcast, but there seems no reason to doubt the statement that not only his bodily health but his mind was very seriously affected. Parliament met on the 14th of Februray, but he did not appear. It was given out that he would come at Easter. Easter arrived, but no Lord Brougham, and when the prorogation took place after a Session considerably shortened by his absence, he was still at Brougham Hall. A debate in the House of Lords during this quiet and dull period was likened "to the play of 'Hamlet,' the part of Hamlet omitted on account of the indisposition of the first tragedian of the company."

Rumors were spread abroad that, like Lord Bacon, when dissappointed by not being made Solicitor-General when he had a right to expect the appointment, he had resolved forever to renounce public life and to devote himself to philosophy; but I believe that his secession is to be ascribed only to his utter incapacity for public business. There can be no doubt that he felt resentment and vowed revenge for the usage he had experienced. He unjustly blamed Pepys. Pepys no doubt owed his advancement to be Master of the Rolls entirely to him. Pepys, however, had not supplanted him by any intrigue, and, on the contrary, had been entirely passive in the movement which

---

[1] It would appear that in the beginning of January, 1836, there was a correspondence between Brougham and Melbourne about bringing in a bill for abolishing imprisonment for debt, but without any allusion to the Great Seal. 30 Hansard, 180.

shoved him on the woolsack. He was selected only to make way for Bickersteth, on whom all the hopes of the party rested. This notion that Bickersteth was to be pitted against Brougham, when at last it reached his ears, exasperated him still more, for he knew that Bickersteth had declined the offer of a seat in the House of Commons from the dread of mixing in debate, and he longed at once to enter the lists with him that he might annihilate him. Though generally plunged in deep melancholy, the recluse at times fired up, and said " he would be off for London," but his medical attendants would by no means permit.him to leave Brougham Hall till his spirits should be more equal.

If he was able to read the newspapers he must have been gratified and even amused by finding that Bickersteth (Lord Langdale) had from the beginning proved an utter failure. Without any opponent the Ministerial champion had actually broken down. Intending to support the Government Bill for bisecting the Great Seal, he made a speech which damaged it exceedingly, and all hope was gone of his ever looking an opponent in the face.

Although Brougham might excusably have enjoyed the humiliation of those by whom he had been injured, and might have been permitted to assist in making manifest their discomfiture, yet if he was capable of reasoning soundly and feeling magnanimously, he must have been glad of an excuse for now avoiding the arena of his former glory. Lyndhurst, whom he must have joined if he was to gratify his vengeance, was acting upon the " obstructive system " in a manner still more outrageous than during the last Session when Brougham had so manfully and so successfully checked him. Lyndhurst's destruction of Ministerial Bills which came up from the Commons can be compared to nothing but the *Massacre of the Innocents.* Brougham, with all his desire to see Melbourne punished, and the heads of his chosen champions, Cottenham and Langdale, knocked together, could hardly have wished to be present at the *open conference* between the committees of the two Houses, when at Lyndhurst's mandate, the Lords insisted on striking out all the useful clauses in a Bill for Amending Municipal Corporations, although Peel had supported them, and they were urgently required for the public good. Yet this was the great struggle of the

Session. The aggravation of Brougham's ill-usage from his own party was that they knew he had no honorable means of being revenged upon them.

The first good news I heard of Brougham in his seclusion was from our common friend Baron Parke, who had gone the Northern Circuit as Judge, and in the month of September found him calm and composed. He was now in the habit of taking long walks in the fields; and, avoiding politics but joining freely in professional gossip about silk gowns, special retainers, fees, verdicts, remanets, and references, he almost seemed himself again. His recovery proceeded steadily, and at the opening of the next Session of Parliament he returned to London in full vigor of body and mind.

Although his sense of wrong remained *altâ mente repostum*, the impetuosity of his resentment had subsided, and he could "bide his time." In the House of Lords he sat on the Ministerial benches, and he talked familiarly, if not cordially, with Melbourne and the other members of the Government. As yet, although he had an intimacy with Lyndhurst professionally, he showed no leaning to the Tory side. At this time he thought that his best game would be to form a connection with the Radicals and to become their leader. The Whigs he intended to represent as having become listless and inefficient. They had fallen into considerable disrepute, and if William IV. had lived much longer he might have had the gratification of ejecting them. The Radicals pressing them still very unreasonably with motions about household suffrage, the ballot, and shortening the duration of Parliaments, they rather too peremptorily declared that the Reform Bill was to be considered a "final measure," and Lord John Russell, their leader in the House of Commons, acquired the nickname of "*Finality Jack*." Brougham thought for a while that the Radicals, who were increasing in influence, might possibly come into office in their turn. However, they had no confidence in him, and although they were flattered to find themselves courted by a man so distinguished, none of them would enlist under him as their leader, with one exception. It was then said in the Clubs, " Roebuck is a joint, and the only joint, in Lord Brougham's tail."[1]

[1] This phraseology originated from Walter Scott's description of a Highland

Lord Cottenham had got on as Chancellor better than was expected. He proved to be an exceedingly good Equity Judge. and while Brougham was absent he had performed tolerably in the House of Lords. But the Lord Chancellor was now in a state of great alarm, and not without reason; despising Brougham's law, he stood in cruel awe of his sarcasms, and would rather have submitted to any insult than enter into a personal encounter with him.

But Lord Langdale, M.R., was more to be pitied. During the negotiation for his promotion it had been kept a strict secret from him that he was expected to be the champion of the Government against Brougham. In truth, he had no taste for public display. He would have preferred the Rolls without a peearge, and he never would have accepted a peerage upon the condition of becoming a rhetorical gladiator. He did not know what was expected of him till he had actually taken his seat on the Barons' bench, when he could not unpeer himself. He was then in a state of great consternation, for " he would as soon have met the devil as Harry Brougham." He was unspeakably relieved for a time by the non-attendance of his adversary. Thus was he induced to try to speak on the second reading of the " Great Seal Partition Bill " and his *break-down* was partly ascribed to a practical joke, in the shape of a rumor circulated through the House that Brougham had arrived in London and was hurrying to the House.[1] Now, when he heard that Brougham actually had arrived, and would regularly attend in his place, he laid down a resolution to which he strictly adhered, that during the Session he would remain silent, contenting himself, upon a division, with supporting the Government either by his vote or his proxy.

William IV. was approaching his end without being able to restore the Tories to his councils, and the thoughts of all were directed to the new reign. The Princess Victoria, the undoubted heir to the Crown, had been reared in great privacy, and nothing was known of her political principles or propensities. The Tories founded their hopes upon the natural instinct of royalty; the Whigs trusted to the feud

chieftain " putting on his tail " when he mustered his clan in military array. Hence the Irish members introduced into the House of Commons by O'Connell were called his *tail*, each of them being reckoned as a joint.

[1] If this be true, it must have been contrived by Lyndhurst, who delighted much in a mixture of malice and fun to be administered to a political enemy.

between the little Court of the Princess and that of the King, which might incline her to like those whom he detested; the Radicals did not despair of captivating royal favor by declaring violently against the aristocracy and the wealthy *bourgeoisie*, whom they charged with encroaching both on the Crown and on the people; and there was a clique looking for promotion under Sir John Conroy, Equerry to the Duchess of Kent, who they supposed might be made Prime Minister on the accession of her daughter. There was an another individual—or in his own opinion "Great Power" in the State—who considered it not impossible, nor very improbable, that a different arrangement from any of these might take place on a demise of the Crown; this was Lord Brougham, who supposed that the Princess Victoria, having necessarily heard so much of him, might have formed as high an opinion of him as the Princess Charlotte had done, and, like that discerning member of the house of Brunswick, might wish to have him for her chief adviser.

In the prospect of the coming change, a cessation of party hostilities in Parliament took place. Brougham laid on the table of the House of Lords three important bills which he had formerly introduced:—" To promote National Education," " To establish Local Courts," and " To put an end to Pluralities in the Church."[1] But he never moved the second reading of any of them; and, contenting himself with irregularly making a few interlocutory observations every evening when the House met, he reserved the great efforts for which his long retirement had prepared him till the effect of what was said and done might, be more accurately foreseen.

When Queen Victoria was at last proclaimed—to do away with the notion which had got abroad that he had been in very bad odor at Court, and that this had been the cause of his exclusion from his office—Brougham was the loudest in commemorating and extolling the virtues and amiable qualities of the deceased sovereign:—

Lord Brougham.—" The situation I had the honor of holding in the councils of his late Majesty during a considerable part of his reign forbids me to be silent on the present occasion [address to her Majesty on her accession]. In all that has been said in his praise I fully agree, and I

[1] 36 Hansard, 79.

particularly honor what I have had the best opportunity
of observing, his gentle disposition, his inflexible love of
justice, and the rare candor by which his character was
distinguished. It is wise and appropriate to the present
occasion to reflect, not only on the virtues of the man, but
also on the glorious, the beneficent, and the auspicious
attributes of his reign; glorious, because it was distinguished by the maintenance of peace abroad and tranquillity at home; beneficent, because it was distinguished by
bestowing the most important boon which a sovereign
could give to or withhold from his people—a wise ameliora-
tion of the laws, and a well-considered improvement in
the institutions of the country; and auspicious, in the
earnest it gave of still greater improvements; greater they
could not be, but they might be increased so as to diffuse
more widely the blessings of those laws and institutions
among the people. These are pledges which have descended with the crown to her Majesty the Queen Victoria;
and I sincerely join with your lordships in hoping that her
Majesty's reign may be long and prosperous, and that in
it, by the blessing of God and the wisdom of Parliament,
these pledges may be redeemed." [1]

Instead of becoming Prime Minister, Sir John Conroy
retired into Wales, and a handsome annuity being settled
upon him, he continued to reside there ever after.

This arrangement left the field open to Brougham, but
the next blasted all his hopes. The Queen "sent for"
Melbourne, and for years he continued to exercise all the
prerogatives of the Crown in her name, subject only to the
control of the Parliament. She had a sort of filial affection
and reverence for him, and she showed that she was pleased
with his captivating manners and with the principles of
government with which he wished to imbue her. Brougham felt that for the present all possibility of his being in
office was gone.

He bore this shock much better than the loss of the
Great Seal when Lord Cottenham was made Chancellor.
Indeed his manner at this time was cool, collected, and
dignified. He continued to sit on the Ministerial side of
the house, and he kept up a speaking acquaintance with
his old colleagues when he encountered them in public,
but he long absolutely refused to meet any of them in so-

[1] 38 Hansard, 1552.

ciety, and he not only would not interchange visits with them, but he would not enter any room where there was a risk of coming in contact with any of them. In his own mind he had vowed their political destruction, and he was indefatigable in the efforts he used to accomplish his object.

In the House of Lords he obtained a most wonderful ascendency, which he was ready at every favorable moment to turn against the Government. Lyndhurst, seeing that Brougham was now in reality a firm ally, no longer fought with him, but, on the contrary, flattered him on all occasions. For conveniently laying down the law in debate Brougham now assumed, and was long permitted to enjoy, unlimited license. Cottenham would sometimes venture to doubt, or to qualify, some of his most extravagant doctrines, but in so hesitating and timid a manner as to persuade the Lords that Brougham had said nothing that could be justly controverted. Langdale remained dumb. Lyndhurst loudly *cheered*.

The nondescript ex-Chancellor likewise made himself formidable by a lavish distribution among all the members of the House of compliments as well as sarcasms; and I am ashamed to say that not only were the latter dreaded, but the former were eagerly coveted. Nearly all who took part in a debate, not only lawyers but bishops, military men and civilians of all parties, looked out with the utmost anxiety to the dole he was to mete out to them. But while he gave pain and pleasure to individual peers by offending or soothing their self-love, he influenced no votes. The practiced rhetorician seemed entirely void of sincerity, and after the division he was regarded with little more respect than a conjuror who has played tricks which excited the wonder of all who beheld them. Nor had his orations more influence out of doors. He was much talked of, abused, caricatured, and laughed at, but, although he had some admirers, he had no followers.

At the meeting of the new Parliament elected on the Queen's accession, Brougham, still sitting on the Ministerial side, took a most determined part against the Government, and showed particular hostility to the Court, as if offended by personal slight. He very early denounced those who had contended (I think very reasonably) that a fair opportunity should be given to test the working of the Reform Bill before any further organic change was hazarded. Said he:—

"The mere corrections and amendments in the details of the bill will not suffice to render it effectual for gaining the great object in view by those who framed the bill, by those who supported it, and by those who adopted it, viz., the securing to the people of this country a full and free representation in the Commons House of Parliament. Experience has already plainly shown the absolute necessity for extending and enlarging the measure especially as to the elective franchise."[1]

He began even to talk respectfully of the *ballot*, which hitherto he had condemned and ridiculed.[2]

The settlement of the Civil List he furiously attacked in debate, and he entered on the Journals of the Lords a long protest against it.[3] When a proposal was made to increase the allowance of the Duchess of Kent to £30,000 a year, he was very bitter and sarcastic because the Tories supported it:—

"In the present state of parties there may be a conflict of rivalry between them; they may wish to outbid one another in the disposal of the income of the people, to show their loyalty. I am well aware of the universal and ardent desire which prevails to make the grant as liberal as possible. I feel great pain, therefore, in making these observations, but no consideration shall prevent me from performing an imperative duty. Why should we act so precipitately when called upon to make an additional provision for the Queen-Mother? [*Lord Melbourne.*—'Not Queen-Mother, the mother of the Queen.'] *Lord Brougham.*—I admit my noble friend is right. On a point of this sort I humble myself before my noble friend. I have no courtier-like cultivation. I am rude of speech. The tongue of my noble friend is so well hung, and so well attuned to courtly airs, that I can not compete with him

---

[1] 39 Hansard, 134.

[2] Although, to throw odium on the Whigs, he then for a time pretended to be ultra-Radical, he was in his heart rather inclined to Conservatism, and he afterwards followed the bent of his inclinations when he took service under the Duke of Wellington. During the present session of Parliament he actually shed tears in the House of Lords, as he deplored the wickedness and folly of those who were for revolutionizing the country by a new Reform Bill.—*Note, April,* 1859.

[3] 39 Hansard, 1370. He likewise published a report of his speech in a bulky pamphlet.

for the prize which he is now so eagerly struggling to win. Not being given to *glozing* and *flattery*, I may say that the Duchess of Kent (whether to be called *Queen-Mother or mother of the Queen*) is nearly connected with the throne ; and a plain man like myself, having no motive but to do my duty, may be permitted to surmise that any additional provision for her may possibly come from the Civil List, which you have so lavishly voted."

Lord Melbourne.—" I took the liberty in the noble and learned Lord's address to suggest that he was confounding two things—that he was making a mistake in a matter not wholly immaterial in its bearing upon the present question. All must be aware that there exists an essential difference between the *Queen-mother* and the *mother of the Queen*, although the noble and learned Lord said this was a distinction only to be learned in courts—a distinction only recognized where there is *glozing* and *flattery*—where tongues are better *hung*, as the noble and learned Lord elegantly expressed it. I do not exactly know what the noble and learned Lord means when he says my *tongue is hung well*. As to the *glozing* and *flattery*, I must be allowed to say I know no man in this country who can more *gloze and flatter* and bend the knee than the noble and learned Lord himself—not one ; and I must say that I should feel myself wholly unqualified to compete with him in these arts, if, from his example, I should acquire a taste for them."

Lord Brougham.—" I call upon the noble Viscount to produce his proofs that I ever in my life was capable of doing that which the noble Viscount has chosen to-night, unprovoked, to fling out as a charge against me. [*Lord Melbourne.*—'Not unprovoked.'] I say utterly unprovoked. My noble friend observed, with a contemptuous air, that I should not say *Queen-mother*, but *mother of the Queen*, as much as intimating, 'Oh, you know nothing of these things; you don't speak the language of courts.' I said, with much humility, 'Far be it from me to enter into competition with the noble Viscount, whose tongue is now attuned and hung to courtly airs.' I meant to dwell chiefly on the attuning of the tongue—the new tune, with recent variations, which he has learned to sing. But the imputation that I ever stooped to *gloze*, or to *bow before*, or to *flatter* any human being, is utterly, absolutely, and, I will say, notoriously without foundation. I have had opportunities to practice such arts, but *I* have never availed myself of them—to the injury of others, to the betrayal of my trust, and to my own shame." [1]

In this first personal encounter between the Premier and the ex-Chancellor, the former was considered to have the advantage. People were well aware of Brougham's powers of vituperation—but had not noticed, till it was pointed out, that he was equally given to *glozing*. I cannot say that he flatters, or that he would flatter for any corrupt or sordid purpose—but merely to make a sensation, to show his power, to add to the effect of his sarcasms by contrast, he is at times extravagantly complimentary. It was said of a very liberal bestower of praise that he laid it on with a *trowel*—but Brougham empties a *hodful* of it on the head of his victim. His success in some instances has been very brilliant.

During the autumn of this year, Brougham found occupation for his leisure and vent for his spleen in preparing for publication a selection of his "Speeches," in four volumes, with "Historical Introductions." His principal object seems to have been not so much to do justice to his own oratorical exertions, as to deal out praise and censure among his contemporaries, according as he then conceived that they had used him well or ill, and above all to hold up to execration the Whig party for having betrayed and abandoned him.[2] The dedication shows the spirit by which he was actuated:—

TO THE MOST NOBLE
RICHARD MARQUESS WELLESLEY,
SUCCESSIVELY
THE GOVERNOR-GENERAL OF INDIA,
BRITISH AMBASSADOR IN SPAIN,
SECRETARY OF STATE FOR FOREIGN AFFAIRS,
AND
LORD-LIEUTENANT OF IRELAND,
THESE VOLUMES ARE INSCRIBED
AS A TRIBUTE
MOST JUSTLY DUE TO SO ILLUSTRIOUS A STATESMAN;
AND IN COMMEMORATION
OF THE RARE FELICITY OF ENGLAND,
SO RICH IN GENIUS AND CAPACITY FOR AFFAIRS,
THAT SHE CAN SPARE FROM HER SERVICE
SUCH MEN AS HIM.

---

[1] 39 Hansard, 972.

[2] I am rather at a loss to account for the bad success of the work. I should

There certainly was some originality in making a dedication the vehicle of sarcasm, and a complaint that the great talents of Dedicatee and Dedicator were not employed in the public service. Lord Wellesley, once a most distinguished statesman, had now fallen into dotage. After the other splendid offices which he had filled, he had accepted that of Lord Chamberlain, to walk backwards with a white wand before the Queen, and had then quarreled with the Whigs because they would not make him Duke of Hindostan. A strict friendship was now contracted between the two discontented individuals, founded upon their common hatred of that party, which with respect to both had so failed in the performance of the sacred duty of rewarding merit.

As a specimen of his " Introductions," I give an extract from that to his "Speech at the Liverpool Election in 1812." Drawing a character of Mr. Creevey, candidate along with him in the Whig interest, thus the ex-Whig Lord Chancellor speaks of Mr. Creevey and the Whigs:—

"He despised the timidity which so often paralyzed their movements; he disliked the jealousies, the personal predilections and prejudices which so frequently distracted their councils; he abhorred the spirit of intrigue, which not rarely gave some inferior man, or some busy meddling woman, probably unprincipled, a sway in the destiny of the party, fatal to its success, and all but fatal to its character; he held in utter ridicule the squeamishness, both as to persons and things, which emasculated so many of the genuine, regular Whigs; and no considerations of interest—no relations of friendship—no regard for party discipline—could prevail with him to pursue that course so ruinous to the Whig opposition, of half-and-half resistance to the Government; marching to the attack with one eye turned to the Court, and one askance to the country, nor ever making war upon the Ministry without regarding the time when themselves might occupy the position, now the object of assault."

If all this were true, it surely comes very ungraciously from one who had been a member of the Whig party

have expected that the *sauce piquante* would have given it a relish. Nevertheless I know, upon the authority of Mr. Black, now M. P. for Edinburgh, who was the publisher, that a large proportion of the edition was *damasked*, *i. e.*, passed through a machine, by which small squares are impressed upon the printed pages before they are sent to line trunks.

above twenty years, and who, within two years, had passionately wished to continue in it. The lady he so uncourteously refers to, is evidently Lady Holland, the wife of his friend Lord Holland, his early patron on his first coming to London—at whose hospitable board I have often met him. Although Lady Holland certainly had considerable influence in Whig counsels, I do not believe that it was ever exercised against Brougham. But he was of a different opinion, and he would never afterwards speak to her, for although he could forgive Lord Melbourne, he could not forgive her, who was supposed to have been Lord Melbourne's adviser in excluding him.

In the Session of 1838, Brougham carried on very active hostilities against Lord Melbourne's Government, still showing Radical colors, but more and more sympathizing and coming to an implied understanding with the Duke of Wellington, Lord Lyndhurst, and the Tories. They accused us of a disposition to revolutionize both Church and State from the proposed measure about Church Rates, and the practical admission of Roman Catholics to a fair share of power and patronage in Ireland, whereas Brougham still denounced us as Reactionaries, Finalists, and Mock Reformers, because we resisted for the present any further organic change. Being taunted by Lord Melbourne for his bitter opposition to those with whom he had so long acted, and whom he had so zealously patronized in the year 1835, when he was no longer in office, and they were pursuing the same policy as at present, he insisted that they had diverged, while he was marching straight forward.

"My Lords," said he, "I indignantly and peremptorily deny that the motive or principle of my conduct is changed. But I know that the changed conduct of others has compelled me to oppose them in order that I may not change my own principles. Do the Ministers desire to know what will restore me to their support, and make me once more fight zealously in their ranks, as I once fought with them against the majority of your Lordships? I will tell them. Let them retract their declaration against Reform, or, without any retractation, only bring forward liberal and constitutional measures, and they will have no more zealous supporter than myself. But in the meantime I hurl defiance at the head of my accuser—I repeat it—I hurl at his head this defiance—I defy him to point out any, the slightest, indication of any one part of my public conduct having even for one instant been affected in any manner of way by feelings of a private and personal nature, or been regulated by any one consideration except the sense of what I owe to my own principles and to the interests of the country."[1]

It is possible that he had worked himself into the belief that he was acting consistently and from purely disinterested motives; but, if so, he stood alone in this belief, for all the rest of mankind agreed that revenge was the main-spring of his conduct, and that his only consideration was how he might most spite and damage those by whom he had been ill used. The Radicals making great play against the Government by the opposition which Ministers offered to the ballot—although he was one of the framers of the Reform Bill who had peremptorily objected to the proposal of his colleagues Lord Durham and Sir James Graham to admit the ballot, and so late as his famous Scottish "Progress," complaining of the unreasonable Radicals, he had intimated an opinion that rather too much had been done in the way of innovation—he now expressly recommended the ballot, and told the Lords that—

"Unless their Lordships made up their minds either to this measure, or some measure of this sort, for the protection of electors, it would be carried against them. The time appeared to him to be come when something must be done. The sooner, therefore, their Lordships made up their minds to some such measure as this, the better it would be for them."[2]

The Tories did not *vocally* cheer, but they showed by their radiant countenances and sparkling eyes with what delight they heard observations which had such a tendency to disparage the Whigs, to deprive the Government of Liberal support, and to accelerate their own return to power. Although they and their irregular ally appeared on opposite sides of the House, there was between them, during the debate, a quick interchange of nods and winks and wreathed smiles, followed by much approving raillery and cordial gratulation when the debate was over.

The great practical measure of this Session was the Bill for the Better Government of the Canadas. There had been

[1] 40 Hansard, 692.   [2] Ibid., 1226.

an open rebellion in Lower Canada, and its Legislative Assembly had thrown off allegiance to the English Crown. The insurgents had been defeated, and tranquillity had been restored; but a change in the mode of ruling the colony was universally allowed to be indispensable, and there was a necessity for conferring extraordinary powers on Lord Durham, who in the emergency had patriotically agreed to go out as Governor. Even the Duke of Wellington and Lord Lyndhurst concurred in the principle of the bill, although they censured some of its details. But Brougham furiously opposed the bill, and every clause of it,—his animosity on this occasion being sharpened by a special grudge fostered by him against Lord Durham, who in the year 1834 had charged him with having become a very cool Reformer, and "little better than a Conservative."

In a great speech upon the subject which, according to his custom, he published as a pamphlet, with a Preface praising himself and vilifying others, he gave a narrative of the measures of the Government at home to meet the spirit of insubordination in Canada, and he thus censured their inaction in the summer of 1837:

"It would seem that just about this time some wonderful change had come over the minds of the Ministers, depriving them of their memory, and lulling even their senses to repose—that something had happened which cast them into a sweet slumber— a deep trance—such as physicians tell us not only suspends all recollection of the past, but makes men impervious to impressions from surrounding objects through the senses. Could this have arisen from the deep grief into which my noble friend and his colleagues were known to have been plunged by the decease of their kind and generous master? No doubt that feeling must have had its day—or its hour—but it passed swiftly away; it is not in the nature of grief to endure forever. Then how came it that the trance continued? Was it that the decease of one monarch is necessarily followed by the accession of another? Oh, doubtless its pleasing endurance must have been caused by the elevation of their late gracious master's illustrious successor— prolonging the suspension of the faculties which grief had brought on—but changing it into that state, inexpressibly delicious, which was suited to the circumstances so interesting of the new reign; or could it be that the Whig party having for near a hundred years been excluded from the banquet of royal favor, and now sitting down to the rich repast with an appetite the growth of a century's fast, were unable to divert their attention from so pleasurable and unusual an enjoyment to mere vulgar matters of public duty, and bring their faculties, steeped in novel delight, to bear upon points so distant as Canada—affairs so trivial as the tranquillity of the most important province of the Crown and the peace of this country—perhaps of the world? All these inconsiderable interests being in jeopardy, were they insufficient to awaken our rulers from their luxurious stupor? . . . . They rush unheeding, unhesitating, unreflecting, into resolutions upon which the wisest and readiest of mankind could hardly pause and ponder too long. But when all is determined—when every moment's delay is fraught with peril—then comes uncertainty and irresolution. They never pause till the season has arrived for action, and when all faltering, even for the twinkling of an eye, is fatal, then it is that they relapse into supineness and inactivity—look around them and behind them, and everywhere but before them, and sink into repose as if all had been accomplished at the moment when everything remains to be done. If I were to ransack all the records to which I have ever had access of human conduct in administering great affairs, whether in the annals of our own times or in ages that are past, I should in vain look for a more striking illustration of the Swedish Chancellor's famous saying to his son, departing to assist at a congress of statesmen, ' *I, fili mi, ut videas, quantula sapientia regatur mundus.*' "

This somewhat cumbrous jocularity may have been produced by pure patriotism, but I must confess it seems to me rather an ebuliition of envy, and that the pseudo-patriot was resenting his own exclusion from the luxurious banquet spread for the famished Whigs at the accession of Queen Victoria.

He had spoken early in the evening, and as soon as he finished he went home to meet a party of dependents whom he had invited to hear his speech, and to dine with him. His absence from the House was severely animadverted upon by those who followed in the debate. Lord

---

[1] 40 Hansard, 202-207.

Melbourne spoke of " the torrent of invective and sarcasm with which the noble and learned lord had overwhelmed the officers of her Majesty's Government, and that most labored and most extreme concentration of bitterness which had been poured forth on this occasion." Lord Glenelg, whom he had personally attacked, joined in the regret that the noble and learned lord had been pleased to remove from the scene of action. "*Abiit, evasit, erupit.* Having vented his thunderbolts with no sparing hand, he shows that he is capable, like the thunderer, of vailing himself in clouds."[1]

At the sitting of the House the following evening, Brougham attempted to reply to these observations, pleading indisposition as the cause of his absence.[2] But I have repeatedly known him follow the same course when he did not mean to call for a division. If he had divided against the Canada Bill he would have had only two other peers to go below the bar along with him. They contented themselves, after opposing it in every stage by speeches, with entering a protest on the Journal against it.[3]

The Canada question recurred in various shapes till the very end of the Session, and kept Brougham in constant employment. He had a prodigious triumph in an illegal act of Lord Durham, professing to be under a power of making ordinances for the good government of the colony. The Governor-General had banished to Bermuda certain persons concerned in a rebellious insurrection. Now, although he might have ordered them to be hanged in Canada, he could not lawfully order them to be imprisoned out of Canada. Brougham denounced this excess of jurisdiction as a most horrible outrage. His law was good, but he could not be justified in magnifying the small slip of the Governor-General into a great crime. Elated with this success, he went on to contend that all Lord Durham's ordinances were unlawful, and he laid down various propositions, both with respect to common law and the construction of Acts of Parliament, which were wholly untenable. But neither the Lord Chancellor nor the Master of the Rolls would venture to contradict him, and Lyndhurst cunningly observed that, concurring in the illegality of the banishment to Bermuda, he thought it more prudent to abstain from giving any opinion upon the other legal points mooted by his noble and learned friend. From the be-

[1] 40 Hansard, 243.   [2] Ibid., 249.   [3] Ibid., 886.

ginning to the end of this Session, Lyndhurst made it a rule to remain silent during the debate, finding it a more convenient course privately to incite Brougham and to praise him.

In addition to his old annual bills on education, charities, and other subjects, Brougham now launched a new one—to give to his Judicial Committee the power of extending copyright to authors when the statutable term has expired; but as it was universally scouted, he allowed it to drop after the first reading, and he has never again brought it forward. Such a discretionary power to tamper with the rights of individuals and of the public could not be endured in a free country.

While Parliament was sitting and he was speaking so copiously, Brougham wrote more than could be expected from a laborious professional bookmaker, who never rises from his desk. Besides revised editions of his speeches, he indited many articles in newspapers, magazines, and reviews, and he brought out several pamphlets to gratify his spleen against the Court and the aristocracy.

He likewise most usefully and laudably employed himself as President of the Society of Useful Knowledge. Under his auspices this Society flourished much for several years, and, selling excellent treatises at a low price, was of essential service to the middle and lower orders. Its most successful publications were the 'Penny Magazine' and the 'Penny Cyclopædia.' The latter, from having often consulted it, I can pronounce a very valuable addition to any library. But the society at last became bankrupt, and was obliged to be dissolved for want of funds by publishing, at his own risk, Lord Brougham's 'Political Philosophy,' the copyright of which he had very generously presented to the Society. This I do seriously and sincerely think is a most excellent treatise, and I have *bona fide* read it through with pleasure and advantage; but I could never find more than one other person who had undergone the same labor, and the fact was that unaccountably it fell still-born from the press. Anticipating a great sale from the reputation of the author, an edition of several thousand had been printed off, and they almost all went to the trunk-makers.[1] The Society had been before in pecuniary distress, and this blow proved its death.

[1] I have been told that the book had much better success in Germany, and

Misfortunes never come single. Of Greek, Brougham, like all others educated in Scotland, had only acquired a slender knowledge. But he flattered himself that he thoroughly understood, as well as relished, Demosthenes. In this belief he ventured to publish a new translation, by himself, of the 'De Corona,' with notes. His ambitious temerity was dreadfully punished; for there came out critiques upon it—particularly an admirable one in the *Times* newspaper, by a profound Grecian—which exposed him most unmercifully, showing that in various instances he had mistaken the meaning of the original, and that he was ignorant not only of the niceties of the Attic dialect, but even of well-known facts in Grecian history. Of all his literary failures this is the one which he took most to heart.

But he might have been comforted by the brilliant success of his 'Sketches of the Statesmen and Philosophers in the Reign of George III.,' now begun, and published the following year, when they at once seized the public attention. Here he really was at home, and he wrote of men with whom he had conversed, and whose merits and defects he was well able to appreciate and to describe. The best of these sketches first appeared in the 'Edinburgh Review.' He afterwards republished them in volumes, with others of very inferior merit, including such characters as Frederick the Great, the Empress Katherine of Russia, and Voltaire, with respect to whom he could state no new facts, and his observations were either vapid or fantastical.

When the Session of 1839 arrived, Brougham continued to speak from the ministerial side of the House; but he now in all parliamentary tactics openly and avowedly coalesced with the Opposition, for the purpose of expelling the Government. He no longer confined himself to speeches which might indirectly disparage the Whigs and bring them into public odium, but, throwing out now and then a little bit of innocent Radicalism, he earnestly and vigoriously made or seconded motions in concert with the Tory leaders. What his hopes or wishes then were, in contemplation of a change of Ministers, I am unable to conjecture. Perhaps he did not look further than the full gratification of his blind revenge.

When he least expected it the long-desired consummation

that a German translation of it was in great demand for two successive Leipsic fairs.

seemed to have arrived. The Government had been going on very smoothly in the Lords. The Duke of Wellington declared to those in his confidence that he had felt rather uncomfortable in 1835, when Peel was Prime Minister; that he would not be at all gratified by seeing such a state of things restored; and as the Queen preferred the Whigs, that he had no objection to their remaining in office if he could induce them to be tolerably moderate in their measures of reform. He had, therefore, discountenanced the intrigues between Lyndhurst and Brougham to precipitate a change of Government. But in the Lower House, where since the passing of the Reform Bill, the Whigs had hitherto been strong, a measure on which they staked their ministerial existence met with such opposition, that they deemed it decent and necessary to resign. This was a bill for superseding the Legislative Assembly of Jamaica, the second reading of which was carried only by a majority of five, although dying members, and members whose near relatives were lying dead, were carried into the lobby to make up this majority.

When Brougham heard Melbourne announce that on account of what he considered the adverse division in the other House, her Majesty's Ministers had unanimously tendered their resignation, and only held their offices till their successors were appointed, he manifested exuberant exultation, and seemed to indicate that then to die would be happiness. However, he decently tranquillized himself and magnanimously "entreated their Lordships, who had under their care the morals, the instruction, and the welfare of the people, not to allow any mere party feeling, any *temporary*, and it may be *only momentary*, gratification to interfere with their highest duty. He considered his Bill for the Repeal of the Beer Act to be of more importance than any change of ministry; and although, under existing circumstances, he would postpone the second reading, he should persist, *whoever might hold the office of Prime Minister*, in endeavoring to obtain the repeal of a measure which he believed to be permanently fraught with mischief to the character of the country."

Alas! he had used prophetic words. The exquisite "gratification" which he felt proved to be "temporary" and almost "momentary." By the clumsy mismanagement of Sir Robert Peel in forming the new Government he failed, and the Whigs remained in office above two years longer.

Brougham, I believe, had an expectation during this crisis that, although Lyndhurst must have had the Great Seal, some high office would be offered to himself, who had so essentially contributed to the victory. However, his disappointment in this respect caused him little grief compared with what he suffered from seeing the restoration of the Whig Cabinet, from which he was ejected. At first he was so overpowered that, to the astonishment of every one, he preserved a deep silence during the whole of the evening when Lord Melbourne announced his return to office, and explained how it arose from a demand having been made upon the Queen that she should dismiss all the ladies of her bedchamber. But when the subject was revived by a question from Lord Winchelsea, Brougham poured forth a torrent of virulent invective against the Whigs, their supporters, the Ladies of the Bedchamber, and the poor Queen. Said he :—

"The private, individual, personal feelings of that illustrious Princess have been made the topic of every riotous meeting, of every mob, and of all demagogues who have set to work to prop a sinking Administration. Their only cry is *the Queen! the Queen! the Queen!* This is the bedchamber crisis. Sir Robert Peel's formation of a Government has been defeated by two ladies of the bedchamber. From all I have ever heard or dreamed of, I never expected to see any, and above all a Whig Government based on a bedchamber question—a question of personal feeling towards the Sovereign. That is the ground for resuming office, after a plain confession that they have lost the confidence of the Commons. The confidence of your Lordships' house, alas! they never possessed. The Government have resumed office only because the Queen has refused to dismiss two ladies of her bedchamber. They stand by the Queen, without the confidence of Parliament. Will this standing by the Queen get back public confidence? I do not believe a word of it. The attempt to pass a falsehood on the nation has signally failed. Considering what an inexperienced person the Queen is, it should be imputed to no fault of her own. She has reigned barely two years. But those who are about her are bound to inform her of the solemn responsibility thrown upon her by the ancient and established principles of the Constitution. There should be no force. Her feelings should be treated with all imaginable tenderness. Even where she may be wrong, every conceivable excuse should be made for her; the most profound respect and veneration of the most devoted courtier should be shown; but duty remains towering above all other and pettier considerations. If the crown fail, as fail it must, a bad service will have been rendered by bad counsellors, bad friends, bad flatterers, and worthless parasites. Let her not be guided by mere lovers of place—wishing to keep place, or only hungering and thirsting after it—whose appetencies have been sharpened by possession, or to whose desire distance makes it more sweet."

Thus continued to roll on almost interminably the turgid stream of his vituperative eloquence. Hansard says, and I make no doubt truly, " The noble and learned Lord sat down amid loud and continued cheers from the Opposition benches."[1]

However, it seems that the *Observer*, a Government newspaper, in commenting upon this speech, had the audacity to make observations, of which Brougham thus complained to the House of Lords as a breach of privilege:—

"' *We are compelled to state*,' says the libeller (now what compelled a man to state a gross falsehood I can not tell except it may be his nature), ' *that there was not a single member of the House who did not leave it disgusted with the speech*.' Not a single member! My noble friend near me (Lord Melbourne) might feel disgusted; but certainly there were some besides myself who did not leave the House from disgust."

He went on to complain of other statements, " that he had shown an inveterate hatred to the monarchy and personal disrespect to the Queen," which he solemnly disclaimed. He concluded without moving to send the libeller to Newgate, or making any other motion.

All the Peers present remained silent except the Marquess of Londonderry, an ultra-Tory Peer, who said that " although the noble and learned Lord had long taken a line in politics which the friends of the monarchy deplored he had at last made a speech which deserved to be

[1] 47 Hansard, 1164.

received with universal acclamation."[1] Such praise from such a quarter must have suggested to the object of it the alarming question, whether, notwithstanding his own consciousness of perfect consistency, he might not have got into a false position. He really was now defending for the Tories that of which they themselves were ashamed. Peel made a blunder when he insisted on the removal of all the ladies belonging to the household on a change of Government; and Peel himself afterwards said that he only meant to stipulate for the *power* of doing so, without meaning to exercise it. Unless the Ladies of the Bedchamber were the Queen's constitutional advisers, it seems strange to say that they must all be removed on every change of Ministers. The principle on which such a rule must rest would go to the preposterous and revolting length of requiring that in a female reign the Sovereign should have a new Consort as often as she has a new Prime Minister. This liberty of retaining mere personal attendants, which Brougham represented as so dangerous to public liberty, has been reserved to the Queen, and has been exercised by her on similar occasions ever since. Yet we still consider ourselves a free people.

From the restoration of Lord Melbourne's Government, Brougham may be considered the leader of the Opposition in the House of Lords. Lyndhurst felt no jealousy of him, full well knowing that his aid would be very useful in the assault, and that the Treasury being stormed, he had no chance of participating in the spoil.

At last Brougham brought forward a motion on which he was promised the whole strength of the Opposition, and which he thought must be fatal to the "Bedchamber Government." Certain political trials had been conducted in Ireland of no great importance, and, after conviction, certain of the defendants had been pardoned upon facts disclosed after the verdict. The charge against the Government was that the Irish Attorney-General had improperly conducted the prosecutions under instructions from the Government, and that the pardons had been granted without the presiding Judge having been consulted. The debate was ushered in by a flourish of trumpets, frequently repeated, to awaken public attention. First came the intention to give notice of motion; then

[1] 47 Hansard, 1232.

the notice of motion; then the postponement of the notice; then the further postponement and peremptory fixing of it for a future day; each accompanied with a long speech proclaiming the importance of the motion, and shadowing forth its probable consequences. When the portentous evening arrived, the orator had a very large assemblage of his friends, male and female, in the House of Lords, to admire him, and a Tory *whip* had secured a decided majority of Peers to vote for him. I copy the prooemium from the "corrected report" of his speech, which he published. It is so very labored and so highly finished, in his peculiar style, that it may, like the famous peroration to his defense of Queen Caroline, have been re-written by him seventeen times. Confidently anticipating a majority, he thought that he had reached a memorable epoch in the history of English party warfare, and he was determined to show himself equal to this great argument. Having slowly risen, solemnly looked round, and taken some time to adjust, not his *toga*, but his *Ettrick check trowsers*, he thus began :—

"If, in addressing your Lordships, I looked only to the paramount—perhaps the unparalleled—importance of the case which I am about to bring under your consideration, as it regards the policy, the welfare, and the constitution of this country, I should feel much less anxiety than I experience at this moment. But I recollect that, unhappily for me, and perhaps unfortunately for the question, it is one of which the indisputable importance is even exceeded by the great interest which it excites; I mean not merely that natural, legitimate, and unavoidable interest which it must raise amongst the people of the country to which it more particularly relates—I allude not merely to the interest which it excites among your Lordships, as the guardians of the pure administration of justice, you yourselves being supreme judges in a court the most distinguished in all the world ; but I am pointing to the personal and the party feelings—the heats naturally kindled among those who on the one hand may suppose that I stand here as the accuser of an individual or of the Government, and amongst those who, on the other hand, may conclude that the parties stand here placed on their personal defense ; and worse than this, I allude, with feelings of a truly painful nature, to that interest which this question is calculated to raise, and which I wish that any effort of mine could lull or delay—I may be supposed to come forward for the purpose of lending myself to personal views, and not merely in the discharge of an imperative public duty. But if the experience which your Lordships have had of me, while practicing before you as a minister of justice at your bar, or as presiding, so far as any Peer can preside, over your judicial proceedings in the house,—if the whole tenor of my not short public life of 30 years and upwards (in which I have constantly—it is perhaps rather the result of good fortune than arising from any merit of my own, by accident I might perhaps say, without deviation or change, or shadow of a turning—proceeded in the the same course, and been guided steadily by the same uniform principles)—if this gives your Lordships no pledge that I appear on the present occasion only to discharge a public and a great responsible duty, then what further pledge can I give, what more can I say than this? Mark how I, this day, perform the duty which I have undertaken; and then whosoever of the accusers may be disappointed, or whosoever of those who are on their defense may be chagrined—whatsoever party feelings may be excited, or whatsoever party objects may be frustrated by my discharge of public duty, at least I shall be able to appeal to your Lordships for my acquittal from the charge of having made myself, on this occasion, what I never did before, an engine of party feeling or an instrument of personal attack."[1]

He then proceeded for three hours to detail his facts very minutely and to read long extracts from printed evidence. His dullness was only relieved by a few passing sarcasms on old friends.[2] What he sought to prove was that the trials had been improperly conducted and that the defendants had been improperly pardoned, and he concluded with moving a long string of inculpatory resolutions, the chief of which was, "that a convicted criminal ought not to be pardoned without consulting the Judge by whom he was tried."

Lord Lyndhurst took no part in the debate, contenting

---

[1] 49 Hansard, 1275. From a corrected report published by Ridgway.
[2] I ought to be a competent judge, for as Attorney-General I was directed to watch the speech, that I might give some hints to the Marquess of Normanby, who was to answer it.

himself with hounding on his noble and learned friends. Lords Normanby and Melbourne ably opposed the resolutions, contending that the Government had acted before, during, and after the trials, according to the well-known maxims of the law and the constitution, and that the motion was a mere ebullition of spleen and factiousness. Although Brougham was informed by the Tory whippers-in that they had a large majority who were impatient for the division, and that several of their men, who had not been able to get pairs, could hardly be prevailed upon to remain longer in the House, he indulged in a very long reply, which he at last concluded with another panegyric on his own consistency. Having enumerated the good measures of the Government while he belonged to it, he continued :—

"Moreover, I have uniformly adhered to one political party; and if at the end of this long period I have found myself under the painful necessity of separating from my former political friends, it has been not on personal but public grounds—it has been—it has *notoriously* been—not because *I* changed, but because *they* have changed their course. When out of the government, in 1835, I zealously supported them; in 1836 I abstained from attendance that I might not embarrass them. But in 1839, when they have utterly forgotten the very name as well as the nature of Whigs, then of course my opposition became habitual, and I heartily desired to see the end of their reign. These Whig ministers under my noble friend. stripping off all decent covering, without one rag of public principle of any kind, stand before the country, naked, as mere courtiers, mere seekers of royal favor; and do not utter a single whisper to show that they have a single principle in their contemplation save the securing a continuance of their places by making themselves subservient creatures of the palace."

Upon a division, the resolutions were carried by a majority of 34—the numbers being 86 to 52. There were 39 pairs, several of which were arranged during the reply.[1] The vulgar custom of loud cheering on the announcement of a majority against the Government on a party question, which is practiced in the Commons, was not now resorted to; but Brougham thought this division was tantamount

[1] 49 Hansard, 1275-1385.

to a vote of want of confidence by one branch of the legislature, and as the other had signified a similar sentiment by the division upon the Jamaica Bill, he considered an immediate change of administration certain. Without any assurance that he himself should be included in the new arrangement, he was for the present contented with being able to say, "I made Melbourne Minister, and I have unmade him."

But he was again doomed to a cruel disappointment, for, instead of the expected announcement next day in both Houses of Parliament, "that Ministers had resigned, and only held their offices till their successors should be appointed," not the slightest notice was taken of the vote upon Brougham's motion, except by Lord John Russell in the House of Commons, who, after stating the Resolution about "pardoning or commuting a sentence without consulting the judge who presided at the trial," said :—

"As this Resolution affects the office which I hold [Secretary of State for the Home Department], I must at once say that it proposes a practice which is utterly inconsistent with that which has hitherto been pursued by Secretaries of State in their recommendations to the Crown, from which it would be exceedingly inconvenient to depart, and in which it is not my intention to make any alteration whatever. If it were a *Bill* instead of a *Resolution*, and it had gained the consent of Parliament, then of course I should be bound to obey it. But till the law is altered I shall consider myself justified in following the practice which has been hitherto pursued, not thinking that a vote of either House can affect the exercise of the royal prerogative of mercy." [1]

Thus the Resolution of the Lords was to be treated as waste paper!

Brougham himself was the only man who had calculated on speedy effects from his victory. The division really disclosed nothing more than what was before well known, —that in the House of Lords the Tories had a majority, which they could command on any question which they deemed it for the benefit of their party to carry, and the only novelty in the last movement consisted in the Tories being led on by a new chief. The Government had been considerably strengthened in the House of Commons by

[1] 50 Hansard, 2.

yielding to a measure of which the Radicals ought to have the credit, and which has conferred immense social benefit upon the world—the Uniform Penny Postage. Melbourne, instead of being crushed, seemed to go on with renovated vigor.

At the conclusion of the Session, however, there was a grand *Review* in the House of Lords when Brougham condescended to restore the chief command to Lyndhurst, but cordially co-operated with him. Lyndhurst, according to annual custom, compared the great things which ministers had proposed by the Queen's opening speech with their discomfiture in having the bills they brought in rejected.

Melbourne, in a very able speech, attempted to prove that ministers had failed in carrying their measures by the factious opposition offered to them, and particularly instanced the bill for reforming the Court of Admiralty.

"I can not advert to it," he observed, "without saying that a rejection of that bill by your Lordships was one of the most disreputable and unprovoked acts of power that I ever knew to be exercised. I deeply lament that the hand which destroyed ought, in reason and right feeling, to have been stretched out to save it."

This bill, which the public good most urgently required, would have been of service to Lushington, the Judge of the Court of Admiralty. Lushington had been Brougham's bosom friend, and had co-operated with him in the defense of Queen Caroline, but had grievously offended him by persevering steadily, as Member for the Tower Hamlets, in supporting the Melbourne Government. Without Brougham's opposition the Admiralty Court Bill, which passed quietly through the Commons, would have passed as quietly through the Lords; for Lyndhurst, left to himself, would not have encountered the odium which the loss of it would have cast upon his party. But Brougham opposed it as a "Whig job," and vowed that he never would let it pass without a clause disqualifying the Judge of the Court of Admiralty from sitting in Parliament. This could not be agreed to by its supporters,—partly from considerations personal to Lushington, and, further, from a sincere belief that the respectability and usefulness of the House of Commons would be materially damaged by excluding from it those whose judicial duties do not clash with the duties o a representative of the people, and who may be of great service in the deliberations of the Legislature from their knowledge of constitutional and international law.

Brougham, in answer to Melbourne, made a speech of enormous length against the Whig Government, which, on some points, he assailed with considerable success; but he was sorely puzzled when he came to his defense on the charge of throwing out the Admiralty Court Reform Bill; and, after some vague compliments to the learning and integrity of Lushington, he condescended to insinuate that the Judge prostituted his judicial character by actively engaging in political strife—" which no Judge ought to have the opportunity of doing "—although he himself was still acting as a Judge in the morning by hearing appeals, and in the evening was the zealous leader of a faction.[1] His new and most telling topic was the conduct of the Government in permitting, for the purpose of pleasing the Radicals, the "Ballot" to be an open question. Now that he was a leader of Tories, he rather wished to wash off the Radical taint which he had contracted while coquetting with the Radicals. He had taunted the Government with their supposed doctrine of *finality*, and now charged them with endangering our institutions by tampering with the Reform Bill, while he represented at the same time that they were hollow in their Liberal professions, and only wished to deceive.

"The reason for making this an open question," said he, "was to hug it to death, to stifle and extinguish it. If it was made an open question, it might be less likely to be carried than if it continued a close question ; it might be made open in order to be strangled. For all these omissions and misdeeds of the Government is it wonderful that Reformers should be hostile—even rancorously hostile, in the exact proportion in which Reformers are heartily and sincerely attached to the cause of Reform ?

> 'Whigs are deceivers ever,
> One foot on sea and one on shore,
> To one thing constant never.'

But you now hear added what was never added before:

[1] There is nothing more strange about Brougham than his seeming forgetfulness in debate of the answer which he might be aware is suggesting itself to the minds of all who hear him, both as to his facts and his reasonings.

> 'Sigh not so,
> But let them go.' "[1]

In spite of these invectives, Melbourne was able again to prorogue Parliament, still continuing Minister, and still basking in the sunshine of royal favor. After the prorogation he proceeded to Windsor Castle, while Brougham was obliged to return, disappointed and forlorn, to his house in Westmorland. He had renounced his Whig connections, and although in public he was closely associated with the Tories, he had as yet little private intercourse with them.

On Monday, the 21st of October, while Brougham was at Brougham Hall, London was thrown into a state of great excitement and consternation by a report of his death. The fact, at first disbelieved, soon gained universal credit, from a letter purporting to have been written to his friend Mr. Alfred Montgomery, by his friend Mr. Shafto, who was on a visit at Brougham Hall, and who professed to have been an eye-witness of the melancholy catastrophe. Such a letter undoubtedly was received by Mr. Montgomery, and, being entrusted to Count D'Orsay, was read by him at a fashionable club in St. James Street, as containing true intelligence. In a few minutes it was spread over the wide metropolis.

All the morning papers of Tuesday, the 22d of October, except the *Times*, contained leading articles on the "sudden death of Lord Brougham," with biographical sketches of him, and comments upon his career and character.

As a specimen of the laudatory, I copy that from the *Morning Chronicle*:—

"DEATH OF LORD BROUGHAM.

"It is with sincere and strong regret that we announce the death of Lord Brougham. So far as the particulars have yet transpired of this unexpected and melancholy event, they are derived from a letter from Mr. Shafto, which we are informed was read yesterday at one of the club-houses. It appears that Lord Brougham, with his guests, Mr. Leader and Mr. Shafto, left Brougham Hall on Saturday, for the purpose of visiting some ruin in the neighborhood; that the axletree of the carriage broke, the horses became unmanageable, the whole party was thrown out, and after his Lordship had received a severe wound

[1] 50 Hansard, 496-543.

by a kick from one of the horses, the wheel passed over his head, killing him on the spot. Mr. Leader it is said was severely bruised, but Mr. Shafto escaped without material injury. Such is the account generally circulated last night. We have seen a frank of Lord Brougham's dated on Sunday, and should have taken it as evidence, notwithstanding the frequency with which Sunday franks in particular are predated, of the falsehood of the report, but for the distinct and circumstantial statement to which we have referred. Of the event itself there is, we fear, no reason to doubt.

"It has been our duty of late to comment with some severity, though not more, we think, than the occasion demanded, on his Lordship's last publication, and on the course of political action which it seemed to forebode. Whatever expectation or apprehension it might suggest is now stilled forever; and the feelings excited by that work are merged in those which embrace his whole life, character, and political career.

"In variety of attainment, facility of expression, energy of purpose; in the grandeur of forsenic eloquence; in the declamation that makes a debater impressive to his audience, and the sarcasm that renders him most formidable to an opponent; in the untiring continuance of intellectual labor; in the fervent championship of many great objects of national philanthropy and improvement; and in that familiar personal acquaintance so important to the practical statesman with the modes of thought and feeling that obtain through all the different gradations of society —Lord Brougham stood pre-eminent amongst all his political compeers. He well earned, by long toil, splendid effort, and gradual ascent, the elevation to which he attained; not that merely of rank and station, but of celebrity and influence. Even before he achieved, and after he was divested of office, no man more surely fixed upon himself the attention of England and of Europe—of the old world and the new; and now while

> 'The extravagant and erring spirit hies
> To his confine—'

there, we devoutly hope, to repose in the bosom of his Father and his God, we feel rising upon us the recollections of many an arduous and vigorous struggle for the right, for unrestricted commerce, for the spread of knowledge, for legal and representative reforms, for the suffering and enslaved African, for freedom, civil and religious, for many a political victim marked for sacrifice, for a persecuted Queen, and for the poor and ignorant—the injured and hopeless—in our own land and all the world over. Such recollections, in spite of all deductions and exceptions, which sink into disregard now that the great account is closed, will endear and enshrine his memory. The Legislature, the country at large, all parties, sects, classes, must feel that a great public loss has been sustained. And in the future annals of our eventful times, conspicuous and illustrious, will stand the name of Henry Lord Brougham."

But the tone of most of the other journals was very hostile, although they professed a wish to be guided by the maxim " De mortuis nil nisi bonum."

The *Times* remained silent on the subject till Thursday, October 24, when there came out the following "stinging" article written by Mr. Barnes, the then Editor, who had been exceedingly intimate with Brougham, and had long been one of his warmest admirers and eulogists, but who had quarrelled with him in the beginning of the year 1834, and had subsequently become his most formidable, because most discriminating, assailant:—

"The intelligence of Lord Brougham's death, believed so generally and with so much confidence throughout the whole of Monday last, and on authority believed to be so unquestionable, owed no part of its circulation to this journal, the only one among the morning newspapers of Tuesday by which the disastrous incident was not assumed for fact, and made the occasion of some sort of obituary article.

" To expatiate at length upon such topics would require an exercise of pen or speech almost as cumbrous as his Lordship's own productions. He has been for a period equal to that of an entire generation the most voluminous of writers, the most voluble of debaters, and of actors, if not the most efficient and successful, at any rate the most restless and indefatigable.

" Had he abstained from writing, speaking, and attempting nine-tenths of that with which he has loaded the name of BROUGHAM, he might have accomplished in each department whereon his multifarious efforts were in a great measure wasted, a success as signal as his failures have been notorious and memorable, and have enrobed himself with a graceful and flowing reputation, not one composed of shreds and patches, here exposing his nakedness, and there oppressing him with a grievous and unwholesome weight.

"There is scarcely a subject on which Lord Brougham has not put himself forward as the author of one or more publications—history, theology, metaphysics, mathematics, political economy, literary criticism, biographical criticism, constitutional dissertation, party controversy without end.

'Omne fere scribendi genus tetigit.'

Alas! we are unable to add 'nullum quod tetigit *non ornavit.*' In fact, there is no one general topic discussed by Lord Brougham with regard to which he has contributed either substance or beauty to the thoughts which preceding writers had expended on it. . . . . . To him the *creative* is not given. He is an advocate, and nothing more; an advocate who gains attention without inspiring any deep or enduring interest, an advocate who entertains his audience, who strives to cut away objections or obstructions by the edge of sarcasm, not by the power of reason; an advocate who can be vehement, but never earnest, who exhibits heat of temper, but not of passion, and could as rarely win the sympathy of jurors as he could the sober sanction of the judge. . . .

"In society, as one of the most agreeable, amusing, kindly, and convivial of associates, there is no individual capable of filling the space which would have been left void by Lord Brougham's untimely exit. There are a multitude of friends who loved him for what he was and is, as there are of observers who have admired him for what he might have been. But solid post in the great political world he has none; followers, he has none; reasonable prospects of influence or power, or gratified ambition, he has none. There is no party, whether 'Movement' or 'Conservative,' that would venture to employ him otherwise than as a transient ally;—as a partner or a colleague, never. Setting aside all affectionate or private feelings, those members of both parties who are best acquainted with Lord Brougham, and have tried him, would, after a little while, have felt his removal a lightening of many cares, and a release from many imminent embarrassments. For it is by impulses of temper or of pique, more of a selfish than even a capricious nature, and abstracted from all broad or distinct considerations of national or general good, that the course of this impetuous, and, in some respects, formidable adventurer, on the scenes of public life, has hitherto been shaped and directed."

This article, although undoubtedly malignant and overcharged in its censure, contains much truth, and displays a very familiar acquaintance with the failings and blunders of Brougham.

The vituperative article next for ability of execution appeared in the *Examiner*, from the pen of Mr. Fonblanque, who likewise once had been a worshipper of the great idol of the Press, and was now disposed to join in demolishing its fragments. He directly charged (what many began to suspect) that Brougham himself was the author of the report, in the hope of enjoying during life the pleasure of perusing posthumous praise.

Thus was the article headed : [1]—

"THE BROUGHAM HOAX.
' And is old Double dead?'—*Master Shallow.*

' She went to the undertaker
To buy him a coffin,
And when she came back
The dog was laughing.'—*Mother Hubbard.*"

The writer went on to observe that, while the report was believed, the general feeling was that *we could better have spared a better man,* and he mixed a little praise, to give greater pungency to his satire; but he concluded with upbraiding the supposed defunct with having been privy to Mr. Shafto's letter, and having committed the crime of *suicide.* No direct evidence of complicity was adduced, except that Brougham, by his own confession, wrote on the Sunday to his family in London not to be alarmed if they should hear a foolish rumor of his being killed by an accident.

This was by no means conclusive; for an accident there had been on the Saturday, when Brougham, with Mr. Shafto and another friend, had been overturned in a carriage while taking a drive in Westmorland, and were ex-

[1] *Examiner*, Sunday, October 27, 1839.

posed to real danger, although they escaped unhurt.
Nevertheless the world believed, and to this day generally
believes, that when the three companions got back to
Brougham Hall, and talked of their narrow escape, and the
sensation which would have been created if the illustrious
ex-Chancellor really had come to his end by the kick of a
horse (like Philip of Macedon, killed by the falling of a
tile), they did agree, by way of a frolic, that Shafto
should write a letter to Alfred Montgomery circumstan-
tially describing the event—Brougham sanguinely believing that it would revive public sympathy in his favor, and
that the contributors to the Press would embrace the
opportunity to make atonement for the abuse which they
had recently lavished upon him. Although Mr. Shafto
denied having written the letter, no explanation of it was
ever given, and it did contain a true statement of some
particulars of the accident which could only have been
known to those who witnessed it. People, therefore, assumed that Mr. Shafto wrote the letter, and the question
was asked, "Would Mr. Shafto, while under the roof of
Lord Brougham as his guest, have written the letter to
Lord Brougham's bosom friend, Mr. Alfred Montgomery,
without the knowledge of Lord Brougham?"

Whether Brougham was cognizant of this piece of bad
pleasantry or not, he was much annoyed by the result of
it. Not only was he mortified by the great preponderance
of abuse which it called forth, but he discovered, to his
great surprise, that he was generally suspected to be the
author of it, and he knew the ridicule which he must have
incurred by killing himself, and reading so many and such
unfavorable characters of himself, written when he was
supposed to have gone to a better world.

No ordinary man who had got into such a scrape could
have rallied and reappeared in society. But by the time
that another session began Brougham was again *upon his
legs* as if nothing had happened. If he received a few
malicious congratulations on his wonderful recovery from
the effects of his accident, most men and women, from
liking him or being afraid of him, refrained from alluding
to the subject, or strongly censured the bad joke which
some enemy had practiced upon him.

The Queen in her opening speech having announced her
intention to ally herself in marriage with the Prince

Albert of Saxe Coburg and Gotha, Brougham showed his ill-humor by expressing—

"An earnest hope that the country might not on this, as on former similar occasions, be doomed to see an indecent and unfeeling race run between conflicting parties at the expense of the interests of a suffering people, for the purpose of paying court in the highest quarters."

Alluding to the riotous proceedings of the Chartists, he continued:—

"With a people full of discontent, and afflicted with distresses such as we know they are now suffering under, with falling wages, rising prices, and diminished profits,—with the country in such a state, to propose any provision beyond what is required by the absolute necessity of the case, would, in my deliberate and conscientious opinion, be a breach of all the duties which either the Government or the Parliament owes to the people. I should revert to the words of one of the wisest of men—I mean Lord Bacon—who, dealing with a matter of the same kind, said: 'Beware if you have to probe popular discontents, and find that they are deep-seated and wide-spreading, beware how you drive back the humors, for they will then only cause the wound to bleed inwards.'"[1]

But Brougham can not be justly accused at any stage of his varied career of deliberately resorting to the arts of a demagogue; he always meant to respect property, law, and order, and he could not on this occasion have sought to seduce the Chartists from their idol, Feargus O'Connor, who told them that they were not only entitled to the five points of the Charter, but to an equal division among themselves of the land, and all its produce. I can not pay a similar compliment to all the Tories. The conduct of the Duke of Wellington and Sir Robert Peel in this respect was unexceptionable, but the subordinate members of the party were always willing to coalesce with the Chartists. If there was to be a public meeting to petition against the Corn Laws, they encouraged the Chartists to break it up by violence, or to join with them in denouncing the conspiracy of the Whigs against native industry. They went so far as to express deep sympathy with Frost and the Welsh insurgents, who had been convicted of high treason; they represented the Whig Poor-Law Reform as

---

[1] 51 Hansard, 22.

a violation of the inherent rights of the lower orders to be
maintained at the public expense; and at parliamentary
elections they often rejoiced in starting a Chartist candidate who, although he had no chance of being returned,
might abuse the Whigs and divide the liberal interest.

During the Session of 1840 there was no ministerial
crisis. Both Brougham and Lyndhurst became milder in
their opposition,—perhaps thinking that ministers were
gradually getting into insuperable difficulties from the de-
crease of the revenue, in spite of additional taxation, and
that the wiser course was quietly to "bide their time."
Another reason was that Peel,—who now had almost unlimited sway in the House of Commons, and without
whom a new Conservative Government could not be
formed,—on one very important question which now
agitated the public mind, had quarrelled with the great
majority of the Conservative party.

This question, which had nearly brought about a civil
war, was whether those who, acting under the authority
of the House of Commons, had printed and published
papers containing criminatory charges against individuals,
were liable to be proceeded against by action for libel in
the courts of law. Lord Melbourne's Government, by my
advice as Attorney-General, adopted the opinion that the
right of ordering such publications for the information of
members of the legislature and of the public was necessary
to enable the two Houses of Parliament to perform their
functions, and that to bring such an action was a breach of
parliamentary privilege. Brougham most passionately
took the other side, partly to spite the Government, partly
to spite the Attorney-General, who was much mixed up
in the Controversy—but, above all, to spite the House of
Commons, an assembly to which he had unaccountably
conceived a strong antipathy. From the time when he
vacated his seat in it by accepting the Great Seal, he had
never been present at any of its deliberations, or for a
moment visited the scene of his former glory; and from
the time of his leaving the Government and going into
Opposition he had systematically caught with eagerness
at every opportunity to sneer at, to ridicule, and to censure its proceedings. When a Committee of the House of
Commons had almost unanimously presented a report
which was adopted by the House, insisting upon this right

of printing and publishing, he contended in pamphlets and in spoken speeches, and in prefaces to printed speeches, that the Commons might as well insist upon a right to order their servants to rob upon the highway. So eager was he, that, when the question came on to be argued in court before the judges, he placed himself on the bench, and several times interrupted the counsel for the House of Commons, who, nevertheless, took occasion in his presence to complain of the manner in which a Peer of Parliament who might have to sit judicially on the question upon appeal, instead of waiting to hear it argued, had as a mere amateur prejudged it, without having heard any argument at all.

The great bulk of the Conservative party in both Houses strongly took part against ".privilege," but Sir Robert Peel gallantly and resolutely was its champion. Things had come to this pass that the Sheriffs of London and Middlesex were imprisoned by the House of Commons for levying damages in obedience to a writ of the Queen's Bench, and the judges of that court had admitted that they had no jurisdiction to grant relief, as the Speaker's warrant of commitment merely stated that it was for a breach of the privileges of the House of Commons without specifying in what the breach of privilege consisted. Brougham presented a petition from the Sheriffs to the House of Lords describing their pitiable condition, but the House of Lords could grant no relief more than the Court of Queen's Bench. The progress of business in Parliament was entirely suspended; motions were talked of to commit Lord Denman and the judges of the Queen's Bench to the Tower, and many who thought that the House of Commons was usurping all the powers of the State meditated petitions to the Queen that she would assist the courts by a military force to administer justice and to enforce their decrees.

Had it not been for the desire to reunite Peel to the Conservative party, the confusion would have thickened, and no one can tell what consequences might have followed; but Lyndhurst perceived that while the existing state of affairs continued he had no chance of recovering the Great Seal, and he consented to resort to legislation—offering that the principle for which the Commons struggled should be conceded, and that an Act should be passed giving power effectually to assert it. This was very distaste-

ful to Brougham, but, as it would hasten the downfall of the
Melbourne Government, he agreed to it. We were thus
in reality to gain all we had been fighting for, and we could
not refuse the offer. So a bill, applying to both Houses,
was prepared, which declared that the disputed power was
indispensably necessary, and which effectually prevented
any action being prosecuted for any such publication.
This bill passed both Houses and received the Royal assent. Although it in reality gave a triumph to the Whigs,
Brougham would not oppose it as he believed it would
hasten their downfall. The swelling waves instantly became smooth, and the liberated Sheriffs at a City feast
amicably related their sufferings to those who had planned
their imprisonment. Brougham was much mortified at
seeing an end put to this " pretty quarrel," and he was not
able to raise up any new cause of embarrassment to the
Government for the rest of the session.

Finding the climate of Westmorland rather moist, he
about this time bought a small estate near Cannes, in Provence, and built a commodious house upon it which he
called Chateau Eleanor Louise, in compliment to his beloved daughter. Here he has since spent several months
in every year—his habit being at the prorogation of Parliament to retire to Brougham Hall, to remain there exercising liberal hospitality till the approach of winter—then
to repair to Paris, where he spends eight or ten days attending the meetings of the Institute and paying his respects to the rulers of France for the time being, Royal,
Republican, or Imperial, and then proceeding to his chateau
by Lyons, Avignon, and the Estrelles. Here he remains
till another session of Parliament is about to commence—
engaged in study, and much pleased to entertain his friends
who are passing by this route between France and Italy.
He is exceedingly popular with his neighbors, the inhabitants of Cannes, not only by reason of the personal kindness and affability with which he treats all classes, but by
his having obtained through his influence with King
Louis Philippe a large *subvention* from the French Government for the improvement of their harbor.

In the beginning of January, 1841, he was summoned to
London by Lyndhurst with an intimation that the Melbourne Government was becoming more and more unpopular, and an assurance that it could not possibly last anoth-

er session. With alacrity he repaired to his old post in the House of Lords on the ministerial side, from which he could most effectually assail his old friends by a flank fire. The Queen's Speech was purposely framed so as to provoke no amendment or opposition, and when the mover and seconder of the address had finished their stereotyped orations there was a general disposition among the peers at once to agree to it as a matter of course, reserving any attack upon the Government to a more fitting opportunity. But Lord Brougham sprang up, and at great length censured the policy and the acts of the Government both at home and abroad. He had most success in giving vent to the feelings which have always most creditably disposed him to cultivate a good understanding between France and England—an object which, from his alternate residence in the two countries and his familiar acquaintance with the disposition of the two nations, he has been essentially instrumental in promoting. Commenting on the great Syrian question which had brought us to the brink of hostilities, he now said :—

"There is no denying that the French are a people of the greatest genius, courage, and military skill. Their brilliant military character makes them 'jealous of honor, sudden and quick in quarrel;' and on these accounts it would have been better if everything like discourtesy, which was calculated to induce them to a course likely to gratify their predilections, had been studiously avoided. To suppose, however, for a moment that any one in this country ever underrated the great military character and renown of the French nation—to suppose that even the noble Duke opposite, or any of his former gallant companions-in-arms ever thought or dreamt of speaking otherwise than most respectfully of the great achievements in arms of that nation—would be in the highest degree preposterous."

Lord Melbourne, in answer, observed that—

"Noble lords, when they studied the whole course of the negotiations, would be persuaded that there had been no want of courtesy on our part, and that we had been guilty of nothing which could justly offend the most sensitive mind. But it would not do for one nation to plead its own irritability as a reason for seeking to govern the conduct of another nation. This would be like what often occurs in private life, where you see that the most ill-tempered member of the family in effect governs the whole household by means of constantly saying, 'Oh, I am very irritable ; I am very ill-humored ; don't make me angry.'"

Hostilities now ceased in the Upper House, for here the Conservative cause had completely triumphed. After repeated divisions, indicating a want of confidence in her Majesty's present ministers, it was not worth while to bring forward new motions to proclaim the same fact. Brougham could not be silent; but for the rest of the session he contented himself with occasional anti-Whig sarcasms as he discussed Bribery of elections, Charitable trusts, Chartists, Church rates, Church of Scotland, Copyhold enfranchisement, Corn laws,[1] Criminal justice, Delay of justice, Petty sessions, Privy council, Punishment of death, Repeal of union, Socialism, Taxation, Universities, and the Welsh language.[2]

In the Lower House the death struggle was now going on, and the ministerial majorities which had been considerably increased after the crisis on the Jamaica Bill, were now slowly but steadily dwindling away. At last came Sir Robert Peel's decisive motion "that her Majesty's Ministers do not sufficiently possess the confidence of the House of Commons to enable them to carry through the House measures which they deem of essential importance to the public welfare; and that their continuance in office is at variance with the spirit of the constitution "—which, after a debate of five days, was carried by a majority of ONE.

The natural consequence would have been an immediate change of Government, but the usual announcement to this effect did not take place, and was not expected, for ministers had intimated their intention in case of a defeat, to dissolve Parliament, and to appeal to the coun-

---

[1] He made many speeches on this subject in presenting petitions for immediate abolition. He had become a convert to free trade in corn, and such was his zeal, that he forgot he had ever been a Protectionist. Having taunted Alexander Baring, Lord Ashburton, who from being a Free-trader had become a Protectionist, with inconsistency, he was told that the taunt came with a very bad grace from him who had become a Free-trader from being a Protectionist. He, as usual on all such occasions, denied the charge, and asserted his steady and uniform consistency on this as on all other questions. But to show his lapse of memory. it is only necessary to refer to his speech as copied in this Memoir.—*Ante*, p. 338.   [2] Index to Hansard.

try. The Queen still retained her attachment to Lord Melbourne, and her dislike of Sir Robert Peel, and it was hoped that the free-trade budget which had been launched would be so popular, as to secure a majority in the House of Commons.

The new Parliament did abolish the Corn Laws, but, alas! not till after the expulsion of the Whigs. The election returns showed a decided majority for " Protection," which was the Conservative cry at the hustings. The famine which followed first gave an ascendency to free trade. Till then it was not only odious to Tories or Conservatives, but to the great bulk of the Whig aristocracy. A number of Whig county members who had abandoned protection, now lost their seats, and other Whig county members, to retain their seats, adhered to protection, and abandoned the Whig Government.

Lord Melbourne went through the form of preparing a speech to be delivered by the Queen, recommending Parliament to consider " whether the laws regulating the trade in corn did not aggravate the natural fluctuations of supply, embarrass trade, derange currency, and by their operation diminish the comfort and increase the privations of the great body of the community "—but he and all his followers well knew that their doom was inevitable.

It seemed to some friends of Brougham that this was a favorable opportunity for reuniting him to the Whig party. The certain anticipation was that Peel must be minister, and it was considered equally certain that " Protection " must be the basis of his Government, for it was from the belief of his being a determined " Protectionist," that he had obtained a majority. Therefore Brougham, the leader of the free-trade faction in the House of Lords, could not accept, and could not be offered, office under such a premier. His attachment to this doctrine would be a good excuse for his returning to the Whigs, who staked their existence upon it. If he had been ill-used by them he had enjoyed his revenge—they were ready to embrace him—and both parties should say, " Let bygones be bygones."

But he was more obdurate and implacable than the son of Peleus. He exulted in contemplating the inevitable destruction of former associates, and he was determined to indulge in the savage pleasure of trampling upon their dead bodies.

In the debate upon the address, Brougham's revenge must have been satiated, unless it was insatiable. Melbourne might have been expected to be roused by the occasion. He might with good effect have taken a review of his administration of seven years, and shown how, amidst many difficulties, he had kept the country in peace —had passed many good measures, notwithstanding a more factious opposition in the House of Lords than any English minister ever encountered—and that he was now to be crushed for supporting the policy of free trade which his opponents would soon be obliged to adopt. But feeling that all·hope was gone, he would not even take the trouble to die decently. His speech was the most perfunctory, jejune, and wretched performance I ever witnessed. Brougham seemed to compassionate him for a moment, but rekindled his ire by reflecting how he had been wantonly thrown aside in 1835, and had been induced to work as the serf of his betrayers for a whole session under the false pretense that time was required to get over the King's prejudices against him. He commented in severe terms on the feeble effort now made by the moribund minister, which seemed to indicate that Jupiter had already deprived him of his understanding. He still eulogized free-trade policy, but argued that it never could have been carried by men who had only suddenly resorted to it as a desperate experiment to keep themselves in power. He denied that the result of the elections afforded any proof of the people being against free trade; they condemned the minister, not the measure. He bitterly censured Melbourne for dissolving Parliament when he might have known that an appeal to the people would only make him more helpless, and for meeting Parliament, instead of resigning, after the result of the elections was known—so that he made the Queen (for whose dignity he affected to be so solicitous) recommend from the throne measures which he knew that both Houses would reject. He hoped that the new ministers would sincerely adopt the great measure of free trade, which had been retarded by the frauds of its pretended friends, and thus only could the country reap the inestimable advantages which it was calculated to bestow.

No answer was given or attempted to this speech, and at the conclusion of it the House dividing, the contents were 96, the non-contents 168; majority against the Whig Government, 72.

The Commons having after a debate of four days come to a similar vote by a majority of 91, Lord Melbourne made the usual announcement that ministers had resigned, and only held their offices till their successors were appointed.

Sir Robert Peel soon constructed his Government, which was supposed to secure the perpetual triumph of "Protection," but which forever established "Free Trade."

CHAPTER CCXXIX.

FROM THE RESIGNATION OF LORD MELBOURNE TO THE RESIGNATION OF SIR ROBERT PEEL.

AT the next meeting of the House of Lords tne two great parties changed sides, the Conservatives (now ministerialists) sitting on the right of the throne, and the Liberals (now oppositionists) on the left. To the surprise of most men Brougham crossed the house along with his old Whig associates, drawn up in line against those whom he had warmly supported, and had resolved warmly to support. This course, I think, was very wrong, as not only being contrary to Parliamentary and party practice and etiquette, but as being actually disingenuous and unfair. In figurative phrase, he was about to fight under false colors, and although I acquit him of all wish ever to overhear the conversation of those whom he meant to attack, I can testify that he sometimes prevented a free communication between them when they were considering how they should defend themselves against his assaults; the continued tone of familiarity and good-fellowship which was kept up between him and us only rendered his presence the more embarrassing. He still felt the same rankling resentment against the Whigs, and he was as eager to disparage and to damage them when reduced to seemingly hopeless opposition, as in their palmy days, when they

could do what they pleased. I have reason to believe
that, although no offer of office was made to Brougham in
the late crisis, he was told, by way of lure, that Peel, who
in his heart was for free trade, entertained a high respect
for him; that if the Great Seal became vacant he might
be asked to accept it, and that Lyndhurst, idle and unwilling to resume labor at his advanced age, and moreover
disliking Peel, would probably soon resign. Whatever
his motives might be, as his intention undoubtedly was
zealously to aid the existing Government, he certainly
ought to have seated himself behind the ministers, thrust-
ing his knees into their backs as he openly and boldly
did when a Commoner in the time of Canning; or to
have taken his place on the ministerial side below the
gangway; or to have joined the discontented and professedly neutral squad on the cross benches. But, while he
was in truth the chief protector of the Government, he
ostentatiously, represented himself as having the inclinations as well as the local station of a leader of Opposition.
Thus, while speaking from his appropriated place on the
left of Lord Melbourne, after commenting on the gross
and universal bribery said to have prevailed at the late
elections, and classing the different parties accused, he observed:—

"The first charge is brought against men who support
the views of the present Government—at that time in opposition—and *over against whom* I have now the honor to
stand. The second case is brought as a charge against
men who supported the late Government—now the Opposition, as it is called—*in the front of which* I have now
the honor to take my place. [*Hear, hear, and a laugh,
from Lord Melbourne.*] My noble friend, the noble Viscount lately at the head of the Government, laughs. I am
at a loss to know what my noble friend meant by the interruption. Was my noble friend annoyed at the term
opposition?"

Lord Melbourne, who was no doubt amused, like others,
by the *false position* of the noble and learned ex-Chancellor,
could not regularly complain of the place from which the
noble and learned ex-Chancellor spoke, as the standing
orders only required all Dukes to sit and speak from the
Dukes' bench, and so of the different grades of the peerage
down to Barons, without mentioning the modern terms of

ministerial and *opposition* sides, which would have astonished our predecessors in the reign of Edward I., although the House of Lords was then arranged as to throne, woolsack, and side benches and cross benches exactly as we now see it. The ex-Premier therefore contented himself with affecting to be shocked at the idea of the ex-Chancellor or any peer coming into the House with the premeditated resolution of opposing any measure proposed by the ministers of the Crown.

"I remember," said he, "when I was a member of the other House, that alluding to a member as one of the Opposition was considered irregular, and the Speaker solemnly pronounced it to be unparliamentary language to say of any member that he had come into the House pledged to oppose the Government; and what he would have said of a member who declared that he *took his place in the front of the Opposition*, the Lord only knows!"[1]

Brougham was much annoyed by my coming into the House of Lords, foreseeing that I should be a sore check upon him when laying down bad law during the debate; but in private we kept up our usual free raillery—even after we were engaged in very sharp personal encounters in public. When we first met in the House he held out his finger for me to shake, and exclaimed, while he made a low bow, "How do you do *my Lord? Jack* no longer." I asked him not to remind me of my misfortunes. *Brougham.*—"Well, there is one consolation for you here; that you may speak when you please, and as often as you please, and on what subjects you please, and you may say what you please." *Campbell.*—"I suppose you expound the rules of the House from your own practice, but this will only suit you. *None but yourself can be your parallel!*"

Brougham was now in exuberant spirits, and seemed to delight in the cherished conviction that the Whigs were forever prostrate. To accomplish this object he was ready to submit to any sacrifice, and he really seemed careless about office for himself. He ascribed the victory which had been won mainly to his own efforts, and till the freshness of the rapture he experienced had passed away, he confessed that he was sufficiently rewarded by the glory he had acquired. Wonderful to relate, he did not at all feel the awkwardness of his own position as the champion of a party which he

[1] 59 Hansard, 1007.

professed to oppose. How deeply is it to be regretted that he did not now retire from party warfare, and, acting with real independence, devote himself to national education, the suppression of slavery, the improved administration of charities and law reform. A party might have formed round him and forced him into power. At all events the remainder of his career would have been straightforward and easy, and would have commanded the respect of mankind. If he could have had a prophetic glance at the difficulties, embarrassments, mortifications and obloquy to be encountered in the course which he was about to adopt, he surely would have shrunk from it with horror.

Sir Robert Peel, being duly installed, proposed no measures to Parliament, most peremptorily refused to give the slightest intimation what his policy was to be, and very speedily put an end to the session, so that Brougham, professing to be in "the front of the Opposition," but eager to show his unmitigated enmity to the members of the fallen Government, was dismissed for a while from parliamentary warfare, in which he always much delighted, to the stillness of private life, which sometimes made him pine for excitement.

In the month of December he found relief in the Judicial Committee of the Privy Council—a very useful tribunal which he had founded, and which, as yet, he continued very assiduously to attend. I myself, ex-Chancellor of Ireland, was now a member of it, and I found him a very agreeable colleague. He used to talk of this tribunal in the House of Lords and elsewhere as *his* court, and represented all the cases that came before it as decided by his own sole authority. But in truth we were all equal, and he was not even *primus inter pares*, although he would represent himself as the chief or president, and the other members as his puisnes or puppets. But when we were sitting together he was very unassuming and docile. He delivered judgment in his turn—never shirking work—and his judgments were often very elaborate and able. He had a scheme for making himself chief, or president, with a salary; but although this was favored by the Duke of Wellington, who thought him a profound lawyer and great judge, it could not be carried, as Peel would not agree to it; and a few years afterwards Brougham grew tired of "his court," and deserted it, under the pretense that Sir Edward Ryan, late Chief Justice of Calcutta, had been improperly made a member of it, although every way better qualified than the individual whom he wished to be appointed.

This was William Courtenay, whom Lord Chancellor Brougham, *proprio vigore*, created Earl of Devon. He was the undoubted male heir to the Courtenays, Earls of Devon, but only collaterally. Now the title had been limited to the grantee and *his heirs male*. This limitation, by the law of England, was only to heirs male descended from his body, and not to heirs male collateral descended from a common ancestor. Therefore, when heirs male of the body of the grantee failed, the title was extinct. So it was universally understood ever since the last Earl died, ages ago, and the true representative of the family laying no claim to the earldom, had been created Viscount Courtenay to him and his heirs male. The Viscount's heirs male becoming extinct, William Courtenay, eldest son of the Bishop of Exeter, bred to the bar, made a Master in Chancery, and afterwards Clerk Assistant in the House of Lords, became the representative of this illustrious house. He made out his pedigree very satisfactorily, and (as he himself told me) he petitioned the Crown that he might have a writ sent to him as Earl of Devon, not with any thought of being entitled to this peerage, but in the hope that, his pedigree being clear, he might be created a peer by favor of the Crown, on account of his distinguished lineage, being of the same blood as the Bourbons and the Emperors of the East. It was referred by the Queen to the House of Lords, and coming before a Committee of Privileges (to the astonishment of all mankind, and particularly of the claimant) Lord Chancellor Brougham expressed a clear opinion that the claim was well founded. Unfortunately for Brougham the point was defectively argued by Sir Thomas Denman, then Attorney-General, who knew nothing of the subject, and omitted to cite the Prince's case from Lord Coke's Reports, which would have been quite decisive against the claim.

Courtenay, from being Clerk Assistant, was now placed nearly at the top of the English peerage, but unfortunately, from having emoluments equal to £5,000 a year, he was reduced almost to destitution, and Brougham, thinking the members of the Judicial Committee were to have salaries, wished to make provision for his "belted Earl," according to ancient royal usage.[1] But the "belted Earl" was very justly considered incompetent, and Ryan, as I have observed, was appointed in preference. Although Brougham gave this as his reason for ceasing to attend the meetings of the Judicial Committee, he must have had reasons more stringent; and a more probable one was that all chance of his being made "President of the Committee of the Privy Council in matters of appeal" had died away.

When Parliament again met he resumed his place in the House of Lords, locally *opposed* to the ministers, but resolved to *back* them most strenuously. Although he always spoke from the opposition side of the house, after the debate began he was seldom in his place, and he moved about very rapidly. His favorite seat was the Woolsack, where he seemed to enjoy *divisum imperium* with Lord Chancellor Lyndhurst. When referring to them in debate, I was obliged to call the latter "my noble and learned friend *on* the Woolsack," and the former, "my noble and learned friend *on the edge of the* woolsack." Lyndhurst, pretending a great deference to Brougham's opinions, now acquired a complete ascendency over him, which he strengthened and continued by hints that he himself was sick of office, and could not go on much longer with Peel, some of whose measures he did not much relish, and whose "cold, stiff, priggish manners" he exceedingly disliked. By these or some other means the two law lords became strictly united, not only as political partisans, but

---

[1] I have often rallied Brougham upon his creating William Courtenay Earl of Devon. He says that he consulted Lord Chief Justice Tenterdon, who agreed with him in thinking the claim well founded. But Lord Chief Justice Tenterdon knew nothing of *Peerage law*, and must have come to a contrary conclusion if he had heard the question properly argued. If the limitation had been "to the grantee *and his heirs*," it is allowed that the collateral heir male could not have taken; and the limitation "to the grantee and his heirs *male*" could not let in the collateral heir. Such a limitation of a landed estate could not be made by the law of England, and therefore could not be made of a dignity. When I was Attorney-General, Brougham was about to create another Earl, by making Mr. Hope Johnston Earl of Annandale; and he had actually congratulated Mrs. Hope Johnston as the Countess; but with the assistance of Sir William Follett, I prevented him from completing the creation, and the claim was disallowed.

as private friends. And they were denominated even in Parliament the " Siamese Twins." [1]

Lyndhurst, although talking in private with the most unbounded license of all things and all men, was exceedingly cautious as to what he said in debate, and I had not any personal conflict with him; but Brougham for some time, in alluding to me, persisted in his restless dictatorial tone. To the surprise of the House, notwithstanding his superior reputation and rhetorical powers, I boldly stood up to him and taught him to respect me. These *logomachies*, by the assistance of newspapers and caricatures, amused the public at the time, but would have little interest for posterity.

The economical and financial measures which Peel now brought forward threw Brougham into some difficulties. Although the commercial tariff was much improved, and the importation of cattle was permitted duty free, a duty on corn was continued with a sliding scale, contrary to the proposal of the ousted Whigs. Brougham had abused them for wishing to retain a small fixed duty, declaring that any tax on the importation of the necessaries of life was an abomination instantly to be swept away. However, he praised the new Corn Bill as "a step in the right direction."

But he had next to meet a measure directly subversive of principles in defense of which he had declared that he was ready to die, and in deference of which rebellion, if likely to be successful, would be justifiable. Soon after his entrance into the House of Commons he had acquired immense credit by resisting the proposal to continue the income-tax for a year subsequently to the conclusion of the general peace, contending that it was an imposition which, on account of its inequality, oppressiveness, and inquisitorial nature ought not to be endured in a free country, unless during flagrant war. Nay, to destroy as far as possible the very recollection of such a tax, and to prevent any wicked minister from ever again attempting to resort to it, he had moved a resolution which was carried, " that all returns, assessments, papers, and documents connected with the income-tax should be immediately burned," omitting " by the hands of the common hangman," only because such an employment of this functionary had fallen

[1] See 78 Hansard, 137.

into disuse. But Sir Robert Peel, after a peace of thirty
years, which still remained undisturbed, when there was
neither war, nor rumor of war, proposed a renewal of the
income-tax as the basis of his scheme for improving the
agriculture, manufactures, and commerce of the country.
What was Brougham to do now? Alas!—*to vote for the
bill!* This was very distasteful to him, but less distasteful than to endanger Sir Robert Peel and to play into the
hands of the Whigs. In the hope of proving his boasted
consistency he moved certain resolutions (which to please
him were met by the previous question) reiterating his old
doctrines about the income-tax; but he argued that this
was an exceptional case, that an income-tax in time of
peace was not so bad as a national bankruptcy, and that
the blunders of the Whigs since he left them had reduced
us to this sad alternative.[1]

He was now amazingly flattered and petted by the Tory
Peers. Without his aid and in spite of his hostility they
could easily have commanded a decisive majority on every
question; but they said truly that, " thanks to him, they
led a very quiet and easy life, and got home to dinner
every evening at a very reasonable hour." They were desirous, therefore, as far as decency would permit (and a
little farther), to comply with all his whims, that they
might keep him in good humor.

Of this I had a remarkable instance towards the close of
the Session. A bill had been introduced into the House
of Commons to disfranchise Sudbury for bribery and corruption, and Roebuck, then a member of that House,
spoke for it and voted for it. When it came up to the
Lords it was to be supported and opposed by counsel at
the bar, and an announcement was made that the same
Roebuck was to argue for the disfranchisement. I mentioned the matter to the Chancellor, to the Chairmen of
the Committees, and to several leading Peers on both
sides, and they all agreed with me that this was a very
unseemly proceeding, which ought to be prevented—that
a member of the other House, who was supposed to have
given an unbiased vote for the bill, should come with a
fee to try to persuade us either to pass it or to reject it. I
accordingly gave notice of moving a standing order, that
" no one be heard at the bar of this House as counsel

[1] 64 Hansard, 39.

for or against any bill depending in this House, who is a member of the Commons House of Parliament." Brougham, through whose patronage this retainer had been sent to Roebuck, was thrown into a transport of rage, ran to Lyndhurst to denounce the proceeding as an attempt to insult Roebuck, " who, though sometimes holding ultra-Radical language, was a very good fellow, and might have it in his power materially to assist or damage the Government." Lyndhurst was immediately convinced that he had taken a hasty view of the question when it was first mentioned to him, and not only promised that he himself would oppose the standing order, but that there should be a Government *whip* against it, so that Roebuck need be under no apprehension. The motion was made; but there was a muster against me as if I had been moving a resolution of want of confidence in the Ministers, and I did not venture to divide. Brougham relied mainly upon what he had done himself in Queen Caroline's case; but allowed that he intended to have resigned his seat in the House of Commons before appearing as counsel at the bar of the House of Lords, and that he had entered into an undertaking not to vote upon the bill or take any part in it when it came into the House of Commons: and that House further passed a resolution against the permission, even on this undertaking, being drawn into a precedent.[1]

For three years following, Brougham's political position and relations remained unchanged. Sir Robert Peel's Government went on very prosperously. The dispute with the United States of America respecting the boundary between Lower Canada and Maine, which had several times nearly led to war, was adjusted by treaty. There was profound peace in Europe. Our disasters in Affghanistan were repaired, and the war with China was terminated honorably and advantageously. To the astonishment of every one, the income tax was paid without a murmur, and made the Minister more popular, instead of proving his ruin. Although "the sliding-scale" still regulated the importation of corn, many other articles upon which there had been prohibitory duties were freely admitted from foreign countries, in exchange for our manufactures, and various internal taxes were repealed which weighed

[1] 65 Hansard, 730-751.

heavily on the springs of industry. The country was in all respects in a better condition than at the expulsion of the Whigs.

Brougham not only patriotically but personally rejoiced in the contrast, and still continuing in "the front rank of opposition," he acted as trumpeter to the Tories. He was ever ready to defend or palliate any mistake they might commit, and to exaggerate their merits and successes.

The boundary treaty with America was very much to be rejoiced in, the disputed territory being of no real value; but Lord Ashburton, our negotiator, acting on the instructions he received, had certainly allowed himself to be overreached by Mr. Webster, the American Foreign Minister, and had agreed to give up a large district which undoubtedly belonged to Canada, and which the Americans had only recently claimed. In the House of Commons the Government was contented with carrying a resolution, generally expressing satisfaction with the treaty. But this was not enough for Brougham, and in the Lords, taking the affair out of the hands of the Government altogether, he, after speaking three hours from the opposition side of the House, moved a resolution—

"That this House doth approve the conduct of the late negotiation with the United States, and rejoiced in the terms, alike advantageous and honorable to both parties, upon which the treaty has been concluded; and doth express its high sense of the ability with which the Lord Ashburton, the Minister sent to treat with the United States, executed his commission."

He took this opportunity of leveling many sarcasms at Palmerston, the veteran Foreign Minister under the Whig Government, showing how much more skill, as well as sincerity, than he could fairly boast of, had been displayed by Lord Ashburton, an ennobled London merchant, who had so completely excelled him in this diplomatic *coup d'essai*. A Peer who spoke against the resolution, having warmly defended Lord Palmerston, Brougham, in reply, "denied that he had intended to sneer at his noble friend, with whom he had the honor of being a colleague for four years."[1]

Peel said truly that his "great difficulty was Ireland." This arose very much from his own imprudent method of

[1] 68 Hansard, 599–678.

meeting the repeal agitation of Daniel O'Connell. He
first allowed the demagogue for several years to hold "monster meetings," which ought at once to have been forbidden
and dispersed, and to make speeches and to publish writings which ought to have been promptly prosecuted and
punished as seditious. He at last, in one "monster indictment" against him, included all the offenses which O'Connell and his associates had actually committed, and charged
as offenses other matters of which the criminal law does
not take cognizance. A conviction having been irregularly as well as unfairly obtained upon this indictment, and
sentence of imprisonment passed, a writ of error was sued
out to bring the case before the House of Lords.

When O'Connell's case came to to be argued at the bar,
Brougham, I believe, formed a clear and conscientious
opinion that the judgment ought to be affirmed. This, of
course, he was bound to act upon, and there would have
been no harm in his privately expressing a hope that what
he considered *justice* should not be defeated by what he
considered *technicality*. But from an indiscreet eagerness
to support the Government, and from personal antipathy
to O'Connell, who had often talked very irreverently of
his doings, particularly of his Scottish "progress," now,
while supposed to be an impartial Judge, he acted as a
keen partisan, and imputed to others the political feelings
by which he himself was palpably influenced. Mr. Baron
Parke having, when consulted by the House of Lords,
given an opinion in favor of O'Connell, Brougham asserted,
in the most direct terms, to private individuals, and insinuated very intelligibly in public, that this opinion of the
Judge was entirely produced by disappointment at his
not having been made Chief Baron, when that office had
been lately vacant. His own opinion for affirming the
judgment he delivered with unjudicial asperity; and
when the judgment was reversed, according to the opinion
of Lord Denman, Lord Cottenham, and Lord Campbell,
he was actually in a furious rage, saying in his place that
"the decision had gone forth without authority, and would
return without respect."[1] He then stepped up to me and
whispered in my ear, "*You* have created a Peer. Tindal
will forthwith be brought in to vote against you, Cottenham, and Denman. Do you suppose that the Govern-

[1] Clark and Finnelly's Rep., vol. xi.; 81 Hansard, 459.

ment will go on with a minority of Law Lords in this House? Tindal has a fair claim to the peerage, having been so long Chief Justice of the Common Pleas. He is a man to be depended upon, and a Peer he will be." I have not a doubt that he recommended this step to Lyndhurst and to Peel, for he is very fond of offering his advice to any Government which he patronizes, but Peel would not listen to it; and Tindal died a commoner.

I ought gratefully to mention the valuable assistance I received from Brougham in carrying through my "Libel Bill," which allows truth to be given in evidence in prosecutions by individuals for defamation, and contains various important provisions for the protection of the Press and for the protection of private character. It was preceded by a Select Committee to inquire into the subject, before which various classes of witnesses were examined, and, among others, the editors of the London newspapers. The *Morning Chronicle* had attacked Brougham rather sharply on various occasions since he had left the Whigs, and Dr. Black, the editor, a gentleman of considerable literary eminence, attending as a witness, Brougham thus began his cross-examination:—" Now, Dr. Black, suppose you resolve to write down a public man, how do you set about it?" *Dr. Black:* "I never knew any public man written down, *except by himself*."[1]

Valuable assistance was likewise rendered me by Brougam in carrying my "bill for giving compensation to the families of those who are killed by the negligence of others"—a most beneficial adoption (with modifications) of the Scotch law of *Assythement*—approved by all except Railway Directors.

Brougham and I heartily coalesced to ward off the impending disruption of the Church of Scotland. He was proud of his relationship to Dr. Robertson, and he took a sincere interest in the prosperity of that Church, of which the celebrated historian had been for many years the ornament and the leader. Having concurred in the judicial decisions against the assumption of power by the General Assembly to repeal the Act of Parliament which recognizes lay patronage, we were willing to concur in any measures to prevent the abuse of that patronage, and all might have gone well. But unfortunately the matter was

[1] 66 Hansard, 395.

left by the Government chiefly in the hands of Lord Aberdeen, a "Ruling Elder," who was said to have exhibited, in a very edifying manner, the gift of extempore prayer in the Kirk Session. But by his vacillation and timidity he brought about the disruption of the Church of Scotland, as some years afterwards he brought about the war with Russia. Producing the impression that his Government would yield and might be bullied, he induced the Non-intrusion party to commit themselves by a step that could not be retraced—like the passage of the Pruth by the Czar Nicholas. When we reproached him for want of spirit, he said, "He had spirit enough to oppose *us*, and that the House was not to be *lawyer-ridden*."

Brougham was still amused by the prospect of holding the Great Seal under Sir Robert Peel, on the long-hinted-at, but never approximating, retirement of Lyndhurst. Meanwhile, as a stepping-stone, he now more eagerly wished for the Presidentship of the Judicial Committee, and Lyndhurst was still willing to humor him, that he might be kept quiet. During the autumn, in his absence, the other members of the Court had worked hard and disposed of every case which was ready for hearing. On coming back to London, at the meeting of Parliament, he moved for and obtained a return of all the cases which stood ready for hearing. The return, of course, was *nil*. Thereupon it was concerted between him and Lyndhurst that this return should be a peg for a discussion on the Presidentship, preparatory to the introduction of a bill for establishing it. In consequence, when there was no motion before the House, Brougham rose, and dwelt upon "the satisfaction which the public must feel in finding that the business before this high tribunal was done with such dispatch."

Lord Chancellor Lyndhurst.—"I take this opportunity of stating my opinion to be unchanged, that it is necessary to have a permanent head of this Court."

Lord Brougham.—"I have no objection to such a plan. The establishment of the Judicial Committee has been unquestionably productive of great benefits; but it is susceptible of improvement, and, if supported, I will endeavor to remedy its imperfections."

Lord Campbell.—"I am of opinion that the system as it now stands, works well. With my noble and learned friend who spoke last, this system originated, and the public are much indebted to the author of it. So well has he framed it, with an inherent power of self-development, that it performs all its functions even when occasionally deprived of its head. How have we the boasted return of *nil?* Because while my noble and learned friend was at his chateau in Provence, enjoying the clear sky of Italy and the soft breezes of the Mediterranean, we, his humble Puisnes, were sitting day by day in the fogs of London, clearing off all arrears. We did miss the good-humored sallies with which he knows how to enliven the dullest drudgery, but still the work was done, and (as he vouchsafes to say) so well *that the public ought to be grateful for our labors.*"

Lord Brougham.—" As my noble and learned friend has been pleased to bestow compliments on me in relation to the Judicial Committee, I beg to reciprocate them—truly and sincerely—although I can not say he throws liveliness on the matters which come before that tribunal; so dry are they, that I defy all the liveliness of all the members to enliven them. But I must say in all seriousness that I feel very great scruples of conscience and much delicacy in calling upon my noble and learned friend, who has other avocations, to come and give his hours and labor in that Court, and to render purely gratuitous services to the public. In the discharge of judicial functions, service merely voluntary is a thing to be abhorred. Here sits my my noble and learned friend in the decision of most important causes, week after week, without either salary or pension. This ought not to be. But a remedy may easily be adopted at a very small expense to the public." [1]

Accordingly he prepared and introduced a bill which created a President of the Court, with a salary of £2,000 a year, and precedence immediately after the Lord Privy Seal; gave the President two puisnes with £1500 and £1200 respectively, and contained several other clauses enlarging the jurisdiction of the Court. On the second reading he again entered at great length into the constitution of the tribunal, and the necessity for having paid judges to serve upon it.

Lord Campbell.—" This House is to consider only what the public good requires; and, getting on very satisfactorily as we are, either with or without my noble friend, I

[1] 72 Hansard, 467.

can not imagine why your Lordships should make any change. For three years I have attended assiduously and contentedly, deeming that I have reward enough in rendering some small service to my country. If we are to have a new head, how do the necessities of justice require that the head should be of the quality here described? I know not who the new head is to be; as to this we can only form a not improbable conjecture. But I discover from the bill that the head is to be of high rank in the Court and out of the Court : he is to take precedence of all Barons, Viscounts, Earls, Marquesses, and Dukes, Knights of the Bath, Knights of the Thistle, Knights of St. Patrick, Knights of the Garter, in this House, in the Privy Council, at Coronations, Levées, and Drawing-rooms, and on all occasions, judicial, social, solemn, or merry. I am and shall continue proud of the tribunal of which I happen to be an unworthy member; but I can not conceive how its dignity or efficiency can depend on its head having such unprecedented heraldic distinction. I shall not object to the bill being read a second time; but unless it be materially altered, I shall not be able to give my assent to it."

The bill being read a second time was referred to a Select Committee.[1] But the job was attacked by the Press in a manner which induced the noble and learned Lord, when naming the Select Committee, to say :—

"I am rather astonished—if indeed, after living so long, I can be astonished by anything—that the motive assigned to me for bringing in this bill is that I want to make a place for myself. However, I ought not to be astonished at this assertion, considering the numerous race it belongs to— engendered by malice and her bastard sister falsehood —both begotten by the father of lies upon the weakness of human nature. The person who put forth the story ought to have reflected that anything more absurd could not have been devised by the wit of man. It is a perfectly notorious fact that I have refused such an offer three times over, and when my noble and learned friend on the wool-

---

[1] 73 Hansard, 691. Brougham said the intention of the bill was to give precedence to the new President only while sitting in Court, but it was anxiously framed to give it in all places and at all times. Indeed, his precedence in Court required no special enactment. Brougham, by no means covetous of money, would have cared very little for the proposed salary, but would have had great delight in the proposed precedence. Such weaknesses are to be found united with high aspirations.

sack and another noble friend pressed me to it, and when,
if I had consented, the bill would have been brought in
with all the weight of the Government, I refused it. I did
not then see the necessity for it as I now do."[1]

Upon this Lord John Russell, leader of the Opposition
in the Commons, put a question to Sir Robert Peel, the
Prime Minister, in the following terms:—

"I wish to call the attention of the right honorable
gentleman and of the House to a very extraordinary
statement which I think the right honorable gentleman
will himself be happy to contradict. It is said that a very
eminent person, some time ago, received an offer no less
than three times repeated to place him at the head of the
Judicial Committee of the Privy Council as a permanent
Judge. It would seem the more wise and usual course, if
the Government considered such a judge necessary, for
them to introduce their own bill and to carry their bill
through Parliament, and to allow it to receive the royal
assent, before an offer was made to any individual of the
new judgeship. It certainly seems a most extraordinary,
—not to call it a suspicious course, to propose to any
individual, however eminent, that he should accept such
an appointment, there being at that time no office of the
kind in existence, and the proposed office being connected
with the Privy Council,—always considered to be so immediately under the control of the sovereign."

Sir Robert Peel was dreadfully puzzled, for he now
heard of this "New President" for the first time. He
would not pervert the truth, and having had such steady
support from Brougham, he was loth to affront him. But
the following sentence contradicts Brougham very flatly,
although not in express words:—

"If the bill in the House of Lords for appointing a
President of the Judicial Committee comes down to this
House, I have as unfettered a right to exercise a discre-
tion with respect to it as the noble Lord himself."[2]

Brougham immediately abandoned the clauses in the
bill about the new judgeship, and the bill passed, merely
altering in some particulars the jurisdiction of the Court.
The newspapers now blamed him for abandoning the
clauses about the new judgeship when he found that he

---

[1] 73 Hansard, 796.   [2] 73 Hansard, 1728.

could not be the judge, and he again complained in the House of Lords—

"That nothing could be more scandalous, false, and audacious, for he had explained in his place that he never had a thought of being a candidate for the judgeship."[1]

I am bound to say that in this affair we have an illustration of the remark I have before made respecting Brougham's strange practice of recklessly making statements in the presence of those who he knew might, if so inclined, have flatly contradicted him. But, to use a favorite phrase of his own, he really seemed at times to labor under a "hallucination," which disturbed his judgment, confused the boundary between memory and imagination, annihilated undoubted facts, and gave him a momentary belief in that which never had existed. Although his statements were not much relied upon, he never had the reputation of a willful teller of falsehoods, and he always maintained his position in society as a gentleman. His supposed entire want of sincerity may perhaps be explained by the diversity of feelings which agitated his mind at different times, rather than by his consciously expressing sentiments, which at the time of expressing them he did not entertain.

I passed the autumn of 1844 at Boulogne. Knowing that Brougham would be passing through on his way to the Chateau Eleanor Louise, I thought that after our recent encounters in the House of Lords he might avoid me, but he found me out—employed upon my biographical work. We were cordial as usual, and he warmly invited me to visit him in Provence,—saying, "Mind, if you do not come, I will write the 'Lives of the Chancellors,' publish before you, and take the wind out of your sails."

We did not meet again till the beginning of the following Session of Parliament. In the interval I received several letters from him, which I have not preserved. Sometimes they contained observations upon individuals, which showed that they were sent on an implied understanding that they should be burnt as soon as read; but generally, they were upon very trifling matters, certainly not written to be published.

[1] 76 Hansard, 778.

The Session of 1845 was exceedingly dull. Peel was now transcendently powerful, and party struggles had almost ceased. In the Lords there was no one to lead the Opposition. Lord Melbourne had suffered from an attack of paralysis, and although he had so far recovered as to be able to come down to the House, he was in such a shattered condition that he was not allowed to speak. Under these circumstances Lord Lansdowne refused to act as leader, and there was no one else who could be recognized in that capacity.

Brougham had an easy time of it as Protector of the Government. However, daily speaking was necessary to him, and I find in the volumes of Hansard for this Session, no fewer than one hundred and seventy-four of his speeches reported.[1] But these were almost all upon subjects of temporary interest.

One great speech he made on Law Reform, detailing, with great minuteness (the Peers thought *tediousness*), what he had proposed, what been had done, and what remained to be done. He concluded by laying on the table nine new bills, for the amendment of the law, and moving that they be read a first time. But, to his great mortification, although there was a numerous attendance of peers when he began, they were now reduced to three besides the orator, viz., the Lord Chancellor on the woolsack, Lord Warncliffe on the Ministerial side, and Lord Campbell representing the Opposition.[2]

I can find no discussions during this Session more interesting than those which frequently recurred about the "New Houses of Parliament." In these Brougham took a leading part, frequently abusing Gothic architecture, Barry the architect, and Prince Albert for protecting him. The Prince thought to appease him by asking him to dine

[1] See Index to vol. lxxxii. I am shocked to say that I found 117 of my own, most of them, I believe, provoked by Brougham. Without his help the House would often have adjourned immediately after prayers, instead of sitting to the late hour of half-past seven.

[2] 80 Hansard, 515. His pet bill of the nine was a bill to establish Courts of Reconciliation, by which no suit was to be commenced in a Court of Law till the parties themselves, without counsel or attorney, had been before the Judge of Reconcilement, forgetting that nineteen-twentieths of the suits commenced are for undisputed debts, and that with respect to the remaining twentieth, the parties themselves would be quite incompetent to state their claims, and the personal altercation would take away all chance of settlement or compromise. Of the nine bills only two passed, and they of a trifling nature.

with the Queen. He went and dined, but widened his breach with the Court, by leaving the palace immediately after dinner, instead of going with the rest of the gentleman into the gallery, into which the Queen had retired with the ladies, and where she is in the habit of conversing with her guests. He afterwards tried to make amends by attending the Queen's drawing-room,—a condescension he had not before practiced since her accession; but here again he was unfortunate (although I really believe he wished to be civil and respectful) by speaking to the Queen *ex mero motu* as he passed her, and telling her that "he was to cross over to Paris in a few days, where he should see Louis Philippe, and that if her Majesty had any letters or messages for the King of the French, it would give him much pleasure to have the honor of being the bearer of them." Her Majesty declined, not entirely concealing her surprise at the offer, and I believe that he has not been at the English Court since.

In the autumn of 1845, Brougham repaired as usual to his chateau at Cannes. When he left England Sir Robert Peel appeared to be established as Prime Minister for life. Chartism was extinguished by the strong arm of the law, and still more by the increased demand for labor in all departments of industry. The Whigs were prostrate, and despaired of ever rising again. An agitation was kept up by the Corn Law League for free trade in corn, but it made little progress, and the "sliding scale" was expected to be permanent. Before Brougham returned to England Sir Robert Peel had resigned; the leader of the Whigs had been entrusted by the Queen to form a new Government, and had failed in the attempt, and Sir Robert Peel, resuming his situation, had, with the concurrence of all his colleagues except Lord Stanley, pledged himself to abandon the sliding scale, and to abolish the Corn Laws. This revolution was caused by a microscopic insect gnawing the roots of a plant which essentially contributes to the food of one portion of the United Kingdom, and constitutes almost the entire support of another. Brougham long heard with incredulity the rumors of the "Potato Famine," and the political consequences which it was likely to produce; but the appalling intelligence at at last reached him that Lord John Russell was at the head of a new Whig Government. Where were now his prospects of being Peel's Chancellor on the retirement of Lyndhurst? The Whigs again in power! Nor had he the consolation of looking forward to an internecine conflict with them, for their Government was to be founded on principles of free trade, of which he had always been the advocate, and there might be serious difficulty in standing up for his boasted consistency if he were now to go over to *Protection*. But he was recompensed for all this mortification and anxiety by the happy tidings that Lord Grey's fantastical objection to Lord Palmerston being Foreign Secretary had demolished the Whig Government, and that he himself might still be the advocate of Prime Minister Peel, and the "hammer of the Whigs." In the beginning of January, 1846, he cheerily re-crossed the Estrelles, impatient for the coming Session, when his consequence would be enhanced by Peel's embarrassments, and the late reward might be expected of his steady partisanship.

It is my duty, however, as a true and impartial biographer, to relate that he was made very unhappy at this time by the successful publication of my "Lives of the Chancellors." There is no disguising the fact that jealousy, even of very inferior men, is a striking defect in Brougham's character, and betrays him into very unbecoming practices. He went about almost in a state of fury, abusing the "Lives of the Chancellors." He wrote himself, or induced others to write, in periodicals over which he had influence, stinging articles against the book and its author. The most formidable of these was in the *Law Review* of which he was, and for years has continued to be, the director. But much coarser abuse was poured out in a succession of "Letters" which appeared in the *Morning Herald*, long the vehicle of his attacks upon those who displeased him. To my great surprise he one day voluntarily assured me that he was not the author of these "Letters." I answered that I was bound to suppose they were written by some one who had maliciously imitated his style. However, the subject was not further alluded to in conversation between us, and we were soon again friends as before.

The repeal of the Corn Laws had been recommended in the Speech from the throne, and the whole Session was occupied with that measure and its consequences. Brougham, although professing Free-trade doctrines, had been very hostile to the Corn-Law League, and had very scurrilously assailed Mr. Cobden and his associates, when they pressed Peel for an utter abrogation of the monopoly of the native corn growers, contending that the "sliding scale" was entirely at variance with the principle on which, by his new tariff, he had admitted so many articles, the raw produce of other countries, to be imported duty free. To show his *consistency* Brougham now said:—

"If am asked, Am I am one of the League or one of followers of the League, or one of the allies or one of the accomplices of the League? I answer, GOD FORBID! From the members of the Anti-corn-law League I differ even more than from those who stand forward as the friends and advocates of *Protection.*"

He then proceeded to argue that under a representative monarchy (the best of all governments), the task of governing the people should be left to the monarch and the representatives elected by the people, without the people themselves interfering, and he strongly condemned a recommendation of Lord Stanley, that before a complete change in our commercial system, there ought to be a dissolution of Parliament, so that the sense of the people might be taken upon it. Being reminded, while speaking, by an irregular interjection, of the dissolution during the "Reform Bill," he said:—

"I do not mean to deny that there are cases of such vast and paramount importance as absolutely to require that the Executive Government should appeal to the people. If I were to single out from all political questions any one upon which it is expedient not to make these constant appeals to the people, I should say it is precisely on such a question as this." [1]

Brougham did not then foresee that when the measure was carried, Peel himself, to spite the Protectionists, would ascribe the victory to the *unadorned eloquence* of Richard Cobden.

At the beginning of the Session, Brougham was sanguine in the hope that the bill being carried by his assistance, Peel would remain in office, and that there might be an official relationship established between them. And so it might have happened if Disraeli had not been raised up

[1] 83 Hansard, 29.

as the unconscious benefactor of the Whigs. But this consummate master of vituperation, thinking to lay the foundation of a great party to be formed from the defeated Protectionists, so exasperated them against Peel, that they were willing to do anything to be revenged upon him, and even to assist in restoring a Whig Government.

Before the Corn-Law Abolition Bill came up from the Commons to the House of Lords, there had been a division there, portentous to the Peelites. I must confess, that upon cool reflection, I feel considerable remorse for the part I took upon this occasion in opposition to Brougham and Lyndhurst, although at the moment, while under factious excitement, I rejoiced in it. The Chancellor had introduced a bill for the "Regulation of Charities," which was very objectionable in some of its details, but which, I am now afraid, was right in principle, and might have been so amended as to be made salutary. However, the Protectionist Peers, in their rage against the Government, offered to vote against it on the second reading, and the Whigs found the temptation into which they were led too strong to be resisted.

The argument was against us, but the Protectionists were with us, and upon a division we had a comfortable majority. This sounded the knell of the Peelites, and Brougham had before him the near and painful prospect of a Whig administration. Still, however, the Corn-Law Abolition Bill had not passed the Lords, and the exact manner in which Sir Robert Peel was to be ejected could not be foretold.

During the great debate on the second reading of the Corn-Law Abolition Bill in the Lords, the House presented a most singular spectacle, and many considered the result doubtful. If the voting had been by ballot, there would certainly have been a large majority of Noncontents. But the Duke of Wellington exerted himself to the utmost to carry the bill, as it had been recommended by the Crown, and was warmly approved of by the Commons. When peers of his party came to him to say how they disliked it, and how they wished to be allowed to vote against it, he said to them, "You can not dislike the bill more than I do, but we must all vote for it." The Peelite peers in the Cabinet made a wretched figure, for in the preceding month of November they had tendered their resignation rather than agree to the measure, and they were then, on principle, sincere and strenuous Protectionists. The Whig leaders alone stood on safe ground, as they had always been for Free Trade; when in office they had proposed to abolish the sliding scale, and they had to defend their own policy, adopted by their opponents. Brougham answered Lord Stanley,—who, having left Peel, and become the head of the Protectionist and high Tory party, had laid himself open to attack by his estimate of the unlimited quantity of wheat which might be suddenly produced in the steppes of Russia, and thrown into the English ports. However, he was treated with much tenderness and courtesy by Brougham, who reserved his sarcasms for the Whigs, and put forth all his strength in a panegyric on Peel. This was his peroration:—

"I should fail of discharging a duty which I owe as a citizen of this country, and as a member of this House—a debt of gratitude on public grounds, but a debt of strict justice as well—did I not express my deep sense of the public virtue, no less than the great capacity and the high moral courage which my right honorable friend at the head of the Government has exhibited in dealing with this question. He cast away all personal and private considerations of what description soever, and, studiously disregarding his own interest in every stage and step of his progress, he has given up what to a political leader is the most enviable of all positions,—the calm, unquestioned, undivided support of Parliament; he has exposed himself to the frenzy of the most tempest-troubled sea that the political world in our days perhaps ever exhibited. He has given up what to an ambitious man is much—the security of his power; he has given up what to a calculating man is much—influence and authority with his party; he has given up what to an amiable man is much indeed—private friendships and party connections; and all these sacrifices he has voluntarily encountered, in order to discharge what (be he right or wrong) he deemed a great public duty. He in these circumstances—he in this proud position—may well scorn the sordid attacks, the wretched ribaldry with which he is out of doors assailed, because he knows that he has entitled himself to the gratitude of his country, and will leave—as I in my conscience believe —his name to after ages as one of the greatest and most disinterested Ministers that ever wielded the destinies of this country." [1]

The second reading was carried by a majority of forty-seven, and thereby the principle of Free Trade was forever established in England, ere long to spread over the globe.

The bill having passed both Houses and received the royal assent, Peel only looked for the first opportunity of decently retiring. It was rumored that Brougham advised him to remain, offering to "stand by him," but I have no sufficient authority for this statement, which may have originated merely from the notion of what was probable. Although Peel's character afterwards rose very much in public estimation from experience of the good consequences of his policy, and from his violent and sudden death,[2] he was not at this time by any means generally popular. Not only was he odious to the landed interest, but the sudden wheel which he made on the question of the corn laws—after that which he made on Catholic Emancipation—lowered him much in the estimation of many dispassionate persons, who thought that if he had sincerely changed his opinions upon such important measures, he ought to have resigned and allowed them to be carried by the party which had always supported them. He discovered even that many of his own subordinates now looked upon him very coolly, complaining that he had encouraged them at the last general election to advocate "Protection" when he had resolved to abolish the corn laws, and that to gratify his fantasy they were all now about to be thrown destitute upon the wide world, whereas they might all have remained comfortably in office for many years to come. Therefore, although he had once hoped to establish Free Trade and to remain Minister, he was now fully aware of his true situation, and he felt

---

[1] 86 Hansard, 1176. The subsequent discussions on the bill were very prolix and very uninteresting.

[2] The fame with posterity of a man's actions during his life depends much upon the time and manner of his death. If Peel had lived on in the common routine of Parliamentary warfare, and died of old age, he would have had no statues erected to his memory. Had Louis Philippe fallen fighting in the insurrection of 1848, he would have been reckoned a great sovereign. Melbourne would have stood much better in history if he had died the day he resigned in 1841, instead of languishing several years a paralytic.

that not only was there a majority against him in the present Parliament, but that upon a dissolution this majority would very probably be increased.

His next measure pressed in the House of Commons was an Irish Coercion Bill, which had passed the Lords though opposed by the Whigs, Brougham shunning all the discussions upon it. The Tory Protectionists might rather have been expected to support it,

"For Tories know no argument but force."

On the contrary, they were impatient to throw it out. The struggle took place on the second reading. The amendment that the bill be read a second time that day six months was taken as a vote of "want of confidence," and after a debate of six nights the amendment was carried by a majority of seventy-three.[1]

A declaration to both Houses of the resignation of Ministers immediately followed, and Brougham had the mortification to see a purely Whig Government re-established with Lord John Russell as Prime Minister. However, I must do my noble and learned friend the justice to say that he bore the reverse with apparent good-humor. On the day when the new Ministers were installed he very courteously congratulated me on my elevation to the Cabinet as Chancellor of the Duchy of Lancaster, telling me I should how have ample opportunity of seeing "quantula sapientia regatur mundus." Hitherto Brougham had never sat on the same side of the house with the Tories; but the Whigs now taking possession of the Ministerial benches on the right of the throne, he did not go over with us, and as he remained behind on the Opposition side, he might at last have truly said in defense of his consistency, "the Tories have come over to me."

The new Government tested its strength by a Free Trade Sugar Bill, making no distinction as to import duties between free-grown sugar and slave-grown sugar. This the Protectionists, headed by Brougham, violently opposed under pretense of an anxiety to put down slavery; but the bill was carried by a large majority,[2] and the session closed with auspicious prospects for the Russell Administration.

[1] 87 Hansard, 1027.   [2] 88 Hansard, 467, 468.

CHAPTER CCXXX.

FROM THE BEGINNING OF THE SESSION OF 1847, TILL THE OVERTHROW OF THE DERBYITES.

WHEN Parliament met in the beginning of the following year, Brougham boldly and openly avowed himself a leader of the Opposition. He took part among the Protectionists in line, fronting the Ministerialists, whom he was assailing. When I congratulatd Lord Stanley upon this accession to his ranks, I warned him against the expectation of finding the recruit well disciplined, and advised him to be contented if he had the "irregular services of a Cossack." No one understood him better than Stanley, who was well pleased while in opposition to court him by all reasonable compliances, but was always cautious not to form any *liaison* with him which might be embarrassing when the time should come for forming a new Government.

Brougham was exceedingly active during the whole of this Session, but he could do no effectual injury to the Government; for as the Peelite peers hated Protectionists more than Whigs, we could command a majority on every division. I now avoided personal altercations with my "noble and learned friend," and handed him over to the new Lord Grey—become a member of the Upper House and Colonial Secretary—who still fostering the notion that Brougham, when Chancellor, had behaved treacherously to the illustrious author of the Reform Bill, took great delight in any favorable opportunity for attacking him.

I was obliged, however, to enter the lists when Stanley and Brougham combined against me respecting the appointment of four extraordinary members of the Council of the Duchy of Lancaster. I successfully turned the matter into ridicule, and said that I wanted assistance to manage the agricultural affairs of the Duchy, for here I was as ignorant as my noble and learned friend, who, when the famous Mr. Coke (afterwards Earl of Leicester) showed him a luxuriant field of drilled wheat, exclaimed, "What beautiful *lavender* you raise in Norfolk." Brougham renewed the laughter against himself by asserting that he was well acquainted with the difference between *wheat* and *lavender*, and that the story was a weak invention of the enemy.

To make it all up I invited him and Stanley to dine with me, that I might introduce them to the new Councillors of the Duchy. They very good-naturedly accepted, and, meeting likewise Lord John Russell, Lyndhurst, and several other leaders of contending factions, we made a "happy family," and had a very merry evening. During a lamentation upon the usual dullness of the House of Lords, Brougham rather took this as a reflection upon himself, who was the most constant reformer there, and he declared that he had made better speeches in the House of Lords than he had ever made in the House of Commons. I could only compare him to Milton, who preferred "Paradise Regained" to "Paradise Lost."

A few days before the prorogation he made a very long and elaborate, but very unsuccessful speech, taking a review of the Session, in imitation of Lyndhurst. He first *heavily* blamed Ministers for all they had done, and much which they had omitted to do in the Upper House. He then descended into the inferior region of the House of Commons, quoting the well-known lines:—

"Ibant obscuri sola sub nocte per umbram,
Perque domos Ditis vacuas, et inania regna."

Where nothing could be seen but the ghosts of slaughtered bills—

"Impositique rogis juvenes ante ora parentum."

He concluded by expressing a hope of better things from the approaching dissolution and general election.

"When the Parliament was again restored to its functions, he trusted he should never again have to witness or to lament over the history of such a Session—a Session disheartening and disappointing to the people; ruinous to the character of the Government; injurious even to the Constitution, and damaging beyond the power of language to describe to the reputation of this great country all over the world."[1]

The truth was that the attention of the Government and of the public had been most exclusively devoted to the measures brought forward to alleviate the sufferings of Ireland from famine and pestilence; and Lyndhurst,

[1] 94 Hansard, 570.

finding that he could on this occasion make nothing of his annual review, cunningly asked Brougham to undertake it, and added to his own fame by the failure of a rival.

Brougham had the mortification to find that the elections went strongly in favor of the Whig Government, and he was so much disappointed that, during the short session of Parliament held in the autumn, he confined himself to a few desultory speeches every evening on presenting petitions.

Sacrificing the pleasure he usually enjoyed at this season of the year in breathing the soft breezes of Provence, he continued amidst the fogs of London till Christmas, attending the sittings of the Judicial Committee of the Privy Council, and watching over the declining health of the Lord Chancellor.

In the end of November Lord Cottenham had burst a blood-vessel, and it was generally supposed that he never would sit in Court again. While I was reading one evening in the Library of the House of Lords, Brougham came up to me, and the following dialogue passed between us: *B.*—" Since Denman's Act makes a witness who is interested competent to give evidence, tell me how Cottenham is." *C.*—" I hear it reported that you are to succeed him." *B.*—" If I were to take the Great Seal again, my first proceeding ought to be to seal a commission of lunacy against myself." *C.*—" Nevertheless some say that you are the only man now fit to be Chancellor." *B.*—" I assure you I never wished to have the Great Seal back again after I had resigned it. If Melbourne had only treated me with common courtesy, we never need have quarreled; and what madness would it be now for me to take such an office when I have no child to be the better for my toils." Here the tears came into his eyes and rolled down his cheeks. *C.*—" But one difficulty is, that Cottenham is recovering, and talks of sitting in Court again next week." *B.*—" If he makes that attempt, a commission of lunacy ought to be sealed against *him.* The blood-vessel, though a small one, was in his lungs. Now is your time." He returned to his difference with the Whigs, which he said was all Melbourne's fault. I observed with perfect sincerity that " I thought it was a most unfortunate occurrence, and that I had always deeply regretted it."

Cottenham grew worse, and a paragraph appeared in

the newspapers stating that I was likely to be the new Chancellor. This brought out a series of scurrillous articles in the *Morning Herald* (Brougham's organ), vilifying me, and attempting to prove that I was wholly unfit for the office. In the morning when one of these appeared, as I was walking through the Horse Guards to the Judicial Committee in Downing Street, Brougham's carriage drove through at a quick pace, and nearly knocked me over without his seeing me. When we met I told him of my narrow escape, adding, "You seem strongly inclined to *run me down*."

It so happened that we now had an Equity appeal from Jamaica to dispose of. With the strange insincerity and inconsistency of his character he whispered in my ear, "You must deliver the judgment in this case. It would have a bad effect at this time if you were to appear to shirk it." And he actually contrived to have the task assigned to me of delivering the judgment.

A few days after, Edward Ellice took me into a corner at Brookes's, and spoke thus:—"Well, I believe all is going right. Johnny has been to consult Melbourne, who I know is on your side. This morning whom did I see at Melbourne's but Brougham? when Melbourne, who is the indiscreetest of mankind, said to him, 'You must lay your account with seeing Jack Campbell Chancellor.' Brougham then inveighed against you, and said he would never sit in the House of Lords with such a Chancellor; declared that it would be a mad appointment, as it would disgust the Equity bar, and a bad one for the public, as you would not venture to overrule the Vice-Chancellors; that Rolfe was the man who would please the profession and the Peers. I said, 'Campbell is the very man to do his duty boldly; although I should have been better pleased to see him Chief Justice of the Queen's Bench, if Denman were to resign.' He declared that you were equally unfit for that office, and that what law you might ever have had you must have forgotten. Melbourne said, 'Nevertheless, Brougham, you must be prepared to see Jack holding the Great Seal.'"

Whimsical change! Brougham and Lord Melbourne in familiar intercourse—gossiping about giving away the Great Seal after their bitter quarrel and mortal enmity, occasioned by this "pestiferous bauble!"

In the beginning of January Cottenham recovered, the articles against me in the *Herald* ceased to appear, and Brougham went to his chateau at Cannes.

Passing through Paris, he, as usual, paid his respects to Louis Philippe, and attended a meeting of the Institute. Paris was a little agitated by the coming political banquets which the Government had prohibited; but although there was a considerable outcry about the "Spanish marriages," no serious apprehension was entertained, and the Orleans dynasty seemed firmly fixed upon the throne of France. The only doubt was whether the aged Sovereign would survive till his grandson, the Comte de Paris, should be of age. Louis Philippe, jumping over a rail to show his agility and strength, exclaimed prophetically and truly, "Il n'y aura pas de régence."

There was no regency; for in a few weeks Louis Philippe was an exile, and his dynasty overthrown.

Brougham was at his chateau near Cannes when the Revolution took place, which placed France under the arbitrary rule of the Provisional Government formed by the contributors to a newspaper. It might have been supposed that he would immediately fly to England, and assist by his advice in guarding his native country from the new perils with which she was threatened. But a strange phantasy entered his brain. The Provisional Government had called a National Assembly, to be elected by universal suffrage, "all Frenchmen of the age of twenty-one years to be electors, and all Frenchmen of twenty-five years to be eligible," with an allowance of twenty-five francs a day to each deputy during the session. The department of the *Var*, in which Brougham's chateau stands, was to have nine deputies. Many candidates came forward, in the hope of being enriched by the promised daily stipend: but Brougham had far loftier views. He counted with certainty on making a distinguished figure in the Assembly by his eloquence, and he sanguinely believed that, from his superior knowledge of parliamentry tactics, he might gain such an ascendency as to be elected President, and so guide the destinies of France, of Europe, and of the world. He announced himself as a candidte for the department of the Var, and he was well received by the inhabitants of Cannes, who were flattered by the preference he had shown for them, who were pleased by his popular manners, and who hoped by his influence to obtain another *subvention* for the completion of their harbor. He knew that Tom Paine, Anacharsis Clootz, and several other foreigners, had sat in the first National Assembly, and, having been long a *propriétaire* in France, he did not anticipate any difficulty from his having been born in Scotland. He was told by the authorities of his department that, before he could either vote or be elected, as he had no qualification by birth, he must produce an "acte de naturalization," but that this might easily be obtained at Paris upon the formal certificates which would be forwarded to the Minister of Justice.

To Paris accordingly he posted—meeting (as he afterwards told me) trees of Liberty planted in every town and village through which he traveled, with the inscription *Liberté, Egalité, Fraternité.* He asserted that during his whole journey he refused the usual homage demanded of travelers—to be uncovered, and to repeat these mystical words—as he foresaw that the madness of the people would be short-lived. Nay, he added that he sometimes harangued them at considerable length, in the hope of bringing them to a better mind. But it is difficult to conceive how at the beginning of his candidature he should be guilty of such imprudence. Although he smarted under the forced payment of the "additional *centimes*," a tax imposed by the Provisional Government under the despotic power which they had assumed—he must have been reluctant to insult the emblems of the *régime* which he was to swear that he would support.

As soon as he reached Paris he addressed a letter to Citoyen Crémieux, Minister of Justice, and the following correspondence passed between them:

"Paris, April 7th, 1848.

"Lord Brougham has the honor to offer his respects to the Minister of Justice; and wishing to be naturalized in France, he has demanded certificates from the Mayor of Cannes (Var), where he has resided for the last thirteen years, and where he possesses a landed estate, and has built for himself a country-house (chateau). Those certificates are to be forwarded directly to the Minister of Justice, and Lord Brougham requests the Minister to transmit to him the act of naturalization with as little delay as possible."

"*The Minister of Justice to Lord Brougham.*

"Paris, April 8th, 1848.

"My Lord,—I must apprise you of the consequences of the naturalization you demand, should you obtain it. If France adopts you for one of her sons, you cease to be an Englishman; you are no longer Lord Brougham, you become citizen Brougham. You lose forthwith all titles of nobility, all privileges, all advantages of whatever nature they may be, which you possessed, either in your quality of Englishman, or by virtue of rights hitherto conferred upon you by British laws or customs, and which can not harmonize with our law of equality between all citizens. This would be the effect, my lord, even did not the British laws possess that rigor with regard to those British citizens who demand and obtain their naturalization in foreign countries. It is in this sense that you must write to me. I must presume that the late British Chancellor is aware of the necessary consequences of so important a demand. But it is the duty of the Minister of Justice of the French Republic to warn you officially. When you shall have made a demand in form embracing those declarations, it shall be immediately examined.

"A. Cremieux."

Brougham was much surprised and mortified by this rebuff. His vision of Gallic greatness vanished; he could no longer even expect the honor of delivering a speech in the National Assembly, and he was afraid of the ridicule to which this unsuccessful attempt might expose him among his friends of the Institute. He therefore resolved to proceed immediately to England. There, at any rate, he must have agreeable excitement, and his abortive citizenship would escape notice in the crisis which seemed approaching, for the 10th of April was the day fixed for the Chartist insurrection in London.

During his passage across the Channel, however, he thought that he might answer the objections to his naturalization, and possibly gain his object, without sacrificing his English peerage and his English pension. Accordingly, the moment he entered his house in Grafton Street, without consulting any human being, he wrote and despatched the following missive:—

"London, April 10th, 1848.

"Monsieur le Ministre,—I have the honor to acknowledge the receipt of your obliging letter of the 8th. I never doubted that by causing myself to be naturalized a French citizen I should lose all my rights as a British Peer and a British subject in France. I will retain my privileges as an Englishman only in England; in France I should be all that the laws of France accord to the citizens of the Republic. As I desire, above all, the happiness of the two countries, and their mutual peace, I thought it my duty to give a proof of my confidence in the French institutions, to encourage my English countrymen to confide in them as I do.

"H. BROUGHAM."

The following answer was received in course of post:—

"Paris, April 12th, 1848.

"MY LORD,—My letter has not been understood. Yours, to my great regret, does not permit me to comply with your demand. You do me the honor to write to me, 'I never doubted," &c. [Copying Lord B.'s letter.] I used the clearest and most positive expressions in my letter. France admits no partition—she admits not that a French citizen shall at the same time be the citizen of another country. In order to become a Frenchman, you must cease to be an Englishman. You can not be an Englishman in England, and a Frenchman in France; our laws are absolutely opposed to it. You must necessarily choose. It was for that reason that I took care to explain to you the consequence of naturalization. In that position, therefore, and as long as you will remain an Engliahman in England,—that is to say, as long as you will not abdicate completely and everywhere your quality of British subject, and exchange it for that of French citizen, it is impossible for me to give effect to your demand.

"A. CREMIEUX."

The correspondence was closed by a short note from Brougham to the Minister of Justice, formally renouncing all naturalization in France.

At the meeting of the House of Lords in the evening of the 10th of April, when by the judicious dispositions made under the advice of the Duke of Wellington, and, still more, by the good sense and spirited firmness of the great mass of the population of the metropolis, the Chartist movement, which many thought would revolutionize England, had proved an utter failure, Brougham presented himself in the House of Lords and took part in the discussion, as if he had never contemplated a divided allegiance, and he gave notice of a motion for the next day, that he might review the recent revolutionary proceedings in France, in Italy, and in Germany.

But the hope that his citizenship would pass unnoticed was disappointed. The Provisional Government having heard that he wished to enter the Assembly with no friendly intentions, not only refused his request, but immediately stated in one of their journals (the *Réforme*) that he had applied to be naturalized as a French citizen, and in a few days published in the *National* the whole of the correspondence between him and the Minister of Justice—to the great amusement of France and of England. In his elaborate speech on the 11th of April, he animadverted with much severity upon the Provisional Government in the country which he had recently visited. Thus he launched his sarcasms at his fellow-citizens with whom he still wished to fraternize:—

"I dispute not the right of five-and-thirty millions to bear the dominion of twenty thousand; and of the things which the chiefs of these men are now doing every day in the name of the whole people we have no right to complain; the fruits, the bitter fruits, will be gathered by themselves. My prayer is that they may be less bitter than I dread and believe." [1]

Lord Lansdowne, in answering him, observed that the expression of these sentiments gave him particular satisfaction, as they showed that there could be no foundation for the strange rumor which had been set afloat, that his noble and learned friend wished to become a naturalized French citizen, with a view of leading the debates in the French National Assembly, instead of continuing the ornament of their Lordships' House in which he had presided with so much luster.

He was treated with much severity by the press, both French and English. I shall give only two specimens. The *National* of April 18, 1848, contained a paragraph, of which the following is a literal translation:—

"So it was really no joke after all! Lord Henri Brougham really wished to become a citizen of France, and ad-

[1] 98 Hansard, 143.

dressed a formal demand to that effect to our Provisional Government! It is incredible, but true nevertheless. His Lordship, however, by no means intended to surrender his privileges as an English citizen. Milord wished to amalgamate the two. France is a beautiful country, no doubt; but England has also its attractions, which are not to be voluntarily abandoned. How to reconcile this double inclination? Milord had discovered a very ingenious plan, the contraction of a second marriage without dissolving the first. We remember hearing the story of the *conducteur* of a *diligence* who had one wife at Paris and another at Toulon, who went on very amicably for awhile, but at last the Toulon wife paid a visit to Paris, and discovered her rival. Lord Brougham conceived an idea not altogether dissimilar; in short, he contemplated the perpetration of a political bigamy! How will prudish England receive such a disclosure? We can not tell; but we confess that were we in the place of milord, we should feel slightly embarrassed. Let him extricate himself as he best can. Fortunately for us, it is his affair, not ours."

And the following is part of a leading atricle in the *Times* of the same date:—

" All who remember English history for the last forty years, speak of Henry Brougham as the most eccentric figure in that eventful period. So much of greatness in words, and so little dignity in action, have never been found in the same individual. Now shaking the House of Commons with his eloquence, and now exciting the laughter of schoolboys, still it is the same marvelous man. Lord Brougham has just thrown the highest somersault that he has ever accomplished. It is not sufficient for him to have played the Edinburgh Reviewer, the English Barrister, to have propounded startling theories in science, to have been created an English Peer, to have translated Demosthenes, and to have passed himself as the greatest orator of his age,—like Alexander, he sighed for other worlds, not to conquer, but in which to display his eccentricities. . . . A National Convention is still open to the *Citoyen Brougham*. He may yet rival Vergniaud in eloquence, and employ the remainder of his life in reconstituting civilization in France. For this turbid pre-eminence we find him almost ready to sacrifice ermine, coronet, pension, and all. When sacrificed at last before the rising demagogues of the new Mountain, and led off to the Place de la Republique in a cart, he will devote the brief minutes of his passage to chanting, with enthusiasm and strong Northumbrian burr,

'——— Mourir pour la Patrie,
C'est le sort le plus beau et le plus digne d'envie.' "

No other man than Brougham could have recovered from the unextinguishable ridicule which now seemed to overwhelm him. But I have already had occasion to celebrate the singular faculty which he possessed of again rising to the surface when it was thought he had sunk to rise no more, and of afterwards pursuing his course as if no misfortune had befallen him. He continued to speak every night upon every subject, except his correspondence with M. Crémieux. The nickname of "Citizen Brougham" did not fix itself upon him, as might have been expected, and at the end of a month it was forgotten that he had ever aspired to lead the debates in the French National Assembly.

During the remainder of this Session his hostility to the Government was much mitigated. He gave me very powerful support in carrying through the House of Lords a bill for amending the marriage law of Scotland. This was framed upon the principle that the parties should be allowed to enter into the most important of all contracts with any religious ceremony, or without any religious ceremony, as they pleased,—but by some palpable form, capable of easy and certain proof. Brougham discussed the subject several times with great force and effect, and although the bill had been strongly opposed at first, it was read a third time with one dissentient voice—that of the Earl of Aberdeen—who (as Brougham asserted) insisted upon marriage being retrospectively established by verbal acknowledgment, out of respect for the memory of his grandmother who had never been married at all, but had been made an honest woman of by acknowledgment long after the birth of her son, the present Earl's father. This joke reached his Lordship's ear and exasperated him so much that he vowed he would have the bill thrown out in the Commons; and as he showed much more vigor in opposing it than he afterwards did in opposing the Czar of Russia, he triumphed. Cunningly appealing to the thrift of the Scottish members, in canvassing them he contrived to persuade them that the registration of the marriage, which the bill required, would bring a heavy pecuniary burden upon Scotland. Thus Gretna Green still flourishes, and many persons in Scotland are unable to tell whether they are married or single, and many others whether they are legitimate or bastards.

Such an *entente cordial* was there now between my noble and learned friend and myself, that I could no longer refuse his often-repeated invitation that I would visit him in Westmorland. So, after the prorogation, accompanied by my wife and one of my daughters, I entered his mansion, formerely " Brougham Hall "—now simply " Brougham."

We were most hospitably and kindly received, and spent several days very agreeably in exploring the romantic beauties of Westmorland, and conversing with my " noble and learned friend." I really believe that both he and I were quite sincere for the moment in testifying good-will towards each other. Indeed I still feel, not only regret, but something savoring of remorse, when I am obliged, as a faithful biographer, to record anything which may seem not altogether to the credit of one with whom I have spent so many pleasant hours.

I did not see him again till the commencement of the following Session of Parliament in February, 1849. He then regularly enlisted himself under the Protectionist banner, and with respect to *whips, proxy, pairing,* and *divisions,* was considered one of that party as much as Lord Hardwicke, Lord Salisbury, Lord Redesdale, or any other of their oldest and most devoted adherents.

A Ministerial crisis was now expected from the proposal of the Whigs to abolish the Navigation Laws. All who had enlightened and disinterested views upon the subject had come to the conclusion that " free trade " could not be said to be established till commodities could be conveyed from one port to another in ships that might sail the fastest and at the lowest freight, whatever country they might belong to, and by whatever crew they might be worked. Therefore, after great deliberation, Lord John Russell's Cabinet resolved unanimously to bring forward a bill to abolish the Navigation Laws, and to stake our existence on its success. But the measure was by no means so popular as the repeal of the Corn Laws. All British shipholders thought that they had an interest in preserving their monopoly; our seamen were told they

would starve when Danes, Swedes, and Norwegians, who
could live on bread made of the bark of trees, were permitted
to come into competition with them; and a very
general prejudice prevailed even among men of education
not engaged in commerce, that our naval greatness depended
upon preventing foreign ships from trading to our
colonies, and requiring that commodities, the growth or
manufacture of foreign countries, should be imported into
the United Kingdom either in British ships or in ships of
the country in which the commodities are grown or manufactured.
As Brougham had always gloried in being the
apostle of Free Trade, and had assumed to himself much
of the merit of at last sweeping away the Corn Laws, it
might have been expected that he would be the philosophic
statesman and powerful orator who would on this
occasion quell the mercenary cry of self-interest, dispel
the delusion of the misguided, and, carrying out the principles
of Free Trade to their legitimate results, would have
quieted the apprehensions of well-meaning ignorance. But,
on the contrary, he placed himself at the head of the opponents
of the Ministerial measure, and, in the most unscrupulous
manner, called sordid self-interest, "crass ignorance,"
and vulgar prejudice to his aid. When the grand
battle was to be fought in the House of Lords on the second
reading of the bill, it had been arranged by Lord Stanley
that Lord Colchester, an old naval officer, should lead
the assault; but Brougham superseded him, his zeal and
impatience being kindled to the highest pitch by the intelligence
he received that, on counting the forces on both
sides, the Protectionists had superior numbers present in
the House, and were sure of victory.

He began, as usual, with a panegyric on his own consistency,
and asserted that from the year of grace 1801,
when he began to write his book on Colonial Policy, down
to the year of grace 1849, when he was addressing their
lordships, he had always stood up for the same doctrines
in political economy as well as in every other department
of political science; he allowed that the best and cheapest
conveyance of goods from port to port should be permitted
for the benefit of commerce—but then he went on to show
at prodigious length that the naval greatness of England,
and the safety of the country from foreign invasion, required

been enacted by the wisdom of our ancestors, and which every succeeding generation of English statesmen had applauded. He, of course, made much of Adam Smith having considered the English navigation laws wise and wholesome, and an illustrious exception to the general rule that trade should be free. A speech of three hours he thus concluded—alluding to the threat of Ministers to resign if they were beaten, and the probability of this threat being carried into execution:—

"I do not, on any account whatever, either public or private, from any feeling whether of a general or personal kind, desire to see a change of the Government. But the risk of any change I am prepared to meet rather than see the highest interests of the empire exposed to ruin. This measure I never can bear, because the national defense will not bear it. All lesser considerations of party policy or parliamentary tactics at once give way; and I have a question before me on which I can not pause or falter, or treat or compromise. I know my duty, and I will perform it; as an honest man, an Englishman, a peer of Parliament, I will lift that voice to resist the further progress of the bill."[1]

After a second night's debate the division took place, and Brougham's anticipation of triumph seemed verified, for of the peers present only 105 said *content* and 119 said *non-content*, giving the Protectionists a majority of 14. But proxies were called, and the Lord-Lieutenant of Ireland, and all the peers holding diplomatic appointments on the continent of Europe, with other noble Government functionaries who were absent, having left their proxies with Lord Lansdowne, there were 44 absentees who supported the Navigation Laws, while 68 absentees condemned them. So the bill was read a second time by a majority of 10.

Articles appeared in the *Morning Herald* on the abuse of proxies, and the lords were threatened, not only with the loss of their anomalous privilege of voting without listening to the arguments for or against the proposition to be determined, but with an entire subversion of all their constitutional powers. Meanwhile, it was felt that the crisis was over, that Free Trade had triumphed, and

---

[1] According to his practice when he had made what he considered a great speech, he published this speech, "revised by himself," as a pamphlet.

that the Government was safe. Brougham and Lord Stanley expressed a confident hope that in the committee on the bill (where, according to well-established usage, proxies are not admitted) they should so mutilate the bill as to render it harmless; and in the committee they moved an amendment to effectuate their object; but this was not considered fair parliamentary warfare; the muster of Protectionist peers fell off, and the amendment was rejected by a majority of 13.

Brougham had been very sanguine, and was deeply mortified, but he affected hilarity, and allowed himself to be ralied by his familiars upon his disappointment. While the Navigation Bill was depending, I happened to call upon him one morning in Grafton street to talk to him about a Scotch appeal, and was shown into his library. He soon rushed in very eargerly, but suddenly stopped short, exclaiming, "Lord bless me, is it you? they told me it was Stanley;" and notwithstanding his accustomed frank and courteous manner, I had some difficulty in fixing his attention. In the evening I stepped across the House to the Opposition Bench where Brougham and Stanley were sitting next each other, and addressing the latter in the hearing of the former, I said,—" Has our noble and learned friend told you the disappointment he suffered this morning? He thought he had a visit from the Leader of the Protectionists to offer him the Great Seal, and it turned out to be only Campbell come to bore him about a point of Scotch law." *Brougham:* "Don't mind what Jack Campbell says: he has a prescriptive privilege to tell lies of all Chancellors dead and living."

Many jokes were circulated against Brougham on this occasion. A few days after his great speech I myself heard Lyndhurst say to him,—" Brougham, here is a riddle for you. Why does Lord Brougham know so much about the *Navigation Laws? Answer.*—Because he has been so long engaged in the *Seal fishery.*"

During the remainder of this session Brougham continued exceedingly factious. He supported the bill I brought in to enable the Government to transport Smith O'Brien, convicted of high treason, instead of hanging and beheading him as the convict himself required; but he vigorously opposed almost every other bill of which I had the charge—particularly the Irish Encumbered Estates Bill—which has done more to tranquilize and to civilize Ireland than any other Saxon measure.

Having acted as Lord Commissioner in proroguing Parliament, I parted with Brougham on rather unfriendly terms, and I laid my account with his continuing pertinaciously in every way to hinder my advancement. But (strange to recollect) he had now formed the resolution that I should succeed Lord Denman in the Queen's Bench; and, if I had been his own brother, he could not more zealously have exerted himself to accomplish that object. During the autumn I received several letters from him on the subject. The last, beginning " My dear C., *vulgo* dearest Jack," contains the following postscript:—

"Between you and me, Denman will never sit again. My own opinion is that you *must* take it. Then if Cottenham goes you can easily slide in there. I have given this as my decided opinion to all inquiring friends. I am ready to stand by you *to the death* in BOTH arrangements, and in H. of Lords. This I do partly for your own sake, partly for the public; and you are at full liberty to quote me if of any use. Yours,

" H. B."

In December the great "Gorham Case" upon "Baptismal Regeneration" stood for hearing before the Judicial Committee of the Privy Council, and Brougham, who was then at Cannes, was very desirous of having it postponed that he might preside when it was adjudged. He had vast delight in playing the judge in any *cause célèbre*. " Il s'amuse à juger," said a Frenchman who had visited England and knew him well. When the occasion required he would boldly plunge into ecclesiastical law, and he had gained much notoriety by a judgment which he wrote upon the question whether a clergyman of the Church of England was bound to read the burial service over a child which had been baptized by a dissenting Minister—not by a priest episcopally ordained. He admitted that the dissenting minister was only to be considered a layman, but he showed that lay baptism in the form prescribed in the Gospels, is, according to the usage of the early Christians, the authority of the Fathers, the decrees of general councils and canons of the Church of England, sufficient to purge original sin and to convey saving grace, *tanquam instrumento*.[1] He would, no doubt, very learnedly have discussed the question whether "prevenient grace" was necessary to give full spiritual effect to the sacrament of baptism; but we could not decently keep the public three months longer in suspense to suit his convenience. I wrote to say that postponement was impossible, and explained to him the difficulty of putting off the hearing of a case upon which so much depended. In truth we were rather glad to dispose of it in his absence, for we were not sure what view he might have taken of it. In the course of the discussion there would have been great danger of his saying something which would have scandalized either the party inclining to Romanism or the party inclining to Calvinism, and for the peace of the Church we were glad to be able to decide, with the approbation of the two Archbishops, that Gorham, notwithstanding his opinion upon the necessiry of "prevenient grace," was entitled to be inducted and instituted.

Brougham was now deeply engaged in a course of experiments upon Light. He had told me that he had made a great discovery which "Newton had nearly approached, but had not reached." In passing through Paris, he explained it in a lecture to the Institute, assisted by diagrams which he drew with chalk on a black-board. I have been told that his brethren all showed great self-command in keeping their countenances while he addressed them in French (or, as Macaulay calls it, in "*Broughmee*"), but that in spite of all their politeness, some of them did smile a little at the supposed discovery, and the fluctional calculations by which it was proved and illustrated. The lecture was afterwards written out by him and published in the "Transactions of the Institute." A copy of it, which he was good enough to present to me, now lies before me, but I must confess my inability to criticise it. This, how

---

[1] Dr. Philpotts, Bishop of Exeter, in talking over this judgment with m allowed it to be *able*, but insisted that it was *defective*, by omitting the qualif cation that lay baptism, to be effectual, must be administered by a lay man c woman *in communion with the Church*, and that it is unavailing if adminis tered by a dissenting minister, who must be considered a heretic or schi matic. Such, however, is not the doctrine of the Church of England; an Brougham's judgment is still considered good law.

[2] Institut Impérial de France. ' Recherches Expérimentales et Analytique sur la Lumière.' Par Henri Lord Brougham, Associé Etranger de l'Institt Impérial, et Membre de la Société Royale de Londres et de l'Académi Royale de Naples.

ever, I will boldly say that Brougham must be a very extraodinary man to have delivered such a lecture, whatever solecisms in language or in science he may inadvertently have fallen into. Neither Lord Bacon nor Newton himself ever performed such a feat, and although Cicero did declaim in Greek, he confined himself to literary subjects without venturing to rival Archimedes.

When Brougham returned to London, in the end of January, 1850, he strove to bring about the resignation of Lord Denman and the appointment of myself to be Chief Justice, as if he had had no other object in this world. The latter event had been settled three months before, upon the contingency of the former, which had become very desirable for the public good, but was extremely doubtful from mental malady. By Brougham's friendly interposition the necessity for any interference of the two Houses of Parliament was obviated, and the succession took place without the public being made aware of the difficulties which had retarded it.

I select from his correspondence at this time the letter containing Brougham's admonitions to guide me on my elevation to the bench, which appear to me very sensible, although it may be thought that they show that he considered himself the *beau idéal* of a perfect judge :—

"Grafton-street, Wednesday Evening.

"MY DEAR C.—As you are now Chief Justice, I will use a *court freedom*. I advised Denman, and also Wilde; the former followed my advice, and benefited; the latter's habits were too strong, and he did not follow, and was the worse for it.

"Don't suppose the *truisms* I am going to give out are therefore valueless. They are really all the better.

"*First*. I beg of you to regard your first week as your most important, even on circuit; certainly in banc. All the impression a man is ever to make does not turn on his start, but nine parts in ten do; and if the start is inauspicious, he has an uphill work to do for long and long.

"I had some luck in immediately on entering Chancery having a good case to start on (an old client of yours, De Tastet), and I overruled bad bankrupt law of Mansfield (Sir J.). The benefit I had hence, and of a judgment in Dom. Proc., the day I first sat there, was inconceivable. My *arrears* prevented me from retaining my first gains.

But I afterwards, by written judgments (quite necessary), recovered lost ground. Therefore I repeat, consider every one matter as a difficult thing to be got over by diligent care, and expend your entire force on every one thing, small as well as great, for the first week or two; afterwards you can afford to take your own ease in your own court.

"*Second.* I need not remind you of the fatal error Scarlett, Pullock, and others made of thinking lightly of judicial difficulties, because they have been leaders, and not pleaders. No doubt your business is to take large views like a leader, but nine parts in ten of your work is akin to the pleader's ways. This is an error you are not the least in risk of falling into.

"*Third.* Politics are not now forbidden ground—but ground rarely to be trodden. However, even party votes, and, in cases of great gravity, debate, are by no means to be considered out of your sphere; for why? those subjects may be such as you most conscientiously deem important, and calling for your interposition.

"*Fourth.* After Denman has set the fashion, and been followed by Lyndhurst, I hardly require a return to the wig and gown, to which my own very decided opinion inclines. Consider this—I am unprejudiced.

"*Lastly.* I really think it right for both yourself and the public that you occasionally attend the Privy Council; for example, in such cases as the ——[1] Shrievalty.

"Excuse these matters, prompted by regard, and wholly consistent with confidence and respect; and wishing you a long and happy reign over learned puisnes and civil barristers, Believe me, &c.,
"H. BROUGHAM."

He presided at the ceremony of my taking leave of the Society of Lincoln's Inn, of which we had long been brother benchers, and on this occasion he delivered a beautiful and well-deserved eulogy upon the talents and virtues of my predecessor, to whom I really think he was attached by the ties of true friendship.

On the 27th of May, Lord Cottenham actually resigned, and the Great Seal was put into Commission. Still, Brougham was as hostile as ever to the Government, and on the 17th of June he spoke and voted for Lord Stanley's reso-

---

[1] Word illegible.—ED.

lution to censure Ministers, on account of their foreign policy, which (being carried by a majority of thirty-seven) almost every one believed would turn out the Whigs. However, Lord John remained firm, and a counter-resolution was carried in the Commons by a majority of forty-six.

The accession of the Protectionists to office was postponed, but could not be very distant.

In the meantime Brougham amused himself by doing all the duties of Chancellor in the House of Lords. Lord Langdale had been appointed Speaker; but he never did more than put the question, as if he had been Speaker without being a peer. I was now too much occupied with my duties as Chief Justice in my own court to take part in hearing appeals or attending to divorce bills, and I cautiously abstained from personal or party contests. Brougham determined that, as far as the House of Lords was concerned, he himself should be Chancellor *de facto*. Formerly he had professed to be of the clamorous party who were for dividing the judicial and the political functions of the Lord Chancellor, and he had actually himself brought in a bill for that purpose. But he now insisted that there was nothing objectionable in the combination of these functions, and that they might all be satisfactorily performed by one individual of competent ability and industry. His theory was to be illustrated by a great example. He therefore took possession of the pending divorce bills (for which he always showed a great relish), and although the arrear of appeals and writs of error had alarmingly accumulated from Cottenham's illness, he resolved to clear off the whole before the end of the session, without any assistance.

Accordingly, he set to work in a most extraordinary manner, assisted by two lay lords, in rotation, to make a house. I know not that any serious injustice was done, but the whole proceeding was considered very unseemly, and much obloquy was thereby brought on the Government. In consequence Lord John Russell resolved abruptly to put an end to the Commission, and pressed the Great Seal on Lord Langdale, arguing that although he could not attend to the judicial business of the House while he was Master of the Rolls and Lord Commissioner, as Chancellor he might stop the complaints upon this subject which had become so loud. Lord Langdale expressed great delight at the prospect of being relieved from his duties as Lord Commissioner, but positively refused to take the Great Seal as Chancellor. He had always had an utter horror of coming into collision with Brougham, and now, from broken health, was more than ever unequal to the *congressus*. Lord John knew well that he need not make the offer to the Chief Justice of the Queen's Bench, who, since his promotion, had openly declared his resolution to refuse the Great Seal if offered to him, and he resorted to the Chief Justice of the Common Pleas, who after much hesitation accepted it.

But the object was not in the slightest degree effected of dethroning the usurper. Brougham said that there were some cases which he had begun to hear, and others which he had appointed to be heard, and which he must finish: he frightened the new Chancellor by saying that they involved some of the most abstruse intricacies of Scotch law; advised him to confine himself for the rest of this session to the Court of Chancery, and held out a hope that he might during the long vacation, with the gigantic industry which characterized him, make himself master of Craig, Erskine, and Stair. Lord Truro, who knew as little of the law of Scotland as of the law of Japan, yielded to the gentle violence, and actually did confine himself to the Court of Chancery for the rest of the session.

Brougham was, therefore, undisputed master of the field, and met with only one check. Resolved to dispose of all the Common-Law writs of error, as well as the appeals, English, Irish, and Scotch, he had summoned the Common-Law Judges to attend in several cases which raised questions of great importance and difficulty. Unwilling that they should be so disposed of, I made a motion in the House that they should stand over till another session; on the ground (assumed, to avoid giving offense) that the Judges, not expecting such a summons, had formed arrangements with respect to their own courts, and the Court of Exchequer Chamber, which could not now be disturbed without serious public inconvenience. Brougham was in a great rage, as if I had been taking a morsel of bread out of his mouth when he was hungry, and accused me of want of courtesy in not giving him notice of the application; but, afraid to divide the House, he ungraciously yielded.

All the other cases he actually did decide, and I believe that all his decisions were defensible, with the exception of one, in an appeal from the Court of Chancery upon the construction of the " Winding-up Acts," and the liability of "provisional committee men." This decision of his caused dreadful confusion, both at law and in equity, and apprehensions were entertained that an Act of Parliament would be necessary to set it right. But, to save Brougham this disgrace, which he himself once proposed to put upon Lord Wynford, we contrived, during the next session of Parliament, by a little straining and ingenuity in a similar case, to draw distinctions whereby the law upon this subject was satisfactorily re-established.

Although no real fault, I believe, could properly be found with the other decisions, Brougham, as a single Judge, certainly did not enjoy the confidence of the bar or of the public; and although he might at last get right, he was in the habit of rashly blurting out observations during the argument which showed that at the time when he made them he had no correct notion either of the facts or of the law on which he was to adjudicate. Accordingly, the newspapers contained letters from correspondents, and even leading articles, complaining of the manner in which the judicial business of the House was transacted in the absence of the Chancellor, who was severely censured for abdicating his duties.

Brougham, who had expected immense applause for the manner in which he had performed his Herculean task, was greatly enraged by these attacks, and a few days before the prorogation made a formal complaint of breach of privilege on account of the libels published upon the administration of justice in their Lordships' House. After a few introductory remarks, he thus proceeded:—

"A more unjustifiable, a more indecent, attack on any court of justice I have never seen in the whole course of my experience. I have been sitting for the last six or seven weeks in the administration of justice in your appellate jurisdiction, assisted by other Peers not law lords. Of law lords I was the only one able to attend. I undertook—I voluntarily undertook—this duty. I sate as the only law lord while the Great Seal was in commission; and on the appointment of my noble and learned friend to the woolsack, hearing that there were heavy arrears of causes in his own court, I felt it my bounden duty still to assist him and your Lordships in getting rid of the arrears before you. I have heard causes as important and difficult as ever came before you. I have sat as many as five and six days in the week, Wednesdays and Saturdays included—contrary to the usage of your Lordships. I have succeeded, and arrears there are none. All the causes ready for hearing have been heard, and all that have been heard have been adjudicated upon. And I will venture to say that even in cases where I have been under the necessity of reversing the decision of the court below, the united opinion of the profession, not excluding those members of the bar against whose arguments I decided, is in favor of the judgments I have delivered. But I am attacked as if I had wantonly entered on a career of injustice—setting law and decency at defiance. First the calumniator says, 'this is the first time that appeals have been heard in this House the Chancellor not being present.' Ignorance of falsehood! When my noble and learned friend Lord Lyndhurst last held the Great Seal, my noble and learned friends Lord Cottenham, Lord Campbell, and myself, sat in turn three times every week, and decided long causes, sometimes in conjuction, and sometimes separately. Then the libeler proceeds, ' The number of cases *knocked off* in the Lords;' as if some one had bragged of the precipitate haste with which cases had been decided. I need not tell your Lordships that I never used so vulgar and low-bred an expression. 'The number of cases *knocked off* in the Lords has been considerable; but whether they have been gravely and attentively heard, maturely considered, and satisfactorily disposed of, is a question which will not be agreeably answered on inquiry amongst the able men who for six weeks past have been pleading at the bar of the House of Lords.' And then comes more stupid ribaldry as to my motives in sitting as judge in the House of Lords. I should regret indeed if now, for the first time, and after a long professional career, and after twenty years of judicial experience, I had afforded grounds for any such remonstrance, betokening, on the part of the bar, a want of confidence in my learning and my honor."

"*Lord Chancellor Truro:* Though I sought no assistance, my noble and learned friend, in his zeal for the public service, was good enough to undertake to hear and decide the appeals in this House, and to leave me more at liberty to deal with the business of the Court of Chancery. I believe generally that the profession is desirous that the person who holds the Great Seal should preside over the judicial business in this House. But I have no reason to doubt that this business has been very satisfactorily disposed of by my noble and learned friend in my absence."

The Duke of Wellington and Lord Lansdowne complimented Lord Brougham for his zeal in the public service, and here the matter dropped without any steps being taken to detect and punish the libeler.[1] Lord Stanley was, unfortunately, present at this exposure on the complaint of "breach of privilege;" and from that time it was pretty certain that, if ever a new Conservative Government was to be constructed, Sugden would be Chancellor.

Soon after, all England rang with the cry of "Papal aggression," in consequence of the Bull of PIO NONO, creating Cardinal Wiseman Archbishop of Westminster, and dividing the kingdom into Roman Catholic dioceses. Brougham, although for allowing all reasonable latitude to religionists of all denominations, had a laudable dislike of ultramontane popery, probably sharpened by his education in Presbyterian Scotland. Therefore, he did not disapprove of Lord John Russell's letter to the Bishop of Durham, which sounded the alarm for Protestantism and national independence; and he afterwards even gave support to the "Ecclesiastical Titles Bill," while he lamented that some defensive measure, less insulting and more effectual, could not be proposed.

When Parliament met in the beginning of February, 1851, Brougham was favorably disposed to Lord John Russell's Government. Lord Stanley, who had hitherto conciliated Brougham's services by all fair means, had lately shown symptoms of alienation as the prospect of being "sent for" became nearer, that there might be no perplexing claim upon him, which he could not refuse without being liable to the charge of bad faith, nor concede without detriment to his party and to the country. There

[1] 113 Hansard, 841.

had even been some sharp skirmishing between them, in which each of them claimed the victory.[1]

But, unluckily, Brougham now quarreled with Lord Truro, the new Chancellor, to whom he at first affected to extend a condescending protection, powdered with a few occasional sneers and sarcasms. The quarrel proceeded on two grounds: 1st. Truro, at last, insisted on taking care himself of the Divorce Bills, and on being present himself at the hearing of all appeals and writs of error. 2ndly. He would not dispose of his patronage as Brougham desired. Flagrant war between them was ultimately occasioned by a vacant Vice-Chancellorship. Brougham had a most amiable passion (if he had not carried it to such excess) for favoring all who were related to him by blood. He had a younger brother, William, of unexceptionable character and rather clever, but not well qualified for a high judicial appointment. Henry, when Chancellor, had made him a Master in Chancery. He now pressed Truro to make him Vice-Chancellor: for this, among other reasons, that he might obtain for him a remainder of the peerage of Brougham, although he was not next collateral heir male. Truro—who during his short Chancellorship displayed much honesty and discrimination in his judicial appointments—absolutely refused to gratify him in this respect. Hence Brougham, *in furore*, declared that "Jonathan Wilde had become a courtier; and, having married the Queen's cousin, laid all his patronage at the Queen's feet. As to her having all the livings in the Chancellor's gift, it does not so much signify; but it will never do to let the Court dispose of judicial appointments." Lyndhurst was now in hot opposition, and he easily prevailed upon Brougham, so incensed, to join in annoying the Chancellor, and doing anything to damage the Whigs.

The Session had made little progress when Lord John Russell was driven to tender his resignation, and Lord Stanley and Aberdeen were successively sent for, and successively tried in vain to form a Government. Brougham was deeply mortified to find that at this crisis no offer was made to him, and he was consulted by no one. In his own opinion

[1] This happened when I was absent on the circuit. When I returned, Stanley said to me, "I have found it necessary to punish the Cossack," and Brougham said to me, "I have been obliged to show up that schoolboy Ned."

the Queen, considering his great experience in public life, his freedom from all party connections, and his high reputation with all sorts and conditions of men, ought to have employed him to form an administration, of which he should be the efficient head, either being Lord Chancellor or First Lord of the Treasury, if not Lord High Treasurer. Not only no messenger came to Grafton Street from Winsdor, but Lord John Russell, by the advice of the Duke of Wellington, was reinstated in office, and all his Cabinet—without Brougham ever having received any communication respecting the pending negotiations from Whig, Peelite, or Protectionist.

I think he may now be considered as having given up the great game of politics at which he had played with almost unexampled boldness and brilliancy above forty years. Henceforth we shall still find him making speeches in Parliament, for speak he must by the necessity of his nature wherever he finds or can make an opportunity of speaking, but he no longer tried any great *coup d'état*, he had no scheme for his own political aggrandizement, and he was guided by the impulse of the moment, merely gratifying a momentary whim without any *arrière pensée*. He even gave up almost entirely " Education," the " Administration of Charities," and " Slavery," confining himself to his favorite hobby, *Law Amendment*. This hobby he did continue to ride "fast and furiously," to the no small annoyance of his brother Peers, and I may say of all the Queen's subjects.

I have diligently looked through the five volumes of Hansard for Session 1851, without being able to find anything in his many speeches with which I could hope to edify or amuse the reader. He supported the important Bill for appointing two Lords Justices of Appeal in Chancery, whereby the office of Lord Chancellor escaped the long-threatened bisection and retained all its patronage, although its salary and its *prestige* were very much reduced. But now he did not care about the office, except in as far as the public was concerned. There were some smart skirmishes between him and me about the Crystal Palace, which amused the House and the town at the time, but were soon forgotten. Having at first violently opposed the erection of this structure in Hyde Park, he afterwards went over to the Paxtonians and resolutely contended that Hyde Park should be permanently sacrificed to it, contrary to a pledge given both by the Crown and the House of Commons. But fortunately he was defeated.

However, by the end of October all our differences seemed buried in oblivion. I then paid him, with my family, a most agreeable visit at the Chateau Eleanor Louise, on the shore of the Mediterranean, as we were returning from Italy. He still talked of " Jonathan Wilde," or " Tom, the Queen's cousin," but did so now without any rancor, and he appeared so mild and gentle and good-humored that no one would have believed that he ever could have had a provoked or unprovoked enemy in the world.[1]

At the opening of the Session in 1852 Brougham was at his post, and, without any ulterior view beyond badgering the Lord Chancellor, joined with Lyndhurst in obstructing the law reforms proposed on the part of the Government. To such a pitch of factiousness did they proceed that they complained of the Common-Law Procedure Act for not going far enough, although it corrected flagrant abuses which had existed without disturbance while the two vituperators respectively held the Great Seal, and it made a greater change in the courts of common law than had been effected by all the statutes that had passed since the reign of Edward I. Lyndhurst even went so far (Brougham cheering him) as to complain that

---

[1] In a short account which my father wrote of his journey in 1851, I find the following mention of his visit to Lord Brougham:—"I felt great curiosity and interest when, after changing horses at Antibes, I drew near to the chateau of ' my noble and learned friend.' . . . I found him quite alone,— that is, with one gentleman (Mr. Vane), who always goes abroad with him as his ' companion.' His place at Cannes is indeed most exquisitely beautiful. He calls it 'Chateau Eleanor Louise,' in honor of his daughter, to whose memory he is still tenderly attached. There are inscribed upon the walls verses in her praise by himself, by the late Lord Carlisle, and by the late Lord Wellesley. I thought the sight of my three daughters strongly revived the recollection of her in his mind, and that he was assailed by the sense of his own derelict condition. He comes, a solitary being, to a foreign land, where there is no one to welcome him, without any occupation to excite him, the projects of ambition which he has been fostering since his fall from power forever blasted, and the infirmities of old age perceptibly laying hold of him. At first he seemed very melancholy, but he gradually brightened up as we talked over our old friends. . . . He conversed very agreeably about the culture of his oranges and his olives, but he chiefly delighted in discussing the bills of the last session and those of the session which is to come. As to the forthcoming new Reform Bill, we were pretty well agreed."—ED.

written allegations of the complaint and of the defense were not entirely swept away,—so that the parties might come before the Judge, verbally state their case, and at once have a final adjudication upon all their differences.

Lord John Russell at last fell by his own imprudence in bringing forward, to please the Radicals, a new Reform Bill, which all parties condemned, the principal enactment being a resuscitation in groups of the rotten boroughs extinguished by himself in 1832. Brougham imagined that his opposition had materially contributed to the change, and for this he quickly felt remorse. Instead of "Jonathan Wilde" he now saw on the woolsack Sugden, whom he disliked more heartily.

Brougham bore the misfortune with apparent magnanimity. In public he affected to be rather cordial with the new Chancellor, but he poured out his griefs pathetically into the ear of a private friend. The truth was that he stood considerably in awe of Sugden, who was infinitely superior to him in professional knowledge and had far higher reputation as a lawyer, while infinitely inferior to him in eloquence and in liberal acquirements. When I returned from the Spring Circuit in April I found that the new Chancellor had been setting all the law lords at defiance, and had threatened to repeal a bill which I had introduced as head of the Real Property Commission, to regulate the execution of wills of real and personal property. I was called in by Brougham to assist in repressing this "aggression," and we gave our "noble and learned friend" a lesson which made him comparatively modest and humble during the remainder of his short tenure of office.

After the prorogation and dissolution of Parliament, Brougham remained in England for the autumn session promised by the Protectionists for bringing forward their measures. But he made no memorable speech during the existence of the Derby Government. The struggle which resulted in its overthrow was carried on exclusively in the House of Commons on Mr. Disraeli bringing forward his rejected budget.

Brougham was rather pleased with the coalition of the Peelites and the Whigs which now took place. He felt no disappointment in not being included in the arrangement, for he sincerely and *bonâ fide* had renounced all hope, and, I believe, all wish of resuming office. Instead of the formidable Sugden he saw on the woolsack the meek and pliable Rolfe, created Lord Cranworth, whom he expected easily to manage. Lord Aberdeen would be more grateful for his support than Lord Derby had been. The only interested object which he now had in view for himself or his family was to obtain a remainder of his peerage for his brother William. He once had a great desire to become an Earl, but this was entirely extinguished by the elevation of Cottenham to that dignity. When Lord John Russell conferred that promotion on the retiring Chancellor, Brougham was very indignant, and either wrote or dictated a pamphlet ridiculing it, to which was affixed, rather felicitously, as a motto " The *offense* is RANK."

CHAPTER CCXXXI.

CONCLUSION.

I HAVE now brought down the life of Lord Brougham to the end of 1852, marked by the fall of Lord Derby's Government.[1] Since he became a Parliament man my narrative has been divided by years or sessions of parliament, and I have hitherto found without difficulty something memorable that he had done, spoken, or written in each of these portions of time. He has retained his mental and physical powers almost quite unimpaired, but his career has become much more quiet and uniform. I will not say that " the flaming patriot who scorched us in the meridian now sinks temperately to the west, and is hardly felt as he declines." But if I were to continue any minuteness of detail I should now have only to relate year by year how he left his chateau at Cannes in the middle of January, and, passing a few days in Paris, turned up in the House of Lords on the first night of the session to make some desultory observations in the debate on the Address in answer to the Queen's Speech; how he presented many petitions to the House every evening, taking

[1] The memoir was resumed at this point by my father in the year 1856, after an interval of three years.—ED.

the opportunity of reminding their Lordships of what he had done and what he still intended to do for law reform ; how he claimed the county courts as his creation, and attempted to give the county-court judges unlimited jurisdiction over all matters civil and criminal, legal and equitable, military and ecclesiastical; how he made repeated speeches on the same subject—when giving notice of a motion, when withdrawing the notice, and renewing the notice—as well as when the motion came on; how he still made himself prominent in the House by a copious distribution of praise and censure among those he mentioned or alluded to; how he was ever esteemed a very delightful companion in private, flattering his friends to their face and laughing at them behind their back; how he affected to attend judicially to the hearing of appeals when he was writing notes to his male and female acquaintances at the rate of a score in a morning ; how he gave pleasant dinners at which he loved to assemble those with whom he had had the bitterest quarrels, and charmed them all with his good humor and kindness; how he delivered speeches at the Law Amendment Society, exalting himself and *vilipending* all competitors in the race of law reform ; how he steadily made the 'Law Review' a tiresome vehicle of self-laudation and vituperation of others; how he would get sick of such occupations about Easter, and run off for relief to rapid motion and the sight of the Mediterranean Sea; how at the end of a month he would return and resume his old course till the end of the session, having in the meantime published various speeches and pamphlets, and prepared new editions of some of his innumerable works ; how he then retreated to Brougham Hall, where he hospitably entertained those whom in his writings he had attacked, was attacking, and intended to attack; how the unceasing rains and mists of Westmorland drove him away in search of a more genial climate; how in Paris he gave lectures on his philosophical discoveries to the members of the Institute, who, notwithstanding their natural politeness and respect for his energy and perseverance, experienced some difficulty in steadily preserving a countenance of admiration; and how he again hybernated in the Chateau Eleanor Louise till awoke by the Queen's proclamation summoning another session of Parliament at Westminster.

The repetition of such matters year by year would be irksome, and for the joint benefit of my " noble and learned friend " and myself it will be better that I should merely, in a few sentences, mention anything that has subsequently occurred respecting him out of the common routine to which I have referred.

Although he might have been very willing to accept the Great Seal from Lord Aberdeen, he did not consider himself aggrieved by being passed over, full well knowing that there were various members in the coalition cabinet to whom he was obnoxious. Himself being excluded, he was much pleased to find, as a companion in exclusion, Lord Truro, on whose stubborn nature he could make no impression when measures were to be framed or places disposed of. Rolfe he considered to be made of more " squeezable materials ; " and he loudly praised the choice of a new Chancellor.

Following the practice to which he had adhered since he first entered the House of Lords, of sitting on the ministerial benches only when he was in opposition, Brougham continued to sit on the opposition benches when the Derbyties came over to the left of the throne ; but, affecting impartiality, he decidedly favored the new ministers. He exercised a sort of protectorate over them, and threw away much good advice upon them in public and in private. Lord Aberdeen, and Lord Clarendon, the foreign secretary, were extremely civil to him, and received his admonitions with seemingly sincere deference. Ever since the year 1827, when he went across the floor of the House of Commons, and " stuck his knees into the back of Canning," his chief delight in life had been to appear the patron of a rickety administration, without condescending to take office under it.

The appellate jurisdiction of the House of Lords now got into great disrepute. The law lords who attended the hearing of appeals were Lord Cranworth, Lord Brougham, and Lord St. Leonards. If the last agreed with the two former, it was generally for different reasons. Brougham coalesced with Cranworth, so as to bring about a decision by a majority ; but when he was absent, the two others disagreeing, the vote was one to one, and they unwisely resolved, instead of having the case re-argued before all the law lords, to allow on such occasions the judgment always to be affirmed. But when Brougham was present, he attended so little to what was going on, and so indiscreetly betrayed his ignorance by irrelevant questions put to the bar, that the joint opinion of himself and the Chancellor carried little weight with it, and the law was more and more unsettled by every fresh decision of the court of last resort. Brougham was disposed to play the tyrant over his *protégé*, and in the exercise of the Chancellor's patronage, and permitting bills to pass the Lords which were sure to be rejected in the Commons, he required very disagreeable concessions. Though none of these were inconsistent with strict honesty on the Chancellor's part, some of them approached very close to the line which separates right from wrong; and, in the Chancellor's situation, I certainly should have resisted them at the peril of a rupture, although not unconscious of the importance, with a view to a quiet life, of Brougham's support in the House of Lords.

I must, however, do Cranworth the justice to record, that he assisted me in withstanding Brougham's scheme to prevent any action being commenced adversely till the parties had first been brought together face to face in a "Court of Reconciliation." Brougham repeatedly pressed upon us this his pet reform, forgetful that of the actions commenced there are not five in a thousand which arise from a personal quarrel, or in which the parties understand or are capable of explaining their conflicting claims,—the far greater proportion of actions being brought to recover undisputed debts; so that the proposed preliminary attempt at reconciliation would mischievously add to the delay and expense of litigation, and would in many cases operate as a denial of justice.

Brougham thought that he would beat us both on a still more important subject,—the framing of a Criminal Code. Commissioners, appointed for this purpose at his instigation, had performed their work in a very rude fashion, and he, turning their Report into a Bill, pressed that it should at once be passed into a law. He had some countenance from Lord St. Leonards, now an ex-Chancellor, who from being a legal *optimist* had suddenly become an ardent reformer, and, to gain popularity for his party, was willing to join in an experiment which would have thrown the administration of criminal justice into utter confusion. But

we succeeded in obtaining a Select Committee upon the
Bill, and a reference upon it to the Judges, who, with entire unanimity, condemned the proposed Code, and pointed
out the fatal consequences which many of its enactments
would have produced. Brougham was highly incensed, and
wrote with his own pen two articles upon the subject in
vituperation of the Judges, one of which he got inserted
in the *Edinburgh Review*, and the other in the *Quarterly*.
He then, in repeated speeches delivered in the House of
Lords and in the Law Amendment Society, asserted that
public opinion was entirely with him, vouching for proof
that the two great antagonistic Reviews for once agreed,
which showed that "all parties were against the narrow-
minded opponents of codification."[1]

In 1854, when England was "drifting" into the Russian
war, I thought Brougham would have been roused to some
great oratorical efforts—particularly as Lyndhurst, who
used to excite his jealousy and envy in debate, had gained
immense applause by very remarkable speeches he had delivered on the aggressive policy of Russia and the timid
policy of Austria and Prussia. But Brougham would not
commit himself by joining either the bellicose or the
pacific,—pretty much imitating the course taken by the
Prime Minister, whom he was inclined to patronize. Although speaking almost every night, he allowed the session
to close in August without leaving anything interesting to
record,—his constant topics still being the excessive costs
of proceedings in the County Courts, and the *desideratum*
in our judicial system—"Courts of Reconciliation."

In October, 1854, when returning from a tour in Germany, I met him in Paris, on his way to Cannes, and I spent
a week with him most agreeably. We were together at

---

[1] While fully aware of the impossibility of reducing the whole law of any
civilized country into a written code in which might be found all that judges
or legal practitioners can require for the due administration of justice, so that
all other law-books might be dispensed with and burned, I was in hopes that
the criminal law, from its simplicity and certainty, was a partial exception;
but having sat for eleven days with one Chancellor and four ex-Chancellors,
Cranworth, Lyndhurst, Brougham, Truro, and St. Leonards, upon the single
title of "homicide," I gave up the attempt in despair. We never could agree
on a definition of murder or manslaughter. Brougham himself was particularly unhandy at this work, and justified the answer given by Maule, J., to the
question whether the attempt could now be safely made:—"I think the attempt would now be particularly dangerous, for the scheme is impracticable,
and there are some who believe that they could easily accomplish it."

Maréchal St. Arnaud's funeral, and he very obligingly carried me to the meetings of the Institute, and introduced me to his literary and scientific *confrères*.

We were then in hopes of speedily hearing of the capture of Sevastopol, although the first intelligence of this event, which had caused such joy, had turned out to be a hoax. Brougham was particularly sanguine, from having been made the depository of Lord Dundonald's secret for taking the strongest place in the world by projectiles assailing the sense of smell. This he had studied and communicated to the Duke of Wellington, and the succeeding authorities at the Horse Guards—and he himself had entire confidence in its efficacy. But, alas! the works to defend Sevastopol were raised with more energy and skill than those to attack it; when Christmas arrived the English army in the Crimea, by mismanagement at home and abroad, had almost melted away, and notwithstanding the glories of the Alma and of Inkerman an appalling dread was entertained of some unexampled national calamity.

Lord Aberdeen was forced to resign, and being speedily followed by all his Peelite associates, a Whig ministry was reconstructed with Palmerston at the head of it.

Brougham had been involved in the most serious personal differences with Palmerston. For years he had bitterly assailed the policy of the Whig Foreign Minister, and in moving a vote of thanks to Lord Ashburton for concluding a treaty with America under Sir Robert Peel, he embraced the opportunity of showing up the alleged unfitness and blunders of "the man who had done his best to embroil us with all the states in the old world and in the new."

Nevertheless no sooner was Palmerston installed than, recollecting Brougham's passion for protecting a minister, he opened a communication with him, and—not offering him a place, but, what was perhaps more agreeable, expressing a deep sense of his great influence in the House of Lords, in the country at large, and all over Europe—asked whether he might not hope for his support in the unprecedently difficult position in which unforeseen circumstances had placed him. There was immediately an *entente cordiale* between them. *More suo* Brougham continued to sit on the Opposition benches, but professing perfect political impartiality, and occasionally criticising the measures of Government so as to maintain his character for independence during the whole of the session of 1855 he played a part which was very agreeable to the new Government. Still he made no great speeches, and his nightly topic was "the heavy tax imposed on suitors in the county courts by the fees exacted from them to pay the salaries of judges."

He continued unaccountably to submit to the drudgery of hearing appeals in the House of Lords. The occupation yielded him neither profit, nor fame, nor amusement, and as I believe he had at last abandoned all notion of again holding the Great Seal, he could no longer be actuated by the wish to retain his acquaintance with juridical proceedings as a qualification for office. Unfortunately he, with Lords Cranworth and St. Leonards, contrived to get the appellate jurisdiction of the House into still greater discredit, and at the end of the session Bethell, the Solicitor-General, brought the matter before the House of Commons, asserting that "judicial business was conducted before the Supreme Court of Appeal in a manner which would disgrace the lowest court of justice in the kingdom." Brougham had left London for Brougham Hall—in his phrase had "*prorogued himself*"—before this explosion, or he would have paid off Mr. Solicitor with usury. According to his annual migration he took wing for Cannes in October, "biding his time" at the opening of another session.

Before this came round, a storm was raised by a heedless step of the Government which involved us all in its vortex. Cranworth, without consulting any one who could keep him straight, thought that his best course would be to have two new Peers who would outvote, if not outweigh St. Leonards, and make him independent of Brougham. One of these was Lushington, Chancellor of the Diocese of London, and Judge of the Court of Admiralty; but who, having a large family and small means, could not accept an hereditary peerage. A life peerage being proposed, he said he could not stand the obloquy of being the first peer for life, but he would not mind following in the wake of another. Baron Parke was fixed upon for the experiment, and in an evil hour he consented to its being made upon him. Brougham was still at Cannes, but he appeared in the House a few days after the opening of the session, and he resisted the claim of Baron Wensleydale to sit in parliament with great zeal and with great talent, distinguishing himself more as a debater than he had done for several years past. On Lord Lyndhurst's motion to refer the patent to a committee of privileges he spoke shortly and admirably; and in the committee he delivered a most excellent argument, which he published in a pamphlet, encountering with skill and force the authority of Lord Coke, which was strong against us. Our triumph was complete, the Lords having by a large majority, "*ordered and adjudged* that neither the patent, nor the writ of summons under it, conferred any right to sit as a peer."

But a considerable mortification followed to Brougham, which is not yet by any means at an end. He has taken a part in hearing appeals in the House of Lords above a quarter of a century, and he fondly hoped that his performance of this character would afford one of the many grounds on which he must enjoy a brilliant and lasting reputation with posterity; but a select committee having been appointed, on the motion of Lord Derby, to consider whether any and what change in the exercise of the appellate jurisdiction of the House is required, grave complaints have been brought forward against his demeanor in hearing appeals, and against various judgments he has delivered. On the adjournment for the Easter holidays he set off in high dudgeon for Cannes, and there he still remains, nursing his wrath.[1] I have received two long letters from him inveighing against those who have offended him, advocating the old system, and expressing his reprobation of the proposed remedy of introducing a Scotch lawyer as a member of the appeal tribunal.

Having thus told all I know that is memorable of him from his birth to the present hour, I must here pause, and this may be the conclusion of my memoir. Although he is a year older than I am, he may very probably survive me, and I shall not resume it unless I survive him. In that event I should like to trace him to his last abode, and try to wind up with an impartial estimate of his character and career. At present I recollect nothing omitted by me which can be supposed to do him honor, except that he has lately published an edition of "Newton's Principia" in conjunction with a Cambridge mathematician; that he

[1] Written 13th of April, 1856.—ED.

has favored the world with a selection, in three volumes,
of his essays in the *Edinburgh Review* (omitting, however,
the most famous of them, his criticism on Byron, which
elicited the poem of "English Bards and Scotch Reviewers"); and that he is carrying through the press a new
edition of all his works, oratorical, political, critical, philosophical, historical, biographical, and miscellaneous (in
how many volumes it is not yet stated). It is rumored
that he is likewise employed upon AUTOBIOGRAPHY. I
hope, most sincerely, that this is true. From his failure as
a novelist in "Albert Lunel"[1] I doubt whether he possesses the tact of presenting an individual personally before
the readers of a book, bringing them acquainted with him,
and making them take a sympathetic interest in his progress and adventures. But he knows a great deal which,
if disclosed, would be found most valuable, and I should
be delighted with the opportunity of comparing his own
with my statement of his acts, his wishes, and his motives.

13th April, 1859.—It is exactly three years since I concluded my Memoir of Lord Brougham. We both survive;
but in the meantime nothing remarkable has happened to
either of us. While I have been carried along as Chief
Justice by the regular revolution of Term, Sittings, Circuit, and Vacation, he has oscillated between Provence and
England, delivering a lecture to the Institute as he passes
through Paris, and making tiresome speeches on Law Reform in the House of Lords. He gave a general support
to Lord Palmerston's Government, notwithstanding former quarrels, but he seldom spoke on foreign politics.

In the year 1856 he retired to Brougham Hall several
weeks before the end of the Session, and thence, when I
was libeled so shamefully after Palmer's famous trial for
poisoning, he addressed the following letter to me:—

"Brougham, 11th June, 1856.

"MY DEAR C. J.,—I have of late been reflecting on
Denman's great alarm about the threatened inroad of
Lynch law. He no doubt regarded the press as the road
for that invasion; and I have had my attention drawn to
the subject by the interference of the press with Palmer's

[1] "Albert Lunel, or the Chateau of Languedoc," published in 1844.

case. No doubt it is after and not before the judgment, and this is a great mitigation; but still it somewhat affects the ultimate dealing with the particular case, and greatly affects judges and juries as to future cases. I need hardly say that if all judges were as much to be relied on as you, little harm would be done. But I could name others who would be much affected by the attacks, which I see with a disgust I have no words to describe, upon your late admirable conduct of the trial. I assure you I have read those attacks with feelings of *general* reprobation quite independent of those which my personal regard for you so naturally inspire. I refer particularly to a pamphlet in the name of the man's brother (a clergyman), and which I have read copied into the daily papers. It clearly is not written by the clergyman, but by some lawyer or half-lawyer, and I am very clear that if it either proceeds from or is countenanced by any of the counsel in the cause (which I can not believe possible), it is as great an outrage as I have ever known in the profession. At the same time, much as one feels the evil of these things, one can not easily check them while full and free discussion of public conduct, including judicial, is allowed—as allowed it ever must needs be.

"If you have seen the foul matter, you certainly have despised it even more than I do. If you have not, there is no harm in your being aware how heartily I both despise and abominate it. There might even have been some talent shown in it, reminding us of your predecessor's rule as to never convicting where the body is not found, and extending this generally to *corpus delicti.* But no such skill appears, only violence and scurrility, excusable in a brother perhaps, not in any professional ally.

"Yours ever,
"H. B.

I am getting so slowly round that I can hardly say I mend at all."

I think the Attorney-General would have done well if he had prosecuted, as there ought to be some limit to the invectives against public functionaries when corruption is imputed to them, but I would not stir in the matter, for vituperation gives me no uneasiness, and it can do me little damage in public estimation to compare me to Jeffereys and Scroggs.

From his retirement at Brougham Hall, Brougham also wrote to me the following letter in reference to the bill which the Lords had passed, aud which was then pending in the Commons, empowering the Crown to create a limited number of peers for life, with a view to the judicial business of the Upper House:—

"Brougham, 14th July, 1856.

"MY DEAR C. J.,—I feel with you how very awkward the condition of the House of Lords is. In truth, the folly of Derby in advertising the inadequacy of the appellate Judicature has been the cause of all the evil, or nearly all. The Parke peerage began it, but there was no occasion for what followed, because I am confident that had they given an hereditary peerage immediately after our decision, and had St. Leonards agreed to give up eternal disputation (he has really been the main cause of the clamor), we might have gone on as before. The vacation will produce some calmer discussion, and it will then be seen how little ground there has been for the main charges against the House of Lords. . . . . As for anything being done now—I mean this session—it is hopeless. I should have made an effort to attend had there been the least possibility of anything. But I have been only very slowly getting round, and I am positively forbidden to go back to business. . . . . . .

"You will see *à propos* of Lynch law and United States abominations, in the next *Law Review*, a full—or at least a sufficient—exposure of the attacks I formerly wrote to you about, and an introductory view of the necessity of making those who attack courts do it in their own name, that it may be seen if they are angry counsel, attorneys, or parties.

"Yours ever,
"H. BROUGHAM."

He had condemned this bill, and every plan proposed for improving the appellate jurisdiction of our court of *dernier ressort*,--thinking it perfect while he sat in it.

I am now glad that the bill was rejected by the Commons, for although the judicial business in the Lords was for some time longer conducted in a very unsatisfactory manner, yet since Brougham has almost entirely ceased to attend to it, and Pemberton Leigh has been created a peer under the title of Lord Kingsdown, public confidence in this tribunal has been restored, and I hope that (Cairns, the new Solicitor-General, becoming Chancellor) it may long be entitled to public confidence.

Having retreated to Hartrigge in the autumn, I invited Brougham to visit me there to meet Philpotts, Bishop of Exeter, whom he abused so terribly in his famous speech against the Durham clergy, but with whom, as well as John Wilson Croker, and almost all his former Tory antagonists, he had long been reconciled. I received the following courteous answer :—

"Brougham, 21st August, 1856.

" MY DEAR C. J.,—Many thanks for your kind letter and hospitable invitation, which, I am sorry to say, I can not avail myself of, as I am here in expectation of what the newspapers call a *succession* of visitors, beginning next week early, and continuing I can not now tell how long, because some are from the other side of the Channel.

" I assure you I should have greatly relished an excursion to your quarter, and had rather have met the Bishop, an old North circuit friend, and a most agreeable companion, than even the Judges of Scotch Assize.

" But I should still more have desired a free conference with you on the House of Lords, and the endless blunders committed there ; and I would fain hope that we still may meet before my southern flight. . . . . .

"Yours ever,
"H. B.

" Kind regards to Lady S., but we really have a right to complain of these *constant* passings by us."

In the course of this year his popularity was much increased. There issued from the press a ponderous volume entitled " Lord Brougham's Acts," with panegyrical notes from the pen of the Editor, Sir Eardley Wilmot. In this were contained all my Acts for the Amendment of the Law of Real Property, and all Lord Tenterden's Acts, and almost all the Law Reform Acts passed for the last thirty years. One man reclaimed a portion of the stolen goods —asserting himself to be the author of the bill for permitting parties in a civil cause to be witnesses—but the rest of the body plundered remained quiescent, and the newspapers placed Brougham as a law-giver above Solon, Justinian, or Napoleon the Great. This volume was dedicated to Brougham himself—with his " kind permission "

—but let us hope that when he kindly gave the permission he was unacquainted with its contents.

For years he had been President of the Law Amendment Society—which he worked as a literary engine by its organ the " Law Review." This Society being comparatively obscure, he panted for a wider field of usefulness, and was gratified by the establishment of the Social Science Society, which embraced among its members Lord John Russell and many other distinguished politicians and authors; which was divided into sections for the consideration of all subjects connected with social improvement, comprehending jurisprudence; and which was to hold aggregate meetings once a year in some great provincial town for lectures and debates. The first meeting was at Birmingham, and here Brougham acquired immense renown. Like Bottom in "Midsummer Night's Dream," he was eager to play all the parts himself. He assigned the Law of Bankruptcy to Lord John Russell, but he retained for himself National Education, the Abolition of Slavery, the Diffusion of Useful Knowledge, and the Advancement of Science. For a week together he extemporized on these topics to crowded and admiring audiences, and at this dead season of the year the editors of all the newspapers in the kingdom were delighted to fill their columns with his harangues.

These exercitations and plaudits had a very salutary effect both on his mind and body. From the languor of rural life he had fallen into a state of deep depression, and his family were most seriously alarmed. Several common friends who came to me from visiting him at Brougham Hall declared that he never appeared till dinner was announced; that he sat silent at table, hardly tasting any food, and that he left them abruptly before the ladies had withdrawn. When I returned to London in the beginning of November, I found him in high health and spirits—delighted with his sociological achievements.

The following year (1858) the Society met at Liverpool, and President Brougham again, for a week, pleased himself and the multitude as much as before—again having Lord John Russell to play second fiddle to him.

In the autumn of this year Brougham likewise obtained prodigious newspaper applause for an oration he delivered on Newton at the inauguration of a statue of the great philosopher, erected at the place of his birth. I really believe that the oration was very well prepared for the occasion, although it can have no permanent interest.

The generation of journalists whom Brougham, when Chancellor, flattered and disappointed, and who long had their revenge upon him by systematically extenuating his merits and exaggerating his faults, has passed away, and the public are now disposed to give credit to his own assertions respecting himself—that he has ever been consistent in his principles and disinterested in his conduct, and that since he resigned the Great Seal, never wishing to engage in party strife, he has patriotically devoted himself to the improvement of our laws and institutions. If he were to die while this impression remains upon the public mind, I should not be surprised if he were to be buried in Westminister Abbey, the two Houses of Parliament attending his funeral.

When Parliament met in the beginning of February in the present year (1859) Brougham, as usual, came from Cannes to be present, and he made several judicious and useful speeches upon the wickedness of France and Austria in going to war without any *casus belli*, and on the importance of the *entente cordiale* between England and France being preserved. To show his impartiality, he lavished his advice both upon the opposition and the ministers. He strongly remonstrated with Lord Palmerston and Lord Clarendon against their visit to the Emperor Louis Napoleon at Compiègne, and he pointed out to Lord Malmesbury, the Foreign Secretary, how the negotiations should be conducted with the continental powers for the preservation of peace. He was disposed to take Lord Derby's Government under his protection; but, his suggestions not being very submissively received, and tired of hearing appeals in the House of Lords, where Lord Kingsdown's opinion now always prevails, about the middle of March he suddenly started for his chateau in Provence, where he now is. He intimated his intention to return to London immediately after Easter, but if he should do so he will find that Parliament has been dissolved, and that the energies of the nation are absorbed in a general election. Before he went he declared himself very emphatically to be against any further organic change in our representative system, and I think he may be considered the leader of the anti-reformers; for the present ministers, although Tories in their hearts, being so weak, dare not venture to profess or to act upon Tory principles.

I here stop for the present. My memoir can not be considered complete without some further account of his writings; an estimate of his character; and a survey of the influence he has exercised upon the times in which he lived.

POSTSCRIPT BY THE ENGLISH EDITOR.

THE summary of Lord Brougham's character which my father had intended to add was never written. I find only a few scattered memoranda in his handwriting of the heads under which it was probably to be divided, as:—"Mental qualities: vigor, elasticity, activity of mind, memory, power of application, power of reasoning." "Moral qualities: amiable in private life, good brother, fond father, obliging, jealous. Ruin of Brougham : his insatiable appetite for present applause, desire to astonish, and to obtain credit for more learning, knowledge, and talent than he possessed." "Literature." "Authorship." "Education, Slavery, and Charities." "His characters a Speaker of the House of Lords." "His judgments." "His marriage;—death of his daughter." "His friendships: Jeffrey, Horner, Sydney Smith, Mackintosh—all broken—Romily an exception—and Denman." One memorandum refers to a "character of Brougham in the ' Life of Romily.'" The following is the passage alluded to:—"March 20, 1816. . . . . Brougham is a man of the most splendid talents and the most extensive acquirements, and he has used the ample means which he possesses must usefully for mankind. It would be difficult to overrate the services which he has rendered the cause of the slaves in the West Indies, or that of the friends to the extension of knowledge and education among the poor, or to praise too highly his endeavors to serve the oppressed inhabitants of Poland. How much is it to be lamented that his want of judgment and of prudence, should prevent his great talents, and such good intentions, from being as great a blessing to mankind as they ought to be." [1]

[1] " Life of Romilly," vol. iii., p. 237. In a codicil to Sir S. Romilly's will,

Lord Brougham's life was prolonged for nine years from the date at which this memoir stops, a few weeks after which my father was himself appointed Chancellor. During the two years that he held the Great Seal perfect peace and amity reigned between him and Lord Brougham, and they were sitting together hearing appeals in the House of Lords on the last day on which my father presided there, and the last but one of his life—Friday, the 21st of June, 1861. This was alluded to by Lord Brougham, in a speech which he made on the Monday following in the House of Lords, warmly bearing his testimony to "the great judicial talents" of his noble and learned friend who had so suddenly been removed from the midst of them.

During his remaining years Lord Brougham retired more and more from political strife, and devoted his energy and activity to the Association for the Promotion of Social Science. He was elected President at the annual meetings of this Society which were held successively at Glasgow, Dublin, London, Edinburgh, York, and Sheffield, and at all these places he delivered long addresses. His strength, however, was gradually declining, and the last gathering of the Association which he attended was at Manchester, in 1866.

He continued his practice of migrating for a part of every year to Cannes. He spent his last winter at his favorite Chateau Eleanor Louise, and there he died on the 7th of May, 1868, in his 90th year.

APPENDIX TO CHAPTER CCXVI.

August, 1857.—Since writing the above account of Queen Caroline's proceedings on her return to England, I have been favored by the Dowager Lady Truro with a perusal of the originals of the following correspondence between the Queen and George IV., respecting her Majesty's name being inserted in the Liturgy, and her pres-

dated October, 1818 (to which also one of my father's memoranda refers), after leaving his papers on Criminal Law to Mr. Whishaw, he adds: "If it were not to suit him to undertake such a task, perhaps my friend Mr. Brougham, who finds time for anything that has a tendency to the advancement of human happiness, would be able, notwithstanding his numerous occupations, to perform this office of friendship."

ence at the King's Drawing-room and at his Coronation. The original letters came into the possession of Lord Truro as one of her Majesty's Executors. The drafts of the Queen's letters are in the Queen's own handwriting, and seem to be her own composition from the bad spelling and ungrammatical English, but they were no doubt afterwards corrected by her counsel or other advisers.

The Queen to Lord Liverpool.

"Brandenburgh House, 18th of March, 1821.

" The Queen Communicates to Lord Liverpool that in Consequence that Queen has not Received any answer relatif to her last letter, which she wrote on the 3th of March, the Queen Requests Lord Liverpool to informe his Majesty the King that the Queens intentions is to present herself in Person at the Kings Drawing-room to have the opportunity of Presenting a Petition of obtaining her Rights that the Queens Name should be Restored to the Liturgy as her predecessors.   CAROLINE R."

Lord Liverpool to the Queen.

"Fife House, 19th March, 1821.

" Lord Liverpool has the honor to inform the Queen that the letter he received on the 3d inst. was immediately laid before the King; but as his Majesty saw no reason for altering his determination upon the principal question of the Liturgy referred to in it, and as the Queen concluded Her letter by saying that 'She submitted Herself entirely to His Majesty's decision,' the King did not consider any answer to be requisite.

" Lord Liverpool is now commanded to state that the King must decline receiving the Queen at His Drawing-room; but he will be ready to receive any Petition or Representation the Queen may be desirous of bringing before Him, through Lord Liverpool, or through the Secretary of State."

The Queen to Lord Liverpool.

" Brandenburgh House, the 19th of March, 1821.

"The Queen is much Surprised at the Contents of Lord Liverpool letter and is anxious to know from Lord Liverpool if his Majesty has Commanded him to forbid the Queen from appearing at his Drawing Room, or merely to prevent her Majesty presenting Her Petition in Person to the King.

"The Restoration of the Queen's name to the Liturgy being first and only favor the Queen has ever Solicited from his Majesty, she trusts he will be graciously pleased to acquiesce in, and she most Ernestly Prays his Majesty to grant. CAROLINE R."

Lord Liverpool to the Queen.

"Fife House, 20th March, 1821.

"Lord Liverpool has the honor to acknowledge the receipt of the Queen's letter of the 19th inst., and as the Queen puts to him the question 'Whether His Majesty has commanded Lord Liverpool to forbid the Queen from appearing at His Drawing Room, or merely to prevent Her Majesty from presenting her Petition in person to the King'—Lord Liverpool is under the necessity of stating that, the King having the clear and undoubted right to regulate his own Drawing Room in such a manner as he may think proper, His Majesty feels it impossible, under all the circumstances, to permit the Queen to be present at it; and Lord Liverpool begs further to add that the King will be ready to receive any communications the Queen may have to lay before Him, as heretofore, through the channel of His Government.

"Lord Liverpool will feel it his duty to lay the Queen's letter of yesterday before the King; but after the determination of His Majesty, so repeatedly and recently announced, on the question of the Liturgy, Lord Liverpool can not hold out any expectations to the Queen that His Majesty's decision on this subject will undergo any alteration."

Lord Liverpool to the Queen.

"Fife House, March 21st, 1821.

"Lord Liverpool has the honor to acknowledge the receipt of the Queen's note of this day, together with a sealed Petition addressed to the King.

"Lord Liverpool has obeyed the Queen's commands in forwarding the Petition immediately to the King."

Lord Liverpool to the Queen.

"Fife House, March 23rd, 1821.

"Lord Liverpool has received the King's commands to acknowledge the receipt of the Queen's Petition.

"His Majesty has commanded Lord Liverpool to inform the Queen, in answer to it, that the decision of the question of the Liturgy in the month of February of last year was not taken by His Majesty without the fullest consideration; and the King regrets to be under the necessity of adding that nothing has since occurred which can induce His Majesty to depart from the decision then adopted."

The Queen to the King.

"Sunday, April 29th, 1821.

"The Queen from Circumstances being obliged to remain in England, Her Majesty requests the King will be pleased to Command those ladies of the first Rank His Majesty may think the most proper in this Realms to attend the Queen on the day of the Coronation, which Her Majesty is informed is now fixed, and also to Name those Ladies which will be required to bear Her Majesty's train on that day.

"The Queen being particularly anxious to submitt to the good Taste of His Majesty most earnestly entreats the King to informe the Queen in what dress His Majesty wishes the Queen to appear in on that day of the coronation. CAROLINE R."

The Queen to Lord Liverpool.

"Brandenburgh House, May 5th, 1821.

"The Queen is much Surprised at Lord Liverpool's answer, and assures the Earle that the Queen is determined to attend at the Coronation, Her Majesty considering it as one of Her Rights and Priveledges which the Queen is resolved ever to Maintain.

"The Queen requests Lord Liverpool to Communicate the above to His Majesty."

"Whitehall, July 13th.

"MADAM,—I have laid before the King your Majesty's letter to me of the 11th of this month, which states that your Majesty considers it necessary to inform me that it is your Majesty's intention to be present at the 19th, the day fixed for His Majesty's Coronation, and you therefore demand that a suitable place may be appropriated for your Majesty; and I am commanded by the King to refer your Majesty to the Earl of Liverpool's letter of the 7th of May last, and to acquaint your Majesty that it is not His Majesty's pleasure to comply with the application contained in your Majesty's letter."[1]

[1] Lord Liverpool's letters are all in his own handwriting; but this, which I presume is from the Lord Chamberlain, is a copy in the handwriting of Queen Caroline, and the signature is omitted.

www.ingramcontent.com/pod-product-compliance
Lightning Source LLC
Chambersburg PA
CBHW020727160426
43192CB00006B/132